German Histories in the Age of Reformations, 1400–1650

This book studies the connections between the political reform of the Holy Roman Empire and the German lands around 1500 and the sixteenth-century religious reformations, both Protestant and Catholic. It argues that the character of the political changes (dispersed sovereignty, local autonomy) prevented both a general reformation of the Church before 1520 and a national reformation thereafter. The resulting settlement maintained the public peace through politically structured religious communities (confessions), thereby avoiding further religious strife and fixing the confessions into the Empire's constitution. The Germans' emergence into the modern era as a people having two national religions was the reformation's principal legacy to modern Germany.

Thomas A. Brady Jr. studied at the universities of Notre Dame and Chicago and Columbia University. He taught for twenty-three years at the University of Oregon and eighteen years at the University of California, Berkeley, where he held the Peder Sather Chair of History, and as a guest at the University of Arizona and the National University of Ireland at Galway. A specialist in central European history from 1400 to 1800, his principal writings include *Ruling Class, Regime, and Reformation at Strasbourg 1520–1555*; *Turning Swiss: Cities and Empire 1450–1550*; *Protestant Politics: Jacob Sturm (1489–1553) and the German Reformation*; *The Politics of the German Reformation*; and *Communities, Politics, and Reformations in Early Modern Europe*. In addition to his PhD from the University of Chicago, Professor Brady holds the PhD honoris causa from the University of Bern, Switzerland. He has held Guggenheim, Fulbright, and Humboldt fellowships and appointments in the Historisches Kolleg at Munich and in the National Humanities Center, North Carolina.

German Histories in the Age of Reformations, 1400–1650

Thomas A. Brady Jr.
University of California, Berkeley

CAMBRIDGE
UNIVERSITY PRESS

CAMBRIDGE UNIVERSITY PRESS
Cambridge, New York, Melbourne, Madrid, Cape Town, Singapore, São Paulo, Delhi

Cambridge University Press
32 Avenue of the Americas, New York, NY 10013-2473, USA

www.cambridge.org
Information on this title: www.cambridge.org/9780521717786

© Thomas A. Brady Jr. 2009

First published 2009

Printed in the United States of America

A catalog record for this publication is available from the British Library.

Library of Congress Cataloging in Publication Data

Brady, Thomas A.
German histories in the age of Reformations, 1400–1650 / Thomas A. Brady, Jr.
p. cm.
Includes bibliographical references and index.
ISBN 978-0-521-88909-4 (hardback) – ISBN 978-0-521-71778-6 (pbk.)
1. Germany – Church history. 2. Germany – History. 3. Reformation – Germany. I. Title.
BR854.B73 2009
274.3′05–dc22   2008037135

ISBN 978-0-521-88909-4 hardback
ISBN 978-0-521-71778-6 paperback

To Kathy

Till a' the seas gang dry, my dear
And the rocks melt wi' the sun;
I will luve thee still, my dear,
While the sands o' life shall run.

Contents

Figures, Maps, and Tables

Figures

Maps

Tables

Acknowledgments

I have striven neither to mock human actions, nor to weep at them,
nor to hate them, but to understand them.

Benedict de Spinoza

This book seeks neither to praise nor condemn the past, neither to justify the present nor to impose a mortgage on the future. It essays to address neither the great issues of German national history nor the current controversies about recent German and European history. The work of a double stranger, neither German nor European, it is written in the first place for fellow strangers, though certainly not for them alone, and in a voice as free as possible from both myths of national superiority or inferiority, and pseudo-theological clouds of guilt, retribution, and incomparability.

While writing this book I have thought especially about other strangers, who might welcome more explanation and orienting information than was available when I began to study this subject. I have written also with a special thought to readers from the lands in which my story is laid, including both those who know the older interpretations and those who come fresh to the subject. In addition to the explanatory notes, therefore, I have added reference materials at the end (references and a glossary).

This book's themes and argument reflect a long road traveled from the time, forty-five years ago, when, as it turns out, my preparation for writing it began. From my teachers, some of them German refugees, I learned a vision of German history as tragedy, the twentieth century's self-destruction of a great people at the height of its achievement. From younger West German scholars I learned in the 1960s and 1970s how to study the local and regional histories, which seemed at the time a retreat into pure particularism but in fact allowed larger histories to be told in new ways. From the East Germans, who came into my ken in the 1970s and 1980s, I learned or relearned how to see German histories in terms of the large continuities and restless conflicts, for the mastery of which the insights of historical materialism proved their worth. And from the Alsatians, the Swabians, and the Swiss, among whom I have lived and worked, I learned that peoples can cope with the complexities of modern life without surrendering their fond sense of even deeper, more complex pasts or lusting after power over others. To all of these guides, living and dead, I owe boundless debts I can never repay.

Not once in this passage have I ever been alone. While the inseparability of teaching and research is often academic life's most treasured cliché, for me it has taken on full flesh in the writing of this book. History – and this is the motto of my seminars – is not a combat sport. It is a collective search whose soul is debate and dialogue. I have always been surrounded by colleagues who have inspired and supported my reach across generations, disciplines, and nationalities. Some have been my students, some my teachers, in the United States or abroad, and some both. They have pushed me year after year to reconsider opinions, received or my own, and to strive for a presentation of German and European histories that is accurate, intelligible, responsible, and fair.

How could I possibly thank all those who aided, many unwittingly, in the making of this book? To render them all adequate thanks would require a roll as long as my story. It would bear the names of my teachers at the universities of Notre Dame and Chicago and Columbia University; of the colleagues who gave me twenty-three happy years at the University of Oregon and eighteen more at the University of California in Berkeley; of historians in North America, Germany, Switzerland, France, the Netherlands, and other countries, with whom I have discussed and debated their work and mine; and of archivists, librarians, staff members, and research assistants who contributed to this book in various, indispensable ways. Among them I single out the colleagues (in alphabetical order) who read parts or all of the manuscript and/or supplied me with references and sources: Margaret Lavinia Anderson, Erica Bastress-Dukehart, Peter Blickle, Miriam U. Chrisman, Luke S. Clossey, Deborah Cohen, Brad Gregory, Carina L. Johnson, Greta G. Kroeker, Howard B. Louthan, Christopher Ocker, Michael O. Printy, Thomas N. Robisheaux, James J. Sheehan, Peter E. Starenko, and Ellen M. Yutzy Glebe. Jeanne E. Grant and Tyler Lange read drafts and completed citations. Very special thanks are due to Julie K. Tanaka, who read the entire manuscript several times with her sharp editorial eye, made many corrections, and gave many helpful suggestions. Katie Russell of Berkeley's Geography Department created the maps. In addition to them all, I am beholden to the students, undergraduates and graduates, who over many years have inspired me to investigate new subjects and to question my ideas about old ones, and who have taught me that nothing is truly self-explanatory.

I owe special thanks to the directors and staff of two special institutions, both of which support resident scholars with exemplary dedication and efficiency. The Historisches Kolleg in Munich, which is dedicated to the advancement of historical studies, was my scholarly home in 1998–99. There I made the first, ultimately decisive, revisions of this book. I am grateful to the Kolleg's curators and staff and especially to Dr. Elisabeth Müller-Luckner for her kindness and help. The second institution is the National Humanities Center, a magnificently organized and superbly operated home of scholarship in the Research Triangle Park in North Carolina. There I completely revised the manuscript again in 2001–2. I am grateful to the director, trustees, and staff, and especially to Dr. Kent Mullikin, for that golden year. For a scholar to work in either of these houses is a foretaste of the Elysian Fields.

In the book's final phase I received most support from Cambridge University Press, and in particular from my editor, Eric Crahan, and my copy editor, Sally Nicholls. To them my heartfelt thanks.

Last and best, my deepest and most enduring gratitude goes to Kathy, my incomparable wife, companion, friend, and collaborator for more than forty years. She is present in all my work as in my thoughts; she lends me her courage when I have none; and she gives me her precious counsel at need. Some time ago and with not a little Swabian hyperbole, Peter Blickle compared our partnership to that of Marx and Engels. "If we are to live up to that mark," I whispered to her, "we must each grow more whiskers."

A Note on Usages

I have tried to avoid unnecessary capitalization and to use English equivalents as frequently as possible. The terms "Empire" and "Imperial" are capitalized only when the historic polity of the Holy Roman Empire is meant. "Church" is capitalized when the entire Western, or Roman Catholic, Church is meant. As the Imperial church is but one branch, it is not capitalized. "Reformation" is not capitalized, except when it refers to the entire movement of Protestant and Catholic reform.

The Holy Roman Empire (of the German Nation) refers to a polity, not a country. It corresponds roughly to "the German lands," which are the German-speaking lands, including Bohemia and, sometimes, the colonized Baltic areas. While the adjectival form "German" is frequently used, the noun "Germany" refers to the post-Napoleonic country. The one exception is the humanists' Roman-inspired use of "Germany" as a collective alternative for "the German lands."

The term "evangelical" is used to mean Biblicist religion in the sixteenth century, either separated or not from the Church of Rome. Protestant is used to mean those people who call themselves "evangelical" in opposition to Rome.

The term "bishopric" normally refers to both the diocese under the bishop's spiritual authority and the territory (*Hochstift*) under his feudal temporal jurisdiction.

The names of members of ruling dynasties take their English forms, those of others retain the original forms.

Place names are given in their usual English forms or, if no such form exists, in the form of the country in which they lie (e.g., Strasbourg not Straßburg), or in more than one form then or now used (to help the reader to locate them).

The words "upper" and "lower" in topographical names always refer to altitude or drainage, so that "upper" is always topographically higher than "lower."

Many of the references used are German-language texts. Where these are quoted, unless indicated, the translations are mine.

In the period around 1600, German monetary equivalents would have been as follows: 1 Gulden (fl.) = 0.85 Thaler (Th.) = 4 "old" pounds (lb.) = 15 Batzen (Bz.) = 20 Schilling (sch.) = 60 Kreuzer (dr.) = 120 pence (d.) = 240 Heller (H.).

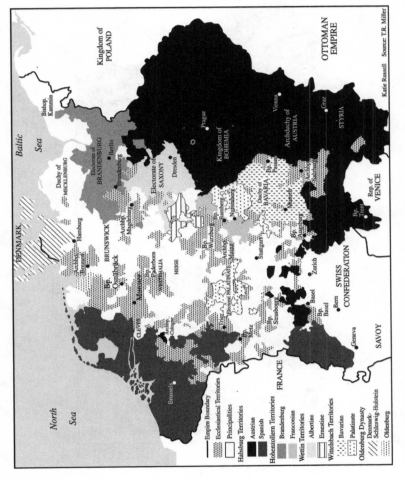

Map 1. The Empire in 1547

North
Sea

Baltic
Sea

DENMARK

Kingdom of
POLAND

Bishop.
Kammin

Hamburg

Duchy of
MECKLENBURG

Elector. of
Brandenburg

Berlin
Brandenburg

Bp.
Bremen

BRUNSWICK

Archbp.
Magdeburg

Electorate of
SAXONY

Dresden

Prague

Kingdom of
BOHEMIA

Vienna

Bp.
Osnabrück

WESTPHALIA

Bp.
Paderborn

HESSE

Bp.
Würzburg

Archbp.
Mainz

Bamberg

Nuremberg

Bp.
Passau

Archbp.
Salzburg

Graz

STYRIA

Archduchy of
AUSTRIA

Münster

Münich

Duchy of
BAVARIA

Rep. of
VENICE

Archbp.
Cologne

CLEVES

Bp.
Metz

Trier

Bishopric PALATINATE

Stuttgart

Augsburg

Bp.
Trent

FRANCE

Bp.
Strasbourg

Bp.
Basel

Basel

Zürich

Bern

SWISS
CONFEDERATION

Geneva

SAVOY

Brussels

Empire Boundary

Ecclesiastical Territories

Principalities

Habsburg Territories

Austrian

Spanish

Hohenzollern Territories

Brandenburg

Franconian

Wettin Territories

Albertine

Ernestine

Wittelsbach Territories

Bavarian

Palatinate

Oldenburg Dynasty

Denmark-
Schleswig-Holstein

Oldenburg

OTTOMAN
EMPIRE

Katie Russell   Source: T.R. Miller

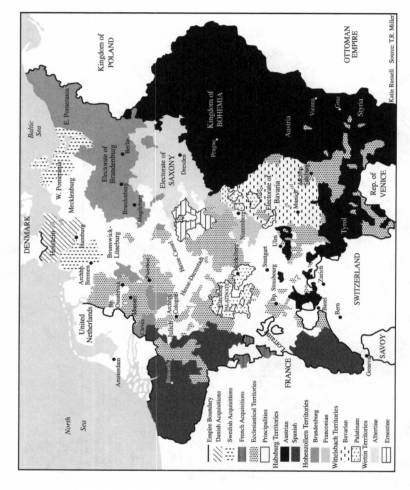

Map 2. The Peace of Westphalia, 1648

Katie Russell   Source: T.R. Miller

xviii

Part I

The Empire, the German Lands, and Their Peoples

> Topography displays no favourites; North's as near as West.
> More delicate than the historians' are the map-makers' colours.
>
> Elizabeth Bishop

If statistics lie with numbers, maps lie with spaces. Their prevarications consist not chiefly in the simplifications required to represent visually physical features, places, and countries in a tiny space, in two dimensions, and in a few colors, for such distortions arise from the inherent limitations on the cartographical representation of geographical and historical realities. Mapmakers do the best they can. The problem lies rather with those makers of national myths who declare polities of distant ages to have been embryonic forms of modern nation-states, and who require maps to support their claims. Consider a map of Latin Christendom in 1400. The map's western tier is after a fashion recognizable today: Scotland and England sit in their places; France lies in the right place, though it is too small; and Iberia presents a recognizable constellation of kingdoms. Eastward, Bohemia, if stripped of its satellite lands, is very nearly the shape of the modern Czech Republic, while a willing eye might see the modern Hungarian Republic in the much truncated form of the old Hungarian kingdom and the Polish Republic as an enlarged, if considerably displaced, version of the old Polish kingdom. The rest is unfamiliar. Only the physical features of mountain, river, and sea enable us to identify Scandinavia, Ireland, and, with a heavier dose of imagination, Italy, that quintessential "geographical expression."

The center, the space of modern Germany and a good deal more, lies at the gradient of recognition's bitter end. Here even the poet Elizabeth Bishop's fine distinction between the historians' and the mapmakers' colors becomes meaningless. The Alps are still the Alps, of course, and the courses of the great rivers still run as they did in 1400, but no other template has anything like a shape recognizable to the untrained modern eye. In the place of Germany we find around 1400 something called "the Holy Roman Empire," the parts of which its peoples called "the German lands." None of its multiple templates – topographical, demographic, ethnolinguistic, ecclesiastical, political, or virtual – sports an obviously ancestral likeness to any of the many Germanys of modern times. Not even the most willing wishful thinking can descry in these landscapes more than a few polities that, even with a great dollop of

1

courtesy, bear likenesses to what later came to be called "states." Bavaria is one, of course, though it is too small, and Austria is another, though it is too large. For the rest, one might be reading a map of China during the Era of Warring States or Greece in the fifth century BC and trying to imagine that they represent ancestral forms of modern counterparts. In such regions, political configuration, historical cartography's bedrock, leads the student of history utterly astray.

There is hope, however. For once we are willing to lay aside assumptions about the genealogies of modern nations and states, other templates come to the rescue. The place to begin is physical topography, the benchmark template for all other shapes in all parts of the world. In the German lands, apart from some canalization of rivers and poldering (filling in) of arms of the North Sea, the physical landscapes remain today much as they were in earlier times. On this template, then, the others may be laid in their order of comprehensibility.

When the theater is built, the company can come onstage. The peoples of the German lands are ranged according to "estates," which are the legally defined status groups according to the notions and practices of the time. Most conventionally they make up two (actually three) lay estates – peasants, burghers, and nobles – and one clerical estate, because the separation of laity from clergy by the church's canon law formed a general principle of legal status in that age. There was nothing static or essential about estates, not only because of the great social mobility that had made medieval society possible, but also because concepts of estates and schemes of estates evolved in response to changes in social realities. Whether one looks at these peoples in terms of estates, which privileges the law, as people then tended to do, or in terms of classes, which privileges the economy, as we tend to do, is a matter of the historian's choice. It depends on whether we intend to look at them in their own time and place or in relation to the world that evolved from theirs. The historian's complete task is, of course, to do both.

It is by no means false to use the lens of classes and proto-classes, for then, as today, tensions and conflicts between such groups drove social change at the most elemental levels. They are classes in our time, but they were estates in their own. In another kind of historical work, one might translate them and their interrelations from the sources' language into the terms modern thought has extrapolated from the class systems of the capitalist age. This entails special problems – the medieval burghers were not really a proto-bourgeoisie, the peasants and lesser artisans were not a proto-proletariat – but class analysis is perfectly appropriate to an investigation of how the social orders came to be and what they portended for the future. In this book the peoples are brought on stage in groups that they might have recognized, and they are arrayed in their cultural multiplicity, their linguistic divisions, and, fundamentally important for this book, their religion.

Part I opens the book with general chapters on the historical setting and modern images of the Holy Roman Empire of the German Nation (Chapter 1) and the various shapes of the Holy Roman Empire (Chapter 2). The following chapters populate this stage with the temporal (Chapter 3) and spiritual (Chapter 4) estates that form the ensuing story's dramatis personae.

I

Reformations in German Histories

> Liberty is characteristic of the Germans.
>
> Justus Lipsius

> Men make their own history, but they do not make it just as they please; they
> do not make it under circumstances chosen by themselves, but under circumstances
> directly encountered, given and transmitted from the past. The tradition of all the
> dead generations weighs like a nightmare on the brain of the living. Karl Marx

In the beginning was Waterloo. Near that small place south of Brussels on 18 July 1815, the armies of two Protestant kingdoms, Britain and Prussia, joined to crush the polyglot forces of a French power thought in Protestant lands to represent both Revolution and Rome. Within a generation Protestants were celebrating their sixteenth-century reformation as the dawn of a modern age of unprecedented prosperity, freedom, and knowledge. In 1827, with Napoleon only six years dead, the Scottish polymath Thomas Carlyle (1795–1881) named the Germans the creators of three keys to modern civilization: the printing press, gunpowder, and Protestantism.[1] (He was right about two of the three.) In 1845–47 his exact contemporary, the German historian Leopold von Ranke (1795–1886), published his *German History in the Age of the Reformation* (1845–47), the single most influential modern interpretation of the German Protestant reformation. Ranke's vision, contrary to much received opinion, was not national but European. "It is one of the greatest coincidences presented by the history of the world," he wrote,

> that at the moment in which the prospect of exercising dominion over the other hemi-
> sphere opened to the Romano-Germanic nations of the Latin church, a religious move-
> ment began, the object of which was to restore the purity of revelation. Whilst other
> nations were busied in the conquest of distant lands, Germany, which had little share in
> those enterprises, undertook this mighty task.[2]

---

1 Thomas Carlyle, *Critical and Miscellaneous Essays*, vol. 1: 32. Carlyle adapted a judgment of Francis Bacon (*Novum Organum*, 1620, Bk. 1, Aphorism 129), who named three great discoveries unknown to the ancients: printing, gunpowder, and the compass.
2 Leopold von Ranke, *Deutsche Geschichte im Zeitalter der Reformation*, vol. 1: 176.

Ranke saw, as Carlyle did not, that the transformation begun in Germany with the Protestant reformation had failed its historic tasks. Far from establishing German or revitalizing European unity, it created the division between Catholic and Protestant that ran right through the middle of Ranke's own nation. "The events of an entire millennium," he wrote, "live on in the conflicts between the Empire and the Papacy, between Catholicism and Protestantism, in the midst of which our age still stands."[3]

I. APPROACHING THE SUBJECT

The twentieth century's events have liberated the two terms in the book's title, "German" and "Reformation," from great, old historical narratives.[4] Just as there was no "Germany," so was there no "German history" or "German nation" before the nineteenth century. There lived, however, peoples whose histories unfolded in what they called "the German lands." They had two things in common: their lands lay in a polity named "the Holy Roman Empire," and they spoke mostly forms of German as mother tongues. In those days, "Germany" was a notion through which scholars tried to conceive, often in confused ways, the pluralities of these lands as possessing a definite if not very concrete unity.

Just as there was no singular idea of "Germany," so there was no singular "Reformation." This hard fact of its plurality has surfaced in recent historical writing, in which "Reformation" refers to a complex set of transformations of Western Christianity – Protestant, Catholic, and others – during the sixteenth and seventeenth centuries. Though often in conflict with one another, they shared a zeal for a more spiritual understanding of the Christian religion and a relative social, if not religious, equality of laity and clergy. The transformations' deeper causes lay far back in the rise of cities and trade, the formation of a monarchical church, the organization of universities and invention of new genres of learning, and the fashioning of bureaucratic forms of governance. Their immediate roots lay in the search for security in the era after the Black Death and in a growing political and spiritual empowerment of the laity.

These two clutches of pluralities were related in a particular way. Whereas the reformations arose from forces identifiable in very many parts of Christendom, they – so this book argues – took the form of popular movements only in places where a general weakness of authority and an intense localization of power endowed them with substantial agency. From this perspective the German lands acquire interest as the sites where, first, the Protestant reformations began and first flourished, and, second, the Catholic reformation displayed, in response to the Protestant challenge, its most striking powers of renewal and recovery. In these lands, too, extreme political diversity both gave scope to these reformations and set limits to their possibilities for success. In consequence, the Holy Roman Empire became the site par excellence of a permanent, legally fixed plurality of religions embodied in a structure of multiple confessions.

---

3 Ranke, *Deutsche Geschichte*, vol. 1: 3.
4 The title offers a modest play on Ranke's title, *German History in the Age of the Reformation* (rendered by Sarah Austin, his translator, as *History of the Reformation in Germany*).

The story constructed in this way can be read in both directions.[5] On the one hand, in the German histories the reformations consolidate religious plurality (without religious tolerance) into a stable, overarching polity, the Holy Roman Empire, thereby completing the reconstruction of governance that had begun in the fifteenth century. On the other hand, German histories radically qualify the western European narrative of reformation religions as cohesive forces in the rise of the typically modern form of the European imperial nation-state. The first reading largely informs this book; the second I must leave to other hands.

The meanings of the story told here will be altered, of course, if its two contexts are expanded into the times that followed those treated here. At the end of this book stands a glance forward into the subsequent history of the Holy Roman Empire and into German history down to the Great War. Brief and of modest scope, it is more a set of suggestions than an argument.

The story presented here does not attempt to integrate fully the German histories into a general European history. To do that would require a conceptual fusion of two quite differently figured narratives. The first, social narrative finds early modern German histories conforming closely to general European norms, regardless of whether one looks at population, family and household, gender relations, or the growth of the market economy. What is called the "old European marriage pattern" of late marriage, household formation, and many celibates dominated the entire zone west of a line drawn from Trieste to St. Petersburg. Zero-growth agriculture constrained the zone's economies and continuously reproduced an unequal distribution of output, although capitalist structures and relations of production were simultaneously taking firm root in both countryside and town. These striking conformities of the German lands to European social patterns lend no support to arguments for German exceptionalism.

An integrated political narrative, on the other hand, uncovers German forms and practices so wildly diverse and particular that they can only with the greatest difficulty be classified at all. The term "political" covers here the entire realm of what may be called "public life," a world in which authority, power, belief, and behavior remained (from the modern point of view) fused and interwoven. Political and religious norms were public, because they generated and reproduced, bounded and informed the terms of governance in units great and small. "Public life" is therefore not to be confused with the modern concept of a "public sphere," which is a creation of bourgeois society in the age of capitalism. The latter's hallmarks are separation of public from private life, centralization of power, uniformity of legal status, and a degree of secularization at least in principle. In the German lands, by contrast, until post-Napoleonic times, public life depended on what subsequently came to be disaggregated into politics and religion, each gaining its own distinct history. "This is the reason," Ranke wrote,

> why church history cannot be understood without political history, and vice versa. Only the combining of the two allows each to appear in its true light and leads perhaps to an intuition of the deeper level of life from which both arise. If this is the case in all nations, it is especially visible in the Germans, who of all peoples have concerned

5 It can also be read in a third direction, hinted at earlier, toward the history of European and post-European Christianity.

themselves with greatest persistence and originality with things ecclesiastical and religious.[6]

Judged by other early modern European histories, those of the Germans represent an extreme in this regard. They therefore require to a special degree a binocular vision that sees both their fundamentally European track from an agrarian-feudal to an industrial-capitalist world and their peculiar patterns of managing power through political and religious diversity. It might be possible to integrate these two ways of seeing into a new grand narrative of European history, but this would require a book of longer scope and broader learning.

2. PECULIARITIES OF GERMAN HISTORIES

This book relates a narrative of authority, belief, power, and tradition. It is typically European in its inner substance but not in its manifestations. It is European in that the early modern Empire, like the western kingdoms, arose fairly rapidly between 1400 and 1650 on foundations laid in an earlier age but ravaged, if not swept bare, by the epidemics and economic depression of the fourteenth century. The story is atypically European in that the German lands' recovery preserved and even enhanced the multiplicity and autonomy of polities, both temporal and spiritual. This book explores how one group of lands, loosely aggregated into a common polity both temporal and spiritual, undertook to reform and strengthen its overarching polity during this era of recovery. It tells how their efforts produced a simultaneous realization of political and frustration of religious reform; how this outcome briefly opened the space for an unprecedented intervention from below into the great issues of politics and religion; how the resulting conflicts led to a negotiated settlement and a provisional stabilization of the entire polity; and how, in the wake of the greatest of Europe's religious wars, the polity reconstituted itself to endure for another 150 years. In sum, the German lands' recovery from the late medieval depression preserved and even enhanced the multiplicity and autonomy of polities, temporal and spiritual. They did not take the road toward the European imperial nation-state.

In writing this book I have tried to shun arguments and judgments based on assumptions about unique experiences and national character. While no one can deny the existence of unique experiences of individuals, perhaps even of specific human groups – beyond the obvious truth that in some sense every human experience is unique and therefore at the deepest level incomparable – such things have no value for the historian who aims to explain. In history, as in physics, the singular cannot be explained, the incomparable cannot be comprehended but only admired or deprecated. Against this incomprehension the historian's chief weapon is comparison or analysis. "Human reality, like that of the physical world, is vast and variegated," Marc Bloch (1886–1944) wrote, and the historian's analysis of it begins when "he seeks out the similarities in order to compare them."[7] This requires a certain assumption, perhaps an act of faith, for, because the assumed uniformity is limited to some very general aspects, "the criticism of evidence relies upon an instinctive metaphysics of

6   Ranke, *Deutsche Geschichte*, vol. 1: 4.
7   Marc Bloch, *The Historian's Craft*, 144.

the similar and the dissimilar, of the one and the many."[8] In other words, the one is not the opposite of but the complement to the many.

The historical record is riddled with claims to uniqueness or incomparability. Some of these were simply expressions of feelings of the time. When the Württemberg jurist Friedrich Carl von Moser (1723–98) wrote in 1765 that "we are a people with name and speech under one common ruler, under laws of a single kind, and bound to a great, common interest in liberty," he was paying (deserved or undeserved) tribute to the hardened dispersal of governance in the Holy Roman Empire.[9] It was not long after that Johann Wolfgang von Goethe (1749–1832) placed a quite contrary notion into the mouth of Frosch, a student at Leipzig: "The Holy Roman Empire, lads, / How can it possibly hold together?"[10] To Heinrich Heine (1797–1856), the defunct Empire was the "moldiest load of junk with all its trumpery";[11] to Gustav Freytag (1816–95) it was a "miraculous creation of a soul without a body."[12] This progressive mystification of that old political order helps to explain why a modern scholar, puzzled by dissimilarity, should wonder why "the fragmented Holy Roman Empire lasted so long in the midst of consolidating, bellicose monarchies. Why didn't it disappear into the maws of large, powerful states?"[13] It is one thing for the historian to recognize and mark off things that are not or perhaps cannot be known. It is quite another thing, however, to elevate the dissimilar into the mysteriously (and pathologically) unique by locating "the origin of what distinguishes German history from the history of the great western European nations" in "the memory of the greatness of the German Middle Ages" and "the earthly reflection of eternity and the ultimate basis of the Germans' mission."[14]

·Another example of hypostasizing dissimilarity into uniqueness is the longstanding dogma of the Germans' political passivity, what is sometimes called "zombie obedience" (*Kadavergehorsamkeit*). A story from Kurt Tucholsky (1890-1935) illustrates the term's meaning. "Mommy! Mommy!" cries a young lad, "Georgie keeps hitting me! He says I should sit in the trash can and sing 'The Watch on the Rhine'! We're playing soldier. I don't want to sit in the trash can, Mommy!" The mother replies, "Why do you do what he says, you lazybones, you yellow-belly?" With sudden enlightenment the young boy says, "Because he's my boss."[15] Like all tales that rest on belief in national character, this one "explains" some modern event or process in terms of a timeless characteristic. It rests on the assumption that the German past was peculiarly burdened by authoritarian governance, which instilled in Germans a peculiar mental habit of obedience. Once again, dissimilarity is escalated into uniqueness. Truth to tell, premodern German governance in the hands of princes, nobles, and magistrates was hardly more authoritarian than France's royal or England's Parliamentary absolutism, but it was authoritarian in a different way.

8 Bloch, *The Historian's Craft*, 115–16.
9 Friedrich Carl von Moser, *Von dem deutschen Nationalgeist*, 5.
10 Johann Wolfgang von Goethe, *Sämtliche Werke: Briefe, Tagebücher und Gespräche*, vol. 7: 90, ll. 2090–1.
11 Heinrich Heine, *Deutschland: Ein Wintermärchen*, 130.
12 James J. Sheehan, *German History, 1770–1866*, 145.
13 Charles Tilly, *Coercion, Capital, and European States, AD 1990–1992*, 65. "Religious organizations" is Tilly's quaint term for the German ecclesiastical principalities.
14 Heinrich August Winkler, *Der lange Weg nach Westen*, vol. 1: 554.
15 Peter Blickle, *Obedient Germans? A Contradiction*, 11.

Absolutist rule in the western style found meager soil east of the Rhine. In the German lands the localization of governance precipitated by the late medieval crisis had dispersed power into and conferred authority on many middling, small, or even tiny polities. The most durable product of post-medieval German politics was not Prussia or the other large states, but Switzerland.

This critique of the exaggeration of dissimilarities into oppositions can be extended into the other major sector of this book's narrative, religion. That the Germans were and are an especially devout people, a long series of observers, German and foreign, has asserted. It was expressed by the Göttingen theologian Carl Friedrich Stäudlin (1761–1826), Goethe's contemporary. "The Germans are still on the whole a very religious people [*Nation*]," he wrote, "and true religious education [*Bildung*] and Enlightenment have attained a higher level among them than among any other nation." In his time, Stäudlin thought, there began "a new revolution in religious knowledge and in the theological sciences" so general that it can "in comparison with other nations be put forth as a general characteristic of the [German] nation."[16] The chief thing to notice in this text is that Stäudlin speaks of religion, not as personal belief, devotion, and praxis – its traditional meaning – but as education, knowledge, and science. Put plainly, religion is culture. His concept shares much with what Ranke meant when he remarked that "the German nation ... has most persistently and independently concerned itself with ecclesiastical and religious matters."[17] The Protestant reformation, Ranke thought, expressed "the maturation of the spirit of Christianity, which had lain latent in the depths of the Germanic nature, to the consciousness of its essence, independent of all accidental forms; in a return to its origin – to those records in which God's eternal covenant with the human race is directly proclaimed."[18] Yet for Ranke the comprehensible aspect of "God's eternal covenant" is not the possibility of individual salvation from the consequences of sin through God's grace, but the welfare of this world. "From the purely historical point of view," he writes, the total triumph of Protestant religion in the German lands "would have been the best thing for the national development of Germany."[19]

Precisely this – the development or the domination of a national religion – did not happen in the German lands either in the age of reformations or thereafter. Instead, there arose a configuration of multiple, transpolitical religious communities – confessions – a configuration that differed from those of other countries chiefly in its longevity. Neither religions nor churches, the confessions fixed the outcomes of the reformations. "The reformation as a historical event," it has been said, "could not have had such far-reaching consequences, had the political system of the Holy Roman Empire of the German Nation not presented it with the possibilities for fixing itself in the territories, despite the emperor's resistance."[20] Whether the confessions survived so long because of a uniquely German devotion to religion, the historian cannot say, but they certainly endured because of their embeddedness in the public life of the German lands under the Empire and, in more recent times, their toughness in the face of the claims of a hegemonic national state.

---

16 Carl Friedrich Stäudlin, *Kirchliche Geographie und Statistik*, vol. 2: 324–5.
17 Ranke, *Deutsche Geschichte*, vol. 1: 3.
18 Ranke, *Deutsche Geschichte*, vol. 2: 111–12.
19 Ranke, *Deutsche Geschichte*, vol. 3: 272.
20 Stefan Ehrenpreis and Ute Lotz-Heumann, *Reformation und konfessionelles Zeitalter*, 1.

3. LISTENING AND TELLING

German Histories is a drama in four parts. Part I (Chapters 1–3) sets the stage and introduces the actors in terms of the physical, political, economic, ecclesiastical, social, and cultural landscapes of the German lands. Part II (Chapters 4–8) recounts the reconstruction of political governance and the programs of religious reform from 1400 to 1520. Part III (Chapters 9–12) examines the movements for religious reform from the beginnings of the Protestant reformation to the consolidation of religious peace around 1580. Part IV (Chapters 13–17) takes the story forward through the formation of the Protestant confessions and the Catholic revival, the treatment of dissenters (Jews, Christian heretics, and witches), and the Thirty Years War. A final chapter presents conclusions and reflections and suggests in broad terms the questions this work raises to historians who write on more recent eras.

This braided narrative sums up the author's participation in the historian's perennial struggle to establish general, explicable similarities among multiple phenomena without destroying their concrete shapes and specific meanings. The topography of the deeper German past, its strong pluralities and weak unities, makes this an especially daunting task, because the oceans of empirical diversity tend to overwhelm the islands of conceptual unity. The resulting liens on coherence menace the historian's native posture between two purposes: achieving understanding and proposing explanation. Understanding or comprehending the past in its own terms requires us to examine the sources truthfully and skillfully. In them lie sleeping, mused Arthur J. Quinn (1942–97), "these shades from time gone, ... geniuses of a certain time and a certain place, ... all strangely requiring only a little of our blood to return to fleeting life, to speak to and through us."[21] "The past will be made more understandable," H. C. Erik Midelfort writes, addressing the same point, if historians "take as a first task the attempt to see a distant world and its problems as people did in the past."[22]

Upon understanding should follow explanation, comprehending the past in the light of and for the sake of the present. Our study of the past, wrote the German Protestant theologian Ernst Troeltsch (1865–1923) nearly a century ago, "for all its striving after exactitude, objectivity, and minuteness of investigation, ... [is] constantly obliged to come back to present experience. The present continually hovers before the backward-looking glance, because it is by the aid of analogies drawn from the life of to-day – however little this may be consciously before the mind – that we reach the causal explanation of the events of the past."[23] We are as much a part of our past as it is of us.

Two purposes, one goal. Like Buridan's ass the historian shuttles back and forth between two equally desirable objects, lured at once by a hunger to understand the past as reported by those who lived it and by a thirst to explain it comprehensibly to one's own age. Getting the events right and embedding the personalities and events correctly in the proper settings should make the past understandable by putting us outside ourselves and allowing us to converse with those long dead. Finding out why

21 Arthur J. Quinn, *A New World: An Epic of Colonial America from the Founding of Jamestown to the Fall of Quebec*, 2.
22 H. C. Erik Midelfort, *A History of Madness in Sixteenth-Century Germany*, 3.
23 Ernst Troeltsch, *Protestantism and Progress: The Significance of Protestantism for the Rise of the Modern World*, 17.

the story should matter then drives us back to our own time, when we see how our times are similar to and dissimilar from times past. Ranke said the same thing in the words of his own day: "Out of the distance of the centuries, we come to know the great combinations that lie within things; acting in present time, however, we cannot depend on this knowing."[24]

24 Ranke, *Deutsche Geschichte*, vol. 4: 50.

2

Shapes of the German Lands

Although the Roman empire once was very powerful, its condition and strength began gradually to decline. It was therefore indicated that, following its translation to the Germans and with the passage of time, the empire should be supplied with special bulwarks and be fortified with princes ...

Peter von Andlau

One morning in the year 1338 as the future Emperor Charles IV lay sleeping, a young knight woke him with the cry, "Sire, get up! The Last Day has arrived, for the whole world is covered with locusts!"[1] Charles arose, dressed, went out to see how large the swarm was, and rode nearly thirty miles without coming to its end. Ten years later, a tremendous earthquake rocked the eastern Alps. A report from Villach in Carinthia said that the castle, monastery, churches, and all the city's walls and towers had collapsed; the earth opened up and poured out water and sulfur; at least 5,000 people had perished. The plague (Black Death) that followed close on this disaster raged so fiercely in Vienna, "that in a single day 1,200 bodies were buried in St. Colman's cemetery. . . . The great mortality was blamed on the Jews, and . . . the common people rose up in the towns of Stein and Krems . . . seized the Jews, and killed them all."[2] At Strasbourg, too, on the western edge of the Empire, Jews were rounded up and killed, and their kinsmen were forbidden ever to reside in the city again. Across the Empire, across Christendom, a declension had begun, the longest and most intense in European history.

If the fourteenth and fifteenth centuries formed an "autumn of the Middle Ages," in Johan Huizinga's (1872–1945) memorable phrase, upon it followed not winter but a new spring. The Black Death and the early Renaissance were not contradictory but complementary forces, companions which stood side by side at the greatest watershed of premodern European history. The plague broke a paralysis in Europe's capacity to improve the ways it produced its goods and promoted new ways more admissive of further development. In short, the patient emerged from the sickness "healthier, more

---

1 Hartmut Boockmann, *Stauferzeit und spätes Mittelalter: Deutschland 1125–1517. Das Reich und die Deutschen*, 228.
2 Karl Brunner and Gerhard Jaritz, *Landherr, Bauer, Ackerknecht. Der Bauer im Mittelalter: Klischee und Wirklichkeit*, 124–5.

energetic, and more creative than before."[3] Then came "the long fifteenth century," when "not only the stars but the whole realm of human society and nature could be investigated, as it were, with new eyes."[4] It was an age of no longer and not yet, a time when social patterns and customs began to assume their early modern forms.

I. TOPOGRAPHY – THE LAY OF THE LAND

The polity known as the the Holy Roman Empire lay at the heart of a Christendom that was beginning to become Europe. It was not "Germany," which was just one name among several names for an agglomeration of lands whose peoples spoke forms of "the German tongue" (*Gezünge*), a word commonly used to translate the Latin "nation" (*natio*).[5] For the lands themselves the common name was a plural, "German lands" (*deutsche Landen*), and a singular form, "German nation" (*deutsche Nation*) did not appear until the later fifteenth century, and then as a name for the body of Imperial estates (*Reichsstände*), just then in the springtime of their early modern consolidation. This linguistic shift "owed more to the artifice of high politics than to any organic growth of a popular national consciousness."[6]

The medieval Holy Roman Empire was not a country but the apex of a universal monarchy called "Christendom," within which dwelt the feudal German kingdom. Head of both was the German king, who was elected "King of the Romans" by his chief vassals, and became by virtue of papal coronation at Rome the putative successor (in the West) to the ancient Roman emperors. The relationships between the two polities – the universal, sacral Empire and the particular, feudal kingdom – were as murky to contemporaries as they have ever since remained.

As the ideal form of Christendom the Holy Roman Empire had no boundaries; as a sacral shell of the German kingdom it did have boundaries, though no one knew precisely where they ran. Very roughly, around 1400 the Empire stretched from the North and Baltic Seas to central Italy, and its shape is better imagined than described. Our best perch for a bird's eye view of it lies high above the St. Gothard massif in the Central Alps between the modern Swiss cantons of Uri and Ticino, where today the railway from Amsterdam, Cologne, Frankfurt, and Zurich plunges into a long tunnel headed for Milan, Florence, and Rome. Facing northward on this perch, at our backs to the south lies Imperial Italy – Piedmont, Lombardy, and Tuscany, but not Venice; to the west, on our left hand, are the lands of the old Burgundian kingdom – Savoy, Burgundy, and Provence – stretching all the way to the Rhone river; and to the east, on our right, lie the lands that today comprise the modern republics of Austria and Slovenia.

Northward from this same vantage point the German lands proper (lands of German "tongues") unfold as far as the northern seas. Downward they roll from the Alps into the tremendous basins of the north-tending Rhine and the east-tending Danube, which together form the great L-shaped aorta of the Empire's old-settled heartlands. To the left, the Rhine's upper tributaries coil out of the Central Alps, unite in Lake Constance (on the modern Swiss-German border), and plunge westward to

---

3 David Herlihy, *The Black Death and the Transformation of the West*, ed. Samuel K. Cohn Jr., 81.
4 Heiko A. Oberman, *The Two Reformations: The Journey from the Last Days to the New World*, 8.
5 As distinguished from the Romance speakers (*Welsche*) to the west and south. The sources are silent about a corresponding linguistic demarcation against the Slavic speakers of the east.
6 Tom Scott, "Germany and the Empire," 340.

Basel, where the river bends rightward to become the greatest highway between Europe's south and its north. Beyond the Rhine, the Empire stretches westward across Alsace and Lorraine's plateau to the old French kingdom's borders. To the right is the basin of the Danube, which rises in the Black Forest near the Rhine and flows eastward across Upper Swabia[7] and Bavaria. At Passau (today on the German-Austrian border) it enters Austria headed for Vienna, Hungary, and the Black Sea. The Alps, the Rhine, and the Danube are the three defining features of the Empire's old heartlands.

To the north in the middle distance, the Main River loops lazily across the line of sight, headed from the Bohemian border westward across the tops of Bavaria and Swabia to join the Rhine near Mainz. Beyond it the land begins to climb again into the Central Highlands, which dribble eastward across modern Germany's waist from west of the Rhine to break on Bohemia's snout and split into the northern and southern mountain ranges that cradle this kingdom. This middle belt of wooded uplands separates the great southern river basins from the northern plains, except in the west, where the Rhine, jogging westward at Mainz, pierces the Central Highlands to emerge on the northern plains near Cologne and begin its final descent to the North Sea.

If we rise high enough to see over the Central Highlands, our gaze sweeps across the tremendous plain that spans the distance from the Rhine delta eastward to the Polish kingdom and beyond. Ground flat by great ice sheets in the deeps of time, it forms the transition zone between central and northern Europe. From its western edge, dominated by the Rhine and its tributaries, the plain's eastward line of march is riven by the lesser but still mighty streams – Ems, Weser, Elbe, and Oder – that drain the Central Highlands' northern slopes and flow northwestward, parallel to the Rhine and down to the seas. At or near their mouths sit the great northern ports – Amsterdam, Bremen, Hamburg, Lübeck, and Danzig – that turn their backs to their hinterlands and their faces across the seas toward London, Bruges, Copenhagen, Visby, and Riga. The northern plain is topographically the least diverse of the German lands' three principal zones, a vast region that pushes eastward over the River Elbe into the great spaces of the Slavic- and Baltic-speaking east.

A huge country, this geomorphologically three-zoned realm, but how huge? Even without the French-speaking far southwest and Imperial Italy, in its narrower sense of the German kingdom alone, until the Polish-Lithuanian Commonwealth formed in 1569, it was Western Christendom's largest country. The Empire was approximately the size (though not the shape) that would be the German state in 1937. A more historically correct sense of its extent, however, can be expressed in travel times, then the only meaningful measurement of distance. Around 1300 a Dominican friar from Colmar in Alsace estimated that in four weeks one could cross Germany, from the Alps to the sea, or from Fribourg (in western Switzerland) to Vienna.[8]

---

7   In Central Europe, "upper" and "lower" refer to topography, not to the orientation of the map. Upper Alsace lies south, because upstream, of Lower Alsace; Upper Franconia lies eastward of Lower Franconia, for the same reason; and Upper Austria lies westward of Lower Austria. Some lands, such as Bavaria, are divided into Upper and Lower by altitude rather than the fall of rivers, while the toponymically anomalous Upper and Lower Swabia lie in different river basins (the Danube and Rhine respectively).

8   Fribourg (German: Freiburg im Üchtland) is a bilingual city-state that joined the Swiss Confederation in the 1450s. It is to be distinguished from Freiburg im Breisgau, a city lying north of Basel on the Rhine's east bank. Since the fifteenth century the latter place belonged to the Habsburgs as part of Outer Austria.

It is not easy to imagine, in the modern world of sovereign states and precisely marked boundaries, polities whose bounds were known so vaguely that today the historian can scarcely beat them. The Empire's western boundary ran from the North Sea southward between the core of modern France and the Empire's western tier of provinces – Lorraine, Burgundy, Savoy, the Dauphiné, and Provence, the latter two of which by 1400 had already been lost to France.

In the south lay the greatest discrepancy between the Empire's legal and its real boundary. In law Imperial Italy embraced the Po River basin (excluding Venice) and Tuscany, but in fact German rulers' attempts to command these rich lands' obedience had long been desultory and episodic. The Empire's practical boundary on the south ran between Switzerland and Lombardy in the west and between the Austrian lands (including South Tyrol and Gorizia) and Venetian territory in the east.

The Empire's long eastern boundary was its most complex. From a point on the Adriatic coast it ran northeastward between the kingdom of Hungary and the Habsburg lands of Carniola, Styria, and Lower Austria. Just above Bratislava/Lemberg (the capital of modern Slovakia), the frontier crossed the Danube and followed the eastern boundary of the Bohemian crownland of Moravia (today the eastern part of the Czech Republic). Bohemia, an independent kingdom, was also an Imperial fief, though its practical ties to the Empire were much reduced by a great revolt in the first half of the fifteenth century. Moving on northward, the Empire included the Bohemian crownlands of Silesia and Lusatia (now southwestern Poland), while the lands ruled by the Teutonic Order in Prussia and Livonia were not of the German kingdom but were closely allied politically to the Empire.

The Empire's northern boundary was its simplest. It followed the Baltic coast westward to the Jutland peninsula, which it crossed between the counties of Holstein to the south and Schleswig to the north (both in modern Germany). It then moved westward along the North Sea coast to the western edge of the Rhine delta to include most of the modern states of the Netherlands, Belgium, and Luxembourg. Most of these Low Countries (hence "Netherlands") lay in both the German kingdom and the Empire, from which they were detached legally in 1548 and politically a century later.

2. LANGUAGES

If the variety of its landscapes distinguished the Empire, so, too, did its linguistic diversity. Languages formed the German lands' oldest template. This Tower of Babel straddled the linguistic boundary zones between Germanic and Romance tongues in the west and between Germanic and Slavic ones in the east. While the realm's heartlands spoke forms of Low and High German, its borderlands spoke French-related tongues in the southern Netherlands, Luxembourg, bits of western Alsace, Lorraine, Imperial Burgundy, and Savoy; Romansh in Graubünden, Vorarlberg, and Tyrol; Lombard dialects of Italian in Graubünden, Ticino/Tessin, and South Tyrol; Slovene in Carinthia and Carniola; Czech, Lusatian, and Sorbian in the central eastern sector; and Kashubian and Polabian, among other tongues, in the northeastern lands. Yiddish was spoken in pockets across much of the Empire, and, after gypsies arrived just before 1500, so was Romany.

Spoken German, like the German lands themselves, existed only in the plural. Very long ago the German tongues had consolidated into three distinct zones: High

German (Swabian-Alemannic and Austro-Bavarian) in the south; Middle German (Frankish and Hessian in the west, Thuringian and Saxon in the east); and Low German (Netherlandish or Dutch in the west, Low Saxon in the east). While the medieval court poets had sung in a courtly language, today called "Middle High German," from 1350, a new written standard, "Early New High German," began to emerge in the south. Shortly after 1400 the Austrian preacher Ulrich von Pottenstein (ca. 1360–1417) wrote of his catechism, "I have chosen to write in the common style of the German language, as it is spoken in our land. For my book, and the teaching within it, are rendered in simple words, just like those one should use in preaching . . . the language of the land is much more useful for the common people than the learned German that scholars know."[9] This "common style of German," which developed in an area defined by the cities of Nuremberg, Eger/Cheb, Würzburg, and Regensburg, was adopted by the Imperial chancery in 1464 and by the Saxon chancery as well. Martin Luther, though he by no means invented the new written standard, did a great deal to spread and standardize it. "I have no special language of my own," he writes, "I use the common German language, so that both High and Low Germans may understand me equally well. In speech I follow the Saxon chancery which is imitated by all the princes and kings of Germany."[10] The invention around 1450 of printing with movable type promoted the new standard's spread. By 1600 this southern speech completed its invasion of the German north, from which only one form of Low German, Netherlandish (Low Frankish), escaped to grow into modern Dutch. Otherwise, in writing and in print the triumph of New High German was total.

Of the Empire's non-Germanic tongues, only one developed and sustained its own written form. Czech, written since the thirteenth century, was never threatened by competition with German. This was not the case for a number of unwritten West Slavic tongues – Sorbian, Polabian, and Kashubian – and Prussian, a Baltic tongue. Slovene, a South Slavic tongue, acquired a written form in the sixteenth century and maintained itself in Carinthia and Carniola, though it died out in neighboring Styria. Romansh, a Romance remnant tongue, was then making its last stand in Vorarlberg, though the lack of a central state in the neighboring Graubünden enabled it to survive there. Yiddish, which also had acquired a written form, survived as well.

3. THE CHURCH

The Church formed, except for language, the oldest human geography of the German lands. It was older than the Holy Roman Empire, even older than the German kingdom. The Church's original geography encompassed the saints in their shrines – the presence of saints' relics in every altar made a shrine of every church – and the monks and nuns in their monasteries. By 1000 the German lands had acquired a second religious geography by virtue of their organization into provinces and dioceses.

These templates mapped a sacred geography of the German kingdom unconnected to the religious character of the Imperial monarchy. The emperor acquired his special role in the Church by virtue not of his ordination as deacon during his

9 Robert James Bast, *Honor Your Fathers: Catechisms and the Emergence of a Patriarchal Ideology in Germany, c. 1400–1600*, 11n. 39.
10 Martin Luther, *D. Martin Luthers Werke. Kritische Gesamtausgabe. Tischreden*, vol. 1: 524.

royal coronation but of the conferral during his Imperial coronation of the office of protector of Christendom. The latter, not the former, stood at the center of the medieval contests between popes and emperors, for even the outspoken Pope Innocent III (r. 1198–1216) recognized the distinction and did not claim authority over Germany as a feudal kingdom. "Thus we recognize," he wrote, "that the right and power of electing the king [of Germany] who afterwards is to be promoted to the imperial office belongs to the princes." Still, "the right and authority of examining the persons elected to the kingship and who is to be promoted to the imperial office belongs to us who anoints, consecrates, and crowns him."[11]

The Imperial church was older by far than the Empire's organization into the feudal principalities and their descendants, the dynastic territorial states. When the states began to emerge from the old patrimonial principalities around 1500, the Empire's ecclesiastical organization was already more than 500 years old. Nearly complete by 1000, this religious geography changed little – except for losses to the Protestants – until the nineteenth century. In its largest conjecturable configuration, the Imperial church comprised the nine provinces of Mainz, Cologne, Trier, Salzburg, Besançon, Bremen, Magdeburg, arguably Prague (since around 1350 seat of a separate Bohemian province), and, by association, Riga.[12]

Neither rhyme nor rule determined the provinces' sizes and configurations. Around 1400 Mainz contained eleven suffragan sees, Salzburg eight, Cologne six, and Magdeburg five, while Trier and Bremen had three, and Besançon and Prague but two each. Five dioceses were exempt (directly under Rome), and nine others lay in five provinces[13] that were neither Imperial nor "German" in any sense. Sorting the Imperial dioceses by principal spoken languages shows that six were entirely French speaking, three mixed French and German, three Italian, three Italian and German, one Danish and German, seven Slavic and German, and the rest German only.

Although the diocese as conceived by the Church's law was perhaps Christendom's most uniformly organized unit of authority, Imperial dioceses varied wildly in size and structure. During the High Middle Ages the larger and middling dioceses had grown subunits, archdeaneries and deaneries, of which the archdeanery of Xanten (in Cologne), with its five deaneries and 148 parishes, may have been typical. The extremes are represented by huge Constance, which divided into ten archdeaneries, sixty-six deaneries, and around 3,000 parishes, and tiny Chiemsee with only a paltry six parishes.

While the Imperial church's bishops served, as did those of other kingdoms, the Church Universal, with its visible apex at Rome, most also played roles in the Empire's temporal governance, which bishops in other lands did not possess.[14] Since

---

11　James Muldoon, *Empire and Order: The Concept of Empire, 800–1800*, 81.

12　In the Church a "province" was (and is) a grouping of dioceses under the jurisdiction of an archbishop (called in this respect a "metropolitan"), who also possesses spiritual jurisdiction over his own diocese (an "archdiocese"). The other bishops in his province are his "suffragans," and appeals from their courts go to his court, from which appeal can be made to Rome. In addition, a few dioceses (called "exempt") stand directly under papal jurisdiction. The "auxiliary bishop" (*Weihbischof*) possesses full sacramental powers (*ordo*) but no jurisdiction (*iurisdictio*) of his own. In practice, many of the sacramental and pastoral duties were performed by bishops of this latter type. This organization differed in only minor features across the lands of western Christendom.

13　Rheims, Tarentaise Aquileia, Gniezno, and Lund.

14　Although not as distinctly as is often assumed. Bishops in some other kingdoms retained at least vestiges of temporal authority, and in France this amounted in some cases to the possession of high justice (capital crimes).

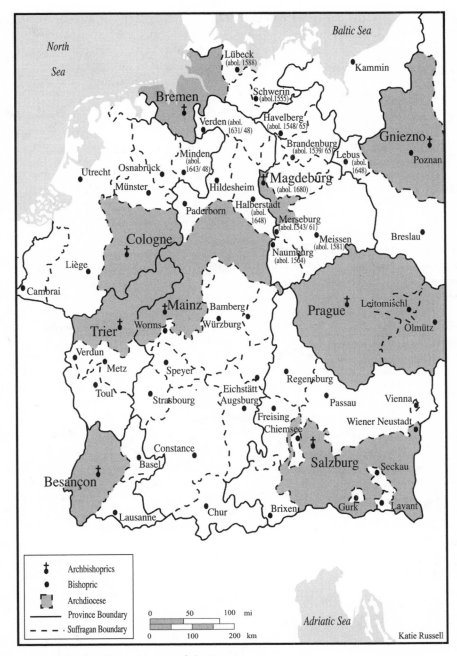

Map 3. Ecclesiastical Organization of the Empire, ca. 1500

the tenth century the emperors had conferred on Imperial bishops lands in fief and later the title of Imperial prince. This kind of spiritual-temporal fusion, widely known in earlier centuries, survived only as remnants in most other Christian kingdoms. It remained the great distinctive mark of the Imperial church until the Empire's end in 1803. Of the nine Imperial archbishops and sixty-eight bishops, only one archbishop and sixteen bishops held neither lands in fief, the princely title, nor (since the fifteenth century) a seat in the Imperial Diet (*Reichstag*).

4. GERMAN LANDS, GERMAN STATES

The fifteenth-century "German lands" were not territorial principalities, much less were they polities, not to speak of "states" in any sense of the word. Most venerable, because they descended from the ancient tribal duchies, were the "four pillars of the Empire": Bavaria, Saxony, Swabia, and Franconia. Of these only Bavaria developed into a principality and then a territorial state bearing the same name on roughly the same site. The late medieval Saxon duchy lay not in ancient Saxony – Westphalia and the lands eastward to the Lower Elbe – but upstream in the middle reaches of the Elbe basin. Swabia and Franconia, both well-defined ethnolinguistic regions to this day, disappeared from the Empire's political map, though not from its collective memories. The duchy of Swabia became extinct in 1266; that of Franconia survived only as a relatively empty title claimed by the bishop of Würzburg. Other lands, notably Alsace, Lorraine, Westphalia, Hesse, and Thuringia, retained some of their Carolingian shapes through the medieval era and beyond but corresponded in shape (as distinct from name) to no principality. The opposite can be said of the archduchy of (Upper and Lower) Austria and the duchies of Styria, Carinthia, and Carniola, which retained their dynastic (Babenberg, then Habsburg) shapes into the modern era.

By around 1200 the German kingdom had grown into a thoroughly feudal monarchy. Organized no longer into tribal duchies but by the institution of vassalage, its lands great and small were now being held in fief from the reigning king in return for loyalty and military service. Although these holdings swiftly became hereditary, frequent extinctions of noble lineages in the male line made for a brisk migration of lands, rights, and titles from extinct to living families. Many leading lineages, many descended from Carolingian counts, had received from Emperor Frederick II (r. 1212–50) the title of "Imperial prince" in addition to whatever older titles they bore: "duke," "margrave," "landgrave," or, simply, "prince." Their descendants, superior in prestige to other nobles, evolved into the ruling dynasties of the institutionalized territorial states of early modern times. Hardly more than a dozen such dynasties survived into the fifteenth century.

Stable, heritable, and increasingly institutionalized dynastic states began to take shape in the German lands during the fifteenth and sixteenth centuries. They lay across the kingdom with a distinct gradient: larger in the east (Bavaria, Saxony, Brandenburg, Mecklenburg, and Pomerania), smaller in the old Imperial heartlands of the south and west, where intensively networked swarms of small lordships, prelacies, and free cities confined dynastic territorial expansion. Very few old comital lineages of the heartlands formed significant territories. Württemberg, raised to a duchy in 1495, was an exception; Nassau, but for its many partitions, might have been another.

The nationalist historians of an earlier age created the notion of "German particularism" for the princely territorial states and lesser members of the Holy Roman Empire in early modern times. In their minds, particularism was a medieval mortgage on the German future, a bogeyman that haunted the Germans' quest for a unified, national state. The term is misleading on two counts. First, institutionalized territorial states developed out of the patrimonial principalities of earlier times only in the course of the fifteenth and sixteenth centuries. They were therefore coeval with the revitalized monarchy and institutionalized Imperial governance of early modern times. Second, these states by no means simply displaced the old German lands, which, even when no longer politically constituted, retained a virtual life in speech, memory, and imagination. Around 1500, when German humanist scholars first tried to map "Germany," they construed the old German lands as zones of common language, customs, and traditions.[15] Such units offered a more stable basis for thinking about the whole than did the fragile, shifting dynastic territories. In an important sense, the lands were the constituting elements of "Germany," which humanists saw as a family of homelands whose shapes, character, and qualities remained stable no matter who might be ruling them. The idea's chief promoter was Conrad Bickel (better known as Conrad Celtis, 1459–1508), son of a Franconian vintner from near Schweinfurt in Franconia. He popularized it in an unfinished, ethnohistorical survey, *On the Fame of Germany*, which he composed to advance the reputation and honor of "Germany." Werner Rolevinck (1425–1502), a farmer's son from Laer in Westphalia who became a Carthusian monk at Cologne, devoted an entire book to the praise of his native "Saxony," a name he used in the old sense for the northwestern land of Westphalia. "I don't know why it is," Rolevinck mused, "that in a foreign place my thoughts dwell happily time and again in Westphalia, my homeland, as though it were – incredible as that may seem – the grandest and richest of all lands."[16] Not polities but homelands, Westphalia and the others outlived every dynasty and state that had colonized their landscapes.[17]

Much larger, less definable unities overshadowed the German lands. The very plasticity of their names bespoke the intensity of local and regional identities. By 1500 there were "the Empire," "the German Nation," and "Germany," no one of which was quite identical with another, nor was any uncontested. In popular usage, happily untroubled by a need for precision, the Empire was sometimes spoken of as a discrete region. Before 1500 "the Empire" meant above all the south and the west, those regions where the medieval monarchy put down its roots. In those days, a traveler from Hamburg, Stettin, or Leipzig to Cologne, Ulm, or Nuremberg journeyed "into the Empire," to which the great territories on and over the Elbe River were not reckoned.[18] For Saxony, at least, this all changed during the age of reformations, when the much closer political ties that arose from the Reformation, plus the

---

15 I use the term "humanist" in the sense associated with the Renaissance, meaning scholars who strove to meet the new, Italian standard of Latin and of learning about ancient Rome and Greece.

16 Werner Rolevinck, *De Laude antiquae Saxoniae nunc Westphaliae dictae/Ein Buch zum Lobe Westfalens des alten Sachsenlandes*, 8–9.

17 This durability warns against putting too much faith in historical maps of the Holy Roman Empire, most of which present early modern German history in terms of an inevitable evolution of the territorial states out of a bewilderingly diverse past.

18 Karlheinz Blaschke, *Sachsen im Zeitalter der Reformation*, 126.

many meetings of the Imperial Diet and other assemblies, bound old heartlands and newer German lands much more closely together. In law, of course, they had already possessed common status under the supreme office of Christendom, the authority and dignity of which the popes – so the story ran – had long ago conferred on the Germans.

By the later fifteenth century, as the new Imperial governance began to take shape, a new term, "the German Nation," emerged. It denoted not a nation in the medieval or the modern sense, but a collection of particular groups of Imperial subjects in their corporate identity as "the Imperial estates" (*Reichsstände*). These princes, prelates, and cities possessed the right to sit and vote in the Diet, and before 1500 they began to advance their corporate claim to cogovernance with the emperor. They were held in some vague sense to represent all the inhabitants of what the Golden Bull had in 1356 called "the German lands": "The Holy Roman Empire was bestowed by popes, cardinals, and other powerful persons on the German land, when it became evidently true that no land of Christendom was more worthy, and there was no more eminent nation and language or a more just people."[19]

Another name which appeared around this time, "Germany," referred at least notionally to this same body of persons. It lay where "Germans" lived, but who was a German? In earlier times this name had expressed the audible difference between a speaker of some form of German and speakers of any Romance tongue. Just as a noble was one whom other nobles recognized to be noble, a German was one whom other Germans recognized to be German. At need this flexible, ambiguous notion could be applied in a very wide sense. The Strasbourg magistrate Jacob Sturm (1489–1553) once referred to Imperial Chancellor Nicholas Perrenot de Granvelle (1486–1550) as "by heritage a German."[20] Granvelle, a Franche-Comtois, was an Imperial subject but a French speaker. Sturm may well have been thinking of ancient Burgundians, speakers of a Germanic tongue, but this, too, suggests a great latitude in his use of the term "German."

Who were "Germans" was one question, another was where "Germany" lay. In 1512 the Nuremberg schoolmaster Johannes Cochlaeus (1479–1552), wrote that "Germany" was bounded "on the south by Italy and Dalmatia, on the east by Hungary and Poland, on the north by the Baltic Sea and the North Sea, and on the west by France and the British [North] sea."[21] These boundaries do describe the Holy Roman Empire of his time, not in its virtual universality but in the real political guise that was just beginning to be called "the Holy Roman Empire of the German Nation." Although Cochlaeus did not settle the question, he and other geographers recognized that contemporary Germany was identical with neither ancient Germany nor the Holy Roman Empire. The geographers did come to recognize the contrast between old-settled lands of the south and west, the *Germania* of the Romans, and the new-settled lands of the east and northeast. A generation or so after Cochlaeus, the Hessian geographer-pastor Johann Rauw (d. 1600) employed the metaphor of city and suburb to make this point. "The German landscape," he wrote in 1597, "makes me think of a great and splendid city with its suburbs, the city itself located within its walls and

19 Ernst Schubert, *Einführung in die Grundprobleme der deutschen Geschichte im Spatmittelalter*, 25.
20 Thomas A. Brady, *Protestant Politics: Jacob Sturm (1489–1553) and the German Reformation*, 10.
21 Johannes Cochlaeus, *Brevis Germanie descriptio (1512) mit der Deuschlandkarte des Erhard Etzlaub von 1501*, 6–7. He was later a principal critic and the first biographer of Martin Luther.

fortifications, the suburbs are without." While all countries where German is spoken "are called German Countries . . . the old, true, real Germany remains within the walls, that is, within her ancient boundaries. The other German regions, however, which are located beyond the Danube and the Rhine, are like suburbs in that they became attached to the real and old Germany, but are not by rights a part of it."[22] This distinction between "real and old" Germany of ancient times and the colonial Germany of medieval times maintained its significance until the eighteenth century.

5. POPULATIONS, ECONOMIES, SOCIETIES

During the fourteenth and fifteenth centuries, the societies of the German lands began to acquire the characteristics they would retain through the early modern era. To the historical demographer they form a subset of what is called "the old European population regime," the patterns that until the eighteenth century governed births, deaths, and marriages of Europeans west of a line drawn from Riga to Trieste. "In the midst of life, behold," sang a Carolingian hymn, "Death has girt us round."[23] Every second adult lost a spouse before ten years of marriage, and a person of fifty was considered "old." When the great killing plagues attacked a population weakened by undernourishment, mortality could quickly multiply by ten- or twenty-fold. The ranks of the living were replenished, to be sure, but their potential fertility was restrained by a set of characteristics called the "European marriage pattern": "one married couple per home; no marriage without a home; no babies outside of marriage."[24] Marriage came late (age 23–27 for women, later for men), and about 10 percent of adults never married. Those who did were expected to separate from both sets of parents and establish a new household, which might include servants and more rarely other resident kin.

The first truly solid evidence for this pattern in the German lands dates to the eighteenth century, but the imprecise and fragmentary evidence from earlier times does suggest that it went back at least to the post-Black Death era. The population movements are outlined by the figures in Table 1.

Table 1. Population of the German Lands, 1300–1800 (in millions)

	1300	1350	1400	1450	1500	1550	1600	1650	1700	1750	1800
Germany	14		9	8–9	9–10	13–14	16–17	10?	14.1	17.5	22
Germany + Austria + Switzerland					11.6		19.2		17.4		26.8

Source: Robert W. Scribner, ed., *Germany: A New Social and Economic History, 1450–1630*, 38–43.

22 Gerald Strauss, *Sixteenth-Century Germany: Its Topography and Topographers*, 41.
23 "Media vita in morte sumus," attributed to Notker (ca. 900), put into German by Martin Luther (1524), and quoted here from the English of Catherine Winkworth (1855).
24 Jan de Vries, "Population," in Thomas A. Brady, Heiko A. Oberman, and James D. Tracy, eds., *Handbook of European History, 1400–1600: Late Middle Ages, Renaissance, Reformation*, vol. 1: 27.

On the eve of the Black Death's arrival, the Empire contained perhaps some 15 million people, around 12 million of whom lived in its German-speaking core lands.[25] By 1450 their numbers had dropped, largely because of epidemic diseases, to something like 12 and 9 million respectively. Then they began to rise again, and by 1500 the Empire contained more than 15.5 million people, very near its pre-plague level. This figure, which includes about 2,350,000 in the Imperial Low Countries, 2,000,000 in Bohemia, and 600,000 in Switzerland, comprised about a quarter of Europe's population. The recovery continued until the mid-sixteenth century – a boom unprecedented since the eleventh and twelfth centuries – but then it slackened and plunged during the Thirty Years War into the second of the two demographic catastrophes that frame this narrative.

In terms of population, therefore, the fifteenth century saw the beginnings of the recovery that replenished the German lands over the next 100 years. The rapid growth did not go unnoticed. Sebastian Franck (1499–1542) wrote in his *German Chronicle* (1538),

> The lands supply plenty of people to everywhere, and yet there is such a surplus that villages and towns run together . . . if God sends no war, and there is no plague, we will once more, as in earlier times, have to admit new people only by lot, or send them out in some other way, just as the gypsies had to leave and seek out other lands. . . . Now, although 100,000 peasants died in the rebellion [1525], so it is said, no one needs new inhabitants, but every hamlet is so full that no one else can enter. In all of Germany it is the same, child upon child. . . .[26]

Within a generation appeared typical signs of flagging growth: exhausted reserves of untilled land, growing proletariats in town and countryside, and widespread overexploitation of the land. These causes, intensified by the cooler mean temperatures and wetter summers of what is called the "Little Ice Age," pushed down crop yields, worsened nutrition, and increased susceptibility to disease. By 1600 the gradient of density measured in households per km^2 ran from the southwest – 10 on the western edge of the Black Forest and 8 in the duchy of Württemberg – downward to the northeast – 2 in the duchy of Mecklenburg and 1 in eastern Pomerania. By the later sixteenth century, such is the overall impression, the German lands were approaching their maximum sustainable levels of population, given the existing social structure and methods of exploitation. Their populations were therefore becoming more vulnerable to disease and famine.

Population trends and economic growth and decline were closely interdependent. The German lands contained three basic types of economic regions: primarily agrarian, mixed agriculture and manufacturing, and mining and manufacturing. In the primarily agrarian region 80 percent of the population was engaged in farming and stock-raising, highly interdependent enterprises. Livestock supplied the farmers with motive power, manure, meat, and milk, and, in some northern regions such as Frisia and the Mecklenburg plains between the Elbe and Oder rivers, large-scale raising of cattle made possible intensive "perpetual" production of grain, chiefly rye. Between

---

25 Demographers commonly use for historical purposes Germany within the boundaries of 1914 (=540,818 km²), which corresponds pretty well to the Empire's German-speaking core around 1300.

26 Sebastian Franck, *Germaniae chronicon: Von des gantzen Teutschlands, aller Teutschen völker herkommen, Name, Händeln, Guoten vnd bösen thaten, Reden, Räthen, Kriegen, Sigen, Niderlagen, Stifftungen, Veränderungen der Sitze, Reich, Länder, Religion, Gesatze, Policei, Spraach, völcker und sitten, Vor und nach Christi gebürt, Von Noe bisz auf Carolum V*, aa iiiiv.

this system and the multi-crop rotation of the Netherlands lay many intermediate forms, the regional prevalence of which was a matter of farming experience and the variable dynamics of transport costs and market demand.

The second type of economic landscape depended on a mixture of agriculture and the manufacture of textiles. A classic region of this type lay on the northern shores of Lake Constance, where the cultivation of flax and the manufacture of linens depended both on the damp climate and the production of milk (for bleaching) in neighboring Upper Swabia. The spread of linen-weaving to other regions, notably Westphalia and Flanders, reflected population growth in the northwestern zone of densest urbanization, where it owed much to the organization of a new, proto-capitalist system of dispersed production, called "putting-out" (*Verlagssystem*), and the strict enforcement of production controls.

The third kind of economic landscape, the industrial type, forged the most direct links between resources and economic forms. The forest belt across the Central Highlands, for example, supported the extractive and metal-working industries of Franconia and Hesse, which required abundant timber. Other branches, notably leather and glass, developed in the same belt because of accessibility to minerals and timber. Of course, the discoveries of ore bodies influenced the locations of metal extraction and refining in the most direct conceivable way, but not absolutely. In Thuringia, a major center of copper production, the mining centers lay in the north, but the smelters in the south, close to the timber of the Thuringian Forest and to the trade routes that linked Leipzig, Nuremberg, and Frankfurt.

Within these broad types, the Empire displayed a hierarchy of complexity ranging from traditional forms of mixed agriculture up to the most advanced areas of specialized industrial production. Sometimes, too, the three types overlapped, as they did in Alsace. On the Rhine valley floor throve cereals, wheat and rye for bread, oats for bran, and barley for brewing; on the higher ground sheep grazed in large flocks, providing wool to the local textile industry; further up, sheltered from the western winds, marched the vineyards that produced the Empire's most prized wine; higher yet, the mountain valleys supported dairying and cheese-making; and above them cattle summered and silver miners delved. This complex pattern of economic zones in a small region supported a highly commercialized economy, the centers of which lay in a network of towns capped by Strasbourg, at 20,000 inhabitants one of the Empire's largest cites. Around this metropolis were strewn middling cities, such as Colmar and Hagenau, plus dozens of smaller towns that specialized in cloth and wine. The great vigor and prosperity of this favored land, therefore, rested on neither agriculture nor industry but on a combination of urban and rural economies. Such complex landscapes sustained the peoples of numerous German lands.

6. UNIVERSITIES

The university ranks among the most durable creations of the great twelfth-century wave of institutionalization in Christendom. "Without these 'republics of scholars' essentially formed during the Middle Ages, modern civilization and today's culture are unthinkable."[27] The German lands were latecomers to this enterprise. Two

27   Rainer Müller, *Geschichte der Universität. Von der mittelalterlichen Universitas zur deutschen Hochschule*, 7.

hundred and fifty years elapsed between the founding of Bologna in 1088 and the founding of Prague in 1348 by German masters who had emigrated from Paris. The Luxemburg and Habsburg emperors felt called upon to found universities in the chief cities of their lands, Prague and Vienna, other rulers followed suit, and over the next 300 years (until 1650) some thirty-six institutions of university or near-university rank were established in the German lands (including two in the Bohemian kingdom). Their fortunes waxed and waned, naturally, with good times and bad. The two troughs in the multiplication of universities in the German lands fall in the first half of the fifteenth century, an era of economic depression, and the first half of the sixteenth, when the Protestant reformations temporarily disrupted university life.

The sites of the earliest institutions of higher learning lay at Prague and in the old Imperial heartlands of the south and west, but very soon universities appeared in the remoter northern lands, at Leipzig in 1409 and at Rostock in 1419. Although the Protestant reformation initially depressed the universities, between 1520 and 1650 twenty new universities (11 Protestant, 9 Catholic) joined the seventeen older ones. The swelling network of higher learning both expressed and enhanced the age's tendency to reduce cultural disparities between the old German lands and the new. When Luther came to teach at Wittenberg in 1510, only seven of the seventeen German universities lay north of the Main and east of the Rhine valley; by 1648 these lands housed seventeen of the Empire's thirty-six universities.

The university, it has been said, arose from "the new scientific scholarship of scholasticism" and "the social revolution of the twelfth century," which supplied respectively its methods and its corporate social form and united ecclesiastical with secular learning and professional training.[28] If elsewhere the founding of universities had been largely a clerical affair, in the Empire it became an enterprise of ecclesiastical and lay rulers, for, although chartered by popes, the older German universities owed their foundations to the initiatives of kings and princes, ecclesiastical and secular. The six earliest (1348–1402) were founded by royal dynasties – Prague (Luxemburgs) and Vienna (Habsburg) – or by princes, lay – Heidelberg (Palatine Wittelsbach) – or ecclesiastical – Cologne, Erfurt,[29] and Würzburg. Eight of the next eleven (1409–1502) were founded by lay princes: Leipzig (Saxony), Rostock (Mecklenburg), Greifswald (Pomerania), Freiburg im Breisgau (Habsburg), Ingolstadt (Bavaria), Tübingen (Württemberg), Frankfurt an der Oder (Brandenburg), Wittenberg (Albertine Saxony). Two more owed their establishments to archbishops (Trier, Mainz); and one to a free city (Basel). The fifteenth century witnessed not just a unique (in European terms) multiplication of universities in the German lands but also a "lasting ... incorporation of the university into the administration of the early modern state."[30] This coordination to state formation lessened both the universities' legal autonomy and the initially cosmopolitan forms of their organization, teaching methods, and curricula. The medieval university arose to serve the Church; the early modern university, in the Empire as in other lands, served the State. Rulers often considered a

---

28 Müller, *Geschichte der Universität*, 10: "erstens die 'neue Wissenschaflichkeit der Scholastik' und zweitens die 'soziale Revolution' des 12. Jahrhunderts."
29 Erfurt lay in the archbishop of Mainz's *Hochstift*.
30 Müller, *Geschichte der Universität*, 45.

local university to be an ornament of their authority. "And even if it had no other benefit," a Basel document of 1459 declares, "it should be highly and dearly honored because of what it is."[31]

The universities of the sixteenth and seventeenth centuries were thus less free and cosmopolitan, more disciplined and provincial, than their medieval predecessors had been. While the overall structure of faculties – Arts, Theology, Law, and Medicine – endured, after 1500 important changes in governance and curriculum took place. Professors, ever more commonly laymen, gradually replaced the college of masters as the chief agents of instruction. At the same time, the movement into the German lands of the new Italianate learning, humanism, brought profound changes into the Arts curriculum of the universities themselves. These changes, especially the new standards for Latin, promoted in turn the growth of new and better Latin schools to better prepare pupils for university studies. The curricula that governed their university students continued to evolve until, by the later sixteenth century, the German universities possessed organizations and curricula that would hardly change for the next 200 years. Around 1500 about 6,000 young men were studying in German universities, of which a few, notably Vienna, Cologne, Leipzig, and Erfurt, grew to supra-regional size and standing, while others, such as tiny Freiburg im Breisgau and Greifswald, could boast a mere 100 students each.

The university remained in some deep sense a religious corporation devoted to the love for learning and the reproduction of itself through the training of masters. Contrary to legend, however, most students did not prepare for careers as clergymen. The overall clerical fraction of student bodies declined all through the fifteenth century to about 10 percent of the whole by 1500, by which point Cologne had shrunk from 45 to around 6 percent clergymen. Around 1500, 10 gulden per year – half a master's stipend – was thought sufficient to cover a student's costs, though for those who could not pay, approximately 15 percent on the average, there were cheap or even free residences and remissions of fees. For the most part, however, the costs had to be covered by the student himself, his family, a benefactor, or an ecclesiastical benefice. Around a quarter of the students matriculated in more than one university. Only a few German universities, including Vienna, Leipzig, and Frankfurt an der Oder, organized themselves according to the Paris practice into "nations," groupings based very vaguely on language and lands of origin.

One way in which the late medieval university resembled its modern descendant in fact rather than in myth was that, whatever their love of learning, students prepared themselves for careers in beneficed or salaried positions. The growth of universities in the German lands multiplied the corps of men educated to serve Church and State. Among the ranks of university men were most of the leading advocates of Church reform and the officials of most territorial and urban regimes. In sum, the spread of higher education in the German lands before 1500 promoted the formation of a learned class that was less cosmopolitan and more bound to region and city than had been the itinerant masters and students of earlier institutions. An institution without deep roots and traditions, the university could respond with impressive speed and thoroughness to the devolution of authority and power that so profoundly characterized the passage of the German lands into the early modern era.

---

31 Arno Seifert, "Das höhere Schulwesen – Universitäten und Gymnasien," 215.

7. PRINTING — THE GERMAN ART

The historical significance of printing with moveable type is difficult to overestimate. It was no coincidence that "this invention, which step-by-step placed the entire system of communications on a new, boundlessly expanded basis, made the Reformation possible and pushed forward the peculiar development of European culture and society, was made in Germany."[32] Proud contemporaries celebrated German inventiveness and detected printing's potential. "More than any other invention or fruit of the spirit," wrote the Alsatian humanist Jakob Wimpheling (1450–1528), "we Germans can take pride in the art of printing, which has raised us up as the new spiritual bearers of Christian doctrines, of all science divine and profane, to be the benefactors of all humanity. What a different vigor now stirs in all classes of people? Who does not wish to remember with thanks the first founder and promoter of this art?"[33] This man, Johann Gutenberg (ca. 1400–67/68) of Mainz, was well aware of what he had begun. The colophon of the *Catholicon*, a Latin reference work printed (perhaps by Gutenberg himself) at Mainz in 1460, boasts of the fact with due thanks to God and understandable national pride: "With the help of the Almighty, by Whose will the tongues of youth oft become eloquent, and Who oft reveals to simple folk what He hides from the learned, this excellent book was printed and completed without the use of reed pen, slate pencil, or quill pen." With patriotic fervor the colophon adds that the work appears "in the Year of Our Lord 1460 in the lovely city of Mainz of the famous German nation, which God in His goodness has preferred and glorified with such a bright light of intelligence and a more generous endowment than to other peoples of the earth."[34] Both Gutenberg and Wimpheling believed that this new art would help to spread the Gospel's light among the masses of the laity. The Augsburg printer Günther Zainer (d. 1478) disdained such a noble intention in favor of national pride: "Lest we seem to linger behind the Italians."[35]

In its beginnings printing was truly what it was named, a "German art." It began in and first spread among the great communes of the old heartlands. From Mainz and Strasbourg printing soon spread to Augsburg, Nuremberg, Basel, and Cologne and, from around 1480, into other parts of the Empire. Frequently, the first printing shop in a new place owed its existence to a bishop who wanted liturgical books produced in the new way, as did Rudolf von Scherenberg (b. ca. 1400, r. 1466–95) at Würzburg in 1479. For quite some time other regions were sparsely represented: Leipzig in the central lands, Lübeck in the north, and Breslau in the northeast. In the 1490s, however, the first presses began to operate at Hamburg, Danzig, and Marienburg in Prussia. By 1500 more than sixty presses were producing books in the Empire, a number approached by no other European country.

In the German lands and elsewhere, the printing industry's organization during its first century of operation (1450–1550) replicated Gutenberg's model. Unrestrained by guild regulations, in the print shops the same man usually combined most or all the

---

32 Heinrich Lutz, *Das Ringen um deutsche Einheit und kirchliche Erneuerung. Von Maximilian I. bis zum Westfälischen Frieden 1490–1648*, 80.
33 Lutz, *Das Ringen*, 81.
34 Lutz, *Das Ringen*, 81.
35 Lutz, *Das Ringen*, 82.

requisite crafts of type founder, printer, publisher, editor, and bookseller, and this adventuresome mobility remained a characteristic of the branch. By 1550 the day of the small, itinerant printer was past, as printing, publishing, and bookselling had become established industries requiring stability, capital, managerial skills, and foresight. The era of experimentation gave way to accepted conventional forms, and the entire industry became capital intensive and geographically concentrated. Only one German-speaking city, Basel, continued to rank among the major European centers of the industry, most of which lay in France (Paris, Lyons, Geneva), Italy (Venice, Rome, Florence), and the Low Countries (Antwerp, Amsterdam, Leiden). The anomalous, almost archaic conditions that governed print shops in the enterprise's homelands are reflected in an attempt of the Imperial Diet in 1570 to limit printing to the capitals of princely states, university towns, and larger Imperial cities. This unenforceable legal straightjacket reflects the stagnation of printing in the German lands, one aspect of their more general cultural provincialization.

8. SHAPES OF THE GERMAN LANDS

From this brief overview of the bewildering variation of economic and social conditions, legal boundaries, and jurisdictions, spiritual and temporal, several generalizations may be drawn. First, the German lands were settings of extreme physical, social, economic, and cultural diversity. The imprecise borders, wherever they lay, rarely coincided with any natural feature, nor did topography pose any significant barrier to mobility. The peopling of the lands conformed to the dominant European pattern of a distinct west-east gradient in density of population and in degree of urbanization. The richest, most developed part, the Low Countries, lay on the Empire's northwestern corner, where it enjoyed close commercial ties to western and northern Europe and came under the influence of French language and culture.

Second, the Empire and the German lands had no political or cultural center. Cologne, the largest German-speaking city, was never a royal seat; Prague, Vienna, and Innsbruck were favored residences of still highly itinerant royal courts; and no princely court enjoyed a greater than local significance. Yet the Empire did possess a political culture, if by this term is understood what has been called "political rules of the game." This is a broader meaning of political culture than the one intended by those who coined the phrase, American political scientists of the post-1945 era. It also differs from the modern concept in specific ways: it depends not on ideas or formal representation so much as on implied consent, which on particular occasions could take or be denied symbolic form. The Empire's traditional political culture had formed in an age when "there was – naturally – no monopoly of power, no statutes, no claim to primacy for public organization, no disjunction of public and private, practically no administration and bureaucracy, nor many other things that we have in mind when we think in terms of 'state' or 'public.'"[36] Absent a state, political culture has to be seen as existing simultaneously on several, perhaps many, linked levels, from the local to the universal (Christian) world. The Empire's political culture opened, therefore, both on the life of Christendom and on all lesser theaters of principality, city, and village. Finally, in order to be useful to early modern history, the concept has

36 Gerd Althoff, *Spielregeln der Politik im Mittelalter: Kommunikation in Frieden und Fehde*, 127.

to include the Church, its priests, and the entire system of official religion as a major force in political, that is, public life, for they were all "political" in this broad, flexible sense of the term.[37]

Third, the German lands and the Holy Roman Empire were never isomorphic. There were German lands outside the Empire (notably the German-colonized Baltic region); Imperial lands that were by no stretch of language German (Imperial Italy, Provence, Savoy, and most of Lorraine); and non-German lands of uncertain relationship to the Empire (Bohemia, and Imperial Burgundy or Franche-Comté). Still, by 1400 the Empire was shrinking down onto the German-speaking lands of its core. This creeping merger of Empire and German lands formed the basis of the Holy Roman Empire of the German Nation, which emerged before 1500 as a newly constituted polity governed by monarch and Imperial estates. To a very great degree, the loss of non-German-speaking lands made the new polity possible, for it enhanced the sense of unity of "the German nation" and of "Germany." Yet the process of shrinkage continued, and by 1650 it had torn away the Swiss Confederation, the seventeen provinces of the Netherlands, Imperial Burgundy, and Lorraine. It is not too much to say that the shearing away of the Imperial west made the Empire's domination by eastern dynasties easier and more durable.

Finally, there existed a notion but no concept of a common Germany before the sixteenth century. In 1400 the German speakers lacked a common written language, their churches had no common ecclesiastical governance, and their supreme polity possessed no core lands that might have provided a central base for a strong German state. This diversity, the early modern Empire's hallmark, displays a durability and a resistance to centralization that present a dramatic contrast to contemporary developments in Europe's western kingdoms.

---

37 My view of this concept has been influenced by Renate Dürr's excellent analysis, which emphasizes how it must be altered to apply to early modern societies. Renate Dürr, *Politische Kultur in der Frühen Neuzeit. Kirchenräume in Hildesheimer Stadt- und Landgemeinden 1550–1750*, 27–31.

3

Temporal Estates – Farmers, Traders, Fighters

> Ill fares the land, to hast'ning ills a prey,
> Where wealth accumulates, and men decay;
> Princes and lords may flourish, or may fade;
> A breath can make them, as a breath has made;
> But a bold peasantry, their country's pride,
> When once destroyed, can never be supplied.
>
> Oliver Goldsmith

> With daring aims, irregularly great,
> Pride in their port, defiance in their eye,
> I see the lords of human kind pass by.
>
> Oliver Goldsmith

The concept of estates or orders – functionally distinct, legally defined social groups – shaped the feudal age's social consciousness as fundamentally as the idea of class does that of the capitalist age. Adalbero (d. 1030), an eleventh-century bishop of Laon in the kingdom of West Francia, expressed in a classic form the three orders that comprise what he called "the House of God": those who pray, those who fight, and those who work. Over the next 500 years, Adalbero's "orders" became "estates," a less normative and more descriptive term rooted in the law. The change reflected such long-range trends as the advance of a money economy, greater social mobility, the decay of kinship, and of Christian notions of equality. Some regretted the results. In 1494 the Strasbourg lawyer-poet Sebastian Brant (1457–1521) condemned the decay of social distinctions as contrary to God's providence: "In every land the disgrace is great/ No longer is there anyone/satisfied with his estate."[1] Brant's lament was perhaps untypical of his age, and when, two generations later, a pair of Nurembergers, the poet Hans Sachs (1494–1576) and the designer Jost Ammann (1539–91), inventoried the estates, they did so in a very different mood. Their spiritual estates include only pope, bishop, priest, monk, and nun; the temporal ones range from emperor, king, and prince through physician, apothecary, astronomer, and lawyer, down to the artisanal trades and persons of low degree. "Thus are shown here," Sachs concludes, "a

---

1 Sebastian Brant, *Das Narrenschiff*, 214, lines 60–2.

hundred and fourteen persons/In offices, arts, and crafts."[2] The Ammann-Sachs catalog of estates lacks entirely the sense of the divinely established totality of Bishop Adalbero's "House of God."

These changes in language reflect the fundamental transformation of European societies during the generations that followed the Black Death. The groups that people this book belong to that age, and in all justice each deserves a large book of its own. Here, however, they play roles in a common drama of governance and belief in the German lands. Seen as estates or as classes, both legitimate ways of viewing them, they are somewhat medieval and somewhat modern, but most of all they are groups of people who were born, worked, loved, reproduced, prayed, and died in their own homes, villages, towns, castles, and churches, convents, and cathedrals.

The Church's law recognized its own scheme of social division into clergy and laity, which formed a universalizing counterpart to the particularizing schemes of estates. The laity, as all such schemes recognized, generated both laity and clergy, which is why in this book they come onstage before the clergy does. Here the laity is arrayed in three broad groups – farmers, burghers, and nobles – set in their typical sites of the village, the town, and the castle.

1. "THOSE WHO WORK" – FARMERS

All humanity, as Bishop Adalbero writes, depends on the labor of the farmer, who "gets nothing without suffering" but "supplies with everything, including clothing. . . . For no one could live without the serfs."[3] Between his time and the thirteenth century there occurred a startling change, as "those who work" fissioned into two closely related social groups, farmers (or peasants) and burghers. Together they comprised the commons, called by their social betters "the common man."[4] They undertook the great enterprise of clearing, and planting around villages, and forming towns between 1050 and 1250. They laid the foundations of an early Europe, which ran up against the limits of its expansibility around 1300, with the beginning of the economic disruptions that preceded the Black Death and introduced the late-medieval depression.

After 1400 the German lands began to recover from the previous century's ravaging of populations and production. Perhaps a quarter of the plowland had been abandoned, entire settlements had disappeared. Farm incomes declined, as the prices of food and manufactured goods fell. The changing land to labor ratio nevertheless meant that farmers could move about, find vacant land, settle, and establish households. An undated document from a western German land stipulates that if a stranger asks for land, the mayor shall take him up on his horse and ride out into the land, and when the stranger sees land he wants, he shall dismount and mark the place, whereupon the mayor shall mark off 15 "morgen"[5] for him to farm. Some rural folk headed

---

2 Jost Ammann, *Das Ständebuch: 133 Holzschnitte mit Versen von Hans Sachs und Hartmann Schopper*, iii.
3 Adalbero of Laon, *Carmen ad Robertum regem*, 20–3.
4 "Farmers" and "peasants" refer to the same persons, the former as members of the agrarian community, the latter as dependents of a seigneur. It is a sometimes useful distinction between what they do and what they owe.
5 Wilhelm Abel, *Agricultural Fluctuations in Europe from the Thirteenth to the Twentieth Centuries*, 79. The *morgen* (South German: *juchart*) is conventionally a morning's work of plowing; highly variable but in modern times this covers perhaps about 0.6 acre.

for the towns and cities, others migrated to the lands of seigneurs who, needing tenants, promised to lease on favorable terms.

These farmers worked the land in ways by now quite traditional. In the zones of classic open-field agriculture, farmers plowed, harvested, grazed, and used the woods and waters together, that is, in common, using a technology that went back at least 200 years: rod and chain to measure land, the heavy wheeled plow and the harrow, manuring and marling, the horse collar, the four-wheeled wagon with movable front axle, and complex schemes of crop rotation. In early times their work had been organized into manors, units commanded by noble seigneurs or landlords, and they worked part of the lands (the demesne) for him pursuant to servile obligations and part for themselves and him (as collector of rents and fees) on leases. In the era of the Black Death, however, many landlords gave up demesne farming with servile labor and leased entire manors on more or less secure, hereditary tenures to peasants who paid rents and other dues.

These changes strengthened enormously the rural social fabric and its central formation, the household, usually a coresidential unit formed by a conjugal pair, children, and servants. The household was self-reproducing, and its rhythms depended on the great act of passage in rural life, the moment when the land, its equipment, and domestic authority passed from parents to children. In German the word "house" (*Haus*) means a dwelling, made of wood and wattle, infrequently of wood alone, very rarely of stone, with a roof of straw, earthen floor, dim windows, and wooden beds, benches, tables, and chests. It also means the community the dwelling housed, whose elaborate division of labor allotted house and garden to the woman, fields and woods to the man. An axiom of rural life held that no single man, much less a single woman, could successfully farm alone. The average German village comprised perhaps twelve or so such households and approximately seventy persons in all, bound to one another by ties of consanguinity, affinity, godparent-hood, parish membership, co-ownership, employment, seigneurial obligations, indebtedness, and friendship (or enmity).

Except in the uplands, where dispersed settlement and pastoral economies pre-dominated, rural landscapes were dotted by nucleated villages divided into farmsteads and gardens clustered around a village square and church and protected by a fence that marked the limits of the village's zone of peace. The farmers lived in separate house-holds but cultivated, harvested, and pastured their stock together. Yet they were by no means equal in standing or fortune, for every village was stratified by degrees of wealth and security. At the top stood the strong farmers,[6] who hired labor and sold some, perhaps most, of their crop. Such big fellows formed the economic backbone of many small territories and some whole regions, such as Westphalia and Franconia, and they sometimes passed their farms down intact for generations. Below them stood the middling farmers, the dominant group in every village. A 1486 tax register from the county of Mark, a smallish territory on the Lower Rhine, reveals that two-thirds of the taxpayers were middling men with holdings worth between 20 and 125 gulden. At the bottom were the cottagers, who rented dwelling and garden and supplemented farming with other work, and the landless, who were often the younger, non-inheriting brothers and sisters of the tenants.

6   This Irish term seems precisely suited to those who in German are called "full peasants" (*Vollbauern*).

The decay of seigneurial exploitation via servile labor shifted many tasks to the villagers. One such task was local governance, which gave rise to the "commune" (*Gemeinde*) of all (male) householders, which assembled at least once a year to audit the commune's finances, fix the rotation of croplands, proclaim and record village law, and elect the commune's officers. Everyday business came before a village council of three to twelve members, who oversaw the common tasks of verifying boundaries, providing the fire watch, enforcing weights and measures, and supervising mill, tavern, smithy, and bathhouse. Over all stood the mayor, a peasant elected by his fellows or appointed by the seigneur, who together with the council possessed limited civil and criminal jurisdiction. Communal forms and practices grew directly out of everyday rural life, though their strength might vary from district to district and region to region.

A long-established interpretation of agrarian history tells of a deep divergence between the agrarian landscapes of western and eastern German lands. It holds that while in the western lands the erosion of seigneurial direct management encouraged communal liberties (and princely authority), in the east direct management and production for distant markets favored the concentration of authority in seigneurial hands at the expense of the farmers (and the princes). The long-term consequence is said to have been a German-speaking world – and a Europe – split between a free west and a servile east. Modern research has largely undermined this stark vision of rural Europe. For one thing, the formation of eastern seigneurialism preceded by as much as two or three centuries the rise of intensified commercial agriculture through lords' direct exploitation; for another, the spread of great-estate agriculture was not uniform (and never exclusive) in Transelbia, the lands of the east; further, the expansion of the seigneurialism associated classically with the Prussian Junkers rested on the taking in of waste and the appropriation of jurisdictions long before the seigneurs resorted to the imposition of labor dues. "The peasant with a family farm," one expert sums up, "the three-field system with rotation by course, or the village commune with its management and allocation of pasture, wood, and forest were not crushed east of the Elbe – and neither was peasant resistance."[7] This does imply uniform agrarian conditions across the German lands during the three centuries that followed the coming of the Black Death. The old-settled lands of the German west experienced a high degree of parcelization, heritable tenures, growing peasant access to the market, and stable legal status, if not the full legal freedom suggested by the classic argument. In the eastern lands of Saxony, Brandenburg, Mecklenburg, and Pomerania, by contrast, large estates did form, with or without a new servility, and nobles did retain their political power and stand between the peasants, on the one hand, and marketplace and princely regime, on the other.

Whatever the peasant and his lord had in common, only before God did they stand on an equal footing. To modern students of history, used to dressing economic extraction in the abstract language of the market, feudal extraction appears nakedly abrupt, brutal, and unpredictable. Brutal it certainly was, though the brutality was systemic rather than simply arbitrary. Some seigneurs could boast of good relations with their peasants, but the irreducible fact was that subjection never disappeared. It

7 Tom Scott, *Society and Economy in Germany, 1300–1600*, 183. Transelbia is a name for the lands east of the Elbe River, which the German speakers colonized after the year 1000.

lies behind the warning of the Swabian knight Hans von Frundsberg, who in 1492 told Kempten Abbey's obstreperous subjects that he did not "care a fig for their griev-ances, but he had come to bring them to obedience with the sword and to make their wives and children into widows and orphans, and their pikes will become their grave-yard."[8]

Recovery from the Black Death and economic depression found villagers more in charge of their own affairs and more responsible for dealing with the recovery's destructive pressures on village life. It brought rising populations, higher prices of manufactured goods, and greater hunger for land. Soaring populations drove up prices. The value of land rose in relation to labor, though in the German lands, unlike in some other countries, favorable tenures limited the seigneurs' power to enclose land by converting arable to pasture. Still, heritable tenures could not protect the farmers against the recovery's other destructive pressures, and even the strong farmers were far less equipped to take advantage of the recovery than were their urban counterparts, the burghers.

To adapt a Russian saying, scratch a burgher, find a peasant. In many respects the average burgher was both a descendant of peasants and, in the nobles' eyes, himself a peasant. Neither in good times nor bad could the cities fully reproduce their pop-ulations, and all towns and cities depended on steady streams of people, especially young people, from the countryside to supply needed labor in the streets and on the rivers, in the shops and in the homes. The city offered opportunities the land could not, especially in the thickly town-dotted Imperial heartlands, where villager and townsman were neighbors.

No document of this era better illustrates how rural folk took advantage of this gradient of opportunity than does the autobiography of Thomas Platter (1499–1582), the poor mountain boy who ended his days as a highly respected schoolmaster at Basel. He came from the upper Rhone valley in the modern Swiss canton of Valais/Wallis,[9] born at a place just north of the Matterhorn. As a boy, little Tömmeli (Tommy) accidentally met Bishop Matthäus Schiner of Sion/Sitten, who asked, "What's your name?"[10] "I am called Master Thomas," the boy replied, and the bishop, himself a poor boy from higher up the valley, chuckled and said, "Surely this child will become something wonderful, soon a priest." Schiner was half-right. At six Tommy became a barefoot herd boy, who defended his goats against great eagles, lived on rye bread and cheese, and slept "in summer on hay and in winter on a straw tick full of beetles and lice."[11] Eventually, after a modest bit of harsh instruction by a local priest, an older cousin promised to take Tommy to "Germany" for schooling. He had learned nothing, Tommy later complained, but how to sing the "Salve regina" as he begged for eggs (just as young Martin Luther had done). They wandered across Switzerland, into Bavaria, and eventually to far Saxony and Silesia. Shoeless and trouserless, Tommy walked much, begged much, pilfered much, and learned little.

8   Günther Franz, ed., *Quellen zur Geschichte des Bauernkrieges*, 27.

9   Now the southwesternmost canton of Switzerland, the Valais was then a free peasant republic, which under the bishop of Sion/Sitten's presidency was associated with the Swiss Confederation. The boun-dary between German and Romance speakers lies just down the valley from Platter's home place.

10 This bishop, Matthäus Schiner (ca. 1465–1522), rose to become cardinal, confidant to popes and emper-ors, European politician of the first rank, friend to the great Dutch humanist Erasmus of Rotterdam (d. 1536), and himself *papabile*.

11 Thomas Platter, *Lebensbeschreibung*, 34.

At last, at age eighteen, he came in 1517 to the Alsatian Imperial city of Sélestat/ Schlettstadt. When the master of the town's famous Latin school discovered Tommy was Swiss, he replied with typically Alsatian prejudice, "there lived only wicked peasant folk, who drive all their bishops from the land. If you want to study properly, you don't have to pay; if not, you have to pay, or I will take the coat off your back."[12] Tommy, by now no fool, thought, "This was the first school, it seemed to me, where things were in order."[13] Here began his transformation from a wandering beggar into a scholar, for when he began, he tells, "I could do nothing, not even read Donatus," the standard Latin primer, "so I sat among the little boys like a hen among the chicks."[14]

The education Thomas received at Sélestat opened the door to a useful and rewarding life as a burgher and schoolteacher. Settling at Zurich, he worked as a rope-maker to support his studies of Latin, Greek, and Hebrew, then moved to Basel where he accepted a call to teach Hebrew grammar at the university. Here the poor goatherd became a citizen, a wealthy man, owner of a country estate, and father of successful sons. But Bishop Schiner was wrong, for Tommy Platter joined the reformation movement and never became a priest.

Thomas Platter's climb from herding goats in the Valais to learning, respect, and wealth as a citizen of Basel hardly made him typical of the rural boys (and girls) who swarmed into the cities, large and small, to find a better life. Yet his pithy, wonderful memoir throws light on the great truth Bishop Adalbero had spoken a half-millennium before – everything came from the farmers – and on the humbler German saying that only his wall separates the burgher from the peasant.

2. "THOSE WHO WORK" – BURGHERS

Burghers and cities hold a special place in the classic narrative of Europe's rise from an economically backward, socially stratified, and politically feudalized world into a market-based, egalitarian, and democratic one.[15] Some of this assertion stands up to scrutiny, for although it stretches the imagination to see in sixteenth-century burghers the progenitors of nineteenth-century citizens (or capitalists), the cities had become and would remain through economic thick and thin the principal forums of economic change. The assertion's political assumptions, on the contrary, do not survive examination. Their powerful corporate institutions and their elaborate regulation of production, consumption, morals, and worship gave little impulse to and probably hindered the most typical political creation of later times, the European imperial nation-state founded on a more or less full market society.

After northern and central Italy and the Low Countries, the Empire's old German-speaking heartlands formed a third great landscape of prosperity and urban autonomy. While the fifteenth and sixteenth centuries witnessed the German cities' golden age, the foundations of their prosperity were laid during the long depression that followed the Black Death. Because food prices fell faster than those of

12 Platter, *Lebensbeschreibung*, 56.
13 Platter, *Lebensbeschreibung*, 56.
14 Platter, *Lebensbeschreibung*, 56.
15 I use the term "burgher" in the broader sense of townsman and, at some places made clear by the context, in the narrower sense of those who belong to the civic commune.

manufactured goods, the towns' economic hegemony over the countryside was strengthened, so that when recovery reversed the "price scissors" – between 1530 and 1600 food tripled in price and real wages fell – the gains and losses cut right across both urban and rural society. Those who had more gained most from the rise, those who had less suffered most from the fall.

The German lands had always been notable for their many towns and their paucity of large cities. Even the largest were surprisingly small. In 1500 only twenty-seven of them housed more than 10,000 persons, and half of these lay in the Low Countries. Cologne, the largest German-speaking city, was a metropolis of 40,000 souls, and Prague was nearly as large, but from these giants the gradient ran steeply down to tiny places with only some hundreds of residents. More than half the German lands' burghers lived in small or middling cities of fewer than 10,000 souls. Large, middling, or small, these cities possessed similar functions as strong places, markets, and nodes of consumption, production, and communications. They also dominated their hinterlands from which they drew food, raw materials, and labor, and over which they sometimes acquired political lordship. Nuremberg had some 35,000 rural subjects, Ulm 24,000, and middling Rothenburg ob der Tauber 14,000. The greatest German-speaking city-state, Bern, was famed far more for military prowess than for commerce and banking. By the mid-sixteenth century its magistrates ruled a city of about 4,800 souls and a territory populated by more than a quarter of a million subjects.[16] Nothing comparable to these southern urban mini-empires appeared in the northern German lands, whose seafaring elites extended their power over the sea, not the land.

The burghers' power began with writing, which they learned from the clergy, and extended to trade, which they mastered by themselves. German merchants operated in two zones, northern and southern, each with its distinctive institutions, business methods, and languages (Low German in the north, High German and Italian in the south). In the north, the great trading alliance known as the Hanseatic League[17] had evolved since the twelfth century out of an alliance between the Baltic merchants headquartered at Visby (on Gotland in Sweden) and the North Sea merchants headquartered at Cologne. They collaborated to improve the terms of trade and to protect their ships and goods from pirates and bandits, though their loosely structured association possessed no permanent organs, fleets, armies, or taxes. The League thus replicated the ad hoc look of the typical northern business firm, which was a small operation of two to four partners formed to organize capital, cargos, and ships for individual voyages. Such firms spread risks by borrowing from rural nobles, clergymen, even harbor workers, and by avoiding specialization in wares. The Hanseatic merchants sailed long distances from London and Bruges via Lübeck to Reval/Tallinn, carrying wax and furs westward and textiles and salt eastward, together with Swedish copper and butter, Danish and Swedish dried fish, Scottish and English wool, Prussian and Polish grain, Hungarian metals and south German metal wares, and French and Portuguese sea salt. The merchants spread their Low German as the northern trade's lingua franca and German-brewed lager beer as its universal lubricant.

---

16 By 1536 Bern was comparable in population to the Florentine Republic of 1427.
17 Its traditional name in English, though the word *Hansa* means "league."

"The Hanseatic merchant had businesses," it has been written, while "the South German merchant had a business."[18] During their great era, the 1480s through the 1560s, the southerners founded long-lived, highly capitalized firms, often based on a single family, in which the principal partners supplied both capital and management skills for a renewable engagement of four to six years. Such firms traded in a zone bounded by the line formed by Rome, Seville, Lisbon, Toulouse, Paris, Antwerp, London, Lübeck, Cracow, Lwów/Lemberg, and Constantinople. The great pioneers were the Nurembergers, who sent their sons and nephews to learn at the Fondaco dei Tedeschi, the German merchants' headquarters in Venice. The young fellows returned to practice such Italian techniques as double-entry bookkeeping (brought to Nuremberg in 1476/84), the bill of exchange, and reckoning with Arabic numerals (the Hanseatic merchants long kept their single-entry accounts in Roman numerals). After Nuremberg came Augsburg, seat of the greatest of all firms, the house of Fugger. Under the management of Jakob Fugger (1459–1525), called with simple justice "the Rich," the firm grew rich enough (245,000 gulden by 1510) to dominate the southern metals trade and to advance nearly a million gulden to grease King Charles of Spain's path to the Imperial throne in 1519.

In the German lands trade and manufacturing went hand in hand, as the firms imported new forms of organization and new technologies from other lands, especially Italy, and spread them through German trade networks. Some manufacturing branches that required small amounts of capital favored intensive regulation of production (through crafts and guilds), but the need for big capitalization favored "putting out" production to non-urban workers.[19] In this practice, an investor, usually a large merchant or a firm, extended credit in cash or materials and tools to the producers in return for an exclusive right to buy the products at a fixed price. Putting out became a powerful instrument for expanding urban economic power over the hinterland, for coordinating whole regions' economies with those of large cities, and for freeing capital from constraints imposed by the cities' elaborate regulation of labor, materials, and output.

In no major branch did capital gain freer play than in mining. During the later fifteenth century, an explosion of mineral production transformed the operations of small, part-time producers, such as the "iron farmers" of Styria and Carinthia, into Europe's greatest industrial sector. Improved technology made possible the exploitation of previously untappable gold, silver, and copper deposits in the Saxon-Bohemian Erzgebirge, in the Alpine lands of Tyrol, Styria, and Carinthia, and in Upper Hungary (modern Slovakia). Europe's insatiable appetite for metals drew Nuremberg merchant-capitalists to Saxony and Bohemia, and those of Augsburg to Tyrol and Hungary.

Most burghers were not great traders and bankers but merchants, shopkeepers, artisans, and servants who made their livings either in homes or shops. The household formed the center of burgher life, and many cities required citizens to "keep fire and smoke," that is, reside locally in a household.[20] Yet alongside secure

---

18   Jakob Strieder, *Studien zur Geschichte kapitalistischer Organisationsformen. Monopole, Kartelle und Aktiengesellschaften im Mittelalter und zu Beginn der Neuzeit*, 97.
19   The German name, *Verlagssystem*, is based on *Verlag*, which comes from a verb (*verlegen*) meaning "to extend credit."
20   I give the form used at Strasbourg, "*feuer und rouch halten*," but there were many others.

house-communities the town sheltered, if not bountifully, all the kinds of persons who could not or would not protect their livelihoods through longstanding bonds to their fellows. Among them were the resident ("housed") poor: the unemployed or chronically underemployed, fatherless families, poor widows and spinsters, orphans, and local beggars, plus practitioners of "dishonorable trades," such as cesspool cleaners, renderers, gravediggers, traveling players, and (universally) executioners. The non-resident ("unhoused") poor were a much more exotic lot: trick riders, acrobats, Hungarian bear-trainers, jugglers, musicians, and singers; gamblers, students, fortune-tellers, and charm-sellers; rat-catchers and mouse-catchers (also mole-catchers); knife-throwers and swordsmen; treasure-seekers and crystal-gazers; and pilgrims, prostitutes, and the occasional werewolf. The poor were numerous and disproportionately female. For example, in 1444 Basel reckoned the propertyless at 20–30 percent of the city's population, and when Strasbourg introduced civic poor relief in 1523, 69 percent of the needy were women, four-fifths of whom (vs. one-fifth of the men) lived alone. Over all such folk the magistrates' hand was tightening, so that no itinerant beggar living in 1600 could have comprehended that the roads had once been open to everyone, and inns open to all social classes, and that travelers in worn-out clothing aroused in the innkeeper's customers not disgust but a hunger for their tales of far-off places, events, and wonders.

Housed or unhoused, the poor lived in the shadows of better-off citizens whose livelihoods were guarded by the city's two most important oath-bound associations, the guild and the commune. Guilds rose to power during their classic age between the mid-fourteenth and the first half of the sixteenth century. Founded both by merchants and by artisans, guilds governed the crafts, gave mutual legal aid, and cared for their members' bodies and souls in life and in death. The typical guild admitted as masters (usually male) householders who could prove free, legitimate, and honorable birth, had performed an apprenticeship and journeymanship (normally 2–4 years) and a probation period (1–3 years), and had executed a masterwork. By 1500 access to the mastership was becoming restricted, later on it commonly became hereditary. Everywhere, the corporately organized guild sought to protect livelihoods of members and families by restricting the size of shops and output. Their control of quality raised the reputation of German manufactures – Constance linens, Augsburg armor, Strasbourg cannon, Ulm fustians,[21] and Nuremberg clocks. The guildmasters also regulated production by restricting the size of shops (1–2 journeymen was usual), the right to practice crafts, and access to raw materials, and by fixing wages.

The need to enforce regulations and the desire for fiscal transparency meant that sooner or later the guilds or crafts began to press for formal representation in the civic magistracies. Their actions often led to gaining guild seats in the city councils: 15 at Basel, 13 at Zurich, 28 (later 20) at Strasbourg, 7 at Überlingen, 17 at Ulm, 12 at Magdeburg, and 16 at Danzig. A guild sometimes combined several (often unrelated) crafts, which tended to proliferate with time. Around 1500 Erfurt had some 206 distinct crafts.

Urban governance – indeed, all governance – was normally a male prerogative. Women were unknown in the councils of civic regimes, and guilds normally excluded

---

21 Fustian, a textile produced in southern German lands, was woven of mixed fibers, normally wool and cotton.

them from the mastership, though some allowed masters' widows to maintain their late husbands' shops. Yet the burghers depended on women's labor in and outside the household. In the retail trades women worked everywhere: at Nuremberg as tailors, shopkeepers, moneychangers, and innkeepers; at Lübeck as masters in many crafts; and at Cologne in their own guilds as yarn spinners, gold spinners, and silk weavers (between 1437 and 1504 their guilds counted 116 masters and 765 apprentices). By the sixteenth century, however, the tide was everywhere turning against working women, who no longer found access to the crafts, much less to masterships. In a world ordered by households, all roles tended to become gender-bound, and the falling price of labor made restrictive notions more potent and more practical.

Politically enabled or not, the guild formed the chief link between producing households and governing magistrates. At the top of the urban corporate order stood the "commune," a real or virtual assembly of the male citizens, often configured as an association of crafts, guilds, and patrician societies. In the sixty to seventy Imperial free cities, those that owned no lord but the emperor, elected or coopted magistrates governed the commune and policed the city under the emperor's (in practice slight) authority. The magistrates of territorial towns, the Empire's other 2,200 or so urban places, did more or less the same, though under the greater restraints posed by princely authority. Magistrates made statutes, admitted new burghers and banished old ones, handed down civil and criminal justice, brought nobles and peasants into forms of associate citizenship, acquired and ruled territories and their rural subjects, sent envoys to the Imperial or territorial diet, and exercised all other "freedoms" under customary law and/or royal or princely statute. In the cities, as everywhere since around 1450, governance was becoming more powerful. Oligarchy became the order of the day, as smaller colleges of magistrates emerged within city councils to take over the most important sectors of civic business. These "secret chambers" or "privy councils" were committees of experienced senior magistrates, who in many cases were coopted for life terms to govern finance, diplomacy, and war. Correspondingly, assemblies of all burghers or representatives of the guilds were reduced to purely consultative roles. Such changes affected most of the cities of the Empire's old-settled south and west. Power to govern in the northern cities had always lain in the hands of the great seafaring merchant families. At Lübeck, a city unencumbered by guilds, the civic regime hardly changed social composition between 1400 and the 1620s.

The city was not just a safer, more comfortable version of the countryside. Its physical features proclaimed its exceptional character and lent it a recognizable identity: walls, towers, bastions, moats, spires, churches, shrines, market squares, city halls, guild halls, and arsenals marked off burghers' spaces. Cities, unlike villages, were truly distinct and individual, and by the later fifteenth century were being represented as such. Printing made it possible for stay-at-home readers to "recognize" by their profiles cities they had never seen. This possibility took a giant step forward with the sumptuously printed *World Chronicle* of Hartmann Schedel (1440–1514) of Nuremberg, which appeared in 1493 in both Latin and German.[22] Among its astonishing images were cityscapes, some conventional and therefore interchangeable, when no description was available, but others quite individual. Rome and Jerusalem

---

22   It is sometimes called the *Nuremberg Chronicle*.

were easy to portray, of course, so were Nuremberg and, presumably, Regensburg, Prague, and other large cities nearby, mostly in forms recognizable today.

From one point of view, whatever the differences between their lifestyles and opportunities, farmers and burghers remained a single group. In the eyes of their social (and political) betters, they remained commoners. "We Germans," wrote Johannes Agricola (1494–1566), a sixteenth-century Lutheran pastor who collected proverbs, "call 'burghers' those who live in walled cities. Peasants live outside the walls. The difference between peasant and burgher is trivial, . . . for the burgher is not truly different, but only because of the walls. . . . The burghers want to be nobler than the peasants, but nothing but a wall separates burgher from peasant."[23] In noble and aristocratic eyes, they were all just peasants.

Against this social prejudice, which lumped them with the ordinary burghers and even, in extreme forms, with the farmers, the urban rich strove to emulate noble ways of life and become noble. The southern German free cities, like their Italian counterparts, housed families who were nobly born, but they also produced would-be nobles. In 1477 Strasbourg's Hans Armbruster spoke for all such thrusters: "He whom God has granted wealth, also wants honor."[24] Having honor meant to live in leisure and to live nobly in dress, manners, and recreations. The Nuremberg lawyer-patrician Christoph Scheurl (1481–1542) identified nobles as those "who lead an honorable life and manner, [and] who get their living from honest and respectable trade, not from disreputable crafts, except for a few artisans who are respectable. . . ."[25] He added that the latter, obviously, could not govern: "The common folk have no power. Since all power comes from God, good government belongs only to those who have been endowed with special wisdom by the Creator of all things and nature."[26]

This general hardening of social discriminations reinforced political tendencies toward oligarchy. The old communal language gave way to the language of lordship, as urban magistrates claimed with greater insistence their right to rule the citizens as subjects. Already around 1450 the city council of Ulm spoke of itself as a "ruler, who is to rule its subjects and the common man in all honor and justice."[27] Still, however extensive their claims, the magistrates had to accord to citizen-subjects their rights under urban law. Hardly any group, no matter how small or poor, could long survive in the town without possessing some right others could be forced to respect. Yet for one community of townsmen, the Jews, the right to protection carried a mortgage of longstanding discrimination and violence.

During the centuries before 1350 Jewish settlement had expanded out of its traditional centers in the Rhine, Danube, and Elbe valleys into nearby regions such as Franconia, Hesse, Saxony, and Austria. In the north, while a few Jews were admitted to the large Hanseatic cities, hardly any lived elsewhere north of a line drawn from Dortmund to Goslar or along the Baltic coast. In this era before the Black Death, Jews lived alongside Christians in more than a third of the Empire's cities, and in a few of

23 Johannes Agricola, *Die Sprichwörtersammlungen*, vol. 1: 190–1.
24 Thomas A. Brady, *Ruling Class, Regime and Reformation at Strasbourg, 1520–1555*, 49.
25 Christoph Scheurl, "Epistel über die Verfassung der Reichsstadt Nürnberg," in Carl Hegel, ed., *Chroniken der deutschen Städte vom 14. bis ins 16. Jahrhundert*, vol. 10: 787.
26 Scheurl, "Epistel," in Hegel, ed., *Chroniken*, vol. 10: 791.
27 Eberhard Isenmann, *Die deutsche Stadt im Spätmittelalter, 1250–1500. Stadtgestalt, Recht, Stadtregiment, Kirche, Gesellschaft, Wirtschaft*, 131.

these – Nuremberg, Frankfurt, and Worms – they sometimes enjoyed rights of citizenship. They also claimed de jure protection from emperor and pope.

The new hard times of the fourteenth century intensified the combination of economic and religious motives – Jews as usurers, Jews as Christ-killers – that stirred Christians to act against their Jewish neighbors, who were themselves suffering demotion from a mercantile into a money-lending and petty trading people. Then came a half-century of terror that peaked in 1349, when the bubonic plague was in the land, in a wave of massacres, expulsions, and extortions. At Strasbourg, when the magistrates refused to accede to the popular demand that the Jews "should be burnt,"[28] they were overthrown in a popular coup that ended in the burning to death of 2,000 Jews. "Money was the reason the Jews were killed," a local chronicler tells, for "had they been poor, and had the lords of the land not been in their debt, they would not have been burned to death."[29] Popular hatred and rulers' indifference colluded to produce disaster for the Jews.

Nuremberg reprised the Strasbourg story with a new twist. In 1349 the city's artisans rose against the patrician oligarchy and established a guild regime. It quickly succumbed to a patrician restoration, under which Nuremberg's Jews were plundered and more than five hundred of them massacred. This happened on the basis of a business deal between the patrician magistrates and the Emperor Charles IV (r. 1348–78), who had mortgaged to them his right to tax the Jews in return for protection. The magistrates proposed to split with Charles the proceeds from plundering Nuremberg's Jews, who were said to be "so numerous and so grasping that everywhere on the face of the earth they possess the most precious places, . . . so that we may wonder whether the victory was won by Christ or by Moses."[30] Nuremberg's great families never forgot the fruits of their Imperial loyalty. "Nuremberg is only Nuremberg," wrote the patrician magistrate Sebald Pfinzing (d. 1543) in 1535, "because she has always been properly loyal to her lords, the Roman kings and emperors."[31]

The stories of Jewish persecution at Strasbourg and Nuremberg in 1349 illustrate the reasons for the instability of Jewish settlement in the German-speaking cities, the vulnerability of Jewish life to popular antipathy and envy, and the inability or even refusal of those, whom the law obliged to protect the Jews, to do so. The resilience of German Jewish life in the face of such conditions is remarkable. Many Jews, true, dispersed to the small towns and the countryside, but the old urban communities quickly reconstituted themselves. They did not live in peace, for while large massacres became a thing of the past, expulsions remained common. A half-century after the Black Death expulsions began anew, moving in three waves (around 1400, 1450–70, and 1490–1520) across the southern German lands from the Upper Rhine to Regensburg.

---

28 Fritsche Closener, "Fritsche (Friedrich) Closeners Chronik, 1362, " in Hegel, ed., *Chroniken*, vol. 8: 127, lines 7–11.
29 Jacob Twinger von Königshofen, "Chronik des Jacob Twinger von Königshofen, 1400 (1415)," in Hegel, ed., *Chroniken*, vol. 9: 763 l. 29 to 764 l. 3. Note that "the lords of the land" probably refers not to the city's magistrates but to the prince-bishop of Strasbourg, who represented both of the higher authorities, pope and emperor, who were responsible for Jewish protection.
30 Gerald Strauss, *Nuremberg in the Sixteenth Century*, 119.
31 Heidi Eberhard Bate, "The Measures of Men: Virtue and the Arts in the Civic Imagery of Sixteenth-century Nuremberg," 196, n. 16.

The stories illustrate another great fact about urban life – indeed, all life – in the German lands. The Jews differed from their fellow burghers in that while for them, too, the city was the place, the only place, that offered the possibility for financial advancement, and while all social life was to some degree insecure, the Jews' inability to protect their rights placed them at the bottom of urban life in terms of security of life, limb, and property. No matter how successful they were, their welfare as individuals always took second place to the paramount goal of communal survival. For Christian burghers, irrespective of their success, this was not the case, and the rhythm of rise and fall could make the story of an individual, a household, a family.

The possibilities of social decline and advancement for industrious Christian burghers are revealed by the story of Burkhard Zink (1396–1474/5). He wrote a "special book about how I, Burkhard Zink, lived since my childhood days, in what ways I have striven, and what were my fortunes."[32] Born at Memmingen into a solid artisan family, he lost his mother at age five and was sent to Carniola, where he lived for seven years with an uncle, the local priest, and attended a German-speaking school at a place south of Ljubljana/Laibach on today's Slovenian-Croatian border. Returning to Memmingen to find his family dispersed and his inheritance disappeared, Burkhard apprenticed himself to a furrier. But schooling had ruined him for hard labor, so he traveled to the nearby town of Biberach, a smaller Imperial city in Upper Swabia, where he found a retired cobbler, "very rich," who "for the love of God wanted me to live with him for a year or longer and to go to school, but I would have to find my own provisions."[33] Burkhard's years as a wandering scholar show the difference between starting as a poor mountain boy, as Thomas Platter did, and as a son of a solid artisan family, even if fallen on hard times. He walked and he begged, as Platter would do, but he also attended schools in important cities, Ulm, Nuremberg, and finally Augsburg. Having intended to become a clergyman, instead he was soon off again to lodge with a rich wine merchant in Nuremberg, a lawyer in Bamberg, and another rich merchant in Augsburg. By age twenty Burkhard had begun his metamorphosis into a settled, respectable, and propertied burgher. It began very modestly. He married Elizabeth, a poor woman, "who," he said, "brought me [as dowry] nothing more than a small bed, a calf, and few pans and other poor things, worth altogether not more than ten pounds. I, too, had little, just a good suit of clothes and not much cash. Yet I was well trained and could earn money, which I would willingly do. Though my master was generous, this is all we possessed, what we'd earned." Burkhard recounts, "I was unsure as to what I should do, for I possessed nothing," but his master said, "my Burkhard, buck up and don't despair. We will help one another, and we will get out of this situation."[34] He found work as secretary to a priest, a Memminger like himself, and in the evenings they sat in their humble quarters, Elizabeth spinning and Burkhard copying. In time, by virtue of their hard work and thrift, Burkhard and Elizabeth became substantial property-owners, comfortably provided for. The twenty years of their wedded life were punctuated by the births of five daughters and five sons, of whom six died before their twelfth year, and by Burkhard's commercial travels. Thereafter, he married three more times and fathered

---

32 Burkhard Zink, "Chronik des Burkhard Zink 1368–1468," 122.
33 Zink, "Chronik," 125.
34 Zink, "Chronik," 128, 129.

in all twenty legitimate children plus two bastards. Having accumulated meanwhile numerous civic offices and honors, he died at nearly eighty in 1468.

Jew or Christian, artisan or merchant, the burgher's security did not and could not protect against all the forces that threatened the urban way of life. Besides the uncertainties of nature – plague, famine, weather – and the market, the main threat to settled life was violence in the forms of banditry, feud, and war. Then, as today, the chief guardians of peace were its chief disturbers, for the major role in governance belonged to the class Bishop Adalbero had defined as "those who fight." In the German lands the nobility, and almost they alone, would determine whether the future would bring better governance or worse.

3. "THOSE WHO FIGHT" – NOBLES

Taken together, farmers and burghers composed the common people – "the common man," in contemporary parlance – or such was the opinion of uncommon people, the nobles. They and their emulators in the towns were the chief guardians of political and social inequality. A fifteenth-century inscription in the ossuary at Kaysersberg in Alsace teaches that in death we are all equal: "Now justice has been done/Here lies the master by his man."[35] Equality before God, inequality before men. In this life the Holy Roman Empire was a feudal kingdom ruled chiefly by nobles, great and small. However poor or ignorant, noblemen strode and rode through the German lands as lords of humankind.

The nobilities of the German lands were numerous and various, and nothing could be further from the truth than to see in them a static, unadaptable relic of the deep medieval past.[36] They had formed before 1250 from a merger of the old free nobility with formerly unfree servitors (ministerials) into an entirely free class eligible for administrative and military posts reserved for the nobility, and for knighthood. With their predominance stabilized by the heritability of fiefs and the patrimonialization of offices (official titles extended to all members of a lineage), the nobles formed a hierarchy that ran from the Imperial princes down through the counts and barons to the untitled knights and simple nobles.[37] During the following generations a political gulf developed between the upper stratum of princely lineages and other ranks of nobles, titled or untitled, who after 1500 or so tended to become subjected to the newly consolidating princely territories. The princes, though not the other nobles, formed with the monarchy the principle agents and bulwarks of Imperial governance. Through all the changes, there nonetheless survived a common noble culture based on eligibility for enfiefment and the honor of knighthood, a noble lifestyle (when they could afford it), a shared military ethos, and a boundless taste for celebrating their lineages in image, word, and deed.

The common denominator of the titled nobility, whether princes or not, was the survival and welfare of the lineage. This was primarily a matter not of territorial

---

35 Walter Hotz, *Handbuch der Kunstdenkmäler im Elsaß und in Lothringen*, 85.
36 This overview rests on Karl-Heinz Spiess, *Familie und Verwandtschaft im deutschen Hochadel des Spätmittelalters – 13. bis Anfang des 16. Jahrhunderts*, 1–4.
37 In what follows I use the terms "aristocracy" and "nobility" to denote respectively the titled and untitled nobles, though, of course, "nobility" in the broader sense applies to them all.

continuity but of successful marriage strategies and biological luck. While the appalling rates of mortality of persons and lineages – the average length of a marriage was about fifteen years – made reproduction a constant problem, the rules of inheritance and the practice of partition made the conservation of resources just as pressing. "Each lineage in each generation had to select anew a plan of action, taking into account both the accumulated experience of one's house and the fates of affiliated lineages of equal rank."[38] A reconstruction of a series of comital and baronial lineages between 1200 and 1550[39] demonstrates the baselessness of the traditional view that noble marriages and partitions of properties reflected an arbitrary, irrational cult of family. What impresses is "how narrow was the foresighted father's freedom to act. The fundamental claim of all legitimate sons on an equal share of paternal and maternal legacies formed the general parameters of action."[40] With good luck, a single surviving, married son with children would receive the lineage's substance undivided; with poor luck, none of five sons might survive to adulthood or, just as threatening, all of them might. Between the blades of these scissors formed by reproductive luck and the laws of inheritance, all lineages lived. Or they did not. Great survivors were the counts of Hohenlohe, who during the fourteenth century produced sons in large numbers (nineteen from two lines between 1305 and 1340) without destroying the family's substance through successive partitions. Indeed, over a number of generations, as the Hohenlohe example shows, the dispersal of properties among numerous progeny tended to be restrained by the extinction of some lines, so that a lineage's total substance was marked by simultaneous dispersal and reconcentration.[41]

This is not to say that choice played no role in a lineage's fortunes. Particularly important were the choices of spouses and the placement of children in ecclesiastical posts and corporations. The Church served as, among other things, a cost-free pasturage for surplus sons (and daughters).[42] This strategy, however, also had its risks. The Swabian noble authors of the *Zimmern Chronicle* remarked on the extinction of the counts of Henneberg: "Thus the great, ancient lineage disappeared, which is a pity, but they could blame themselves and not fortune, . . . for the cause of their extinction was sending most of their sons to be priests in order to gain them benefices."[43]

Balancing security of reproduction with dispersal of assets, a problem that faced all lineages of the upper nobility, posed special problems for the handful of great princely dynasties on whose success the future of the German lands depended. During the age of reformations a handful of high noble lineages of princely status emerged from the layered body of the German-speaking nobilities. These were the lineages that became territorial state-formers – dynastic rulers of territorial principalities – and significant players in Imperial political life, and on their successes and failures would depend much of the German lands' fate during the early modern era. By the fifteenth century they numbered fewer than a dozen: Habsburg (Austria, Burgundy), Wittelsbach (Bavaria, Palatinate), Wettin (Saxony), Hohenzollern (Ansbach, Brandenburg),

38 Spiess, *Familie und Verwandtschaft*, 273.
39 Only the male lines, because the rules of inheritance were dominantly patrilineal.
40 Spiess, *Familie und Verwandtschaft*, 272.
41 Based on charts in Spiess, *Familie und Verwandtschaft*, 227–8.
42 The subject is explored later in this chapter for its bearing on the Church.
43 Froben Christof von Zimmern, *Zimmerische Chronik*, vol. 4: 21.

Welf (Brunswick), Zähringen (Baden), Greifen (Pomerania), Pribislav (Mecklenburg), and Brabant (Hesse). Such was their concentration that by 1582 eight of these dynasties held all four lay electorates and twenty-seven of the thirty-five lay seats in the princes' council of the Imperial Diet.

The distinctive mark of the Empire's great princely lineages, what set them off from the rest of the German-speaking nobilities, titled or not, was their adaptation to the political model, from the fluid medieval politics of lineage and proximity to the king to the more stable early modern politics of institutionalized territorial power. The most important sign of this change was the transformation of bundles of patrimonial holdings and rights into territorial states of fixed extent and regular administration. In the process, the old lineage became a territorial dynasty, whose (real or alleged) descent from ancient times merged with the identities of the lands they ruled. The fixed association of territorial names (Austria, Saxony) with dynastic ones (Habsburg, Wettin) marked this transition, and chroniclers, monastic and others, zealously jumbled fact with fiction to proclaim the antiquity, continuity, fame, and honor of princely lineages through their associations with the histories of lands and peoples. Their recording work lent legitimacy to princes who possessed neither crowns nor inherent sacral power, and for whom the chroniclers fashioned fictional tales of dynastic unity against real histories of intradynastic rivalry, feud, and partition.

The union of land (in the form of territorial lordship) and lineage introduced special problems into the world of the great dynasties. For one thing, the custom of partition posed a constant threat to a lineage's unity of planning and action. Armed intra-dynastic conflict formed the great political plague of the German lands after the Black Death, and, its damage to others apart, it often brought best-laid plans to naught. Louis the Bearded (1365–1447), a fifteenth-century duke of Bavaria, ordered that Ingolstadt's new parish church should become the sacred resting place for his Ludovician line of the Wittelsbach dynasty. Alas, in a tragedy of Shakespearean quality, his own son revolted and held him to ransom, his kinsmen invaded his lands, and, when the old duke died, his cousins of the Landshut line – already so wealthy that the last three of them were nicknamed "the Rich" – inherited everything he had possessed. Far into the sixteenth century, intra-dynastic strife was as much the norm as the exception among the dynasties of this rank. First to abandon the practice of partition was Bavaria, whose duke told the king in 1496 that "although the previous partitions have caused the House of Bavaria to be regarded as more than a single principality, now there is no more than a single house of all Bavarian princes."[44]

Strategies of marital alliance also took on new importance among the royal and princely dynasties.[45] Marriages balanced the localization of a princely lineage by placing it into an immense network that crossed all conceivable boundaries. Status and power counted, ethnicity and language hardly did. This was especially true of royal marriages. Emperor Charles IV of the house of Luxemburg, son of a French-speaking prince and a Bohemian royal princess, married four times in a west-to-east

44 Jean-Marie Moeglin, *Dynastisches Bewußtsein und Geschichtsschreibung: Zum Selbstverständnis der Wittelsbacher, Habsburger und Hohenzollern im Spätmittelalter*, 24. The speaker was Duke Albert IV (1447–1508). The problem of territorial partition is treated at greater length in the discussion of the formation of territorial states in Chapter 5.
45 It is worth pointing out that German "royal" dynasties – Luxemburg, Wittelsbach, and Habsburg – were simply very powerful (and fortunate) princely dynasties.

succession: a French royal princess, a Palatine princess (daughter of an elector), a Silesian princess, and a Pomeranian duchess. His first son, Wenceslas, married a Bavarian Wittelsbach, while his second son, Sigismund, married an Angevin (a Capetian cadet line that ruled Naples and Sicily from 1266 to 1435) royal princess of Hungary and Poland and a countess of Cilli in Slovenia. Sigismund's daughter married a Habsburg archduke of Austria (later German king).

The Habsburg network was even larger and more far-flung. Frederick III married a Portuguese royal princess; his children married into the houses of Burgundy, Milan, and Bavaria; his grandchildren into the houses of Castile/Aragon (2), and Savoy; and his great-grandchildren into those of Portugal (2), France, Denmark, and Hungary/Bohemia (2). Frederick's son and successor, Maximilian I, commissioned a work that portrayed his lineage as a mega-dynasty of Christendom, in which the charisms of all earlier dynasties converged, only to be redistributed to various royal and princely lines. In his fictional "autobiography," the *White/Wise King*, the rulers' names are coded: Maximilian is the Young White/Wise King and his father the Old White/Wise King, France is the Blue King, Scotland the King of the Wild Men, and so forth. Non-royal princes, here raised to royal rank (Milan as the Serpent King, Cleves-Jülich as the Swan King, and Burgundy as the Flintstone King), join this family of sovereigns under Maximilian's leadership. The same notion of Christendom as a royal kindred inspired the saying, "let others make war, while fortunate Austria shall marry."[46]

From these aristocratic heights to the lower levels of the untitled nobles was a long way down. Whether causally or coincidentally related, the rise of the great princes and the decline of the knights had always been coupled in traditional accounts of the period. The fact, at least, of the lesser nobles' decline in wealth, status, and, above all, political significance is well documented. As its symbol may stand a grim, haunting woodcut of 1513, *The Knight, Death, and the Devil*, by the Nuremberg artist Albrecht Dürer (1471–1528). It shows an aging veteran of many a raid, feud, and battlefield, mounted, in full plate armor, with lance in hand and sword at his side. His companions are Death mounted and the Devil on foot.

The knight, like all mortals, was doomed to die, but so, believed many sixteenth-century observers and most modern historians, was his entire estate. The lesser nobles, with their small holdings and their inability to forge their limited judicial authority over peasants into a kind of proto-sovereignty, had certainly lost much economic substance during the agrarian crisis. The price scissors caught them, as it did peasants, between falling farm prices and rising ones for manufactured goods. Whether the nobles' incomes were declining in absolute terms is difficult to say, but they were surely falling behind those of wealthy burghers. In 1474 the Saxon nobleman Hans von Honsperg of Klöden allotted annually for his family's clothing the rye equivalent of 41,700 kg, half for himself, a third for his wife, and the rest for his daughters.[47] This sum was less than half the limit prescribed by Regensburg's sumptuary law for a single dress for a burgher's wife or daughter. Constrained by custom from increasing rents, now increasingly fixed in cash rather than produce, the nobles adapted to shore up their incomes. Some hitched their wagons to princely stars, others imitated the

---

46 "*Bella gerant alii tu felix Austria nube.*" Derived from Ovid (*Her. Ep.* xiii. 84) and ascribed to the occasion of Maximilian's first marriage in 1477.

47 Historians of price movements in this period normally translate prices into one of two standard equivalents: grams of silver or kilograms of rye.

Figure 1. The Knight, Death, and the Devil

burghers by getting educations, and yet others moldered away in their old lifestyle of ignorant banditry, hated by the common people and bullied by princes.

Many lesser nobles came willy-nilly into military and political service to princes. Their service could be individual and familial, as when Franconian knights served as officials and creditors of the (Hohenzollern) margraves of Brandenburg-Ansbach; or it could be collective, as when nobles made up an estate in a territorial parliament. In Austria, Bavaria, Saxony, Brandenburg, Hesse, and other principalities, the nobles gradually became directly subordinate to their princes and only indirectly, through him, to the emperor.

In the older, politically fragmented regions of the southwest and west, including Swabia, Franconia, and the Rhine valley, many lesser nobles remained the emperor's vassals, called "Imperial knights." Locally they jostled with a myriad other small powers – Imperial cities, abbeys, and even peasant associations – in political landscapes not yet much threatened by expansive princely dynasties. Like other estates, they banded together in noble associations, some ninety-two of which have been identified for the fifteenth century. These jousting societies, which bore such colorful names as "the Ass," "the Falcon," and "the Bear," staged tournaments as arenas for acquiring honor and markets for acquiring wives. Some were organized to fight, notably the League with St. George's Shield, which formed between 1406 and 1414 to fight Swiss expansion into what is now northeastern Switzerland. Between the Black Forest in the west and the Lech River in the east, boasted one of its commanders in 1433, "fewer than a tenth of the counts, barons, knights, and squires in Swabia are not in the league."[48] Yet the day of independent noble leagues was brief, and in 1488 the League and the free cities of the southwest ganged together under royal sponsorship to form the Swabian League. Within thirty years this body, too, came under princely domination. New corporate associations of Imperial knights and Imperial counts did emerge from royal patronage in the mid-sixteenth century, but they possessed no independent military power.

Fifteenth-century writers wondered whether these nobles should not lend their only obvious asset, military skill, to the Empire's service, as King Maximilian proposed to the Imperial Diet at Worms in 1495. When the princes balked – they wanted no standing royal army – Maximilian turned back to his mercenaries, the famed German lansquenets (*Landsknechte*) who were more numerous and much easier to train and arm to fight in the modern style. A very few of the knights did make fine careers as military enterprisers.[49] One such fellow was the Tyrolean Georg von Frundsberg (1473–1528), who in the early 1520s took perhaps 10,000 lansquenets over the Alps to fight the emperor's wars against France and, incidentally, to storm the walls of Rome in 1527. To fight for pay was to move with the times.

Most attempts to generalize about the lesser nobilities' fortunes in this era founder on the reefs of regional differences and individual fates. The Cologne Carthusian Werner Rolevinck, a farmer's son, admitted that his native Westphalia was notorious for its bandits, who are "generally persons of noble descent" whom "great poverty has . . . seduced to commit their many crimes."[50] Describing the brutal training of young, poor nobles, he sighed, "I cannot stop thinking of these martyrs! For they are truly martyrs; if not God's martyrs, then the Devil's! In earlier times I was often in their company, though not to rob but to sit at table with them."[51]

Franconia, a richer land than Westphalia, was dotted with the castles of Imperial knights. Their sons might serve princes, such as the prince-bishops of Würzburg and Bamberg and the margraves of Brandenburg-Ansbach, or they might work

48 Hermann Mau, *Die Rittergesellschaften mit St. Jörgenschild. Ein Beitrag zur Geschichte des deutschen Einungsbewegung im 15. Jahrhundert*, 249.
49 A military enterpriser was someone who contracted with a warlord to raise an army, which he also took on campaign and commanded in battle. See Chapter 16.
50 Werner Rolevinck, *De Laude antiquae Saxoniae nunc Westphaliae dictae/Ein Buch zum Lobe Westfalens des alten Sachsenlandes*, 205.
51 Rolevinck, *De Laude antiquae Saxoniae*, 209.

independently, for the Main valley was the southern home of the classic noble feud. In his old age, Götz von Berlichingen (1480–1562), one of his generation's most avid feuders, looked back on a happy upbringing: "In my childhood I behaved and acted in such a manner that many persons concluded that I would become a fighting man or a knight."[52] Having little taste for school but much for horses and riding, as he confessed, Götz launched a remarkable career of feuding, raiding, kidnapping, and arson for honor and profit.

While country life suited Götz when he was not feuding and fighting, for others of his class the rural noble's traditional way of life proved a crucifixion. Ulrich von Hutten (1488–1523), another Franconian, was a veteran of ten German and Italian universities and one of the best educated nobles of his age. He chose princely service to escape the relentless monotony, the squalor, and the stinks of the country life Götz so loved. "Do not imagine that your life has anything in common with mine," he wrote to a Nuremberg friend, for country gentlemen spend their days "in the fields, in the woods, and in fortified strongholds," leasing their lands to "a few starveling peasants who barely manage to scratch a living from it. From such paupers we draw our revenues, and income hardly worth the labor spent on it."[53] It was dangerous to leave his fortified residence, it was disgusting to live in its "dark rooms crammed with guns, pitch, sulfur, and other materials of war," where "the stench of gun powder [is] mixed with the smell of dogs and shit and other such pleasant odors."[54] The decades around 1500 were a time of betwixt and between, when one nobleman could be satisfied with a traditional life of feuding and plundering, another could find no honorable employment for the fruits of his excellent education. In the ideal scheme of things, the knights stood at the acme of the social order, just under the aristocrats and the king. In the world of their time, they were hated and ridiculed by the commoners, bullied and lorded over by princes, and harried by merchants and markets that exacted rising costs but provided no corresponding means to meet them. This world seemed to offer no way into the future consistent with honor, lineage, and tradition.

Around 1500 in the old Imperial heartlands, with their politically broken landscapes, strong peasantries, and wealthy towns and cities, noble power, of which seigneurial rights over peasants formed the bedrock, ought to have been a ripe target for revolution. And so it was, for seigneurial power lay at the heart of the great storm that swept over those lands in the mid-1520s. Yet that revolt did not, on the whole, succeed. Instead, at the same time there arose a related but different storm against another target. The reformations of the sixteenth century aimed to change not social relations in the southern and western countrysides but the operations everywhere of the Church, its personnel and the religion it taught.

---

52 Götz von Berlichingen, *Mein Fehd und Handlungen*, 53.
53 Gerald Strauss, ed., *Manifestations of Discontent in Germany on the Eve of the Reformation*, 193. This famous letter's recipient was the Nuremberg humanist-patrician Willibald Pirckheimer (1470–1530).
54 Strauss, ed., *Manifestations of Discontent*, 194.

4

The Church and the Faith

There are the sacraments, which are both illuminating and purifying; there
is the pastoral priesthood, which is both purified and purifying; and there is the
faithful people, which is purified and does not purify . . .

Nicholas of Cusa

The clergy, Bishop Adalbero's "those who pray," belonged to the Church in a special
way.[1] These men and women embodied and tended the channels of grace between the
two realms of St. Augustine's concept, the earthly city and the City of God. The
clergy normally took pride of place in medieval schemes of social hierarchy and
commonly formed the first estate in parliamentary bodies. One tradition of medieval
teaching conceived the clergy in the broadest sense as a complete clerical society
parallel to but distinct from the laity ordered into temporal or secular estates. This
status was warranted, it was argued, by the clergy's guardianship of the sacramental,
penitential, and intercessional ties both between God and His creatures and among
His creatures.

The Church was the most regularly structured and best understood institution in
late medieval Christendom. Its foundation comprised the medieval Church's greatest
creation, which was not the papal monarchy or the universities but the network of
territorial parishes that blanketed Christendom with a church in every place and a
priest in every church. From this base the ecclesiastical system arose in tiers through
territorial dioceses and their subunits (deaneries and archdeaneries), through provinces, and the papal government in Rome. Above them all stood the Church Universal
of the living and the dead, represented on this earth by the papal monarchy and the
body of Christian bishops assembled in the general council. Parallel to this structure
had grown up the regular clergy, members of the religious orders, each with its
abbeys, monasteries, and convents, its provinces, and its general assembly, which
convened under a presiding general.

---

1 The term "clergy" is used here not in the narrow sense of those who have received the ecclesiastical
   tonsure, nor in the even narrower sense of those who are ordained, but in the general sense of all to
   whom clerical privileges have been extended. In this sense it includes bishops, canons, and priests, and
   also monks, nuns, lay brothers, novices, and some other groups that lived under vows approved by the
   bishop.

1. PARISHES AND PASTORS

By the fifteenth century the work of localizing the means of grace was nearly complete in Christendom as a whole. In the villages and rural districts of the German lands, in their cities and their neighborhoods, a people's church was served by a priest provided (nominated) by a bishop, abbot, collegial chapter, noble, or civic regime and ordained and installed by the diocese's bishop (or, very often, by his auxiliary bishop). The priest thereby acquired a legal right (benefice) to certain incomes attached to his new pastoral office, above all from the parishioners' tithes.[2] In return he was obliged to say Mass, administer the sacraments, preach, bury the dead, occasionally collect taxes, and in later times keep records. It was a matter of both good pastoral service and local pride for each village to have its own church and priest. Otherwise, the people of a churchless village or district had to trudge down the road or over the hill through the snow and mud to hear Mass in a neighboring village; their young boys and girls had to walk in the night to fetch the priest for a dying grandparent or sibling; and their dead lay among strangers. A village without a church and pastor was like a body without a soul or a town without walls, market, and town hall.

Villagers often felt acutely the need for their own parishes staffed by good priests. During the fifteenth century in some southwestern lands – the Palatinate, Swabia, and Switzerland – those lacking priests were doing something about it. If the village already had a church building, it had merely to ask the bishop to send a priest. The commune agreed to support him, providing that the tithe, which was now going to the priest in a neighboring village or to an abbot or to a lay seigneur, be repatriated. This was harsh music to the ears of lay impropriators (owners or usurpers) of tithes, harsher yet to those of neighboring priests, who might be able to survive on the incomes from several villages but not from one only. Just like the nobles who had founded churches in earlier times, rural communes regarded their pastors as servants and often claimed the right to elect (but not ordain) them and to depose unsatisfactory ones.

While a beneficed rural pastor might attain an income comparable to that of an artisan master in town, many did far more poorly. One-quarter of the clerical livings in the late medieval diocese of Osnabrück produced less than a minimum for survival; in many Brandenburg parishes the nobles had simply seized the tithe, leaving the priest nothing on which to live; in the diocese of Worms the bishop encouraged his priests to assume, albeit illegally, several beneficed posts in order to secure a living income; and in Würzburg approximately three or four benefices were required to support adequately a single village priest. Urban priests did better if beneficed, but an increasing proportion was not. Many were hired not to serve congregations but to say the Masses endowed by the pious for the repose of their own souls and those of their dead. Thousands of "Mass priests" performed their duties at numerous altars in urban churches or in specially built chapels.[3] In some cities such benefices existed in great numbers: 60 in the great church at Ulm, 236 at 105 altars in two Breslau churches.

By 1500 young priests who had studied at universities were leaving poor regions to look for beneficed posts in richer ones. In the diocese of Strasbourg the influx of

---

2　In most places two tithes were owed: the "great tithe" levied (nominally 10 percent, usually less) on the principal crop, and the "small tithe" on other products.
3　In England these chapels were called "chantries."

strangers, mostly Swabians and Bavarians, was so great between 1450 and 1520 that of 529 parish priests whose place of origin is known, 400 came from other dioceses. Alsatians, who generally did not like Swabians, no more than Austrians did Bavarians, grumbled against "these damned foreigners" and their incomprehensible sermons.[4] Prejudices were, if anything, more pronounced between Swiss and Swabians. Huldrych Zwingli (1484–1531), Zurich's future reformer, once expressed his outrage that a Swabian priest would be preferred to him for a benefice. "I was indeed compelled to think," he wrote, "that a prophet has no honour in his country if in place of a Swiss a Swabian is preferred, a man to whom I would not yield even in his native land. . . . If they take this foreigner, they can see what he will produce from his pig-pen."[5]

The formal price for becoming one of the Church's sacramental mediators between God and Man was celibacy, remaining unmarried and sexually abstinent. Though the rule was old, in the agrarian world of medieval Europe it could not be much enforced, and many priests chose to live in uncanonical marriages (concubinage). Their sons, however, could not simply follow them into the priesthood. Because of their defect of birth (*defectus natalium*), these bastards needed to receive a dispensation before they could receive ordination. Fortunately, the Church that was hard in principle was often reasonable in practice. By the later fifteenth century dispensations were easy to obtain via petitions to the Penitentiary, an office of the Roman Curia.[6] The Penitentiary received 37,916 such petitions between 1449 and 1533, of which 60 percent came from sons of clergymen. In the Empire the petitioners were heavily concentrated in the southwestern and northwestern ecclesiastical provinces, ten times more from Mainz (34 percent) and Cologne (35 percent) than from Salzburg (11 percent), Trier (7 percent), Magdeburg (4 percent), and Bremen (3 percent). The attitude toward bastardy seems to have been generous, the practice of concubinage among the lower clergy widespread. The availability of dispensations, a byproduct of celibacy, tended to ease the problem of conserving clerical learning and skills by allowing sons to succeed fathers. The Protestants would very much improve the efficiency of this conservation by approving, even insisting on, a married clergy.

For those who entered the priesthood bent on making it a career, the best posts, like the best of almost everything, lay in the cities. Most desirable were individually beneficed canonries in well-heeled collegiate churches,[7] but these were few, and most were hogged by nobles and well-to-do burghers' sons. Far more accessible to the ordinary aspirant were the urban parishes, the number of which in any one city bore no discernible relationship to the local population's size: Erfurt had 28 parishes, Cologne at least 20, Strasbourg and Regensburg each 9, Nuremberg 2, and Frankfurt am Main, Bamberg, Freiburg im Breisgau, and Ulm only 1. Collegiate and monastic

---

4 Francis Rapp, *Réformes et reformation à Strasbourg. Église et société dans le diocèse de Strasbourg (1450–1525)*, 451–2.

5 Hans J. Hillerbrand, ed., *The Reformation: A Narrative History Related by Contemporary Observers and Participants*, 113–14. The comment plays on epithets – "Pig-Swabian" and "Cow-Swiss" – with which Swiss and Swabians customarily flattered one another.

6 The following figures come from Ludwig Schmugge, *Kirche, Kinder, Karrieren. Päpstliche Dispense von der unehelichen Geburt im Spätmittelalter*, 262–73.

7 A collegiate church (*Stiftskirche*) resembled an abbey in being staffed by a corporately organized body of priests, but it differed from monastic communities in that the individual members, called "canons," were individually beneficed. In this era their religious duties were often performed by salaried vicars.

churches often competed with parishes for burghers' loyalties, and the chief episcopal cities, the "German Romes," housed religious communities in truly astonishing numbers. By 1350 Cologne contained 11 collegiate churches, 20 religious houses,
20 parish churches, 44 chapels, and 62 houses of beguines and beghards.[8] Erfurt,
which was either a free city or belonged to the archbishop of Mainz (depending on
whom one asked), was possibly the most churched town in late medieval central
Europe: it contained a cathedral and an adjoining collegiate church, 22 monasteries,
23 other churches, 36 chapels, 6 hospitals, and 28 parishes. In such cities the numbers
of clergy and their servants reached high levels, totaling perhaps 10 percent of the
residents at Augsburg and nearly 8 percent at Würzburg. They ranged from noble
cathedral canons down to humble Mass priests, monks, and nuns. The patrician
families, the guilds, and the religious confraternities all had their favorite chapels
and churches.

2. THE REGULAR CLERGY

Of the two great sectors of the Christian clergy, the "regulars" were so called because
they lived a common life under a rule (*regula*), while the "seculars" worked individually in "the world" (*saeculum*). Not only did the regulars live under a prescriptive,
papally approved set of rules, but, in addition to celibacy, they also took perpetual
vows of chastity and obedience. Many but not all male regulars were also ordained
priests. The eleventh and twelfth centuries had been an age of glory for the great, old
religious orders, above all the Benedictines but also the Cistercians, Brigittines, and
Premonstratensians, whose abbeys and priories dotted the countrysides of the German lands. Most such orders also included female branches, whose members, like
their male counterparts, lived cloistered in community.

A whole new branch of the regular clergy arose in the thirteenth century with the
founding and papal approval of the mendicant (begging) friars, most notable of whom
were the Franciscans and the Dominicans.[9] They were urban orders, founded during
the great wave of urbanization in the High Middle Ages, and their principal tasks of
pastoral work, preaching, and teaching were all associated with towns, burghers, and
universities. The general spirit of this movement was truncated in practice by
medieval attitudes toward gender. Like the great, old monastic orders, the mendicants
also had female branches, whose members, however, were not permitted to work in
the world but lived in enclosed communities, just like the nuns of the older orders.
Therefore, whereas the male mendicant communities represented a transitional form
between cloistered communities of medieval abbeys and the noncommunal societies
of a later time (most notably the Society of Jesus, called "Jesuits"), their female

---

8 Beguines (female) and beghards (male) were persons who, beginning in the twelfth century in the Low
   Countries, lived alone without vows and devoted themselves to prayer and good works. Since the early
   thirteenth century they (especially the women) had grouped their dwellings together in a community
   called a "beguinage." The male communities usually held their meager properties in common. While
   the reputation of being irregular, disorderly, and unruly attached to both female and male communities, in the later Middle Ages they played significant roles in the religious and social life of some cities,
   especially in the southern Netherlands (modern Belgium).
9 The word comes into English from Latin, *frater* (brother) via Old French. It was generally reserved for
   members of the mendicant orders, of which the four most prominent in this era were the Franciscans,
   Dominicans, Augustinian Hermits, and Carmelites.

counterparts were allowed only to practice the old, cloistered way of life, though in urban settings. In time, the friars took on a great deal of pastoral work, which in many places brought them into conflict with the local secular priests who served the urban parishes.

Taking all these groups together, in the German lands around 1500 there were to be found more than thirty constituted orders living in communities that ranged in size from highs of 300 to 500 members down to tiny priorates of no more than ten. Alongside them lived the canons of many dozens, perhaps hundreds, of individual collegiate chapters (whose members were often not regulars but secular clergy), not to speak of a vast infrastructure of small informal and unrecognized communities.

The ethos of the regular clergy before 1500 was characterized by a tension between devotion to the active life in the world and withdrawal from the world into the cloister. The latter could be involuntary, as was the case more commonly for women than for men, but for both the communal life fluctuated between relaxation and restoration of the respective monastic rule's prescriptions for the conventual life. Some houses and orders, particularly the Cistercians and Carthusians, remained relatively strict, while others were generally lax, notably the many foundations of canonesses who lived under versions of the Augustinian or Benedictine rule but sometimes kept private servants and property.

The Black Death's ravages, exacerbated by the ensuing depression, plunged many monastic and mendicant convents, male and female, into hard times and less strict ways of life. During the fifteenth century counter-movements began in many of the old monastic orders and among the mendicants. The struggles for strict return to the rules were especially pronounced among the mendicants, whose programs went under the name of "Observance," and a comparable movement enjoyed great success among the Benedictine abbeys in the German lands.

The Benedictine reform began in the north. From Clus Abbey near Gandersheim in Lower Saxony sprang a Benedictine reform movement, which spread, much as the Burgundian abbey of Cluny had done from the late ninth to the early twelfth century. In 1433 Otto (d. 1463), the one-eyed duke of Brunswick-Göttingen, called Abbot Johann Dederoth (d. 1439) of Clus to undertake a reform of Bursfeld Abbey, which lay on the Weser River west of Göttingen. Johann soon died, but his successor spread the program of strict observance of the rule and restoration of the liturgy to other abbeys. In 1446 a group of six reformed abbeys received approbation from the Council of Basel as the Bursfeld Congregation, which speedily spread to other Benedictine abbeys, especially in the northern German lands. Laden with patronage and favors by popes, bishops, and temporal rulers, notably the dukes of Brunswick, the program continued down to the beginnings of the Protestant Reformation, by which time the congregation embraced 136 abbeys.

The conditions of monastic life were to become one of the most visible targets of criticism, polemics, and invective in the Protestant movement that arose during the 1520s. It told tales of tyrannical popes, warrior bishops, grasping monks, and wanton nuns. Often the writers simply recycled images and charges deployed by the monastic reformers of the fifteenth century. All of the sharpest critics down to and including Martin Luther were themselves monks or friars. Prominent among them stands Johannes Trithemius (1462–1516) from Trittheim in the Mosel Valley, who became at the age of twenty-one abbot of Sponheim, which lay on the Nahe River in the

Rhine Palatinate. There he labored to turn a poor, lax, and physically ruinous abbey into an important center of learning.[10] In one of his writings Trithemius posed these questions to his order's founder, St. Benedict of Nursia (ca. 480–543):

> Where is now your earlier beauty, your adornment? Where is a holy way of life? . . . Where are learned and holy abbots and monks who dedicate themselves to the rule? Woe, you possess more than 10,000 cloisters in your order, of which, I believe, scarcely 1,000 come close to obeying the rule. Your abbots scorn the rule's discipline, neglect pastoral work, give themselves over to worldly vanities, strive for temporal wealth, and drown in carnal pleasures.[11]

To Trithemius's complaints many others could be added. The intensification of worldly life, the multiplication of worldly opportunities, the availability of worldly pleasures all contributed to what must have seemed a great conspiracy against religious life. Failing centralized governance and strong reform movements, an initiative to reform could come only from without, say, from a bishop or a prince. Against this possibility the Church's past held it in an iron grip, for not only were the convents in general immune from episcopal authority, the bishops themselves tended to be as worldly as the unreformed religious communities.

3. BISHOPS

"Where the bishop is," ran the oft-quoted dictum by St. Ignatius of Antioch (d. before 117), "there is the Church."[12] Zealous or lax, learned or unlearned, resident or absent, princely or pastoral, in the Church's eyes the bishop stood in an unbroken succession to Christ's Apostles. Once elected, confirmed, and consecrated, he possessed ordinary jurisdiction[13] over all churches in a bounded area (his diocese), where he could legislate in all ecclesiastical affairs, ordain priests, teach Christian doctrine, exercise authority in the first instance over ecclesiastical disputes, crimes, discipline, and persons, and excommunicate. He also possessed the right to sit and vote in a general council of the Church.

Bishops had been chosen by popular or purely clerical assemblies in ancient times and later by Carolingian kings, but in the High Middle Ages the popes had attempted with some success to wrest their appointment from the kings and aristocracies and repatriate it to the Church. The weakening of papal power after the Black Death reversed this trend in favor of the kings, whose treaties (concordats) with the papacy gave them greater powers over episcopal appointments. In the Empire, by contrast, the monarch did not have formal rights to the nomination of bishops. Instead, the concordat of Vienna in 1448 affirmed the rights of cathedral chapters to elect bishops,

---

10 Having had difficulties with his convent, in 1505 Trithemius accepted the bishop of Würzburg's call to the Irish Convent (*Schottenkloster*) at Würzburg, where he was buried with a splendid tombstone by Tilman Riemenschneider (ca. 1460–1531). Among his pupils were two outstanding figures: Heinrich Cornelius Agrippa of Nettesheim (1486–1535) and Theophrastus Bombastus von Hohenheim, called "Paracelsus" (1493–1541).

11 Peter Dinzelbacher, ed., *Handbuch der Religionsgeschichte im deutschsprachigen Raum: Hoch- und Spätmittelalter*, 367.

12 St. Ignatius of Antioch, "Letter to Smyrniots," VIII, 2.

13 In the Christian West an "ordinary" is an ecclesiastical officer holding both pastoral and governmental jurisdiction over a defined group of persons; in the Christian East such an officer is called a "hierarch."

who, once confirmed by Rome and consecrated by other bishops, possessed full rights over their dioceses.[14]

One might assume that a bishop's chief duties were to ordain parish priests and install them in parishes, to teach and exercise spiritual lordship over their parishioners, and conduct visitations of the parishes and administer the sacrament of confirmation. True enough according to canon law, but reality displayed a wild variety of practice and great extremes of behavior. For one thing, episcopal authority over the parishes was often enforceable only indirectly, sometimes not at all. Because of lay patronage and the incorporation of parishes into monasteries,[15] bishops often lacked the legal right to appoint many parish priests in their own dioceses. In the diocese of Worms, 187 of the 243 parishes were incorporated into monasteries and other ecclesiastical bodies, 55 stood under lay patronage, and only 1 parish benefice was directly controlled by the bishop. Once installed, however, priests and parishes were subject to periodic inspections (visitations), though bishops normally delegated this task to a senior official who visited the urban and rural churches, interrogated priests and people separately, admonished them to improvement, and made recommendations to the bishop, usually in writing.[16] Visitations tended to be made fairly regularly by zealous bishops and desultorily or not at all by uninterested or incompetent ones. Nearly all of the fifteenth-century reform writings recommended an intensification of visitations as the best means for restoring clerical and lay discipline.

The bishop was also a judge. His authority over the clergy was comprehensive, though as often as not a clergymen could document exemption (immunity) from the bishop's judicial authority. Over the laity, too, the bishop's jurisdiction was incomplete and in many matters contested. Marriage cases were litigated sometimes in episcopal courts, and sometimes in secular courts of customary law, while the damages caused by sin and the sinner's restoration to the Church's fellowship generally took place through not judicial but penitential channels. The general tendency was to moderate the harsh discipline of earlier times through the commutation of penances to fines and to replace public acts of penance by private ones.

These powers and functions were common to all of the Western Church's bishops. The fusions of these spiritualia with temporal offices and jurisdictions had long been common in other lands, in some of which, notably France, they survived well into early modern times. The extreme case of such a fusion is to be seen in the Imperial church, many of whose bishops wielded the "two swords" of spiritual and temporal authority and ranked as Imperial princes.[17] Beginning in the later tenth century under the Ottonian emperors, a bishop, once elected by the cathedral chapter of his diocese and confirmed by the pope, became a feudal vassal of the emperor. He received

---

14 See Chapter 6.
15 Lay patronage (Latin: *ius patronatus*) was a set of rights and obligations pursuant to a giving of land to the Church (benefice). The rights included that of presentation of a candidate for a vacant benefice, though if the benefice involved pastoral duties (the "cure of souls"), the patron had to choose from qualified candidates, and his choice had to be confirmed by the bishop. Incorporation of a benefice into an abbey or collegiate church gave the latter the right to collect the tithe and to choose the pastor, who became in effect the abbey's vicar.
16 As with most records, visitation reports are scantier and more fragmentary from the Empire than from some other countries. They become a regular source of reliable information only from the sixteenth century.
17 The application of the image of "two swords" (Luke 22:38) to governance is attributed to Pope Gelasius I (d. 496), who in 494 wrote to the emperor that the world is governed by two powers, spiritual and temporal.

investiture with temporal authority of various kinds over specific lands, which constituted his *Hochstift* (territory).[18] In the fifteenth century some 55 archbishops and bishops ruled *Hochstifte*, plus about 75 Imperial abbots and abbesses and the masters of the Teutonic Order and the Knights of St. John.[19] The perhaps 15 percent of the Empire's lands that stood under clerical rule was unevenly distributed, greatest in the northwest and west, least in the northeast and in the Austro-Bavarian southeast. Some prince-bishops, such as those of Brandenburg, Chur, Metz, Sitten/Sion, Gurk, Lavant, Seckau, Merseburg, and Naumburg, either possessed tiny *Hochstifte* or had lost their lands to princely dynasties. Others, notably those of Würzburg, Bamberg, Salzburg, Münster, and Paderborn, still ruled wide lands and became sufficiently centralized to be comparable in secular power to all but the greatest lay princes. Yet bishops were on the whole weak rulers, and resistance to their temporal authority by burghers and cathedral canons convinced quite a number of prince-bishops to depart their cathedral cities for other, safer residences. By the late fifteenth century the bishop of Constance lived at Meersburg, Strasbourg at Saverne, Mainz at Aschaffenburg, Worms at Ladenburg, Speyer at Udenheim, Basel at Porrentruy/Pruntrut and Délémont/Delsberg, and Augsburg at Dillenburg. If the Church existed where the bishop was, it was very often found in a small country town or even a castle.

4. A NOBLE CHURCH

The Imperial church was a noble church, and on its green pastures routinely grazed the sons and daughters of the mighty and the not so mighty. The roots of this exploitation lay, at least in arguments for it, in the distant past, when the Church had developed in the German lands under noble protection and patronage. The nobles in turn came to regard the Church as, to be sure, a way of life for especially devout progeny, but also as a reservoir of substance from which to support their families and provide a hedge against extinction of their lineages. The Church's law, true, qualified in principle the noble families' management of their futures by prohibiting intensive endogamy and by insisting on the consent of partners to make a valid marriage. In practice, while the prohibition seems to have been relatively effective, its insistence on consent "could in praxis hardly be exercised by young candidates for marriage"[20] because of the patriarchal family's power to break their resistance and its ability to prevent many children from marrying at all.

In this light it may have seemed only just that the Church, which heightened some threats to noble lineages' survival, should provide livelihoods from its substance – much of which went back to nobles' gifts – for the many who did not or could not marry.[21] And so it did, as generations of noblemen and noblewomen streamed willy-

---

18 Against my usual practice, I retain the German term, because the alternatives – "ecclesiastical states" and "episcopal territories" – imply misleading similarities to lay dynastic principalities.

19 Here are meant not the grand-masters of these two military-religious orders but the subordinate masters of the orders within the Empire, each of whom held a seat in the Imperial Diet.

20 Karl-Heinz Spiess, *Familie und Verwandtschaft im deutschen Hochadel des Spätmittelalters – 13. bis Anfang des 16. Jahrhunderts*, 534.

21 This is not to suggest that noblemen and women did not enter the Church from a genuine sense of religious calling, but the picture drawn by Spiess is compelling. It shows that young nobles had choices among three possible statuses – lay unmarried, lay married, and clerical – and not just the latter two.

nilly into abbeys, convents, and collegiate chapters. By the fifteenth century many such institutions lay fast in the grip of the regional nobilities, which defended their possession by requiring genealogical proofs for admission. Written documentation of noble descent was required for admission to the Rhenish and Franconian cathedral chapters: the "four-ancestor rule" was used at Freising and Regensburg, the "sixteen-ancestor rule" at Bamberg, Würzburg, and Mainz.[22] At St. Alban's Abbey in Mainz, "they exclude men who could be admitted to the College of Cardinals. Yes, to speak in jest, if the Lord and Saviour came back to earth, he would be excluded from the community of St. Alban's on the grounds that his non-noble descent on both sides endangered the honor and prestige of the monastery."[23]

For the princely dynasties the stakes rose much higher. They parked surplus children in clerical posts and communities, as lesser nobles did, but they also sought to place their sons and nephews in the prince-bishoprics, especially the rich, politically significant sees. Regensburg, Freising, and Constance were poor, but Speyer, Würzburg, Cologne, Strasbourg, and Salzburg were rich, and, better yet, Mainz, Trier, and Cologne brought with them electoral offices. Some dynasties turned to their advantage Rome's relaxation of the Church's law against accumulating benefices.[24] The Palatine Wittelsbachs at Heidelberg played the game with great abandon: a son and three nephews of Elector Palatine Louis III (r. 1410–36) accumulated an archbishopric and five bishoprics; five sons of Elector Philip, called "the Upright" (b. 1448, r. 1476–1508), gained sees, including one who held three sees simultaneously without the benefit of ordination, much less episcopal consecration. What such worldly prelates could not do, at least not before the Protestant Reformation, was to secularize and retain episcopal *Hochstifte* for themselves and their dynasties. It was not for want of wishing, for the logic of curbing episcopal power promised both accretions of lands and incomes and the possibility for ecclesiastical restructuring to fit the newly formed territorial states. Once princes began to regard their lands as a single territory and to claim greater powers over the lands' churches, the fragmentation (from their point of view) of ecclesiastical jurisdictions over the churches constituted a hindrance to this goal. Along the Lower Rhine below Cologne, the scattered lands of the dukes of Cleves-Jülich lay in eight different dioceses and three ecclesiastical provinces; the Brandenburg elector's relatively compact lands lay in nine dioceses and three provinces; Mecklenburg was divided among six dioceses and two provinces; and the Bavarian duchy lay in seven dioceses, none of whose bishops were in any way subject to ducal authority.

The map shows an acute case of the general lack of fit between the templates of spiritual and temporal authority, which rarely became troublesome before the formation of institutionalized dynastic principalities, but which stood directly in the way of consolidations of a prince's desire, from whatever motive, to consolidate his lands in an ecclesiastical sense.

Finally, there was the question of money. For the great lay dynasties, weakening episcopal rule would make easier a reduction of the clergy's immunity from secular

---

22 Such rules required that a candidate for a canonry in the cathedral chapter offer proofs of the noble status of his grandparents, great-grandparents, or even great-great grandparents (the "sixteen-ancestor rule").

23 Aloys Schulte, *Der Adel und die deutsche Kirche im Mittelalter*, 248. The Dutch humanist Erasmus cracked the same joke about the cathedral chapter of Strasbourg.

24 The Church's law forbade "accumulation," which meant holding simultaneously two or more benefices bearing the care of souls. The papacy often departed from this rule.

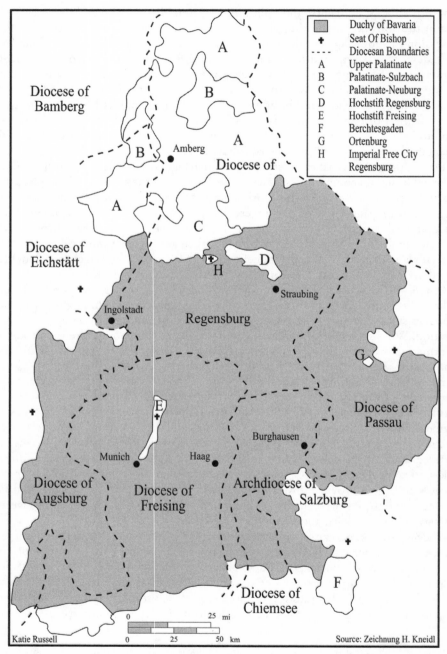

	Duchy of Bavaria
✛	Seat Of Bishop
----	Diocesan Boundaries
A	Upper Palatinate
B	Palatinate-Sulzbach
C	Palatinate-Neuburg
D	Hochstift Regensburg
E	Hochstift Freising
F	Berchtesgaden
G	Ortenburg
H	Imperial Free City Regensburg

Diocese of Bamberg

A

B

A

B   Amberg

A

Diocese of

C

Diocese of Eichstätt

H

D

Straubing

Ingolstadt

Regensburg

G

Diocese of Passau

E

Burghausen

Munich   Haag

Diocese of Augsburg

Diocese of Freising

Archdiocese of Salzburg

F

Diocese of Chiemsee

0   25 mi

0   25   50 km

Katie Russell

Source: Zeichnung H. Kneidl

Map 4. Bavaria at the Time of the Reformation

taxation. In 1480 Margrave Albert Achilles (1417–86) ordered the clergy of his Franconian lands to contribute to the taxes for the Ottoman War. The prince-bishops of Bamberg and Würzburg objected that this would violate clerical immunity from temporal jurisdiction. "If God had wanted there to be only one sword," growled Albert, "He could have created one instead of two. He was a very wise fellow."[25] He called the clergy's representatives to him and read them the riot act: "You call me 'prince' and 'lord,' and rightly so, for so I am. Do you know what I have done to you? I have created an example to other princes, so they will treat your fellows likewise."[26] "The German Fox," as his contemporaries called Albert, made the priests pay. "If this has been done by an old, wasted man," the vicar-general of Bamberg wondered, "what will his tall young sons do?"[27] What, indeed? It was a sign of the times. Lay rulers longed to liberate the lands and incomes from the Church's "dead hand."[28] This was reasonable, but so was the clergy's expectation of a continuation of past practice. Reasonable, surely, but not compatible with the times.

The Church's dilemma arose from its success. The more deeply it penetrated the structures of Augustine's "earthly city," the more thoroughly its freedom of action became ensnared in the complexities of local life. The very assets that guarded its freedom – powerful bishops, rich monasteries, and clerical immunity from lay impositions – promoted its own secularization and compromised what remained in principle its primary mission, the salvation of souls. This experience, while by no means peculiar to the German lands, was heightened there by the tremendous strength of local institutions and the weakness of large ones, plus the extreme degree of fusion of leaders of the Church with lords of the world. Against these fragmenting forces, however, stood the powerful forces of the common religion. It had proved its adaptability when it broke out from small, sectarian communities into Graeco-Roman society, and again when it addressed the agrarian world that succeeded the passing of Roman rule in the west. The challenge of adaptation it faced around 1500 was, if not so dramatically obvious, nonetheless impressive enough.

5. RELIGION – THE BOND OF SOCIETY

"Religion is the bond of society," taught early modern German lawyers.[29] Ancient in origin, this recognition of religion's social function was a commonplace in late medieval and early modern Europe. "Governance is preserved chiefly by religion," wrote the Strasbourg priest Johannes Hug in 1504, "and the emperor holds the body public together more by means of religious rites than by the performance of duties or by public works."[30] Just as commonplace was the contrary view, that disunity in religion

25 Julius von Minutoli, ed., *Das kaiserliche Buch des Markgrafen Albrecht Achilles. Kurfürstliche Periode 1470–1486*, 347.
26 Minutoli, ed., *Das kaiserliche Buch*, 378.
27 Minutoli, ed., *Das kaiserliche Buch*, 381.
28 Under the principle of the "dead hand" (*mortmain*), the Church's property could not be alienated or sold.
29 Heinz Schilling, "Confessional Europe," in Thomas A. Brady, Heiko A. Oberman, and James D. Tracy, eds., *Handbook of European History, 1400–1600. Late Middle Ages, Renaissance, Reformation*, vol. 2: 642.
30 Johannes Hug, *Quadrivium Ecclesie / Quatuor prelatorum officium / Quibus omnis status tum Secularis tum vero Ecclesiasticus subijcitur*, fol. 49r.

breeds discord and civil conflict. "In our times," sighed the eloquent Strasbourg magistrate Jacob Sturm in 1534, "scarcely anything else so unites people's minds or drives them apart as unity or disunity in religion does."[31] From a theological point of view, of course, maintaining civil peace and solidarity was but the secondary role of religion, for the Church taught that "the salvation of souls is the highest rule."[32] The Church also promoted the idea that at death God would judge each individual according to His promise to "show mercy to all those who depart this life with true repentance."[33] Otherwise, the love of God was held to be the central bond in the triadic relationship among God, the individual, and one's neighbors. The Church stood as common broker in this triad, mediator and dispenser of grace, guaranteed by Christ to endure until the end of time.

What, then, was religion? First of all, to be "in religion" meant to have taken up the ascetic life in a religious community or order bound by vows. "Religion" could also mean piety in the sense of "true piety," which meant both an idea and a practice: an acceptance of the central teachings of the faith and a willingness to perform the acts prescribed by that acceptance.

At the heart of Christianity stood the idea of personal salvation through atonement for sin.[34] As expounded by St. Anselm of Canterbury (1033–1109), the principal medieval explanation of what this meant held that when Adam and Eve disobeyed God, they formed a condition of offence between themselves and Him, that led to their expulsion from Paradise. This condition – the central point – had been transmitted to their descendants, whom God could in all justice not restore to His favor until the debt was repaid and His honor repaired. Humanity, however, lacked the wherewithal to pay this limitless debt, which could be repaid only by One who was both God, and therefore of infinite worth, and Man, and therefore a kinsman to God's debtors. The existence of such a person, the gospels testified, was a fact of history. After much thought, the Church determined that His existence entailed a plurality of persons in God, of whom One, the Son, had gratuitously taken it upon Himself to be born into the human kindred and to offer through His death due satisfaction to the Father in the name of His human kin. Infinite sin gained infinite compensation, when Christ transferred His righteousness to his helpless kinsmen and women. Since the Father could not in justice refuse this free offer, the state of offense could be overcome and humanity restored to favor and future blessedness. For the Christian the possibility of individual salvation depended on kinship and ultimately on the matrilineal kindred of Jesus. He was kinsman to humanity through the Virgin Mary, who "had the most right to rail against the rest of mankind for the killing of her son ... [and] was bound to represent the first member of the redeemed human race."[35] Salvation thus depended fundamentally on Christ's humanity far more than on His divinity.

How could one participate in the righteousness that Christ, through His death, had won for His human kindred? The answer to this question depended absolutely on

31 Hans Virck et al., eds., *Politische Correspondenz der Stadt Straßburg im Zeitalter der Reformation*, vol. 2: 237, n. 59.
32 In Latin: "*salus animarum suprema lex*," Codex iuris canonici, c. 1752.
33 Berndt Hamm, *The Reformation of Faith in the Context of Late Medieval Theology and Piety. Essays by Berndt Hamm*, 136. This text is spoken by God in a painting, *Das Vorbild des Ulrich Schwarz, d. J.*, Hans Holbein the Elder (1508).
34 This summary rests on John Bossy, *Christianity in the West, 1400–1700*, 3–4.
35 Bossy, *Christianity in the West*, 8.

belief in the presence of God in the world and how that sacred presence could be accessed and benefits be drawn from it. The manifestations of the sacred within the profane world "enabled people to establish relations with the sacred and to create from them a form of 'cosmic order.' This cosmic order encompasses human relationships with the sacred, with other persons and with the natural world."[36] Salvation, though individual, was worked out in the midst of two aspects of the world's life, social reproduction of the household and community and biological reproduction of animal and plant life. They defined the ritual cycles of the life of an individual and of the year of seasons, through which holiness could be imparted. They also demonstrated a pragmatic understanding of sacred power and confirmed God's presence in the world.

In the main, therefore, religious life played out against the background of a mental world the Church had influenced to varying degrees but not fully determined. This mentality partook of "an essentially sacramental view of the world" braided of three strands: first, "a pragmatic, inner-worldly understanding of the efficacy of sacred power;" second, "the development of a sensual connection with sacred objects;" and third, "a materialist conception of the workings of the sacred."[37] During the fifteenth century, rich in religious novelties, this worldview was falling under criticism from advocates of a more spiritual, interior, and personal religion, but it would be a mistake to regard this tendency – so obviously related to the Protestant reformation – as dominant. The demand for a more personal and spiritual religion stood in a many-sided tension with the rich world of ritual practice the agrarian world had created in the deeper past. What had not appeared before was the striving of laypeople to invent, promote, and protect ways to live a spiritual life in the world. Such efforts did not lead directly to the Protestant attempt, "with its radically different understanding of the sacred," to make "a firm break between the sacred and the secular worlds."[38] Yet it did try to dispel illegitimate superstitions by devaluing image and symbol in favor of the word audible or visible.

The most forceful teaching of spiritual religion in this sense came from the Dutch humanist Erasmus of Rotterdam (1466–1536). He argued for spiritual religion as a sublimation, not an obliteration, of the religion of pure practice. "What is the use of being sprinkled with a few drops of holy water," he asks,

as long as you do not wipe clean the inner defilement of the soul? You venerate the saints, and you take pleasure in touching their relics. But you disregard their greatest legacy, the example of a blameless life. No devotion is more acceptable and proper to the saints than striving to imitate their virtues. Would you like to win the favour of Peter and Paul? Imitate the faith of the one and the charity of the other, and you will accomplish more than if you were to dash off to Rome ten times.[39]

In the *Enchiridion*, one of his most widely read books – and Martin Luther was his contemporary – Erasmus spoke with authority to the devout, literate laity, whom he

36 Robert W. Scribner, "Cosmic Order and Daily Life: Sacred and Secular in Pre-industrial German Society," in Robert W. Scribner, *Popular Culture and Popular Movements in Reformation Germany*, 1. His ideas have strongly influenced my comments here.
37 Scribner, "Cosmic Order and Daily Life," in Scribner, *Popular Culture*, 13.
38 Scribner, "Cosmic Order and Daily Life," in Scribner, *Popular Culture*, 15.
39 *Enchiridion militis christiani*, in Desiderius Erasmus, *Collected Works of Erasmus*, vol. 66: 144. My thanks to Greta G. Kroeker for this and the following quote.

taught a spiritual redaction of the traditional Catholic ideal of striving for virtue. "Perfect piety," he writes,

> is the attempt to progress always from visible things, which are usually imperfect or indifferent, to invisible [ones]. This precept is most pertinent to our discussion, since it is through neglect or ignorance of it that most Christians are superstitious rather than pious, and except for the name of Christ differ hardly at all from superstitious pagans.[40]

By raising "the ethical demands of the Gospel" from the periphery to the center of religion," Erasmus spoke to the educated clergy and laity of his day as few others had done.[41] His teaching represents a turbocharged version of one of the principle tendencies of fifteenth-century religion: individual spiritual growth through progress in virtue. Only the success of Luther's revolutionary attack on this principle diminished Erasmus's stature as the leading spiritual teacher of his day.

While this spiritualizing, moralizing critique of ordinary religion flourished in the German lands well before 1500, so did the modes of religion it attacked as external and superstitious. Some Christians searched for a more meaningful spiritual life within, others strove through actions to make the Church's blessings and privileges their own. The satisfaction of their common desire, a more Christian way of life, could work in seemingly contradictory ways. It could express both a reaffirmation of traditional practices and hierarchical authority or "a determination not to leave the church to prelates, orders, or princes."[42]

Was there ever a common religion at all? Did the beliefs and notions about the Christian life have a common core, or did they mark a religion of two separate tiers, a formalistic, external one for ordinary people and an ethical, spiritual one for the educated? Many historians believe they did. Yet the concept of "two tiers" is, by definition,

> timeless and faceless, because it exhibits modes of thinking that are unintelligible except in terms of failure to be something else – failure through the pressures of anxiety, failure through the absence of the cultural and social preconditions of rational thought, failure through that hard fate that has condemned half of the population of any age, through accident of gender, to being members of "that timorous and pious sex."[43]

Hard fate also condemned nearly all of the other half, the allegedly less timorous and less pious sex.

The various modes of Christian life certainly did not correspond to the distinction between clergy and laity, who were, on the contrary, becoming more alike. While the clergy was being laicized by its accumulation of property and participation in the market, the laity was being clericalized through its mastery of writing, statute law, and the ability to think about abstract and spiritual things, such as the market and divine grace. As the differences between them lessened, relations between them became more competitive and less complementary than they earlier had been. Indeed, a more devout laity corresponded to a clergy who was more worldly in both senses of

40   Erasmus, *Enchiridion*, in Erasmus, *Collected Works*, vol. 66: 65.
41   James D. Tracy, *Erasmus, the Growth of a Mind*, 133.
42   John Van Engen, "The Church in the Fifteenth Century," in Brady, Oberman, and Tracy, eds., *Handbook of European History, 1400–1600*, 313.
43   Peter Brown, *Society and the Holy in Late Antiquity*, 12.

the term, active in the world and captive to the world. The more worldly in these senses the clergy became, the less clear were its special functions and the weaker the perceived legitimacy of its privileges. These changes belong to the prehistory of the Protestant reformers' desire to redraw the boundaries between clergy and laity by mobilizing the laity and demonizing the old clergy. Victory in this endeavor depended, however, on the possibility of giving the grievances of all classes of the laity a distinctly anticlerical focus. "If the revolution of a people and the emancipation of a particular class [*Klasse*] of bourgeois society are to coincide," wrote Karl Marx,

> so that one group [*Stand*] stands for all social groups, then the contrary is also true: a particular group must be despised by all others, it must embody that which blocks the desires of the others. In this case, one particular social sphere [*Sphäre*] must be the locus for the notorious crimes of the entire society, so that the liberation of this sphere may appear to be a general self-emancipation.[44]

Another helpful way to acknowledge, without exaggerating, the different kinds of religion is to classify their local and supra-local elements. The Church contained "two levels of Catholicism – that of the Church Universal, based on the sacraments, the Roman liturgy, and the Roman calendar; and a local one, based on particular sacred places, images, and relics, locally chosen patron saints, idiosyncratic ceremonies, and a unique calendar built up from the settlement's own sacred history."[45] In the German lands, as elsewhere in Christendom, Christians high and low lived a religious life configured by the life-cycle of baptism, puberty, marriage, and death and by the annual liturgical cycle of the sacred year. The ordering of time had three parts: a main cycle ("the Lord's year") centered on the feasts of the Incarnation, Crucifixion, and Resurrection of Christ; a cycle of Marian feasts; and the feasts of the saints, both the universal apostles, virgins, martyrs, doctors, and the purely local saints. What unified the churches, local and universal, was thus neither ideas as such nor practices as such, but the acting out of efficacious relationships between cosmic order and daily life. The year's ritual observance combined sacred times with sacred space and sacred actions to constitute the chief performances of the local church in this world, but they also united the local with the universal Church in all three of its aspects: the Church Militant struggling against sin and evil here on earth; the Church Suffering enduring punishment in Purgatory for sins until the release to eternal life; and the Church Triumphant protecting and interceding for the other two sectors. Together the three formed a timeless body known as "the Communion of Saints." Around this endless cycle of common rites, however, sacred notions, rites, and individual actions of most varied kinds and tendencies swarmed with abandon. In the German lands, core and context together lent Christian piety its special, kaleidoscopic character.

6. CHRISTIAN PIETIES IN THE FIFTEENTH CENTURY

The "long fifteenth century" was a landscape "full of ruptures and booby traps," through which no direct paths ran.[46] Its rich variety of religious notions and practices

44 Karl Marx, *Werke*, vol. 1: 501.
45 William A. Christian Jr., *Local Religion in Sixteenth-Century Spain*, 3.
46 Heiko A. Oberman, "The Long Fifteenth Century: In Search of its Profile," 1.

reveals no unambiguous road signs. The picture's obverse displays forms more sensual, emotional, concrete, and communal than the individualized practices of "modern" religion. The same picture's reverse, however, reveals apparently "modern" forms more spiritual, disciplined, literate, and individual than the communal, ritualized practices of "medieval" religion. For the historian the bewildering diversity and inventiveness of popular religiosity in this age creates staggering problems of comprehension, for "feelings often remain hidden, and in many cases what one believes to have discovered is frequently in fact hypocrisy... he must be satisfied to register the expressions of piety and to proceed from the postulate that fear and love, true piety and hypocrisy, are bound together in indeterminate relationship."[47] It is commonly said that most fifteenth- and sixteenth-century reformers, Catholic and Protestant, favored "modern" spiritualizing and individualizing modes of religious practice over "medieval" concrete and communal ones. Yet the former was no more truly "new" than the latter was truly "old," for "new" practices arose from earlier forms, while "old" ones were being constantly invented. There was no direction to this picture, in other words, until the sixteenth-century reformations' disciplining projects took the matter in hand.

For something under four centuries before the reformations, popular practice and belief emphasized the real presence of Christ in the world. It was the object of images, prayers, and rites, of which the Eucharist loomed over all others. To the discussion, however, of how this presence was possible, there was no end. "All those in the first half of the sixteenth century," one historian has written, "who took up discussion of Christ's presence ... had grown up within a rich density of representations of Christ's person and agency and within so many different conceptions of 'presence.' In the sixteenth century, Christians would divide violently on the question, How is Christ 'present' and where?"[48]

By the fifteenth century Eucharistic piety held pride of place among the older cults, holy practices, and minor rituals, on which so much of traditional religious life depended, yet it did not discourage the people's religious inventiveness. This energy is revealed in all its complexity by the Modern Devotion as a way of life, by the cult of Wilsnack Blood, and by the Drummer of Niklashausen's apocalyptic pull. These display respectively the individualizing, sacramental, and prophetic tendencies in fifteenth-century Christian life in the German lands.

The Modern Devotion (*devotio moderna*) was one of the greatest success stories of central European religious history. Netherlandish in origin, the movement produced a loose association of communities known as the Sisters and Brothers of the Common Life. Other participants organized a monastic society based on the rule of St. Augustine (Windesheim Congregation, est. 1378),[49] and still others entered the third orders of the mendicant friars or lived in informal communities without vows. The movement's three main branches[50] – Sisters, Brothers, and the Windesheim Congregation – spread from the Low Countries' Ijssel valley into the northwestern German lands and far up the Rhine, forming in the process a network of around 250

---

47 Francis Rapp, *Christentum IV: Zwischen Mittelalter und Neuzeit (1378–1552)*, 205.
48 Lee Palmer Wandel, *The Eucharist in the Reformation: Incarnation and Liturgy*, 45.
49 The Canons Regular of St. Augustine, whose rule was attributed to the bishop of Hippo, were distinct from the Augustinian Hermits, who were mendicant friars.
50 Not including those who joined third orders of the mendicants.

communities, 113 of women and 139 of men. The Devotion traced its origins to Geert Groote (1340–84) of Deventer, a highly educated man who taught that "to love God and worship him is religion, not the taking of special vows," and those "who despise temporal honors, leading chaste lives, obedient and poor: they are religious people."[51] All currents of the Devotion followed the spiritual program captured by its famous manual, the *Imitation of Christ* by Thomas à Kempis (1379/80–1471), one of the most widely printed, translated, and read books of that or any other age.[52] The *Imitation* teaches a strongly Christocentric but not mystical piety, which is oriented toward virtue and charity and remains wary of the quantitative piety of pilgrimages, multiple Masses, and indulgences. Its touchstone is experience, "so, if we desire to have a true understanding of His gospels, we must study to conform our life as nearly as we can to His."[53]

While the Modern Devotion formed in the most densely urbanized landscape north of the Alps, the sacramental wonder known as "the Wilsnack Blood" erupted out of the deep countryside in the Empire's far northeastern region. In 1383 in Brandenburg's Prignitz district, a pastor discovered three bleeding hosts in the remains of a village church destroyed during a local feud. As its fame grew, Wilsnack soon became the most lively pilgrimage site of a relatively new piety centered on the blood of Christ. Although not unrelated, the cult of Christ's blood was identical neither with the new Eucharistic piety nor with anti-Jewish blood libels and charges of host desecration.[54]

Local motives played an important role in promoting the Wilsnack Blood. The village became a boom town that supplied both the local people and the bishop of Havelberg with considerable incomes. Among the theologians, however, its authenticity did not go uncontested, for the issue of the resurrected Christ's blood in this world challenged some strongly held positions in the academic theology of the day and engaged some quite prominent theologians. The complexity of the issue can be seen in the views of the Bohemian theologian Jan Hus (ca. 1369–1415), who condemned Wilsnack (as did many other theologians) as a fraud, "that red thing" that makes no miracles.[55] Yet Hus's theology of the chalice was also a theology of blood, and he composed a special treatise on the blood of Christ. "[T]he blood of Christ," he wrote, "which flowed out from his body in the circumcision," and the blood that "drained out on the cross and converted to vapor by the heat of the sun . . . reverted then by his power on the day of resurrection to its proper form."[56] Thus can the Christians "wait happily for the glorification of our blood, even if it has been poured out for the dogs to drink in the name of our Lord Jesus Christ."[57]

---

51 Albert Hyma, quoted by Lawrence G. Duggan, "The Unresponsiveness of the Late Medieval Church: A Reconsideration," 17.
52 More than fifty editions appeared between the first printing in 1472 and 1500 and more than 1,800 editions and translations by 1780.
53 Thomas à Kempis, *The Imitation of Christ*, 31.
54 It was quite well known that crucifixion had killed Christ through suffocation rather than exsanguination.
55 Caroline W. Bynum, *Wonderful Blood: Theology and Practice in Late Medieval Northern Germany and Beyond*, 37.
56 Bynum, *Wonderful Blood*, 37.
57 Bynum, *Wonderful Blood*, 37.

Jan Hus, of course, was later condemned and executed for heresy, but no one could question the orthodoxy of some of the Wilsnack Blood's other critics.[58] Heinrich Tocke (ca. 1390–ca. 1455), canon of Magdeburg and former court preacher to Brandenburg's elector, spent much of his life attacking the Wilsnack Blood and other blood miracles as frauds perpetrated by local priests. About one such (confessed) fraud he declared, "How many would he and his followers have tricked, how many pious Christians would they have deprived of their worldly goods through this evil fraud, how many miracles would they have fabricated to the shame of the diocese!"[59] Any number of proven frauds, however, could hardly establish the impossibility of such miracles, which is what theologians critical of Wilsnack had to undertake. They paid no attention to the argument, approved by a papal bull in 1453, that the Wilsnack pilgrimage was essentially a Eucharistic cult (and therefore licit). Among Wilsnack's critics emerged a consensus that "something 'separated' or 'left behind' [by Christ] was problematic both as object of veneration and means of salvation."[60] None of this extensive criticism led to any official action against the Wilsnack Blood, which did not lose its power until after 1552, when the church's first Protestant pastor burnt the miraculously bleeding hosts.

The story of the Wilsnack Blood illuminates many aspects of religious life in the fifteenth-century German lands. Perhaps the most important for present purposes is how clearly it shows that the popular religion and official religion belonged to the same culture. The theologians were well aware that new practices, because of the beliefs they implied, had to be scrutinized for their agreement with the received faith. The pilgrims, of course, had no such worries. "Pilgrims voted with their feet, theologians with their tractates."[61] Yet the central issues bound the two together, for the controversy over the presence of the blood was not just about practices, the proper Eucharistic piety, or the authenticity of venerated relics. Rather, it concerned two essential ideas: "on the one hand, a matter of the relation of the body and blood of Christ to each other and to his person, and on the other hand, a question of how Christians gain access to the *sanguis Christi* that saves."[62]

The story of the Drummer of Niklashausen adds a third, prophetic, mode of religion to the individualizing-moralizing mode of the Modern Devotion and the hyperbolically sacramental mode of the Wilsnack wonder. It unfolded in yet a different kind of landscape, the intensively mixed rural-urban land of Franconia in the Empire's old heartlands. In May 1476 a young shepherd named Hans Behaim surfaced in the Franconian village of Niklashausen, which lay in the diocese of Würzburg. Inspired by his accounts of a vision of the Virgin Mary, a chronicler records, "there arose a great movement into the Tauber valley . . . which expanded tremendously day by day, so large that no one could survey it."[63] Hearing that "the Virgin Mary, God's Mother, appeared to him," tens, possibly hundreds of times, thousands came to hear the Drummer's sermons at Niklashausen, where they camped in the surrounding

58 Among them was Nicholas of Cusa, who in 1451–52 was active as papal legate in the Empire.
59 Bynum, *Wonderful Blood*, 33.
60 Bynum, *Wonderful Blood*, 40.
61 Bynum, *Wonderful Blood*, 86.
62 Bynum, *Wonderful Blood*, 110.
63 Klaus Arnold, *Niklashausen 1476. Quellen und Untersuchungen zur sozialreligiösen Bewegung des Hans Behem und zur Agrarstruktur eines spätmittelalterlichen Dorfes*, 253–4, 189–90.

fields and woods. Most of them, sources agree, were loosely attached and "unhoused" folk, youth and servants, including many women.[64]

The pilgrims heard the Drummer prophesy that "the priests say I am a heretic and want to burn me. . . . If they do burn me, woe to them, for they will truly see what they have done when they themselves are attacked."[65] His prophecy came true one July evening, when Würzburg troopers seized the Drummer from among his sleeping flock and carried him away. "To Würzburg," went up the cry, as ten or twelve thousand pilgrims streamed northward with banners and tall candles in their hands and Marian hymns on their tongues. Having arrived at the bishop's mighty fortress, perched high above and across the Main River from the city, they demanded Behaim's release and told his marshal that "if His Grace would not grant this, they intended to recover him by force."[66] Whether this was bravery or bravado, their spiritual siege collapsed at the first show of force. Rumors flew about

> also about the grave, intolerable, reckless, and terrible words some men and women have said against Our Gracious Lord of Würzburg and his clergy. Namely, the men . . . announced that they would come here and kill them; the women called Our Gracious Lord and his priests lazy rascals who have put in jail that pious man, the young fellow in irons.[67]

On 19 July, as Würzburg's armed burgher militia looked on, the Drummer sang his Marian hymns until the rising flames stopped his voice. Much in the Drummer's sermons was offensive, to be sure, but his attraction arose less from his own ideas than from the Virgin's prophecies.

The Modern Devotion, the Wilsnack Blood, and the visions of Niklashausen show three faces of fifteenth-century religion, each with its own fervent followers. They do not on the face of them convey the union of deep devotion with strong criticism of the Church that would form the signature of the sixteenth-century reform movements. Occasionally, however, the bewilderingly variegated landscape of fifteenth-century religion does flash what in retrospect can be seen as a powerful longing for a life more godly, more devout, and more self-aware. For those who thought this way, one great object of their longing was a restoration of the Christian clergy to its pastoral tasks, free from its entanglements in worldly affairs. Johann Dränsdorf (d. 1425), a Hussite priest who in 1425 was arrested at Heilbronn, interrogated, and then executed at Heidelberg, expressed this desire. His deposition targets in the first place clergymen who hold temporal lordship.[68] The "pope, cardinals, archbishops, bishops . . . and other prelates," the doomed priest asserts, are heretics "in a state of damnation, because they . . . possess full lordship and wield both swords." Indeed, "all religious who possess temporal lordship are in a worse state of damnation than the bishops, who are secular clergy." Holy priests are needed, he says, because "souls can be purified in purgatory through the prayers of holy priests," and "the Hussites do no good when they burn images and destroy monasteries." "Where," he asks, "are

---

64 Arnold, *Niklashausen*, 189–90.
65 Arnold, *Niklashausen*, 205.
66 Arnold, *Niklashausen*, 196.
67 Arnold, *Niklashausen*, 207–8.
68 Hartmut Boockmann, *Die Stadt im späten Mittelalter*, 254–5.

there bishops today who preach, hear confessions, and administer the Church's sacraments?" This fervent priest wanted a more disciplined, a more pastoral, and in the end a holier Church to replace the one governed by unworthy bishops corrupted by temporal power. His desire may be taken as a signature of fifteenth-century religious reform in general and of reform in the German lands in particular.

Part II

Reform of the Empire and the Church, 1400–1520

> A mortal disease has befallen the German Empire; if it is not speedily
> treated, death will inexorably ensue. Men will seek for the realm of Germany and
> will not find; and in time strangers will seize our habitations and divide them
> among themselves. So we shall be subjected to another nation.
>
> Nicholas of Cusa

Part II begins the narrative that fills most of this book. Its central theme is the problem of the reform of the Empire and the Church during the decades between 1400 and 1520. The chapters play out two great stories. The first story consists of the actual reforms in governance, successful in the Empire but not in the Church. The reforms emerged not under the inspiration of ideas, such as the Church being a model for the Empire, but as a series of concrete changes inspired by political and military needs. The possibility of change depended on the king-emperor and his leading vassals coming willy-nilly to terms as co-regents of the Empire. One great change made political reforms: the institutionalization of dynastic power over specific, feudal but heritable lands, or, in a word, territorialization. Unlike their Luxemburg predecessors, the two Habsburg king-emperors of this era managed to consolidate their rule over a cluster of dynastic territories. The Austrian lands served them as a base for advancing dynastic interests in the Empire as a whole. On the other side, the other Imperial princes, none of whom was strong enough to deal alone with the monarch, formed a corporate force, an estate, within a new Imperial parliament, the Diet. Out of these changes came the corporate forms of royal-aristocratic cogovernance that characterized the Empire in its early modern form.

Part II's second story is the failed reform of the Church, the counterpart or even the complement of the successful reform of the Empire. The fundamental cause of failure was a lack of agency or leadership for reform. The end of the Western Schism left the papacy reunited but with gravely weakened authority. The general council's bid to reform the Church in "head and members" dribbled into the sand. And while things were better in several of the western kingdoms, in the Empire there was no dedicated, persistent leadership on behalf of a reform of the Imperial church. The most plausible reason for this failure was that the Imperial political reform locked the church into the hands of a feudal aristocracy whose growing power, the fruit of territorialization and corporate organization, gave the princes power over the church without responsibility for it. No extra-Imperial agency, particularly not a weakened papacy preoccupied with Italian affairs, would or could intervene in the name of the Church Universal. For all practical purposes, therefore, the Imperial church remained the spiritual guise of a thoroughly feudalized fusion of temporal and spiritual governance. Until this fusion could be disaggregated, there could be no meaningful reform of the Church.

The peculiar combination of successful political and failed religious reform in the Empire goes far toward explaining why its public life in early modern times differed so deeply and extensively from those of the proto-national kingdoms of western Europe. If there was a "German problem," it began in this era, and it was not a question of the German lands abandoning European norms. The Empire's dispersed governance and its (in retrospect) hyper-pluralities of institutions, laws, and claims to almost everything conformed to earlier European governance more closely than did absolutist rule based on the western European combination of centralized state power, mobilization of peoples as nations, and imperial ventures. Whether regarded as backward or fortunate, the Empire took a path that was certainly no deviation.

The Imperial political reform that began in the fifteenth century did not restore the medieval German monarchy but created a substantially new one based on the dispersed territorialization of power. This change frustrated a corresponding reform of the Imperial church by depriving it of an episcopacy capable of collaboration to create the chief object of reform, a more pastoral church. The breaking of this dead-lock began with Martin Luther, whose revolutionary theology, against his own intentions, opened the way to a reform of the church that worked with, not against, the massive intensification of aristocratic power that territorialization engendered.

Part II begins with the failed reform of Empire and Church under the Luxemburg dynasty (Chapter 5), followed by the territorialization of the princely lands in general and in the Habsburg dynasty's Austria in particular (Chapter 6). There follow the reforms: the successful Imperial reform in the time of Maximilian I (Chapter 7), and the failed church reform down to the accession of Charles V (Chapter 8).

5

Reform of Empire and Church

The emperor is one ruler of the world exercising his authority over the
others in the plenitude of power, and in his own sphere he is the equal of the
Roman pontiff in the temporal hierarchy on the model of the sacerdotal hierarchy.

Nicholas of Cusa

On Christmas Day 1414 at two o'clock in the morning, King Sigismund (b. 1368,
r. 1410–37) and Queen Barbara (ca. 1390–1451) of Cilli/Celje arrived by boat at the
docks of Constance, a middling free city at the western end of Lake Constance. They
had come to open a general council of the Church, called to end the festering Western
Schism, and to undertake a reform of the Church, as the common phrase ran, "in head
and in members." The undertaking had begun, records the Constance burgher Ulrich
von Richental (d. ca. 1438), when "our lord King Sigismund sent word to Our Holy
Father, Pope John XXIII, that he should fulfill his promise to give peace and rest to
Holy Christendom."[1] The king had further announced that the council "should not
be delayed, [so that] the princes spiritual and temporal would take notice that Holy
Christendom will suffer great harm, and the holy ship of St. Peter will founder in such
weather."[2] As churchmen streamed in from the four corners of Christendom, "everyone looked for the arrival of our lord King and the electors, and no session was held,
and no man would take part in one"[3] until the king should arrive. Despite his irregular
royal election and his lack of the Imperial title, Sigismund's claim to be lord of
Christendom and protector of the Church could hardly be disputed, least of all by
the three claimants to the papal throne.

Pope John XXIII (r. 1410–15), second and last pope of the Pisan line,[4] awaited King
Sigismund and Queen Barbara in Constance Cathedral, where for nine hours after
their arrival he celebrated the three Masses of Christmas Day, interspersed with the
hours of the Holy Office. Sigismund, an ordained deacon, assisted the pope. Decades
later, when a miniaturist illustrated Richental's chronicle, behind the robed king he

1 Ulrich von Richental, *Chronik des Constanzer Concils 1414 bis 1418*, 17.
2 Richental, *Chronik des Constanzer Concils*, 17.
3 Richental, *Chronik des Constanzer Concils*, 35.
4 The Pisan line of popes began in 1409 as the last stage of the Western Schism. It ended with John
XXIII's abdication in 1415.

71

placed the elector of Saxony holding a bared sword to signify that this figure was no ordinary deacon. He certainly was not, for on this royal clergyman depended to a very great degree the Council of Constance's successes and failures.

Like a Constantine or a Theodosius, Sigismund dominated the general council. Once it had ended the papal schism, he undertook a stupendous journey to sell its decision to the other rulers of Christendom. Westward he went via Geneva, Nîme, Narbonne, Avignon, and Lyons to Paris; next across the Channel from Calais to Dover, Canterbury, London, Windsor, and Leeds; and then back over the Channel to the Low Countries and up the Rhine to Constance. Everywhere Sigismund proclaimed the Church's restored unity. The king's journey for Christian unity was perhaps the last time a Holy Roman emperor actually performed his role as protector of the Church Universal in the medieval sense. Christian unity was his one great success, for in nearly every other important respect, Sigismund's reign was marked by failure. He failed to avert an extinction of the Luxemburgs in the agnatic line; he failed to gain for them a secure territorial base from which to rule the German lands; and, except for his leading role at the Council of Constance, he failed to accomplish much for reform of Empire and Church. On one project, however, thinking about Empire and Church in their similarities and differences, real progress was made in his time. The realization of Sigismund's proposal for reform required another 200 years.

1. THE IMPERIAL MONARCHY – LUXEMBURG PROJECTS

The later history of the Luxemburgs as an Imperial dynasty supports the argument that a new era for the German lands began in the fifteenth century. French speakers, they belong to the last wave of Imperial lineages who migrated out of the west to hunt for opportunity in the less densely settled east: Habsburgs from the Upper Rhine to Austria, Hohenzollerns from Swabia to Franconia and thence to Brandenburg, and Wettins from Eastphalia[5] to Upper Saxony. The dying off of native central European royal dynasties during the thirteenth and fourteenth centuries – Bohemia's Presmylids, Poland's Piasts, Hungary's Arpadians, and the German Hohenstaufens – opened space for new blood. Royal successions became tontines, in which each aristocratic marriage bet on inheriting from biologically less fortunate relations. The Luxemburgs rose via marriages to royal princesses of two eastern dynasties that failed in the male line: John (1296–1346), called "the Blind," ruled as elected king of Bohemia following the Presmylid extinction; Sigismund, his younger grandson, ruled Hungary in succession to King Louis I (r. 1342–82) of the house of Anjou.

Marriage and/or election could create a new royal dynasty, but legitimacy without wealth meant to reign without ruling.[6] Emperor Henry VII (r. 1308/12–13), John's father, had proved the point. He had sought wealth and power in the old way, in Italy, and had died in the attempt. Henry lacked what his predecessors for a century had lacked, a royal demesne. The king, a widespread maxim held, should "live of his own." This was impossible in the Empire, because the once considerable domain of

---

5 This ancient name has disappeared from the maps. It lay approximately between the Middle Weser and the Middle Elbe rivers.

6 The conventional distinction between hereditary and elective monarchy is a lawyers' fiction. Many monarchies – the Empire, Hungary, Bohemia, Poland – were both, elective in law and often hereditary in practice.

castles, towns, tolls, and taxes had been mortgaged and never redeemed or usurped and never disgorged. Emperor Charles IV (r. 1346/49–78), Henry's grandson, sold or mortgaged nearly all of what remained. Sigismund estimated his Imperial incomes at only 15,000 gulden per year when he succeeded in 1410, and by 1417 this sum had fallen by two-thirds.[7] "Alas," he sighed, the Empire's "rights are everywhere weakened and torn to pieces."[8] He was right, for the Bavarian duchy alone brought in about 20,000 silver marks annually, or about three times as much as the emperor's regalian (royal) rights yielded. The Bohemian kingdom, by contrast, brought in about 100,000 silver marks annually, enough to make Bohemia and its crownlands (Moravia, Silesia, and Lusatia) wealthy enough to make German mouths water.

Bohemia offered a promising base for Imperial ambitions, thrusting westward as it did like a great spearhead into the heart of the German lands between Bavaria and Franconia to the south and Saxony and Thuringia to the north.[9] The kingdom possessed strong traditions of royal rule, its own written language (Czech), an unrivaled center at Prague, and a flourishing trade based on its central position and its extensive mining industry. King John had also obtained from Rome the elevation of Prague to an archbishopric, and sponsored the transformation of the city's church of St. Vitus into one of central Europe's great Gothic cathedrals.

From these beginnings John's elder son, Charles, "deliberately aimed to build up Bohemia as the core land of the Empire."[10] Creating a dynastic base in the middle of the Empire, the royal hand could reach westward and northward from Prague, which, with a population of 40,000, was one of Europe's largest cities. This was the project of Charles, the first emperor in 118 years to rule by unchallenged right. In 1356 he issued the Empire's first fundamental law, the Golden Bull, named for the golden seal it bore. Despite its opening, a patchwork quilt of prayer, classical allusions, moral theology, and fancy words from Charles's chancery, the law's intent is plain enough. It aimed to end contested royal elections – the German kingdom's bane – by fixing "the true and legitimate Electors of the Holy Empire" as seven in number: the archbishops of Mainz, Cologne, and Trier, the senior Count Palatine, duke of Saxony, and margrave of Brandenburg, plus the Bohemian king.[11] The law also spelled out the electoral procedure in considerable detail, including an all-important provision for majority rule, and declared the lay electorates to be hereditary and the lands of all electors indivisible. The Golden Bull also fixed the rules that governed all royal elections from Sigismund (1411) to Francis II (1792).[12] It ended disputed elections and made the electors into the first permanent, non-royal component of Imperial governance, a project on which no further progress was made for the next 130 years.

7 Francis Rapp, *Les origines médiévales de l'Allemagne moderne: de Charles IV à Charles Quint (1346–1519)*, 87.
8 Jörg K. Hoensch, *Kaiser Sigismund: Herrscher an der Schwelle zur Neuzeit 1368–1437*, 13.
9 Whether Bohemia itself may be counted as one of the German lands is a matter of definition. The kingdom did function, in some eras, as part of the Holy Roman Empire, of which it was a fief. The ethnolinguistic argument is relevant but not decisive. For one thing, many German speakers lived in Bohemia, which was in this respect less distinct from the German-speaking lands than were, say, Savoy, Imperial Burgundy, Lorraine, Gorizia, or Carniola. For another, as has been noted, the very term "German" was sometimes used in the sense of "an Imperial subject."
10 Hoensch, *Kaiser Sigismund*, 15.
11 Not coincidentally, two of these electorates – Bohemia and Brandenburg – currently reposed in Luxemburg hands.
12 There is no evidence it had any practical significance before around 1400.

The Luxemburg project halted under Charles IV's elder son, Wenceslas (r. 1363–1419 in Bohemia, 1376–1400 in Germany), who inherited a Bohemian kingdom endowed with a population of some 2 million, a written vernacular of its own, a great capital city, and a royal stream of silver from the mines at Kutna Hora. He proved incapable of meeting two challenges: opposition from the 150 baronial families who held local power and mounting enmity between the native Czech speakers and immigrant German speakers.

From the perspective of his sons' reigns, Charles IV's Bohemia seems to have basked in the light of a golden age. This is a grossly one-sided impression that makes the most of Wenceslas's notoriety for being in his cups. There are worse things than the rule of an incompetent king. One of them is terror. The most startling recent revelation about Charles's Bohemia is that underneath the glitter of his court, the prestige of a newly independent archbishopric, and elegance of his chancery's Latin, humbler folk, most of them immigrants, suffered what can only be called a "reign of terror." It was conducted by an inquisitorial agency, the composition, organization, and powers of which remain more than murky. What is certain is that during the middle third of the fourteenth century, some thousands of suspects were questioned about their religious beliefs, and perhaps some hundreds were convicted and executed for heresy. Most of the known suspects seem to have been alleged Waldensians, mostly farmers and burghers, and nearly all of them bore German names. In Bohemia, "hardly a day went by in which people were not tried, condemned, and burned" by inquisitors, and although the evidence is very incomplete, "terror was an ongoing phenomenon – the fragmentary evidence reveals this with clarity."[13] These revelations place the subsequent history of Bohemia under the Luxemburgs in an entirely new, if quite uneven light. Although these events do not point clearly to the constellation of forces that developed in early Hussitism, and although the ethnic character of the dispositions is hardly transparent, the religious agitation that seems to mark the descent from the heights of Charles IV's reign to the wars of Sigismund's was by no means a reversal of fortunes. Possibly, the inability to deal with religious tensions associated with the wave of German-speaking immigrants in Charles's time weakened the stability of public life and undermined the Luxemburg project's chances for success.

2. SIGISMUND – THE LUXEMBURGS' SECOND CHANCE

In 1368 Empress Elizabeth (1347–93) proudly announced to Strasbourg's magistrates, "God took mercy on this fatherland of Bohemia, because it is large and had only one surviving heir, and presented it with a second one."[14] Sigismund, his dynasty's insurance policy against biological misfortune, became a master of languages – he was bilingual in Czech and German and a speaker of Latin, French, Italian, and a second Slavic tongue. He rivaled his father as a patron of art and culture, and married well, taking as his wife the daughter of King Louis I of Hungary, called "the Great," who had no surviving sons.

---

13 Alexander Patschovsky, ed., *Quellen zur böhmischen Inquisition im 14. Jahrhundert*, 23. Patschovsky judges this wave of persecution to have been equal in extent to the somewhat earlier wave in southern France.

14 Hoensch, *Kaiser Sigismund*, 32.

The resemblances between the Hungarian and Bohemian kingdoms around 1400 are very impressive. Founded around 1000 under a native dynasty, Hungary, too, possessed a royal saint, St. Stephen, as well as a powerful baronage, a numerous lesser nobility, a united and influential national church, and a distinctive national language. Upon King Louis's death in 1382, succession fell to Princess Mary (1371–95) and her betrothed, Sigismund, who married in 1385. Two years later, on Palm Sunday (31 March) 1387, Sigismund swore to respect the kingdom's "ancient good customs," to select councilors from among the prelates, the barons, and their heirs, and to bestow no office or estate on a foreigner.[15]

Hungary, which unlike Bohemia undoubtedly lay outside the Empire, faced formidable threats from its powerful magnates, rival Polish claims, and the rise of the Ottoman power. Not until Timur (Tamerlane, 1336–1405) advanced against the Ottomans did Sigismund gain respite to deal with German and church affairs. His chance came in 1410 with the death of King Rupert (r. 1400–10), a Wittelsbach of the Palatine line. Yet because the electors were badly divided, Sigismund's election on 20 September 1410 was irregular. "In Frankfurt behind the choir stool," quipped a jokester, "a king was elected by a child and a fool."[16] Sigismund, who got only two votes, later had to be re-elected.

Forty-three years old at his election as German king, Sigismund possessed a breadth of vision and a sense of grandeur unseen in a German monarch since the thirteenth century. He promised to halt Venetian expansion and recover Imperial Italy, to resolve the papal schism, and to take up the cross against the Ottoman power and recover the Holy Land from "infidel and barbarian peoples,"[17] to reconcile the Latin and Greek churches, and to undertake the reform of Empire and Church. This vision seemed to be nothing but high words from a king who not long ago had fled from the Ottomans and suffered captivity at the hands of the Hungarian barons and bishops. However high his intention, Sigismund faced a grave financial obstacle, for already in 1412 he was complaining that "the incomes and taxes from all German lands are so much diminished and usurped, that they hardly yield 13,000 gulden per year, as an audit has determined."[18] By contrast, his Hungarian revenues, managed for him by Florentines and Neapolitans, brought in some 300,000 gulden per year, plus a good deal more from extraordinary revenues.

On one point the new king was as good as his word. He called the general council to Constance to end the schism begun by the double papal election of 1378, the healing of which he named "the highest, most useful, and most necessary" of all his duties.[19] This he accomplished, and the rest he hoped to finance with the revenues of a third kingdom, Bohemia, where his incompetent brother Wenceslas's interminable 56-year reign was ended by his death in June 1419. Wenceslas had fully disqualified his father's confidence in his fitness to rule. Fond of his cup, he had badly mismanaged the kingdom's finances and carelessly tolerated growing religious unrest in Prague. As the unrest became revolt, Sigismund had to fight his way into Prague to be crowned

15 Pal Engel, *The Realm of St. Stephen: A History of Medieval Hungary, 895–1526*, 199.
16 Hoensch, *Kaiser Sigismund*, 151.
17 Hoensch, *Kaiser Sigismund*, 157.
18 Hoensch, *Kaiser Sigismund*, 160.
19 Hoensch, *Kaiser Sigismund*, 173.

on 28 July 1420. It was the beginning of the Hussite Wars, a long struggle that destroyed all hopes of employing Bohemia as a base for larger dynastic ambitions.

The Bohemian trouble-makers called themselves "Hussites" after Jan Hus, a Czech-speaking master of theology in the University of Prague. After the Council of Constance had condemned him for heresy, King Sigismund had ordered his execution, and the news touched off the revolt. It led not only to wars but to a permanent schism in the Bohemian church, a foretaste of what the Empire would experience after 1520.

The connections between the Bohemian and the German reformations lie in their critiques of the Holy Roman Church. Since 1402 Hus had been preaching in Czech in Prague's Bethlehem Chapel that the papacy and its administration, the Roman Curia, were to blame for the schism. This was no heresy but a common discourse of the day, and many critics said far worse. Dietrich Vrie (ca. 1370–after 1434), a German monk who attended the Council of Constance, lamented, "The pope, the wonder of the world, has fallen. The first years of the Curia were golden, this gave way to the baser age of silver, the papal Curia then deteriorated even further. The iron age laid its yoke upon the obstinate neck. Then came the age of dirt. After the dirt, could anything be worse? Yes, shit, and in shit the Curia sits."[20]

For several generations, critics had been arguing that while the pope held highest rank in the Church, he did not possess "the power of the keys," the Church's mandate to command and forbid, and that disregard for this truth had allowed greed for money to wreck the Church. Some were abusive in the extreme, and many belonged to the party – the historians call them "conciliarists" – that at Constance supported the teachings that a pope could fall into heresy, and that a general council could limit and modify papal authority. The council said as much in its reform canons.

Hus was called to explain his teachings. He arrived at Constance on 3 November 1414 under royal safe-conduct, confident that he could convince the council of his orthodoxy. It was a bad misjudgment, for the council – the same that proclaimed its supremacy over the pope – charged him with heresy, tried and condemned him, and sent him to the stake. While recent opinions disagree about the heterodoxy or orthodoxy of Hus's teachings, he was clearly a theological conservative. For Hus the central issue was the nature of the Church, which he held to be primarily the body of the faithful in all ages – past, present, and future – rather than the hierarchy of pope and bishops and, only secondarily, the people. He taught, following the Englishman John Wycliffe (d. 1384), whose condemned writings he had read, that being in a state of mortal sin canceled all legitimate lordship, whether of pope, bishop, king, or prince. Hus also taught that no one who lives in mortal sin may be acknowledged as a temporal ruler or bishop. This ecclesiology (theory of the Church) helps to explain why Hus's deeply Catholic thought centered on Christ's Real Presence in the Eucharist, the full reception of which in both kinds, bread and wine, he held necessary for the laity as well as the clergy. This position, called "Utraquism,"[21] became the master symbol of the movement that formed in his name.

Even if no theologian, King Sigismund certainly understood what Hus's views on holiness and authority meant. There is no evidence, to be sure, that he wanted Hus to

---

20 Thomas A. Fudge, *The Magnificent Ride: The First Reformation in Hussite Bohemia*, 33, slightly revised.
21 From the Latin "*sub utraque specie*" (in both kinds).

die and every reason to believe that he feared the consequences in Bohemia if the master should. Yet Hus's refusal to retract his statements frustrated Sigismund, who at last declared that "if he [Hus] does not recant those errors, swear his renunciation of them, and affirm the contrary, he should be burnt to death."[22] And so it came to pass. Defrocked and handed over to the temporal authorities, on 6 July 1415 the Bohemian master, bearing on his head a paper crown embellished with images of two demons and between them one word, *"Heresiarch,"* was taken to the harbor. There, Richental reports, Sigismund said to Elector Palatine Louis (b. 1378, r. 1410–36), "I hold here the temporal sword, dear Uncle Louis, . . . so take him and in our stead treat him as befits a heretic."[23] Louis delegated the task to the bishop of Constance's governor, and so it was done. Before a huge crowd – Richental says 3,000 armed men, not counting the unarmed men or the women – Hus was taken over a bridge to a small field. After he had prayed, "Jesus Christ, Son of the living God, have mercy on me," he was asked whether he would confess his sins. He would, but the priest refused to hear his confession unless he admitted his heresy, which he refused to do. Then Hus was bound, the fire was lighted, and "he gave forth terrible cries and was soon burnt to death."[24] His ashes were dumped into the Rhine. King Sigismund, under whose guarantee of safety Hus had come to Constance, presided over the man's execution, just as he presided over the ending of the schism.

Whatever the thousands thought who witnessed Hus's death, the martyred preacher's followers knew precisely what had happened: Sigismund the oath-breaker had sent Jan Hus, that holy man, to his death following an illegitimate condemnation by the general council. Falsely claiming to speak for the entire Church, the council had failed, as the papacy had earlier failed, and if hope for the council's reform agenda remained, it rested with the local churches. The Hussites were by no means alone in their disappointment, humiliation, and desire for revenge. An anonymous observer of the Council of Constance offered a bitter remedy for the situation:

> Recipe for the stomach of St. Peter and for his total healing, given at the Council of Constance. Take 24 cardinals, 100 archbishops and prelates, the same number from each nation, and as many priests as it is possible to get. Immerse in Rhine water and keep submerged for three days. This will be good for the stomach of St. Peter and for the removing of all his afflictions.[25]

Unlike the papacy's other critics, the Bohemian Hussites followed words with deeds. They organized the first separatist reformation of the western Church and, through their rejection of Sigismund's Bohemian succession, dashed all hope of using Bohemia for the Luxemburg project in the Empire. In the ensuing wars the Bohemian rebels became for a while a major force in the public life of Christendom. And while it is idle to speak of "nations" and "majorities," the active engagement of a large and various population in the Hussite movement had no precedent in Christendom's history.

Unlike the contemporary English dissenters called "Lollards," the Hussites were fighters, and in 1419 King Sigismund, with the new pope's approval, made his

22 Hoensch, *Kaiser Sigismund*, 206.
23 Richental, *Chronik des Constanzer Concils*, 80.
24 Richental, *Chronik des Constanzer Concils*, 81.
25 Fudge, *The Magnificent Ride*, 36.

preparations for war against them. The Hussite movement, though divided into parties, had united on the "Four Articles of Prague": free preaching throughout the kingdom; communion under both kinds for all Christians; expropriation of the Church; and punishment of mortal sins. When Sigismund moved on Prague "in order to punish the Hussites for their unbelief,"[26] his army was beaten (14 July 1420) by an inferior force. The rebels followed their first victories with a declaration of Sigismund's unfitness to govern Bohemia. "Because of great cruelty and injustice brought about by Sigismund, the king of Hungary," announced an assembly – with Catholic participation – "the entire Kingdom of Bohemia has endured great harm. . . . We have never accepted him as king nor recognized his right as lord, [for] by his own unworthiness he has demonstrated himself unfit to wear the crown of Bohemia. We will never accept his claims as long as he lives unless the will of God should be otherwise." Furthermore, Sigismund "is notorious and has despised the sacred truths clearly demonstrated from Holy Scripture. He is the deadly enemy of the honour of people of the Czech nation."[27]

For more than a decade the fighting went on, invasion for invasion, murder for murder, atrocities on both sides, the memories of which lived on for generations. "Around the year 1430," a Franconian chronicler records, "the Hussites from Bohemia burned Kulmbach and Bayreuth and committed great cruelties on the common people and the notables – just like wild animals. The clergy, monks, and nuns they put into the fire, or they took them onto the ice of the streams and rivers in Franconia and Bavaria and killed them by drenching them in freezing water."[28] After five failed crusades against the rebels, in 1431 the Council of Basel stepped in to mediate a peace. It invited the Hussites to present their case, which would be judged – an unprecedented concession – by the law of God, the practice of Christ, and the witness of the apostles and the primitive church as contained in the Bible, and not by "the knife of ecclesiastical authority."[29] Even Giovanni da Capistrano (1385–1456), a half-German Franciscan from Italy and one of their foes, confessed, "I have consistently avoided a debate with the Czechs . . . on account of the fact that they have studied well in order to justify their heresy from the scriptures and ancient practices," and they possess "a perfect knowledge of these numerous texts which do favour communion in both kinds."[30]

The Compacts of Basel won over the larger, stronger Utraquist party, which in May 1434 ended the Hussite revolution with a slaughter of the radicals. In August 1436, King Sigismund, now seventy years old, rode into Prague for the first time since 1420. Even in victory he made a mistake typical of his regnal style. His vengeful execution of rebel hold-outs sealed Sigismund's reputation as "the murderer of the Czechs."[31] Three months later, death relieved King Sigismund, "elected by divine providence to be a head of Christendom," from the torture of gout. He was the last of tens of thousands

26 Hoensch, *Kaiser Sigismund*, 209: "die Hussen stroffen umbe den ungelöben."
27 Fudge, *The Magnificent Ride*, 100–1.
28 Martin Zeiller, *Topographia Franconiae, das ist, Beschreibung und eygentliche Contrafactur der vornembsten Stätte und Plätze des Franckenlandes/und Deren die zum hochlöblichsten Fränkischen Craiße gezogen warden*, 39. My thanks to Christopher Ocker for this text.
29 Fudge, *The Magnificent Ride*, 110. This phrase first appeared in the official sentence against Jan Hus at Constance.
30 Fudge, *The Magnificent Ride*, 112.
31 Fudge, *The Magnificent Ride*, 120.

of dead from the wars his political folly had begun. Pursuant to his orders, the king-emperor's body, clad in Imperial robes and crown, sat on the throne for three days, so that all could see that the world had lost its rightful lord. With him ended the Luxemburg line and its Imperial project. As for his opponents, during the following 180 years no king could rule against the Bohemian nobles' will. Under their leadership and because of their victory, Bohemia had become a kingdom ruled by king and estates, among which the nobles had the preponderant voice. When this outcome was next threatened, generations later, it led to war.

"About Hussitism, which lies deep in the past," writes the subject's reigning master, "there are almost as many proposed interpretations as historians."[32] According to whether one holds with Christian theologians, Czech nationalists, or historical materialist historians, the Bohemian movement that bore Hus's name was a first Protestant reformation, a national revolution, or the first social revolution in the movement toward European modernity. Here it is unnecessary to say more than a little about these global interpretations, none of which bears directly on the theme of this book.[33] As to the first, it is true enough that Luther not only acknowledged Hus as a forerunner of his own protest but also took up significant elements of Hus's program: the chalice for the laity, worship in the vernacular, secularization of ecclesiastical property, and rejection of the inquisitorial procedure for dealing with dissent. What Hus, much less John Wycliffe, did not do – here Luther is the best witness – was to attack the Church's doctrine in a radically theological sense. Still, one must ask whether the drawing of a very sharp distinction between the Bohemian Hussite and German Protestant movements is not a fiction "founded by German Protestant historiography."[34] This becomes obvious once we recognize the deep roots of both movements in medieval ideas and programs of and demands for reform of the Church in head and members. That these roots were entwined is hardly surprising, given the contiguity of the Bohemian to the German lands, the intermingling of Czech speakers with German speakers, and the larger Christian religious discourse on which reform-minded writers in both kingdoms drew.

Much the same is true from a social-historical perspective. The case for the bourgeois or proto-bourgeois character of the Hussite revolution is not stronger than for the Protestant reformations in the German lands, including the great insurrection of 1524–26. This judgment by no means disproves the historical-materialist concept of European history as a series of stages of development connected by social revolutions, but it does mean that the origins of capitalist development and, therefore, of a bourgeoisie capable of becoming a ruling class must be sought in other places and other times. "Except for the religious-utopian projections, the qualitative accord between the social programs of the Bohemian and the German reformations did not disrupt the mental world of the feudal order and its social structure."[35]

32 František Šmahel, *Die Hussitische Revolution*, vol. 1: 1. Although *German Histories* is meant to present, not to evaluate, the current state of discussion on its chief topics, it seems important here to take notice of the state of the question concerning "the Hussite revolution."
33 I set aside the Czech national and nationalist interpretation as only marginally significant for this book.
34 Šmahel, *Die Hussitische Revolution*, vol. 3: 2001.
35 Šmahel, *Die Hussitische Revolution*, vol. 3: 2001.

3. THINKING ABOUT IMPERIAL REFORM

The problem of reforming the Church in the post-Basel era, when neither papacy nor general council could or would assume a role of leadership, assumed an unusually acute form in the Empire. Among literate laity, "especially in Germany, people did not remain content simply to complain of abuses, they demanded a fundamental restoration of the Church."[36] To think about the Church was difficult, to think about the Empire seems to have been nearly impossible. The difficulty began with the belief that in the German lands Empire and Church were not distinct entities but two aspects of a single body. King Sigismund expressed this notion, declaring at the beginning of his reign:

> We intend with God's help, as soon as possible to dedicate ourselves to seeing how we can bring the affairs of the Holy Church and of the Holy Roman Empire into good, sound order, to attend to justice and the common good, both long suppressed, to protect the roads, and with the help of yourselves and other loyal members of the Empire to bring peace and order to the lands and to preserve you and others of the Holy Empire's subjects in your rights, privileges, and liberties.[37]

The king repeated the idea in calling for the general council to be assembled at Constance. "If We take up the matter not only of the Church but also of the Empire and the common good," he announced, "the counsels and aid of both are sorely needed, . . . for which reason We ask to send your principal envoys with plenipotentiary powers to Us and to the common assembly of the Empire on the aforementioned All Saints' Day [1 November] to advise and to help as best they are able."[38] Sigismund thus proposed simultaneously to preside over the deliberations on reform of the Church and to negotiate with the princes about reform of the Empire. His belief was reasonable both on conceptual grounds, as tradition taught a unitary concept of Church and Empire, and on practical grounds, for fully 70 percent (90 of 130) of the Imperial princes were churchmen.

Sigismund's concept of a reform of both Church and Empire certainly suggested that the two were in some sense a single body. Well before his time, however, this old idea had run its course. The debates on reform at the Council of Constance, over which King Sigismund in some sense presided, tended to discriminate between the reforms of Empire and Church as separate projects. The principal discussion aimed to clarify that

> the long, painful process of separating a united Church and State had historically become problematical at the time of the eleventh-century reform of the Church. In the eyes of the High and Late Middle Ages, the unified political order of Church and State appeared as a corpus mixtus of spiritual and secular elements. Recognition of this hybrid and, therefore, the necessity of reform remained living over the centuries. . . . How should we understand the notions of reform in an age when a reform council such as Constance had burnt a radical reformer such as Jan Hus?[39]

36 Francis Rapp, *Christentum IV: Zwischen Mittelalter und Neuzeit (1378–1552)*, 83.
37 Dietrich Kerler, ed., *Deutsche Reichstagsakten unter Kaiser Sigmund. Erste Antheilung 1410–1420*, 56, n. 38 (21 January 1411).
38 Kerler, ed., *Deutsche Reichstagsakten unter Kaiser Sigmund*, 270 (6 August 1414).
39 Ivan Hlaváček and Alexander Patschovsky, eds., *Reform von Kirche und Reich: zur Zeit der Konzilien von Konstanz (1414–1418) und Basel (1431–1449): Konstanz-Prager historisches Kolloquium (11.–17. Oktober 1993)*, 8.

The men who served Sigismund possessed a good practical grasp of the Empire's political complexity, and they did not easily absorb the idea of separation. Still, they no longer spoke of a mystical fusion of Empire and Church into the one body of Christendom. The Golden Bull of 1356 had spoken of the emperor's subjects not as a "Roman people" or a "German people," but as a "Christian people." By contrast, a royal declaration of 30 January 1412 addressed "all princes (spiritual and temporal), counts, barons, knights, squires, burgraves, wardens, district governors, territorial judges, judges, headmen, mayors, councilors, and communes of all cities, valleys, and villages, and all other subjects and servitors of Ourselves and the Holy Roman Empire who receive this letter."[40] These words suggest an early version of the notion of "emperor and Empire," in which "the Empire" meant the Imperial estates composed in the Diet.

Did a reform of Church and Empire require their disaggregation? Probably, it did, for the traditional Christian idea of reform knew two times, a normative past and a utopian future, but no space. This had presented no problems, so long as the political order of the German kingdom and its superstructure, the Empire, depended on the proximity to or distance from the king-emperor's person. The fifteenth century saw a major shift in the Imperial political order, the greatest innovation in which can be suggested by a single word, territorialization. Beginning with the general heritability of fiefs, the emergence of a firm bond between princely lineages and specific lands had begun to shift the basis of power from symbolic action to the possession of territorial holdings. This materialization of princely power was making the Empire's governance ever more different from that of the Church, in which prelates, whatever their temporal power, could not convert their unions of office and territories into permanent assets of their dynasties.

To recognize the coming order of things and adapt Imperial politics to it proved a nearly impossible task. There were writers, to be sure, who attempted to describe the Empire in relatively secular terms. One of them was a Benedictine abbot, Engelbert Pötsch (ca. 1250–1332), who studied at Padua and had long ruled Admont Abbey in his native Styria.[41] Engelbert, who was a Thomist, described the Empire in terms of an Aristotelian vocabulary of "nature," "the common good," and "divine law and human law." He hoped to square nature's bias for plurality with the divine law's norm of unity to prove that among men, as among beasts, nature's rule is that "one will be king and lord of all."[42] The happiness of "one natural kingdom and empire," he concluded, is "the one, last, and best salvation and happiness of all."[43] Neither Engelbert's Thomism nor tags from Roman law nor the old idea of a translation of the Roman imperium in the West from the Romans to the Germans was of much help in coming to grips with the new reality, an Empire composed not of royal followers and servitors but of territorial rulers.

A more likely source of ideas and practices useful for an Imperial reform lay in the Church. On the practical side, the Church's officers were deeply experienced in governing through corporate institutions, which could be found at nearly all levels

---

40 Lorenz Weinrich, ed., *De reformando regni teutonici statu in medioaevo posteriore fontes selectae/ Quellen zur Reichsreform im Spätmittelalter*, 44, §3.
41 He is normally called "Engelbert of Admont."
42 Engelbert of Admont, "On the Rise and End of the Roman Empire," 64.
43 Admont, "On the Rise and End of the Roman Empire," 73–4.

of the Church, from the college of cardinals through the religious orders, the metropolitan and diocesan synods, to the chapters of cathedral and other collegiate
churches. Their culture of governance dictated rule through representation, consultation, consent, and voting. Since the twelfth century it had taken root in the Church's
canon law and become the common property of all churchmen who had studied the
law. It received a great boost from the movement to heal the papal schism through
corporate action of bishops and university teachers. Their ideas lay in the Council of
Constance's decree *Sacrosancta*, which set conciliar above papal authority. Constance
and its successor held at Basel also brought together educated clergy of similar educations but different countries and promoted an exchange of ideas and knowledge.
Forty to fifty percent of the participants belonged to bodies that practiced a collegial
form of governance, and nearly one-fifth of them were university graduates. Drawn
disproportionately from France, the German lands, and the Low Countries, many of
them came from cities where collegial government was an everyday affair. These men
"were steeped in the *moeurs* of collective, consultative, and constitutional government," and they were perfectly familiar with the chapter, the college, the cloister, and
the university as realizations of a single model of governance. It is no wonder that the
council sometimes called itself "the college of priests."[44]

The most obvious links between the ecclesiastical culture of collegiality and the
problem of Imperial reform were the German conciliarists. They faced numerous
problems, of which the most notable was the difficulty of conceiving the Empire as
a polity rather than as the protective shell of the Church Universal, the custody of
which God had conferred on the Germans. The standing of this ideal does not seem to
have suffered much from the circulation at Constance of the ideas of Marsiglio of
Padua (ca. 1290–ca. 1343), a most notorious defender of the political supremacy of
temporal authority against the papacy. No one cited Marsiglio's writings by name,
of course, but ideas from his condemned writings were certainly discussed. Yet antipapalism did not lead automatically either to caesaropapism, the doctrine of the
emperor's supremacy over the Church in all but purely spiritual matters, or to defining the Empire as a German kingdom of limited extent. Dietrich von Niem, the
Westphalian conciliarist who at Constance brutally attacked the papacy, read and
quoted Marsiglio (though without citing him) in his advocacy of conciliar authority.
When he came to the Empire, however, Dietrich reproduced the golden ideal of a
universal, sacral Empire ruled by great emperors – Charlemagne, Otto the Great,
Frederick I – as custodians of Christendom. He could not and did not want to translate Marsiglio's ideas into a non-universalist concept of the Empire.

It bears asking why the Italians from Marsiglio to Leonardo Bruni Aretino (ca.
1369–1444), Dietrich von Niem's Florentine contemporary, were able to think about
polities as particular social organizations while the Germans were not. Some Italians
thought about polities and politics in an Aristotelian, secular way that enabled them
to treat the local polity (usually the city) as a singular, comparable, and human entity.
It was to be understood in terms of law, human and natural, and also, by Bruni and
other writers, of history. The Empire could hardly be treated in this way because, as
the worldly shell of the Body of Christ, it occupied most of the space in which the
Aristotelian idea of a purely human organization might have flourished. Over the

44 Antony Black, *Council and Commune: The Conciliar Movement and the Fifteenth-century Heritage*, 37.

course of the fifteenth century, to be sure, the German kingdom as "the German Nation" gained increasing visibility and weight in the governance of the German lands. It was not, however, conceptualized as a particular, complete polity distinct from others. The fusion of sacral universalism with temporal authority in the monarchy, as in the prince-bishoprics, produced a tough, long-lived mentality.

The peculiarity of the Empire can be seen in terms of a contrast with the world that gave rise to Italian, and later western European, thinking about politics. For Marsiglio the human legislator was sovereign; for Bruni the commune was sovereign. In effect they produced an idea of the state as sovereign, that is, natural, complete, and purely local. This had the consequence that a local ruler or commune could act in a sovereign way without disturbing or being disturbed by the intimate bonds between local and universal religion. This is why the Italian city-states of this age experienced no serious attempts to fuse temporal with spiritual power.[45]

The situation in the German lands presents a very great contrast to the world of the Italian theorists of politics. Here the parts – dynastic principalities, episcopal *Hochstifte*, and Imperial cities – were structurally secular in that their legitimacy was purely temporal, but they were nested in a monarchy that claimed to be sacral, universal, and, if not eternal, guaranteed existence by God until the End of Days. The parts had no universal significance; the whole, having no local power, could not become natural, mutable, and thus comparable to other polities in the Aristotelian sense. There was, however, nothing essential or unchangeable about these relationships, and the mood of the conciliar age favored thinking about reforms of Church and Empire as comparable tasks.

When German conciliarists turned their thoughts to Imperial reform, they began to suggest that the Empire's (vaguely defined) comparability to the Church might enable reformers to undertake a reform of the former in the image of the latter. Job Vener (ca. 1370–1447), a Strasbourgeois of Swabian background, had studied theology and law at Paris, Bologna, and Heidelberg and settled at Speyer as a beneficed canon and councilor to the Elector Palatine. At Constance, Vener represented the German Nation in the papal conclave of 1417 and even received a few votes for the papal office. In his *Avisamentum*, a memorial on ecclesiastical reform drafted during the council, Vener turns from the present business of reform of the Church to a future reform of the Holy Empire. "For in many respects," he writes, "in the reform of the Holy emperorship the same principle is valid as for the reform of the papacy."[46] This comment suggests an unspecific comparability which might allow analogies to be drawn between Church and Empire. Over this bridge the conceptual riches of ecclesiological theory and jurisprudence might be applied mutatis mutandis to the Empire. This said, a general council's assumption of the task of reforming the Church might be followed by a comparable assumption of the comparable task in the Empire.

In the heady days of the Council of Basel, before it was crippled by a split with the pope, Nicholas of Cusa developed Vener's suggestion into an almost fully analogical view of the relationships of Church and Empire. A fisherman's son from Kues in the archbishopric of Trier, Nicholas had studied at Heidelberg and Padua, and he came to

45 They did know the converse fusion, spiritual with temporal, of which the supreme example existed at Rome.
46 Job Vener, "Avisamentum (1417)," *in Die Vener von Gmünd und Straßburg 1162–1147*, ed. Heimpel, 1309, lines 529–30.

Basel in 1432 as the archbishop of Trier's delegate. He began writing his *Catholic Concordance* in the following year, while Hussite envoys to the council were negotiating peace, and finished at year's end, when the Emperor Sigismund, newly crowned, took up residence at Basel. Several months later, Sigismund worked his magic once more, as Pope Eugenius IV (r. 1431–47) declared his adherence to the council. "And the emperor became very happy and pleased," an envoy wrote home to Frankfurt, "because this act made him mighty and won him great power."[47] In this atmosphere of hope for unity and reform, Nicholas wrote his book.

The *Concordance* is a deceptively uneven work. Book I offers philosophical arguments for a cosmos ordered into hierarchical ranks based on the heavenly hierarchy that leads to God. The world's order thus mirrors heaven's. Book II, however, takes a stoutly conciliarist view of Church, pope, and council: "The council has power both over abuses and the one who causes abuses, [and] its power is immediately from Christ and it is in every respect over both the pope and the Apostolic See."[48] A council represents all the various groups in the Church, and therefore voices the consent of all the faithful, and "rulership comes from God through men and councils by means of elective consent."[49]

In Book III, where Nicholas broaches the problem of Church and Empire, he tries to have his cake and eat it, too. He asserts a strict parallel between the pope's spiritual authority and the temporal authority of the emperor, who is "one ruler of the world exercising his authority over the others in the plenitude of power, and in his own sphere he is the equal of the Roman pontiff in the temporal hierarchy on the model of the sacerdotal hierarchy."[50] One body, two hierarchies. Yet, although Nicholas does call the emperor "the minister of god" and "the vicar of Jesus Christ on earth,"[51] he concedes that "his power to command does not extend beyond the territorial limits of the empire under him."[52] This is a crucial step, for it makes the Empire a temporal and particular rather than a sacral and universal polity. The emperorship "is only rightly possessed through the elective agreement of the subjects, . . . he is only lord over those who are actually subject to him, and we should conclude that the emperor is lord of that part of the world over which he exercises effective authority."[53] The emperor thus stands under the law, and he is obliged by his election to consult through councils his subjects about laws. Nicholas makes one exception. When he exercises his "highest responsibility" in calling a general council, the emperor acts as a "minister of God." His universal authority is limited to this one act. Only at that moment does he differ from other monarchs, so that the traditionally distinctive quality of the imperium, its sacrality, is reduced to an infrequent if necessary anomaly. Otherwise, "the king should not think that he is freed from the laws, for if a law is just it is binding and not otherwise, and therefore it also binds the king himself who is obliged to rule justly."[54]

47 Hoensch, *Kaiser Sigismund*, 407.
48 Nicholas of Cusa, *The Catholic Concordance*, 113.
49 Cusa, *The Catholic Concordance*, 194.
50 Cusa, *The Catholic Concordance*, 216.
51 Cusa, *The Catholic Concordance*, 234.
52 Cusa, *The Catholic Concordance*, 235.
53 Cusa, *The Catholic Concordance*, 236.
54 Cusa, *The Catholic Concordance*, 248.

For Nicholas, the pope thus stands under the law of the Church, the emperor stands under the law of – what? Is there an "Empire" distinct from the emperor, and, if so, can it make law? Nicholas's answer is representation. The emperor is not the Empire, he represents the Empire, which comprises his subjects who act through *their* representatives. In his concept these princes, bishops, and urban magistrates *are* "the Empire." They are much like the Church's representatives in council vis-à-vis the pope or a cathedral chapter vis-à-vis the bishop. Assembled together, they are the emperor's partners in Imperial governance. This is a brilliant insight. Within a quarter-century of Nicholas's death, although no scrap of evidence connects this innovation with Nicholas's book, when the Imperial Diet began to take fixed shape and procedures, the phrase, "the emperor and the Empire" (*Kaiser und Reich*) appears and is first attested in the 1480s.

Nicholas also sketched a model for the Imperial governance of the future. He recognized that neither emperor nor electors alone could make and enforce law. As in the Church, only representative bodies, councils, could do that. "Just as the universal council of priests is properly organized along similar lines," so there is a "universal council of the empire," in which sit princes, "heads of provinces representing their provinces," rectors of "the major universities and professors," and "those of the senatorial rank which qualifies them for the imperial assembly," presumably the patrician magistrates of the free cities. Nicholas's inclusion in Imperial governance of the universities and their professors and of "heads of provinces" resembled nothing in the real existing Empire. He simply translates ecclesiastical into Imperial institutions: emperor and kings are like pope and patriarchs, archbishops like dukes, counts like bishops, "and so on with the rest."[55] Nicholas could fashion a *concept* of Imperial governance because churchmen had already fashioned one for the Church. He did not understand how the territorialization of lordship, then in its infancy, would make an Imperial parliament a body of lords rather than of subjects.

The moment of Basel proved brief indeed. By 1437, when Nicholas shifted his loyalty from the general council to Pope Eugenius, the moment was past, and with it passed the moment of Nicholas of Cusa's *Catholic Concordance*. There would be no new discourse of Imperial reform free from the whining nostalgia for ancient glories that marred nearly all other fifteenth-century German treatises on reform. Fifty more years would pass until, in the 1480s, work began on a program of Imperial governance that in some sense resembled though, so far as we know, was not influenced by Nicholas's concept. Still, his book suggests how the Church's political culture, in which practical experience could be analyzed and criticized through the application of concepts, could be brought to bear on problems of Imperial governance in general and the need to create permanent institutions in particular. "All general laws affecting the commonwealth," Nicholas writes, "should be adopted and ordained in a council of primates and rulers of both [the spiritual and temporal] estates." Thereupon the king executes "what is enacted with the agreement of the council, since this constitutional arrangement is the way in which the subjects wish the authority of the king to be limited."[56] If this does not quite describe a "state" in the modern sense, neither does it fit any traditional, patrimonial polity.

---

55 Cusa, *The Catholic Concordance*, 283–4.
56 Cusa, *The Catholic Concordance*, 248–9.

Nicholas's scheme of Imperial reform attempts to transfer a template of authority and power from the Church to the Empire. This project was perfectly in keeping with the tendencies of the age:

> Partly thanks to the twilight ratiocinations of the medieval papacy, the new monarchies had the benefit of Minerva's owl from the start of their development. The doctrine of monarchical sovereignty issued as a clear and mature idea from the complexities of late medieval ecclesiastical thought, and was wholly in line with the interests and aspirations of national and territorial monarchy.[57]

Well and good, but as a polity the Holy Roman Empire was neither national nor territorial, which is the chief reason why Nicholas's ideas seem so remote from political reality. Yet he did manage to avoid the constant complaint – the Empire is weak because the papacy is strong – that runs mantra-like through writings on reform from Sigismund's time right through to the reign of Charles V. It would have been more realistic to say that "the Empire must become strong because the papacy is weak." This was the ultimate lesson of conciliarism: the papacy could not heal the schism, but if fully restored it could not govern the Church. The problem had changed entirely since the eleventh century when Pope Gregory VII (r. 1073–85) had asserted the Church's liberty against a strong emperor. The post-conciliar papacy lacked the ability to reform itself, much less the Church Universal.

4. THE PASSING OF THE LUXEMBURGS

Except for Sigismund's support for the general councils, reform of the Church did not and could not rank high on the Luxemburgs' list of ever-pressing problems. Their two ablest monarchs had ruled lands – Charles IV's Bohemia and Sigismund's Hungary – over whose wealth they enjoyed relatively unchallenged command. Each endeavored to exploit his kingdom as a base from which to gain a secure hold on the German kingdom and Holy Roman Empire. Each failed. It is easy to overestimate the power of personal ability and even substantial revenues to promote lasting dynastic power, especially in kingdoms where hereditary claims could not permanently neutralize the nobles' asserted electoral rights. This was true above all in the German kingdom, where no sense of national cohesion balanced the feudalization. Its practices were nearly impossible to alter from outside the realm, and the Luxemburgs never established a stable dynastic base within. Much like their predecessors, they encouraged for short-term gains the parcelization of royal power into princely hands.

One can easily be puzzled by the tough resilience of the traditional ways of feudal politics. Two examples from Sigismund's reign illustrate how the tradition of feudal parcelization had created its own logic of governance. In each case Sigismund traded something of great long-term value – extensive lands plus an Imperial electorate – for immediate political support or money. The first case involved the margraviate of Brandenburg, a large but poor northeastern land, which had come to the Luxemburgs through a history more bizarre than any make-believe tale. The Ascanian margraves, who had numbered nineteen males in 1290, became extinct in 1319. Well after Emperor

57 Antony Black, *Monarchy and Community: Political Ideas in the Later Conciliar Controversy 1430–1450*, 131.

Louis IV (r. 1314/28–47), called "the Bavarian," had conferred the vacant fief on his own Wittelsbach kinsman, Charles IV backed the claims of a mysterious "last Ascanian," who turned over Brandenburg to him in exchange for a pension and then conveniently died. Other German princes grumbled but did nothing, and Brandenburg remained in Luxemburg hands for nearly seventy years. Sigismund, however, granted it in fief to the Hohenzollerns, who thereby gained the title of Imperial prince. In 1413/17 Sigismund enfiefed Margrave Frederick VI (ca. 1371–1440) with the electorate and the Brandenburg lands in return for 400,000 gulden. The Hohenzollerns, Swabian upstarts without royal ancestry or expectations but having patience and extraordinary biological luck, became 300 years later kings in Prussia and, 180 years after that, emperors of Germany.

The second case involved Saxony, a duchy rich in silver from the mines in the Erzgebirge and endowed, like Brandenburg, with an Imperial electorate. In 1423, in return for support against the Hussites, Sigismund conferred the electorate and lands on a prince of the Wettin dynasty, Margrave Frederick IV (1370–1428), called "the Belligerent," of Meissen. His dynasty briefly became the greatest power in the German east. Dreamers of a royal crown, 400 years later they became kings of Saxony.

These two stories reinforce some fundamental lessons of late medieval German political history. First, so long as reverted fiefs were exchanged for cash or military aid, a royal dynasty could not replace the already squandered Imperial domain. Sigismund, who traded long-term prospects for short-term gains, was in this respect, as in others, truly his father's son. Second, the eastern lands, where kings were more powerful but dynasties less secure than in the west, offered tempting bases from which the Empire's highest office might be gained and held. The plasticity of royal and princely authority marked the entire zone that stretched from Bohemia, Hungary, and Poland westward to Austria, Bavaria, Saxony, and Brandenburg. This situation offered opportunity. Yet electoral risks and biological misfortune could quickly ruin dynastic projects and even the dynasties themselves.

The fragility of dynastic rule appears with great clarity in the aftermath of Sigismund's death in 1437. All three crowns passed to a neighboring prince, Archduke Albert II (r. 1438–39). This prince of the Habsburg dynasty married Sigismund's only surviving child, Elizabeth of Luxemburg (1409–42), whose two sisters had married the rulers of Saxony and Poland. When Albert died only two years after his election, the hope of a joint Luxemburg-Habsburg future lay in Elizabeth's womb. The failed succession of this boy, the last male Luxemburg, illustrates both the fragility of dynasties and the relative importance of legitimacy and power in successions to allegedly elective thrones.

The tale is wonderfully told by one of its chief actors, the Viennese Helene Kottannerin (ca. 1400–58?), a noble lady-in-waiting to Queen Elizabeth.[58] Immediately following Albert's death on 27 October 1439 at Neszmély/Langendorf on the Danube, about halfway between Buda-Ofen and Bratislava/Pressburg, the pregnant queen sped from her husband's funeral southward. She aimed to make certain that the royal crowns and other coronation regalia still lay secure within Castle Visegrád/Plintenburg, a fortress north of Buda-Ofen. Aided by a brave Croatian nobleman,

---

58 Hers is the oldest extant memoir by a German-speaking woman. Helene Kottannerin was married to a Hungarian nobleman. Elizabeth was not empress, because Albert had never been crowned.

Helene snuck into the castle on the night of 20–21 February 1440, replaced the crowns and other items with copies, and fled upstream to Komárom/Komorn, where they crossed the frozen Danube. One week later, Elizabeth's son was born and baptized Ladislaus (Hungarian: Lazlo) (1440–57), called "Posthumous." In May the party traveled to the coronation city, Székesfehérvár/Stuhlweissenburg in southern Hungary, in whose cathedral on 15 May, the tiny 11-week-old heir was lifted from his cradle and gently crowned with the crown of St. Stephen. All this came to pass because Helene, who "has given service to Her Grace [Queen Elizabeth], also the noble king [Albert], and Their Graces' children of this noble, princely line,"[59] and her brave Croatian companion had lifted "Her Grace's crown, her collar, and all of her other regalia" from under their guardians' very eyes.[60]

Crowned as a helpless, fugitive infant swathed in his grandfather's cut-down coronation robe, Ladislaus owed his chances solely to his mother and to the redoubtable Helene Kottannerin (and her Croatian accomplice). His chances were never good, because a strong party of Hungarian nobles rejected the coronation and supported the Polish king's claim. The young man did live to become king of Hungary and Bohemia, but only briefly, before he died in 1457 at age eighteen. Following his death the Bohemian and Hungarian lords chose to live under native dynasties much as they had done before the coming of the Luxemburgs.

The failure of the Luxemburg project mirrors the failure of projects to reform Church and Empire. The Luxemburg aim, to build a strong, external territorial base from which to gain and retain the Imperial crown and the rule of the German lands, was not unpromising. Biological luck was against them, true, but so was politics, for the partly elective nature of the Bohemian and Hungarian crowns made royal successions subject to political chance, such as rebellion (the Hussite revolt) and the growing nativism of the nobilities. The Luxemburgs failed to gain a secure territorial base, just as they failed to perpetuate their line.

Still, by the rules of the time – primacy of the agnatic line – Ladislaus, the luckless late-born, was a Habsburg more than he was a Luxemburg. His father's dynasty possessed the assets his mother's lacked, fecundity and a secure base in a large, hereditary Imperial principality. They came into play in the hands of Ladislaus's guardian, Archduke Frederick of Styria. With this unprepossessing Habsburg prince, the future Emperor Frederick III (r. 1452–93), began a continuous, with but one brief interruption, dynastic possession of the Holy Roman emperorship that lasted 479 years. Now, with a ring only audible in retrospect, struck the time of the Austrian house of Habsburg.

59 Helene Kottanerin, *Die Denkwürdigkeiten der Helene Kottannerin (1439–1440)*, 28.
60 Kottanerin, *Die Denkwürdigkeiten*, 13.

6

The Empire and the Territorial States

> Whoever concludes that Germany's undertakings will be powerful and
> will always succeed does not consider that it suffices to block the emperor, when
> the princes do not support him in the execution of his plans. Those who do not
> dare to make war against him, deny him the troops; those who deny them also
> have the courage not to send them to him; and those who don't dare to deny them,
> dare to delay their sending so that they come too late to help him. . . . Germany's
> might is great, but is such that it cannot be used.
>
> Niccolò Machiavelli

Frederick III, the strange, eccentric man who came to the royal throne in 1440, would reign over the Holy Roman Empire for fifty-three years, longer than any other emperor. After him came Maximilian I (r. 1493–1519), his only son, who ruled for another twenty-six. Longevity and fecundity, Habsburg hallmarks, preserved the dynasty's reign over the Empire and its Austrian successor state for nearly 500 years. Had anyone predicted such a future at Frederick's accession, or at any other point in his long life, that person could today be considered certifiably mad.

There is truth behind Frederick's image as a monarch weighed down by isolation and lethargy, though he did not deserve the nickname of "the Empire's Arch-Sleeping Cap."[1] His isolation did not reflect ignorance about his realm, for no emperor in 250 years had better first-hand experience of the German lands.[2] His reign began with a tremendous, 371-day journey through vast reaches of his new realm. Starting from Graz in Styria, his favorite residence, and ending at Wiener Neustadt in Lower Austria, Frederick crossed the entire Empire from southeast to northwest to be crowned at Aachen. His progress then took him up the Rhine to Frankfurt am Main, where he consulted his princes, and to Basel, where the general council was still sitting. Finally, he traversed the entire southern rim of the Central Alps from Savoy to Tyrol before returning home over the Brenner Pass through Innsbruck and Salzburg to Vienna. He kept to the old Imperial heartlands, true, but no monarch in human memory had ever so nearly beaten their bounds as he did. He did not travel in the younger lands of the

---

1 Hartmut Boockmann, *Stauferzeit und spätes Mittelalter: Deutschland 1125–1517*, 327. The epithet plays on his dynastic title of "archduke," unique to the Austrian princes.
2 I count since Frederick I Barbarossa (r. 1152/55–90).

north and east, of course, where an emperor's writ hardly ran. No monarch in this era ever showed his face in Bremen, Hamburg, Rostock, Berlin, Magdeburg, Leipzig, or Dresden.

This long, cumbersome journey – the royal entourage numbered some 700 persons and a thousand horses, plus an armed escort of hundreds to several thousand cavalry – contributed greatly to Frederick's education. Although he had been to Jerusalem, at his election the German lands beyond Austria were still terra incognita. A member of his chancery kept a record of marches made, places visited, ceremonies endured, amusements enjoyed, relics viewed, and notable buildings admired. In the small Imperial city of Donauwörth on the Danube the writer noted the towered ring wall, and also a local cheese. At Nuremberg he recorded that the city councilors, bearing holy relics, greeted the king and took him to St. Sebald's Church, and at Speyer he visited the tombs of the Habsburg kings, Rudolph I and Albert II, and asked for the Latin inscriptions to be translated for him.

On this journey Frederick also learned that a monarch could exercise power where he visited, but he often could not even feed himself or his companions. Everywhere a stranger, he could be secure only where he resided. After he returned to his own Austrian lands, Frederick did not leave them again during the next twenty-seven years.

1. A HABSBURG COMES TO THE THRONE

The fundamental problem of Frederick's long life was not his rule over the Empire but his struggle to become master in his own Austrian house. He had to fight the bane of all the great German dynasties, an entropy of lordship caused by frequent partitions of lands and by brutal intra-dynastic quarrels and noble revolts. The house of Habsburg tried to guard its unity by means of a rule of seniority, whereby the eldest archduke exercised the guardianship of all minor males of the lineage until they reached majority at sixteen, and a rule against new partitions. Around 1395 the latter rule failed, and strife among heirs progressed by 1407 into civil war. "Now arose in Austria a more terrible strife than had ever before been witnessed," a chronicler tells, "the son felt compelled to rob his father, who responded in kind, and neighbor to rob neighbor."[3] Hard men streamed in from all the surrounding lands to help the natives take knives to one another, while in Vienna two factions took turns sending one another's leaders to the scaffold. Peace eventually came, as one chronicler wrote, but the marauding, feuding, and murdering had "lasted that time for nearly ten years."[4]

The dynastic peace of 1411 ended scattershot partitions by dictating a durable triple division of the Habsburg lands into the western lands of Tyrol and Outer Austria,[5] the three southern duchies of Inner Austria,[6] and the two halves of the Austrian

---

3   Thomas Ebendorfer (1388–1464), in Günther Hödl, *Habsburg und Österreich. Gestalten und Gestalt des österreichischen Spätmittelalters*, 150.
4   Hödl, *Habsburg und Österreich*, 154.
5   Called "die Vorlande" (capital at Ensisheim in Alsace, later Freiburg im Breisgau), they included modern Vorarlberg, Austrian Swabia, and a chain of lands that stretched from around Einsielden in Switzerland northwestward through the Breisgau and Sundgau (southern Alsace) into Imperial Burgundy.
6   Styria (capital: Graz), Carinthia (capital: Klagenfurt), and Carniola (capital: Ljubljana/Laibach).

archduchy proper.[7] It took Frederick nearly sixty-five years to unite the three Austrias in his own hands. Only once in their entire subsequent history (in 1564) would they again be partitioned among heirs. The reunion of the Austrian hereditary lands, the fruit of some political skill and much good luck, was the most important achievement of Frederick's rulership, for it created a secure base for the long Habsburg hegemony over the German lands.

The archduke-emperor himself cut a homely figure. Tall and slim, he inherited his father's large, strongly hooked nose; he wore his wavy, dark blonde hair long; and his small, deeply set eyes gave him a perpetually sleepy look. With increasing years the famous undershot jaw of the Habsburgs and the gaps in his teeth would become more prominent. Frederick often gave an impression that fit his appearance – stolid, taciturn, and deliberate, even mistrustful. The Florentine humanist Giovanni Poggio Bracciolini (1380–1459), who met him in 1452, thought him "no emperor but a lump of lead, who was interested only in money."[8]

Frederick had received a superior education for a German prince of his time. He could read and write German and had some Latin, though he ignored the advice of his Italian secretary, Enea Silvio Piccolomini (1405–64) of Siena,[9] who urged him to practice his Latin for speaking on public occasions. He had read law and history and avidly studied alchemy and astrology. Pious as was his fashion, Frederick built churches and convents; he promoted the cult of St. George, he treated the Church's substance as his own, and he endowed 30,000 Masses for the salvation of his soul.

From an early age this unprepossessing young man had an idea: the advancement of his dynasty. On the first page of his journal, dated 27 April 1437, he wrote down the meaning in Latin and German of the not-yet-famous Habsburg device, AEIOU, an acronym for, "All the earth is subject to Austria" (*Austriae est imperare orbi universo* or *Alles Erdreich ist Österreich Untertan*).[10] Although this has a ring of pure bombast, the fantasy of a provincial prince moldering in the Austrian backwoods, the device expresses an imagination about power and a dynastic pride that could find freer play in the Empire's eastern rather than in its western lands. The east was younger, less fixed in its ways, more open to ambition, and perhaps for this reason it early awakened ambitions for territorial unification and expansion. Perhaps Frederick knew of a prescient document called the "Greater Privilege." This fourteenth-century forgery envisaged Austria as a practically autonomous state, subject to the emperor only in the most limited respects. It declared the dukes, as "archdukes," free of all Imperial service and judicial authority and introduced primogeniture and indivisibility of lands: "These lands shall forever have as their ruler the eldest of the dukes of Austria, to whose eldest son the rule shall pass by the law of inheritance, though without leaving this lineage. And at no time shall the duchy of Austria be divided."[11] If not the text, Frederick knew the vision, for he was himself suspected of plotting to introduce

---

7 Upper and Lower Austria (capitals respectively at Linz and Vienna).
8 Brigitte Haller, *Kaiser Friedrich III. im Urteil der Zeitgenossen*, 122.
9 The future Pope Pius II (r. 1458–64).
10 According to the military cadets of a later age who studied in the Imperial residence at Wiener Neustadt, the motto meant "The State's food is often inedible" (*Aerarisches Essen Ist Oft Ungenießbar*). Boockmann, *Stauferzeit und spätes Mittelalter*, 327–8.
11 Lorenz Weinrich, ed., *De reformando regni teutonici statu in medioaevo posteriore fontes selecta/ Quellen zur Verfassungsgeschichte des Römisch-Deutschen Reiches im Spätmittelalter (1250–1500)*, 399, n. 95.

primogeniture. In 1444 two nobles from the Austrian archduchy, then nominally under Ladislaus's rule, were heard to charge that "Our Gracious Lord, the Roman King, had secured a charter from the electors to the effect that from now on the eldest of [the house of] Austria should rule and govern, for which purpose His Grace as Roman King has granted himself a Golden Bull."[12] A canard, perhaps, but nonetheless a suggestive one.

2. A MEETING OF MINDS WITH ROME

Frederick's reign commenced as the specter of schism began once again to haunt both Empire and Church. In 1439, after the Council of Basel elected a rival pope – a Savoyard duke, as Felix V (1383–1451, r. 1440–49) – the Imperial electors, meeting at Mainz, supported the council and adopted a modified version of Basel's reform decrees.[13] The Rhenish electors warned that if Pope Eugenius would not recognize and obey conciliar authority, they would call a "national" council of the Imperial church – what this unprecedented step meant, none could say – and recognize Felix V as true pope. Appreciating the situation's stakes, the wily Frederick hedged his bets. While he strove to heal the new schism he also made a separate peace with the pope. To this end in 1445 he sent Enea Silvio, a conciliarist who had turned his coat, to tell Eugenius of his readiness to make a deal and come to be crowned at Rome. In return, he demanded and got in February 1446 nomination rights to six bishoprics and a number of Austrian abbeys. Frederick also discarded, permanently as it turned out, any idea of sponsoring a reform of the Roman Catholic Church in head and members.

This was a realistic policy, for he did not want to split the Imperial church, any more than did the German princes, who signed their own agreements with the papacy in 1447. As a capstone on this strategy, in February 1448 Frederick signed a treaty (concordat) "on behalf of the German Nation" (*pro natione Alamanica*). It regulated the papal claim to "reserve" appointments to all vacant ecclesiastical benefices and stipulated 1) free, canonical election of all archbishops and bishops, plus the heads of abbeys standing directly under the pope; 2) filling of vacant canonries in cathedral and other collegiate churches by the pope in odd- and the emperor in even-numbered months; and 3) payment by bishops of the usual tax for confirmation by the Roman Curia. Although never published as such, the Concordat of Vienna carried the force of Imperial law, and it governed the legal status of the Roman Catholic Church in the Holy Roman Empire until 1803. Over the next quarter century, the Imperial estates one after the other consented to the treaty, until the very last city, Strasbourg, followed suit. The concordat's implications for the German lands can hardly be overstated. It ended the schism in the Empire, and by further embedding the Imperial church in Imperial governance, it effectively shifted responsibility for reform from pope and/or council to emperor and princes.

The concordat opened Frederick's way to Rome, where he was to be crowned and wed. The bride to be was Princess Eleanor (1434–67) of the Portuguese royal house of Aviz. Small, dark, and beautiful, just as Enea Silvio had described her, we can imagine that her elegance, fine manners, and friendliness put her tall, taciturn groom into the

---

12   Karl-Friedrich Krieger, *Die Habsburger im Mittelalter von Rudolf I. bis Friedrich III.*, 186.
13   This act is called the "Acceptance of Mainz."

shadows. The couple's peaceful journey to Rome formed a dramatic contrast to the tumultuous progresses of the medieval emperors. Frederick's was to be the last Imperial coronation at Rome and the last but one by a pope.[14]

Accompanied by 5,000 armored German cavalry commanded by his younger brother, Duke Albert VI (1418–63), the royal couple entered the Eternal City on 9 March 1452 along a way lined by papal soldiers to the steps of Old St. Peter's. Dismounting, Frederick knelt before Pope Nicholas V (r. 1447–55) to kiss the pope's foot and hand. Ten days later, young King Ladislaus of Hungary escorted the couple to St. Peter's for the coronation Mass. Following the Gradual, Pope Nicholas crowned Frederick – the wobbling of the pope's tiara was taken as a bad sign – and the occasion ended with the couple's exchange of marriage vows. The newlyweds then set off for Naples to visit Eleanor's brother, King Alfonso (1396–1458) – he impudently asked his new brother-in-law whether the marriage had yet been consummated – and via Venice, through whose gates no emperor had ridden since Frederick Barbarossa, over the mountains to the Austrian lands.

Frederick had secured what he wanted, greater autonomy for the Imperial church and his interests therein. The conciliar movement lay in ruins, and his new comity effectively removed reform of the Church from the political agenda for the next two generations. The schism overcome, the fresh-crowned emperor now had to deal with his own hereditary lands.

3. THE TERRIBLE DECADES

Frederick found his own possessions once more in turmoil. The key to all success lay in getting a secure grip on the Austrian lands; the difficulty of subduing them explains why for the next quarter of a century he rarely left his hereditary Austrian lands. It cannot have been easy, even given the huge discrepancies between authority and power that were everyday fare, to identify the real, rusticated Frederick in a desperate fight to rule his own lands with the emperor's image as the pope's partner in a dual lordship over the world. Yet the German lands had become quite accustomed to a monarch who did not intervene in their affairs, but who continued to represent the Christian imperium in German hands. The Nuremberg publisher Hartmann Schedel portrayed it so in his *World Chronicle* of 1493, placing Frederick side by side with Pope Pius II, who as Enea Silvio had once been his own secretary. Once master and servant, now dual lords of the world.

Frederick's progresses through German and Italian lands did not impress the turbulent Austrian nobilities, a perpetual thorn in Frederick's side. At King Albert II's death in 1439, the nobles of Upper and Lower Austria had demanded to be recognized as co-governors of Albert's legacy. They staged a wave of feuds and raids that attracted outsiders – old Hussite warriors in Upper Austria, Moravians and Slovaks in Lower Austria – who roamed the countryside in gangs in search of prey. Meanwhile, the leaders rallied their fellows against their Imperial archduke. They held assemblies, one of which called for Frederick's crucifixion, and asserted their right to control provincial governance, at least when the prince was absent from the lands. The Viennese burghers, the Empire's most obstreperous, joined the fray with glee.

---

14 The last papal coronation of an emperor took place at Bologna on 24 February 1530. See Chapter 11.

Eneas pius der babſt   Fridericб der dritt ein römiſcher kaiſer

Figure 2. Pope Pius II and Emperor Frederick III

The formal cause of this revolt was a dispute over custody of Ladislaus, the young Hungarian king. In 1447, disregarding Habsburg dynastic law, the Austrian estates had demanded that the boy reside in Vienna Castle, not at Frederick's court in Styria. Four years later – Ladislaus was now seven – the Mailberger League of nobles had met at Vienna to declare feud against Frederick in a huge document bearing no fewer than 254 seals. Unperturbed, Frederick had embarked on his planned journey to Rome to be crowned and wed. The leaguers tried but failed to kidnap Ladislaus at Rome, but at home the nobles and abbots and a Viennese faction managed to seize the government of Lower Austria. Lacking troops and money, Frederick, now returned home, had to give in. On 4 September 1452 his envoys – Enea Silvio was one – appeared at Wiener Neustadt's Stone Gate and handed Ladislaus over to the Austrian nobles. The emperor noted in his journal: "Happy is he who can forget what he cannot alter."[15]

15 Hödl, *Habsburg und Österreich*, 209.

Frederick's next challenger was his younger brother, Albert, who correctly suspected his brother of aiming to reunite the Habsburg lands. When civil war flared anew in 1461, the burghers of Vienna at first sided with Albert and besieged the Imperial family in Vienna Castle. Only Albert's sudden death in late 1463 ended this conflict. Frederick, who was no fool, drew the correct lesson from these years: "If a prince would rule forcefully according to his own interests and desires, he should beware of assemblies of his estates and the nobility."[16]

The Austrian revolts formed but one phase of a wave of feuds, wars, and revolt that swept through whole regions of the Empire during the mid-fifteenth century. "On St. James's Day [25 July] 1449," records the Augsburger Burkhard Zink, "began a great war in Franconia."[17] It was a familiar story, a local feud metastasized into a great regional war between a cities' league headed by Nuremberg, Augsburg, and Ulm and a princes' league of Brandenburg, Baden, Württemberg, Bamberg, Eichstätt, and Saxony, plus some counts and nobles. At the center of this bloody brawl stood the "German Fox," Elector Albert Achilles of Brandenburg, the age's most formidable Imperial warlord. "He was a master in counsel," writes Hans Ebran von Wildenberg (d. by 1503), a Bavarian who had been in the field against the margrave, "he was a master on the march, he was a master in the field, he was always among the first and foremost in attack and in combat."[18] Ferocious and implacable, Albert liked to say: "Burning adorns war as the Magnificat adorns Vespers."[19]

The Imperial cities who went to war, Zink freely admits, badly misjudged Albert. "The whole affair could have easily been kept in hand and settled, a knowledgeable man told me, so that it would not have led to war," but "the Nurembergers were too confident and arrogant to yield to a prince," and "all the cities, including us Augsburgers, had promised the Nurembergers more aid and support than they actually rendered once the war began."[20] There were no pitched battles, only a long, wearisome campaign of raid and counter raid in and around Franconia. Albert plundered Nuremberg's villages and castles, Nuremberg troops repaid him by burning eighteen villages and driving off 2,000 head of stock in a single day's work. Although in the end Albert wore the burghers down, victory by no means cooled his temper. In 1462, looking back on the Cities' War, he wrote to his brother, Margrave John (1406–64), that "if the bishops, those scoundrels, are not burnt, we and our lordship will never flourish like the green tree. Therefore, don't hesitate to burn both men and women, day and night, and spare no one, priest or layman."[21] That such a dangerous man held the office of Imperial elector and took a leading part in the counsels of kings and princes, suggests the utterly violent condition of life in the fifteenth-century Empire. Albert and his allies taught the cities a lesson they never forgot, for never again did the southern Imperial cities league together to fight princes.

---

16 Hermann Wiesflecker, *Kaiser Maximilian I. Das Reich, Österreich und Europa an der Wende zur Neuzeit*, vol. 3: 386.
17 Burkhard Zink, "Chronik des Burkhard Zink 1368–1468," in Carl Hegel, ed., *Chroniken der deutschen Städte vom 14. bis ins 16. Jahrhundert*, 187. This tremendous struggle, formerly called "the Princes' War," is today usually called the "Cities' War" or "Second Cities' War."
18 Zink, "Chronik," in Hegel, ed., *Chroniken*, 187.
19 Zink, "Chronik," in Hegel, ed., *Chroniken*, 187.
20 Zink, "Chronik," in Hegel, ed., *Chroniken*, 188.
21 Ernst Schubert, "Albrecht Achilles, Markgraf und Kurfürst von Brandenburg (1414–1486)," 153.

4. THE CULTURE OF VIOLENCE

The German wars of this era were more like feuds than wars in the usual sense. For centuries feuding, not a crime or a private war but a prerogative sanctioned by customary law, had been habitual in all of the Empire's governing classes. The commoners learned from the nobles. By the fifteenth century, revolts by burghers and peasants – always in the name of justice – had become common across a great arc that stretched from Upper Swabia across Outer Austria and the Black Forest to the Upper Rhine. The rebels aimed to defend property and livelihood by forcing rulers, including their own seigneurs and magistrates, to negotiate grievances with and acknowledge the rights of their subjects. Revolt was, in effect, a mass feud conducted by common people.

Although burghers could often sit in safety behind their walls, it is a serious error to think of them as essentially peaceful people. They were violent because their world was violent, and burghers took an astonishingly active part in the culture of feud and war. Everywhere – in the murals painted in city council chambers, in the funeral monuments erected in the urban churches, and in the miniatures created to illustrate urban chronicles – wealthy burghers are depicted as warriors. And so they were. Clergy also feuded. Prince-prelates, bishops, and abbots secured Roman dispensations from the Church's prohibition against a clergyman shedding blood. The anonymous priest who composed (ca. 1438) the most famous reform tract of the time, *The Reformation of Emperor Sigismund*, spoke truly when he declared that the bishops "make war and cause unrest in the world; they behave like secular lords, which is, of course, what they are."[22]

Not the burghers but the lesser nobles made the German lands notorious for violence. A Roman cardinal once remarked: "All Germany is a gang of bandits and, among the nobles, the more grasping the more glorious."[23] German commentators said much the same. Most notorious for its feuding nobles was the land of Franconia – the Main River basin between Swabia and Bavaria to the south and Hesse and Thuringia to the north. Here in 1522–23 Franz von Sickingen (1481–1523) mobilized the Franconian knights for revolt to fulfill his dream of becoming a prince; here lived and reaved Götz von Berlichingen, the infamous "Knight with the Iron Hand," who once defied the authorities with the memorable saying, "Kiss my ass"; and here dwelt and plundered Cuntz Schott (d. 1526), the fellow who collected hands from the Nurembergers he caught on the road.

Well before 1500, in Franconia and in other highly parcelized lands, sentiment was mounting for an end to the feud. Foremost among its foes, surely, were not the peasants – no one asked them – but the merchants whose wagons and goods attracted greedy nobles like flies to a banquet. "How can you give yourself out as so upright," asks the merchant in Ulrich von Hutten's dialogue called *The Robbers*, "and yet you have robbed so many, also killed some, for flimsy reasons and with no right to do so?"[24] His enraged antagonists, two noblemen named Ulrich (von Hutten) and Franz (von Sickingen) protested that they and their fellows used force only to protect the poor.

22   Gerald Strauss, ed., *Manifestations of Discontent in Germany on the Eve of the Reformation*, 11.
23   Hillay Zmora, *State and Nobility in Early Modern Germany: The Knightly Feud in Franconia, 1440–1567*, 1.
24   Zmora, *State and Nobility*, 1–2.

Yet the merchant knew what "protection" meant. So did the historian Sebastian Franck, who remarked that "those who should be the sheepdogs at the enclosure are often the wolves themselves, seizing with violence whatever they can, so that the people must be protected from the protectors."[25]

The pressure against the feud drew strength from a growing hope that stronger governance would make its suppression possible. Clergymen's entreaties and oaths aside, only a new configuration of power could realize this hope. The princes, above all, had to agree to new laws and enforce them. In 1486 Emperor Frederick proposed to the Diet a Public Peace, which was later accepted by the Diet of Worms in 1495. The new law declared that "no one, whatever his rank, estate, or position, shall conduct feud, make war on, rob, kidnap, ambush, or besiege another, . . . nor shall he enter any castle, town, market, fortress, villages, hamlets, or farms against another's will, or use force against them, illegally occupy them, threaten them with arson, or damage them in any other way."[26] Well and good, but might deeds follow words? For the time being, apparently not. When Charles V (1500–58, r. 1519–56) first came to the German lands in 1521, merchants from several southern free cities begged him to act against the endemic plague of robbery and murder on the Empire's roads, for, despite the law of 1495, the burghers were being "captured, kidnapped, imprisoned, tortured, and charged sums of money larger than we can pay, [and] our goods are blocked by land and by water, attacked, seized, burnt, and destroyed."[27] The criminalization of the feud depended on a concentration of power in the hands of princes and urban regimes. Their weapon was the statute, an innovative act of authority that could "break" custom. The statute was law permanent not temporary, commanded and not negotiated, and it defined the boundaries of power in the territorial state.

5. THE ORIGINS OF THE GERMAN TERRITORIAL STATE

The solution to the problem of weak, ineffective government lay in a double movement: on the one hand, the early transformation of the late medieval patrimonial principalities into institutionalized territorial states; on the other, a complementary growth of Imperial governance through the collaboration of emperor and Diet. The agents of governance were not the king's own men but these same princes, nobles, and magistrates who commanded their own armies and levied their own taxes. Gradually they came to support the suppression of feud, because thereby their own power was enhanced. Without them, there could have been no Imperial governance at all.

The German territorial state displays a variation on what Max Weber (1864–1920) called the "rationalization of domination" that lay at the heart of state formation in early modern Europe. European rulers did not abandon their predecessors' program of "protection" – guarding subjects and extracting fruits of their labor – but, learning from one another, they brought into use a toolkit of newly fashioned or newly adapted practices: bureaucracies of specialized functions staffed by lawyers and scribes, regular taxation and audits, mercantilist trade policies, standing armies, and regular

25 Zmora, *State and Nobility*, 2, slightly altered.
26 Johann Jakob Schmauss, ed., *Neue und vollständigere Sammlung der Reichs-Abschiede, welche von den Zeiten Kayser Conrads des II. bis jetzo auf den Teutschen Reichs-Tagen abgefasset worden*, vol. 2: 4.
27 Peter Blickle, *The Revolution of 1525: The German Peasants' War from a New Perspective*, 243.

diplomacy. Toward the end of the sixteenth century there appeared a new term, sovereignty, to describe a polity so equipped. A sovereign state possessed a well-defined, continuous territory, commanded a relatively centralized governance distinct from other social organizations, and advanced at least a claim to monopolize the means of physical coercion within its boundaries.[28]

Understanding state formation in the German lands requires us to keep in view the two principles that define respectively how the German lands resembled and how they differed from the western kingdoms. First, making feuds and wars and making states were not alternatives but two sides of a process that transformed feudal violence into state violence. Both "war making and state making – quintessential protection rackets with the advantage of legitimacy – qualify as our largest examples of organized crime."[29] The operative word, "protection," did imply a notion of lordship as contract, which was far older than the early modern concept of the contractual state. *The Mirror of Swabia*, a thirteenth-century German lawbook, summed up this notion perfectly: "We should serve our lords for they protect us, and if they do not protect us, justice does not oblige us to serve them."[30] Yet "protection" also assumed the inequality of the contractual relationship, which the lord could understand as giving him a right to employ force at will. This double meaning, custody and force, is neatly captured by the word's meanings in both English and German (*Gewalt*). European state formation entailed not a fundamentally new creation but a reconfiguration of lordship and its practice of protection, in which the prince claimed to be the sole lord, who possessed alone the right to "protect," that is, to define the common good and to coerce those who refused to obey. In a sense, the prince captured the noble feud and folded it into his own prerogative.

The second peculiarity of early modern state formation in the German lands is more familiar: the Imperial monarchy never monopolized this conversion of the nobles' culture of feud into the state's power to make war. This fact was neatly summed up by King Maximilian I, who once joked that while he was a "king of kings," whose vassals did as they pleased, his brother of France was a "king of animals," whose subjects had to obey.[31] Niccolò Machiavelli (1469–1527), who had visited Maximilian's court, made the same point: "Whoever concludes that Germany's undertakings will be powerful and will always succeed . . . does not consider that it suffices to block the emperor, when the princes do not support him in the execution of his plans."[32] Maximilian knew this; the Florentine understood it.

These observations show that the classic formulation of how German and Western (in fact, French) state development differed, dispersed power versus centralized power, is not incorrect. In France the monarchy gradually appropriated and absorbed the jurisdictions of aristocratic lineages, noble seigneurs, abbeys, and cities; in the German lands similar programs foundered on durable reefs made up of some thousands of polities. The political culture of dispersed "protection" – negotiation,

---

28 Charles Tilly, "Reflections on the History of European State-Making," 27. It has been argued that this idea was not established in the German lands until the eighteenth century, and some historians believe that the German territorial polities were never states, at least not in the Italo-Franco-English sense.
29 Charles Tilly, "War Making and State Making as Organized Crime," 169.
30 Otto Brunner, *Land and Lordship: Structures of Governance in Medieval Austria*, 219.
31 Wiesflecker, *Kaiser Maximilian I*, vol. 5: 5.
32 Wiesflecker, *Kaiser Maximilian I*, vol. 5: 529–30.

arbitration, threats, conciliation, and compromise – endured, even flourished. "It is not possible to understand the German state without taking into account its symbiosis with this corporative system of local interest groups."[33] In a European context, one of the German lands' most distinctive formations was the territorial state. Indeed, the monarchy itself survived only by becoming linked to Austrian territorial state formation. The emperor's authority may have been legitimized by history, Roman law, and the Church, but his power came from his own position as a territorial prince.

The early modern Holy Roman Empire thus became an agglutination, not a federation, of territorial rulers, for whom emperor and Imperial governance formed a kind of umbrella. Successful rule depended on monarch and estates acting together. Without an effective king, the princes could be no more than the greatest warlords in a world filled with war; without territorial states, the Empire could be no more than a set of symbols painted on the walls of city halls and portrayed on drinking cups. The key point is that for the overwhelming majority of the peoples of the German lands, central authority entered their lives, if at all, only through the mediation of local authority. Only one serious challenge to this settlement would ever be mounted. It came during the Thirty Years War, and it failed utterly.[34]

6. THE TERRITORIAL STATE – CHARACTER AND GROWTH

The dynastic territorial state evolved from the medieval patrimonial principality. Its hallmarks included the indivisibility of lands, an educated bureaucratic class of agents, and formal negotiations between prince and subjects. Of these the first is most obvious. So long as lands and rights remained in some sense the hereditary feudal property of a lineage, the division of patrimonial holdings among a prince's heirs was encouraged by the Germanic rule of partible inheritance and by an Imperial mandate of 1231 on the heritability of fiefs and offices. From this combination of custom and statute, the Golden Bull of 1356 excepted only the electors' lands.

The fifteenth century witnessed the first attempts to introduce indivisibility of patrimonial lands, a principle long before asserted by the Austrian forgery known as the "Greater Privilege." In this, as in most other stages of state formation, Bavaria led the way. In 1506, following 250 years of partitions and recombination and a bloody war in 1504, Duke Albert IV (b. 1447, r. 1465–1508) gained his estates' consent to the rule of primogeniture in Bavaria. Most other major dynasties followed suit, each at its own pace. The Habsburgs fissioned in 1379, 1396, and for a last time in 1564. Very highly addicted to partition were the Welf dukes of Brunswick, who between 1202 and 1495 partitioned their dynastic lands twelve times. The most fateful partition, surely, occurred in 1485 in Saxony, then a power second only to Austria. It left the two Saxonies much weaker in Imperial affairs than their population (of roughly 400,000) and mines warranted. A similar division of Baden by Margrave Christoph I (r. 1475–1515) turned a second-class power into two third-class ones. The Imperial counts preserved the practice of partibility much longer, some lineages until the French Revolution. The counts of Nassau, who since the twelfth century had held possessions along the Middle

33 Sheilagh C. Ogilvie, *State Corporatism and Proto-industry: The Württemberg Black Forest, 1580–1797*, 200.
34 See Chapter 17.

Rhine in the midst of lands belonging to Mainz, Trier, and Hesse, divided in 1255 into two lines, each of which underwent six subsequent partitions.[35]

Declaring a dynasty's lands indivisible did not in itself transform patrimonial holdings – partible bundles of rights, incomes, immunities, and jurisdictions – into a unified territorial state. The decisive step was the prince's assertion of his right to legislate, to make law rather than simply to enforce it, and to do so uniformly for all of his lands, regardless of their local traditions. Such laws, or statutes, began to appear in the mid-fifteenth century: Thuringia (1446), Bavaria (1440s), Lower Bavaria (1474), Saxony (1482), Württemberg and Baden (1495), and Hesse (1497, 1500). The coming of this kind of "territorial ordinance" (*Landesordnung*), a term first documented between 1489 and 1499, coincided fairly neatly with the onset of the Imperial reform. The term expressed a highly important innovation. Traditionally, a land was defined by language and common customs, not by a prince's authority. Historic entities such as Swabia and Franconia knew many lords but only one land. The coming of territorial ordinances implied, therefore, a supersession of the old "land" by the new "territory," just as old "custom" yielded to new "statute." At the root of both changes lay the prince's authority, by virtue of which land became territory and custom statute.

By 1500 a term had appeared to denote such regulating statutes. "Good governance" (*gute Policey*) uniformly forbade gambling, restricted exports, set standards for brewing (the famous Bavarian "purity law"), established dress codes, and fixed the wages of servants and day-laborers. As often as not, the obstinate multiplicity of customs and traditions frustrated the unity such statutes both assumed and asserted. Yet gradually the aggregate weight of territorial statutes came to influence Imperial legislation. Imperial statutes of 1530 and 1548 concerning servants and wages followed a chain that ran from a Tyrolean law of 1352 and a Thuringian ordinance of 1446 down through laws in Bavaria, the Silesian duchies, and Prussia. These statutes targeted the apprentices, journeymen, servants, and day-laborers, also beggars and other "traveling folk," in short, all whose condition made their relationship to the local authority temporary or doubtful. The transformation of old polities into new states regularized and strengthened lordship over those who, possessing neither subjects (dependents) nor permanent masters, could be regulated only by means of a new kind of law. It is easy to oversimplify this process, for a long and crooked path led from personal to supra-personal lordship, and what now are seen as fifteenth-century beginnings marked at the time no obvious way into the future. Some writers, such as the author of *The Reformation of Emperor Sigismund*, still understood "law and justice" as attributes not of one authority, the state or the prince, but of many – Empire, prince, bishop, seigneur, and city.

Behind the new regulations lay less a legal evolution than an administrative transformation of the late medieval principality. The first step was to identify the objects of rule by inscribing on the prince's various holdings a new map of invented districts (*Ämter*). Such units appear in most territories by 1500. Each district originally stood under a noble official (*Amtmann*), who was supported by a literate assistant knowledgeable in law. The growing importance of reading, writing, and reckoning skills gradually made the assistant more useful than his noble superior, and during the sixteenth century burghers commonly replaced nobles as district officials in most territorial states.

35 Gerhard Köbler, ed., *Historisches Lexikon der deutschen Länder*, 401–4.

At the very center of the institutionalizing project lay the creation of permanent organs of governance – a bureaucracy. The passage from the princely jurist of the fifteenth to the lawyer-bureaucrat of the seventeenth century was neither swift nor direct. German universities did not teach civil law until the middle of the fifteenth century, and around 1400 there may have been only one person, the Bologna-trained Swabian priest Job Vener, who held an earned doctorate in both canon and civil law.[36] Educated lawyers were by no means common at the courts of Imperial princes in the fifteenth century, though some larger free cities had begun to appoint them as civic attorneys. By the mid-fifteenth century the typical German holder of a coveted Italian law degree sold his services ad hoc to multiple employers in exchange for fees and gifts. The Franconians Gregor Heimburg (ca. 1400–72) of Schweinfurt and Martin Mair (ca. 1420–80) of Wimpfen typify the tiny elite of these adepts of the civil law. A hundred years later, such freelancers had been replaced by lawyers who worked exclusively for one prince or one city and drew salaries in addition to suits of clothes for summer and winter and reimbursements for travel expenses. They were forbidden to take "gifts" (bribes) from other rulers because, as a Saxon observed, "it seldom happens that the ruler is well served thereby, when his privy councilors accept gifts."[37] This domestication of learned servitors spread south to north from court to court, ending the freedom in which the old freelancers had lived. In the mid-fifteenth century, the Brunswick dukes had no interest in hiring lawyers and never consulted the one canonist they did retain. Over the course of the following century the Brunswickers conformed to the general trend so that by 1550 more lawyers than nobles sat in the duke of Brunswick-Wolfenbüttel's privy council.

The history of administration in the early modern state may be envisaged "as a history of social networks."[38] The social history of the Habsburg courts between 1480 and 1530 supports this statement. Men flocked into Habsburg service from Swabia and the Upper Rhine (31 percent), Tyrol (24 percent), the other Austrian lands (21 percent), and others lands ranging from Bavaria and Franconia to the Low Countries (24 percent). Most remarkable is the speed with which these officials' families intermarried to form an enormous connubial network. The integration of the royal court arose from presence and service and "also their marriages forged the lands into a political unit."[39] The nobles, three times as endogamous as the burghers, were far less well educated. Well paid or not, service was grueling work, especially the great amount of traveling officials had to undertake. The Tyrolean Blasius Hölzl (ca. 1470–1526), long head of the treasury at Innsbruck, declared in 1511 that he was tired of this "gypsy" life.[40]

A princely regime was built of men and also of paper, and its growth required ever more men who produced ever more documents and collected ever more records. The chancery was the head, if not the heart, of every state, and its chief, the chancellor, usually a university-trained jurist, emerged after 1500 as the most important officer in

36 Hermann Heimpel, *Die Vener von Gmünd und Straßburg 1162–1447*, vol. 2: 164.
37 Ernst Schubert, "Vom Gebot zur Landesordnung. Der Wandel fürstlicher Herrschaft vom 15. zum 16. Jahrhundert," 28.
38 Heinz Notflatscher, *Räte und Herrscher. Politische Eliten an den Habsburgerhöfen der österreichischen Länder 1480–1530*, 74.
39 Notflatscher, *Räte und Herrscher*, 262.
40 Notflatscher, *Räte und Herrscher*, 207.

every princely regime. Justice and administration came to depend less on the prince's personal presence and the collective memory of nobles expert in the customary law and more on the disembodied memory of the state lodged in the archive. The growth of the archive is a kind of index of the written word's supersession of the spoken in the everyday work of governance.

The point of institutionalization is to preserve governance and policy through the deaths, minorities, and successions of rulers, and through changes of administrative personnel. Institutions give governance memory. Their formation meant the creation of permanent commissions through which professional servants administered the prince's justice, committed his commands to writings, and watched over his money. By 1500 such administrative and judicial bodies were beginning to appear in some territorial regimes. King Maximilian's reforms in the Austrian lands followed Burgundian models: collegial organs separated by competences into chancery, treasury, and judicial administration; learned advisors and judges; and a much greater density of record keeping and control. Bavaria had a centralized judicial system based on Roman legal, that is written, procedures by 1520; Baden acquired its first chancery regulations in 1504 and a central court in 1509; in Hesse the high court (*Hofgericht*) was finally separated in 1500 from both the state council (*Rat*) and the chancery; and in Mecklenburg Duke Magnus II (r. 1477–1503) created a regime that lasted until the nineteenth century.

Reading territorial ordinances, which speak in the prince's name only, easily suggests a profoundly misleading conclusion that by the sixteenth century the German territorial state was becoming a proto-absolutist polity. Bureaucracy and central control alone did not make a principality into a state. Although the prince's grasp was generally stronger if narrower than the king's, no matter how deep his financial pockets and complex his bureaucracy, he required the collaboration of his estates. Estates consisted of a territory's notables constituted in a territorial diet. Long before princes began to hire lawyers and employ the written word as an everyday tool of lordship, they recognized the need to get leading subjects' consent to their principal actions. By the fourteenth century a land's notables, those worth calling, comprised more than the nobles, and the multi-chambered diet became a standard feature of princely governance.

The estates met at the prince's call, supplied him with advice and money, pressed him for the relief of grievances, and demanded that law be made only after consultation. In most principalities the practice of princely governing with estates fell somewhere between two imaginable extremes: the estates as the prince's tool; the estates as a permanent opposition. Estates did sometimes supply the impulse for new legislation. In Tyrol, where the nobility was weak and the commons strong, a series of general laws issued between 1404 and 1474 owed their origins to the estates' grievances. Even in lands where the estates' collaboration was by no means the rule (Bavaria) or was unacknowledged (Jülich-Berg), grievances and pressure lay behind the comprehensive ordinances of the later fifteenth century. Most grew out of conflicts among the estates – nobles, clergy, towns – or between the estates and their princes. In 1569 Duke Heinrich Julius of Brunswick-Wolfenbüttel (b. 1564, r. 1589–1613) declared his estates' advice to have been indispensable to "the territorial ordinance and policing."[41]

---

41 Schubert, "Vom Gebot zur Landesordnung," 31.

Like its Imperial counterpart, a territorial diet followed customary rules, the recording of which tended to transfer the authority for the rules' validity from the collective memory of participants to the document – an example of how the codification of custom contributed to legality. A Saxon document from this time affords a rare glimpse into how these bodies operated. In Electoral Saxony[42] the prince "determines the day and place, when and where he wants the diet to meet. He then sends out a general, written summons to his territorial estates – prelates, counts, barons, knights, towns, and universities – to appear personally."[43] The prelates and counts appear in person or send proxies, the towns, depending on size, send two to four persons each and the districts send two or three nobles, each with full powers to present their grievances. Meanwhile, the prince "has his wishes and whatever else he wishes to propose formulated in a formal, written proposition, on which his councilors deliberate as necessary and consider well each and every point."[44]

On the appointed day, after the diet is assembled, the prince, flanked by his courtiers, councilors, and servants, enters the hall and speaks to the assembly through a councilor. He commends their obedience to his summons, explains why he called them, orders the proposition read to them, and reminds them of their duty to be obedient. The chambers deliberate separately on the proposition and prepare a common reply, to which, if he is dissatisfied, the prince responds by demanding more. Now the estates present their grievances to be redressed before any aid is approved. When agreement on the money is reached, the estates are thanked, and the official record of the actions is read and signed. Finally, the estates "are also reminded to keep these matters secret, . . . and so the whole thing comes to an end, having once again taken its proper course."[45]

Most other German territorial diets will have followed procedures similar to those just described. As a contemporary saying suggested, deliberations on the land's welfare tended to become deliberations on money. Occasionally, as in the Brunswick duchies, a diet's decisions could supersede a territorial ordinance, but the heroic image of estates resisting princely tyranny is belied by the presence among the estates of the prince's principal creditors, who were deeply interested in his paying his debts at the subjects' expense. It is easy to see how this collaboration tended to level differences and create a general category of dependents, the taxpaying subject. A Prussian territorial ordinance of 1529 recognized "the peasant, of whatever status he might be," as simply a taxpayer.[46] By the seventeenth century the circle closed, as the territorial state had become a corporate collectivity of elites headed by the prince and his regime at its center, all supported by the body of subjects.

No idea or plan, and certainly nothing which smacked of absolutist notions, lay behind these changes. Everything grew out of practice, experience, experimentation, and imitation. Institutionalization on this scale suited the social formations and

42 Until 1547 Electoral Saxony comprised the lands of the elder, Ernestine line following the division of 1485; the younger, Albertine line, which ruled Ducal Saxony from its seat at Dresden, acquired the electorate and lands associated with this office in 1547 as a reward for aid in the Protestants' defeat by Charles V. This act reversed the pre-1547 distinction between what are called "Electoral Saxony" and "Ducal Saxony." See Chapter 11.
43 Paul Sander and Hans Spangenberg, eds., *Urkunden zur Geschichte der Territorialverfassung*, 68.
44 Sander and Spangenberg, eds., *Urkunden*, 69.
45 Sander and Spangenberg, eds., *Urkunden*, 72.
46 Schubert, "Vom Gebot zur Landesordnung," 32.

political configurations of the German lands, and it also made the reform of Imperial governance possible.

7. FREDERICK AS EMPEROR AND HIS END

No one in the German lands who lived through Frederick III's long reign, and surely not the emperor himself, could have recognized, much less understood, what tendencies lay behind the hundreds of small incidents and petty struggles of the age. Yet even while the consolidation of princely territorial states lay mostly in the future, the Imperial reform, which would reshape the early modern Holy Roman Empire of the German Nation, had already begun.

It had begun with the emperor's reappearance in Imperial affairs in the mid-1470s. His action concerned the most important matter any emperor or king could address, the continuation of his own dynasty. Frederick had business with Duke Charles (r. 1467–77) of Burgundy, called "the Bold."[47] Over the previous century a branch of the French royal house of Valois had risen to wealth and power by consolidating lordship over the province of Burgundy[48] and most of the seventeen provinces of the Low Countries. This composite polity had no proper name, though it was sometimes called "the grand duchy of the west" (*le grand duché d'Occident*). Its lands, which straddled the Romance-Germanic linguistic boundary in the basins of the Lower Rhine, Maas/Meuse, Scheld, and IJssel rivers, contained some 200 walled cities and produced incomes far greater than those of any Christian king. Duke Charles thirsted after a royal crown, something the emperor could grant. He thus suggested a marriage of his only child, Duchess Mary (1457–82), to Frederick's only son, Archduke Maximilian, a match Enea Silvio had proposed years before when Mary had been but six and Maximilian five.

The encounter between Frederick III and Charles the Bold at Trier in 1473 throws a strong light on the economic and cultural contrasts between Latin Christendom's richer west and its poorer east. Frederick and Maximilian entered first with a cortege of 2,500 horse. The duke's party followed with 3,000 armored cavalry, 5,000 light horse, 6,000 infantry, and an artillery park so fine it made the German nobles drool. Charles's golden cloak alone, rumor ran, was worth 100,000 gulden. With this "Latin upstart" came the flower of the Burgundian nobility, his bishops, and a tremendous collection of treasures and relics to dazzle the Germans. The Burgundians, in turn, marveled at the Germans' long hair, heavy armor and weapons, and poor equipment.

In return for his daughter, Duke Charles wanted a Burgundian kingdom extending from the North Sea to the borders of Savoy. Frederick hesitated, for the German princes wanted the matter referred to the Imperial Diet. Documents were prepared for the elevation of Charles to royal rank – Frederick was paid 80,000 gulden for feudal investiture with the provinces of Gelderland and Zutphen – but there the matter ended. The wily emperor left Trier, his purse filled with Burgundian coin, leaving behind beaten and baffled the splendid creature who had expected to enter Trier as a duke and leave it as a king.

47 Conventionally so called in English, though "the Rash" is a better translation of "le Témeraire" – and better fits his fate.
48 The duchy of Burgundy, a French royal fief, and the Franche-Comté (free county) of Burgundy, an Imperial fief, had their capitals respectively at Dijon and Besançon.

Not for nothing was Duke Charles nicknamed "the Bold." His army, the wonder of Christendom, invaded the *Hochstift* of Cologne and invested the archiepiscopal town of Neuss on the Rhine. Fifty-six times the Burgundians assaulted Neuss's walls; just as many times the burghers threw them back. Charles had misjudged his foe, for the stolid emperor raised an army and marched it westward under Elector Albert Achilles's command. They forced Charles to break off the siege (June 1475), sign a truce, and promise his daughter to Maximilian. The canny emperor got what he wanted – the Burgundian marriage – the Imperial estates bore the costs, and the foolish duke, Frederick's superior in all but rank and patience, slunk home with empty hands, humiliated but not humbled.

It was not the emperor who stopped the Burgundian project but typically German regional federations of small and tiny powers. After Duke Charles purchased the duchy of Lorraine, which closed the large gap between his Low Countries and his southern lands, he moved his court to Nancy and prepared to serve up the Alsatians next on his bill of fare. They were ready for him. In December 1473, the Alsatian free cities, the free nobles, and Strasbourg's bishop had formed a defensive league, the Lower Union, which then allied with the Swiss (called "the Upper Union") and with Duke Sigismund of Tyrol. In the ensuing war (November 1474 to January 1477), this triple alliance fought a series of fierce battles against Burgundian forces. At Grandson they seized Charles's famous treasure as booty; at Murten/Morat they drove an entire Burgundian army to its death by drowning in Lake Murten; and at Nancy in January 1477, they routed Charles's army, plundered his camp, and left his naked corpse on the frozen field. Through it all, Frederick calmly went forward with his plans for the Burgundian marriage.

From the 1420s to the 1470s, a half-century of war – the Hussite Wars, the Austrian civil wars, the Cities' War, and the Burgundian Wars – shook the Empire's old heartlands and provoked a mounting cry for stronger governance. Satisfying this demand required not only greater collaboration and willingness to pay among the Imperial estates but also a readiness of those who made feuds and wars within the Empire – princes, nobles, prince-prelates, and free cities – to decide that keeping peace would serve their interests better than making war. Finally, in the later 1480s, fifty years after Jan Hus's death by fire at Constance but only a decade after the relief of Neuss, a movement got underway to curb the Empire's culture of endemic violence.

In his last years, Frederick III presided over the initial measures of the Imperial Reform, the main phase of which unfolded under his successor. The old emperor was and is an enigmatic figure. Maximilian's fictionalized biography portrays him as

> an especially noble king, who in his times stood highest in royal honor in the whole earth. He was extremely powerful in realms, lands, and peoples, and he possessed great ability, deep intelligence, and especially foresightedness and deliberate wisdom. For these reasons, everyone gave him and called him by the name of "the Old White King" in later years, when he ruled royally and well and had reached a sufficient age.[49]

The Italians, politically wise and practiced in the mockery of foreigners, had another view. Archbishop Antonino (1389–1459) of Florence, who met Frederick en

---

49 Reinhard Rudolf Heinisch, "Das Bild Kaiser Friedrichs III. in der frühen Neuzeit," 504. The name given to Frederick plays on the German words for "wise" (*weis*) and "white" (*weiss*).

route to Rome in 1452, thought "he had nothing at all Imperial in his appearance" and possessed "neither generosity nor wisdom, for he always spoke through his orators. His great greed for gifts was always evident, and when he returned to his quarters he left behind a very poor impression."[50]

We cannot know how Frederick looked back on his long reign as he lay dying at Linz in Upper Austria in the summer of 1493. His mind was on the state of his soul, of course, but also on a more immediate problem. Even as the surgeons were cutting away his gangrenous leg, he remarked that it was better to be a healthy peasant than a sick emperor.

Frederick had been born in the year of Jan Hus's death at the stake in Constance; when he died, ten-year-old Martin Luther was studying Latin grammar at Mansfeld in Thuringia. Unlike his unlucky predecessor, this emperor had a son, 34-year-old Maximilian, already for five years king of the Romans, that is of the German lands, and experienced in both government and war. Frederick bequeathed to him two legacies of utmost importance to the Imperial reform just begun: a secure grip on the Austrian lands as a dynastic base and a credible Habsburg claim to the Imperial succession.

It may seem odd to locate the beginnings of both the Imperial revival and the rise of the territorial state in the reign of Frederick III, "the Empire's Arch-Sleeping Cap," or, as others called him, "the peasant king." It is perhaps odder yet to see his Austrian lands, remote from the old Imperial heartlands, as central to putting the Imperial monarchy on a secure territorial base. Frederick nevertheless achieved the crucial preconditions – unity and indivisibility – of Austria's passage from a gaggle of medieval patrimonial principalities into an early modern territorial state. Austria's importance to this story lies less in the priority or strength of its state formation than in the timing of it. It occurred at precisely the right moment to underpin the monarchy's role in the Holy Roman Empire of the German Nation. United with the Habsburgs' fabulous biological luck, their Austria – not the Luxemburgs' Bohemia and Hungary or the Wittelsbachs' Bavaria – filled the space of the long-lost German royal domain and thereby made possible a stable monarchy for the next 300 years. The process remained obscure, so long as the classic, state-centered narrative of German history remained vital. The narrative's central message – state formation by the Imperial dynasty *or* by the princes – has yielded to a quite different story, in which the early modern Empire and the princely territorial states appear as nearly simultaneous and complementary foundations of the early modern Empire. It was a story of old bottles and new wines, the superior vintage of which bore the Habsburg label.

50 Wiesflecker, *Kaiser Maximilian I.*, vol. 1: 61.

7

The Reform of the Empire in the Age of Maximilian I

> The popular and aristocratical powers in a great nation, as in the case
> of Germany and Poland, may meet with equal difficulty in maintaining
> their pretensions; and in order to avoid their danger on the side of kingly
> usurpation, are obliged to withhold from the supreme magistrate even
> the necessary trust of an executive power.
>
> Adam Ferguson

Fifteenth-century Germans who traveled southward to Italy or westward to the Low Countries saw wondrous things and suffered deeply hurtful jibes at their backwardness. A Pole or Hungarian journeying in the German lands might feel the same, but Italians who traveled in them gave far more injury than they endured at native hands. Giovanni Antonio Campano (1429–77), a humanist-poet and bishop who worked in the Roman Curia, came as a cardinal's secretary to the Imperial Diet at Regensburg in 1471. It was his first venture outside his native Italy, and what he saw, and smelled, and what he had to eat and drink appalled him. "Nothing is filthier than Germany," where "there is no life except drinking," and each glass of the sour wine "makes me cry."[1] The muses have no homes here, he adds, for there "reigns a monstrous spiritual barbarism, [as] none but a few know literature, and no one elegance." In Italy Italians treated Germans as country bumpkins, barbarians who knew nothing about how to live.

When Maximilian and his father met Duke Charles of Burgundy at Trier in 1473, Latin elegance as usual trumped German solidity. They heard Charles's wondrous choir, watched his gorgeous troops, and inspected the treasures – plate, reliquaries, the famous Burgundian sideboard, glorious tapestries, the twelve Apostles in solid silver, and a bejeweled golden lily as tall as a man. The Holy Roman emperor may have been lord of the world, but at Trier he was seen as a poor, dowdy bumpkin.

The splendor of the west did not cast the same reflection on Archduke Maximilian. He admired and envied the elegant duke. Charles, whatever he thought of the dumpy father – his own liege-lord – liked the son, a strongly built youth, tall for his

---

1 Klaus Voigt, *Italienische Berichte aus dem spätmittelalterlichen Deutschland. Von Francesco Petrarca zu Andrea de' Franceschi (1333–1492)*, 177.

fourteen years and wearing his blondish hair shoulder-length in the German manner. He invited the young prince to his quarters, introduced him to a talking parrot, and showed him the famous Burgundian artillery. Frederick, who soon grew weary of dealing with this arrogant Latin prince – his own vassal many times over – grumbled, "One day the duke makes a promise, next day he takes it back."[2] Maximilian, riding at his father's side as they left Trier for home, had found a second father in his future father-in-law. He would one day honor the flamboyant duke by taking Charles's motto as his own: "I dared it!" (French, *"Je l'ay emprint!"* German, *"Ich hab's gewagt!"*).[3]

As king and emperor, Maximilian I would become a westernizer. From a German king of German lands only, as his father had been, he would become a power on the battlefields of the Low Countries, Italy, Hungary, and the German lands; he would attempt to refashion the Imperial office from a feudal lordship into a modern – one might say "Renaissance" – monarchy; and he would favor in all things, from administration to entertainment, models he had learned in the Burgundian Netherlands. His father had rebuilt Austrian power, now Maximilian aimed to rebuild German power in the image of the great emperors of the past.

I. YOUNG MAXIMILIAN

On Holy Thursday (22 March) 1459 at Wiener Neustadt, legend later told, at the moment of the young archduke's birth a great comet passed overhead like the Star of Bethlehem. In his fictional autobiography (*Weisskunig*), Maximilian's alter ego is called both "the Young White King" and "the Young Wise King." This prince learns easily all the military, political, linguistic, and artisanal skills a future monarch might need. From the old books he reads the great lesson for all rulers, that great deeds, inspired by the memory of the past, must be fixed in memory for the future. That story was fiction; the reality was a troubled boyhood. His teacher Johannes Cuspinian (1437–1529) tells us that Maximilian did not speak until his ninth year, "so most people thought he was mute," and when he did speak, "he said words with much difficulty, which greatly distressed his mother."[4] Once speaking, however, the prince hardly stopped, and "in later years his ability at languages astonished everyone, especially foreigners."[5] He learned his native German, Latin, French, and Italian "very well," and at assemblies and audiences "he often spoke himself, not through the customary orator, and delivered very long extemporaneous speeches about complicated matters."[6] Awed, Emperor Frederick told some princes at Frankfurt in 1486, "I don't know how this happened that he reads and speaks so; I know very well that when he was twelve years old, I was afraid that he would be either stupid or mute."[7]

Maximilian learned from his beautiful Portuguese mother, whom he adored, that the appearance of power is itself a kind of power. In 1462 she had shown her mettle

2 Hermann Wiesflecker, *Maximilian I. Die Fundamente des habsburgischen Weltreiches*, 40.
3 Hermann Wiesflecker, *Kaiser Maximilian I. Das Reich, Österreich und Europa an der Wende zur Neuzeit*, vol. 1: 112.
4 Inge Wiesflecker-Friedhuber, ed., *Quellen zur Geschichte Maximilians I. und seiner Zeit*, 3, n. 3.
5 Wiesflecker-Friedhuber, ed., *Quellen zur Geschichte Maximilians I.*, 33, n. 3.
6 Wiesflecker-Friedhuber, ed., *Quellen zur Geschichte Maximilians I.*, 33, n. 3.
7 Wiesflecker-Friedhuber, ed., *Quellen zur Geschichte Maximilians I.*, 33, n. 3.

during a seven-week siege by Viennese rebels, at the end of which the royal family had to ride out of the city under the protection of Bohemian mercenaries with the burghers' shouts ringing in their ears: "King of the Jews" and "Get the hell back to Graz!" The queen supposedly told Maximilian, "If I had known, my son, that you would become like your father, I would have regretted having born you for the throne."[8] "The emperor does not deserve to have his crotch covered by a skirt," the bold queen added, "for he does not punish injustice with the severity it requires."[9] Frederick was a negotiator, Eleanor was a fighter.

In time Maximilian came to experience, but never to accept, the reason for "the Old White King's" quiet tenacity of purpose and patient bearing of disappointments. Money, or the lack of it, was the bane of lordship. It was a very hard lesson to learn. Frederick, a notorious pinch-penny, once called his son "wastrel."[10] In 1494 a priest inscribed his presentation copy of Engelbert of Admont's *De regimine principum* with the words, "Wisely order your governance and your life: / Collect all you are due and spend it wisely!"[11] If only he could have heeded the abbot's words – an apt summary of the era's idea of good governance – but he could not trim his ambitions or his pursuit of personal and dynastic glory to his means. Many shrewd observers recognized in this disparity between ends and means the great weakness of Maximilian's reign. The Venetians nicknamed him "Maximilian Empty-Pockets," and the Augsburg merchant Wilhelm Rem (1462–1529) looked back on his reign as a grave mismatch between ends and means: "The emperor was lord of Austria, he was honest, not very intelligent, and always poor.... He always wanted to make war, but he never had any money."[12] Western ambitions, eastern incomes.

The splendor of the west, which he had glimpsed four years ago at Trier, drew the young Lochinvar out of the east in August 1477 to claim Duchess Mary for his bride. Down the Rhine he came, into the late Duke Charles's lands, where Netherlandish burgher wealth and French aristocratic culture combined to support and animate a rich culture unrivalled except in the great Italian cities. The experience overwhelmed him. "We came on Monday, St. Agapitus's Day [18 August] to my gracious lord's bride at Ghent," relates an anonymous companion, "which is a large city, probably half a [German] mile long and larger than Venice. We were well received by about 522 mounted men, all in white, and the streets were hung with tapestries, . . . on which sheets of paper were pinned. On one was written, 'You are our ruler and prince, fight our fight,' and on another, 'All that you desire, we will do.'"[13] At Ghent he met his bride, and the next day they were married in the presence of the papal legate, the future Pope Julius II (r. 1503–13).[14]

Maximilian spent twelve years in the Netherlands. Mary died after five years of married life, leaving him a son, Philip (1478–1506), called "the Handsome," whose regent Maximilian became. In these years the German bumpkin-prince transformed into, in his modern biographer's words, "a complete Burgundian," who "saw and

8   Wiesflecker, *Maximilian I.*, 26, 28.
9   Wiesflecker, *Maximilian I.*, 28.
10 Wiesflecker, *Kaiser Maximilian I.*, vol. 5: 564.
11 Wiesflecker, *Kaiser Maximilian I.*, vol. 1: 413.
12 Wilhelm Rem, "Cronica newer geschichte 1512–1527," 99–100.
13 Wiesflecker-Friedhuber, ed., *Quellen zur Geschichte Maximilians I.*, 35, n. 5. The German mile equaled about five statute miles.
14 A papal legate is a representative endowed with specified powers in ecclesiastical matters.

judged the politics of the hereditary lands, the Holy Roman Empire, and Europe with a Burgundian's eye."[15] His "Burgundian eye" registered two things, both more important than the lavish entertainments – dances, masques, and tournaments – he loved so much. He learned how to make war in the modern style, and he learned the most advanced methods of government.

The ablest royal warlord of his generation, Maximilian learned the trade while defending the Netherlands for his wife and their small son against the French king's forces. He counts as a major figure in what has been called "the renaissance of infantry," the shift to solid phalanxes of pike-wielding heavy infantry, who, if well drilled and their flanks guarded, proved more than a match for armored, mounted knights. The Swiss had blazed this trail, but the Germans came close on their heels.[16] In the Netherlands Maximilian created a force of German mercenaries, lansquenets, trained and armed in the Swiss manner, and their successors fought under his standard on battlefields against all of his foes. Under his tutelage, the Germans became pioneers in the world of Renaissance warfare. The Lombard physician Alessandro Benedetti (ca. 1450–1512) describes with wonder the stunning German formations he saw paraded at Milan in 1495:

> All eyes fixed on the German phalanx, which formed a quadrangle of 6,000 men. . . . Following the German custom, such troops have so many drums that it nearly breaks one's eardrums to hear them. Armored only with breastplates, they march in close formation, the foremost with long, pointed pikes, those behind with lances raised upright, followed by halberds and broadswords. At the appropriate sign from their standard-bearers, the whole troop moves right, left, or backwards, as though it were on a raft. On its flanks are gunners and crossbowmen. Parading before Duchess Beatrice, this troop instantaneously converted itself into a wedge, then it divided into two wings, which moved, one fast and one slowly, so that one part revolved around the other, and they seemed to form a single body.[17]

Order and discipline, the hallmarks of a new era. The commander of such troops, plus a good artillery park, might rule the battlefields of Christendom.

2. A NEW WAY OF GOVERNANCE – AUSTRIA

Maximilian's notions of governance can be inferred from his intermittent, often desultory attempts to reshape the reunited Austrian lands. Elected king of the Romans at his father's wish in 1486, he returned from the Netherlands in 1489 to find Frederick a wandering fugitive from the eastern lands, a large part of which lay in the hands of King Matthias Corvinus (b. 1443, r. 1458–90) of Hungary, who now sat in Vienna's castle. In the following year came two strokes of luck: the Hungarian king died, and Maximilian purchased Tyrol and the other western Austrian lands from his childless, spendthrift uncle, Duke Sigismund. With the dynastic lands united for the first time in nearly a century, the king took up residence at Innsbruck, Tyrol's capital, which lies at the northern foot of the Brenner Pass, closer to Augsburg, Nuremberg, Venice,

---

15 Wiesflecker, *Kaiser Maximilian I.*, vol. 1: 228, 389.
16 This distinction is conventional, for most of the Swiss of this era were also Germans in every respect but one – they opposed Imperial interference in their affairs.
17 Hans Delbrück, *Geschichte der Kriegskunst im Rahmen der politischen Geschichte*, vol. 4: 15.

and Milan than to Vienna, and much further west than his father's favorite seats. He settled there at the peak of Tyrol's great age, when the mines and smelters around Schwaz and Hall were pouring out rivers of silver, copper, and gold. Most of it, alas, flowed not into the king's treasury but into the purses of Augsburg merchants, who advanced the king cash in return for monopolies of the selling of metals to the world at large and of foodstuffs to the miners.

The governance of the Austrian lands lay chiefly in the hands of their prickly, deeply conservative provincial nobilities. Gradually, against heavy odds, some of his own making, Maximilian and his councilors introduced what came to be called "the Netherlandish [i.e., Burgundian] government."[18] They brought the two northern (Upper and Lower Austria) and the three southern (Styria, Carinthia, and Carniola) provinces under a single regime, called – a Burgundian-style title – "the lower Austrian lands." This eastern unit and a western one (the "upper Austrian lands" of Tyrol and Outer Austria) were given parallel governments under a central regime at Innsbruck.

The central government's heart comprised three parts: a new high court (1497/98), a chancery (1498), and a financial administration and treasury (1491, 1496). Maximilian's men struggled to create at each level – provincial, regional, and central – a set of specialized councils staffed by salaried councilors and judges. During the 1490s a new vocabulary of Burgundian administrative language came into use at Innsbruck,[19] the sign of an intention to create permanent institutions that would function also in the prince's absence or between reigns. Instead of threatening the noble-controlled provincial estates, Maximilian imposed the new institutions on the old bodies. This was precisely how the Valois dukes had created their Burgundian state.

These creations, islands of relative order in a sea of bricolage, suggest a desire to rationalize governance. Other changes point in the same direction, of which the most important targeted the heart of Maximilian's (and every other) regime, the chancery.[20] At the beginning of Maximilian's reign, his court chancery at Innsbruck stood in competition with the Imperial chancery, which functioned under the authority of the senior Imperial chancellor, the elector-archbishop of Mainz. Maximilian began to refer Tyrolean, Austrian, and Imperial business alike to his own chancery, which became "the most influential body in Maximilian's government."[21] The two chanceries were united in 1502, after Maximilian demanded that the elector of Mainz return the Imperial seals. From this measure and the new ordinances for separate departments of the Innsbruck regime a reasonably direct line led to the first comprehensive ordinance, Archduke Ferdinand's statute (*Hofordnung*) of 1527.

The centralizing tendencies in themselves pointed to a stronger Austrian governance but not to using Austria as a base from which to strengthen royal command over Imperial governance. This idea did surface, however, in two projects of the king's last years, well after he had tried and failed to undermine reform dominated

18 Wiesflecker, *Kaiser Maximilian I.*, vol. 5: 209.
19 Examples: finances, tresorier, tresorier-général, greffier, argentier, estat, journal, controlleur, régent-erie, chambre des comptes. Wiesflecker, *Kaiser Maximilian I.*, vol. 2: 198.
20 A chancery (also, chancellery) is the administrative office that prepares, seals, transmits, and archives official documents. The ultimate model of such offices was the chancery of the Roman Curia.
21 Elaine C. Tennant, "An Overdue Revision in the History of Early New High German: Niclas Ziegler and the Habsburg Chancery Language," 257.

by the Imperial estates. The first scheme, formulated in 1516, aimed to raise the Austrian lands to a kingdom within the Empire – just what Charles of Burgundy had sought at Trier in 1473 – which Maximilian might leave to his younger grandson, Archduke Ferdinand (1503–64). Two years later, he unveiled before representatives of all the Austrian lands assembled at Innsbruck the idea of a combined Austrian-Imperial state council, the membership of which the king would control: with five members from the eastern Austrian lands (the five duchies), four from western Austria, four royal nominees, and a mere five named by the Imperial estates. He also promised to establish separate regional regimes at Vienna, Innsbruck, and Ensisheim in Alsace, plus a central treasury and chamber of accounts for all Austria. These projects remained on paper, but they show that the king never forgot what he learned during his twelve years in the Netherlands. He never lost his "Burgundian eye."

The projects of 1516–18 also suggest that the idea of connecting a more centralized Austria to royal influence over Imperial governance was "in the air" at court during Maximilian's last years. Securing the Imperial princes' acceptance of a joint Austrian-Imperial regime was probably a pipe dream, but there was another way. At Innsbruck in 1518 the king told the Austrian estates of his wish to promote "our own welfare and that of our lands and subjects" by establishing "at the proper time and place a neighborly union, agreement, and league with the estates of the Holy Empire, or, if that is impossible, at least with the principalities and lords who border on our Austrian lands."[22] Hardly novel, the idea of expanding Austrian influence over the neighboring lands through a system of clientage had animated the founding of the Swabian League in 1488. A simpler version, a royal league of Imperial cities, went back to Sigismund's time. The idea of consolidating Austrian lands and Habsburg clients in the fragmented regions of the south offered a possible way around the Imperial Diet, in the chambers of which sat many a prince and city the emperor could never coerce.

At the heart of all of Maximilian's schemes for centralization and royal patronage lay the fundamental problem of his reign, money. On this subject the king had no idea or morals, only need. "I am not a king of money," his alter ego in *Weisskunig* says, "but I want to be a king over the people, especially those who have money. . . . A warlike government and fame are worth far more than money."[23] Although he understood quite well the ancient Roman commonplace, "money is the sinews of war" (*pecunia nervus belli*), Maximilian remained nonetheless perfectly heedless, even reckless, about how it was obtained in order to serve his quest for fame and glory.[24] The best that can be said of his financial practices is that he borrowed democratically from rich and poor alike and defaulted with the same even-handedness.

Maximilian's exploitation of the Austrian lands suggests how he would have governed the Empire had the Imperial estates been at his mercy to the degree that the Austrian subjects were. In 1509 the king spoke to them of the problem of financing his emperorship from his dynastic base. "The estates should in all fairness remember," he told his councilors,

22 Thomas A. Brady, *Turning Swiss: Cities and Empire, 1450–1550*, 90.
23 Wiesflecker, *Kaiser Maximilian I.*, vol. 3: 229.
24 "*Pecunia nervus belli.*" Cicero, *Phil.* 5.12.32. The saying is also known from Horace, Terence, Varro, and Tacitus.

that as ruler of Austria and Burgundy, I have had to bear and suffer many long years of heavy expense, burdens, and effort in countering the opposition of the French, Swiss, . . . Hungarians, and Turks. I have survived them all through my own strength and inherited treasure, and against all such threats I have always thought it most essential to retain my House of Austria and Burgundy, forging them into a shield to protect the Empire from such attacks.[25]

The facts do bear him out. In the king's later years, Austria yielded annually between half and 1.2 million gulden, as against something over 50,000 gulden from the rest of the Empire. Most of this money – at least 70 percent if the accounts for 1516 are typical – went for war. Over his entire reign, Maximilian may have spent something like 25,000,000 gulden, leaving at his death debts amounting to more than 6,000,000 gulden. The vast bulk of the difference, some 19 million gulden, Maximilian squeezed from the Austrian lands. None contributed more in proportion to their wealth than did his Tyroleans, most loyal of his subjects, who paid heavier taxes and suffered more than others did from Maximilian's friends, the Augsburg merchants who monopolized the smelters and the sale of imported foodstuffs. They suffered, too, from the stags and the boars that destroyed their crops. As if in delayed compensation, on news of the king's death, the Tyrolean uplanders attacked the wild game, Maximilian's beloved playthings. The old king, they joked, had bequeathed to them his favorite beasts.

Moneys collected both flowed through and into the hands of the men who staffed Maximilian's treasury at Innsbruck, where some thirty persons toiled to find money, quaintly called "finances." One of the ablest was Blasius Hölzl, who called himself "Sir Blasius," but was in fact a peasant's son from the Puster Valley in South Tyrol. For years this "voracious finance fellow" combed the land for cash for his lord, terrorizing one and all. "If you throw him out the front door," complained the archbishop of Salzburg, "he backs right back in."[26] Long on cunning, short on polish, Sir Blasius scoured the realm for funds, struck deals with the moneybags of Augsburg, and plugged with his fingers a hundred holes in the financial dikes that stood between the king and ruin.

Venality was the soul of Maximilian's court. Dr. Erasmus Topler (1462–1512), provost of St. Sebald's Church in Nuremberg, spent the last five years of his life at court. "As I have earlier told you several times," he wrote home, "the nature of this court [is] dedicated to deals [*finanzen*]."[27] Everyone at court, the saying went, knew how to "carve a good joint." This was not the institutionalized venality of the early modern French and Spanish courts but a good, oldfashioned taking of bribes by officials who were paid irregularly or not at all.

In another important respect – the recruitment of officials – the court at Innsbruck favored competence over birth.[28] Compared to the chief officials of any past German royal or Imperial regime, those who worked for Maximilian seemed like upstarts, burgher and peasant boys, some formed in universities and others in the school of life, who flocked to Innsbruck for advancement and fortune. Of seventeen outstanding

25 Alphons Lhotsky, "Was heisst 'Haus Österreich?'" 169.
26 Wiesflecker, *Maximilian I.*, 199.
27 Brady, *Turning Swiss*, 87.
28 See the discussion in Chapter 6.

figures, eight were lesser nobles, seven burghers, and two peasants born. All but one of the nobles came from the Austrian lands, all but one of the burghers from southern Imperial cities. Even the greatest personalities were of relatively low degree. Jakob Villinger (ca. 1480–1529), son of a petty burgher in Sélestat/Schlettstadt in Alsace, rose to be treasurer-general and the king's leading financial strategist and cultivated excellent relations with the great Augsburg firms. At his death the king owed Villinger some 190,000 gulden. Paul von Liechtenstein (ca. 1460–1513), from an old Tyrolean noble family, came from Duke Sigismund's court to Maximilian's, where he had authority over all Austrian incomes, lent the king more than 100,000 gulden, and became a knight of the Order of the Golden Fleece. Matthäus Lang (1468–1540), from an impoverished patrician family at Augsburg, educated in arts and law at Tübingen, Ingolstadt, and Vienna, enjoyed incomes estimated at up to 50,000 gulden per year, masterminded the French alliance in 1501–5, proclaimed Maximilian's Imperial title at Trent in 1508, and became archbishop of Salzburg, cardinal, and the king's decoy as papal candidate. Finally, Florian Waldauf (ca. 1445–1510), son of peasants in the Pustertal, entered Sigismund's chancery and played a major role in the transition to Maximilian, mediated the Augsburg merchants' takeover of the mines and foundries, and in 1501–2 leased the entire Austrian revenues. These men were capable, ambitious, and grasping, and though the court's reputation for venality, trickery, and fraud was very bad, the regime they ran, judges the king's biographer, "was an improvement on the noble governments of earlier days."[29]

3. IMPERIAL REFORM

In his dreams Maximilian might absorb Imperial governance into a reformed Austrian central regime; in reality he had to deal constantly with powerful Imperial estates whose vigilance against royal domination never flagged. In the space between them during the years from 1486 to 1521, a jointly enacted series of laws did establish in law, if not yet in fact, an order of governance under which the Empire would live all through the early modern era. The idea of restoration, returning the Empire to its pristine condition as it had been ruled by the Ottonian, Salian, and Hohenstaufen dynasties of the eleventh to thirteenth centuries, belonged in the well-used toolkit of every fifteenth-century writer on reform. The real world prescribed something quite different.

The restorationists were by no means incapable of adapting their discourse to current conditions. The Magdeburg clergyman who in 1495 wrote *The Dream of Hermansgrün* describes how his title character dreamt he saw the Empire, flanked by two deadly enemies, the Ottomans and France, falling into decay because of the princes' immorality, selfishness, and crimes. They are rich, the Empire is poor; they are mighty, the emperor is weak; they are corrupt, their ancestors were virtuous. Help could be had only if the princes at the coming Diet at Worms would vote taxes for two large armies and promise to abolish the feud. There was the rub, for there could be no reform without the princes' collaboration and consent, and they had no desire to strengthen the royal hand. Yet better Imperial governance clearly required permanent institutions dedicated to creating and enforcing new laws. The only way forward was

29 Wiesflecker, *Kaiser Maximilian I.*, vol. 5: 224.

to fix rules of representation, negotiation, and consent for which past practice offered no precedents. Nicholas of Cusa had thought of such things, but no one seemed to have heard of his words.

The fifteenth century's instrument for securing law and order was the Public Peace, a fixed-term (ten years was common) agreement to cease fighting and suppress feuding. In 1442 and again in 1486 Frederick III proposed such laws, precedent for which went back at least to Emperor Frederick II (d. 1250). Under neither Frederick did an apparatus exist for enforcing the peace. The feud could not be controlled, much less suppressed, unless the peace was enforced by a new executive power. But in whose hands? The only hope lay in the Imperial Diet, which in the course of the fifteenth century had begun to take on a relatively fixed form. While it descended from the old assemblies of the king's vassals, it was becoming a corporate institution possessing a fixed form and standard procedures and capable of negotiating with the monarch who convened it. In it even the Imperial cities finally gained seats, though no votes. A Strasbourg envoy described in 1481 how the electors and princes deliberated and decided, "while the burghers sit outside the door like snuffling dogs."[30] The princes spiritual and temporal gave the tone, and from their chamber of the Diet – not from the king – came all the innovations that made up the Imperial reform.

Whatever Maximilian intended when he called the estates to assemble at Worms on 2 February 1495, it certainly was not Imperial reform. He wanted money, enough to finance a campaign to Italy, where a war sparked by a French invasion had just begun. He would ask for money, take the money, and go over the Alps on campaign. "My dear cousin," he wrote to Duke Sigismund,

> We have shortened the meeting [Diet] at Worms on the Rhine and translated it into the mountains among the wild chamois.... We hope to invite you in the near future to join us for a tremendous chamois hunt.... To this hunt will come from the Rhine many electors and princes, who will never believe that they might see such mountains or such unusual ways to hunt. I hope to God, that the horns will sound so loudly and the wild hunting calls so wildly, that they will ring in the ears of the Turks and all other evil Christians.[31]

Flush with credit secured by new funds the Diet would grant him, Maximilian would lead Sigismund and other princes to battle with his beloved stags and chamois. With them would go the little green tent that shrouded the royal chaise percée. As for "the Turks and other bad Christians," well, the king would have his joke. They could wait while Maximilian prepared for a triumphant invasion of Italy to keep King Charles VIII (b. 1470, r. 1483–98) from making good on an old French claim to the kingdom of Naples. "Whoever during his lifetime makes no reputation," the Young White King in *Weisskunig* says, "will leave no memory and will be forgotten even as the bell tolls for him."[32] "Money flows away," Maximilian once said, "but honor lasts forever."[33]

30 Eberhard Isenmann, "Reichstadt und Reich an der Wende vom späten Mittelalter zur frühen Neuzeit," 117–18.
31 Heinz Angermeier, ed., *Reichstag von Worms 1495*, 142–3.
32 Wiesflecker, *Kaiser Maximilian I.*, vol. 1: 29.
33 Wiesflecker, *Kaiser Maximilian I.*, vol. 1: 29.

The king envisaged not new laws but new taxes and, above all, the power to share in his subjects' wealth with a recurring tax to finance the standing army. Then he would defeat and scatter his enemies. Maximilian knew that the Imperial princes – those "German sheep" (*deutsche Hammel*), he called them – feared nothing more than his achieving such power. They targeted more the office than his person, and it was said later of Charles V: "He will teach the Germans to pay obedience in the Latin and French manner and bring them under his yoke – which is intolerable to all the princes."[34] Only the king's penury, the German princes knew, kept him from becoming, like his brother of France, a "king of animals."

The princes assembled in the Diet thus faced a problem analogous to what the conciliarists had earlier faced in the Church: how to strengthen the Empire without strengthening the king's hand. At their head stood Archbishop Berthold of Henneberg (b. 1441, r. 1484–1504), elector of Mainz. Born the son of a Thuringian count and a Rhenish mother and elected archbishop of Mainz in 1484, Berthold was known as "the Nightingale" for his lovely singing voice. As senior elector, Imperial arch-chancellor, and primate of the Imperial church, he was, after the king, the Empire's leading officer. Maximilian came to hate this great prelate who sat "at the bottom of the entire matter [of reform],"[35] and his royal hatred pursued Berthold beyond the grave. The Milanese ambassador more thoughtfully described Berthold as "the ranking prince and elector of the Empire, who possessed great intelligence and vigor."[36]

Elector Berthold certainly touched the sensibilities and mobilized the wills of powerful men behind his vision of law and order for the German lands. He represented a collective desire for stronger governance against Maximilian's desire for great military enterprises, two goals that expressed two quite different understandings of the Empire and its needs. While the king aimed to recover the Empire's lost territories and glory outside the German lands, the estates that followed Berthold felt themselves to be something more bounded and limited, for which a phrase – "the German Nation" – had since the 1430s and 1440s been coming into use for the Empire in its narrower, territorial sense.

The critical phase of confrontation between the two visions, a warlike Imperial Christendom and a peaceful German kingdom, lasted nearly four years, from 1495 to 1498. In this time the Diet assembled four times in an atmosphere progressively soured by Maximilian's expensive military adventures in Italy. At Worms in 1495, the estates responded to Maximilian's demands with an elaborate reform agenda of five points:

1. a jointly staffed (by king and estates) Imperial council to govern the Empire;
2. a Perpetual (of unlimited duration) Public Peace and abolition of the right of feud;
3. a jointly staffed supreme judicial body, the Imperial Chamber Court;
4. a police system to enforce the Public Peace; and
5. the "Common Penny," a direct property tax on all Imperial subjects.

These points formed the Diet's price for an immediate levy for Maximilian's army.

---

34 Joseph Edmund Jörg, *Deutschland in der Revolutionsperiode von 1522 bis 1526, aus den diplomatischen Correspondenz und Original Akten bayrischen Archive dargestellt*, 14.
35 Heinz Gollwitzer, ed., *Reichstage von Lindau, Worms und Freiburg 1496–1498*, 90.
36 Gollwitzer, ed., *Reichstage*, 90. The envoy, Erasmo Brascha, blamed Elector Frederick of Saxony and Count Heinrich of Fürstenberg for making Berthold the king's "inimico desperato."

The idea of an Imperial executive council had figured prominently in Nicholas of Cusa's recommendations, and it stood at the heart of Berthold's program. His draft proposed a council of seventeen members seated at Frankfurt, of whom the king would appoint only one, the six electors one each, and the other estates ten. Its proposed powers – a new treasury at Frankfurt, annual budgeting, raising armies, and negotiating with the Roman Curia – show how thoroughly Berthold's party intended to kill two birds with one stone. They would simultaneously provide the Empire with a new central government and curb the king's power. No wonder that an angry royal councilor wrote in the document's margins, "not accepted" and "this the king has refused to allow."[37]

The king and his councilors took the point immediately. Such a council, the royal orator told the estates on 23 May, could be allowed to function only during his planned expedition against the Ottomans, "since in our absence we cannot deal personally with other affairs of Empire and business," but he alone would appoint the members, "organize them, and give them also our full powers."[38] When the king was personally present in the Empire, "we reserve our free administration and [our powers] to deal with and carry out each and every one of Ours and the Empire's affairs and business, such as pertains to a ruling Roman king or emperor. And [we will] do so with advice and in sound order in the manner and degree that we shall prescribe to the councilors in our instructions and commands."[39] This is the clearest statement of Maximilian's attitude toward Imperial reform: he accepted, even welcomed, the participation of the princes, bishops, and cities in his royal government – but by his appointment alone and under his instructions.

The great Diet at Worms in 1495, Strasbourg's Sebastian Brant believed, produced "such a powerful unity . . . as was never before seen in the Empire."[40] United, perhaps, but unwilling to pay for unity. Predictably, the only proposal the king liked was the Common Penny, which, if collectible, would support the Imperial army. Several treasurers were appointed, headquartered at Frankfurt, and, there being no Imperial local officials, parish priests were saddled with the task of collecting moneys at the local level. Its sponsors estimated the tax (part poll tax, part graduated tax on real property and incomes) would yield 2 million gulden over four years. In fact, by 1499, when the treasurers of the Common Penny disappeared from the historical record, the tax had brought in something between 106,632 gulden and 136,632 gulden, or a little more than 6 percent of the projected sum. About a third was paid to the treasurers, the rest came through other channels, as shown in Table 2.

One can attribute the failure of the Common Penny to a lack of realism on the part of its advocates, Elector Berthold and his allies. But if the tax was financially unrealistic, even utopian, politically it was a fiasco. At the Diet of Augsburg in 1500 it was reported that with respect to the tax "everyone is so hostile to it," and in fact this Diet found no means for making the laggards pay.[41] Nor did any future Diets, and the project of an Imperial property tax faded from the scene for the next forty years. The political cost to the Imperial reform and the reformers was colossal. Berthold soon

37 Eduard Ziehen, *Mittelrhein und Reich im Zeitalter der Reichsreform 1356–1504*, vol. 2: 478–82.
38 Angermeier, ed., *Reichstag von Worms 1495*, 358.
39 Angermeier, ed., *Reichstag von Worms 1495*, 358.
40 Wiesflecker, *Kaiser Maximilian I.*, vol. 2: 241.
41 Schmid, *Der Gemeine Pfennig von 1495*, 573.

Table 2. Payment of the Common Penny, 1495–1499 (in gulden)

Via the Imperial Treasurers	42,254
King Maximilian	50,000/80,000
Princes	12,351
Others	1,026
Total	106,632/136,632

Source: Peter Schmid, *Der Gemeine Pfennig von 1495. Vorgeschichte und Entstehung, Verfassungsgeschichtliche, politische und finanzielle Bedeutung,* 564. The uncertainty about the king's (relatively paltry) payment stems from the difference between the sum he reported (50,000 gulden) and what the estates reported (80,000 gulden).

feared such an outcome. There are very few, he wrote with resignation in early 1499, "who have paid the Common Penny, otherwise no one, regardless of whether he had especially obliged himself to pay. People laugh about it."[42] The Diet soon reverted to the traditional matricular levy, a specific sum apportioned among the estates according to their (self-) estimated wealth.

The king's campaign in October 1496 to drive the French out of Tuscany ended as another fiasco, this one before the walls of Livorno. Maximilian called the Imperial estates to assemble at Lindau on Lake Constance and fought his way through rain and snow across the Alps to bully them for funds. All his tricks and wiles – printed propaganda, patronage and favors, personal charm, savage attacks on the French king, and slander of the opposition – were stymied by the estates' wariness and Elector Berthold's leadership. When the Diet reassembled at Freiburg in mid-1497, Elector Berthold rose to the king's provocation and explained to the Diet's plenary assembly why they must not bend before royal pressure. "Look," he implored, "how the Empire is diminishing so rapidly and how much it has lost." Bohemia, Moravia, Silesia, and Lombardy no longer contributed to the Empire's costs, while "the burdens on the remaining members persist and even increase, for they must carry the burden of the entire Empire."[43] If the remaining estates "do not participate and unite more zealously and loyally than in the past, one day a foreigner will come to rule us all with an iron rod. See, nobody takes this to heart, one after another simply takes his leave." And now Berthold comes to his chief point. In the past, he says, "we spoke and agreed that when major lordships and lands belonging to the Empire fall vacant and revert to the Empire, they should not be granted anew in fief without the electors' consent. But God knows how things have actually gone."[44] This speech displays clearly Berthold's central aim to strengthen the Empire, not its head. Maximilian, for his part, continued to speak only of money.

The deadlock over Imperial reform continued until the Diet assembled at Augsburg in December 1499. Maximilian, still chasing victory over the French in Italy, painted the Empire's situation in the darkest possible tones: the Ottomans were pushing up toward the head of the Adriatic; the French king and his Venetian ally

42 Schmid, *Der Gemeine Pfennig von 1495*, 573.
43 Gollwitzer, ed., *Reichstage*, 385.
44 Gollwitzer, ed., *Reichstage*, 385.

were making a second attempt on Milan. The princes, however, stood firm behind Berthold's program of granting taxes only in exchange for the creation of an Imperial council. Maximilian erupted in fury. "By the Lombards I am betrayed," he howled, "by the Germans deserted. But I will not let myself be again bound hand and foot as at Worms. . . . I must and will make war. . . . And this I must say, even though I might have to throw my crown on the ground and trample it under foot."[45] It did not work, for at Augsburg the estates voted to establish the executive council. Sitting at Nuremberg without royal approbation, this body attempted to assume some of the king's rights and the Diet's functions in military affairs and diplomacy. It was a total failure. Incapable of managing itself, much less the Empire, and dogged by Maximilian's obstructions, by 1503 the council had run its short course. A year later Berthold, the very soul of the reform, died at the very moment of Maximilian's greatest triumph.

The major test between the king's ability to command Imperial resources and the ability of particular German powers to resist him took place in 1499. His opponents were the Swiss, folk determined not to be taxed without their consent. At the end of 1498 armed strife flared between the Graubündeners and the Austrian regime at Innsbruck, whereupon each party called for help from respectively the Swiss Confederation and the Swabian League.[46] As the fighting spread all along a line from Tyrol to Alsace, Maximilian came storming up from the Netherlands to the front at Lake Constance. There he unfurled the Imperial standard and called on the estates and the league to help him crush these "wicked, crude, contemptible peasants, who despise virtue, nobility, and moderation in favor of arrogance, treachery, and hate for the German nation."[47] Thus opened the Swabian War.[48]

Maximilian had chosen his foes unwisely. "Ferocious by nature, . . . the Swiss are shepherds rather than farmers," wrote Florence's Francesco Guicciardini (1483–1540), and "as a result of their innate ferocity and their disciplined organization, not only have they always valiantly defended their own country, but they have been consummately praised for their military service in foreign wars."[49] His countryman Machiavelli put it more pithily: "Rome and Sparta for many centuries were armed and free. The Swiss are heavily armed and wholly free."[50] Most alarmingly, the armed opposition of these "peasants" threatened to spread northward – who could say how far? The king sensed this danger. On one occasion he flung his glove to the ground and cried, "You can't fight Swiss with Swiss!"[51] Indeed you could not. All along the front, the "wicked, crude, contemptible peasants" trounced the Austrian and Imperial forces. After peace came, in 1501 the Imperial free cities of Basel and Schaffhausen "turned Swiss," and although the Confederates long continued to regard themselves as members of the Empire, they never again submitted to "emperor and Empire."

45 Wiesflecker, *Kaiser Maximilian I.*, vol. 2: 285.
46 Graubünden, now the southeasternmost canton of Switzerland, was at this time an autonomous republic under the bishop of Chur's presidency, allied to but not a member of the Confederation.
47 Wiesflecker, *Kaiser Maximilian I.*, vol. 5: 29.
48 The war of 1499 is called the "Swiss War" by German historians but the "Swabian War" by Swiss ones. It seems right that the victors should name the war.
49 Francesco Guicciardini, *The History of Italy*, 240.
50 Niccolò Machiavelli, *The Chief Works and Others*, vol. 1: 48.
51 Wiesflecker, *Kaiser Maximilian I.*, vol. 2: 347.

In 1499 Maximilian's preference for force over negotiation – so unlike his father – led him to utter defeat at the hands of the Swiss. Five years later, it brought him to the acme of his power in another German civil war. In 1504 the king's fortunes stood at a crossroads. He wanted to make war on Venice, which blocked his way to Rome, and wanted it so badly that he did the unthinkable: he made peace and "eternal friendship" with King Louis XII (b. 1462, r. 1498–1512) of France. Together they would carve up the new Venetian mini-empire, but not before Maximilian settled a new German question in the way he preferred, by armed force.

The road to the War of the Bavarian Succession began at the end of 1503 with the death of Duke George of Bavaria-Landshut (1455–1503), called "the Rich." In violation of Wittelsbach dynastic law, George bequeathed his lands to his daughter, Elizabeth (1478–1504), and her husband, Count Palatine Rupert (1481–1504), heir to the Elector Palatine.[52] The Palatine capital at Heidelberg had long been the chief center of anti-royalist intrigues. Rather than arbitrate between the two Wittelsbach lines, as a feudal overlord was obliged to do, Maximilian sided with Duke Albert IV (1447–1508) of Bavaria-Munich. He raised the Swabian League's army and took it westward to the Rhine, where he and his allies plundered the elector's lands. Then he marched the army back eastward to deal with the forces raised by George's heirs (in fact, Duchess Elizabeth, whose husband had died). In September their forces met near Regensburg, where a wild charge led in person by the king, followed by stout infantry from the Imperial cities, broke the wagon-forts of Elizabeth's Bohemian mercenaries and "slew them like hogs."[53] The deed had been done. Maximilian collected his "interest" (his term), the lands that guarded the passage from Bavaria southward through the mountains into Tyrol.[54] At their strongpoint, Kufstein Castle, Maximilian promised the garrison mercy and then had its officers beheaded before the eyes of his assembled lansquenets. Over this scene, his modern biographer writes, the king presided "like a prehistoric barbarian prince."[55] Could such a king be trusted to bring law and order to the Empire?

Trustworthy or not, Maximilian now seemed true lord of the Empire. He summoned the Imperial estates to Cologne, where in June 1505 he entered the city on foot, pike on shoulder at the head of his beloved lansquenets. He had come to the pinnacle of his glory: Elector Berthold was dead – of grief or the new French disease, depending on who was reporting – the broken Palatine elector approached to make his submission; the French had made peace, and the Ottomans remained quiet; and on the death of Queen Isabella (b. 1451, r. 1474–1504), Maximilian's daughter-in-law, Princess Juana (1479–1555), succeeded to the Castilian throne. "The king is so powerful among the German princes," a Venetian envoy reported, "no one dares to oppose him."[56]

As an Otto or Frederick of old might have done, Maximilian settled the Bavarian question. With Solomonic gravity he partitioned Duke George's legacy and handed

52 The war of 1504 was intradynastic in two senses: it began over a dynastic rule within the Bavarian line of the Wittelsbachs; it continued against the Palatine line of the same dynasty.
53 Wiesflecker, *Kaiser Maximilian I.*, vol. 3: 189.
54 Kufstein in Tyrol, which lies where the Inn River debouches from the Bavarian Alps to start its run down to Passau and the Danube, was one piece of Maximilian's "interest," his share of the Landshut spoils.
55 Wiesflecker, *Maximilian I.*, 146.
56 Wiesflecker, *Maximilian I.*, 146.

over the major part – minus his own "interest" – to Duke Albert. Then he dealt with the estates. He offered them an Imperial executive council, but only under his command and subject to his veto. The cowed, leaderless estates meekly responded that "they cannot wish to prescribe to His Royal Majesty the form and scope of his regime."[57] They voted him enough to pay 4,000 men for a royal expedition to Hungary, then on to Rome for an Imperial coronation. "His Imperial Majesty," wrote the Venetian ambassador, "is now a true emperor of the empire and ruler of Germany."[58] A loyal German voice went on to prophesy a future Habsburg "lordship over Europe, Asia, and Africa."[59] No one now spoke of the lost Imperial reform.

His coffers for the moment full, Maximilian began preparation for an invasion of Hungary in summer (1506), but catastrophic news interrupted his plans. On 23 September 1505 came from Burgos in Spain a letter reporting the death of Philip, his only son. "My God, my God," Maximilian scrawled in the crucified Savior's words, "why hast thou forsaken me?"[60]

Despite all appearances and the predictions of Maximilian's supremacy between 1504 and 1507, Berthold's project did not die. It lay dormant until fortune ripped victory from Maximilian's grasp and ground his dreams to dust. The rod of war, which he trusted far more than he did law and government, betrayed him, and in ten years of war in Italy, he lost everything he had gained.

4. THE IMPERIAL WARLORD

War, the principal business of states, was also the chief recreation of kings. From his years as regent of the Burgundian Netherlands down to 1504, Maximilian had focused his ambitions and his enmity on one target: France, the toughest, most resilient great power of the age. His late father-in-law, Duke Charles, was known to have said that he loved France so much that he wished for it six kings instead of one; Maximilian formed a "great plan of war" that called for the kingdom's permanent partition. When the struggle for Italy began in 1494, he found a loyal and rich ally in Duke Lodovico Sforza (1451/52–1508), called "the Moor," of Milan. In terror of the huge French army, the duke dowered his sister, Bianca Maria (1472–1510), to Maximilian with 1 million gulden. This naive, good-hearted, and badly neglected queen lived surrounded by exiled Lombard countrymen – the French held Milan from 1499 to 1511 – whom the German-speaking courtiers mocked as "the children of Israel."[61] Yet all the wealth of Lombardy could not fill Maximilian's bottomless purse. Throughout the dragging decades of the Italian Wars, his penury always stood between him and his goals: recovery of Milan, subjection of Venice, coronation at Rome, restoration of Imperial Italy, and victory over the Ottomans.

Maximilian perhaps fooled himself – he certainly tried to fool others – into believing that victory in one of these endeavors would bring success in the others. The French invasion of Italy in 1494, he claimed, had struck from his own hand the sword

57 Wiesflecker, *Kaiser Maximilian I.*, vol. 3: 211, paraphrased.
58 R. G. D. Laffan, "The Empire under Maximilian I, 1493–1520," 211.
59 Wiesflecker, *Kaiser Maximilian I.*, vol. 3: 205; Brady, *Turning Swiss*, 78.
60 Wiesflecker, *Kaiser Maximilian I.*, vol. 3: 304.
61 Wiesflecker, *Kaiser Maximilian I.*, vol. 5: 382.

he raised against the Ottomans. In truth, his goal was not Constantine's New Rome but Old Rome and Italy.

The central problem of Maximilian's military operations was that, while in the east he could easily handle the Magyar nobles, who feared him "worse than the Turks or the Devil,"[62] in the west he could not beat the French and seldom the Venetians. It was his fate to stand at the midpoint of a descending gradient from Paris/Venice toward Moscow in terms of population densities, degrees of urbanization, volumes of trade, and levels of literacy. The joker in this deck was, of course, the great Ottoman power, though even without serious Ottoman pressure on his eastern flank, Maximilian could do no more than block (and at that only with Spanish aid) French expansion in the west.

At the end of 1503, Maximilian and King Louis of France agreed to seal their newfound comity with the destruction of Venetian power in Italy. This project would require money, lots of it, and in May 1507 Maximilian called the Imperial estates to Constance to vote him an army of 30,000 to defeat Venice and open the way to Rome. It was one of his best performances. "I have spent 10 million gulden on the Empire's behalf," he declared,

> a tenth of which the Empire has given me. No king has ever done so much for the Empire as I have. Only Frederick Barbarossa can compare. There is a man, whom I shall not name, who has until now hindered me from taking the road to Rome to regain Milan and to receive the Imperial crown. The French poisoned my son. Now it is the Empire's task to ward off the French attacks. I will not stint to earn the gratitude of the Empire and the German Nation for all time.[63]

After deliberation the Diet voted him a force too large for the Venetians to allow safe passage and too small to defeat them.

Venice proved the reef on which Maximilian's quest for Italian glory foundered. He opened the Venetian (or Second Italian) War with a characteristic gesture. On 6 February 1508 in Trent's cathedral, he proclaimed himself "emperor-elect," an act for which he possessed no authority. Besides, the pope was his ally in the League of Cambrai against Venice. Maximilian's task in this war was to take and hold the fortresses of Brescia, Vicenza, Verona, and Padua. When Padua's walls stymied his army, the emperor retreated, and this time the Imperial estates listened to his request – 50,000 men for ten years – in silence. They had heard this song before.

As the League of Cambrai crumbled, Maximilian found his scapegoat in Pope Julius, who had shifted sides during the war. Maximilian tried to force Julius to recognize the validity of his self-coronation at Trent, demanded a permanent papal legation in the Empire, and entertained the bizarre notion of succeeding Julius II, that "cursed pope [and] traitor," in St. Peter's chair.[64] Through most of the 1510s, Maximilian's military position sank to a humiliating level. When he came to Milan in 1516, his own lansquenets mocked him as "a king of straw."[65] The end came the next year, when his garrison at Verona, for nine years stalwart guardians of his passage into

62 Wiesflecker, *Kaiser Maximilian I.*, vol. 1: 286.
63 Wiesflecker, *Maximilian I.*, 154.
64 Wiesflecker, *Kaiser Maximilian I.*, vol. 5: 173–4.
65 Wiesflecker, *Maximilian I.*, 182.

Italy, gave up the dead city and trailed their pikes back over the mountains to Tyrol. Nine years of war in Italy had cost millions of gulden, tens of thousands of lives, the substance of Austria, the peace of the Imperial church, and the southern Germans' Venetian trade. All for naught.

5. MATTERS OUT OF HAND

In these years, when the Italian War brought Imperial political life to a standstill, violence and unrest flared in region after region of the neglected Empire. It was the Indian summer of the feud. "It seems to me," Götz von Berlichingen looked back on these happy days, "that I just moved from one war to another. Only yesterday I made peace with Nuremberg; today it begins again [with Mainz]."[66] Clouds of tough mercenaries, back from the Italian Wars, scoured the poorly policed southern regions to make up their lost pay by robbing peasants and merchants. In 1517 rural insurrection flared once again on the Upper Rhine. Its leader was the mysterious, charismatic Joss Fritz, formerly a serf in the prince-bishopric of Speyer, whose banner flew the Bundschuh, the peasant's laced boot, as a symbol of resistance. Fritz's failure was not the end but the beginning of a great wave of rural insurrections.

At the same time the era's most terrible feud, as brutal as the Austrian conflicts of the mid-fifteenth century, burst out in the north. It began with a prudent act of a conscientious bishop. In 1504 Duke John of Saxe-Lauenburg (ca. 1478–1547, r. 1503–27) was elected in succession to his brother as prince-bishop of Hildesheim. A thrifty lord, his policy of paying off the see's heavy debts was fiscally sound but politically dangerous, for when he sought to recover the mortgaged episcopal lands and castles, his own vassals declared feud against him. In 1516 the Hildesheim Feud became a regional war, in which sixty episcopal vassals allied with the heads of two Brunswick lines (Wolfenbüttel and Calenberg) against the bishop and the head of a third line (Lüneburg). Their forces met at Soltau in the heart of the modern state of Lower Saxony on 28 June 1519, just as a new emperor was being elected at Frankfurt.[67] The rebels' crushing defeat at Soltau ought to have been decisive, but when peace finally came in 1523, the bishop's enemies gained a complete victory. The two Brunswick dukes retained Hildesheim's "Large *Stift*," two-thirds of the episcopal territory – six counties, nine towns, twenty-three castles, and a great many villages – leaving Bishop John with only his cathedral city and two other towns. "The good, pious bishop," a chronicler lamented, "thus tragically and miserably lost his *Stift* through the words and deeds of evil advisors, . . . for the princes of Brunswick retained what they had conquered, and he found no favor from His Imperial Majesty."[68] Vast tracts of the north had been laid waste, villages burnt, and towns besieged, taken, and plundered, sometimes several times over. This terrible civil war remained in living memory for generations. Although Bishop John acted with "the best of intentions and with complete honesty" and ruled "with great deliberation and did so effectively and well," just these qualities "in the end brought him and the bishopric injury and ruin." John's

66 Götz von Berlichingen, *Mein Fehd und Handlungen*, 106.
67 Soltau lies south of the Lüneburg Moor on the road from Hamburg to Hanover.
68 Hans Wildefuer, *Die Hildesheimer Bischofschronik des Hans Wildefuer*, 193–4.

vassals hated him, because "it was his policy and intention to free the bishopric from all of its debts."[69]

Northern events were regional history; great Imperial events occurred in the old heartlands of the west and south. Here the miserable end of Maximilian's Italian Wars was provoking an important change of mood. The new spirit surfaced at the Diet of Augsburg in 1518, when for the first time appeared a convergence between the Diet's debates and the opinions then circulating among literate circles. The mood of this new "public opinion" – a mere twenty years ago it had not existed – was anti-Roman and anti-Italian. The humiliation felt at the Italian defeats was accomplishing what Maximilian's hectoring, fables, and braggadocio had never been able to do, for it focused attention on the foreign foes responsible for German woes.

A decade of wars, revolts, feuds, and famine had prepared this change in mood, but its trigger was the printing press. Printers now churned out by the hundreds a new genre, the pamphlet, a cheap, small-format, unbound booklet graced by a title-page illustration and written to inform a literate public, to propose, criticize, or condemn. The pamphlet both created and served large new audiences for the written word. The possibilities may be represented by a contrast. In 1461 Gregor Heimburg, an excommunicated lawyer-priest, wrote of Enea Silvio Piccolomini, then Pope Pius II, that "the absolute lordship over slaves is the imperial sway that he desires to exercise over us."[70] Shrewd, but Heimburg's text had to be reproduced laboriously by hand and could therefore at best make its weight felt only over time. It was quite another thing for an anonymous author to publish in many copies and in German a *True History of Emperor Frederick I with a Long Red Beard*, which was for sale in 1519. One passage portrays Frederick Barbarossa as reconciling himself with the pope. "The emperor then humiliated himself by lying at the pope's feet," the author wrote, whereupon "the pope stepped on the emperor's neck and said, 'It is written [Luke 10:19]: on the serpents and reptiles will you walk and tread on the lion and the dragon.'" The emperor replied, "I am obedient not to you, but to Peter, whose successor you are."[71] Though only moderately inflammatory, such texts were much more widely accessible than before, and more skillful hands could turn phlegm into savage mockery.

At Augsburg in 1518, reform stood on the agenda once more. Some progress had been made during the war years. The Imperial Chamber Court, voted in 1495, had gotten on its feet, and in 1512 the Diet had created a system of districts, called "circles" (*Kreise*), to nominate judges to the court.[72] The plan of 1512 divided the Empire into ten circles, of which two (Austrian and Burgundian) comprised only Habsburg lands, two (Electoral Rhenish, Upper Saxon) were dominated by electors, and the others comprised the Imperial estates of specific regions, four in the south (Franconian, Bavarian, Swabian, Upper Rhenish) and two in the north (Lower Rhenish/Westphalian, Lower Saxon).[73]

69 Wildefuer, *Die Hildesheimer Bischofschronik*, 186.
70 Kurt Stadtwald, *Roman Popes and German Patriots. Antipapalism in the Politics of the German Humanist Movement from Gregor Heimburg to Martin Luther*, 46.
71 Franz Pfeiffer, "Volksbüchlein vom Kaiser Friedrich," 266.
72 The new plan, which had ancestral forms going well back into the fifteenth century, derived from a scheme of 1500.
73 Outside the circles were the Swiss Confederation, Bohemia-Moravia-Silesia-Lusatia, Imperial Italy, and the Imperial parts of the Low Countries.

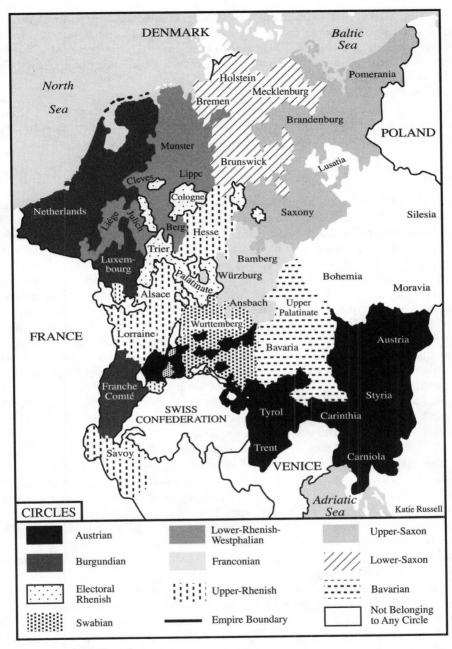

Map 5. Imperial Circles of 1512

Although very slow to take form, the circles gradually acquired political, military, and fiscal responsibilities, formed their own diets, and came to play important roles in Imperial defense and justice. When this system matured, "it imparted a different character to regional politics, where the lesser counties, bishoprics and imperial cities had proportionately more weight."[74]

When Maximilian addressed the Diet, he sang the only note he knew, money, this time for a crusade against the Ottomans. Yet, when he cried to them "Turk! Turk!" they responded with "Rome! Rome!" Now it seemed as if the Germans – the Imperial estates – would at last unite against a foreign foe. That foe was Rome.

6. MAXIMILIAN'S END

While the Diet seethed with harsh words and charges against the pope, the Curia, Rome, and the Italians, Maximilian took care of other business. On 28 June, the day after his arrival in Augsburg, the emperor received Albrecht Dürer, who "in the little room upstairs in the tower painted his portrait."[75] This marvelous work shows the emperor at age fifty-nine, dressed in Renaissance style in the robes and velvet hat of a great aristocrat. Around his neck hangs the collar of the (Burgundian) Order of the Golden Fleece. His look is distant, reflective, even somber, for he almost certainly knows, in those days without anodynes, that he has not long to live. His sad mien bears the marks of disappointed hopes, grief for his dead son, humiliations on a dozen battlefields, endless worries about money, a lifetime of hyperbolic bravado, and the wear and tear of thousands of jousts, dances, fêtes, balls, and hunts.

Still, Maximilian was no invalid. For the Augsburg Diet's most festive occasion, the marriage of his niece, Duchess Susanna of Bavaria (1502–43), to Margrave Casimir of Brandenburg-Ansbach (1481–1527), he mounted up one more time and rode out with 3,000 Imperial and Brandenburg cavalry to bring the 16-year-old Wittelsbach princess into the city. The wedding feast went on for four days.

On the emperor's mind weighed his last great project: the election of his grandson, Charles of Spain, to the Imperial office. Grandfather and grandson had met only once, in the Netherlands a year earlier, and, while Maximilian found the 18-year-old cold and diffident, "like a statue,"[76] Charles found no more to like in the grandfather than he had in his own father. Dynasty, however, would be served, even if the heir-apparent and the prospective realm were utter strangers to one another.

Advancing this project required mending old fences and tons of cash. Maximilian spent, it was said, some 900,000 gulden to grease the royal election, most of it borrowed from the Augsburg banker Jakob Fugger. Only Saxony and Trier held out, arguing that no king could be elected before Maximilian was canonically crowned as emperor. They enjoyed the backing of Pope Leo X (r. 1513–21), who was coming to realize that the papacy would be more endangered by an Imperial-Spanish hegemony in Italy than by a French one. Finally, the deal was sealed. In a touching farewell address, Maximilian admonished the electors to choose Charles as king after his own death, for he himself could not go to Rome to be crowned. Once again he told the

74 Peter H. Wilson, *From Reich to Revolution: German History, 1558–1806*, 183.
75 Wiesflecker, *Kaiser Maximilian I.*, vol. 4: 421.
76 Wiesflecker, *Kaiser Maximilian I.*, vol. 4: 381.

estates how much his beloved Austrian lands had suffered for the Empire's sake. Maximilian possessed a magical skill with such scenes, full of solemnity and emotion, and the electors, deeply moved, assured him that his services to the Empire would remain unforgotten. As he made ready to leave Augsburg for the last time, the favorite city where he had so often danced and dallied with the burghers' wives and daughters, only one enemy remained. "As long as I have lived," he alluded bitterly to Leo, "no pope has kept his word to me."[77] Then he was gone.

The dying emperor headed first for his beloved Tyrol. He had suffered a stroke, and Georg Spalatin (1484–1545), the Saxon elector's chancellor, noticed how the emperor dragged his leg when he said goodbye to Elector Frederick. Maximilian also suffered from a sore throat, a stubborn stomach complaint, and, possibly, the French disease. At Innsbruck came the next-to-last humiliation, for the innkeepers there said they would not take in the royal entourage because of 24,000 gulden owing in arrears. This affront sums up the entire reign of the Young White King who had boasted of not being "a king of money." Maximilian then came by litter down the Inn River to Kufstein, the site of his vengeful act of cruelty in 1504, onward by boat down to Rosenheim, and thence eastward toward Austria. On 10 December 1518 he came to Castle Wels on the Danube. It was his last station.

An emperor could not be allowed to simply die in peace. The best Austrian physicians gathered to treat Maximilian, mainly with strong purges which probably hastened his death. He suffered from gall stones, intestinal inflammation, perhaps ulcers, he was jaundiced, and he had pneumonia. Ever the monarch, he received foreign envoys and read documents right down to the end. In the night from 30 to 31 December, he dictated his will, a bricolage of politics and piety, by which he left his grandsons the Austrian lands and endowed room and board for retired Tyrolean salt-makers. On Epiphany (6 January), when his physician-confessor, the Swabian Carthusian Gregor Reisch (ca. 1467–1525), arrived, the royal patient said, "You come just in time to help me into heaven."[78] Five days later, Reisch gave him Extreme Unction, anointing the backs of his hands, as for a bishop, because the palms had been anointed at his royal coronation. "I am thoroughly prepared by God's grace for this last journey," Maximilian sighed, and next day, at three in the morning, he got underway.[79]

Money, the bane of Maximilian's life, dogged him in death, for he was buried on borrowed funds. After the corpse had been displayed for two days, the coffin was taken to the town church of Wels, followed by a weeping Archbishop Matthäus Lang, Maximilian's longtime confidant. After lying in state for three days in St. Stephen's Cathedral in Vienna, Maximilian's body was laid to rest in St. George's Church in Wiener Neustadt.

For eighteen years, beginning in the dark days around 1499, Maximilian had planned his funeral monument. The design called for forty statues of legendary Germanic heroes, German kings, Austrian princes and princesses, kings of Spain, Bohemia, and Hungary, and dukes of Burgundy; twenty busts of Roman emperors; and 100 statues of saints associated with the house of Habsburg. The tomb's concept was a

77 Wiesflecker, *Maximilian I.*, vol. 4: 414.
78 Wiesflecker, *Kaiser Maximilian I.*, vol. 4: 427.
79 Wiesflecker, *Kaiser Maximilian I.*, vol. 4: 429.

funeral procession of the figures from the Germanic sagas down through the Roman emperors, and old German kings and emperors to the Habsburgs. By the time of Maximilian's death, twenty-four of the main bronze statues were finished, plus one of the kneeling emperor. Alas, the choir of St. George's in Wiener Neustadt would not bear the weight, and the work was broken off until 1585. Today the court chapel at Innsbruck displays the monumental bronzes, cast by Dürer or his school, of the kneeling Maximilian surrounded by personages ranging from his parents to King Arthur. The ensemble forms a fitting representation of this emperor: it is incomplete; it mixes real with fictive ancestors; and even his tomb and his grave are at opposite ends of Austria. Nothing ever turned out as Maximilian had planned.

Maximilian I was the first Holy Roman emperor in 250 years who ruled as well as reigned. His royal power rested on the Austrian territorial base formed by Frederick III and reformed by his son. Together they solved the problem that had brought the Luxemburgs' Imperial projects to naught. As in reality, so also in representation, a new era had begun. Much of Maximilian's influence depended on his image makers, the humanists, artists, and printers who created for him a virtual royal self of hitherto unimagined quality and intensity. They half-captured and half-invented a rich past, which progressed from ancient Rome through the line of Charlemagne to the glory of the house of Habsburg and culminated in Maximilian's own high presidency of the Christian brotherhood of warrior-kings. Devout after his fashion, Maximilian was no reformer of the Church, and his image as a crusader was entirely bogus. So often he pledged to take the cross against the Ottoman power – just as soon as he got his hands free of other matters. But Maximilian knew too much about warfare to take the field against the great Ottoman warrior-sultans of this era. The crusade was his ultimate illusion, the final trick in every performance by this royal magician.

Everything about Maximilian bears the feel of makeshift and ad hoc. He spun his illusions to distract attention from his long string of miserable failures – Livorno in 1496, against the Swiss in 1499, Padua in 1509, Milan in 1516, and Verona in 1516 – while his successes in war came against lesser folk, the Palatine Wittelsbachs in 1504 and the Hungarians two years later. Even his emperorship bore the taint of illegitimacy, as several electors pointed out in 1518 at Augsburg. Behind the illusions stood the bleak reality of thriftlessness, a grinding, humiliating penury, and a constant worry about money, all swathed in a haunted feeling that only the lack of cash prevented his dreams from coming true. Maximilian truly was not "a king of money," for money was hardly less mysterious to him than was the Holy Trinity.

Today, freed from the husk of national narratives, the apparent contradictions of Maximilian's behavior and style of rule can be seen to have been very much in tune with his age. They teach, above all, that territorial dynasticism and imperial universalism were not opposed but complementary tendencies and motives. The Empire, a soul without a body, and the territorial principality, a body without a soul, formed a composite capable of life. The emperor's rule had to be symbolic because he had little power to coerce; the local and territorial rulers had to acknowledge the emperor because, however powerful, their authority was partial and uneven. Between them they created over the past eighty years the Holy Roman Empire of the German Nation, now truly a body but, unlike France, not the monarch's body. The ancient monarchy may have been sacral, but the new, corporate German Nation certainly was not. It negotiated with its emperor; it did not simply obey him.

By 1519, on the eve of the Protestant reformation, nearly all the essential features of the early modern Holy Roman Empire had come onstage: the Imperial Diet, the supreme court, the administrative districts (circles), a primitive scheme of taxation, an Imperial army raised by levies on the estates, and cogovernance of monarch and Imperial states through negotiations at meetings of the Imperial parliament. The product – still more ideal than real – resembled in some respects the monarchical polities of Europe's western tier, and in others the loosely integrated, elective polities of East Central Europe. For 150 years and more, nationalist historians dramatized the formation of the early modern Empire as a conflict between (good) centralizing and (bad) particularist forces represented respectively by the monarchy and the princely territories. From our longer view, this dichotomy neither fits the actual story of how new governmental forms evolved in the German lands nor helps to explain the new polity's remarkable longevity and stability. The Imperial reform realized one part of King Sigismund's projected reform of Empire and Church, though perhaps at the cost of the other part, the Church in the German lands.

8

Ideals and Illusions of Reforming the Church

> I never saw, heard, nor read, that the clergy were beloved in any nation where Christianity was the religion of the country. Nothing can render them popular, but some degree of persecution. Those fine gentlemen who affect the humour of railing at the clergy, are, I think, bound in honour to turn parsons themselves, and shew us better examples.
>
> Jonathan Swift

The Council of Basel had one great achievement, the peace made in 1439 with the Bohemian Hussites. Thereafter the council skidded toward its unhappy demise a decade later. Well before then, Pope Eugenius IV's "ill-judged, hasty, and abortive" attempt to dissolve the council created a state of affairs "that was to render impossible the achievement at the council of truly significant and permanent church-wide reform."[1] Ideas there were aplenty, for the councils had promoted an intensive and fruitful exchange of reform principles, arguments, and agendas among the churchmen of Christendom. The central problem was agency. The pope's actions and the general council's failure presented reform-minded churchmen with a vexing question: How could a reform of "head and members" be achieved without either a pope or a general council at its head? How, especially, could it happen in the Empire, this vast kingdom with its weak monarch and its bishops deeply ensnared in its feudal governance? This was the German variation on a greater question: How could the Church be one and the churches many? On the reef of this conundrum most movements for reform foundered.

The story of church reform in the Empire during the eighty years from the death of Sigismund in 1439 to the accession of Charles V in 1519 is a tale of three great illusions disguised as three solutions to the post-conciliar deadlock. First, the caesaro-papist illusion held that the emperors could restore the old fusion between sacral and temporal authority and enable a reform of both Church and Empire. Second, the national illusion held that severing the Imperial church from Rome would enable a reform carried out by "the people" in their guise as the "German nation." Third, the communalist illusion held out the possibility of a local reform by local communities

---

1 Francis Oakley, *The Western Church in the Later Middle Ages*, 227.

responding to their churches' needs. While none of the three views was politically realistic, each supplies a glimpse into existing relations of power and political tendencies within the Empire, and each contributed to the swelling demand for making the Church more responsive to its peoples and more pleasing to God.

I. THE CAESAROPAPIST ILLUSION – EMPEROR AND CHURCH REFORM

The caesaropapist[2] solution to the dilemma of reform developed in the writings (and presumably the speech) of dedicated German churchmen while the council still sat at Basel. It took up two conciliarist themes: the papal monarchy had failed in its duty to promote the common good of the Church; the churches needed a more pastoral and more disciplined clergy. To these the Germans added a third: the emperor, as God's agent, must assume his rightful authority over things sacred as well as things temporal. This solution is clearly laid out in an anonymous tract called *The Reformation of Emperor Sigismund*, which was composed around the time of Sigismund's death in 1439. Although it cannot be directly connected to him or his court, as the title suggests it probably does reflect ideas discussed in his milieu. Issued in eight printed editions between 1476 and 1522, *The Reformation* enjoyed the widest circulation of any reform document of this era.

The Reformation begins with what had been a central issue for generations, the proper relationship between spiritual and temporal authority. "This book indicates," it declares, "how spiritual and secular authorities ought to conduct themselves and how they must govern," and the author prays God's grace "to accomplish and undertake a true ordering of spiritual and secular affairs."[3] This sounds very much like Sigismund's declaration of 1411, though with an untraditional addition, for the author repeatedly speaks of a political role for "the people," a term he does not define.[4] Perhaps this is a sign that the author, like Nicholas of Cusa, perceived the need for a broader basis of Imperial governance and reform than that provided by the traditional combination of personal networks and sacral charisma.

The bishops, those natural heirs to the mantle of leadership discarded by pope and council, receive, by contrast, shortest shrift in *The Reformation*. The author flatly condemns the fusion of spiritual and feudal powers in their hands as a source of ills for both Church and Empire. "Take a good look at how bishops act nowadays. They make war and cause unrest in the world; they behave like secular lords."[5] "No bishop ought to own a castle," he continues, "he ought to take up permanent residence in the principal church of his diocese and lead a spiritual life there. He should be an example to the clergy in his bishopric."[6] Further, "a bishop should be a doctor of Scripture and

---

2   "Caesaropapism" is the customary, if unlovely, name for the subordination of the spiritual power of the Christian church to the ruler or government.
3   Gerald Strauss, ed., *Manifestations of Discontent in Germany on the Eve of the Reformation*, 4, slightly revised.
4   No term employed in this text has given rise to greater debate than "the people." The term probably owes something to the concept of "the legislator," also undefined, in Marsiglio of Padua's *Defender of the Peace*. This work had circulated at the general councils of the fifteenth century, and several other writers borrowed freely from its ideas, always silently, because Marsiglio had been condemned for heterodoxy.
5   Strauss, ed., *Manifestations of Discontent*, 11.
6   Strauss, ed., *Manifestations of Discontent*, 11.

a scholar in theology and canon law," and he should be salaried, not beneficed.[7] Finally, "a bishop is to conduct himself piously and honestly and to have no worldly concerns."[8] This agrees almost precisely with Nicholas of Cusa's observation that those bishops who "devote themselves to secular concerns and decisions in opposition to church law ... neglect to offer prayers and supplications for their own offenses and for the ignorance of the people."[9] The reason why they don't, Nicholas adds, could be expressed in one word: property. "What good are the temporal possessions of the church to the commonwealth," he asks, "what good are they to the Empire? What good to its subjects? Little or none."[10] The anomalous character of the Imperial prince-bishoprics was even more striking to a keen-eyed foreigner than to German reformers. It astonished Enea Silvio, Nicholas's friend and fifteenth-century Italy's best student of German affairs. He marveled at the "more than fifty episcopal churches [dioceses], which are ruled by rich, powerful bishops. Compared to them, our Italian bishops are more like parish vicars."[11] The most compelling inference from this discussion was the principle that a good prince made a bad bishop, and a good bishop made a bad prince.

The author also took up the problem of local reform. While the bishops were to be reformed by separating spiritual from temporal authority, in his view the parish clergy were to be integrated into their local communities by allowing them to marry. Clerical marriage, natural and illicit, was already common. It was called "concubinage," and if contemporary charges about it were exaggerated, "it is undeniable that the phenomenon of the 'priest's whore' was commonplace."[12] In some dioceses the episcopal officials simply gave up punishing such priests and instead collected a fine – in Constance it was called a "cradle fee" – from priests who lived in concubinage and fathered bastards. Lay opinion about irregular clerical marriage was divided. To some people, especially in the countryside, it was clear that solitary priests had domestic needs, and a happy priest served his people better than did an unhappy one. To others, especially in the towns, concubinage seemed an intolerable offense against both the vow of celibacy and the institution of marriage. Around 1500 "the institution of marriage seemed to many contemporaries to be under a state of siege," and "sexual promiscuity, according to critics, ran rampant in all areas of society" and made "a mockery of the Church's traditional teachings on both marriage and celibacy."[13] This left reformers with two options, stricter enforcement of the rule of celibacy or its abolition. The author, and a number of German reformists after him, chose clerical marriage over celibacy.

Lurking in the background of this discourse of reform lay a growing unease about the power of money in the Church. It was perceptible in the traffic in benefices that

7   Strauss, ed., *Manifestations of Discontent*, 12.
8   Strauss, ed., *Manifestations of Discontent*, 14.
9   Nicholas of Cusa, *The Catholic Concordance*, 171.
10 Cusa, *The Catholic Concordance*, 291.
11 Enea Silvio Piccolomini, *Germania und Jakob Wimpheling: "Responsa et replicae ad Eneam Silvium,"* 59.
12 Robert W. Scribner, "Anticlericalism and the Reformation in Germany," in Robert W. Scribner, *Popular Culture and Popular Movements in Reformation Germany*, 247. He notes that one Reformation polemicist alleged that in the diocese of Constance 1,500 priests' children were born each year, an unbelievable figure, given that the diocese contained only 17,000 religious persons.
13 Joel F. Harrington, *Reordering Marriage and Society in Reformation Germany*, 25.

had burgeoned in the papacy's Avignonese period (1309–78), in the collecting of crusade taxes and the granting of indulgences, and in the "stole fees" charged by priests for administering the sacraments. Money, like Nature, seemed a power vast, impersonal, unpredictable, and capable of working miracles.[14] Consider the miracle of credit, by means of which the market could absorb materials and labor at one place and move them by mysterious means to other places near and far, whence new goods just as inexplicably returned. To the serious Christian, making money was necessary to life but a danger both to the individual who might gain the world but lose his soul and to the community, his fellow citizens and neighbors who suffered from manipulations of the market for personal gain. Christ taught us to protect and sustain the poor, the weak; the market enables us to exploit them for gain.

The Reformation of Emperor Sigismund offers a classic formulation of the problem of money. The roots of our evils, the author declares, are "among the clergy terrible simony, which is comparable to usury and has poisoned the entire clerical estate; but among the laity greed, which destroys all friendship and gives rise to rebellion, disloyalty, and much injustice."[15] "Simony arose at the papal court," he alleges, "more than two hundred years have passed since the papal Curia was in good and honest order."[16] Then it spread via the Curia to the bishops and from them right down to the parishes. The result was that although Emperor Constantine and Pope Sylvester saw to it that the churches were well endowed with property and tithes, "now the monasteries have got hold of it all, and parish churches must go begging. And yet the meanest parish church is worth more than the grandest of monasteries."[17] The author's solution to this impoverishment of local churches is global, practical, and foresighted. If a salaried pastorate replaced the beneficed clergy, a priest could concentrate on his office, which is to conduct the divine service and to study, read, write, preach, and protect his flock. This is approximately the direction in which Protestant princes, magistrates, and churchmen would transform the Christian clergy.

The Reformation of Emperor Sigismund may stand as a relatively sober statement of the essential themes of caesaropapist reformism: the emperor is lord of Empire and Church; the bishops are corrupted by (feudal) property; the parish priests should be salaried and married; the Church is corrupted by the simoniacs and their money; Rome is the source of most evils; and the hope for reform rests on the shoulders of a coming emperor.

The chief change in the caesaropapist reform agenda over the course of the fifteenth century had to do with the emperor. As the real, existing Habsburg emperors disqualified themselves by exhibiting minimal interest in sacrificing other goals to a reform of the Imperial church, the great emperor became a mythic figure revealed by prophecy. This figure of a savior-emperor features in a remarkable treatise completed around 1509 under the title of "The Book of the Hundred Chapters and the Forty Statutes." Its anonymous author was a learned jurist, probably from Alsace, who served emperors Frederick III and Maximilian I. Never printed, the work survives in a single manuscript.[18] Its author, who now hides under the (modern) name of

---

14 This had surely been St. Francis of Assisi's point, as it was of the conservative post-Basel reformers.
15 Heinrich Koller, ed., *Reformation Kaiser Siegmunds*, 60.
16 Strauss, ed., *Manifestations of Discontent*, 6.
17 Strauss, ed., *Manifestations of Discontent*, 9.
18 His identity has been the subject of a lively scholarly discussion.

"The Upper Rhenish Revolutionary," was no man of revolution but merely a worried and forlorn voice on the margins of public affairs. He did show up at the Imperial Diet in 1495, he tells us, and again in 1498, but no one paid him any attention.

The author of "The Book of the Hundred Chapters" also stands squarely in the post-Basel tradition. He, too, advocates an end to the temporal authority of bishops and to clerical celibacy. For the present state of things he, too, blames the pope, the bishops, and the egotistical princes, to whom he adds new culprits, the Jews and the monks. And he, too, is a dyed-in-the-wool caesaropapist. "The emperor should be lord of the whole world," he writes, and "when he sees that the Roman church approves things which are harmful or contrary to custom, he is obliged to suppress them. The emperor is elected over all lords of the whole earth to promote the common good, just like the eagle."[19] He instructs Emperor Maximilian, whom he served, that "His Imperial Majesty is called a shepherd over all the clergy. His Imperial Majesty possesses the power to elevate and depose a pope."[20] The emperor also requires support from others, in this text the "common men," as "it is high time for common men to raise to the throne one like themselves so that an end might be made of the depredations of the priests. God and the law will be on his side . . . . Better one pious priest than eleven thousand useless ones, as Emperor Sigismund used to say."[21] The meaning of "the common men," who in this text replace "the people" of *The Reformation of Emperor Sigismund*, is unclear, but it certainly does not refer to the princes and other nobles[22]

Between 1439 and 1509, the times of these two anonymous texts, a practical Imperial reform had gotten well underway. Nothing comparable had happened in the Imperial church, and by around 1500 the prospect of action seemed so remote that the author of "The Book of the Hundred Chapters" pushed the figure of the great, reforming emperor into the realm of prophecy. "Our future king," he writes, "is sent us by God. He is great in wisdom but small in power, not rich but endowed with reason, strict in giving judgment, loving justice and hating those who transgress the written law." This future emperor will punish usurers, protect the land, emancipate the peasants, feed the poor, and protect widows and orphans. And his name shall be Frederick. How does our author know this? Because, as he states in his preface, "Michael, archangel and worthy messenger of Almighty God, appeared to this pious man and made revelations to him."[23]

2. THE NATIONAL ILLUSION — BLAMING ROME, DISCOVERING GERMANY

Blaming Rome for the Imperial church's ills formed the most convenient inference from the caesaropapist concept of the emperor's universal authority. The charge of greed and simony, though irrefutable in fact, by no means explained the situation, for the fiscalization of the Church since the fourteenth century signaled not the strength

19 Strauss, ed., *Manifestations of Discontent*, 242.
20 Strauss, ed., *Manifestations of Discontent*, 245.
21 Strauss, ed., *Manifestations of Discontent*, 245.
22 There is no agreement on what he meant by "common men." My inference rests on the writings of Peter Blickle.
23 Strauss, ed., *Manifestations of Discontent*, 234.

but a weakening of papal power. It offered a way around the unwelcome truth that emperor and bishops alike disdained to sponsor a comprehensive reform of the Imperial church. Indeed, when he concluded the Concordat of Vienna in 1448, Emperor Frederick promised that nothing like this would happen.[24] The concordat's terms dealt reform a crushing defeat by burying the levers of ecclesiastical governance even more deeply than ever in the snares of local noble interests. In effect, it nested the feudal character of the Imperial church in Imperial law and thereby neutralized its bishops as possible agents of reform.[25]

The conciliarists' anti-Romanism raised its head once more in 1451, when Nicholas of Cusa, an old Basler who had made his peace with the pope, returned as papal legate to the German lands. He was charged with selling a papal reform plan to a series of provincial (archiepiscopal) and diocesan synods in the Empire. The reception was very mixed, and somewhere, perhaps at Mainz, a list of German grievances (*gravamina*) against Rome was put into his hands. This classically conciliarist piece calls on "the German nation" to approve reform decrees presented only by a general council, not a legate speaking for the pope, and to press for a new general council. Since "practices vary widely in the church, and faithful observance of divine laws would vary from province to province if they were to be reformed separately, . . . both a general council and a national council for Germany must be called into session, so that the German nation, if reformed, will not deviate in its ways from the practices of other nations." In any case, reform "must begin with the pope and the Roman Curia," whose trafficking in benefices brings "a hoard of gold and silver to Rome, and the pope, in his haste to fill his money bags, is heedless of what the rest of us know, namely, that the higher a man's place, the graver his sins."[26] The churchmen who composed this document shrugged off the task of self-reform by insisting that reform could only come from above, for "if pope and curia were to reform themselves, or if a general council were to bring about a universal reformation of the Church, there would be no difficulty in reforming every Christian in his own estate."[27] A national council – for which no precedent existed – proved merely an empty suggestion.

The *gravamina* of 1451 were the hardcore Baslers' revenge on Nicholas the Turncoat and also on the Italians, for at this time anti-Italian sentiment was becoming prominent in a new way. One advocate for it was the Franconian lawyer Gregor Heimburg, whom the Italians drove to fury by their condescension to Germans. "His manner of speech and gestures were unruly," Enea Silvio remembers,

> and, stubborn as he was, he heeded no one, living, as was his wont and prizing freedom above all else. There was something offensive in his behavior, for he was shameless and cynical . . . . With his drooping boot tops, bare chest, bare head, and rolled up sleeves, he

24 See Chapter 6.
25 Over the century that followed the Concordat of 1448, the proportion of commoners in episcopal sees increased, reaching a peak of 21 in the sees with *Hochstifte* and 26 in those without. Thomas A. Brady, "The Holy Roman Empire's Bishops on the Eve of the Reformation," 26. In the Empire's Rhenish-Danubian heartlands, only 5 of 38 bishops were commoners in 1517, when Luther's public career began. Eike Wolgast, *Hochstift und Reformation. Studien zur Geschichte der Reichskirche zwischen 1517 und 1648*, 20–1.
26 Strauss, ed., *Manifestations of Discontent*, 49.
27 Strauss, ed., *Manifestations of Discontent*, 51.

showed his displeasure, and he constantly mocked Rome, the pope, the Curia, and Italy's hot weather.[28]

A man born for politics, Heimburg successively served King Sigismund, Emperor Frederick III, the city of Nuremberg, and Duke Sigismund of Tyrol. While in the duke's service he had the pleasure of hounding Nicholas of Cusa out of his South Tyrolean bishopric. Yet Heimburg was more than a post-conciliar thug, he was also a perceptive political realist. In 1461 he circulated to the German princes his *Appeal from the Pope to a Future Council*, in which he makes three points. There is nothing new in the first two, which charge the pope with bleeding the German lands dry through his crusading tax and striving for "the imperial sway that he desires to exercise over us."[29] Heimburg's third point, however, recommends that the Germans' best defense against Rome lies not with the emperor but with the princes, bishops, and nobles, who possess "the experience to inspire the army to shatter the enemy."[30] This statement departs markedly from the caesaropapist view that the growth of princely power was a threat, not an asset, to the Empire.

Heimburg's appeal to the Imperial princes complemented his fierce anti-Romanism. It is easy to fathom how he and others exploited such sentiments, even though outside Italy the great advance of papal power was largely a myth. Far from essaying to gain the lordship of the German lands, in these days the popes turned their attention to the task of building a secure Italian base for themselves and the Curia. They struggled to combine "the concrete exercise of power in the universal Latin Church during the decline of the medieval respublica christiana" with an adaptation to "the overpowering ascent of the political system of the modern states and of the new economy."[31] The adaptation sought to build a secure state in Italy through methods more advanced than any a fifteenth-century emperor possessed: stronger bureaucracy and more effective fiscal management. An alliance of Italian princes, brokered by the pope, protected this state-building effort for nearly a half-century until the Italian Wars erupted in 1494. The result was the modern Papal State, a centralized territorial state nested within the popes' spiritual monarchy over the Western Church. Papal success contrasted dramatically with Imperial failure.

Under these conditions it is hardly surprising that around 1500 there arose a new wave of German anti-Romanism. Writers schooled in the Italianate learning of neoclassicism aimed to hoist the pope and his Italians with their own petards, that is, beat them at their own game. Called "humanists" by modern scholars, they took up the standard against Rome and Italy during the Italian Wars (1494–1518) that occupied Emperor Maximilian's entire reign. The money and men the emperor spent on his Italian ventures brought the Germans little more than new humiliations at the hands of the "Latins." Smarting, they presented themselves as speakers for their people's wounded pride against the pope, his Curia, and the Italians in general. They bore new

28 Heinz-Otto Burger, *Renaissance, Humanismus, Reformation: Deutsche Literatur im europäischen Kontext*, 81.
29 Kurt Stadtwald, *Roman Popes and German Patriots. Antipapalism in the Politics of the German Humanist Movement from Gregor Heimburg to Martin Luther*, 46.
30 Stadtwald, *Roman Popes and German Patriots*, 46.
31 Paolo Prodi, *The Papal Prince: One Body and Two Souls: The Papal Monarchy in Early Modern Europe*, vii.

weapons in this fight, above all historical documents and methods adopted from Italians, through which they could prove that their ancestors had been victims of ancient Rome, just as they themselves were of modern Rome. Though heirs to the older caesaropapists, they also introduced a new element, claiming to speak not just for the emperor, but for a "German nation" and "Germany," which the emperor represented.

One advocate of this new, historicizing anti-Romanism was the learned Heinrich Bebel (1472–1518), the son of Swabian peasants, who became professor of rhetoric and poetry at Tübingen, and by repute the finest German Latinist of his generation. In 1501, when King Maximilian crowned him poet laureate at Innsbruck, Bebel responded with an oration cast in the humanist idiom. Named *In Praise of Germany*, it dispenses the typical caesaropapist message of praise for the emperor and blame for the Imperial princes. "I am certain," Bebel flatters his king, "that you have before your eyes a clear picture of what needs to be done. When I see how our German princes neglect the public weal in favor of their private interests, and . . . waste their days in feuding and pleasure-seeking . . . I should be fearful indeed of our future as a nation were it not for you . . ."[32] In a passage that drips with christomimetic figures, the poet tells how Mother Germany had come to Bebel in a dream and asked him to tell Maximilian, "he is his grieving mother's only refuge and consolation, having been my hope since the time I carried him in my womb."[33] Bebel must remind the king of how the ruin of mighty states of antiquity lay in the "license given to personal greed and ambition, in the search for private gain and advantage, and in internal dissensions resulting from these."[34] Like the Drummer of Niklashausen's Virgin, Bebel's Mother Germany offers consolation and hope to her downtrodden children. Still, all is not lost, for

> We Germans can hold our own with any nation under the sun. . . . We are an autochthonous people, born from the soil of the land on which we now make our home. . . . Our best claim to honor and glory, however, is founded upon our superior virtue, a trait in which we excel all the other nations of mankind. What people, pray, shows a greater devotion to justice? What people is more steadfast and sincere in its faith? . . . Where may clearer evidence be found of a people's love and respect for divine worship and the Christian religion? Where are signs of greater devotion than the wars we have fought for the protection and propagation of our faith?[35]

"We who possess virtue and faith," Bebel trumpets with an overcompensating bombast, "are greater than all other nations."[36]

Bebel did not take the next step, which was to deploy the new contrariety of ancient Germans and Romans against the heirs of Rome, the Italians in general and the papacy in particular. The man who did take it was a boisterous and learned Franconian nobleman named Ulrich von Hutten. He studied at no fewer than seven German universities before traveling via Vienna to study law at Pavia and Bologna.

32 Strauss, ed., *Manifestations of Discontent*, 65.
33 Strauss, ed., *Manifestations of Discontent*, 66.
34 Strauss, ed., *Manifestations of Discontent*, 66–7.
35 Strauss, ed., *Manifestations of Discontent*, 70.
36 Strauss, ed., *Manifestations of Discontent*, 71.

Later, following a brief period in the service of Elector Albert of Mainz, in 1515–16 Hutten went back over the Alps to study at Rome and Bologna.

Living in Italy transformed Hutten from an ambitious striving man seeking the main chance into a literary hammer of papal Rome. His "mature" works (he died at age thirty-five) blend the caesaropapist discourse of the reforming emperor and the national discourse of German victimization by Italians with the old anti-Romanism. The result appears in his savage anti-Roman diatribes of 1518–19, when the controversy over Martin Luther was stirring up some folk and depressing others. For Hutten, to be German is to be anti-Roman, to hate in the same breath the ancient Romans as ancient Germans' oppressors and papal Rome as a tyranny over the Germans and their churches. Most effective is his *Roman Triads* (*Trias Romana*), a list of fifty-eight three-part satirical "praises" of the city of Rome, the Curia, the clergy, and the pope. Among its more pungent lines are these:

> Three things are honored at Rome: shrines, papacy, and indulgences.
> Three things are valued at Rome: women, horses, and letters. . . .
> Three things are commonly brought from Rome: a bad conscience, a sour
>   stomach, and an empty purse. . . .
> Three things are mortal sins at Rome: poverty, fear of God, and devotion.[37]

In another widely read dialogue, *Vadiscus, or the Roman Trinity,* a speaker named "Hutten" announces that "the German nation has recovered its eyes and now recognizes how unjustly it has been led around by the nose and defrauded, and how the people has been tricked, and a free, warrior nation, a courageous people [with] many proud nobles and princes, [has been] exhausted and treated with contempt."[38] At Rome the popes "make doctrines and weaken us more and more, . . . and they even slay us with the power of their thunder." The pope is "a betrayer of the people."[39]

Ulrich von Hutten represents a measurable radicalization of the post-Basel reformist tradition. He aimed not to renew the church, local or universal, but to liberate the German nation as a whole from the papacy's spiritual and financial tyranny. Some of his ideas are conventional: the need for a spiritual and poor clergy, the invasion of the faith by money, and Roman interference in German affairs. His brilliant meld of style and stridency, however, struck a pitch far more extreme than any previous reformist had achieved. What was still lacking was agency, for his staunch caesaropapism combined fawning praise for the often hapless emperor with inadvisable contempt for the German princes as mere selfish foes of the German common good.[40] Yet his timing was brilliant, for his heaviest blows fell just at the moment when German anti-Romanism was mounting to a new peak. Still, Hutten's call for national and anti-Roman reform of the Imperial church voiced but another illusion about reform. Who would take the initiative in this enterprise?

---

37 Ulrich von Hutten, *Opera quae reperiri potuerunt omnia,* vol. 1: 148–51.
38 Hutten, *Opera,* vol. 1: 61–2.
39 Hutten, *Opera,* vol. 1: 112.
40 It should be mentioned that the murder of his cousin, Hans von Hutten, at the behest of Duke Ulrich of Württemberg, fueled his hatred of princes.

3. THE COMMUNAL ILLUSION – JOHANN GEILER VON KAYSERSBERG

A person who strolls up the left aisle of Strasbourg's tremendous Gothic cathedral today might stop at the first of the crossing piers to marvel at the gorgeous Gothic pulpit. The gift of a leading politician – Jacob Sturm's grandfather – it was fashioned for the man who came to the city in 1478 to be cathedral preacher. He was Johann Geiler (1445–1510), called "von [of] Kaysersberg" in central Alsace, though he had been born at Schaffhausen, a small Imperial city just north of the Rhine, today a Swiss border town.[41] For thirty-two years Geiler preached to burghers of Strasbourg, correcting their morals and entertaining them with his folksy language, wit, and learning. Geiler must have been a striking figure in the pulpit. A priest who knew him reminisced, "He was of upright stature and had curly hair, a lean face, and a healthy, well-formed, and handsome body."[42] Geiler preached whole cycles of sermons, each interconnected by a theme, such as the world's folly (drawn from Brant's *Ship of Fools*), or a metaphor, such as human society as an anthill. Many, printed in his lifetime, circulated to spread his fame as a preacher, a moralist, and an outstanding wit.

Johann Geiler was one of the best-known, most outspoken, and most respected social critics of his day. Behind his folksy, entertaining manner of preaching stood a priest who knew the great world as well as his smaller one. He had been rector of the University of Freiburg, he had in person pressed the cause of reform (without success) on Emperor Maximilian and on Strasbourg's bishop, a worldly, uninterested son of the Elector Palatine. He counted among his friends and correspondents many important writers of the day. As to the issue of an agency of reform, Geiler's ideas were neither caesaropapist, national, nor anti-Roman, but communalist. They flowed from Geiler's understanding of the Church as communal and corporate, not feudal and hierarchical. While he did not ignore the local church's invisible bonds to the universal Church, he spoke chiefly to Strasbourg's burghers as though they were, should be, or soon might be serious, devout Christians who treated their neighbors as Jesus had instructed his followers to do. At the center of Geiler's reforming activities stood his flock, the city, and the diocese. This local concentration formed Geiler's great strength, but also his weakness, as a reformer.

Of all the dangers that threatened Christian communities, in Geiler's eyes the most pressing was hatred and strife between the Church's two estates, clergy and laity. He understood that, however the matter had stood in earlier times, in affairs of this world as he knew it, clergymen had to serve laymen. This was so because, without the laity's respect and support, the clergy, from the pope down to the humblest novice in the poorest religious community, could not survive. Geiler understood, too, that the root of anticlericalism in his day lay in the Church's accumulated wealth and the temptations it posed. "You laymen hate us priests," he preached around 1508,

and it is an old hatred between you and us. Whence comes this hate that makes you our enemies? I believe it comes from our foolish way of life, that we live so wickedly and

---

41 Together with Basel, Schaffhausen, which lies on the Rhine's right bank below Lake Constance, entered the Swiss Confederation in 1501 following the Swabian War of 1499. See the discussion in Chapter 7.

42 Matern Berler, "Chronik," in Louis Schnéegans, ed., *Code historique et dipomatique de la Ville de Strasbourg*, vol. 1, 2: 115.

thereby give scandal. This cannot be the sole reason, but I don't know any other. Why is it that when there is an assembly of honorable priests, who have never given scandal, you hate them just the same? And many say that the priests have too much.[43]

Geiler saw that the most provocative of clerical faults were swollen if not entirely caused by their involvement with the market, that mysterious power that competed with the equally mysterious power of their own sacramental office.

For Geiler the worst enemies of Christian life among the burghers were not the scandalously living priests but the big merchants and moneylenders with whom, it had to be said, clergy were often in cahoots. Geiler calls on Jesus Christ to take action against the merchants, whose secret knowledge enables them to profit from their neighbor's losses. They ought to be cut away from the community, for they "stand alone in the trough like an old sow who won't let the other hogs in. As though they want to possess all the wares, and everyone has to take his light from their light."[44] The Holy Sacrament should be refused, he says, "to those who buy as cheaply as possible and those who sell as dearly as possible . . . for this is against brotherly love. You should add a modest profit, also your trouble and effort, but to buy as cheaply and sell as dearly as you can, that is false!"[45] Geiler spoke for the wave of hatred of what were called "monopolies," powerful persons and firms who exploited their neighbors' needs by means of secret knowledge and a disregard for Christian teachings. They set their prices, on an unprecedentedly large scale, without regard to cost or risk – this was the canonical definition of usury.[46] After Geiler's death this wave would rise to a peak at the Diets of the early 1520s, only to break in 1525 on the emperor's refusal to banish the "monopolies."

Geiler spoke for the great exchange between local and universal community. In his great sermon cycle named *The Ants* he created one of his most remarkable tropes, Christian society as an "anthill." Its division of labor, from which each and every member lives, creates both the exchange of material and spiritual goods within the local Christian community and the exchange of spiritual goods between clergy and laity within the Church Universal. The Imperial church and the Roman Church are both anthills, and their mutual participation in the universal exchange of spiritual goods protects Christians against domination by the exchange of material goods and its instrument, money. "Participation," Geiler's keyword, is essential to his idea that both laity and clergy take part in both divisions of labor. The local division of labor is experienced, its universal counterpart must be believed in. At the local level, Geiler admits, "We clergy, monks, priests, and nuns thus eat up your work," but "you nourish us, so we should repay temporal with spiritual goods."[47] This exchange supports and is protected by the universal economy of grace, which the Church shares through its prayers. When a priest at Rome says Mass in a state of grace, Geiler tells

43 Johann Geiler, *Die Emeis: Dis ist das buch von der Omeissen, und ouch her der kunnig ich diente gern*, 27b.
44 Jakob Strieder, *Studien zur Geschichte kapitalistischer Organisationsformen. Monopole, Kartelle und Aktiengesellschaften im Mittelalter und zu Beginn der Neuzeit*, 190.
45 Johann Geiler, *Die brösamlin doct. Keiserspergs vffgelesen von Frater Johann Paulin*, 47b. This was very much the view Martin Luther would express some years later.
46 The sin of usury, it must repeatedly be said, was not simply the taking of interest, it was the taking of interest in the manner indicated here. That this was illicit was a teaching that hardly changed from Thomas Aquinas through the Protestant reformers.
47 Geiler, *Die Emeis*, 9a.

his flock, "you benefit from his action. And when you here at Strasbourg pray the Our Father in the state of grace, the priest at Rome benefits from it. This is *participium*, that is, mutuality."[48]

Two things prevented the proper working of these exchanges. One was obvious: the (seemingly) unbridled exchange of money and goods driven by greed. The second was the failure of rulers, especially bishops, to serve their people rather than play the lord over them. "Now look at the prelates," Geiler preached, "how they behave in the cities in both spiritual and temporal affairs, and you see how they wear the bell. Don't you see how the prelates and princes through their bad example are the cause and source of destruction of the whole earth? They mislead the poor sheep who follow them."[49] A true bishop, he asserts, is one "who serves the whole community," for a bishop is the community's man, not the emperor's. With these words Geiler attacks the feudal captivity of the Imperial episcopate, of which he had bitter personal knowledge. In his sermon cycle based on Brant's bestselling *Ship of Fools*, he condemns the predictable effect of this captivity, the favoring of nobility over virtue in the episcopal elections.

> The fifth [fool's] bell means to elect rulers for their family and their nobility. This is a sign of great foolishness, to fill offices out of friendship and because of nobility, and to disregard the pious and the wise. All Germany is filled with this foolishness, for bishops are elected not for their chastity or their holiness; magistrates are not elected for their wisdom, but because of their nobility and their families. Thus come fools, mischievous and stupid men, into the government. . . . Bishops are elected not for their learning, holiness, or piety . . . [but] in former days it was different, . . . for then bishops were elected by the whole people and with their consent from among the holiest and most pious. . . . Nowadays, however, are elected young men, who are unlearned, very crafty, incapable of governing in both spiritual and temporal affairs, and they are elected only because they are nobles and have pals.[50]

Against the feudal graveyard of episcopal initiative and leadership, Geiler set his populist conception of the active Christian community. "The Son of Man is come not to be served but to serve," Geiler quoted St. Matthew. "All who command, spiritual and temporal rulers," he preached, "should believe that the community belongs not to them, but they to the community. The community does not exist for them, but they for the community, whose servants and dependents they are."[51] Bishops are not lords but servants, just like the parish priests.

With his ideal of a Church devoted to "participation" and service, Geiler was proposing to translate the ideal of Christian asceticism into a new social setting. What may be called his "worldly asceticism" is founded, unlike Max Weber's concept, on an obligation to mutuality and a concern for both personal salvation and the welfare of neighbors.[52] This ideal, by no means Geiler's alone, was a burghers' ideal. The

48 Geiler, *Die Emeis*, 9b.
49 Thomas A. Brady, "'You Hate Us Priests': Anticlericalism, Communalism, and the Control of Women at Strasbourg in the Age of the Reformation," 222. The phrase "wear the bell" alludes to Sebastian Brant's *Das Narrenschiff*, from which Geiler took his themes for this sermon cycle.
50 Johann Geiler, *Narrenschiff so er gepredigt hat zu straßburg in der hohen stifft daselbst ... uß latin in tütsch bracht*, 194v–95r.
51 Brady, "You Hate Us Priests," 181.
52 It can be pointed out here that Geiler's ideas belong to the prehistory of Weber's "Protestant ethic," though not to that of the "spirit of capitalism."

Dutch humanist Erasmus grasped its significance vis-à-vis the old monastic asceticism in these days, when monks had become men of the world. "And yet on account of their attire," Erasmus wrote to a friend in 1518, "on account of some title, they arrogate so much virtue to themselves that in comparison they do not regard others as Christians. Why do we so limit the profession of Christ, which he wished to extend most widely? If we are moved by splendid appellations, I beseech you, what else is the city but a great monastery?"[53] In truth, a great deal more. Huldrych Zwingli, the leading Protestant reformer of Zurich, did grasp it a few years later. "The kingdom of Christ is also external,"[54] he wrote in one place, and at another, "a Christian city is nothing more than a Christian commune."[55]

Where was the illusion in all this? Like the caesaropapist and the anti-Roman-national visions, Geiler's illusion lay in its passing over the problem of agency, the most fundamental political fact about the Imperial church. This yawning hole unfilled by pope, general council, emperor, or national synod meant that no agent possessed the authority and the power to effect the reforms that, as many dedicated persons agreed, were urgent and necessary. This lack could not be served by Geiler's commune, the people in their real-existing form, not by the "German people" fantasized by the publicists. Nowhere, with the single exception of the Swiss Confederation, did there exist a set of communes and communal federations that could act with full sovereignty unchecked by other powers. If such powers existed, they lay in another quarter, in the Imperial princely dynasties whose status as vassals masked true rulers unburdened by the traditions of monarchy and the aura of sacrality. Neither the post-Basel caesaropapists, the advocates of the German nation, nor Geiler the communalist looked toward the princes for agents of reform.

Johann Geiler knew that neither the emperor nor the bishops would take up the cause of reforming the churches. And he, faithful and intelligent Catholic that he was, quite realized that if local communes were to undertake serious reform without reference to the Church Universal, they would shatter it to pieces. The Waldensians and the Bohemian Hussites had blazed this path into schism. Absent any sign of leadership from responsible authorities, one could only hope. Preaching before King Maximilian and Queen Bianca Maria in August 1504 at Strasbourg, Geiler warned that "if neither pope, bishop, emperor, nor king will reform our unspiritual, insane, godless way of life, God will raise up one who will have to do it and raise up the fallen religion once more. I have hoped to see that day and become his disciple, but I am too old. Many of you will experience it, and I ask you to think on me and what I said."[56] In 1527, sixteen years after Geiler's death, Caspar Hedio (ca. 1494–1552), his successor-but-one in the cathedral pulpit, reflected on his legacy. "The more I read Dr. Kaysersberger," he wrote, "the more he pleases me, for when I read his writings, I find that he identified and understood the problem quite well. The time, however, was not yet ripe."[57] It was not ripe, because for a hundred years reformers had sought effective

53 Desiderius Erasmus to Paul Volz, Basel, 14 August 1518, in Desiderius Erasmus, *Collected Works of Erasmus*, vol. 66: 22. This is the dedicatory letter to Erasmus's *Enchiridion militis christiani*.
54 Huldrych Zwingli, *Huldrych Zwinglis sämtliche Werke*, vol. 9: 454, line 14.
55 Zwingli, *Huldrych Zwinglis sämtliche Werke*, vol. 14: 24, line 21.
56 Daniel Specklin, "Les Collectanées," *Bulletin de la Société pour la Conservation des Monuments Historiques d'Alsace*, 14: 297, no. 2190.
57 Brady, "You Hate Us Priests," 175.

agents of reform in persons who could not supply that need. Of none was this truer than of the emperor; of no emperor was it truer than of Maximilian.

4. MAXIMILIAN I AND THE IMPERIAL CHURCH

Little happened under Emperor Maximilian to gladden the heart of either a sincere caesaropapist or a reformist of any other stripe. The emperor trumpeted his rights and duties as lord of Christendom, but mainly he lobbied new Austrian dioceses from Rome, milked half the vacant benefices' revenues, grabbed monastic incomes, and robbed indulgence chests. He and several German princes plundered more than a third of a million gulden from the jubilee indulgence of 1500 and the crusade indulgences of 1501–3. Yet the emperor was by no means impious. He practiced elaborately and punctiliously the Catholic faith as he had learned it from his deeply devout parents. He heard Mass every day, even on hunting trips; he observed fasting times; he frequently deployed Biblical images and Christocentric metaphors; he discovered hitherto unknown saints in his own lineage; and he loved sacred music and grand religious ceremonies. In the matter of church reformation, however, he had only one interest: the churches' wealth belonged to him, and reforms should bring him fiscal or political advantage. Maximilian was merely a practical caesaropapist who regarded popes, bishops, priests, and abbots as his own servants under God. From the pope he wanted control of ecclesiastical appointments and incomes in Austria and the Empire comparable to those his late father-in-law had enjoyed, and to those his brothers of France, Aragon, and Castile continued to enjoy. He also wanted a permanent papal legate for the Empire and an Imperial party in the college of cardinals. In all modesty, he even proposed himself as a candidate for St. Peter's chair.

For most of his reign, control of Imperial Italy and Rome stood far higher in Maximilian's hierarchy of desires than the condition of the Imperial church. In 1494 the crack of doom for Italy sounded for the papally led "Holy League" that guarded the peninsula from foreign threats. King Charles VIII of France crossed into Italy with an enormous army to vindicate his hereditary claim to the crown of Naples. Thus began the Italian Wars, in which for the next seventy years France, Venice, the Empire, and Spain strove for the lordship of Italy, and the popes strove to prevent the success of any of them. This reflected papal self-interest in security, of course, but also a fear for the Church. Subservience to any Christian monarch, it was thought in Rome, would crush the papacy's independence and provoke other rulers to break with Rome.

Except when they combined in 1508 to smash Venice, pope and emperor sailed on collision courses. Maximilian, who regarded himself as Italy's true and rightful lord, wrote in his rough but fluent Latin, "I don't want that Italy, which is mine, should fall into other hands."[58] After Pope Alexander VI (r. 1492–1503) abandoned in 1495 the alliance against the French, Maximilian called him "Mohammed" and "Antichrist."[59] He hated Pope Julius II's "betrayal" in 1509 of the League of Cambrai against the Venetian Republic.[60] And although Maximilian snorted in disgust when Pope Leo X

58 Hermann Wiesflecker, *Kaiser Maximilian I. Das Reich, Österreich und Europa an der Wende zur Neuzeit*, vol. 2: 26.
59 Wiesflecker, *Kaiser Maximilian I.*, vol. 5: 170.
60 Wiesflecker, *Kaiser Maximilian I.*, vol. 5: 168.

opposed Charles's succession to the Imperial crown, Leo knew what he was doing. "Do you know," Leo asked his cardinals in 1519, "how many miles it is from here to the border of Naples? Forty!" he exclaimed to the Venetian ambassador, "therefore, Charles must never become King of the Romans!"[61]

With or without the pope, Maximilian was bent on having his way with the Imperial succession. This, not reform of the Church, was his motive in calling the Imperial Diet to Augsburg in 1518. The great assembly nonetheless formed the final act of the drama in which Sigismund, Frederick III, and Maximilian I, Nicholas of Cusa, Gregor Heimburg, and Enea Silvio Piccolomini, and the last of the Empire's armored bishops had all played their apparently fruitless roles. The Diet assembled to the tunes of venomous antipapal and anti-Italian polemics played by the learned patriots, of whom Hutten was by far the most eloquent and by some measure most effective. At Augsburg the cacophony of voices ranged from old-style, post-Basel conciliarist gravamina to anti-Roman predictions of the apocalypse. They were not orchestrated by Maximilian, whose relations with Rome had for the time being improved. The papal legate acknowledged this fact when he announced Leo's creation of two new German cardinals, Archbishops Albert of Mainz and Magdeburg, and Matthäus Lang of Salzburg.[62] This made four German cardinals. At Maximilian's accession, fifteen years before, there had been none.[63]

The Diet of Augsburg opened with grander than normal ceremonies. On 1 August 1518 in the city's great Gothic cathedral, the legate conferred the cardinalate on Archbishop Albert and rich papal gifts on Maximilian. After a declaration of the Diet's agenda, a crusade against the Ottomans – the old refrain echoed once more – the ceremony closed with a *"Te Deum"* sung to the sounds of organ, drums, and trumpets. The aged emperor now retired into seclusion to manage his chief business of smoothing his grandson's path to the Imperial crown.

The assembly's unsettled, unpredictable mood at Augsburg is well represented by Elector Albert of Mainz (b. 1490, r. Magdeburg 1513–45, r. Mainz 1515–45). When Erasmus heard of the archbishop-elector's red hat (the cardinalate), he grumbled that Albert had become "the pope's monk."[64] Well said, for, whoever he was, Albert was never his own man. The last child of the elector of Brandenburg and his Saxon consort, Albert had been tutored in Latin, rhetoric, law, philosophy, and music. In 1506, after his sister-in-law produced an heir, he entered the church, another piece of dynastic life insurance. Or, rather, he collected benefices: cathedral canon of Frankfurt, Trier, and Mainz; administrator of Halberstadt and archbishop-elect of Magdeburg (1513); archbishop-elect and elector of Mainz (1514); Imperial vassal (1516); and cardinal (1518). Albert presents to our eye an archetype of the prelate who replaced the armored bishop of earlier days – a German Renaissance prince, well educated, a patron of music and the arts, a sybarite, and a womanizer. Albrecht Dürer's portrait of 1519 captures the man perfectly: clear-eyed, well fleshed, already jowly at age twenty-nine, and looking very much a man of the world he loved. Although a good

61 Wiesflecker, *Kaiser Maximilian I.*, vol. 4: 455.
62 Lang was long one of Maximilian's principal advisors.
63 Counting as a German the Netherlander Adrian of Utrecht (1459–1523), who succeeded Leo as Pope Adrian VI (r. 1522–23). The fourth was Matthias Schiner (d. 1520), often called a Swiss, but in fact a native of the Valais, an independent republic.
64 Wiesflecker, *Kaiser Maximilian I.*, vol. 4: 389.

administrator, as a politician Albert was mercurial and timid. With one hand he signed the Diet's grievances against Rome, with the other struck a deal with the Roman Curia to sponsor an indulgence campaign in his jurisdictions. Hither and yon he swam with the tides in a sea of mounting excitement and agitation. Albert's vacillation suggests why neither before nor during nor after the Diet at Augsburg in 1518 was any progress made toward the mobilization of its leaders behind a national, orthodox reform of the Imperial church. The very ferocity of the gravamina provides a precise benchmark for the leaders' inaction. The gravamina, one historian has written, "did not become the starting point for a national church system, because the Imperial estates acted only defensively, referred to the unbearable [financial] burdens, and were united only in their rejection of Roman demands."[65] Nearly one hundred years ago the general council had risen at Constance; nearly sixty years had passed since the Council of Basel had closed; but only fourteen years had gone by since Johann Geiler had warned King Maximilian of God's coming man who will "raise up the fallen religion once more."

In the midst of these agitations, while the king-emperor expended his failing energy on assuring his grandson's succession, one figure calmly stood above the storm. Some thought Elector Frederick III (b. 1463, r. 1486–1525) of Saxony, called "the Wise," a better candidate for the Imperial throne than this unknown Charles of Spain. Frederick, a sober, reflective man of fixed principles, nonetheless had reason to be worried. One of his professors was in trouble with Rome.

5. MARTIN LUTHER — FRIAR, PROFESSOR, AND PROPHET

On 12 October 1518 a professor of theology in the eight-year-old University of Wittenberg in Saxony entered the great Augsburg mansion of the Fuggers, the Empire's greatest banking family. Martin Luther (1483–1546) had been summoned to give the papal legate, Cardinal Cajetan, an account of his teachings.[66] Nearly one year before, on All Hallows' Eve (31 October), this unknown professor in an obscure university had publicly attacked both the practice of collecting fees for issuing letters of indulgence and the efficacy of indulgences themselves.[67] According to the Church's teaching, these extremely popular acts of grace could, if performed in an attitude of true contrition, lessen the time one would expect to spend in Purgatory for the punishment (not the guilt) owing to sin. The benefit could be transferred to others who were already in that state of existence. Like many other acts of grace and favor, indulgences had been fiscalized as a most successful species of quantified grace. Although authorized by the pope alone, indulgences could not be preached, much less fees collected for issuing them, without the collaboration of the local authorities – emperor, princes, archbishops, and bishops. A campaign of preaching indulgences resembled a business partnership, in which each participating lord received a share of the incomes, and so

65   Georg Schmidt, "Luther und die frühe Reformation – ein nationales Ereignis?" in Bernd Moeller and Stephen E. Buckwalter, eds., *Die frühe Reformation in Deutschland als Umbruch: Wissenschaftliches Symposium des Vereins für Reformationsgeschichte 1996*, 63.
66   Tommaso de Vio (1469–1534), called "Cajetan" after his birthplace, Gaeta, in the kingdom of Naples. A Dominican, he was a philosopher and theologian of note.
67   It is possible, perhaps even probable, but unproved, that the Ninety-Five Theses were nailed to a door of Wittenberg Castle's church.

did the firm that managed the collecting. Theologically, of course, it was sinful to sell sacred things, so the fee was declared an administrative charge, but, as Luther pointed out, this distinction was often lost on the common people.

Professor Luther's four-session interview with the papal legate was not a success. By the professor's own account, Cajetan initially assured him "that he would proceed in a mild and fatherly manner, though in fact he treated me with force of the purest and hardest kind."[68] "Recant, admit your error," the legate said, "for the pope requires it, whether you will or no."[69] When the discussion came to the treasury of merit, accumulated grace dispensed by the Church to the penitent, Cajetan bluntly asked Luther, "Do you or don't you believe it?"[70] In the following session the two men debated whether Christ's merits formed a treasury of grace that the Church could distribute by means of indulgences (Cajetan), or were simply the fruits of Christ's death on the cross (Luther). Finally, the legate, weary – as many have been – of being lectured by a professor, dismissed him with the words, "Go, and don't come again into my sight unless you intend to recant."[71] Luther's appeal, "from a pope ill informed to a pope better informed," was posted on the cathedral's door, but only two days after he had departed for home on 20 October.[72] Eight months later, on 15 June 1520, there appeared a papal bull of excommunication under the opening words, "Arise, O God, and judge Your own cause" (Ps. 74:21).

In 1518 at the Diet of Augsburg, Martin Luther rose out of his provincial obscurity into the Empire's public life. A marginal man from the Empire's margin, when he began to be talked about in distant places probably not one German speaker in twenty-five could have said where Wittenberg lay. Three years later everyone knew, for he had become the most talked-about person in the German-speaking world.

Luther's origins offer no clues to what he became. He was born in 1483 in the country town of Eisleben in the county of Mansfeld, a small principality that in the following year became a Saxon fief. Martin was the first (or second) son of the seven (or nine) children of Hans Luder (d. 1530), a son of Thuringian peasants, and Margarethe Lindemann (d. 1531), a townswoman from Eisenach. Hans was a striving man, an ambitious partner in several copper-smelting combines, incomes from which made the family, now settled in the county town of Mansfeld, prosperous and respectable. The town's substance came not from the soil but from beneath it, and to this day the surrounding landscape is dotted with odd knolls that mark where the copper miners dumped their tailings.

The family's success enabled Martin to become an educated man. From 1490 to 1497 he attended the town school and went for one year to the Brethren of the Common Life at Magdeburg before transferring to Eisenach, where three years of study (1498–1501) gave him a mastery of Latin. In 1501 Martin entered Erfurt, an old university and the only one in the land of Thuringia. Come to prepare himself for a

68 Luther to Georg Spalatin (a Saxon court preacher), Augsburg, 14 October 1518, in Luther, *D. Martin Luthers Werke. Kritische Gesamtausgabe. Briefwechsel*, vol. 1: 214, ll. 8–13.
69 Luther to Georg Spalatin (a Saxon court preacher), Augsburg, 14 October 1518, in Luther, *D. Martin Luthers Werke. Briefwechsel*, vol. 1: 214, ll. 13–14.
70 Luther, *D. Martin Luthers Werke. Briefwechsel*, vol. 1: 214, ll. 16–17.
71 Luther, *D. Martin Luthers Werke. Briefwechsel*, vol. 1: 214, ll. 38–9.
72 During the medieval period, one faced with an unpalatable papal judgment or command might appeal "from the pope ill informed to the pope better informed," a joke but also a reminder that popes are mortal men who come and go.

career in the law, by 1505 he had gained a master of arts, the ticket to advanced studies in the other faculties. But an experience in July of that year changed his life forever. On the way home to Mansfeld, Martin was overtaken near the village of Stotterheim by a thunderstorm, in terror of which he made a vow to St. Anne, the Virgin's mother and patroness of miners. "Help me, St. Anne," he later told the story, "I will become a monk."[73] And so he did, for the obligation a vow created could be neglected only at the peril of one's soul. Ten days later, braving his father's wrath, Martin pounded on the gate of Erfurt's "Black Cloister," the house of the Austin Friars[74] and home to around fifty monks.

Luther's hidden time proved surprisingly brief. Two years later, now a fully professed friar, he was ordained a priest and said his first Mass (2 May 1507), and though he continued his studies at Erfurt for three more years, he read not law but theology. In 1510, after a brief journey to Rome on his order's business, Luther received his doctorate in theology and a call to a professorship in theology in the new university of Wittenberg. Here, after four years of quiet reflection and lecturing on the Bible, he emerged into public view in the autumn of 1517, when he announced his opinions on indulgences and offered to debate them with all comers. From this point on, given Luther's refusal to back down and Archbishop Albert's timidity, Luther's progress to the Diet of Augsburg took a relatively direct path.

Those who criticized or condemned Luther's views on indulgences as heterodox knew whereof his views spoke. By 1518 his critique had both expanded to other teachings of the Church and become quite radical. His budding theology did not replicate the ideas of such alleged "forerunners" as Wycliffe and Hus, for although they, too, were scholastic theologians, they came from a different tradition. Luther's teachers belonged to a tradition of critical thinking that descended from William of Ockham (ca. 1280–ca. 1349). This legacy had little to do with the differences between the various traditions of scholastic philosophical thought, and everything to do with the late medieval theology of salvation. The nominalist theology of salvation began from a specific configuration of the three theological virtues, faith, hope, and charity (love). Faith is essentially cognitive, accepting as true the teachings of the Holy Scriptures and the Church, but it cannot be authenticated by individual experience. Oriented to the authoritative word of the divine truth, faith is always receptive, not active, in contrast to love, which operates on and qualitatively changes the innermost heart. Love is the highest stage, "the way by which God comes to dwell in his [the Christian's] heart."[75] Faith, by contrast, is the lowest stage of the Christian's step-by-step climb toward hope, the root virtue that underlies progress toward sanctity and divine acceptance. The distinction between faith and hope shows clearly "why in the Middle Ages faith could not be the central concept of Christian life since the humility and hope of a spiritual life was not yet contained in the truth reference of faith alone."[76] This theology

---

73   Luther, *D. Martin Luthers Werke. Kritische Gesamtausgabe. Tischreden*, vol. 4: 440, ll. 9–10.
74   This is the traditional English name for the Order of Hermits of Saint Augustine (O.S.E.A). They were neither hermits nor cloistered monks, but mendicant friars who worked actively in the world, notably as teachers.
75   Berndt Hamm, *The Reformation of Faith in the Context of Late Medieval Theology and Piety. Essays by Berndt Hamm*, 156.
76   Hamm, *The Reformation of Faith*, 162.

defined two levels of spiritual experience, faith and love, linked by hope, and they could not be unified.[77]

Luther, who learned this theology from his teachers, expounded it as his own until the early 1510s, when he began to revise it under the influences of a radically Augustinian theology of grace and a philologically empowered Biblicism, both of which were spreading through the German universities. Although the precise genesis of Luther's own theology of grace remains, and probably will ever be, controversial, its consequences are clear enough. Luther taught that faith is not only the beginning of but also the gateway to salvation. It is neither a kind of knowledge nor an earned possession but an undeserved gift from God, by which He chooses freely not to regard us, despite our sins, as worthy of damnation. Hope and love are therefore consequences, not causes, of salvation, which is not a possession or a quality but an act of God's judgment.

Luther's unification of the modes of Christian experience – faith and love, intellect and will, and doctrine and prayer – offered an immense simplification to those who wanted to understand how the Christian might be saved in accordance with the Scriptures. Of course, had Christians not already accepted the divine and therefore infallible authority of the Bible, few would have listened to his theology as distinct from his other ideas.

Luther's new theological coign of vantage enabled him to reconfigure well-known issues, hopes, goals, and resentments in new, startling, and appealing ways. In its light, each issue acquired a new visage. Luther taught that the Christian lives at the End of Time, those Last Days before Christ comes again in glory to judge the living and the dead. When Luther looked to the horizon, he saw:

> the dark clouds of divine judgement gathering over a world nearing its end, a world fettered and enslaved in a thousand ways, that insisted on self-determination before God, that dared to speculate about the "meaning of history" and to speak of freedom of the will without being able to free itself from the paralyzing primeval fear of being trapped helplessly in the cage of an impenetrable world history.[78]

While this vision recapitulated some ideas of the great medieval apocalyptics, Luther focused it in an entirely new way on the practical problems of Christian life. His understanding of St. Paul's doctrine of faith and grace – faith is given, not acquired; grace is conferred, not earned – was deeply personal, but he was driven to focus it as well on the lives of others. What Luther wanted – a believing, devout, and literate laity served by well-informed clergymen who lived regular, chaste lives and preached and otherwise ministered to their flocks – was neither radical nor novel. Entirely radical, however, was his prescription for breaking the century-long deadlock over reform through basing everything on the Word. With this slippery term he meant Christ as the essential Word (the Johannine sense), the Scriptures as the prescriptive Word, and true doctrine truly preached as the operative or instrumental Word. The three senses, different but not separable, bring everything else under their united judgment.

---

77 One does not have to share Hamm's teleological assumption, "yet," to grasp the divergence's implication for personal piety.

78 Heiko A. Oberman, *Luther: Man between God and the Devil*, 218.

The Church lives under the judgement of the Word. Luther's theological absolutism enabled, perhaps forced, him to relativize all other things by denying them an authority or meaning independent of what God had *demonstrably* decreed in the Scriptures. This applied most of all to the Church, whose adaptations to and comprises with the world he saw as betrayals of Christ's great commission to carry the Word to all nations. The brilliance of this insight, which did not blame Rome as the cause of the Church's evils, weaknesses, and corruptions – something done aplenty by critics from the conciliarists to Hutten – lay in Luther's redefinition of the Christian Church. He disemboweled the fundamental distinction between clergy and laity and rejected Christian asceticism as defined in terms of monastic vows, the regular clergy, and clerical celibacy. His rejection, it could be said, targeted most of what had enabled the Latin Church to survive the transition from the Roman Empire through the Dark Ages and into the era of tremendous growth after the eleventh century. In a step that required a good deal of fictional history, Luther made war on historical time in the name of the End of Time. Getting history right – an obsession of many German humanists – hardly interested him.

Luther's vision of time shaped his definition of the Church as a "priesthood of all believers," though it could with equal justice be called "the laity of all priests." The phrase sounds truly populist and was mistakenly so taken by many of his hearers. Luther's populism (*pace*, those who would remove his friar's habit and his professor's gown to clothe him in good democratic trousers) was skin-deep. He trusted "Lord Everybody" (*Herr Omnes*, as he called the common people) little more than he did Rome, the bishops, and the monks, and this mistrust liberated him from the stagnant pool of postconciliar reformism. Although poorly informed about politics, thanks either to naivety or sublime intuition, Luther nonetheless resolved the problem of agency, the Gordian knot of reform. In real German politics of his day, Luther discovered agents who could, and should, effect reform where pope and general council had not and the emperor would not. He conceived the German princes (he called them "the German nobility") both as a corporate estate and part of the German Nation and later, when this failed, as mini-emperors responsible to God alone.

6. LUTHER'S APPEAL TO THE CHRISTIAN NOBILITY (1520)

During the three years between the Diet of Augsburg and the Diet of Worms in 1521, the obstreperous professor became a public prophet. In a frenzy of work in 1520, he delivered the writings for which he is best remembered: *On Good Works* (end of May, in German); *On the Papacy at Rome against the Very Famous Romanists at Leipzig* (June, in German); *To the Christian Nobility of the German Nation* (mid-August, in German); *On the Babylonian Captivity of the Church* (October, in Latin); and *On the Freedom of a Christian* (November, in German and Latin). A tract of 1523, *On Temporal Authority, How Far One Is Obliged to Obey*, completed this blitz of print that made Luther famous. His near manic capacity for quick study and rapid writing partnered with presses in major German cities enabled the circulation of the wave of criticism, debate, and enthusiasm that made him famous well before his public debut at Worms in 1521.

Of these formative writings, Luther's biographer writes, *To the Christian Nobility of the German Nation* enjoys "a unique place among his other publications."[79] In form it owes much to two genres, the postconciliar reform tract and the gravamina against Rome. "The time for silence is past," Luther opens, "and the time to speak has come."[80] He intends his words "to be laid before the Christian nobility of the German nation, in the hope that God may help his church through the laity, since the clergy, to whom this task more properly belongs, have grown quite indifferent."[81] This is the central idea: given the clergy's default, God may reform His Church through the nobility constituted as the German Nation.

Luther's theological vision informed his program in ways that departed from all traditions of German reformist writing. His opponents were defined not in ecclesiastical or moral but in theological terms: the "Romanists" are not just greedy Italian clergy (à la Hutten); they are "the princes of hell."[82] Luther draws the line, therefore, not between the Germans and Romano-Italy but between faithful Christians and demonic "Romanists," and the struggle between them turns not on power, reason, history, or law, but on faith alone. The first and most important thing to do, he writes, is not to trust "in great power or human reason. . . . For God cannot and will not suffer that a good work begin by relying upon one's own power and reason."[83]

Luther's theological critique is far more important intellectually, if not necessarily rhetorically, than his catalog of grievances against Rome. It enables him to desacralize his opponents' defenses by portraying them as purely human and offensive to God. These are the "three walls" that "the Romanists have cleverly built around themselves," so that "no one has ever been able to reform them."[84] This powerful metaphor is the tract's rhetorical masterpiece, for the three walls of Rome rest not on money, immorality, or injustice but on false doctrines: 1) subordination of the temporal to the spiritual power; 2) exclusive papal authority to interpret the Bible; and 3) exclusive papal right to convoke a general council. One by one, Luther attacks and, in his mind, razes them. His negation of spiritual authority leaves temporal authority alone as rightful and just. Because it is "ordained of God to punish the wicked and protect the good, it should be left free to perform its office in the whole body of Christendom."[85] The papal claim to authority over the Bible, by contrast, is "an outrageous fable," for "it is clear enough that the keys were not given to Peter alone but to the whole community."[86] "There is no authority in the church except to promote good," Luther adds, for "no Christian authority can do anything against Christ" except by "the power of Antichrist and the devil."[87] Luther's attack on the fusion of powers of the papacy and also implicitly of the Imperial episcopacy simply sweeps away the conceptual barrier that had stymied all German reformers before him.

One of the most compelling features of Luther's tract is his argument from necessity. Because the Church's officers will not act, he writes, "ordinary people and the

79 Martin Brecht, *Luther*, vol. 1: 369.
80 Martin Luther, *Three Treatises*, 7.
81 Luther, *Three Treatises*, 7.
82 Luther, *Three Treatises*, 10.
83 Luther, *Three Treatises*, 9.
84 Luther, *Three Treatises*, 10.
85 Luther, *Three Treatises*, 15.
86 Luther, *Three Treatises*, 20. This seemingly populist idea reflects an Ockhamist ecclesiology.
87 Luther, *Three Treatises*, 24–5.

temporal authorities" must do so "without regard to papal bans and fulminations."[88] This political argument had deep roots in Christian reform traditions. The conciliarists had deployed it against the papacy and in favor of the general council of the whole Church. Luther is much more radical, for he transfers the title of "church" to the world and calls on it to reform the Church. Luther barely nods in the new emperor's direction. He declares it to be "God's will that this empire should be ruled by the Christian princes of Germany, no matter whether the pope stole it, got it by force, or established it afresh."[89] In conferring the duty of ecclesiastical reform on the German princes, Luther broke the spell of caesaropapism that had so long enchanted German reformism. His discovery of the princes as divinely approved rulers rather than mere vassals was his most radical innovation.

It was Luther's genius to snatch a realistic sense of Imperial politics out of the prevailing swamp of royalist patriotism. His catalog of specific reforms – suppression of pilgrimages to Rome, the mendicant orders, clerical celibacy, endowed Masses for the dead, excommunications and interdicts, most feast days, prohibited degrees for marriage, shrines to the saints, begging, all Mass endowments, the schism from the Bohemian Hussites, and the Aristotelian curriculum of the universities – resemble an advanced Hussite reworking of the post-Basel reform tradition. His doctrine of salvation, however, enabled him to relativize all forms of earthly authority, spiritual as well as temporal, and to outflank the mystical union of Empire and Church that had frustrated reform since Basel. He thereby opened the way to a step long prepared in practice: the assumption by princes and magistrates of authority over the local churches. It may have made some difference, of course, that Luther's homeland belonged to those German lands in which the Imperial presence was distant and largely symbolic. Out in the east, where city halls did not display Imperial symbols, and where royal agents were hardly ever seen, the Empire was more virtual than real to a degree far greater than in the old heartlands. Whatever their legitimacy, the eastern and northern princes governed their lands free of interference from anyone except their neighbors or their own nobilities. Whether in Thuringia and Saxony or in the entire northern tier from Westphalia across through Brunswick, Mecklenburg, Brandenburg, and Pomerania, and on into the Baltic lands, within a span much longer than living memory, no emperor had ever been seen. Nor would Professor Luther have seen one had he not left home for the south, in 1518 for Augsburg and in 1521 for Worms.

7. CHARLES V AND LUTHER AT THE DIET OF WORMS (1521)

History has moments when the normally invisible forces that propel become visibly represented by – Hegel would have said embodied in – the actors of a particular drama. Such a moment occurred at Worms on the Rhine on 18–19 April 1521, when Emperor Charles V and Martin Luther met for the first and only time. Charles had sailed in 1520 from Spain to his native Low Countries. Pausing for his royal coronation at Aachen, he then moved up the Rhine to Worms, whither he had summoned the Imperial Diet. The young emperor-elect, reared to age sixteen at the French-speaking

88 Luther, *Three Treatises*, 26.
89 Luther, *Three Treatises*, 103.

court in Brussels, had succeeded to the Spanish thrones in 1516.[90] A true cosmopolite, he was also polyglot, and a tradition credits him with joking, "I speak Spanish to God, Italian to women, French to men, and German to my horse." Well said, except that, while he had some Netherlandish (Dutch), he could not understand the High German in which the Empire conducted most of its business and horses, allegedly, conversed.

Charles came to preside over the Imperial Diet, an assembly that had taken its final shape in his grandfather's time, though without Maximilian's initiative. By 1521 the Diet had assumed the shape it would retain for nearly 300 years: an agenda set by the emperor or his deputy; three chambers sitting by rank and taking decisions by majority vote; negotiations within and between chambers; and plenary sessions to ratify decisions. Table 3 shows the structure of the chambers and the strength, nominal and actual, of each chamber. While the electors stood first in prestige, the great weight of the Diet lay in the princes' chamber, with its 45 ecclesiastical princes and its 27 lay dynasties and lineages. The Imperial cities were important, because of their wealth, but politically less powerful.

Taken together, these estates formed the Empire's ruling class, and their assembly, if well attended, displayed the Empire itself. At Worms in 1521, the first and one of the great assemblies of his reign, the young Charles V would have to confront a troubling case of a stubborn theology professor from the Empire's edge, who refused to obey his ecclesiastical superiors. That such a case came before the Diet at all suggests how little the Church in the Empire was able to govern its own affairs.

Professor Luther was among the most provincial of Germans. Except for brief journeys to Rome, Heidelberg, and Augsburg, he had never been outside his native region, and he spoke none of Charles's languages except Latin. The professor's road to Worms began with a citation by Charles on 6 March 1521 to appear under Imperial safe-conduct at Worms for a hearing before emperor and Diet. It was an ominous invitation, for everyone around Luther knew about Jan Hus and royal safe-conducts.

Table 3. The Imperial Diet according to the Register of 1521

Estates	Listed	Valid	Votes
I. Electors' Chamber	7	6	6
II. Princes' Chamber			
A. Ecclesiastical Princes	51	45	45
B. Lay Princes	32	29	27
C. Prelates, Abbesses, & Teutonic Knights	91	48	2
D. Counts and Barons	137	93	2
III. Cities' Chamber	86	59	59

Source: Information is based on the register (*Reichsmatrikel*) of 1521, which was revised but never superseded. The differences between listed and valid standing reflect the archaic state of the register.

90 The Germans always called him "the king of Spain," though in fact "Spain" was a union of two kingdoms, Castile and Aragon.

He arrived in Worms on 16 April about supper time, the papal legate reported, escorted by just under 100 cavalrymen. When he stepped down from his wagon, a gift from the city of Wittenberg, a priest hugged him, touched his garment three times, and went away as though he had held a relic of a great saint in his hands.

On 18 April came the professor's first hearing in the episcopal palace, where the emperor-elect was lodged. The archbishop of Trier's chief judge put two questions to him: Do you acknowledge your writings? Do you retract them? The titles in question were now read and acknowledged by Luther, who then asked for time to consider the second question. On the next day, when the hearing continued, Luther was told to answer the question clearly and frankly. This he did, switching back and forth between German and Latin. "If I am not overcome," he declared,

> by the testimony of the Holy Scriptures or the clear arguments of reason – for I believe in neither popes nor councils alone as witnesses, since they have often erred and contradicted themselves – I remain overcome by the Bible as I have explained it. My conscience is captive to the Word of God, and I can and will recant nothing, because it is always burdensome, unwholesome, and dangerous to act against one's conscience. God help me! Amen.[91]

Even if confident of Frederick of Saxony's power to protect him, Luther displayed astonishing courage in defending his views before emperor and estates. Yet his famous statement was but the first of the pair of utterances that defined the new situation. On the following day, the morning of 19 April, Charles consulted the electors and princes about what should be done with Luther. The princes asked for time to deliberate, and many of them went pale at the young monarch's reply.

Charles, now twenty years young to Luther's thirty, was bearded and slim to Luther's clean-shaven burliness, and he was gorgeously attired to Luther's plain monk's habit. His orator – emperors do not speak, they are spoken for – read a statement in Charles's own French, then in German translation. It stated the emperor's position as forcefully as Luther had his the day before. "You know," Charles begins, "that I am descended from the Most Christian emperors of the noble German Nation, the Catholic kings of Spain, the archdukes of Austria, and the dukes of Burgundy, who all remained until their deaths loyal sons of the Roman Church."[92] These ancestors "were defenders of the Catholic faith, the sacred ceremonies, decretals, ordinances and holy rites to the honor of God, and propagation of the faith and the salvation of souls. After their deaths they left, by natural law and inheritance, these holy Catholic rites for us to live and die by following their example."[93] For his part, Charles declared his resolve "to maintain everything which these my forebears have established to the present, especially that which my predecessors ordained at the Council of Constance and at other councils."[94] With these words Charles framed the central issue: one man's conviction against the Church's unbroken traditions. For him it was a clear choice, for "it is certain that a single monk errs in his opinion which is against what all of Christendom has held for over a thousand years to the present.

---

91 Adolf Wrede, *Deutsche Reichstagsakten unter Kaiser Karl V.*, 581, line 23, to 582, line 2. The famous sentence, "Here I stand," etc., is probably apocryphal.
92 Wrede, *Deutsche Reichstagsakten unter Kaiser Karl V.*, 595, ll. 7–10.
93 Wrede, *Deutsche Reichstagsakten unter Kaiser Karl V.*, 595, ll. 10–15.
94 Wrede, *Deutsche Reichstagsakten unter Kaiser Karl V.*, 595, ll. 17–20.

Figure 3. Martin Luther as Augustinian Friar with the Holy Spirit

According to his [Luther's] opinion all of Christendom has always been in error."[95] The king closed by declaring his decision "to proceed against the said Luther and his false doctrines."[96]

That Luther, though he did not retract his condemned views, departed Worms untouched on 26 April, is a sign of how the Empire had changed since Jan Hus died at Constance just over 100 years before. On 8 May the emperor's Edict of Worms outlawed Luther and forbade Imperial subjects to print, sell, or read his writings, which were to be gathered up and burnt. Yet the channels that had made Luther a public figure now made him a sensation, as news of the events at Worms spread across the

95 Wrede, *Deutsche Reichstagsakten unter Kaiser Karl V.*, 595, ll. 20–3.
96 Wrede, *Deutsche Reichstagsakten unter Kaiser Karl V.*, 595, ll. 34–5.

Empire like a rising wind. The printers reproduced the reports, along with his writings, like loaves and fishes for hungry audiences – the enthusiastic, the interested, and the hostile. Christian Germans of that day knew their Bible history, and many saw immediately that if Luther were not a damnable heretic, as Church and Empire had pronounced, he was perhaps a great new prophet of the Lord, a new Elijah. A contemporary portrait shows a tonsured Luther in his Augustinian habit, while above him hovers the Holy Spirit.

By the time Luther arrived at Worms, some half a million copies of his writings were circulating in the Empire, an explosion of print unfathomable in its uniqueness and its power. This reception and this reception alone – not the consistency of Luther's words but the response to them – burst the hardened logjam of reform and at last made possible reformations of the church in the German lands. The day of illusions was over.

Part III

Church, Reformations, and Empire, 1520–1576

> Religions are kept alive by heresies, which are really sudden explosions of
> faith. Dead religions do not produce them.
>
> Gerald Brenan

The reform of the Church and religious life presented the greatest leftover problem associated with Western Christendom's recovery from the fourteenth-century crisis and depression. It is neither coincidental nor merely interesting that the most luxuriously creative set of solutions should have appeared in the Holy Roman Empire. Of all the major kingdoms of Western Christendom, the Empire had experienced in the previous 100 years the least successful attempts at reform of the Church and religious life. Of all the sixteenth-century reformations, it proved easily the most tumultuous, most varied, most creative, and, therefore, least decisive. For these reasons, the Protestant reformation forms the obvious, even unavoidable, centerpiece of any account of the German lands in this epoch. Some have called it the dawn of Europe's modernity, others a failed German national revolution. About its causes, too, there is no consensus. Did it happen because of Luther's unique personality, the corruption of the Church, the formation of nation-states, or the rise of the middle classes? Each explanation founders on the reefs of the known facts or on the shoals of ignorance. We do not even know whether the Protestant reformers attacked a Church fallen from the higher standards of medieval (not to mention ancient) times; whether a more devout laity was placing higher expectations on its clergy who could not fulfill them; or whether (some) Christian people revolted against the old Church because it burdened their consciences, their pocketbooks, or both. One thing is certain. Now that the European twentieth century has cast a pall over all teleological interpretations of Western history, the reformations in the German lands seem to belong far more to their own age than to ours.

Part III examines the movements and outcomes that are classically designated by the phrase "the Protestant Reformation" in the German lands. Standing at the center of this book's three-part narrative, it begins with what are called "the evangelical movements"[1] of the 1520s in town and countryside. It moves into the crucial decade between the mid-1520s and the mid-1530s, when princes, nobles, and magistrates joined a new Protestant party, the members of which pledged to reform their churches and to defend them by peaceful means if possible and armed force if necessary. This led, following two brief wars, to the initial pact (1555) that permitted two forms of Christian religion in the Empire. For two more decades the advance of the Protestant faith continued, until around 1580 intra-Protestant strife and Catholic resurgence slowed its advance.

The central argument of Part III is that whatever the evangelical reformers' opinions, the possibility of a deep and lasting reform of religious life depended fundamentally on the unprecedented claims to actions and voice from social groups who in more settled times possessed little or none. Of these, the townsmen or burghers stand prominently at the center of the religious, though not the political, culture of the Reformation. The importance of printing to the formation of the evangelical movement, the domestication of its clergy by means of marriage, household, and citizenship, and the overwhelming role of both words and the Word to its spirituality, all these mark the Protestant reformation as originally burghers' work. The intervention of communally based farmers and their allies, on the other hand, determined in its very failure the transformation of the larger movement into an agglomeration of allied but separate reformations from the top down. The German Protestant reformation thus stationed itself between the fact of Rome and the possibility of a revolution, which became sublimated into an apocalyptic vision.

Originally with little aid from state power, the mobilization of these social groups depended on an intersection between their own experiences and communal traditions and two potent, fruitful beliefs. The first stated the problem in a perfectly traditional way: there is a more or less serious gulf between the Church's operations and the mission Christ had laid upon it. The second belief posed the remedy in terms that were radical if not entirely novel: Rome is not only to blame for this situation, Rome is its irreformable source. This pair of opinions could be, and was, held by some Christians who did not abandon the old faith to follow Luther. Yet the Wittenberg reformer proved a powerful catalyst to the growth of an anti-Roman movement for independent, even separatist, reform. As powerful as his teachings on faith, grace, works, reason, and free will may have been for individuals, the central issue he placed on the docket for public life was the Church and its management. The logic of his argument dictated that reformation of the Church depended on weakening its authority but above all its power.

Part III opens with two chapters on the upheavals of the 1520s, the urban reformation (Chapter 9), and the Peasants' War (Chapter 10). Chapter 11 takes up the narrative of the Reformation in the Empire, which Chapter 12 continues down to the mid-1570s, the time

---

1   In Part III the term "evangelical" refers to the broad set of religious ideas and movements that called on the Bible and/or the Word as the normative authority for Christian life. It included Biblicist streams of thought and sensibility in the Roman Church. "Evangelical" is thus not synomous with "Protestant," which refers to the politically constituted and sponsored movement that since around 1530 undertook reforms of the Church in opposition to Rome. This identity later merged into that of "Protestant."

when the Protestant advance began to slow and the Catholic recovery to emerge. This unconventional breaking point is dictated by the view that the book's most important theme is not the evolution of the Imperial constitution but something that long outlived it, the growth of the religious confessions and their configuration into what may be called "the old confessional order."

9

Urban Reformations

Had I but Venice's might
Augsburg's splendor,
Nuremberg's skill,
Strasbourg's cannon,
And Ulm's money,
I would be the richest man in the world.

Traditional saying

The citizen's first duty is unrest.

Günter Grass

One day in 1524 an Augsburg ropemaker named Ott was overheard to curse "the dishonorable priests and the rich . . . , who pile up goods and money and keep the truth from us. We have always been evangelicals, and we still are today, but, truly, we have been fed many lies. If we truly followed the gospel, we would all have to be like brothers."[1] At the center of the unprecedented storm of words and deeds that broke over the German cities during the first half of the 1520s stood precisely Ott's principle: Christians follow the Gospel as brothers. In this evangelical movement, collective hopes of a better, more just future mingled with personal hopes of salvation. For this reason, and because for a while the cities became the nurseries and schoolhouses of religious change, it is hardly going too far to say that the Protestant reformation was, at least in its youth, "an urban event."[2] The cities served the whole society as concentrated points of knowledge, technology, literacy, wealth, communication, and power. In their milieus new ideas could gain a hearing and new practices support. Secure within their walls could take place the mobilization of movements for change.

I. CONTOURS OF URBAN REFORMATION

Between 1520 and about 1535 the evangelical movements in German towns and cities, large and small, northern and southern, followed a strikingly common pattern:

---

1 Thomas A. Brady, *Turning Swiss: Cities and Empire, 1450–1550*, 157. The late Hans-Christoph Rublack generously gave me this text.
2 A. G. Dickens, *The German Nation and Martin Luther*, 182.

1. the tremendous explosion of the printed word spread new ideas with unprecedented speed to reach remote audiences;
2. the convents came under attack, as the urban elites sought to repatriate their religious women, often against resistance, while the male religious communities mostly dispersed voluntarily;
3. destructive acts against sacred objects, places, and persons aimed to purify the cities' public spaces of idolatry;
4. the urban clergy, domesticated through marriage and citizenship, became full members of the urban communities; and
5. the civic magistrates acted, often under popular pressure, to control the convents, discourage acts of violence, and protect married priests against episcopal retribution.

Evangelical ideas found their first urban audiences in the elites, the educated patricians, merchants, professional men, and clergy, who by 1520 were reading and discussing Luther's ideas at home and abroad. At this earliest stage, opinions were often sharply divided. The Strasbourg ammeister (mayor) Claus Kniebis (1479–1552) wrote to Peter Butz (d. 1530) from the Diet of Nuremberg in March 1522,

> Sir Hans [Bock] and I were sitting at table with three princes, but I couldn't speak about Luther. They were all against him, including Hans Bock, and they thought he would be burnt. I feared that if I spoke up for him, they would have damned me to the flames, too. I therefore kept silence, for I fear the fire. . . . If they had tortured me, I would also have confessed. There are many, however, who are not his enemies.[3]

Spirits were just as divided at this time among the magistrates and other leading figures in Nuremberg, Augsburg, Ulm, and other southern Imperial cities.

Within several years the discussions spread into public space and engaged ordinary burghers. Now the pulpits came into play, and actions followed words: priests took wives; laymen and laywomen criticized and attacked priests and monks, convents and chapels, relics and images. As the agitation mounted, citizens organized – usually through guilds in the south and ad hoc citizens' committees in the north – and demanded that their magistrates allow free preaching of the Gospel, introduce a reform of worship, and abolish clerical privilege. Official reactions varied. At Augsburg the magistrates long resisted major changes; at Zurich, Strasbourg, and Hamburg they quickly mandated reforms. City councils protected married and heterodox priests from their bishops, suspended the prosecution of iconoclasts, ordered clergy to become citizens, and took over the administration of monastic properties. Such changes accelerated during the Peasants' War, and the symbolically supreme moment came with the magistrates' suppression of the Mass, the premier Catholic symbol and means of God's grace to His people.

By the mid-1530s such movements for religious change, and often for social change as well, had engulfed most of the free cities in both south and north. Such changes swept across almost all of the Imperial free cities, except for a few small ones, and all Hanseatic cities but one (Cologne). The visible religious and social changes progressed at blazing speeds: five years or less at Zurich, Nuremberg, and Lübeck; under

---

3 Jean Rott, *Investigationes historicae – Églises et société aux XVIe siècle – Gesammelte Aufsätze zur Kirchen- und Sozialgeschichte*, vol. 1: 112. These were important figures at Strasbourg: Butz (d. 1530) was city secretary, Hans Bock (d. 1542) held the patrician office of Stettmeister and was later father-in-law to Jacob Sturm, the city's leading politician from the late 1520s.

ten years at Strasbourg, Constance, Ulm, Hamburg, and Bremen. The teenagers of 1521, when news of Luther at Worms raced through the German lands, had become young grandmothers in 1555, when the Religious Peace of Augsburg was signed. To them the Mass was a living memory, good or bad; but to their children it was an alien, exotic rite performed by false priests for ignorant people, in fact, mostly old women.

The urban movements' speed and degree of success was governed by the participation of solid, respectable burghers, who possessed full rights of citizenship and, strongly networked through guilds or other kinds of corporate associations, engaged in a process of push-and-pull with their magistrates. They were not necessarily a numerical majority but might be a majority of those who counted. If such men (and some women) could not be mustered again and again to demand changes from the government, an urban movement could fail. This happened most famously at Cologne, the great metropolis of the Lower Rhine Valley, where the tight integration of parishes, craft associations, and merchant patriciate afforded the evangelicals no secure institutional base from which to operate. By 1530 the evangelical movement was but a memory in Cologne, which remained the seat of a major Catholic university and (since 1584) of a papal nuncio.[4] All through the age of reformations, Cologne stood as the greatest Catholic stronghold in the northwestern German lands.

If civic magistrates resisted the changes strong burgher groups pressed upon them, sooner or later those groups might seek to secure their demands with force. This did not happen at Nuremberg, where the patrician oligarchy assumed the leadership of the movement, staged a public debate between the parties, and in 1525 undertook to suppress the old religion. At Augsburg, by contrast, the magistrates began (3 August 1524) by banishing a fiery Franciscan preacher named Johannes Schilling. Three days later some 1,000 burghers gathered before the city hall and demanded Schilling's freedom. When asked whether they would support the city council, as the merchant Wilhelm Rem (1462–1529) reports, "Some said they would, others only if it was not against the Gospel, and they would be glad to swear an oath, so long as it was not against God's Word."[5] These burghers, he declares, "were good evangelicals and good Christians, as one says, but the majority of the magistrates were on the side of the priests."[6] With the help of 600 mercenary troops, the magistrates arrested and executed two old men, both weavers, and staved off the crucial decision for nearly a decade.

Some urban reformations were purely domestic affairs, others had important external implications. At Hamburg in January 1526, four parishes decided to accept in the future no parish priests appointed without their congregations' consent. Their resolve was tested in April, when the magistrates tried to bar Johann Zegenhagen (d. 1531) from preaching at St. Catherine's on the grounds that he had caused disturbance in his previous post at Magdeburg. They banished Zegenhagen as Augsburg's magistrates had banished Johannes Schilling. But at Hamburg the burghers resisted, Zegenhagen stayed, and in September the burghers protested the city council's refusal

4   A papal nuncio (officially, Apostolic Nuncio) was not a permanent diplomatic representative to a single state, as in modern times, but a representative of the pope resident either in an important capital city (Vienna, Munich, Graz) or other city (Cologne).
5   Ruth Kastner, ed., *Quellen zur Reformation 1517–1555*, 178.
6   Kastner, ed., *Quellen*, 178.

to seat the preacher at St. Catherine's. Once again the magistrates yielded, and with this capitulation the struggle in Hamburg was over.

What took only one year at Hamburg took six in the southern city of Basel, a great bastion of powerful guilds. In May 1525 the magistrates clashed with the weavers, who tried to remove their guild's lamp from St. Martin's Church with the justification, "God Himself is the light and heat of the true, passionate love of our hearts and our longing for Him and from Him."[7] The agitation continued until Christmas 1528, when all of Basel's guilds petitioned the city council for the "exclusive proclamation of the pure and true gospel" and the abolition of the Mass in order to secure "the peace of the entire city."[8] Five weeks later, 800 armed burghers surrounded city hall, locked the city gates, took over the arsenal, and demanded a final decision. Next day they stormed the cathedral and smashed the images and altars. This was the end. On 1 April 1529 Basel became officially an evangelical city.

Basel, since 1501 a full member of the Swiss Confederation, could do as it pleased without external complications. The opposite was true of the great Hanseatic city of Lübeck, where the evangelical triumph led directly to a disastrous foreign adventure. The evangelical party gained power through a peaceful coup in July 1530, ejected the patricians from the regime, and over the next ten months undertook an extensive reform of the city's religious worship, clergy, schools, and poor relief. Yet victory did not bring stability. In 1533 a merchant named Jürgen Wullenwever (ca. 1492–1537), head of the popular party, became mayor of Lübeck. Inspired by a vision of restoring Lübeck's old glory as mistress of the Hanseatic north, Wullenwever led his city into an adventure in Denmark, where he hoped to intervene in a royal election.[9] Soon, the Danish fleet appeared before Lübeck, the old patricians returned to power and made peace, and in 1537 Wullenwever went to the block at Wolfenbüttel in Brunswick. Lacking a foundation in stabile institutions, at Lübeck the evangelical cause's victory unhinged regime and policy and ruined the popular party that had brought it to power.

2. THE POWER OF THE WORD, PRINTED AND SPOKEN

The remarkable circulation of ideas, beliefs, and demands among the urban evangelical movements depended on words. They flew in every direction, traveling long distances in weeks, crossing all boundaries, and multiplying in the telling and retelling. One might say, given how thoroughly this spectacular eruption depended on printing with movable type, that the early German reformation might be characterized in terms of "justification by print alone." In 1520 the sixty-two presses operating in the German lands were concentrated in just six cities: Cologne, Nuremberg, Strasbourg, Basel, Augsburg, and Wittenberg. Except for ever-anomalous Cologne, each became a principal site of evangelical agitation, religious innovation, and, eventually, Protestant religion.

The unchallenged star of this drama of the printed word was Martin Luther. During the quarter-century of his public life, German presses may have produced

7 Peter Blickle, *Communal Reformation: The Quest for Salvation in Sixteenth-Century Germany*, 71.
8 Blickle, *Communal Reformation*, 72–3.
9 In his folly Wullenwever attacked Duke Christian of Holstein (1503–59), who as Christian III of Denmark destroyed the Catholic cause in his kingdom.

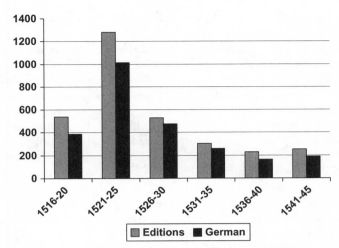

Figure 4. Printings of Luther's Writings, Total and Vernacular Editions, 1516–45 (in 5-year increments)
Source: Based on Mark U. Edwards Jr., *Printing, Propaganda, and Martin Luther.*

some 3.1 million copies of his writings, not counting whole and partial editions of his German translation of the Bible.[10] This tremendous surge peaked very early. It rose from 275 editions in 1520 to 390 in 1523 and then stabilized at about 50 editions a year after 1528. Three-quarters of the 7,000 editions of his works appeared between 1520 and 1526. Adding the writings of other evangelical reformers printed during Luther's lifetime brings a current estimate of the total volume of evangelical comment, instruction, and agitation in print to 6.3 million items produced, sold, and read.

Among the vectors of this flood, pride of place belonged to a fairly new genre, the pamphlet.[11] Easily concealed and transported, the handy pamphlet was a perfect carrier of ideas and opinions to and among a literate laity. At around eight pence it cost one-third of a journeyman's daily wage, or as much as a hen, two pounds of beef, or a pound of wax. Some 10,000 pamphlets issued from the German lands' presses between 1499 and 1530, about nine in German for every one in Latin. The absolute peak came, as with Luther's editions, in 1523.

By far the most important topic in this tsunami of print was religion, the subject of 84 percent of the 498 German titles printed in the year 1523. As the fronts formed, the two parties emulated one another in polemic savagery and racy language, in which neither had the clear advantage. They gave tit for tat. The Strasbourg Franciscan Thomas Murner (1475–1537), one of the most folksy writers of his age, attacked Luther in a satire of 1530, which portrays the reformer as "seven-headed Luther," each head labeled with an insulting epithet, such as "heresiarch" and "antichrist." Luther

10 His figures on printing do not include editions and translations published beyond the German lands.
11 The expressive modern German term, *Flugschriften* (literally, "flying writings"), is an eighteenth-century borrowing from French. See also Chapter 8.

retorted with an attack, not on Murner, but on the "seven-headed papacy" as the beast described by St. John in his Apocalypse.

While in Murner's case a defender of the old religion[12] struck the first blow, more often Luther and his followers gained and retained the initiative. Luther attacked the pope, friars, bishops, the Mass, images, relics, and indulgences; the Catholics attacked him and his followers as frauds, deceivers, egoists, disciples of the Devil, and antichrists, men degraded by lust, avarice, and pride. Though determined to give as good as they got, the Catholics nonetheless fell behind in both quantity and quality. Between 1518 and 1544, Luther alone outproduced his Catholic opponents about five to one, and the ratio worsened after 1539, when Leipzig and Dresden were taken over to the new religion, leaving Cologne the only Catholic center of big-scale printing.

The Catholic polemicists also fell behind in quality in this war of words and images. In the main, they failed to grasp the propaganda value of merging text and images and/or supplied texts that were too academic, sometimes in Latin. Most of these features can be seen in anti-Lutheran broadsheets.[13] One, called "Luther's Game of Heresy," features Luther and the Devil. Luther, clad in his friar's habit and assisted by three devils and a diabolical raven perched on his shoulder, cooks up a huge pot of vices: falsehood, unbelief, pride, envy, disobedience, heresy, blasphemy, and sexual license. Each figure has a block of text, and there are three large blocks of text at the foot of the page; a good idea, except that the texts are not coordinated with the images. The piece relied "heavily on the literacy of the reader and had an unimaginative visual message, [and] even the good ideas for propaganda were not fully exploited."[14] Even worse, the broadsheet appeared tucked into a Latin work that enumerated all the heretics since the beginnings of Christianity, hardly popular fare. The Catholic defenders did not yet understand the print culture's explosive potential.

One has only to examine one of the best evangelical efforts to see why the Catholics lost the first round in the battle of print. The "Passions of Christ and Antichrist" is a set of twenty-six woodcuts produced in May 1521 by Lucas Cranach (1472–1553) with texts by Philip Melanchthon (1497–1560), Luther's Wittenberg colleague. It juxtaposes scenes from the life of Christ with fictive moments in the life of the pope. The layout in facing images (Christ on the left, Antichrist on the right) drives home the main message, even to an illiterate: the true Christ and the false Vicar of Christ are opposites. Some pairs are brilliantly conceived. Christ wears His crown of thorns; the pope bears his triple tiara;[15] Christ refuses to be acknowledged as king of the Jews; the pope defends his lordship with sword and cannon. A particularly effective pair shows Jesus driving the money-lenders from the Temple, while the pope by means of taxes and indulgences brings the usurers back into the Church.

In the final pair, Christ ascends into heaven, the pope descends into hell. This powerful little pamphlet was both accessible and complex. It could be read as an

---

12 I use the contemporary terms "old religion" and "new religion" in a sense that survives in the German terms "old-believing" (*altgläubig*) and "new-believing" (*neugläubig*).

13 The broadsheet is a large, one-page combination of images and text.

14 Robert W. (Bob) Scribner, *For the Sake of Simple Folk: Popular Propaganda for the German Reformation*, 231.

15 The text falsely ascribes to Emperor Constantine the triple crown, which in fact evolved over nearly a millennium.

Figure 5. Seven-headed Luther

illustrated morality play, as a contrast between true and false Christianity, as a primer of anticlericalism, as a guide to papal pretensions with respect to the Holy Roman Empire, and as a meditation on the meaning of the Biblical Antichrist. The multiplicity of possible readings explains its effectiveness as propaganda: the "Passions" went through one Latin and ten German editions within a few years and set the standard for a favorite Protestant genre.

It was not literacy alone that ensured the spread of ideas. Print did not replace speech; it collaborated with and fueled the spoken word in all of its many genres – conversation, dramas, singing, group reading, prayers, and sermons. The sermon was particularly well equipped to cross the boundary between spoken and printed

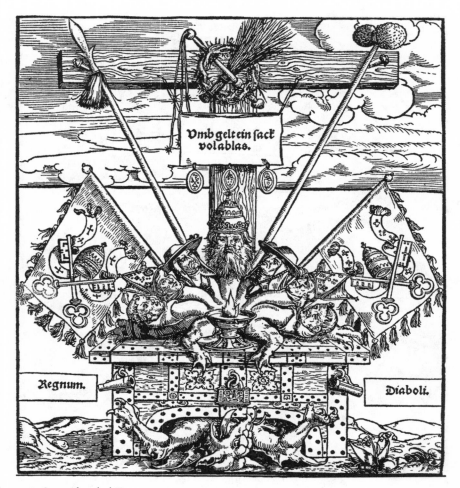

Figure 6. Seven-headed Papacy

expression. The Strasbourg preacher Mathis Zell (1477–1548) wrote in 1523 that he was now putting to paper what he already taught in person to more than three thousand persons. Locally, the evangelical movement was first and foremost a preaching revival. Often the first sign of interest in an evangelical message came when a parish or other community asked to be supplied with a preacher to proclaim "the pure Word of God."

Messages could also be acted out. The traditional time for popular theater was carnival, the season of inversion and indulgence that preceded Lent, the season of asceticism and penitence. Evangelicals mobilized the traditional carnival play to good propaganda effect. Some were extremely harsh. The plays of Nuremberg's Hans Sachs (1494–1576), the genre's most famous practitioner, pale into blandness beside those of the Bernese magistrate Niklas Manuel (1484–1530), called "Deutsch" (the German). One of Manuel's pieces, *The Corpse-Eaters*, attacks in very colloquial speech and with great violence the Church's management of relations between the

Figure 7. Luther's Game of Heresy

living and the dead. It ignores Luther's theological objections to indulgences and attacks them as a purely commercial venture. The first scene portrays the pope and his splendid court on one side of the stage and the source of their wealth, a rich man's corpse in his coffin, on the other side. The man's death benefits everyone, from the churchwarden up to the pope, who is attacked in each scene from a new point of view

Figure 8. Jesus Drives the Money-lenders from the Temple

as exploiter of the laity, as warlord, and as robber of the crusade taxes and thus an Ottoman ally. Through the scenes the pope continues his dinner, rising only to plot new outrages with his henchmen. The play closes with a prayer that proclaims the Gospel to be the only means of Christian salvation. Though technically clumsy, the play treats a highly topical theme in a most sensational way, and it was often reprinted by Swiss and south German presses.

Inversion as mockery, the soul of carnival, had many other uses, and the printers who produced evangelical pamphlets redeployed existing images against new targets. One such image was the well-known "Jewish Sow." The image shows a large sow

Figure 8. (*Continued*) The Pope Welcomes Them into the Church

suckling or being otherwise fondled and licked by Jews. It plays both on the specific character of the hog as unclean and forbidden by Jewish law, and on the more general image of the hog as filthy and unclean. Such images were to be found carved on churches and other buildings, mostly in Central Europe, since the High Middle Ages, and they also circulated in print. Evangelical publicists or printers converted this shameful image into the "Papal Sow," in which the pope rides a large sow, which he urges forward by holding a huge turd over its nose.

The image's point is to transfer the image of filth from the Jews, usurers who suck the people's blood, to the pope, who is lord of the new, Christian usurers. Evangelical pamphlets attack pope and friars overwhelmingly in terms of money

Figure 9. The Jewish Sow

and greed: the begging friars, dedicated to poverty, pick the people's pockets; the popes, vicars of Christ, live in great splendor; and the indulgence preachers, those "corpse-eaters," coin the dead into money. The mighty, mysterious energy of money had polluted and degraded the Church into a mighty engine of fraud and spiritual destruction. It threatened the entire Christian community; it endangered every household.

3. PATRICIANS, NUNS, AND MONKS

The household formed the most basic unit of the burghers' way of life. A burgher household depended on the management of its money and of its children, and the conservation of its integrity involved training for marriage, marriage itself, the payment of dowries, and management of inheritance. But not everyone married, and the wealthier burghers, like the nobles, commonly placed some daughters in convents. There they lived among their new, spiritual siblings, their "sisters," out of sight of, though usually near, their natural families, with whom their ties were never entirely broken. They did their part in the economy of salvation by praying for the souls in Purgatory, for their relatives by blood, for their sisters in religion, and for themselves.

Martin Luther, who knew first hand the ascetic life in community, condemned it as socially useless and dangerous to the soul. "I have clearly proved," he writes, "that the whole institution of the vow is fictitious both in its first principles and in its most important essentials, namely, obedience and poverty. Even though it is vowed and kept by most holy and godly men, it is really a lie, and to those who are not holy and godly it is by its very nature impious, sacrilegious, and blasphemous. What more do you want?"[16]

16   Martin Luther, *D. Martin Luthers Werke. Kritische Gesamtausgabe. Schriften*, vol. 8: 651.

Figure 10. The Papal Sow

Luther's condemnation far exceeded in vehemence and force the earlier critics of monastic life. They had demanded that bad monks and nuns should become good monks and nuns; Luther demanded that monks and nuns, bad and good, should not be tolerated at all. His attack touched in a special way the noble and merchant families, whose heads ruled the cities, and whose daughters, sisters, nieces, and aunts populated the female convents, especially those of the mendicant orders. Individual families tied themselves to particular convents in life, by giving their dowered daughters to the communities, and in death, by Mass endowments for souls and burial in conventual churches. In the convents, therefore, especially the women's houses, there converged a whole series of issues: monastic vows and ascetic life; prayers for the dead in Purgatory; the Mass; and burial in sacred spaces. Soon, spurred by the words of

Luther and others, patrician families began efforts to recover their daughters from convents, whether lax or strict. For these women the evangelical message brought not liberation, as it did for many of their male counterparts, but repatriation.

Among all the special targets of the evangelical movement in the cities, the female religious communities stand out for posing the most vigorous resistance to the campaign to abolish their communities. The most spectacular case is surely that of the Poor Clares of Nuremberg, which admitted girls and young women who, had they not come to live in religious community with one another, would have been attending the same balls and vying for the favor of the same young patrician men. The convent's prioress, the learned and redoubtable Caritas Pirckheimer (1470–1530) recorded in 1524, for which a great flood had been predicted, "experience has taught us that the stars did not indicate water as much as misery, fear and distress, and later, bloodshed. In the year noted above it happened that many things were changed by the new teachings of the Lutherans and much dissension befell the Christian faith." "And so it came to pass," she explains, "that many nuns and monks made use of such freedom and ran away from their cloisters and threw off their robes and habits; some married and did whatever they wanted. "Each day at St. Clare's," she relates, "many of the powerful as well as simple people came to their relatives who resided in our cloister. They preached to them and spoke of the new teachings and argued incessantly that the cloistered were damned and subject to temptations, and that it was not possible for them to attain salvation there. We were all damned." All of these visitors, among whom were matrons from some of Nuremberg's greatest families, "wanted to remove their children, sisters and aunts from the cloister by force and with many threats and also with many promises half of which, without doubt, they could hardly keep."[17] Soon, the day arrived – it was Corpus Christi Eve (14 June) – when "the ferocious wolves, both males and females, came to my precious lambs, entered the church, drove out all the people and locked the church door." The invaders of the cloister demanded that their young nuns be handed over, for "here their children were in the jaws of the devil, and in good conscience they could no longer allow that." To this the daughters replied, the prioress relates, "they did not want to leave the pious, holy convent. They were not in hell at all," and although begged by their own mothers, "their daughters owed them no obedience in those matters that could damage their souls."[18]

Here, on a summer day in 1524, the central theme of the Protestant reformation was acted out in a small convent. Conscience versus authority, the drama of Worms, but this time with the parties' roles reversed. The point that moved the actors, both parents and daughters, was not clerical corruption, church property, or the sins of the papacy, but the claims of conscience. Bravest of all was Katharina Ebner, now twenty years old. Six years earlier, she and her closest friend, Clara Nützel, had professed on the same day. Katharina addressed her mother, who led the patrician women come to claim their daughters: "You are a mother of my body, but not of my spirit, for you did not give me my soul. For that reason I owe you no obedience in matters which my soul opposes." Lecturing them on the Scripture, "she found errors in all their statements and told them how much their actions ran contrary to the Holy Gospel.

17   Caritas Pirckheimer, *Caritas Pirckheimer: A Journal of the Reformation Years, 1524–1528*, 11–12.
18   Pirckheimer, *Journal*, 89–90.

Afterward outside the men said they had never heard anything like that their whole lives. She had just spoken the whole hour without interruption. Not a word was wasted." When at length Caritas Pirckheimer agreed, as she must, to release the young women to their parents, Katharina Ebner spoke up once more: "Here I stand and will not yield. No one shall be able to force me out. If I am removed by force, however, it shall never be by my will in eternity. I will appeal to God in heaven and to all the world on earth."[19] Everyone in Nuremberg, of course, had heard the story of Luther at Worms. Then, with much quarreling, scuffling, and noises of dragging over the children's howls and cries, each was dragged away by four men.

Scenes comparable in meaning if not in publicity or scope unfolded at contemporary Strasbourg. Ammeister Claus Kniebis told the prioress of the Dominican convent of St. Nicolaus-in-Undis of his desire to remove his 14-year-old daughter, Margarethe, from the house, for "his wish is that she live in his house for a time and test herself in the world."[20] Margarethe reminded her father, "I've said to you many times that I don't want to leave, that I don't want to be in the world. If you force me, God will forgive me, for my will is never again to be in the world." Angered by her show of will, Kniebis retorted, "even if you don't want to leave, you must leave. You must leave, even if you do so in the Devil's name." "In his name I won't leave," Margarethe responded, "but in God's name and in obedience to God's will. For you brought me into this house and offered me to God with your own hands."[21] Five months later, when Kniebis returned to claim his daughter, the prioress submitted. "This is your daughter," she said to him, "whom I give from my hand into your hand, from my care into your care. Please God, that you care for her well. I give you a good, devout, innocent child. Please God, that you keep her so, and if you do not, then we are absolved of responsibility before God and before you."[22] Nine days later, Margarethe was fetched home; three years later she was married to a well-to-do cloth merchant's son. Her community, however, and two other Dominican convents resisted heavy pressure to convert and disband. The magistrates, declining to close the houses with force, sent the preacher Martin Bucer (1491–1551) to convert them, expelled their confessor from the city, and forbade the nuns to allow anyone else to preach to them. The nuns were forced to attend the preaching of Bucer, an "apostate from the [Dominican] order," and were threatened with dissolution if they refused.[23] They did refuse, and yet they were not dissolved, because "neither the nuns nor the people of Strasbourg wanted them to. The members of the ruling class continued to have close connections to these institutions through the sixteenth century, often despite their own religious conversions."[24]

The Strasbourg Dominicans' story, like that of Nuremberg's Franciscan women, is quintessentially a tale of resistance by women, those who, by contemporary norms, should not resist. The nuns resisted because, in their view, the evangelicals had nothing to offer them better than the religion they knew. This is clear from another

19 Pirckheimer, *Journal*, 90–2.
20 Thomas A. Brady and Katherine G. Brady, "Documents on Communalism and the Control of Women at Strasbourg in the Age of the Reformation," 210.
21 Brady and Brady, "Documents," 210.
22 Brady and Brady, "Documents," 212.
23 Amy E. Leonard, *Nails in the Wall: Catholic Nuns in Reformation Germany*, 80.
24 Leonard, *Nails in the Wall*, 155. Two of the communities survived until the French Revolution.

Dominican story, this one from Augsburg. In 1523 the organist Bernhard Rem (b. after 1472) hectored his sister, Katharina (b. after 1475), and a second sister to abandon their useless way of life. Katharina knew just what to reply. "There you have also come with many good words," she retorts, "and wanted to lead us astray and makes us despondent. You should not think that we are so foolish that we place our hope in the convent and in our own works. Rather we place our hope in God. He is the true lord and rewarder of all things. Him do we serve more willingly in the convent than in the world, with the grace and help of God."[25] Katharina Rem, too, was an evangelical, no less than her brother a follower of the Gospel. Such resisters rejected not the Gospel but Luther's argument that vows and a life of celibacy were both useless and contrary to the Gospel. This is why the strongest resistance came from the strictest communities of the mendicant orders.

The male monastic houses displayed, on the whole, far less resistance to dissolution, though they, of course, had better chances than the women did outside the cloister. Chiefly at risk were the houses of the four mendicant orders: Franciscans, Dominicans, Carthusians, and Austin Friars. They were easier targets than the older abbeys and priories, many of which possessed considerable property and enjoyed powerful protectors outside the city. In general, magistrates proceeded with caution, but in most cities sooner or later the time for decision arrived. Once the magistrates asserted their own competence over the definition of true religion, in most places the end swiftly followed. At Nuremberg, following the public disputation of 1524, the magistrates decided to close all the monasteries within one year. The Bernese took a similar step in 1528 following an important disputation between the two parties' theologians.

The story of the urban convents "dramatized and focused the divisions within the elite," from whose daughters the urban convents traditionally recruited.[26] The evangelical attack on the ascetic life as social parasitism and a false path to personal salvation offered the nuns' families a resolution of the tension between two teachings of the Church: the sanctity of the ascetic, celibate life and the sanctity of marriage and the procreation of the race. The attack on the female communities signaled the immense power of the ideal of the patriarchal household, of which the urban upper class was the chief guardian and greatest beneficiary. But it also expressed a new attitude toward the world of sex and money, and hence toward the Church. No class felt more keenly than did the patricians and other rich burghers that if the world, and hence the Church, were to continue, the ancient ascetic ideal must be revised with respect to the three evangelical counsels, poverty, chastity, and obedience. In effect, it was proposed to revise ancient Christianity's great compromise with the world, which had led to a distinction between two ways of Christian life, strict for those "in religion," moderate for those "in the world." Henceforth, this dual standard could give way to a single standard, a burghers' standard, for managing sexuality, property, and authority. The new standard took its model from the burghers' household rather than from the cloister, and while Luther's movement did not create the new model, it certainly removed obstacles to its elevation. The subsequent history of

25 Merry Wiesner-Hanks, ed., *Convents Confront the Reformation: Catholic and Protestant Nuns in Germany*, 29.
26 Lyndal Roper, *The Holy Household: Women and Morals in Reformation Augsburg*, 210.

Catholic reformation shows that accepting this ideal was not irresistible at the time; the history of the European bourgeoisie suggests that in the long run it probably was.

4. BURGHERS AND PRIESTS

Ordinary respectable burghers did not often send their daughters to convents. For them the evangelical attack on the clergy and its ideal of celibacy found its way into their households from another forum, the parish congregation. Reformist writers had long argued that congregations would be better served by a married clergy. An affair at Worms in 1524 illustrates how the evangelical movement radicalized this idea. The people of St. Michael's parish expelled their priest, Johann Leininger, and installed a married ex-monk in his place. Leininger complained to the dean of Worms Cathedral, who spoke to the city council, which in turn called on the parish to account for its action. The congregation's response offers a rare insight into relations between pastor and people at the parish level in these times. Leininger, the parishioners replied, lived in sin with a woman by whom he had a son and had for a time installed her in the post of parish sexton. This gave outsiders the opportunity to ridicule with the double-entendre that "the parson of St. Michael's sleeps with his sexton."[27] Worst of all, when a gravely ill woman of the parish asked for the Sacrament, Leininger said he would not come until he was paid the customary Mass-penny. It was Leininger's bad fortune that over at St. Magnus the priest was preaching that every Christian community had the power, indeed the responsibility, to elect its own pastor. Hearing this, the people at St. Michael's decided to remove Leininger and elect in his place another, married priest, who honorably served his flock. Their ideal came straight down from post-Basel reformism, but their actions belong to the evangelical movement of the 1520s. It was a matter of agency. Parishioners acted where their magistrates failed to act, and in their acts such phrases "the gospel pure and simple" and "godly law," innocuous in themselves, became fighting words. The end of this fight would be the communalization and domestication of priests.

Where the evangelicals succeeded, the urban priests simply moved from episcopal into civic jurisdiction. By his willingness to take the oath of citizenship, the priest signaled his will to become a burgher and share, often as member of a guild, communal privileges and duties. By his willingness to marry, the priest signaled his adherence to the evangelical movement. In the past, citizen-priests were not unknown but rare; the evangelical movement made them the norm. At Strasbourg the city council, which in 1452 had first mandated citizenship for its priests, ordered in March 1523 that the clergy must "join a guild, just like other burghers . . . [and] bear all the burdens of a citizen, except that they are freed from the duty to ride [i.e., travel] in the city's service, and they may pay a fee in lieu of service in the night watch."[28] Thirty-five of them, including all future leaders of Strasbourg's evangelical church, obeyed by the end of 1524; during the Peasants' War another 113 clergymen discovered compliance to be a reasonable act. Only the cathedral chapter stood on its immunity and remained aloof.

27 Robert W. Scribner, "Preachers and People in German Towns," in Robert W. Scribner, *Popular Culture and Popular Movements in Reformation Germany*, 123.
28 Bernd Moeller, "Kleriker als Bürger," 45. These stipulations were added to the text of a law first issued in 1322.

After so many generations of clerical immunity from secular law, compliant priests felt a need to justify their actions. In August 1523 Martin Bucer declared to his fellow priests that they should, "true to their new name and estate, zealously devote themselves to nothing else than the common good and spiritual welfare of others."[29] Wolfgang Capito (1478–1541), provost of St. Thomas's chapter, declared that "it is a characteristic of the Christian to live in community and not to seek a separate way [of life]."[30] At Zurich, Huldrych Zwingli taught much the same. Although Christ was Lord and King over all lords, he wrote, "He nonetheless gave us an example, that we should all help one another to bear the common burden and also give the emperor his denarius [Matt. 17: 24–27]. Which example the clergy refuse to learn. They do not help the common people pay taxes . . . or sustain the common good. They claim that they are exempt."[31] In these preachers' views, community was local. They preached and practiced Johann Geiler's ideal of participation (*participatio*), but with an all-important revision, for in their version the local church claimed to need nothing from a Church Universal. The communalization of the clergy became a hallmark of urban reformations.

As with the commune, so with the household, for once the priests' sacramental powers were denied, there remained no barrier to their becoming husbands. Domestication and repatriation of the clergy (to which the nuns also belonged) defined at the deepest level an evangelical defense of the household's sexual and spiritual integrity. So did communalization, for the new police of sexuality also targeted the women who sold or gave illicit sex. Zwingli, accused of abetting adultery, retorted that he was being slandered by the prostitutes who, "by virtue of God's Word . . . have been expelled from the city, and naturally these whores don't leave the city without cursing us mightily."[32] All have been expelled, he reported, first "the public whores who are known to have consorted with adulterers, then those who live from the trade,"[33] though he said nothing about their customers. Moreover, such laws proved difficult to enforce. In June 1534 a group of burghers asked the city council of Strasbourg to suppress the brothels in their neighborhood, "in order that their honest wives and children not be so deeply offended."[34] The councilors decided that "the houses there shall be abolished and no others allowed," but – a second thought – added that "we should discuss whether a house should be established at another place, where it will give least offense, in order to supply necessity and prevent greater evils. . . . The world must be allowed a bit to be the world."[35]

The power of granting of citizenship lay entirely in the magistrates' hands. Clerical marriage, however, meant conflict with the bishop, for "the marriage of a priest was a much more unambiguous mark than the vague charging of 'Lutheran' preaching."[36] It was the act by which priests provoked episcopal punishment, to which the local

29   Martin Bucer, *Deutsche Schriften*, vol. 1: 54, ll. 28–30.
30   Wolfgang Capito, *An den hochwirdigen Fürsten vnd herren Wilhelmen Bischoffen zu Straßburg vnd Landtgrauen zu Elsas. Entschuldigung*, iiiv.
31   Huldrych Zwingli, *Huldrych Zwinglis sämtliche Werke*, vol. 4: 306.
32   Kastner, ed., *Quellen*, 366, n. 119.
33   Kastner, ed., *Quellen*, 366, n. 119.
34   Kastner, ed., *Quellen*, 387, n. 123.
35   Kastner, ed., *Quellen*, 387, n. 123.
36   Stephen E. Buckwalter, *Die Priesterehe in Flugschriften der frühen Reformation*, 14.

authorities had to respond and resist, for if the old concubinage had gained a certain legitimacy from the Church's recognition of natural marriage and, often enough, local opinion, Christian marriage for priests was another thing entirely. It meant open, public defiance of the canon law and ecclesiastical authority from which there was no returning.

The priests who married all knew this, but they also knew that for generations reformists had been recommending a married, salaried clergy for the parishes. Priests who married forced their magistrates to decide whether to protect them against episcopal punishment. Public, demonstrative marriage was "a provocative innovation" by the priests, and, if successful, it was contagious.[37] At Strasbourg, Mathis Zell, first to marry, touched off a wave of marriages that peaked in January 1524, encouraged by rumblings from the congregations and the regime's hesitancy to act before the Diet rose at Nuremberg. Even when the regime officially "approved the bishop's efforts to punish the married priests, it did nothing to aid the spiritual jurisdiction to this end."[38] The bishop, after all, resided at Saverne; the priests' supporters were agitating within the city's walls.

Many pamphlets appeared for clerical marriage, some against. Martin Luther might well say in a reflective moment, "if you are married ... for this you are neither saved nor damned; if you are unmarried, you are also for this neither saved nor damned. This is all free, free."[39] Notions of freedom hardly belonged, however, in the urban cockpits where in the early 1520s the immediate fate of the new faith would be decided. Here it was laid on with hammer and tongs. And with good reason, for the vehemence with which the evangelical pamphlets charged the old faith's clergy with whoredom and praised clerical marriage as chaste makes it likely "that they had to convince an audience who believed the contrary."[40] No one stated the case for clerical marriage more forthrightly or with simpler elegance than did Katharina Schütz Zell (1497–1562), daughter of a master cabinet-maker at Strasbourg.[41] On 3 December in Strasbourg's cathedral, Martin Bucer presiding, she married Mathis Zell (1477–1548), son of a Kaysersberg vintner and now pastor of the cathedral parish. In the following year the 26-year-old Schütz felt compelled to defend in print her unusual marriage to a priest. That clergymen may marry, she writes, "is taught in Holy Scripture in both the Old and New Testament, not in obscure but in clear, plain language, so that even children and fools can read and understand it."[42] Why, then, does the rule of celibacy exist? Schütz begins her answer with the burghers' favorite complaints: money, sex. She targets the "whoring tax" (the fine priests paid to the bishop for concubinage). "If a priest has a wife, he behaves like any other honest, pious burgher, and he pays the bishop no tax for it, since God has allowed him to be free," whereas "if they have whores they become bondsmen to the popes and bishops."[43] Her second target is "the unchaste chastity, the diluvian, sodomistic, noachistic whoredom," which popes and

37 Buckwalter, *Die Priesterehe*, 300.
38 Buckwalter, *Die Priesterehe*, 237.
39 Buckwalter, *Die Priesterehe*, 301.
40 Buckwalter, *Die Priesterehe*, 300.
41 This is the woman also known as Katharina Zell. It was very common for married women to be called not by their husbands' but by their own names, to which, at least in the south, the feminine ending "in" was often added.
42 Katharina Schütz Zell, *Katharina Schütz Zell, vol. 2: The Writings. A Critical Edition*, 34.
43 Schütz Zell, *The Writings*, 35.

bishops "do not punish . . . but have protected."[44] The laity are now resolved, she adds, no longer to "tolerate such whoresons of priests in their midst."[45]

Schütz's second line of argument repeats another classic point of the fifteenth-century reformists. Married priests will also be more effective pastors, she declares, for they "would be obliged to punish adultery with great severity," whereas now people say, "if I should not do it, why does my pastor do it? If he will forbid it to me, he must first be free of it himself."[46] Schütz adds from her own experience of marriage to a priest, "I had made up my mind not to marry, but then I witnessed the great fear, the raging opposition, and the great lewdness. When I nevertheless took a husband, I meant to give heart to and show the way to all Christians, as I hope to have done."[47] In defense of her marriage, Schütz attacks the priests as greedy, sexually (and not only heterosexually) licentious, and without authority as pastors, against whom and against their concubines the legitimate, respectable, and sexually exclusive household ought to be defended.

By no means did all burghers agree with Katharina Schütz's advocacy for clerical marriage. In the spring of 1524 a controversy broke out at Strasbourg over whether priests might marry. Augustin Drenss (d. 1552), a respectable master in the gardeners' guild, complained to the city council against the wedding of his sister, Margarethe, to Dr. Caspar Hedio, the cathedral preacher (and successor to Geiler). This had taken place with the complicity of Ammeister Claus Kniebis and Augustin's (and the bride's) mother, Agnes. The gardener demanded that his sister "give up the priest and marry a good, honest citizen," for clergymen "are forbidden to marry not only by local law and custom, but also by the laws according to which Christendom has lived for a thousand years and more."[48] Otherwise, Drenss warned, "if it should happen that it were considered proper and permissible for any priest or monk to take with impunity and by fraud and trickery a child or other relation from a respectable citizen, without his knowledge and against his will, that would be a scandalous thing. What that might lead to, my lords can well imagine."[49]

Agnes Drenss responded to her son's charge by saying that Dr. Hedio had courted her daughter, Margarethe, "as a pious, upright gentleman ought to do," and she hoped her son would come to recognize "that holy matrimony is permitted and even recommended by God to everyone, and that just because the clergy have been forbidden to marry, scandal and vice have flourished and flourish still."[50] This was the standard evangelical argument against celibacy: marriage is God's universal restraint on human concupiscence. Son and mother, to be sure, upheld the same idea, the integrity and security of the Christian household, but differed drastically as to meaning and means: for him the household was threatened by clerical marriage, for her by clerical celibacy.

If the integrity of the burgher household lay at the center of the struggle for clerical marriage, then the integrity of the civic community lay at the heart of the

---

44 Schütz Zell, *The Writings*, 36.
45 Schütz Zell, *The Writings*, 37.
46 Schütz Zell, *The Writings*, 37–8.
47 Schütz Zell, *The Writings*, 39–40.
48 Thomas A. Brady, "'You Hate Us Priests': Anticlericalism, Communalism, and the Control of Women at Strasbourg in the Age of the Reformation," 214.
49 Brady, "'You Hate Us Priests,'" 214.
50 Brady, "'You Hate Us Priests,'" 223–4.

war against idols. It began with iconoclasm, attacks on images, common events during the heyday of the urban reformation in the 1520s. The chief theorist of iconoclasm was the Franconian Andreas Bodenstein von Karlstadt (1480–1541), Luther's sponsor for the doctorate at Wittenberg. In *On the Removal of Images* (January 1522), Karlstadt denied the common belief that pictures are the Bible of the illiterate and defended the absolute and exclusive hegemony of the Word as the link between the human condition and God's justifying grace. "Is it not truly a papist teaching," he writes, "and prompting of the Devil to say that Christ's sheep may use forbidden and deceitful books and examples? Christ says: My sheep listen to my voice. He does not say: They see my image or the images of the saints."[51] "Even if I might admit that the laity could learn something useful of salvation from images," Karlstadt the Biblicist argues, "nevertheless I could not permit what is contrary to scriptural prohibitions and against God's will. Scripture clearly states that God hates the pictures which the papists call books."[52] He calls on the temporal rulers to command the purging of the churches, for "by divine right they may force and compel priests to expel deceitful and damaging things."[53]

Because advocacy of iconoclasm struck at the heart of Catholic piety, it could not go unchallenged. When the Catholic publicist Hieronymus Emser (1478–1527), a Swabian from Ulm and another of Luther's teachers, took pen in April 1522 to defend the religious value of images, he deployed the standard argument: images, permitted by natural law and by the Old and New Testaments, are useful aids to meditation and teachers of the illiterate. Emser did not yet understand, however, that the polemical definition of "idolatry" was being expanded from images in the strict sense to mean any object – images, practices, money, and persons – that competed for the attention the Christian owed to God alone. The views of two Strasbourg writers illustrate this expansion. The nobleman Mathis Wurm von Geudertheim argued in 1523 that "we should have no visible images and we should not represent any spiritual pictures for we cannot see a likeness of God. He speaks to us in our hearts through his holy speech, so he must be understood only spiritually."[54] The truck-gardener Clement Ziegler (ca. 1480–1535) went further in his *Short List and Extract from the Bible in Which One Can Learn What Is Idolatry* (1524). He collected Old and New Testament texts to demonstrate that God "said we should not make any images nor pray before them (Levit. 25),"[55] for He is not to be worshipped by means of material objects but only through prayer and service (Matt. 4). Images, things, practices, and persons, all could be idols.

The evangelical burghers who invaded churches understood quite well the expanded notion of "idol." They heckled preachers during sermons, defaced sacred images, destroyed relics, and desecrated holy objects by, among other acts, urinating and defecating in sacred vessels. Sometimes they terrorized their priests. On

51 Bryan D. Mangrum and Giuseppe Scavizzi, eds., *A Reformation Debate: Karlstadt, Emser, and Eck on Sacred Images. Three Treatises in Translation*, 26–7. He attacks the teaching of Pope Gregory I (r. 590–604) that images are the "Bible of the poor" (*Biblia pauperum*).
52 Mangrum and Scavizzi, eds., *A Reformation Debate*, 27, slightly revised.
53 Mangrum and Scavizzi, eds., *A Reformation Debate*, 37.
54 Miriam Usher Chrisman, *Conflicting Visions of Reform: German Lay Propaganda Pamphlets, 1519–1530*, 143 (translation slightly revised).
55 Chrisman, *Conflicting Visions of Reform*, 164.

Christmas Day, 1524, Jacob Megerich, pastor at Our Lady's Church in Memmingen, was incensing the altars. "As I went to St. George's altar," he reports,

> a great murmur arose from the Lutheran women and men, . . . [who] drove me into the sacristy with great violence and there reviled and scolded me with their fists and many words of abuse, beat me about the head and shoulders with their fists kicked me in my side and threw me down onto my hip, pelted me with stones in the sacristy, smashed and tore out the window panes, damaged the picture on the retable, overturned the altar light, broke off and carried away the candles on the altar.[56]

Megerich reports that the crowd ravaged the church for two hours, and "if Mayor Hans Keller and six town councilors had not arrived, I would have been struck dead in the sacristy."[57] He had to pay for official protection, for "I had to promise the Lutherans that I would afterwards present myself before the worthy town council and dispute with the preacher Christoph Schappeler."[58]

Idols and idolatry seemed to touch everyone and everything, and Nuremberg's Hans Sachs warned that all were implicated in the evil. The clergy, he wrote in *The Wittenberg Nightingale Now Heard Everywhere* (1523), had strayed by

> becoming monks, nuns, and pastors, wearing habits [and] tonsures, [and] screaming day and night in church at matins, prime, terce, vespers, and compline; with vigils, fasting, lengthy prayers, . . . flagellation, kneeling, bowing, nodding, genuflection; with ringing bells, organ playing, relics, candles, carrying flags, . . . blessing bells, lighting lamps, selling grace; [and by] blessing churches, wax, salt, and water.[59]

The laity, for their part, had strayed from the Gospel:

> with offerings and lighting candles; with pilgrimage and worshipping saints; fasting in the evening, then celebrating the next day; confession routinely; with confraternities and rosaries, indulgences, missing mass, the kiss of peace, viewing relics; by buying masses and building churches; equipping the altar with expensive vessels; making French votive images, velvet vestments, golden chalices, monstrances, [and] silver figures.[60]

The civic magistrates had to bend willy-nilly with the tide of sentiment against idolatry. In 1520 Zurich's regime beheaded Uly Anders from the Toggenburg for blasphemy, a capital crime, after he destroyed a painted crucifix with the words, "the idols bring nothing, and they will help nothing."[61] By 1522 the preaching of Zwingli and others had "inspired no other actions in Zurich as immediate, as violent,

---

56 R. W. Scribner, "Anticlericalism and the Cities," 148n. 2.
57 Scribner, "Anticlericalism and the Cities," 148n. 2.
58 Scribner, "Anticlericalism and the Cities," 148n. 2. Within weeks Schappeler would become co-author of the *Twelve Articles of the Swabian Peasantry*. See Chapter 10.
59 Paul Russell, *Lay Theology in the Reformation. Popular Pamphleteers in Southwest Germany, 1521–1525*, 172.
60 Russell, *Lay Theology*, 172–3.
61 Lee Palmer Wandel, *Voracious Idols and Violent Hands: Iconoclasm in Reformation Zurich, Strasbourg, and Basel*, 53n. 2. The Toggenburg, the upper valley of the Thur River, was the homeland of Huldrych Zwingli, principal reformer of Zurich. It lay in the prince-abbey (and in the modern canton) of St. Gallen.

and as widespread as the attacks on the idols."[62] The magistrates did what magistrates do best, they temporized. By 1524, however, the pressure to purify had grown too strong to resist, and the magistrates permitted the removal of images, but a few days later they decided "to do away with the images or idols in all places where they are worshipped. . . . And the goods and expenses that have been laid upon these images should be turned to the poor, needy human beings, who are the true image of God."[63]

Attacking symbols rather than persons is the urban reformation's hallmark, for it testified to a sense of distance between spiritual realities and their material and personal representation. In this burghers differed from country people, whose religious life sprang from a sense of interconnectedness among cosmos, sacrality, and fortune. The burghers might and sometimes did qualify or even deny the interpenetration of the invisible and visible worlds. The targets of their ire varied accordingly. Farmers knew precisely that their enemies were the seigneurs, lay or clerical, who claimed to be their lords; burghers could believe that their foe was the far-off pope who seemed to control the world through money. The farmer needed protection from nature, the burgher from the market, each, in other words, from the respective source of his livelihood.

It is of the greatest importance to our understanding of the stormy years of the early Protestant reformation that at some deep level these two mentalities represented separate redactions of a single worldview. This is hardly surprising, for the cities sustained their numbers by turning village folk into burghers, and the humbler burghers retained much in common with their rural ancestors and kinfolk.

Finally, the urban reformation was not a mass movement, nor did it anywhere mobilize all burghers or even majorities among them. What it did, and did effectively, was to mobilize within the brief span of fifteen years groups of respectable citizens strong enough to push through, with clerical inspiration and sometimes leadership, their demands for change. The methods continued, true, those of the civic political movements' bodies of earlier times, but their program, however strongly it drew upon fifteenth-century ideas, bore a radically spiritual, desacralizing justification no previous urban movements had possessed. Their actions melded for a while social and individual strands of grievances and goals into a powerful but unstable religious mentality. One of its two strands carried a social vision of Christians as a spiritual family living in justice, equality, and love, to whom faith was the handmaiden of love, and for whom striving for holiness through service marked the path to salvation. The other strand held forth a spiritual vision of the individual living in godliness and obedience to the Scriptures, to whom love was the product of faith, and for whom the key to salvation was the unmerited, unmediated grace of God.

62 Wandel, *Voracious Idols*, 62, slightly altered.
63 Wandel, *Voracious Idols*, 97.

10

A Revolution of the Common Man

> Injustice, poverty, slavery, ignorance – these may be cured by reform or revolution. But men do not live only by fighting evils. They live by positive goals, individual and collective, a vast variety of them, seldom predictable, at times incompatible.
>
> Isaiah Berlin

Between 1524 and 1526 the southern and central German lands experienced the greatest rural insurrection in European history. Whether conceived as "the greatest natural event of the German state"[1] or as "the first attempt of the popular masses to create a unified national state from below,"[2] the Peasants' War was a moment of decision. The shocked reactions to it provoked a debate among the German rulers about Luther's movement – was it the cause of or the remedy for the upheaval? – and thereby initiated the transformation of the popular evangelical movements into the Protestant reformation. The insurrection itself has been called "a revolution of the common man."[3]

The ability of farmers, joined sometimes by burghers and miners, to carry out a large-scale insurrection depended fundamentally on their experience of communal government. Enabled by this heritage, in the first decades of the sixteenth century there arose a movement for village rights, against serfdom, and in favor of stronger governance with popular participation on a territorial level. The rebels justified their demands by an appeal to a "godly law" taught by the Bible, which, though it gained vigor from the religious ferment in the cities and towns, was actually older than Luther's movement. Their movement resonated with the general mood of political reformism in the Empire, which rose to its peak in 1524–25. Although their revolution was not in any sense "Lutheran," for a moment the movements interacted in what seemed to many observers a single revolutionary wave.

1 Leopold von Ranke, *Deutsche Geschichte im Zeitalter der Reformation*, vol. 2: 126 (Bk III, ch. 6).
2 Max Steinmetz, "Theses on the Early Bourgeois Revolution in Germany, 1476–1535," 17.
3 "The common man" (*der gemeine Mann*) was a contemporary name for those who, because of their status, lack of noble lineage, or wealth, were considered by others to be unfit for participation in governance.

I. THE MAKING OF A REVOLUTION – 1525

The Peasants' War was the culmination of a generation of rural conspiracies in the southwest. It began in 1493 with an Upper Rhenish conspiracy that flew the sign of the laced farmers' boot, the Bundschuh, from which the conspiracy took its name. In such groups first appeared a new slogan, "the godly law." In the heavens would appear the sign. The astrologer Johann Lichtenberger (1440–1503) had predicted that 1524 would witness a great mutation in things. He was not wrong. In summer an anti-seigneurial revolt erupted in the southern Black Forest. Over the following winter and into the spring revolution spread into the Upper Rhine, Swabia, and Franconia, long deeply fragmented hotbeds of rural revolt, and thence northward into Hesse and Thuringia and southeastward across the Austrian duchies to the borders of Hungary. Revolt spilled over the language lines into Romance-speaking villages in Lorraine and Slavic-speaking ones in Carinthia and Carniola. Over this zone regional armies of rebels sprang into being, six each in Upper Swabia and Franconia, and one in Thuringia, of which the largest counted perhaps 10,000–12,000 fighters. They swore oaths, unfurled banners, armed themselves, called on burghers and miners to join them, and were determined to teach nobles and clergy the justice of their demands. Sometimes they established their headquarters in towns, such as Memmingen in Upper Swabia, Heilbronn in Franconia, and Mühlhausen in Thuringia. By Easter 1525 perhaps 300,000 rebels lay under arms; by high summer most of their formations had either been defeated in battle (Alsace, Württemberg, Franconia, and Thuringia), dispersed without major fighting (Salzburg, Styria, Tyrol), or pacified through negotiations (Upper Swabia, Baden). About a third of the rebels – 130,000 by a contemporary estimate, somewhat fewer by modern ones – were shot, cut down, blasted, skewered, smashed, hanged, or tortured to death. Most were farmers, though in the ranks stood also burghers, miners, priests, officials, professional soldiers, and a few noblemen.

The causes of this insurrection can be inferred from the numerous lists of grievances and demands that were composed all across the affected regions. Their archetype, the *Twelve Articles of the Swabian Peasantry*, was drafted around 1 March 1525 at Memmingen in Upper Swabia by a priest and a local furrier. Circulated widely and in many local redactions, the document portrayed a way of life assaulted by the seigneurs' fiscal pressure and by competition for land generated by rising rural populations. Most numerous are grievances about what may be attributed to economic matters. Some arose from the penetration of the countryside by market relations, as when seigneurs tried to appropriate the village commons, which yielded such marketable commodities as timber, livestock, and fish. Less numerous are grievances against the wild game, which the lords protected for hunting and forbade the farmers to kill. Bears, wolves, and aurochs (a huge, black wild ox) still roamed the land, and one wild boar overnight could make a mire of a planted garden.

Grievances classifiable as political aimed to decouple local governance from seigneurial rights in human labor and land. They targeted serfdom, the long-term decline of which made it all the more onerous and unbearable. While it was burdensome but not dishonorable to be unfree when most of your fellows were unfree, it was dishonorable when your neighbors were free, and you could not move when and where or marry whom you wanted. In addition, as the economy recovered seigneurs attempted to reimpose legal servility, a kind of "second serfdom," on their tenants. Their agents scoured charters for evidence of lapsed obligations that could be restored. Theirs was a law inscribed in writing, against which the peasants' customary law, the ancestors' "good old law," afforded no defense.

When custom had failed to defend them, the peasants discovered the "godly law," the oldest and greatest of all laws. It trumped the seigneurs' customary law and charters, at least in their eyes, because the Bible, holiest of all charters of liberties, prescribed it. The godly law expressed not a traditional belief in original peasant liberty, nourished by grandfathers' tales, but a decree of God, Who willed all to be free, and Who had sent His only beloved Son to pay the price of their freedom. Against the seigneur's documents, God's law decreed that no man should own another. Article 3 of the *Twelve Articles* planted the case for universal freedom on this spot: "It has until now been the custom for the lords to own us as their property. This is deplorable, for Christ redeemed and bought us all with His precious blood, the lowliest shepherd as well as the greatest lord, with no exceptions . . . the Bible proves that we are free and [we] want to be free."[4] Christ's death on the cross had purchased universal freedom for His kinsmen and -women, rescuing them from bondage both to sin and death and to other men. One consequence of this equality, another article stipulates, is that "What the lords possess is to be held according to the agreement between the lord and the peasants."[5] The *Twelve Articles* gave Biblical justification for the culture of equality, harmony, consent, and negotiation that made local life possible by restraining egoism and promoting collaboration and solidarity. The authors meant it to be generally valid for everyone, not just for peasants. Indeed, in 1525 their armies invited lords and princes to enter their associations as brothers. Egalitarian communalism was a powerful idea, but it did not solve the practical problems of winning the struggle.

2. REBEL FORCES — THE ARMIES

The rebel armies took part in at least 60 military engagements: 13 pitched battles, 19 skirmishes, 11 raids and ambushes, 6 sieges, 7 storms of walled places, and 4 bombardments. They commonly organized themselves into companies under captains and subunits under sergeants, much like professional lansquenets. The rebel troops elected their officers and their officials: a paymaster, baggage master, a master of spoils, a master gunner over the artillery, and a wagon master to manage transportation and war wagons (a borrowing from the Hussites). Each army also possessed a chancery – several seals survive to attest this – and one or more chaplains.

Most of the rebels lacked experience with weapons, and though some had served in territorial militias, a bare familiarity with a simple defensive weapon was not much by lansquenet standards. Some professionals served in their ranks and fought either for pay or gratis. One of them, Hans Müller of Bulgenbach (d. 1525), a Black Forest man and veteran campaigner in France, was "most eloquent and forward of speech – he had no equal as an orator: God had clearly provided [the peasants] with a capable man."[6] During the second half of May 1525, he led the Hegau army from west of Lake

4 Günther Franz, ed., *Quellen zur Geschichte des Bauernkrieges*, 176.
5 Franz, ed., *Quellen zur Geschichte des Bauernkrieges*, 178.
6 Tom Scott and Bob (Robert W.) Scribner, eds., *The German Peasants' War. A History in Documents*, 233, no. 107a.

Constance over the Black Forest to besiege the city of Freiburg im Breisgau. Before his beheading he declared "that if things had gone their way the Hegau peasants would have allied with the Swiss peasants."[7]

Nobles, too, rode with the rebel armies, whether voluntarily or under coercion is not always easy to tell. The wily Götz von Berlichingen would have served the Palatine elector against the rebels, he said after the fact, had his mother-in-law and his pregnant wife not destroyed a summons that came from Heidelberg. The leaders of the Odenwald army then "persuaded" Götz, he later alleged, to serve with them. They had him so closely watched that "if God had come down from heaven, He would not have been able to speak to me without ten to twelve standing around to listen." As the Swabian League's army approached the rebels near Würzburg, Götz slipped away, leaving 5,000 corpses of "evil folk" – his comrades in arms – on the battlefield.[8]

While the urban magistrates everywhere stood against the rebels, not a few common burghers favored their cause. Some served in the ranks, others helped to open the gates of towns to the rebel forces. This happened in the middling free city of Heilbronn in Franconia, which the Odenwald army occupied on Easter Tuesday (18 April 1525). The Strasbourg magistrate Jacob Sturm wrote an eyewitness account of how Heilbronn burghers, "especially the women," forced the magistrates to open the gates to the rebels. Their commander, an innkeeper named Jörg Metzler from Ballenberg, "posted a placard ordering all citizens and journeymen who want to join the army to assemble at one of the gates. The council has to let depart anyone who will."[9] When Metzler's men marched out of Heilbronn, the mayor wept at the gate to see his fellow citizens stream out with them.

Insurrection was men's work; women managed things at home. But not always. Margarete Renner, known as "the Black Courtier," whose husband was steward to the Teutonic Knights, served with Jäcklin Rohrbach's Neckar Valley army. Something of a wise woman knowledgeable about magic, she "continually and often consoled the band that they should march boldly, [for] she had blessed them so that neither pikestaffs, halberds, nor firearms could harm them."[10] At Weinsberg, Renner boasted, she had stabbed the count of Helfenstein and smeared her shoe with his blood. Then she marched with the band "over the moors to Heilbronn," where she scolded the burghers and "especially spoke ill of the worthy town council, calling them rogues and knaves. Note that she said, 'no stone must remain upon another here in Heilbronn, it must become a village like Böckingen.'"[11]

Time worked against the rebel forces since the princes with their vassals and credit outlasted the rebels, but the latter's poor military skills proved to be their downfall. They lost every engagement except one, a mere raid at Schladming in Styria on 16 July. Slack discipline and rotation of men between army and village also hurt their fighting effectiveness, as did deficiencies in firepower and cavalry. The first problem, guns,

7 Scott and Scribner, eds., *The German Peasants' War*, 233, no. 107c.
8 Scott and Scribner, eds., *The German Peasants' War*, 205, no. 85.
9 Hans Virck et al., eds., *Politische Correspondenz der Stadt Straßburg im Zeitalter der Reformation*, vol. 1: 197.
10 Scott and Scribner, eds., *The German Peasants' War*, 225, no. 101a.
11 Scott and Scribner, eds., *The German Peasants' War*, 226, no. 101a. Böckingen lies on the Neckar River's west bank across from Heilbronn, into which it is now incorporated.

could be and was to some degree redressed, as the rebels seized or captured field guns from towns and castles and learned how to serve them. The results can be read from campaigns of the Swabian League's army commanded by Jörg Truchsess of Waldburg (1488–1531),[12] which campaigned in Upper Swabia, Württemberg, and Franconia. When Waldburg faced the Baltringen rebels at Leipheim (4 April), he outgunned them, but at Böblingen a month later, the two sides were about equal in guns at eighteen each. Two months later at Königshofen in Franconia (2 June), the rebel force's front ranks were protected by forty-seven guns, their rear by a circle of 300 war wagons. While the artillery and infantry repulsed the League's initial assault, a flank attack by Waldburg's cavalry (ever the bane for inexperienced infantry) broke the infantry and turned a solid defensive position into a field of slaughter. Only at Leubas in Upper Swabia (16 July) did the rebels give as well as they got. The Allgäu army, its flanks protected from Waldburg's cavalry by bogs, blasted away at his lines, and the battle ended in a draw. Another deficiency, lack of cavalry, could not be overcome. The opposing armies had plenty; they had little or none. In Waldburg's army the ratio of cavalry to infantry varied between 1:2 and 1:5; in the forces of Duke Antoine (1489–1544) of Lorraine, who crushed the Lower Alsatian rebels, it was a remarkable 6:5. In the field, an iron law of warfare held: infantry had to be protected from enemy cavalry, whether by terrain, cannon, cavalry, or all three.

The rebels' specialty was not pitched battles but capturing castles and abbeys and spreading terror across whole regions. In the Bamberg lands alone, they took 200 castles and 6 abbeys. In the Kraichgau farther west, the Bright Band under "Pastor Iron-hat" (the priest Anton Eisenhut) took a place named Hilspach, where the Palatine elector had built a new wine cellar. They "seized the cellarer and plundered the cellars and the houses of priests and nobility."[13] At Sinsheim in the Palatinate, where there was "a fine collegiate church," the rebels, after "they were let into the town by the burghers without resistance, attacked the canons in their houses, smashed the windows, stripping some of them out, devastated the houses, seized and plundered what they found inside."[14] Luther's vicious diatribes to the contrary, the rebels rarely slaughtered their enemies. The one exception, important because of its notoriety, occurred on 16 April 1525 at Weinsberg Castle in Württemberg.[15] The town and castle surrendered after the burghers opened the gates. Then men of Jäcklin Rohrbach's Neckar Valley army took twenty-four persons, including the castellan and thirteen other noblemen, out into a field on the Heilbronn road, where they were "driven through the lances" of the gauntlet, a lansquenet regiment's standard rite of execution. Afterward, reports Johann Herolt, the local priest, "contrary to all the rules of war the bodies were dragged out naked and let lie there."[16] The "treacherous and vile treatment" and "tyranny" of Weinsberg was a deed of blood, an act of fury much like King Maximilian's vengeance on the Kufstein garrison in 1504.[17] It was a unique deed, at least on the rebels' side.

---

12 "Truchsess" is a title, equivalent to "seneschal" in English. For his role in defeating the rebels this man was subsequently called "Peasant Jörg" (Jörg being a South German form of George).
13 Scott and Scribner, eds., *The German Peasants' War*, 236, n. 110.
14 Scott and Scribner, eds., *The German Peasants' War*, 236, n. 110.
15 Weinsberg lies in the Neckar Valley between Heilbronn and Stuttgart.
16 Scott and Scribner, eds., *The German Peasants' War*, 158, n. 54.
17 See Chapter 7.

Instead of killing them, the rebels commonly humbled their opponents, sometimes in the topsy-turvy manner of carnival. When his Odenwald army occupied Heilbronn, Jörg Metzler sat in the mayor's chair in the town hall, surrounded by his captains, while local nobles, including women, came to plead for their lives and make peace with the victors. "Daily come many nobles to make alliances with them," reports Jacob Sturm, "to whom safe-conducts are given. The counts of Leonstein have also made peace with them, together with the city of Wimpfen."[18] It was a world turned upside-down, in which free cities and nobles, titled and untitled, sued commoners for peace. The counts of Hohenlohe and Löwenstein came before the commanders of the fierce Bildhausen army – named for an abbey they had plundered – doffed their caps, and suffered to be addressed by rebels as "Brother." The same thing happened to William von Henneberg-Schleusingen (1478–1559), a powerful count of princely rank and a kinsman of the late Elector Berthold of Mainz. These events belie the tales that the rebels desired only to rob and slaughter the nobles, the clergy, and the rich burghers, though possibly the idea did not escape some of them. Erasmus Gerber (d. 1525), chief rebel commander in Lower Alsace, was reported to have confessed (probably under torture) that "it was their purpose that when they had conquered castles and towns, they should take from all rulers . . . whatever they had; abuse their wives before their husband's eyes, and afterwards strike dead all rulers, lords, nobles, [with their] wives and children, and [so] wipe out the nobility and rich burghers, plus many other wicked words and opinions."[19]

This is not to say that the rebels committed no atrocities. At Frankenhausen in Thuringia, where Thomas Müntzer (ca. 1488–1525) was later taken, interrogated, and executed, the magistrates reported that Müntzer had staged a trial of three emissaries of Count Ernest of Mansfeld (1479–1531), in the course of which the men were interrogated "by torture . . . very cruel, swift, and intense, and then were beheaded with a sword."[20] A captured rebel confessed that when Rohrbach's Neckar Valley army "found a knight, a priest, or an idler, they would strangle them."[21] Rohrbach himself was caught and roasted over a slow fire – revenge for Weinsberg.

Whether in battle or acts of retribution, the rebels bled and died in far greater numbers than their opponents did. They were amateurs at killing; their foes were professionals. Much the worst slaughters took place in Lower Alsace. Wolf Füll of Geispolsheim, Strasbourg's bailiff in Herrenstein Castle, reported on 16 May that "today the Lorraine cavalry and foot attacked Dossenheim, where they smashed open the gates of the churchyard, broke open all the chests in the church and the powder tower, burned the powder therein, and caused much distress in the village, ran after the womenfolk and struck some of them. . . . Things are indeed in a sorry state in these parts."[22] Next day Duke Antoine's forces crushed one large rebel band outside of Saverne (17 May) and the next day another at nearby Scherwiller (18 May). "Wasn't

18   Virck et al., eds., *Politische Correspondenz*, vol. 1: 198.
19   Virck et al., eds., *Politische Correspondenz*, vol. 1: 182–3. This excerpt from a letter to the city council of Strasbourg from the prince-bishop of Strasbourg's councilors reports that no written confession was recorded. Presumably, following normal procedure, Gerber was questioned under torture.
20   Scott and Scribner, eds., *The German Peasants' War*, 239, n. 112c.
21   Scott and Scribner, eds., *The German Peasants' War*, 237, n. 111.
22   Scott and Scribner, eds., *The German Peasants' War*, 308, n. 147a.

that a terrible price to pay," an anonymous poet sang, "ten thousand on a single day?"[23] A balance sheet of Duke Antoine's brief, brutal campaign tells that "after he slew up to thirty thousand men at Saverne and in those parts, and plundered towns and villages, the duke . . . headed back to Lorraine with fifteen hundred wagons of booty."[24] Payment and overpayment for Weinsberg.

3. POLITICAL PROGRAMS OF THE GERMAN PEASANTS' WAR

Had the will to change been empowered, how could the peasants' grievances have been redressed and a better, more just future for them, their families, and their neighbors assured? Certainly, in their view, not from the center. The Holy Roman emperor, much less the Imperial Diet, hardly appears in the programmatic documents from the Peasants' War. To the peasants the Empire was vague, the emperor distant and shadowy, and the Church hardly noticed above the local and regional levels. The rebels' demands for good governance nonetheless resonated with the spirit of the fifteenth-century reform tradition; they focused it on their own regions. The rebels wanted territorial governments more responsive to the peasants' needs and governed according to the rules the peasants knew from communal life: consultation, representation, and consent. The *Twelve Articles* denied revolutionary intentions: "Not that we wish to be completely free and to have no authority, for God does not teach us that. . . . We will gladly obey our elected and appointed rulers (whom God has ordained over us) in all reasonable and Christian matters."[25]

If not political revolution, then what? A series of important programmatic documents emerged from the movement. Building on the existing order of things, they envisage two types of political reform, territorial and associative. Where a constituted territorial regime already existed, the programs accepted princely rule but proposed to alter the composition and powers of its government. Much depended on the character of existing institutions. At one pole lies the county of Tyrol, where the towns and rural districts already dominated the territorial diet. In June 1526 the estates abolished the clergy's temporal authority, curtailed that of the nobles (though not their economic privileges), and repartitioned governance between prince and commons. The old and new constitutions compare as follows:

- Regime: prince + governing council (unchanged);
- Governing Council: appointed by prince → appointed by nobles/burghers/peasants;
- Parliamentary Estates: nobles/clergy/towns/rural districts → nobles/towns/rural districts/miners;
- Local Officials: appointed by prince → elected by communities.

The reform agenda also improved peasant property rights, lowered servile dues, and removed restrictions on hunting rights and the export and import of food. Many of these measures survived the new constitution's nullification in 1532.

Some states allowed no popular participation in territorial governance. In the Franconian prince-bishoprics of Bamberg and Würzburg, the rebels demanded

---

23 Thomas A. Brady, *Protestant Politics: Jacob Sturm (1489–1553) and the German Reformation*, 41. The village of Scherwiller lies 33 miles southwest of Strasbourg.
24 Scott and Scribner, eds., *The German Peasants' War*, 308, n. 147b.
25 Scott and Scribner, eds., *The German Peasants' War*, 254–5, n. 125.

deep structural changes: secularization of the abbeys, abolition of the cathedral chapter's role in governance, and expansion of communal rights. At Bamberg a reform commission established at the end of April 1525 recommended the following changes:

- Regime: bishop + cathedral chapter → bishop + governing council;
- Council: cathedral chapter → 18-member governing council (9 bishops' men, 3 nobles, 3 burghers, and 3 peasants);
- Local Officials: appointed by bishop → elected by communities.

The disempowerment of the cathedral chapter was realistic; that of the powerful landed nobility was not. Very similar proposals appeared in the neighboring prince-bishopric of Würzburg. In both *Hochstifte* all reforms disappeared with the insurrection's suppression.

Where no constituted territorial polities existed, programs were proposed to create their popular equivalent in the form of associative polities based on communal institutions, regardless of the existing structures of lordship. A new kind of popular, communally based, territorial polity under the generic name of "Christian Union" was proposed by the rebel forces in the field. The idea of an associative polity was by no means utopian, for models of associative territorial governance were known to exist in the Swiss Confederation and its associated rural republics, the Graubünden and the Valais.

The idea of "turning Swiss" had long existed in the lands neighboring the Confederation, an agglutination of small polities dominated by burghers and farmers. A pamphlet attributed to Christoph Schappeler (ca. 1472–1551), a St. Gallen priest resident at Memmingen and co-author of the *Twelve Articles*, pointed to the Swiss model during the insurrection of 1525 in Upper Swabia. "What indescribably great deeds," the author wrote at the peak of the Peasants' War,

> were often performed by the poor peasants, your neighbors, the Swiss, for whenever they had to defend their land, wives, and children against arrogant violence, they mostly won and earned great honor thereby. This has doubtless happened by God's power and decree. How else could the Confederation, which daily grows in strength, have arisen from only three simple peasants?[26]

The established authorities in the southwest knew very well about this attractive model, and they feared its spread among their own subjects. "I fear," wrote in 1519 the Augsburg magistrate Ulrich Arzt (1460–1527), one of the Swabian League's commanders, "that we will be pushed from behind toward the Swiss. Then the old proverb will come true: when a cow stands and moos on the bridge at Ulm, she'll be heard in the middle of Switzerland."[27] And perhaps from further away, for another version of the saying puts the mooing cow in Franconia, much farther north, where "a

26 Siegfried Hoyer and Bernd Rüdiger, eds., *"An die Versammlung gemeiner Bauernschaft." Eine revolutionäre Flugschrift aus dem deutschen Bauernkrieg (1525)*, 117–18. The "three simple peasants" are Uri, Schwyz, and Unterwalden, the founding members of the Swiss Confederation.
27 Heinrich Lutz, *Conrad Peutinger. Beiträge zu einer politischen Biographie*, 147.

cow will stand on top of the Schwanberg in Franconia and will bellow, and she'll be heard in the middle of Switzerland."[28] To the lords "turning Swiss" meant anarchy and an end to lordship; to the common people it meant securing more responsive government by ending seigneurial power based on property rights in land and labor.[29]

Upper Swabia formed a fertile region for thinking about new, associative polities. In January 1525 the subjects of Kempten Abbey, resolute veterans of years of conflict with the prince-abbots, formed a new territorial assembly to debate resorting to law or to arms. A month later, when their neighbors in the Allgäu region rose to demand "the holy gospel and the godly law,"[30] the Kempteners joined them in a new Christian Federation of the Land of Allgäu. The more radical Baltringen army moved in a similar direction.[31] By mid-February 7,000 to 10,000 peasants had streamed into their encampment from many small territories in the lands south of the Danube. They directed their demands not to the seigneurs but to the Swabian League in the name of their Christian Assembly and by the authority of God's Word. "Whatever this same Word of God grants us or takes from us," they assert, "we will gladly accept and suffer whatever good or pain comes from it."[32] This was the higher law to which they appealed against the lords' claims that servile labor obligations were "of ancient origin" and death taxes were "not newly invented but . . . in force for many years."[33]

Out of the Upper Swabian movement formed the coalition that gave the movement its manifesto. In March representatives of three armies met in the merchant guild's hall at Memmingen to frame a federal ordinance for the Assembly of Bands from Allgäu, Lake Constance, and Baltringen. It took its norms from "the Gospel," "the divine Word," and "justice and godly law"[34] as expressed in *Twelve Articles*. When they failed to agree on abolishing seigneurial authority, they decided to recognize existing governmental and seigneurial rights within the framework of godly law, though they also declared – a rare reference – to own no lord but the emperor. Neither this nor any other notion of an associative polity could be in any way realized. Absent the power to force the seigneurs from the land, a communally based territorial polity à la Suisse simply had no chance. The rebels could not conquer this power, nor could they obtain it through negotiation with the princes, who were themselves seigneurs.

Besides strong military power, the rebels sorely needed what have been called "organic intellectuals," those who put the intellectual skills of one social class in the service of another.[35] Men of this sort drafted at least five projects for new or reformed polities. The authors – three officials, one clergyman, and one artisan – developed

---

28 Thomas A. Brady, *Turning Swiss: Cities and Empire*, 1450–1550, 39. The Schwanberg is a hill that lies southeast of Kitzingen in Lower Franconia, approximately 185 miles from the nearest piece of Switzerland.
29 The two points of view have nothing to do with modern discussions of the relatively democratic or authoritarian character of contemporary Swiss governance.
30 Peter Blickle, *The Revolution of 1525: The German Peasants' War from a New Perspective*, 91.
31 The village of Baltringen lay in Upper Swabia just north of the small Imperial free city of Biberach an der Riss.
32 Blickle, *The Revolution of 1525*, 91.
33 Blickle, *The Revolution of 1525*, 92.
34 Blickle, *The Revolution of 1525*, 98.
35 The term is attributed to Antonio Gramsci (1891–1937), Italian political theorist and co-founder of the Italian Communist Party.

their ideas within one of three political settings: Imperial, territorial, and utopian. A brief examination of two Imperial, one territorial, and two utopian programs illustrates the scope and variety of this genre, in which similar ideas were adapted to very different circumstances.

The two Imperial projects stand in the fifteenth-century tradition of agendas of Imperial reform. Both were drafted by Franconians: Wendel Hipler (ca. 1465–1526), a university man and former secretary to the counts of Hohenlohe, served with the Odenwald army and drafted a reform agenda for the rebel envoys who gathered in May 1525 in the liberated city of Heilbronn;[36] and Friedrich Weigandt, a district bailiff in the archbishopric of Mainz, may have written the second program.[37] Hipler proposed a supra-regional federation of armies to move "against the Palatinate, Brandenburg-Ansbach, and Baden . . . and the same with the Bavarian princes and Hesse" and to act "with severity" against the prince-bishops of Trier, Cologne, Mainz, and Würzburg. Against these southern princes, Hipler thinks, they could "seek support from princes outside the region, such as the Saxon elector, etc., who has shown more moderation toward the common man than other princes have done." He is nonetheless uncertain about "how and in what form we should act towards the Emperor" or "whether and in what measure of form we want to bring the foreign nobles in other lands into this association." Hipler was no revolutionary but a moderate. He advocates the redress of peasant grievances, "though not to excess, but rather according to the judgement of those appointed for that purpose, . . . so that the princes, lords, and nobles will thereby have the same right to the same fair settlement as their subjects, and no one will take any liberties, but [treat] the poor the same as the rich."[38] Hipler proposed to open the bounds of Imperial public life to the common people, a cause that pitted the logic of the reform tradition against the facts of class relations.

The second Imperial program, perhaps by Weigandt, also stands squarely in the fifteenth-century tradition. The author proposes to reform everyone and everything: clergy, princes and nobles, towns and communities, courts of law, regimes, jurisprudence, security of roads, taxes, mines and coinage, weights and measures, trading firms, and alliances and associations. He would abolish the clergy's temporal authority and replace clerical benefices with salaries, so the priests can devote themselves as "good pastors who tend the sheep with the Word of God alone," noting that "needy folk and the common good may be cared for from any surplus income."[39] As for the princes and nobles, each should be supported "according to his rank" in return for his "maintenance of Christian peace and the augmentation of the Empire" and the protection of the rights of all, especially the poor.[40] Weigandt also assumes that emperor and Imperial estates will collaborate to provide good government with "only Imperial peace and protection."[41] Weigandt's ideas, like Hipler's ideas, are fully in tune with fifteenth-century reformism.

---

36   The county of Hohenlohe in southwestern Franconia is today divided between northeastern Baden-Württemberg and northwestern Bavaria.
37   Weigandt's authorship of this document is disputed. It develops ideas from an anonymous pamphlet, *The Needs of the German Nation*, which had appeared in 1523.
38   Scott and Scribner, eds., *The German Peasants' War*, 258.
39   Scott and Scribner, eds., *The German Peasants' War*, 259.
40   Scott and Scribner, eds., *The German Peasants' War*, 259–60.
41   Scott and Scribner, eds., *The German Peasants' War*, 264.

The territorial reform program was drafted for the county of Tyrol by Michael Gaismair (1490–1532), a university man from Stertzing[42] in South Tyrol and secretary to the prince-bishop of Brixen. It conceives the county as an autonomous territorial polity without regard to emperor or Empire. The land was to be reformed into a radically populist, Gospel-based society with centralized governance and an autarchic economy. Gaismair was elected in May 1525 to be chief speaker for the Tyrolean rebels, to whom he handed over his bishop's palace. His *Tyrolean Constitution*, drafted in 1526,[43] shows, unlike the Franconian programs, clear evangelical influence, especially in his insistence on the godly law. "You will spare no effort to establish a wholly Christian constitution," he exhorts, "which is founded in all things on the Word of God alone, and live wholly according to it."[44] The new order must be committed to preach the Word of God "faithfully and truthfully everywhere," to destroy all images, shrines, and chapels, and to abolish "the Mass, which is an abomination before God and wholly unchristian."[45] All other changes are to be based on a commitment "to seek ... first the honor of God, and then the common good" and to root out the "godless men who persecute the Word of God, burden the common man, and hinder the common good."[46] Gaismair proposes a thoroughgoing social revolution: expropriation of the nobility and clergy, razing all walls and castles, centralizing manufacturing (at Trent), socializing trade in commodities, and ridding the land of usury, unjust prices, and social injustice.

Michael Gaismair's program represents the reform of Empire and Church refitted for a single land, his own Tyrol. He marshals the popular movement's leading values – solidarity, equality, obedience to legitimate authority, godly law, and God's honor and the common good – in support of a communally structured, territorial polity. Each citizen of this commonwealth is to swear:

> to pledge body and goods for one another, not forsake one another, to do or to die together but always to act on orders, to be loyal and obedient to your superior authorities, and in all things to seek not self-interest but first and foremost the honor of God, and then the common good.[47]

Like the others, this most clearly evangelical of all the programs associated with the Peasants' War came to naught. Fleeing the failed revolution, Gaismair was murdered at Venice in 1532.

Michael Gaismair makes an interesting comparison with Martin Luther, he from an old Imperial heartland and Luther from a much more recently colonized region. They nonetheless came from "remarkably similar backgrounds and lived and worked in landscapes which were undergoing profound economic and social transformations ... areas stamped by large-scale mining enterprises."[48] This is so, but the two men differed utterly on whether the world could be or should be governed by Biblical

42 Stertzing, today the Italian town of Vipiteno, lies at the southern foot of the Brenner Pass.
43 Tyrol was one of the few lands where the insurrection continued into 1526.
44 Scott and Scribner, eds., *The German Peasants' War*, 265–6.
45 Scott and Scribner, eds., *The German Peasants' War*, 266.
46 Scott and Scribner, eds., *The German Peasants' War*, 265.
47 Scott and Scribner, eds., *The German Peasants' War*, 265.
48 Tom Scott, "The Reformation and Modern Political Economy: Luther and Gaismair Compared," in Thomas A. Brady, ed., *Die deutsche Reformation zwischen Spätmittelalter und Frühe Neuzeit*, 175.

principles. Gaismair nonetheless did agree with Luther – against the caesaropapist reformers – in seeing the territory, not the Empire, as the politically practical forum of public life.

For all of their improbabilities, the reform projects of Hipler, Weigandt, and Gaismair seem highly realistic when compared with the two utopian programs. The first comes from Thomas Müntzer (1489/90–1525), a native of the Harz Mountain region in Thuringia, who studied at Frankfurt an der Oder and became a Franciscan friar and a priest. Although an early advocate of Luther's ideas, he quickly displayed his radicalism – he ridiculed Luther as "Doctor Soft-Flesh" – and began to preach apocalyptic religion and social revolution. Müntzer's program, which brought him into prominence in the Thuringian movement of 1525, does honor to his Franciscan background. He teaches a spiritual gospel that holds that the believer should be guided not by Church or Bible but directly by the Holy Spirit. Faith, far from being merely individual, marshals God's chosen ones in opposition to the ungodly powers of this world. In these Last Days, believers will "come together and make a league," for the time has come "when God will no longer suffer the temporal lords' flaying, fleecing, fettering, shackling, grinding, binding, and other tyranny."[49] They will make "an ordinance according to God's Word" and choose their own territory in this manner: "when the people is foregathered, it shall vow together to keep God's word, and from twelve men put forward by the peasants shall choose one, with no special regard to be given to the nobility."[50] In dramatic contrast to all of the southern programs, Müntzer's lacked roots in everyday communal experience, ignored the specific problems of agrarian life, and betrayed no interest in stable, responsive governance. The abolition of property, the former friar confessed under torture, was not a goal of revolution but a sign of the end of this world and the beginning of a new one. In 1525 Müntzer led the rebel forces gathered at Mühlhausen, perhaps 7,000 strong, to Frankenhausen, very near where Emperor Frederick Barbarossa lay sleeping in the Kyffhäuser Mountain until his people would need him again. There, on 15 May 1525, about 6,000 of them fled or died – the princes lost only 6 men – and twelve days later Müntzer, too, met his end.

A second utopian program is attributed to Hans Hergot (d. 1528), an itinerant peddler and sometime printer, who in May 1527 was arrested, tried, and executed for peddling a pamphlet he may have composed. Called *On the New Transformation of a Christian Life*, it is set in the old Joachimite framework of the Three Ages of Father, Son, and Holy Spirit. The imminent passage into the Third Age will be a "transformation of the world out of the terrible state in which it now exists."[51] There will come a great mutation of things "to the promotion of God's honor and the common good" – the classic pair of communalist thinking – "and in the new order no one will say, 'This is mine.' The lords and the cities will disappear, but the villages will become populous and wealthy. Both spiritual and temporal authority will be dissolved," and "it will be pointless for anyone to try to maintain his estate." Hergot claims that his "little book does not encourage revolt but shows those, who are now

49　Tom Scott, *Thomas Müntzer: Theology and Revolution in the German Reformation*, 133.
50　Scott, *Thomas Müntzer*, 133.
51　Adolf Laube and Hans Werner Seiffert, eds., *Flugschriften der Bauernkriegszeit*, 547. Joachimism (also Joachism) is so called from Joachim of Fiore (ca. 1132–1202), an Italian Cistercian abbot, whose highly influential concept of the Three Ages rested on his doctrine of the "eternal gospel" (Rev. 14: 6).

captive to evil, how to recognize who they are and to ask God for His grace."[52] Hergot's new order is an autonomous community of farmers and artisans; its polity is a republican and theocratic pyramid of villages, provinces, and "twelve nations," in which spiritual and temporal authority are completely fused. Its interest lies not in his quaint utopianism but in his absolutizing of the leading ideas of 1525: an end to individual property and feudal society; universal political rights secured through representation and election; the transformation of territorial government into a representative parliament; and the rule of freedom, brotherly love, and the common good in public life. Hergot's version of the ideas of 1525 universalizes a fusion of the communal tendencies of village life with popular aspirations for security and good governance. In his imagination the world will become, to adapt Erasmus's dictum, "a great monastery."[53]

4. THE GOSPEL OF SOCIAL UNREST

What had the rebels' aspirations and the programs inspired by their movement to do with the earliest stages of the Protestant reformation? This question has long been a controversial one. Those who followed Luther and stuck with him repudiated the rebels of 1525 one and all. They feared the rebels as agents of armed revolt, though later generations would condemn the movement for its alleged misunderstanding of Luther's teaching. Other interpreters see in Luther's savage polemics a betrayal of his own movement. In fact, Luther did not betray the peasants; he was never with them, though some of them were briefly with him. Quite apart from modern speculations about ideas, the Peasants' War played a highly important role as a turning point in the transformation of the early evangelical movements into the Protestant reformation.

To contemporaries, the central question asked whether the rebels were inspired by Luther. They understood what was happening but differed over the causes. In February 1525, Chancellor Leonhard von Eck (1480–1550) wrote to Duke William IV (b. 1493, r. 1508–50) of Bavaria about the rebellious Hegau peasants, who "all let it be heard, that they want to live under the godly laws. The other peasants proclaim that by 'godly law' they understand nothing less than freedom, and they want neither to pay nor be obliged to give anything to anyone."[54] The entire movement, Eck believed, was "begun to suppress the princes and nobles, and it has its origin in the Lutheran doctrine; for the majority of the peasants justify their demands from God's Word, the gospel and brotherly love."[55] He was right about the Christian coupling of liberty, relief, and godly law, and right to connect them to "Lutheran doctrine," but only in the vague sense that heresy and rebellion were long held to be bedfellows.

The southern rebels, just as Eck said, appealed to godly law. They meant God's will as it was revealed in the Bible, which taught the Gospel as a set of prescriptive norms for Christian life. The Bible authenticated the godly law much as a royal

---

52 Laube and Seiffert, eds., *Flugschriften*, 547, 557.
53 See Chapter 8, 143. It is worth noting that here, as in the Anabaptist communities, the monastic ideal is adjusted to the needs of the household.
54 Wilhelm Vogt, *Die bayrische Politik im Bauernkrieg und der Kanzler Dr. Leonhard von Eck, das Haupt des Schwäbischen Bundes*, 380. The Hegau is the area just west of Lake Constance.
55 Brady, *Turning Swiss*, 187–8.

charter authenticated an ordinary legal right. The idea of godly law did not derive from Luther. Strictly speaking, it contradicted his theology of salvation by uniting two things Luther radically separated: human law and divine law, that is, the Gospel. The idea of godly law had surfaced during the 1510s in the Upper Rhenish Bundschuh movement. It accompanied the Peasants' War from its very beginnings in June 1524, and it inspired the *Twelve Articles'* claim that Christ "redeemed us all with his precious blood, the shepherd the same as the Emperor."[56]

This is not to deny that genuine evangelicals were to be found in the rebels' ranks. Christoph Schappeler and the Memmingen furrier Sebastian Lotzer, authors of the *Twelve Articles*, were such men. Their presence helps to explain why the Upper Swabian armies' assembly voted to seek advice from six evangelical theologians – Luther, Zwingli, and four others – though in this case the reformers' reputations for fearless dissent clearly trumped their theologies. The same language appears in articles drafted in mid-May 1525 in Tyrol's Thaur and Rettenberg districts. Their anonymous author writes that "although up until now the holy, divine Word has been obscured by human teachings, . . . now the divine Word has by God's will appeared clearly, fully, and unadulterated in the light of day."[57] The articles ask Archduke Ferdinand to permit his subjects "to search for learned, godly men to serve our churches, who will proclaim to us the holy, godly, true Word of God, clear and unadulterated, in no other form than that which agrees with and conforms to these new teachings."[58] This language is evangelical, comparable to what urban parishes employed when they rejected old and called new pastors. The phrase, "Word of God," while not semantically evangelical, was contextually so. It is no coincidence that when the Christian Association of Upper Swabia named "Christian teachers," they named priests from Eisenach, Nuremberg, Nördlingen, Strasbourg, Ulm, Schwäbisch Hall, Augsburg, Zurich, Reutlingen, Constance, and Kempten – all evangelicals in the strict sense.[59]

If representatives of the rebels sometimes thought Luther one of theirs, he never thought the rebels some of his. This contradiction was productive, but its revelation enraged Luther, to whom the idea that universal *human* freedom was a teaching of the Gospel was both blasphemous and dangerous. Yet it is also true that teachings of those who honored Luther did penetrate into villages, at least in highly urbanized areas. Martin Kiefferknecht of Rappoltsweiler/Ribeauvillé in central Alsace testified under torture on 6 August 1525 that his "Lutheran opinions" came from hearing "Master Mathis [Zell]" at Strasbourg. From Zell he learned, among other things,

That one should neither honor nor invoke the Virgin and the saints. That he was not obliged to confess or to fast, and that all days were the same, except for Sundays . . . that the Masses and good deeds done for the benefit of the dead were of no account and in

---

56 Scott and Scribner, eds., *The German Peasants' War*, 254, n. 125. Scott quotes not from the printed version but from the written version presented to Memmingen's city council.
57 Hermann Wopfner, ed., *Quellen zur Geschichte des Bauernkriegs in Deutschtirol, part I: Quellen zur Vorgeschichte des Bauernkriegs, Beschwerdeartikel aus den Jahren 1519–1525*, 3: 70.
58 Wopfner, ed., *Quellen*, 3: 70.
59 Plus from more distant places: Luther, Melanchthon, and Bugenhagen. The list betrays, of course, a clerical hand.

vain. . . . Finally, Master Mathis said to him that these teachings and opinions would win out and must do so, for Duke [Elector] Frederick of Saxony will push the cause forward and draw the people with him, and that he will gather all Lutherans under his banner.[60]

Of course, he also reported that Zell had taught that one should obey no authority except the emperor, for which, if the report were true, Strasbourg's magistrates would have taken the priest by the heels. Yet Kiefferknecht's reported confession did not touch directly on what Luther thought most essential, his teaching on salvation, and it bears asking how farmers and their wives might have received Luther's message that their labors – "good works" – had no value in the eyes of God.

The report on Mathis Zell's preaching suggests that he emphasized the negative, purgative side of the new religion, its attack on the old ways. The impression is supported by a story from Stertzing in South Tyrol, Gaismair's hometown. On Palm Sunday (25 March) 1525, some peasants, gathered in an inn, sent for their preacher, who told them that "their oath and whatever they had sworn to their territorial prince was not valid before God. . . . And the Mass was of no value – the priests merely practiced sorcery thereby."[61] There is no reason to believe that the peasants and burghers did not believe everything they were told. A good many priests taught ideas both evangelical and subversive. Yet village people often thought for themselves and did not simply obey their priests, whether heterodox or orthodox. Pastor Jörg Mentz at Neuler near Ellwangen, it is reported, "said to Veit Eberhart he should unlock and share out the parson's goods, and afterwards they would all go from house to house, and whoever had more than another should share it out with them."[62] The priest's gesture hardly impressed Neuler's hard-handed peasants, who truly understood property. They told one freeholder that if he did not help them to convert their leaseholds into freehold, "they would take his from him."[63]

Whatever their sympathies, few of the urban priests who had been teaching the new faith sided openly with the rebels. For the majority position may perhaps stand the Strasbourg preachers' reply to the rebel commander Erasmus Gerber, who had appealed to the "Christian brothers and preachers in Strasbourg" to support the peasants and represent their cause to the lords. Although "we have always faithfully striven to help lighten the burdens upon the common man," the city's preachers replied, "we cannot see that you have cause either in [the name of] God or in your interests" to reject the Strasbourg magistrates' proposal "and to remain assembled en masse."[64] "It is not in accordance with the gospel to resist," they wrote, "for that is a sign that you place your trust in no one, which is contrary to Scripture, or that you desire the temporal more than the eternal, which is also contrary to the gospel," for "God . . . commands the faithful not to put our trust in temporal power."[65]

It is fair to say that the Peasants' War unmasked the hitherto hidden incompatibility between the idea of earthly justice and Martin Luther's theology of salvation. Ranke, who saw this better than many a later interpreter, wrote:

60 Franz, ed., *Quellen zur Geschichte des Bauernkrieges*, 238.
61 Scott and Scribner, eds., *The German Peasants' War*, 106.
62 Scott and Scribner, eds., *The German Peasants' War*, 107.
63 Scott and Scribner, eds., *The German Peasants' War*, 107.
64 Scott and Scribner, eds., *The German Peasants' War*, 109.
65 Scott and Scribner, eds., *The German Peasants' War*, 110.

It seems clear what sort of nourishment ideas of this kind must find in the reformation movement, which had so deeply shaken the clergy's authority. Yet it is no less
clear how evangelical preaching, which in and of itself represented other points of view,
could already have so mightily been stirred by them. The preaching had not given birth
to these ideas but was carried along with them. Not all could test the spirits, as Luther
could.[66]

This is exactly right. Luther knew what he thought. How could others have
mistaken it? With his incomparable verbal violence he came down with special vehemence on those who claimed the Gospel as sanction for rebellion against their lords.
Legend to the contrary, Luther did not change his mind on this score in 1525. Two
years earlier he had said the same thing in *On Temporal Power, Whether It Should Be
Obeyed*. What he did during the Peasants' War was to repeat his opinions three times
with ascending levels of cruel hyperbole. He warned both sides of danger to their
souls; he attacked the peasants alone; and he then called for murder of the peasants.
Luther's harsh sayings dispel any doubt about the compatibility of his doctrine of
justification by faith alone with the peasants' belief in godly law. There was a shared
but superficial Biblicism, but the Gospel, which for him freed Christians from the
law, for them *was* the Christians' highest law. This was the sin for which, Luther
declared, "they have abundantly merited death in body and soul . . . ten times over."[67]
Luther's time was Müntzer's time, the End of Days. The peasants' time was the time
of everyday life, interrupted by occasional extraordinary efforts to improve it.

5. RECKONINGS, RETRIBUTION, AND RESTORATION

By late summer 1525 the insurrection was over except in Tyrol and other Austrian
lands, where the aftershocks lasted into 1526. Now the bills began to fall due. To the
slain the victors added many others they now executed or maimed; they confiscated
weapons and other property, curbed rights, and assessed fines. In early June Margrave
Casimir of Brandenburg-Ansbach (1481–1527), a fierce and pugnacious lord by any
account, took his troops on an avenging sweep through eastern and central Franconia.
His executioner, Master Augustin, who bore the nickname of "Master Ouch," earned
1 gulden per beheading, a half-gulden per blinding. At Kitzingen on 8 June, he blinded
sixty-two men; at Rothenburg ob der Tauber three weeks later, he beheaded twenty-
five, among them a pastor, and displayed their bodies for shame and warning in the
marketplace. In the Black Forest, notes the Bernese chronicler Valerius Anshelm (ca.
1475–1546/47), "the lords, having gained their victory, became more ungracious and
unjust than before, for they believed that 'the ass would be kept in check and tamed
with a tighter girth and a sharper bit.'"[68] They stripped the peasants "as rebellious
perjurers, of their honor and weapons, especially their firearms and armor, their fine
clothing, berets, and leather shoes, prohibited them from visiting inns on pain of life
and property," and fined every household 6 Rhenish gulden "under threat of fire and

66 Ranke, *Deutsche Geschichte*, vol. 2: 109 (Bk III, ch. 6).
67 Martin Luther, *D. Martin Luthers Werke. Kritische Gesamtausgabe. Schriften*, vol. 18: 357. This is from
    Luther's "Against the Murderous and Thieving Hordes of Peasants."
68 Scott and Scribner, eds., *The German Peasants' War*, 302, no. 142.

pillage, while the rich, the officials, and the ringleaders were punished more heavily."[69] Many, Anshelm reports "came out [shorn] like sheep," and even the innocent and those who had opposed the rebels "were secretly and publicly shorn and butchered."[70]

Whether from calculation, pity, or both, free cities' magistrates acted more moderately than did princes. Along the Upper Rhine's west bank, Strasbourg's magistrates tried in vain to head off the devastation of Lower Alsatian villages by Lorraine and Palatine troops. On the east bank they and other cities' magistrates mediated peace between the rebels and the margrave of Baden. The Treaty of Renchen in the Ortenau, signed on 25 May 1525, actually incorporated much of the substance of the *Twelve Articles*. Urban magistrates, safe within their walls, could afford to take the longer view that a mild peace might avert another great rising.

The German Peasants' War ended in bloody vengeance but, myth to the contrary, not in mute obedience and the loss of all peasant freedoms. Little changed in the Rhine valley's middling stretches, or in Saxony-Thuringia, Bavaria, and certainly not in the Swiss Confederation. Where things did change, sometimes they favored the peasants. In Tyrol, in Baden's Markgräflerland, and in some other southern principalities, the peasants preserved or even expanded their right to participate in territorial governance. Nowhere else in Europe, except Scandinavia, did peasants enjoy this right to a comparable degree. In the longer run, the insurrection's settlements also promoted judicialization – resort to lawcourts rather than arms – of the peasants' grievances and defense of their property rights. In the chief theaters of conflict, the communes gradually learned how to fight fire with fire, that is, law with law. In the eastern German lands, by contrast, hardly touched by 1525, rural revolts continued through the seventeenth and into the eighteenth century.

The common people's bid to enter the Holy Roman Empire of the German Nation ended in near total failure. For the German reformations' course the insurrection's consequences were not trivial. It deeply shocked princes, nobles, and magistrates in the Imperial heartlands, turning minds from liberty to order, and it encouraged some people to seek stricter religious paths in the interstices and shadow zones of society.

6. PEACEABLE KINGDOMS – ANABAPTISM

The dissenting religious separatists of the sixteenth-century German lands were and are commonly lumped together under the originally perjorative name of "Anabaptists." Meaning "re-baptizers," the term refers to the practice of adult or believers' baptism practiced by many of the groups. Such people are often taken to be refugees from the failed insurrection of 1525, who gathered in little bands to practice religion, since they could no longer make revolution. In a literal sense, this is hardly credible, for the groups lumped by their Protestant foes under this title were by no means chiefly veterans of the lost cause. Yet the most important streams of congregationally organized, separatist religion, Anabaptists, did assemble either in theaters of the Peasants' War (Thuringia, Upper Swabia, Tyrol) or around Zurich. In their midst

69   Scott and Scribner, eds., *The German Peasants' War*, 302, no. 142.
70   Scott and Scribner, eds., *The German Peasants' War*, 302, no. 142.

lived and worked persons whose ideas in some important points resembled or agreed with those expressed in documents of 1525. The Seven Articles of Schleitheim, which were formulated near Schaffhausen in February 1527, and in which "the principles of early Swiss-generated Anabaptism were formalized, . . . recall the programs of the recently concluded Peasants' War."[71] Indeed, on one central issue, community of property, "all Anabaptists until 1535, the first expulsion of the Anabaptists from Moravia and the fall of [the Anabaptist kingdom of] Münster, fretted, brooded and experimented with the grandest social vision of all, that *omnia sunt communia*, everything belongs to everyone, just as in the Jerusalem church described in Acts 2 and 4."[72] Perhaps the most nearly common mark of these groups, and the belief that distinguished them from all of the programs of 1525, was their doctrine of a gathered church distinct, even separated from, the parish. They desired not to reform the governance of their world but to escape it. This desire not only resonated with the ancient tradition of Christian communal asceticism, it set them apart from all other reformations in the German lands.

In 1525, as the storm of insurrection was raging in neighboring lands to the north, what became the archetypal Anabaptist group began to form in small towns and villages near Zurich. The leaders of the people called "Swiss Brethren" cut their dissenting teeth on Huldrych Zwingli, whom they thought to have halted partway on the road to purely Biblical Christianity. A young patrician named Conrad Grebel (ca. 1498–1526) and several village priests attacked Zwingli's defense of tithes and infant baptism. The Swiss radicals were not followers of the spiritual gospel but Biblical literalists, committed to restoring the practices of the faith as prescribed by Christ in the New Testament. Unlike the more radical central German spiritualists, who gave the two testaments equal weight, the Swiss held entirely to the only Bible they could read, the New Testament, which they did read, ironically, in Zwingli's German translation. They hoped to convert Zurich's church to adult baptism, and only the magistrates' obduracy forced them to begin forming their own small, illegal congregations.

Official rejection and repression helped to make the Swiss Brethren into separatists. In February 1527 a group led by Michael Sattler (ca. 1490–1527), a former Benedictine monk from Staufen in the Black Forest, drew up the Schleitheim Articles, a confession of faith that became normative for the Swiss Brethren and influential among other groups. Summing up their experience of persecution, the co-signers renounced temporal governance as applying to Christians, approved congregational leadership and excommunication, and refused to swear oaths, bear arms, or hold office. They also repudiated rebellion or violence of any kind, though Sattler, faced with death at the hands of Catholic officials in the town of Rottenburg am Neckar (in presentday Württemberg), declared that if he did take up arms, he would sooner do so against the persecuting Christian authorities than against the Turks. Rulers, he declared, are "Turks according to the spirit."[73]

During the diaspora years following the Peasants' War, the central German spiritualist and Swiss Biblicist streams flowed together. They mingled first at Augsburg

71 James M. Stayer, "Radical Reformation," in Thomas A. Brady, Heiko A. Oberman, and James D. Tracy, eds., *Handbook of European History, 1400–1600: Late Middle Ages, Renaissance, Reformation*, vol. 2: 257.
72 Stayer, "Radical Reformation," vol. 2: 276.
73 Stayer, "Radical Reformation," vol. 2: 258.

and, expelled from there, from 1528 at Strasbourg on the Upper Rhine. Others had earlier begun the first migrations to the margraviate of Moravia, where they found haven on the lands of easygoing seigneurs who welcomed them as quiet folk and good farmers. Among the first to arrive was Balthasar Hubmaier (ca. 1480–1528), a Bavarian priest who in his younger days had preached against the Regensburg Jews. Moving to Waldshut, an Austrian town on the Upper Rhine, he went over to the evangelicals, took part in the Peasants' War, and linked up with the Zurich radicals. Hubmaier came to Moravia on the run in 1526 and settled down under noble protection. Soon, however, hordes of poor Anabaptist refugees arrived from all parts of south Germany and Switzerland, perhaps 5,000 at their peak, and in the ensuing sectarian disputes the upper hand was gained by Hans Hut (ca. 1490–1527), a disciple of Thomas Müntzer. Moravia became "the melting pot of early Anabaptism,"[74] where the various streams became relatively united in their practice of community of goods and nonresistance to force, which together formed the glue of the Moravian way.

These German-speaking sects took shape between 1526 and 1529, just when the Empire's princes and Imperial cities were beginning to organize the religious parties that would dominate Imperial politics for several generations to come. Persecution began almost immediately, as Anabaptists were hounded out of city after city and from land after land.[75] Both Protestant and Catholic rulers persecuted Anabaptists far more cruelly than they persecuted Catholics or Protestants. There was never any chance that Anabaptists would convert whole communities, because their doctrines of strict separation seemed to endanger all but their own kinds of communal obligations and solidarities. Still, their ideas crept quietly through the lands, attracting many who never joined an organized community. The vale of tears through which they labored is suggested by a song of martyrdom, "How Precious Is a Holy Death," by Leonhard Schiemer (d. 1526/27), who won a martyr's crown in his native Tyrol. It runs:

> We sneak around in the forests.
> We are hunted with dogs.
> And like voiceless lambs
> We are caught and bound.
> They show us to everyone
> As though we were rebels.
> They look upon us
> As sheep for the slaughter,
> As heretics and seducers.[76]

Persecution drove many Anabaptists onto the roads. Harried from place to place, many groups gravitated toward Strasbourg, the metropolis of the Upper Rhine. It seemed a likely choice, for the magistrates of Strasbourg had decisively protected their evangelical clergy in the early 1520s, pursued a policy of arbitration during the Peasants' War, joined the protest at the Diet of Speyer in 1529, and suppressed the Catholic Mass at the beginning of 1530. The city's leading evangelical clergymen, Wolfgang

---

74 Stayer, "Radical Reformation," vol. 2: 261.
75 The figures and consequences of the repression are examined in Chapter 15.
76 Heinrich Lutz, *Das Ringen um deutsche Einheit und kirchliche Erneuerung. Von Maximilian I. bis zum Westfälischen Frieden 1490–1648*, 245.

Capito and Martin Bucer, both Alsatians, were known to have had good relations with Karlstadt, to be favorable toward Zwingli, and to admire the devout of all streams of belief.

All through the years 1528 and 1529, Anabaptists and spiritualists of every stripe streamed into Strasbourg, where initially the local church leaders received them relatively well. The spiritualist chiliasts from the central lands and the Swiss Biblicists were soon joined by two lone spiritual teachers: Caspar Schwenckfeld (1489–1561), a fashionable Silesian nobleman obsessed with the meaning of the glorified Christ; and Sebastian Franck, a Swabian ex-priest, whose great *Chronicle* (published 1531) demonstrated historically the futility of seeking authority in an institutional church, a book (including the Bible), a movement, or a body of thought.

Schwenckfeld and Franck were pesky but relatively innocuous fellows, but the same could not be said of the Swabian furrier Melchior Hoffman (ca. 1495–1543). He had wandered through the Baltic lands during the mid-1520s, preaching (one wonders in what language) first as a Lutheran, then as a Zwinglian, and in mid-1529 he landed in Strasbourg. Here Hoffman encountered Anabaptism for the first time and was converted once more, this time by a group of local prophets who convinced him the Last Day had arrived. Soaking up teachings from all sides like a sponge, Hoffman began to teach that Strasbourg was to be the New Jerusalem, where Christ would soon establish a new kingdom and pour out His Holy Spirit on the true believers. From Strasbourg would go out the 144,000 apostolic missionaries to evangelize the whole world and prepare it for Jesus's second coming.

Between 1530 and 1533 Hoffman moved back and forth between Strasbourg and the lands along the North Sea, but on his fourth visit to Strasbourg, he was denounced, arrested, and thrown into a prison from which only death would free him. His arrest was part of a general sweep of dissenters following a synod held in 1533, Jacob Sturm presiding and Martin Bucer preparing the agenda. One by one, the dissenting teachers and clergy were questioned and their opinions condemned, and those who refused to conform were warned to leave Strasbourg and never return, under pain of death.

The fate of the Anabaptists at Strasbourg illuminates the transformation of the evangelical movement of the 1520s into the Protestantism of the 1540s and beyond. Catholic rulers, who, after all, created most of the Anabaptist martyrs, did so under a law that clearly justified their actions. Most evangelical rulers (the major exception was Bern) preferred to punish dissenters by exile rather than death, perhaps because the sects so pointedly reminded them of how their movement had begun – preaching the Gospel in defiance of the law. Pilgram Marpeck (ca. 1495–1556), who had abandoned substantial property and a promising political career in his native Tyrol to join the Brethren in Bohemia, came to Strasbourg in 1528, purchased citizenship, and joined a guild. In 1532, when the magistrates called him to debate Bucer in council chamber, Marpeck declared that "between the papists and the Lutherans the dispute is largely a temporal quarrel," for the evangelicals preach "in the presence of princes and urban magistrates, instead of preaching freely before the cross of Christ."[77]

This was a powerful indictment, especially of such as the Strasbourg magistrate Jacob Sturm, architect of his city's religious cleansing. At heart an Erasmian who held

77 Manfred Krebs et al., eds., *Elsaß, parts 1–4: Stadt Straßburg 1522–52*, vol. 1: 351–2.

that "God promised us Christians not happiness in this life (as He did to the Jews in the Old Testament) but only suffering and persecution,"[78] Sturm believed that "laws make hypocrites."[79] By policy, however, he accepted the official clergy's admonition that the magistrates "are obliged to help us all they can . . . [so] that Strasbourg, too, will at last have one doctrine and religion."[80] In 1533–34 he decided that the time had come "to combat the sects, hold a disputation, and hold to one [i.e., infant] baptism."[81] "The magistrates do not intend to force anyone in matters of faith," Sturm told the synod, "but only to suppress conspiracies that might lead to division of the commonweal."[82] Faced with one of the perennial conundrums of Christian history – free preaching of the Gospel versus a perceived need for public morality – Sturm made his choice "to further the honor of God and the welfare of this city" through coercion.[83]

The cat jumped out of the bag before Strasbourg's magistrates could close it. On his trips to the northwestern German lands, Melchior Hoffman had been able to plant his brand of apocalypticism there, with the consequence that Melchioritism became "the major tradition of the Radical Reformation in north Germany and the Netherlands."[84] Hoffman's followers played a leading role in founding the Anabaptist kingdom at Münster in Westphalia in 1533–34.

The story began with a Lutheran reform in the episcopal town of Münster in February 1533, to which the prince-bishop was forced to accede. It was a coup carried out with little popular support by some wealthy families and a local group of radicals led by Bernhard Rothmann (ca. 1495–1535). Soon, in response to his calls, Melchiorites were arriving from the Netherlands, among them Jan Matthijs (d. 1534), a baker from Haarlem, and Jan Beukelszoon (John of Leiden, 1509–36), a journeyman tailor from Leiden. These two chose Münster because, as Beukelszoon said, he had heard that the word of God was being preached there best and most powerfully. These Netherlandish Melchiorites brought the news that not Strasbourg, where Hoffman lay in jail, but Münster was the promised heavenly Jerusalem.

When Münster's political elite split over Matthijs's baptism of Rothmann and others in January 1534, Rothmann's people took power and packed the city council. This second coup began the Anabaptist reign at Münster, which for sixteen months withstood a siege of the city by the prince-bishop's army, supported by money and troops from other Imperial estates, Protestant and Catholic alike. The siege convinced many that the last days had begun, and among the thousands who trekked to join the saints at Münster, about 2,500 Netherlanders and Westphalians actually reached the city. The high tide came at Easter 1534, and when the promised divine deliverance did not come, Matthijs died in a suicidal sortie from the city. With the succession of Jan Beukelszoon a revolutionary regime was installed, based on the Twelve Elders and the Davidic kingship with Beukelszoon as king. To his notorious institution of polygamy, which reflected the preponderance of women over men (around 5,000 to 2,000), Jan

78 Virck et al., eds., *Politische Correspondenz*, vol. 1: 264.
79 Krebs et al., eds., *Elsaß*, vol. 2: 354.
80 Krebs et al., eds., *Elsaß*, vol. 1: 357–8.
81 Krebs et al., eds., *Elsaß*, vol. 1: 577.
82 Krebs et al., eds., *Elsaß*, vol. 2: 178.
83 Krebs et al., eds., *Elsaß*, vol. 2: 43.
84 Stayer, "Radical Reformation," vol. 2: 267.

added a severe system of rationing, a kind of war communism. All came tumbling down on 25 June 1535, when the bishop's troops forced their way into the city. Some prominent figures escaped, and prophecies circulated about the advent of a new king in 1538, but Münster lay occupied by troops until 1541, and the city only recovered its limited self-government in 1553.

Anabaptist Münster did not represent a revolution of the poor and oppressed, for behind the coup stood from first to last a faction of substantial local burghers. Stripped of its leaders' boasts about the coming kingdom of Christ and its enemies' warnings about the Anabaptists' desire for world hegemony, Münster does not look so different from other communalist experiments in godly governance. Yet the undertaking's symbolic and rhetorical impact should not be underestimated, for in some nearby lands the regimes, Catholic and Protestant, began in response to undertake reforms and to institute new levels of surveillance. More significant, perhaps, was Münster's role in the spread and growth of Anabaptism in the Netherlands. From the 1540s onward, the majority party among Dutch Anabaptists comprised followers of Menno Simons (ca. 1496–1561), a West Frisian priest, who accepted Melchiorism but opposed its literal apocalypticism and its advocacy of force. After Münster he led the remnant of Dutch Anabaptists away from violence and preached to them a near-Catholic spirituality of inwardness which aimed at producing a new man in Christ. His leadership continued through various divisions and disputes until his death in 1561, but his project to unite with the southern German Anabaptists failed in 1557–59, though later it did partly succeed.

The fortunate Anabaptists were those who migrated eastward to remote Moravia, where, tolerated by local lords, they organized dispersed small settlements that lived from handicrafts. Here Anabaptism experienced its golden age, and by 1600 there were perhaps 20,000 of them living in seventy settlements, some of whom were practicing communalism under "a sort of theocratic oligarchy selected from the ranks of the brotherhood."[85]

The sixteenth-century German-speaking sects were radical in practice in a medieval way, not theologically radical in Luther's way. Their religious sensibilities centered on a communal Christian life, not on justification by faith alone, and they were ascetic in the classical sense, shunning the world and worldliness for the sake of following Christ. Of the great conundrum of asceticism – some must be worldly so that the godly may live – they were well aware, but unlike the Protestant reformers, they stoutly resisted being dragged into the worldliness of government, oaths, taxation, and war. In many ways they represented the noblest tendencies of popular Christianity *before* the Reformation. That in the end they had little influence on the course of other reformations, the singular scandal of Münster aside, says more about the severity of their persecution, which drove them from the cities into rural provincialism, than about the representative character of their original sensibilities. The Anabaptists belonged to the reformations but not to the Protestant reformation in the Empire, the fate of which was to be determined by Imperial, territorial, and civic politics.

85 Stayer, "Radical Reformation," vol. 2: 266.

Imperial Reformations in the Age of Charles V

> Every human benefit, every virtue and every prudent act, is founded on
> compromise.
>
> Edmund Burke

A prophesied age of peace and unity arrived in 1519 with the election of Spain's young king to the Imperial throne. The Archangel Michael himself, the author of "The Book of the Hundred Chapters, " had announced, "proposes . . . to reestablish a firm Christian faith on earth, so that the words of our Savior may be fulfilled: 'There shall be one flock, one shepherd.'" [John 10:16][1] When news of Charles's election at Frankfurt came to the royal court in Spain, Grand-Chancellor Mercurino Arborio di Gattinara (1465–1530) announced that the work begun by Charles the Great (Charlemagne) would be completed by Charles the Greatest, who would give the world one pastor and one flock.

Every sun shone on fortune's darling. Brightest of all glowed the great golden disk of Moctezuma II (ca. 1466–1520), sent to the king by Hernán Cortés (1485–1547) from the sack of Tenochtitlán. Albrecht Dürer viewed this wonder at Antwerp in 1520: "I also saw the things sent to the king from the new, golden land, a sun entirely of gold a klafter wide, a silver moon just as wide."[2] "In all my life," he marveled, "I have seen nothing that so gladdened my heart as these things, for I saw there wondrous works of art and marveled at the subtle skills of those men in foreign lands."[3] Made for the last Aztec emperor, the golden sun now shed its radiant glory on the Holy Roman emperor-elect. Charles's reign opened in that bright sunlight; it would end thirty-nine years later in a grim mood of defeat, his grand personal empire in tatters, his Holy Roman Empire in a state of precarious peace, his beloved Church wallowing in one of the deepest crises in its long history.

I. THE HABSBURG BROTHERS AS LORDS OF THE EMPIRE

On the first day of June 1520, Charles returned to his native Netherlands. Once crowned German king at Aachen, Charlemagne's residence, he came upriver to

---

1 Gerald Strauss, ed., *Manifestations of Discontent in Germany on the Eve of the Reformation*, 235.
2 Albrecht Dürer, *Schriften und Briefe*, 3.
3 Dürer, *Schriften und Briefe*, 32. Like all weights and measures, the *klafter* varied in size, but it was something less than two meters.

Worms to open his first Imperial Diet. On that assembly's agenda lay the task of putting a capstone on the Imperial Reform by creating an executive Governing Council, reforming the Imperial Chamber Court, and compiling a new Imperial tax roll (it would remain in use for nearly 300 years).[4] When the Diet rose at the end of May, Charles and his court returned down the Rhine to his Low Countries, then governed by his Aunt Margaret (1480–1530). One year later he shipped for England, where he visited another aunt, Queen Catherine (1485–1536) and negotiated with her husband. In July 1522 he sailed for Castile.

Event piled upon fortunate event at a dizzying pace for the young sovereign. Six months before he left England, the cardinals' conclave at Rome elected his old tutor to the chair of St. Peter. Pope Adrian VI (r. 1522–23), born as Adriaan Floriszoon (1459–1523), the son of an Utrecht carpenter, had studied with the Brethren of the Common Life and at the University of Leuven/Louvain, where he became professor of theology in 1493. Tutor to Charles since 1507, Adrian accompanied him in 1516 to Spain, where he served as the king's top advisor. Adrian's elevation to the papacy in 1522 represented the dream of every king-emperor since the eleventh century – an Imperial client on Peter's throne.

During the golden decade of the 1520s, the young emperor's armies marched from victory to victory. On 23 April 1521 near Villalar in Castile, his troops defeated the rebel association of the *comuneros*; in July 1522, as he sailed home from England, his Italian army crushed the French and their Swiss mercenaries (Huldrych Zwingli witnessed the battle) at La Bicocca near Milan; two-and-a-half years later, on Charles's twenty-fifth birthday (24 February 1525), his commanders defeated the French king, Francis I (r. 1515–47), at Pavia and took him prisoner; and in 1527 Pope Clement VII (r. 1523–34) learned who was master in Italy, as Charles's unpaid and mutinous troops stormed the walls of Rome and indulged themselves in a sack that shocked the age. In that same year Charles married Isabella (1503–39), royal princess of Portugal, who in 1527 bore him Philip (1527–98), his only legitimate son. Even the most terrible event of this decade brought Charles advantage. The death of King Louis II (b. 1506, r. 1516–26) of Hungary at Ottoman hands on the field of Mohács (29 August 1526) triggered a residual Habsburg claim to the crowns of Hungary and Bohemia. The two kingdoms came (permanently, as it happened) under Habsburg rule. In summer 1529 King Francis bowed to the Habsburg hegemony in Italy and made peace with Charles. The Italian question settled (for the time being), Charles took up two other unfinished matters. In February 1530 at Bologna, Pope Clement crowned him Holy Roman emperor, whereupon Charles crossed the Alps to Augsburg, whither he had called the Imperial estates to settle the religious question. Finally, in 1531 his brother, Ferdinand of Bohemia and Hungary, gained a third crown as king of the Romans (German king).

It was an incredible decade, the interval between Charles's first visit to the German lands in 1521 and his return in 1530. Tradition and good fortune transformed Charles of Ghent from a shy, homely, awkward youth into a mighty emperor, worthy successor to his Ottonian and Hohenstaufen ancestors. His new splendor hid his

---

4   This register lists 384 Imperial estates: 7 electors, 4 archbishops and 45 bishops, 31 lay princes, 65 prelates, 14 abbesses, 4 district commanders of the Teutonic Order, 137 counts and barons, and 84 free cities. The Imperial standing of quite a number of them was debatable.

unhappy youth, just as his new beard disguised his jutting jaw, his dynasty's physical signature. He seemed truly to deserve Gattinara's prophetic accolade, "Charles the Greatest." He was master of all he surveyed, except in the Empire, where hardly anything had gone right since his departure from Worms in 1521. Then he had left behind the Luther problem; he returned in 1530 to an Empire riven by a full-blown schism.

2. EMPIRE AND REFORMATIONS – THE BEGINNINGS, 1521–1524

Before Charles left Worms in early summer 1521, he had made arrangements for the Empire's governance in his absence . Nine years would pass – the storm years of the German Reformation – before the Germans saw his face again. He left Archduke Ferdinand behind as his Imperial vicar and lord of the five eastern Austrian duchies (Upper and Lower Austria, Styria, Carinthia, and Carniola), plus Tyrol and Outer Austria. He had little time to devote to this dynastic legacy or to his grandfather's project of expanding the Habsburg influence over the southern German lands. Following the Burgundian Wars of the 1470s, a grand Habsburg position in the southern lands had begun to take shape in 1488 with the founding of the Swabian League under Habsburg sponsorship; it took an important step forward in 1504 with Maximilian's victories in and settlement of the Bavarian War. A vast network was forming. It linked the patronage of small powers to the Habsburgs' Austrian base to make a gigantic arc of dynastic power from the borders of Hungary to those of France.

Charles's principal opportunity to expand Habsburg power came at the beginning. There were two important territorial powers in the German southwest, the Palatinate, which his grandfather had humbled in 1504, and Württemberg, which fell into his lap in 1519. In that year Duke William of Bavaria raised the Swabian League against Duke Ulrich of Württemberg (his brother-in-law) and marched its forces westward to drive the prince from his lands. The victory left the league with Württemberg on its hands, the costs of the campaign unrecompensed, and but one potential buyer for the duchy. The leaders offered the land to the new king, who at the end of 1519 sent a Brabanter named Maximiliaan van Bergen (d. 1521) to Augsburg to make the deal. It was the opportunity of a lifetime, for the compact land of Württemberg, a perfect base from which to dominate the German southwest, could be had for the mere bagatelle of 210,000 gulden. Van Bergen urged his master to consider "that this land of Württemberg is a large and important territory, and that Your Royal Majesty can procure no greater advantage than to bring it into Your Majesty's hands. This is so because it lies in the middle of the Holy Empire and borders on some of Your Royal Majesty's hereditary Austrian lands."[5] As archduke of Austria, Charles would then "possess adequate power *vis-à-vis* the disturbers of the peace in the German lands . . . [and] could thus all the better maintain law and order in the Holy Empire."[6] Charles accepted his councilor's proposition but gave little further thought to his grandfather's vision of a great Habsburg system from Vienna to Besançon and Metz. He never paid the price he had pledged. Charles did assign Württemberg and the other Austrian lands to his brother, Ferdinand, whose officials governed at Stuttgart until

5 Thomas A. Brady, *Turning Swiss: Cities and Empire, 1450–1550*, 107.
6 Brady, *Turning Swiss*, 108.

they lost the duchy at the old duke's restoration in 1534. Maximilian's legacy, the project of a powerful Austrian southwest, now followed him into the grave.

Eighteen years old when he came to Austria as his brother's vicar and vassal, Ferdinand was small of stature (five feet, six inches), slim, and clean-shaven. He possessed a good deal of what a modern biographer has called "the unself-conscious bonhomie that marked his grandfather, the Emperor Maximilian I."[7] Born in 1503 at Alcalá de Henares in Castile, after the death of his father, King Philip I (1478–1506), the boy was taken off to be reared at the court of his maternal grandfather, Ferdinand of Aragon (r. 1479–1516). From the day the two brothers first met in 1517 at Mojados, a dusty Castilian town west of Valladolid, Charles began to teach Ferdinand his place. Yet he needed his only brother, for Maximilian had negotiated a Habsburg-Jagiellonian double marriage of their sister, Mary (1505–58),[8] to King Louis II, and of Ferdinand to Princess Anne (1503–47).[9] First, however, Ferdinand had to be outfitted with the titles and lands. On 27 May 1521, one day after the Diet rose at Worms, Anne and Ferdinand were married at Linz in Upper Austria.

Don Fernando, archduke of Austria and Infant of Spain, was built of sounder royal timber than his elder brother, whose upbringing at court in Mechelen/Malines in the Netherlands had encouraged his gluttony and other faults he never mastered. More moderate in his habits than Charles, Ferdinand was also better educated and more clear-headed about what he believed. He spoke Latin, Spanish, Italian, and French fluently, and he learned German. A good Habsburg, devoted to the reputation and welfare of his dynasty, living and dead, he once told his sister Mary that "honor and reputation were the things that most marked a man in the world."[10] Spoken as a true grandson of Maximilian. In religion Ferdinand was punctilious about his duties and firm in his Catholic beliefs. In politics he was tactful and careful in his dealings with the touchy German aristocrats, unlike Charles, who never adjusted to this alien world in which great lords felt free to say "yea" or "nay" to their monarch. All in all, Ferdinand suggests what a Renaissance education might have done for Maximilian I, the kinsman he most resembled.

As Charles's vicar Ferdinand had initially little to do, for in the 1520s Habsburg governance outside Austria presents a picture of immobility, even torpor. Within the Austrian lands, however, Ferdinand quickly took things in hand. Perfectly amazed at what could be tolerated in this backwoods of Christendom, Ferdinand ordered marauding provincial nobles to be caught and hanged, and he made quick work of Viennese rebels. He slowly put the lands' governance in better order than it had ever been under his grandfather, and his administrative ordinance of 1527 laid the foundation of the lands' future governance.

Effective Imperial governance proved a much harder nut to crack. If the emperor's authority over the Governing Council created at Worms in 1521 seemed ambiguous, that of Ferdinand as his vicar was a pure mystery. Modeled on the failed council of 1500, the new body's twenty-three members comprised the six electors (in fact, their

---

7 Paula Sutter Fichtner, *Ferdinand I of Austria: The Politics of Dynasticism in the Age of the Reformation*, 2.
8 This is Mary of Hungary, who in Charles's name governed the Habsburg Netherlands from 1531 to 1555. She succeeded in this office their Aunt Margaret (b. 1480, r. 1507–15), and preceded her niece, Margaret of Parma (b. 1522, r. 1559–66), who was Charles V's (illegitimate) daughter.
9 Anne and her younger brother, Louis, were the only surviving legitimate children of King Vladislav/Lázló II (1456–1516) of Bohemia and Hungary and Anne de Foix (1484–1506).
10 Ferdinand to Mary, 27 July 1549, in Fichtner, *Ferdinand I*, 4.

deputies), princes, nobles, and envoys from two Imperial free cities, plus several royal nominees. One of its immediate tasks was to enforce the Edict of Worms against Luther, his followers, and his printers. Despite intensifying evangelical agitation at Nuremberg, the Council's seat, in January 1522 it commanded all estates to suppress innovations and abuses in their jurisdictions and to punish priests who "undertake to change the Mass . . . and in the German language consecrate the most worthy Sacrament."[11] Hans von der Planitz (d. 1535), the Saxon elector's representative, reported from Nuremberg that Duke George of Saxony (1471–1539), called "the Bearded," and the bishop of Bamberg had threatened to inform the emperor about "such occurrences in Your Electoral Grace's lands, . . . [and] one knows the temper of His Imperial Majesty and those around him in this matter."[12] Still, nothing much happened.

One year later the Governing Council tried again. It ordered the clergy "to shun everything that might stir up the common man against the rulers or confuse the ordinary Christian; but they should preach and teach only the holy Gospel as interpreted by the writings that the holy Christian church has approved and accepted."[13] Yet many Imperial estates hesitated to act, preferring to wait until a council, national or general, or the Diet settled the dispute. "Things are quite deplorable among the princes," wrote Duke Ernest of Bavaria (1500–60), administrator of the see of Passau, "for some stand firmly on Luther's side, some not; yet they are all agreed on negotiating with His Holiness to the effect that our province should not be abused. . . . I worry that nothing good will come of this, and God alone knows what will."[14]

In the years between the Diet of Worms and the Peasants' War, no one could foresee the situation's outcome, least of all the southern cities' magistrates, who were caught between the rock of the Edict of Worms and the hard place of mounting agitation for illegal religious changes. While no prince had openly declared for Luther and against the edict, many did support proposed Imperial laws to suppress the large trading firms ("monopolies") and introduce an Imperial customs duty, measures that could only damage the rich burghers and worsen the magistrates' position. When the Diet of Nuremberg in 1523 approved limits on the size and capitalization of firms, plus the customs duty, the urban envoys predicted that if the measures were enforced, they "may in time well achieve the annihilation of general trade and exchange through the ruination of all the honorable free and Imperial cities."[15] To whom could the cities turn? Perhaps to the king, for the stage seemed neatly set for a royal-urban alliance to promote stronger central governance. Chancellor Eck of Bavaria saw the import duty in just this light. "This money, which will come to many hundreds of thousands of gulden," he wrote to his prince, "will go to the House of Austria and stay there" to help Charles to reduce the German princes to servitude.[16]

In response to these threats, internal and external, the southern urban regimes (plus Cologne) came together, just as they had in the 1440s. Between 1522 and 1525 they met ten times to deliberate on a common policy. The magistrates of four large

11 Ruth Kastner, ed., *Quellen zur Reformation 1517–1555*, 489.
12 Kastner, ed., *Quellen*, 491.
13 Brady, *Turning Swiss*, 158.
14 Georg Pfeilschifter, ed., *Acta reformationis catholicae Germaniae concernantia saeculi XVI. Die Reformverhandlungen des deutschen Episkopats von 1520 bis 1570*, vol. 1: 420–1.
15 Brady, *Turning Swiss*, 136.
16 Brady, *Turning Swiss*, 131.

southern cities – Augsburg, Nuremberg, Strasbourg, and Frankfurt – decided to petition the emperor against "the [proposed] customs duty, . . . which . . . is considered to be so grievous and entirely injurious, that we think it will in time prove ruinous to all powers, but especially to the honorable cities."[17] When the cities' embassy came to Valladolid in mid-1523, they were asked what their masters "would do for him, should His Imperial Majesty take the government into his own hands and abolish both the customs duty now proposed and the Governing Council."[18] Charles seemed open to solidarity with the cities, but while the envoys were told that His Majesty did not intend to diminish or harm commerce in any way, they also heard of his displeasure over the fact that Augsburg, Strasbourg, and Nuremberg "adhere to the execrable, damnable, seductive, false, heretical Lutheran doctrine."[19]

There the matter stood until January 1524, when the Diet assembled at Nuremberg for the third time in two years. The Empire's virtual capital had become a cockpit of religious strife, in which the patrician magistrates played a double game: they protected both the evangelical preachers against the bishop of Bamberg and the Catholic Mass against the evangelicals. The arrival of great Catholic dignitaries for the Diet upset this strategy by rousing the preachers to new heights of vehemence. It was reported that in Easter Week, the holiest season in the Christian calendar, "the preachers here preach more sharply than ever before against the pope, cardinals, and bishops."[20] The local preacher Andreas Osiander (1498–1552), it was said, "is now also attacking the lay authority to the degree that the subjects might well rise up against it."[21] At Forchheim in Nuremberg's territory the peasants were out, and local artisans were plotting to make common cause with them. The Devil was loose in Nuremberg, and the magistrates had him by the tail.

On 14 February, Archduke Ferdinand called before him Nuremberg's senior magistrates. Only four appeared, and they were told, the Saxon elector's envoy related, that "His Princely Grace takes it badly that they permit Luther's doctrines and his writings to be sold, his perverted teaching to be preached, the runaway monks and the priests to take wives and reside in the city, and peasants to preach."[22] The magistrates responded with an eloquent gesture. Since 1349, when their ancestors had crushed the guilds, on the Feast of the Holy Lance (the second Friday after Easter) the sacred objects in Nuremberg's custody were displayed to burghers and visitors, so that "all believers who have reverently venerated these insignia may the more joyfully greet Christ when he comes to judge the earth."[23] The treasures, stored in the chapel of the Holy Ghost, included the Holy Lance that pierced the Savior's side, St. Anne's arm, chains that had bound St. Peter, Paul, and John the Evangelist, St. Maurice's sword, St. John the Baptist's tooth, and the sword, spurs, orb, scepter, dalmatic, coat, crown, belts, and stockings of Emperor Charlemagne. In this year, 1524, the magistrates decided to forgo the customary display of these treasures. While their decision

---

17   Brady, *Turning Swiss*, 137.
18   Brady, *Turning Swiss*, 141.
19   Brady, *Turning Swiss*, 142.
20   Brady, *Turning Swiss*, 171.
21   Brady, *Turning Swiss*, 171.
22   Günter Vogler, *Nürnberg 1524/25: Studien zur Geschichte der reformatorischen und sozialen Bewegung in der Reichsstadt*, 54.
23   Heidi Eberhard Bate, "The Measures of Men: Virtue and the Arts in the Civic Imagery of Sixteenth-century Nuremberg," 137.

did not in itself signal taking a definite side in the religious conflict, the gesture took its meaning, as gestures will, from the situation.

The pressure at Nuremberg also began to crack the large free cities' solidarity. Lazarus Spengler (1479–1534), the host city's secretary, favored no action by the urban envoys, because the longer the religious ferment went on, "the more, praise be to God, the Word of God will spread to and take root in all parts of the land, so that nothing can be undertaken against it."[24] Strasbourg's Hans Bock (d. 1542) demurred. His masters, he said, would "support and accept [whatever] a free council or Christian assembly might ... decide."[25] Bock held the day, and the cities' envoys decided to admit to Charles V that "this same mandate is framed in such a way and with such difficult demands, that many of the honorable cities cannot enforce all of its articles. Their attempt to do so would give rise to severe resistance, the destruction of law and order, and dissension between the regimes and their subjects, both lay and clerical, and would lead to murder and bloodshed."[26] They were right to be worried in this high summer of the year 1524, for in the southern Black Forest rebels were already swearing solidarity.

A glance at what happened between the Diet of Worms and the Peasants' War reveals three things about the situation. First, whatever happened, even with a united will (which did not exist) the Governing Council at Nuremberg could not enforce the edict against Luther, the magistrates could not obey it, and the Imperial vicar, Ferdinand, could not begin to take the violations in hand. Second, thrown on their own resources the Imperial cities' magistrates could neither defend urban interests in the Diet nor pacify agitation among their burghers. The day of mighty urban leagues had passed. Third, though some princes – George of Saxony, William of Bavaria – supported the edict and others – Frederick of Saxony, perhaps Philip of Hesse – did not, as yet no real parties had formed among them and the other Imperial estates. The dilemma's horns were real enough. On the one hand, Luther had defied both pope and emperor, who made him and his active followers prosecutable; on the other, the spread of enthusiasm for Luther summed up more than a century of criticism and protest by voices high and low against the papacy and its practices. What was a Christian or, more to the point, a Christian ruler to do? What did the common good of Empire and Church require? Into this mare's nest thrust, in 1525, the powerful coagulant of insurrection.

3. IN THE SHADOW OF REVOLUTION – THE BIRTH OF PROTESTANTISM, 1525–1529

Archduke Ferdinand called the Imperial Diet to Augsburg for the end of 1525 but had to prorogue it to Speyer four months hence. When finally assembled in mid-summer 1526, the estates faced a dilemma. Should emperor and Empire suppress the evangelical movement as the cause of insurrection or defend it as the remedy? While all lords claimed a duty to protect true religion, conscience, and the common good,[27] the insurrection posed

---

24 Brady, *Turning Swiss*, 169.
25 Brady, *Turning Swiss*, 169–70.
26 Brady, *Turning Swiss*, 173.
27 When public documents of the time refer to "conscience," they almost always attribute it to rulers, rarely to individual subjects. The theologians recognized conscience as individual, of course, but only Anabaptists and other sectarians condemned in principle coercion in matters of religion.

decisions for which their customs and practices had not prepared them. The Catholics argued that the evangelicals, under the cloak of religious reform, had aroused the subjects against their lords, just as they themselves rebelled against God and His Church. "Do not allow the Lutheran scoundrels to begin preaching," Leonhard von Eck warned Duke William on 12 February 1525, "for they alone are the cause of this insurrection."[28] The evangelicals argued the contrary: the papacy, bishops, and priests had caused the rebellion, for which evangelical religion offered both a remedy and a prophylactic. "The gospel now called 'Luther's doctrine,'" wrote Landgrave Philip of Hesse (1504–67) to his Saxon father-in-law, Duke George, "brings forth not peasant revolts but every form of peace and obedience."[29] On one thing, of course, the proto-parties in the Diet could and did agree: the debate about true religion aside, rebellion was always a wicked thing. Yet this did not push them together on the religious question.

At Speyer in 1526, Ferdinand charged the estates to listen to the peasants' grievances. Taking the easy way out, they blamed Rome. The papacy and its taxes, they declared, were a "cause of rebellion and other forms of disobedience."[30] This was the excuse offered in 1518, echoing 1451. In its point-by-point commentary on the *Twelve Articles of the Swabian Peasantry*, the Diet's committee kept to this line, asserting that since Rome was chiefly to blame: "many of the pastors are so ignorant and so uneducated and preach and proclaim God's Word so incompetently that the common man is outraged"; and the cure of souls would be improved if the princes took over benefices now reserved to Rome.[31] How this step might redress peasants' grievances, the committee did not say. The committee piously appealed to the seigneurs to treat their subjects consonant with their (the lords') "consciences," the "law of God and of nature," and "fairness."[32] The committee declared the dispute over religion to be "not the least important cause of the late insurrection of the common man, as also of all unrest now present in the German lands," for which the remedy would be "a unanimous, common understanding of the Christian faith."[33] This could be achieved by "a free general council or at least a national assembly, which should be held in the German lands within one year, eighteen months at the most."[34] No one knew what a "national council" of the Empire might be or who might be represented in it.

The best one can say about these measures is that they combined self-serving silence about the insurrection's causes with dissimulation concerning religion. A commoner might have sooner agreed with the Catholic Johannes Salat (1498–1561), town clerk of Lucerne, who did not blame the evangelicals, whom he strongly opposed, for the Peasants' War. "It can be concealed from no one," he writes, "that the origin of the peasant uproar, dissension, and affliction lies with the transgressions and oppressions of the clergy and nobility who have serfs."[35] The seigneurs have

28 Wilhelm Vogt, *Die bayrische Politik im Bauernkrieg und der Kanzler Dr. Leonhard von Eck, das Haupt des Schwäbischen Bundes*, 381.
29 Thomas A. Brady, *Protestant Politics: Jacob Sturm (1489–1553) and the German Reformation*, 56.
30 Peter Blickle, *The Revolution of 1525: The German Peasants' War from a New Perspective*, 166.
31 Blickle, *The Revolution of 1525*, 166.
32 Blickle, *The Revolution of 1525*, 168.
33 Johann Jakob Schmauss, ed., *Neue und vollständigere Sammlung der Reichs-Abschiede, welche von den Zeiten Kayser Conrads des II. bis jetzo auf den Teutschen Reichs-Tagen abegefasset worden*, vol. 2: 273.
34 Schmauss, ed., *Neue und vollständigere Sammlung*, vol. 2: 273.
35 Tom Scott and Bob (Robert W.) Scribner, eds., *The German Peasants' War. A History in Documents*, 95.

burdened their peasants "with unaccustomed grievances and have subjected them to intolerable coercion in many ways . . . and have imposed upon them much which is neither proper, just, godly, nor tolerable."[36] In Salat's view, Luther, Zwingli, and the other preachers merely took advantage of a situation they had not created.

The Diet of Speyer in 1526 closed with the era's most pregnant act of political weaseling. Its recess declared that until a general council decided the matters at issue, every Imperial estate should act "in such a way as he will be responsible for to God and the emperor."[37] Whether the Diet meant in this passage to legitimize wholesale religious change by the rulers, as it came to be interpreted, is surely a moot point, for no one could say what intentions lay behind it. Perhaps panic, for two days after the Diet rose on 27 August 1526, the main battle army of Sultan Süleyman I (r. 1520–66) met the Hungarian king's forces at Mohačs and slew King Louis, 28 magnates, 7 bishops, around 500 nobles, 4,000 cavalry, and 10,000 infantry. From this moment the Ottoman power became a powerful and constant force in Imperial political life.

The formation of religious parties among the Imperial estates was a fruit of the Peasants' War. On 19 July 1525, five Catholic princes agreed to form an alliance against what George of Saxony, easily their commanding figure, called the "damned Lutheran sect" and the "root of this insurrection."[38] The evangelicals countered by clustering around George's first cousin, Elector Frederick, and, following his death in 1525, around his brother, John (1468–1532), called "the Constant." In the very midst of the great insurrection, Elector Frederick and Duke John met Landgrave Philip of Hesse at Kreuzberg on the Werra River, where the handsome young Hessian declared he would defend the Gospel at all costs. In February 1526 he and John (Frederick having died) founded the League of Gotha. Although the princes invited the leading southern Imperial cities to join this first evangelical alliance, their magistrates politely declined to do so.

When the Diet convened again at Speyer in the spring of 1529, all eyes were fixed on Hungary, where a huge Ottoman army was preparing to besiege Vienna. Charles and Ferdinand (in the meantime elected king of Hungary and Bohemia), frantically sought new taxes to finance the salvation of their realms. The Saxon elector's party responded that this issue could not be isolated from "the dispute about our Holy Christian faith."[39] They saw now that the desperate situation – Ferdinand expected an Ottoman invasion of Lower Austria by late summer – placed a new weapon, tax refusal, into their hands. Approached for support of this policy, Jacob Sturm of Strasbourg balked, for although at Speyer, as he wrote home, "Christ is handed over to Caiphas and Pilate," yet "we should approve this recess in temporal matters, so that others are shown that in our protest we seek no material thing."[40] Soon enough, the evangelical cities' isolation – "even the Jews are looked on with more favor here than are the cities who adhere to the gospel," groused a Strasbourg envoy[41] – swept away Sturm's reservations. When the Diet's majority voted to revoke its vague

36 Scott and Scribner, eds., *The German Peasants' War*, 95.
37 Schmauss, ed., *Neue und vollständigere Sammlung*, vol. 2: 274.
38 Walter Friedensburg, *Der Reichstag zu Speier 1526 in Zusammenhang der politischen und kirchlichen Entwicklung Deutschlands im Reformationszeitalter*, 56. Members were Duke George of Saxony and Elector Joachim I of Brandenburg, Duke Eric of Brunswick-Lüneburg, Duke Henry the Younger of Brunswick-Wolfenbüttel, and Elector Albert of Mainz.
39 Schmauss, ed., *Neue und vollständigere Sammlung*, vol. 2: 293.
40 Brady, *Protestant Politics*, 68.
41 Brady, *Protestant Politics*, 68.

decision of 1526, which had left the religious issue to the individual estates, the fateful protest came. On 19 April five princes and envoys of fourteen cities protested the decision and demanded that "the recent recess [of Speyer 1526], which was … unanimously approved, should in essence and substance remain in effect."[42] Otherwise, they declared, they would refuse to sign the Diet's recess (or pay the taxes), or yield to the majority, for "in matters concerning God's honor and the salvation of our souls, each must stand alone before God and give his account of himself."[43] From this demonstrative act arose a new party name, "Protestant." Although it at first referred only to the signers of the Speyer protest, gradually it displaced "evangelical" as the appellation of those who rejected Rome's religious authority.[44]

Upon the heels of this victory rode defeat. A dark cloud hung over the pledge to form a defensive league, which Nuremberg, Strasbourg, Ulm, the Saxon elector, and the landgrave had agreed to form at Speyer. Its ranks should be open to all who adhered to "the divine Word." What did that mean? It meant a standard by which to define that faith, something no one had the authority to make. At Speyer Jacob Sturm, who agreed with Philip of Hesse's view that they were already "in agreement on the chief doctrine," the Eucharist or Lord's Supper, "though differing in their understandings of it,"[45] naively gave the Saxons a written account of what was being preached at Strasbourg. Naively, because since the mid-1520s Luther and Zwingli and their supporters had been engaged with mounting heat in a debate about precisely this question. The Eucharist or Lord's Supper emerged as the central issue in this quarrel. Clerical parties formed, and while they agreed in the negative – all rejected the Catholic doctrine of transubstantiation – the theologians could find no generally acceptable alternative.[46] Luther hammered at the Zuricher, well aware that the Strasbourgeois and other southerners were trying to play on both sides of the fence.

The legacy of the Peasants' War colored this quarrel, as it did most others of this era. Melanchthon charged the southerners with teaching the spiritual Gospel: "Müntzer taught the same thing."[47] Strasbourg's Martin Bucer denied that Zwingli was teaching "the repudiation of Christ, the abolition of the pulpit, the abandonment of Holy Writ, and the destruction of all good discipline and obedience – as though the spirit of Müntzer reigned there, the most intolerable and terrible that can be imagined."[48] Heresy and rebellion were twins, Melanchthon insisted, and from Zwingli would come, as had come from Müntzer, "a terrible and great butchery," disruption of the churches, and "the erosion of government, which could not be repaired in a hundred years – nay, not for the rest of time."[49]

The political significance of this dispute is easily described. The coupling of the projected alliance with the doctrinal dispute supplied John of Saxony with a perfect

---

42 Kastner, ed., *Quellen*, 499.
43 Detlef Plöse and Günter Vogler, eds., *Buch der Reformation. Eine Auswahl zeitgenössischer Zeugnisse (1476–1555)*, 446–7.
44 Excepting the sects (Anabaptists and others), who were not in any meaningful sense Protestants.
45 Brady, *Protestant Politics*, 69.
46 Luther taught that the spiritual Body of Christ is present in and with the elements of bread and wine, which, however, did not lose their former substance. Zwingli taught that Christ is spiritually present in the sacrament, but only to those who possess faith. His view was followed in the main by the entire Protestant tradition that calls itself "Reformed."
47 Brady, *Protestant Politics*, 69.
48 Brady, *Protestant Politics*, 69.
49 Philipp Melanchthon, *Opera quae supersunt omnia*, vol. 2: 93, no. 718.

reason to scuttle the former because of the latter. Landgrave Philip, supported by Sturm, tried to break this coupling in September 1529, when Luther and Zwingli met at Marburg Castle in Hesse. What seemed, as the saying goes, a good idea at the time, proved a disaster. The landgrave cajoled, Sturm pled, and Bucer lent soft words, but Luther remained adamant, Zwingli obdurate. At one point, it is reported, Luther dramatically flung aside the tablecloth to reveal words he had written on the table, "This *is* My Body."

The project to form an armed party of Protestant powers had come to its critical point. After the Saxon elector vowed no union with heretics, the Hessian landgrave wrote with bitterness to Sturm: "It is time. If we sleep and let the lamps burn out, the Bridegroom will not let us in [Matt. 25:1–13]."[50] When first Strasbourg's regime and then the landgrave allied with the evangelical Swiss cities – Zurich, Bern, and Basel – they merely confirmed the Lutheran theologians' dictum: the Sacramentarian heresy and Swiss revolution went hand in hand. Yet time pressed, for Charles V, now lord of Italy and emperor crowned, was coming back to settle the German schism. He would find the Protestant party riven by conflict.

4. A MOMENT OF DECISION – AUGSBURG, 1530

Early summer sun was melting the Alpine snows as Charles V and his huge entourage rode up from the plains of Lombardy, crossed the Brenner Pass to pause for rest at Maximilian's Innsbruck, and then made their final crossing down into the Lech River valley.[51] He was headed for Augsburg, whither he had summoned the Imperial estates. The emperor, freshly crowned, meant to settle the Empire's religious schism. On 15 June 1530 his party approached the gates of the mighty Swabian metropolis, a city burgeoning with population, wealth, and pride. Once over the Lech bridge they were met by the electors, princes, and other lords on foot, whereupon Charles and Ferdinand dismounted, and all their train with them. After the young emperor gave his hand and a few friendly words in Latin or French to each prince, the archbishop-elector of Mainz greeted him in the name of all the Imperial estates, to which Count Palatine Frederick (1482–1556) replied in Charles's name. The emperor remounted, trumpets blared, drums crashed, and a tremendous cry went up in many tongues "from many lands of all Christendom, as though the entire earth gave back its echo."[52] Now came the host city's turn to shine, as its senior magistrates appeared, all in Augsburg's white-and-black, at the head of 1,000 guild militiamen armed with guns, spears, and halberds, plus twelve light cannon. After the city secretary, the noted humanist Dr. Conrad Peutinger (1465–1547), greeted the royal personages in Augsburg's name, all guns and cannon thundered in greeting.

The monarch now entered, like a Roman emperor of olden times, his realm's richest city, if not quite yet its largest.[53] The Holy Roman Empire of the German

50 Brady, *Protestant Politics*, 71–2.
51 My account of the emperor's entry into Augsburg in 1530 owes much of its inspiration to Ranke's brilliant portrayal in Leopold von Ranke, *Deutsche Geschichte im Zeitalter der Reformation*, vol. 3: 146–50.
52 Rosemarie Aulinger, *Das Bild des Reichstages im 16. Jahrhundert. Beiträge zu einer typologischen Analyse schriftlicher und bildlicher Quellen*, 333.
53 The entry was portrayed in ten sheets by Jörg Breu the Elder, an Augsburg artist. This account is based on the chronicle of a local Benedictine, Clemens Sender, who is quoted at length by Aulinger, *Bild des Reichstages*, 335–6.

Nation was on parade. At the procession's head marched Charles's 1,000 infantry bearing two great banners, followed by "the Spanish lords, [dressed] lavishly in gold or black satin coats, and they had large golden chains around their necks."[54] Then came Duke John Frederick (1503–54, r. 1532–47), the elector of Saxony's son, with his troopers, more Spanish nobles, and the escorts of Duke George of Saxony, the archbishops of Mainz, Cologne, and Trier, Dukes William and Louis of Bavaria, Counts Palatine Ottheinrich and Philip, and Margrave George of Brandenburg-Ansbach. They were followed by the two monarchs' escorts of young Netherlandish and Austrian nobles on fine horses, plus young princes and counts from the Habsburg courts, "who rode the finest horses, called jennets, and others from Turkey, North Africa, England, and Poland."[55] After them came the main body, led by Elector John of Saxony as high marshal of the Empire, in his hand the bared Imperial sword. On his flanks rode the two other lay electors (Brandenburg and the Palatinate), then the three spiritual electors, followed by Emperor Charles "under the canopy ... in a golden coat adorned with arms, and he gazed on every part of the city with a happy smile, doffing his hat . . . to every church he passed."[56] On his right rode King Ferdinand, on his left the papal legate,[57] followed by the cardinals of Salzburg and Trent, two archbishops, and "the other bishops, prelates, princes, and ambassadors, also great lords, each in the order befitting his estate."[58] Following the Imperial prelates came Spanish churchmen and nobles, trailed by 300 Spanish riders and a large number of King Ferdinand's troopers. Augsburg's cavalry, infantry, and cannon brought up the rear of this fabulous cavalcade of more than a thousand riders and many more horses.[59] When Charles, Ferdinand, and the legate came to city hall, the clergy greeted them in full vestments and then escorted them into Augsburg's cathedral, where the canons and Bishop Christoph von Stadion (b. 1473, r. 1517–43) awaited. Charles knelt before the high altar, while behind him stood "many princes and lords in a big crowd."[60]

The entry's chronicler, the Benedictine Clemens Sender (1475–1537), mentions no women, nor does he take notice of the huge corps of cooks, armorers, chamber servants, keepers of wardrobes, secretaries, teamsters, huntsmen and falconers, nor the emperor's 200 Spanish hunting dogs. The entire entourage represented half the churches, nobilities, and peoples of Latin Christendom, speakers of Portuguese, Castilian, Catalan, Italian of all varieties, French, Dutch, many forms of German, Hungarian, Czech, and Croatian, plus probably a few Ottomans, Aztecs, and other true exotics.

Charles's entry dramatized the Empire's many identities, at once a German feudal kingdom, a partnership of emperor and estates, a dynastic world-empire, and a sacral protectorate over Christendom. At this moment Augsburg became *the* Imperial city, for so long as Charles resided in the bishop's palace, his law trumped local law, and

---

54 Aulinger, *Bild des Reichstages*, 336.
55 Jennet means here not a female donkey but a small Spanish saddle horse.
56 Aulinger, *Bild des Reichstages*, 337.
57 Vincenzo Pimpinella (1485–1534), archbishop of Rossano (now Rossano-Cariati) in Calabria, and nuncio to Ferdinand.
58 Aulinger, *Bild des Reichstages*, 337.
59 The escorts of Electors John of Saxony and Joachim of Brandenburg comprised 200 and 150 horsemen respectively.
60 Aulinger, *Bild des Reichstages*, 335.

the Augsburgers wanted no trouble. The visitors filled the city's inns, stables, and taverns, and the burghers' pockets, a bonanza for the city's landlords, innkeepers, provisioners, stablemen, entertainers, beggars, pickpockets, gamblers, and prostitutes.

The Diet of Augsburg was to the sixteenth century what the Council of Constance had been to the fifteenth, a moment at which the virtual Empire assumed flesh and blood in color, sound, and pageant. It was literally "the day of the Empire" (Imperial Diet, *Reichstag*), when the emperor's presence set the world in order.

In the background of this brilliant display of order lurked the schism in its bitter local configuration, for neither Lutherans, Catholics, nor Zwinglians had the upper hand in Augsburg. Yet on this great day the preachers of all three held their tongues. The guests did, too, though the Hessian landgrave's men openly displayed a badge bearing the evangelical motto, V.D.M.E. Evangelicals eagerly explained this device as meaning "God's Word endures forever"; it really meant, the Catholics mocked, "you'd better get the hell out of town."[61] The schism lay near the surface of all minds on the emperor's entry day, for no one doubted that a moment of decision was near. If the Diet of Augsburg adopted the guise of the "national council" for which some had been calling since 1523–24, Charles V was its Constantine. Anticipating a future general council's approval of the results, he announced that his (twenty) theologians would inspect and judge the statements of belief he had solicited from the estates. The evangelicals responded with alacrity in three different voices: the Lutherans under the Saxon elector; Strasbourg and three associated cities; and Zwingli alone (his statement was ignored).

On the surface the Diet was a great success. There were tournaments, balls, and endless dinners, some in the Latin manner (two hours) and some in the German (six hours). Aristocrats and lesser folk, many peoples exchanged clothing fashions, jousting techniques, music, and, surely, beds. The festivities peaked in one of the era's most brilliant ceremonies, as Charles formally enfiefed King Ferdinand with the Austrian lands. Having made his peace with dynastic logic, Charles set in motion plans for his brother's election as King of the Romans and, presumably, his own successor.[62] Still, the emperor's great matter, the unity of the Church, made no progress, and by early autumn it was clear that Augsburg was to be no German Nicaea. The theologians, Catholic and Lutheran, could reach no agreement, the Zwinglians lingered at the edges of negotiations.

The Diet's recess (proclamation of decisions) tells the tale of what had happened during Charles's nine-year absence: 66 of 143 articles deal with the schism, 35 with governance, 32 with the Ottoman war, and 10 with other matters. While the Peasants' War was receding into still anxious memory, the schism deepened. The Catholic majority stated in the recess the emperor's irenic intention, acknowledged its failure, and gave the Protestants until 15 April 1532 to say "whether they wish to confess and make peace concerning the disputed articles with the Christian Church, His Holiness, Us, and the other electors, princes, estates of the Holy Roman Empire, and other Christian rulers and subjects of the common Christendom until a future Council shall meet."[63] In the interim, nothing new concerning the faith "shall be printed or sold in

---

61 A joke impossible to translate: "*Verbum Dei Manet In Eternum*" vs. "*Vnd Du Musst Ins Elend.*"
62 He did so with some reluctance, for he wanted to leave everything – the Austro-Burgundian inheritance, the Iberian kingdoms (with Naples), and the Imperial crown – to his son, Philip.
63 Kastner, ed., *Quellen*, 503–4.

their principalities, lands, and territories."[64] Charles promised to secure a general council within six months, announced his intention of enforcing the Edict of Worms, and declared that he and the Catholic estates

> have agreed and promised for Ourselves and Our subjects, to remain firmly faithful to the old, true, traditional Christian faith and religion, and by the honorable, praiseworthy ceremonies and usages which have always been performed in all the churches. And We will allow no alteration in them to be made prior to the decision by a future General Council.[65]

Step by step the recess details abuses, invasions, violence, and false teaching and condemns nearly every evangelical departure from Catholic doctrine and usage. The Diet had spoken, the Protestants had heard. Recognizing their party's political weakness, they never again demanded the convocation of a national council.

5. THE RISE AND FALL OF THE SMALKALDIC LEAGUE

The Diet of Augsburg drove the two Protestant factions back together. Before leaving the city Elector John told a nonplussed Jacob Sturm of his hope that, by God's grace, the Protestant princes and cities would unite in alliance. Within five weeks their envoys assembled in Smalkalden, a small town in Thuringia, to draft an agreement. Their purpose, it declares,

> is to give praise and due honor to Almighty God, to foster and spread His holy Word and the Gospel, and, while remaining obedient members of the Holy Empire, to guide and keep our subjects in a Christian manner to all that is good, Christian, honorable, just, and conducive to their salvation, and to prevent by God's grace unjust, illegal violence and damages.[66]

Duly signed and sealed, the treaty brought into being the Smalkaldic League, whose members pledged to defend one another against all comers, not excluding the emperor.

The Smalkaldic League operated for fifteen years until it was defeated in war and dissolved in 1547. Its constitution, approved at Smalkalden on 23 December 1535, adopted the common forms of late medieval German urban and noble associations, but with several innovations. For one thing, the alliance's immense extent, nearly conterminous with the Empire itself, portended an entirely new integration of north and south. The league's structure reflected this novel arrangement of the members into two geographical divisions, a northern district under the Saxon elector and a southern one under the Hessian landgrave. In each division princes, nobles, and cities sat and voted together. New also was the league's stated principle of unity, an exclusive faith defined by the Confession of Augsburg. The constitution of 1535 stipulated a total of nine votes in the assembly, increased in the following year to thirteen, under

---

64 Kastner, ed., *Quellen,* 504.
65 Kastner, ed., *Quellen,* 507.
66 Ekkehart Fabian, *Die Entstehung des Schmalkaldischen Bundes und seiner Verfassung 1524/29–1531/35: Brück, Philipp von Hessen und Jakob Sturm,* 358, line 17, to 359, line 6.

the copresidency of the Saxon elector and the Hessian landgrave. It met twenty-six times during the league's fifteen-year history.

Over the Smalkaldic League's birth shone a lucky star. In the early days it withstood two major challenges. The first was a heated dispute over the right of active resistance to (the emperor's) authority. Officially, the league was purely defensive: "this alliance has . . . no other reason, cause, or intent than to defend and afford protection to ourselves and our subjects and dependents, in case we are invaded, attacked, or in any other manner . . . interfered with because of the Christian, just, and righteous cause for which our Christian alliance has been formed."[67] Following the Diet of Augsburg, Luther, who had stood for non-resistance, discovered that resistance was in fact a matter for the lawyers and not the theologians. More consistent was Nuremberg's Lazarus Spengler, who insisted that "for the sake of the Gospel no Imperial estate . . . may protect itself with force or resist force with force against the emperor as his legitimate overlord."[68] Landgrave Philip mocked him and the other faint-hearts. "It seems to me, a poor German fifer who is innocent of Latin and learning," he scoffed, "that if it is all right to resist in one case, it is all right in the other."[69]

Far more difficult to surmount was the schism within Protestant ranks. While the Lutherans condemned the Swiss evangelicals' teachings, many clergymen, especially in the southern cities, shared Zwingli's position on the disputed points. A Saxon who stopped in Strasbourg on his way to Paris in late winter 1531 reported being told that the city "is divided into three groups. Many are Zwinglian, many Lutheran, and also many papists. There is no sign that the preachers are backing away from the Zwinglian teachings, and they are very much hated."[70] Indeed they were, and they were encouraging the same policy at Augsburg, where the situation was far more unsettled. Although committed Zwinglians stilled preached in some Upper Swabian cities, such as Memmingen and Kempten, outside Switzerland the Zwinglian party fell into decline. Strasbourg had defaulted on its Swiss alliance when it signed the treaty of Smalkalden, and in 1532 its preachers subscribed to the Confession of Augsburg. Eventually, the city of Augsburg came over and discord formally ended, except concerning the Swiss, with the Wittenberg Concord of 1536.

The 1530s were the Smalkaldic League's halcyon days, when the Protestants advanced from strength to strength: in northern cities, such as Bremen, Hamburg, Göttingen, Lübeck, Magdeburg, and Bremen; and with northern princes such as Dukes Barnim IX (1501–73) and Philip I (1515–60) of Pomerania. Augsburg joined, and so did Württemberg after Landgrave Philip drove out Ferdinand's Austrian regime from Stuttgart in 1534. Ulrich, the restored duke, had evangelical religion introduced into his duchy with rigor and system. Each new admission increased the League's military potential. So did the successions of Protestant sons to the two most powerful Catholic princes in the north: in 1535 Joachim II (1505–71) to Joachim I as elector of Brandenburg; and in 1539 Henry II (d. 1541), called "the Pious," to Duke George of Saxony.

67 Brady, *Protestant Politics*, 144.
68 Brady, *Protestant Politics*, 74.
69 Brady, *Protestant Politics*, 75.
70 Brady, *Protestant Politics*, 80.

By the end of the 1530s the league went over to a forward policy under the young elector of Saxony, John Frederick. His father, a devout, relatively pacific prince and the very model of a Lutheran patriarch, had left belligerent posturing to the league's pile driver, Landgrave Philip. At first cautious like his father, by 1539 John Frederick had turned to a policy of preventative first strike, while his chancellor, Gregor Brück (1482–1557), was talking up a French alliance. "Just remember," Brück declared, "what help the Swiss got from this crown for the preservation of their own freedom."[71] One day, he speculated, "our party could set up its own king of the Romans, to whom the whole Empire could be made subject."[72] In 1541, when the forceful and inventive Duke Maurice (b. 1521, r. 1547–53) succeeded at Dresden, the two Saxonys were one in commitment to the Protestant cause.

The Protestant tide's sweep across the Empire maintained its energy right into the 1540s. Between 1525 and 1545 the cause gained ascendancy in 27 principalities, 30 counties, and 19 lordships. In addition, the evangelicals gained 5 bishoprics, 1 Imperial abbey, and the Prussian lands of the Teutonic Order, which in 1525 became a secular duchy under Hohenzollern rule.[73] In addition, a number of prince-bishops lost their spiritual authority over their dioceses outside the limits of their *Hochstifte*. In the mid-1530s the league's growing might attracted foreign rulers, the French and the English kings, who courted the German Protestants as potential allies. Their interest peaked late in December 1535, when French and English embassies came to Smalkalden to request their respective kings' admission to the league. Elector John Frederick rebuffed the French king as a Catholic and his English brother, based on the Six Articles of 1539, as a crypto-Catholic.

During the league's glory days, its assembly functioned as a Protestant diet. So thoroughly had the schism overcome Imperial life that for a decade from 1532 to 1541 the Imperial Diet did not meet, and the Smalkaldic leaders negotiated directly with the emperor through his agents. Mapping the frequency of Imperial Diets during Charles V's reign shows two major peaks in the 1520s and 1540s divided by a trough in the era of his absence from the Empire. King Ferdinand could have called the Diet in Charles's absence, true, but not without permission, which his elder brother did not grant him. And by the time of Charles's return in 1541, the League had arisen, fleshed out its constitution, created a military council and a financial system, and learned how to deal directly with the monarch.

In the free political space during the emperor's absence the Protestant powers established through action a right of reformation (*ius reformandi*) they did not legally possess, and suppressed Catholic institutions and worship in their lands and cities. Some, including especially the urban regimes, turned the Church's properties toward support of the evangelical clergy and schools; others, mostly princes, just gathered them into their own treasuries, as the kings of England and Sweden were doing. Confiscation strengthened the Protestant party and depleted the Catholics' resources for weathering the Protestant storm. Against such moves, however, stood the Imperial courts, especially the Imperial Chamber Court, a creation of 1495. For thirteen years from 1531 to 1541, the Smalkaldic League waged a campaign of resistance to the

---

71 Brady, *Protestant Politics*, 222.
72 Brady, *Protestant Politics*, 222.
73 According to Hubert Jedin, Kenneth Scott Latourette, and Jochen Martin, eds., *Atlas zur Kirchenge-schichte. Die christlichen Kirchen in Geschichte und Gegenwart*, no. 73.

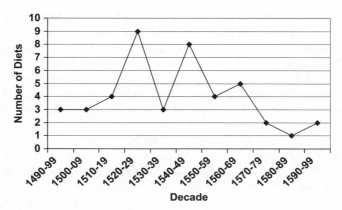

Figure 11. Imperial Diets per Decade, 1490–1599
Source: Based on information in Johann Jakob Schmauss, ed., *Neue und vollständigere Samm-lung der Reichs-Abschiede, welche von den Zeiten Kayser Conrads des II. bis jetzo auf den Teutschen Reichs-Tagen abegefasset worden,* vol. 2.

stream of writs and judgments for restoration of properties that issued from the court's seat at Speyer. It was a bitter time for those who staffed the court, for whom the religious division seemed to be bringing Imperial governance down around their ears – or, rather, starving it to death, for the Protestants refused to help pay the judges' salaries or the court's other costs. One of the assessors (judges), Count Wilhelm Werner von Zimmern (1485–1575), lamented the court's decline. In better days, when he had lodged and boarded in Speyer with other assessors, it was as "open, happy and charming a society as I have ever met."[74] By 1541, however, all was changing. "Because the Protestant Estates had prevailed and spread so much," he wrote,

> the members of the Chamber court lived in a state of heightened insecurity and at times were in danger when they dared to venture out. In addition more than a few adherents had infiltrated the assessors, doctors, and procurators, which cause a great distrust to develop within this once commendable group. Because of this insecurity and disquiet, the count [of Zimmern] no longer wanted to remain.[75]

Emperor Charles, who needed the princes' support for his wars, suspended the court's operations in 1544.

Their crippling of what the Protestants took to be a biased court in the name of a higher law proved a dangerous policy. Because Imperial princes' authority rested on feudal law alone, Protestant rulers could adduce no very convincing appeal to their consciences while denying the same appeal to their subjects. The Smalkaldeners understood this problem very well, and the very last thing they wanted was to con-cede to their subjects' consciences a weight comparable to their own. In 1542–43 the embattled evangelical minority that ruled the city of Metz in Lorraine asked to be admitted to the Smalkaldic League. Strasbourg's magistrates, asked for support,

---

74 Erica Bastress-Dukehart, *The Zimmern Chronicle: Nobility, Memory and Self-representation in Sixteenth-century Germany,* 179.
75 Bastress-Dukehart, *The Zimmern Chronicle,* 183.

weighed the minority position of Metz's Protestants against the tempting possibility that if the city turned evangelical, "a large part of France, Brabant, Flanders, Luxemburg, and also Lorraine and Burgundy could be brought over by means of the common [French] language." [76] The Wittenbergers, who were having none of such pipe dreams, responded that taking risks for the Gospel's sake was a matter for "the rulers, as those who through God's grace understand these matters better and have more to do with them than we do." [77] By the end of 1543 the matter was dropped. It never arose again. The Smalkaldic League might have become a political association of German Protestants; it remained an alliance of German princes and urban regimes.

By the late 1530s Protestant princes ruled the northern German lands. East of the Rhine and north of the Main, only the northwestern prince-bishops and one lay prince, the duke of Brunswick-Wolfenbüttel, still held to the old faith. After 1539 the Smalkaldic chiefs began to meddle in these Catholic principalities, notably the archbishopric of Cologne, the Lower Rhenish duchies of Cleves-Jülich, and the Westphalian prince-bishoprics. At most they aimed to drive the Catholic Church out of the northwest and strike at the seat of Habsburg power in the Netherlands. The Protestants now possessed two electoral votes, Saxony and Brandenburg, and hopes of a third, the Palatinate, where the next elector in line seemed to be mildly pro-Protestant. If Cologne fell, giving them a 4 to 3 majority, what would happen at the next Imperial election?

In 1539 war loomed over the Imperial Chamber Court's outlawry of Minden, a smallish city just north of where the Weser River debouches from the Central Highlands. Elector John Frederick favored a preventive strike. His allies demurred, but the evangelical advance continued. The Pomeranian pastor Johannes Bugenhagen (1485–1558), chief traveling salesman of Lutheran church ordinances, traveled back and forth across the northern lands. He spent much of a year (1534–35) in Pomerania and another (1537–38) in Denmark, and meanwhile he served as Luther's confessor, worked on Luther's publications, translated Luther's Bible into Low German, and preached his funeral sermon. In the south, meanwhile, the Swabian Johannes Brenz (1499–1570) composed a common church ordinance (1535) for two traditional rivals, the city of Nuremberg and the margrave of Brandenburg-Ansbach, while in 1538 Strasbourg-based Martin Bucer oversaw the drafting of a church ordinance for the landgraviate of Hesse.

One great shadow loomed over the Smalkaldic League during the early 1540s. Landgrave Philip of Hesse was in love. In 1539, after sixteen years of marriage to a Saxon princess, Duke George's daughter, he fell head-over-heels for a 17-year-old Saxon noblewoman, Margarethe von der Saale (1522–66). Her shrewd mother forbade her to share his bed except as a wife. German princes were no wife-killers à la King Henry VIII, and Philip, not to be denied, married Margarethe. The potential damage, once the news got around, was incalculable, since his Protestant allies might, and his Catholic enemies surely would, condemn a bigamist. If the Hessian's allies did not stand by him, Chancellor Brück told Jacob Sturm in early April 1540, the landgrave "will leave the Christian alliance," and "if such a division, split, and bad will arise among us now, this will come at truly a bad time." [78] It certainly would, and

76 Brady, *Protestant Politics*, 178.
77 Brady, *Protestant Politics*, 178.
78 Brady, *Protestant Politics*, 219.

Strasbourg's Martin Bucer, ever flexible in a good cause, openly defended the land-grave. Meanwhile, news of the Hessian bigamy spread far and wide, evoking ridicule at Rome, amusement at Munich, and rage at Wittenberg.

The landgrave's bigamy cut to the bone against the Protestant defense of Christian marriage against the Catholic rule of celibacy. Bigamy was also a capital crime, though for this, as for most crimes, a prince could be prosecuted only if a powerful superior made it a point to have him prosecuted. Charles V was possibly such a superior, and during the first half of the 1540s the princely bigamist grew unsurprisingly more attentive to the emperor's wishes and cooler toward those of his fellow Smalkaldeners. The landgrave's shift is one reason why Imperial politics began to fall back into its old patterns during the early 1540s, the chief sign of which was a resumption of the Imperial Diet's sessions.

In 1541 Emperor Charles returned to the German lands. He was once more at war with the French king, and, to paraphrase an Irish saying, the emperor's difficulty was the Protestants' opportunity. Charles convoked the Diet frequently between 1541 and 1546. He followed a double strategy of pressing, on the one hand, the entire Diet for money and troops to fight the Ottomans and the French king, while he courted, on the other, the Smalkaldeners in a series of special meetings ("colloquies") intended to forge an interim agreement on doctrine. Although the German schism could not be settled permanently within the Empire alone, the prospect of an interim arrangement encouraged the Protestant princes to support Charles's military aims. This strategy worked fairly well until the theologians reached an impasse at the Diet of Regensburg in 1546. Until then, the Diet met, princes supported Imperial wars, taxes were voted, subjects paid them, and theologians discussed differences. In time, the flow of Imperial politics returned to its old bed.

The mood of the half-decade of calm that preceded the Empire's first religious war is suggested by an incident in March 1546. On his way to the Diet of Regensburg, Emperor Charles stopped at Speyer. In rode the Hessian landgrave, hawk on arm, with 200 men. After they had hunted together, emperor and vassal dined, and Charles asked Philip how things stood with the Smalkaldic League. "My Gracious Lord Emperor," the Hessian replied, "I am missing only one man." To the emperor's query, who that might be, he replied: "Why, I mean to have Your Imperial Majesty among the pious folk." The two men chuckled, and Charles retorted, "No, no, I will not join the party of error."[79] The dinner ended, presumably, in friendly spirit, though by high summer quite a different mood would prevail.

Meanwhile, behind the scenes there was a growing determination, at least on the Catholic side, to settle the schism by force. Some years previous, Pope Paul III (r. 1534–49) had decided to settle the schism via a general council, just as in the 1410s, and he called the bishops to Mantua in 1539, then to Trent in 1542. For his part, Charles was losing patience. Having just ended a war (his fourth) against the French king, the emperor made up his mind to meet Protestant disobedience with deeds rather than words. During the Diet at Regensburg in 1546 he made his alliances, checked with his bankers, and began to mobilize his troops. When the Protestant princes refused to send their envoys to Trent, Charles outlawed them and told his commanders to concentrate at Ingolstadt on the Danube in Bavarian territory. The emperor's

79 Brady, *Protestant Politics*, 292.

Germans and Spaniards, plus the pope's Italians, comprised about 36,000 foot, 6,000 horse, and 70 guns. From the north came against them the Smalkaldeners' army, which, though somewhat weaker in men, brought more than 100 cannon. The Protestants had to hurry, for at their backs Maximilian of Egmont (ca. 1500–48), count of Buren, was on the march with 12,000 Netherlandish foot and 8,000 horse. His army slipped past the Smalkaldeners' shadowing forces, crossed the Rhine unhindered at Bingen, and marched southeastward to play hammer to the emperor's anvil.

Rarely in sixteenth-century warfare did a strategic plan so nearly succeed as did the emperor's Danube campaign. Time was on his side, for the league could win only by risking an early battle of decision. Count William of Fürstenberg (1495–1547), a tough, ruthless veteran commander of mercenaries, told them as much after inspecting their troops. "Dear lords and friends," he said, "you have laid your preparations very well. But Emperor Charles is a warrior not for a summer but for several years, if he must. You are lost, for Charles is a fighter and can stand a long war, which you cannot. In the end, though you don't see it now, you will not prevail against him."[80]

Count William's words spurred the Smalkaldic chiefs to action. Well aware of Buren's oncoming Netherlanders, on 31 August and 1 September they ordered a furious bombardment of the emperor's army as it lay before Ingoldstadt. The emperor's chroniclers present in camp declared it to be a bombardment more terrible than any they had ever seen. Dr. Bernabé de Busto (d. 1557) reports that the ground shook as in an earthquake, "as if the hellish furies, the true authors of this pestilent invention, had sallied forth from their abyss of darkness," in the midst of which the emperor stood "as if made of marble."[81]

Upon this terrible cannonade must follow the storm, the Smalkaldeners' only chance for victory. John Frederick and Philip hesitated, and in that moment they lost the war. Sebastian Schertlin von Burtenbach (1496–1577), a Swabian veteran who commanded the southern Smalkaldic cities' troops, described the scene. "Despite my many pleas, my cries, and my oaths, also my loyal advice," he remembered, "the landgrave would not attack. He defended himself with hands and feet and cried that I wanted to depart with my troops, and that in two hours the Saxons would also leave the field."[82] Philip ran to fetch the elector, and the two princes took Schertlin out into a field before the league's lines and told him of their fears to attack. "To sum up," Schertlin sighed, "our commanders would allow us under no circumstance to attack. May God forgive them! I wonder that I did not go insane in these days, for everything else happened!"[83]

Ingoldstadt was the moment that, once past, history would never give back. Having declined to attack, the league's chiefs now decamped to move up the Danube's left (northern) bank. Charles followed, and there ensued a running play of feint-and-duck, the Protestants afraid to stop and give battle, Charles unwilling to risk his entire force in an attack. To the astonishment of all observers, there was no more combat.

80   I conflate two versions of this story from Froben Christof von Zimmern, *Zimmerische Chronik*, vol. 3: 19–20, 425.

81   James D. Tracy, *Emperor Charles V, Impresario of War: Campaign Strategy, International Finance, and Domestic Politics*, 213.

82   Sebastian Schertlin von Burtenbach, *Leben und Taten des weiland wohledeln Ritters Sebastian Schertlin von Burtenbach*, 64.

83   Schertlin von Burtenbach, *Leben und Taten*, 64.

The two armies went into winter camp, where bad weather, poor rations, lack of pay, and disease ground down their effective forces.

The Smalkaldic chiefs' failure allowed Charles to play his high trump. In late winter King Ferdinand invaded the Saxon elector's lands from Bohemia, joined by none other than Duke Maurice of Saxony. Although a Smalkaldener and a Lutheran, Maurice now seized the main chance to bring down Elector John Frederick, his second cousin. Meanwhile, as the Smalkaldic chiefs headed northward to their own lands, Charles and his forces slowly trailed them. In March 1547 the emperor linked up with his brother and Maurice on the River Elbe, where on 25 April 1547 they beat John Frederick's army in the battle of Mühlberg. On 23 May the victorious emperor rode into Wittenberg, the spiritual capital of the German Protestants. He paused to visit Luther's grave in the Castle Church and then prepared to render judgment on his rebellious vassals. He deprived them of lands and titles, but, against his original intention, not their heads. The Empire was no England, and a German prince was no mill-run European aristocrat. As for Maurice, for betraying his fellow Protestants and old allies he got his price – the electoral title and lands.[84] Other Protestants named him "the Judas of Meissen."[85]

The judgment day at Wittenberg announced to the German lands that Charles V was now truly lord of the Empire. And so Titian painted him about this time, a conquering Roman Caesar in Renaissance dress, splendidly mounted and ready for war. Truth to tell, Charles was suffering so horribly from gout that he had to be carried about in a litter. He nonetheless called the estates to assemble at Augsburg and traveled southward to meet them at the end of 1547. To this "armored Diet," as it was named, he proclaimed provisional settlement to the schism (the Interim of Augsburg), which would remain in force until a decision of the general council, already sitting at Trent in South Tyrol. That might have settled the matter, but it did not. The Protestant powers did send envoys to the council, but only under duress, and at that only briefly.

6. THE BITTER FRUITS OF THE EMPEROR'S VICTORY

Had Emperor Charles known of Machiavelli's judgment that fortune rules half our affairs, he would have found the estimate far too low. In 1552, four years after Mühlberg, the triumphant Imperial warlord became a fugitive in his own kingdom. Duke Maurice turned his coat once again and signed a treaty with King Henry II (1547–59) of France to make war on the emperor. If successful, Maurice promised, the young French king would ascend to the Imperial throne. In summer, as Henry moved his army eastward toward the Rhine, Maurice and his German allies drove southward toward Tyrol. From Innsbruck the disheartened and helpless emperor fled to Italy, whereupon Ferdinand stepped in to negotiate with Maurice the Treaty of Passau. This document contained the formula that would be enacted into Imperial law in 1555.

---

84 The lands in question were those attached to the electoral title (*Kurkreis*) with their capital at Wittenberg.
85 The name is from a parody on the song, "O, you poor Judas, what have you done? / Why have you betrayed your Lord? / For that you must suffer in Hell / And be eternally Lucifer's man / May the Lord have Mercy." Based on the melody for the Latin hymn, "Laus tibi, Christe," it became a favorite among the Protestants. "Meissen" refers to Maurice's new title as margrave of Meissen. Another version of the parody (stanza 4) runs: "Maurice, you true Judas / What have you done? / That you bring the Spaniards to us / who defile both woman and man / into our fatherland/also the Italians/Is your eternal shame."

"In order to prevent the permanent division and the ruin of the German nation, our beloved fatherland," the treaty says, "we have agreed . . . [that] His Imperial Majesty and we, the estates . . . shall maintain this following religious peace, together with all provisions of the . . . established public peace."[86]

Thirty years after the Peasants' War, the German Reformation came to a standstill, though not an end. Its cumulative achievement was truly impressive. Princes, nobles, and civic magistrates had mastered the variegated evangelical movement of the early 1520s and disciplined its energies into an Imperial political party. Based on the Confession of Augsburg of 1530, the Protestants had forged an ideological unity that remained intact despite notable setbacks. More than any other event, the reversal of Charles's fortunes in 1552 demonstrates how fragile was an emperor's power over the German lands. The Protestant party, beaten in battle and stripped of its leaders, rose again to achieve an unforeseeable change of fortune. In 1555, when the treaty between King Ferdinand and Duke Maurice was written into Imperial law, the evangelical faith (in its Lutheran redaction) became a second legal religion in the Empire. This law sheltered, with one spectacular failure, the Empire's civil peace for centuries to come.

86   Kastner, ed., *Quellen*, 525.

12

Imperial Peace, 1555–1580

It's a maxim not to be despised, "Though peace be made, yet it's interest
that keeps peace."

Oliver Cromwell

At fifty-six, Charles V was spent in spirit and body. On 25 October 1556, one hand on a crutch and the other on the broad shoulder of Prince William of Orange-Nassau (1533–84),[1] he stood before the Netherlandish notables, knights of the Golden Fleece, and members of his own family in the great hall of the palace at Brussels. After a reading of his formal declaration of intent to abdicate in favor of his son, Prince Philip, Charles himself began to speak. He reminisced about his youth in these beloved Low Countries and spoke of the purpose that had gripped his life during these past forty years. "I sought the Imperial office," he said, "from a desire not to rule over other kingdoms, but to watch over Germany, my dear fatherland, and my other realms, especially those of Flanders, as well as over the peace and unity of Christendom. I have gathered all my forces and all my lands to strengthen the Christian religion against the Turks."[2] Yet "because of the difficulties and confusions created partly by the heresies of Luther and other heretical innovators in Germany and partly by neighboring princes and others who . . . embroiled me in perilous wars, I have not attained these goals to the degree that I have always desired."[3] Therefore, "I have come to the irrevocable decision to give up all my lands."[4] Having announced he would retire to Spain, Charles continued to say, "I have decided . . . to hand these lands over to my son and the Empire to my brother, the king of the Romans. I commend you to my son and ask that you show him the same love you have always shown me."[5] Charles, tears flowing down his face, blessed his kneeling son, raised him into an embrace, and kissed him.

With Charles V's abdication and the partition of his many lands and titles ended the final incarnation of the Holy Roman Empire in its universal guise. For the vast

1 He was later the leader of the Dutch Revolt against King Philip II of Spain.
2 Heinz Schilling, *Aufbruch und Krise. Deutschland 1517–1648*, 253.
3 Schilling, *Aufbruch und Krise*, 253.
4 Schilling, *Aufbruch und Krise*, 253–4.
5 Schilling, *Aufbruch und Krise*, 254.

congery of lands of which he was lord, Charles had no concept of all of them being connected, except through him, to one another. In this he differed markedly from some of his contemporary rulers. One was his sister, Mary of Hungary, regent of the Netherlands from 1531 to 1555, who "clearly grasped the importance of strengthening the commercial relations of the Netherlands" and tried without success to divert her brother from damaging them through a hopeless war to put his niece on the Danish throne.[6] Another such realist was King Francis I, who aimed to expand French commerce through the port of Savona into the Mediterranean basin.

Charles had no such vision. There is no evidence that he was aware of the need for his realms' trade or agriculture to be promoted and protected to the crown's ultimate advantage. He neatly summed up his view in a speech on his projected Italian campaign to the Council of Castile in 1529: "It is very pusillanimous for a prince to forgo undertaking a heroic course of action merely because money is wanting, for in matters of honor a prince must not only risk his own person but also pledge the revenues of his treasury."[7] Spoken like his paternal grandfather come to life once more. In a document of 1548, Charles enjoined his son and heir, Prince Philip, that because his realms were physically separated from one another and the objects of envious neighbors, the prince ought to maintain friends and informants everywhere. Sound advice, perhaps, but containing no speck of what historians call a "grand strategy."

Charles's limited views help to explain the logic of his legacy to Philip. With one hand, he ordered a strategically realistic union of his Italian lands to Spain; with the other, he decreed a senseless linking of the Low Countries to Spain.[8] The latter disposal guaranteed a trouble-filled century for his direct successors in the Spanish line. It removed, on the one hand, the Habsburg Netherlands from the jurisdiction of Imperial law and thus from the terms established by the Religious Peace of 1555. It created, on the other hand, a Spanish logistical nightmare once the revolt of 1568 had begun. Of Charles V's many errors, this was surely the worst.

In the fall of 1556 Charles sailed for Spain. He had chosen to live in the monastery of San Jerónimo de Yuste in the Estramadura, where cool mountain air flowed down to moderate the fierce summer heat, but where, as his physicians pointed out, the rainy, foggy climate in spring and fall made the place a bad choice. Charles, as usual, stuck to his decision. Although the climate did him good, nothing could relieve the terrible pain of his gout, made all the worse by his love of beer and shellfish. King Henry of France contemplated the ex-emperor's life and remarked, "now the emperor is as good as dead, he has retired from the world of men, and he suffers from the same sickness his mother had."[9] That was a patent exaggeration, for Charles had not lost his mind, merely his reputation. Surrounded by a court of some fifty persons, he lived a life that, modest by Imperial standards, clashed with the Hieronymite monks' ascetic severity.

On 21 September 1558 the former emperor lay dying. At his bedside stood Bartoloméo Carranza (1503–76), archbishop of Toledo. "Your Majesty," he said, "set your

---

6 James D. Tracy, *Emperor Charles V, Impresario of War: Campaign Strategy, International Finance, and Domestic Politics*, 20.
7 Tracy, *Emperor Charles V*, 21.
8 The decision to make the Burgundian Netherlands part of Philip's inheritance had been announced to the Diet at Augsburg in 1547–48.
9 Alfred Kohler, *Karl V. 1500–1558. Eine Biographie*, 358.

entire trust in the sufferings of Christ, our Savior. All else is foolish."[10] Then Charles died, true to the last to the faith he had defended at Worms so long ago. Later, when Carranza was being hounded by the Inquisition on suspicion of Lutheran views, some said that he had converted the dying monarch. It was a sign of the times.

1. THE RELIGIOUS PEACE OF AUGSBURG (1555)

When the report of his brother's decision to abdicate came to King Ferdinand at Augsburg in September 1555, it was hardly welcome news. Charles's long-time vicar feared that "a transfer of the Imperial office during Charles's lifetime, an innovation under Imperial law, would provoke the eruption of an acute political crisis in the Empire, the consequences of which, given the current situation of the European war, could not be foreseen."[11] The Protestants were still refractory, the Ottomans still fearsome, but the immediate danger lay in Italy, where any day war could break out anew between the Habsburgs and the pope. Still, Ferdinand had waited a very long time. Now came his reward, as with electoral approval he assumed the Imperial title in 1558. He did so, as his grandfather had done at Trent fifty years before, without a papal coronation. That rite would never be performed again.

Perhaps the most important act of Ferdinand I, this patient, long-underestimated monarch, was to shepherd the Religious Peace through the Diet of 1555. The new law represented a compact of non-intervention among the princes, prelates, nobles, and urban magistrates who constituted the Empire's immense governing class. Ferdinand strove to secure this settlement. He knew the German situation, though he was probably still puzzled as to why, unlike their Netherlandish, French, Italian, and Spanish counterparts, German princes could claim a right to resist their monarch. He nonetheless pressed forward, assisted by two electors as his commissioners to sell the peace, the Catholic archbishop of Mainz and Elector August (b. 1526, r. 1553–86) of Saxony.

The Religious Peace, the Empire's most important statute between 1356 and 1648, guaranteed toleration for those Imperial estates that adhered to the Confession of Augsburg, so that – the pious hope ran – "we might come the more speedily to a Christian, friendly, and final composition of the disputed religion."[12] The Catholics agreed to treat "the disputed [evangelical] religion in no other way than by Christian, friendly, peaceful means and paths to a unanimous, Christian understanding and conciliation."[13] They thereby accepted the principle, formulated at Speyer in 1526 and confirmed at Regensburg in 1532 and at Frankfurt in 1539, that princes, nobles, and civic regimes were responsible for their churches' governance and their subjects' consciences. "Whose the rule," ran a tag later coined by a Greifswald jurist, "his the religion" (*cuius regio, eius religio*).[14] Subjects, who had no such rights, must at their ruler's command conform to his faith or emigrate.

10 Kohler. *Karl V.*, 366.
11 Heinrich Lutz, *Christianitas afflicta: Europa, das Reich und die päpstliche Politik im Niedergang der Hegemonie Kaiser Karls V., (1552–1556)*, 444.
12 Heinrich Lutz, *Das Ringen um deutsche Einheit und kirchliche Erneuerung. Von Maximilian I. bis zum Westfälischen Frieden 1490–1648*, 353.
13 Hanns Hubert Hofmann, ed., *Quellen zum Verfassungsorganismus des Heiligen Römischen Reiches Deutscher Nation 1495–1815*, 205.
14 It was coined in 1612 by the Greifswald jurist Joachim Stephani (1544–1623).

To this the king appended on his own authority two supplementary provisions: the Declaration of King Ferdinand provided limited toleration for Lutheran subjects of Catholic prelates; and the Ecclesiastical Reservation provided that Catholic bishops and abbots who turned Protestant must surrender their offices, spiritual and temporal. The clear purpose of the latter rule, which the Protestant estates never recognized, was to preclude the secularization of additional ecclesiastical principalities. In a final exception to the Peace's general norm, sharing of offices and churches was ordered in a few bi-confessional cities. The enforcement of this settlement was integrated into the Perpetual Public Peace which had been established at Worms in 1495.

The Religious Peace embodied one of those historical moments when the awareness of realities and the estimation of possibilities combine to shape a rule of law that, because it sums up the situation, helps to preserve it. The peace marked the end of the idea, now 150 years old, of a simultaneous reform of Church and Empire. It also confirmed the Empire's character as an aristocratic corporation whose head could never be more than a "king of kings," to use Maximilian I's pithy phrase.[15] Every principal organ of Imperial governance came to be subject to the rule of "parity," equal representation of the majority Catholic and the minority Protestant parties.

The Religious Peace was from the beginning an act of Imperial politics, for attitudes toward the schism remained unchanged, and a positive rule of toleration was not intended. Emperor and estates reached agreement on a (in principle provisional) two-tiered order – toleration for rulers, coercion or exile for subjects – only by laying aside the issues of illegality the religious reformation had raised. Except for its political utility, what the Peace meant depended on which side one stood.

The principle of parity, on which the Peace of 1555 stood, "arose not from the [Protestant] religious revolt against [Imperial] law but from the legal schism caused by the religious schism," which had altered the very meanings of such words as "Empire," "Church," and "law."[16] There could now be no agreement on the sacral character of the Empire and hence on the basis of law, while the Church had become two mutually exclusive churches. Furthermore, the purely instrumental principle of political parity created ipso facto a kind of politics of religious neutrality. It "consisted of an unprecedented situation of coexistence between what were in principle two hostile bodies which, while each understanding itself as absolute, were bound together in a subordinate political order."[17] This political fiction offered three mutual advantages: a guarantee of external security; freedom to regulate the particular churches; and the provision of new norms and decisions for delimiting political and ecclesiastical spheres of influence and organizing procedures for Imperial institutions. The introduction of parity thus permitted the Imperial estates to act for more than a generation as though their irreconcilable differences had little or nothing to do with Imperial public life. It was a deal, like all peaces, and it remained to be seen whether and how long it could hold, for plenty of voices on each side declared the price to be too high.

15 See Chapter 7.
16 Martin Heckel, *Gesammelte Schriften. Staat, Kirche, Recht, Geschichte*, vol. 1: 127.
17 Heckel, *Gesammelte Schriften*, vol. 1: 135.

2. SECURING THE PEACE

The Imperial Peace of 1555 held without serious challenge for a generation. Around 1580 two things began to threaten the balance of confessional power on which it rested. First, in the early 1560s there appeared in Imperial public life a third confession, the Reformed (Calvinist) faith, which in the Empire was illicit and thus not covered by the Peace of 1555. Second, and in the long run far more serious, in the 1570s and 1580s a revival of the Catholic faith in the Empire began, which by 1600 was making its weight felt in Imperial public life. It was only for about four decades, therefore, that the Empire enjoyed a respite from religious strife, under three emperors: Ferdinand I, Maximilian II (b. 1527, r. 1564–76), and (for the first decades of his long reign) Rudolph II (b. 1552, r. 1576–1612). These were the halcyon days of the Imperial *convivencia* (coexistence).[18]

The cautious mood of these years attests the reluctance of both sides to renew the conflict, or to intensify their subjects' uncertainty about the Church's future and confusion about the differences that divided the Empire into parties and milieus. Boundaries could still be crossed that would later harden. Friendships continued across religious divisions, and intermarriage was more common than it would later be. The dire dichotomy between true and false religion was nonetheless spreading from the churches into the streets and taverns and right into the bedrooms of the great. Young Duke Eric II (r. 1540–84) of Brunswick-Calenberg wrote in 1549 to his wife, Duchess Sidonia (1518–75) of Saxony, that until she returned to "the old, true Christian faith" and abandoned her Lutheran heresy, he could not continue to live with her as man with wife, even if he must abandon all he had in this world.[19]

Living together occurred in a form, mandated by the Peace, in four southern "parity cities" – Augsburg, Biberach, Ravensburg, and Dinkelsbühl – where the two confessions shared the magistracies, the churches and schools, and the welfare institutions. In such conditions, marriages across religious boundaries remained fairly common. As in all situations of *convivencia*, the burghers had to develop codes to regulate the conduct of everyday life among citizens who were divided by religion. While such codes by no means presupposed greater tolerance of the other party's religion, they could and did encourage cooperation. At Ravensburg in 1584, when a spring storm set the church tower on fire, Catholics and Lutherans, who shared the church's use, set up a common fund for repairs. Still, the divisions were hardening as the process of fleshing out identities gave substance to the divisive repertory of images, epithets, and prejudices, the custody of which lay in clerical rather than lay hands.

It is wishful thinking to assume that the coexistence of plural religious communities in a single polity would in time necessarily go beyond formal *convivencia* to mutual acceptance and tolerance. It is more nearly nonsensical to assume that religion ipso facto generates violence. In general, violence between religious communities is not some hidden, essential potency but a concentration and redeployment of the fundamentally violent character of social life. Intercommunal religious violence

18 *Convivencia* (Spanish: living together) is the usual term for the coexistence of Muslims, Jews, and Christians in the medieval Iberian kingdoms. "Imperial *convivencia*" in my usage refers only to the settlement among emperor and Imperial estates and does not imply any rule of general toleration.
19 Johannes Hermann and Günther Wartenberg, eds., *Politische Korrespondez des Herzogs und Kurfürsten Moritz von Sachsen*, vol. 4: 510, n. 438.

frequently represents an interruption of a *convivencia* guarded by ritualized but often fragile codes of behavior. Hostile words and gestures may lead to violent acts or not, depending on the situation, for inherited discourse "acquired force only when people chose to find it meaningful and useful, and [the discourse] was itself reshaped by these choices. . . . Discourse and agency gain meaning only in relation to each other."[20] "Toleration," it has been said, "is possible only among tolerant people, and in the mid-sixteenth century [in the Imperial cities] the principle of tolerance would have destroyed the confessional unity between magistrates and citizenry."[21] Stable *convivencias* are created not by laws, though laws may be a condition for their survival, because "the capacity for and will" to tolerance is gained "only at the cost of time and disappointment."[22]

It remained nearly impossible for local, internally strong *convivencias* to form in the German lands until the power relations between the religious communities became stable, a condition that hardly occurred until after 1648. The few exceptions were makeshift local arrangements vulnerable to disruption both from within and without, notably in the Empire's far northwest and the southern cities of mandated power sharing. Elsewhere, for a hundred years local minorities were haunted by the threat of aggression by majorities in the form of demonstrations, disruptions, riots, insults, ridicule, boycotts, and outright violence. The rhythm of confessional aggression mirrored the fortunes of the religious parties: as the Protestant cause flourished from the 1520s to the 1570s, the Protestants were the principal aggressors, but by the early seventeenth century the Catholic revival enabled the Catholics to assume that role and to repay the Protestants in kind. All through this cycle of Christian persecution of Christians, the will to persecute Jews was ebbing.[23]

The fate of minorities who lacked effective protection from without is best documented for the southern Imperial cities, of which Strasbourg provides an instructive example. The emperor's victory over the Protestants in 1547 brought a ray of hope to the city's Catholics, "survivors of more than twenty years of underground religious life."[24] Almost immediately, however, the magistrates' negotiations with the victorious emperor over the Interim sparked resistance that nearly brought down the civic regime. Day by day, an eyewitness recorded, as the magistrates debated about the Interim, "two or three thousand citizens were gathered constantly before the town hall, and nobody knew what to do. Again and again the regime asked the people to trust them and to go to their homes."[25] Some magistrates, in "fear for their own skins and afraid of the emperor, wanted to flee, but Sir Jacob Sturm stood at the door and wouldn't let anyone leave until a decision had been reached."[26] When the decision fell to accept peace with the emperor, "these men renounced their citizenship and went abroad until the crisis was over. The people cursed them and charged them with cowardice, following them through the streets with insults."[27] The chief issue in this

20 David Nierenberg, *Communities of Violence: Persecution of Minorities in the Middle Ages*, 6.
21 Erdmann Weyrauch, *Konfessionelle Krise und soziale Stabilität: Das Interim in Straßburg (1548–1562)*, 59.
22 Weyrauch, *Konfessionelle Krise*, 59.
23 See Chapter 15.
24 Amy E. Leonard, *Nails in the Wall: Catholic Nuns in Reformation Germany*, 118.
25 Thomas A. Brady, *Protestant Politics: Jacob Sturm (1489–1553) and the German Reformation*, 340.
26 Brady, *Protestant Politics*, 340.
27 Brady, *Protestant Politics*, 340.

encounter was simple: the magistrates judged that the restoration of Catholicism in some form was regrettable but politically necessary, the opposition believed that it was intolerable under any circumstance. Although fired on by their preachers, the opposition lost the fight. The magistrates negotiated the local terms of the Interim with the bishop, who acted for the emperor. The cathedral and several other churches were restored to Catholic hands, and on Pentecost Sunday 1550 the Mass was openly sung once again at Strasbourg. The patient faith of Strasbourg's small Catholic minority had been vindicated, and every loyal Catholic must have been heartened when the magistrates, bowing to an episcopal command, sent Martin Bucer off into exile in far, rainy England, where he died in 1551.

There was no rush to Catholicism, though for a time the ceremonies, especially at the cathedral, drew burghers out of antipathy, curiosity, or both, along with some genuine Catholics. The city secretary Heinrich Walther (d. 1564) minimized the rites' attraction: "Few burghers, and none of any standing, attend their doings beyond those who come for the spectacle. [Otherwise] they are only the sorts of men and women who always follow this tribe [the priests]."[28] Three years later Konrad Huber (1507–77), Martin Bucer's ex-secretary wrote much the same thing: "I know of no magistrates and only a very few burghers who attend the papist idolatries, which greatly riles them [the priests]. Only priestlings, whores, crazy old women, and epicureans and such attend their sermons. For a city of this size, the figure 200 or a few more adherents of their errors is not surprising."[29] In 1556 the magistrates repeated this assessment in a letter to the bishop: "in our city the [Catholic] clergy have few hearers and hardly any who are truly attached to them. The churches remain empty."[30]

However deliberately confident these reports sound, they did not express wishful thinking. Strasbourg's Catholic community never existed long enough or grew large enough to constitute a true minority confession. Yet they were not fugitive or negligible as a presence in the city. The widow Katharina Zell called them "lost children and a few old, malevolent women, who in their youths served priests and students and have long since taken the Devil's ha'penny."[31] In fact, these "lost children" and "old women" were "drawn from all of the city's classes."[32] Catholic nobles and merchants sat in the city council; noble families maintained Catholic priests as private chaplains; and the recusant community contained notaries and other professionals, but also fishermen, hod-carriers, boatmen, and truck-gardeners. Some attended Mass at the house of the Knights of St. John; some went out to villages outside the civic territory. Three communities of Dominican nuns, who were protected by the magistrates, earned their livings by educating daughters of good families, including some Protestants.

Despite the Catholics' small numbers, the passage of a decade did nothing to soften the general population's "latent hatred of Catholics."[33] The Reformation had

---

28 Hans Virck et al., eds., *Politische Correspondenz der Stadt Straßburg im Zeitalter der Reformation*, vol. 5: 37.
29 Traugott Schiess, ed., *Briefwechsel der Brüder Ambrosius und Thomas Blarer 1509–1548*, vol. 3: 200. If Huber's estimate was anything near accurate, the Catholics who openly showed their faith amounted to about 1 percent of the population. Bucer, exiled by the regime in 1549 as a condition of the peace, had died in 1551 in England. "Epicurean" was a favorite term for the religiously indifferent or inconstant.
30 Weyrauch, *Konfessionelle Krise*, 162n. 63.
31 Katharina Schütz Zell, *Katharina Schütz Zell, vol. 2: The Writings. A Critical Edition*, 182.
32 Leonard, *Nails in the Wall*, 118.
33 Weyrauch, *Konfessionelle Krise*, 247.

grown strong from the vilification of Catholic rites, images, and clergy in images and allegations that very much remained in living memory. For a time, to be sure, the magistrates protected the restored Catholic clergy against aggression, keeping one eye on the restive burghers, the other on the emperor and his local representative, the bishop. They also watched carefully the Protestant preachers, who had most to lose from the restoration, and whose relations with the regime reached in the mid-1550s a nadir for the whole century.

For nearly a decade this situation seemed stable, as the burghers came to terms with the new situation, even though they loathed the pope and his minions, while the magistrates steadily chipped away at the Catholic establishment's protections, just as their fathers had in the 1520s. This culminated in their refusal to renew the treaty with Bishop Erasmus von Limburg (r. 1541–68), unless he removed their obligation to protect the Catholic clergy. The tactic worked, and the apparent stability crumbled on a Sunday morning in November 1559. When the Catholic preacher climbed into Geiler's cathedral pulpit, he found himself surrounded by a howling crowd, and as he fled into the safety of the church's choir, snowballs and rocks were thrown at him. At the midday Mass the tumult was worse, as again the preacher had to flee a larger, noisier demonstration. The evening service simply did not take place, as the crowd made it impossible to sing vespers. Only the intervention of three magistrates allowed the priests to leave the cathedral, whereupon the besiegers began to plunder the great church "as though they wanted to destroy the entire cathedral."[34] In the recriminations and apologies that followed, the magistrates blamed foreign artisans and unknown young people. The old religion had within one generation become to many, perhaps most, Strasbourgeois an alien, bizarre, and dangerous faith. Its suppression in public life satisfied all Protestant parties – magistrates, burgher activists, and preachers – and Catholicism slipped back into a quiet, marginal existence at Strasbourg. There was, to be sure, no serious religious cleansing of the city, which continued to house many faiths but only one official church. In the 1570s the Jesuit Johann Jacob Rabus (d. 1585) surveyed the religious identities of his fellow Strasbourgeois: "In poor Strasbourg you now have five or six sects among the common people. One fellow is an out-and-out Lutheran, the second a half-Lutheran, the third a Zwinglian, the fourth a Calvinist, the fifth a Schwenckfelder, the sixth an Anabaptist, and the seventh lot is purely epicurean."[35]

The story of Strasbourg suggests that in these times a religious minority could expect to suffer provocations and discrimination on a routine basis, punctuated by irregular, sometimes politically important, acts of violence and, sometimes, voluntary or involuntary exile. The use of coercion was asymmetrical between the two confessions, as Protestant rulers normally did not persecute Christian minorities as ruthlessly and efficiently as their Catholic counterparts (beginning some later) did, or as their ancestors had persecuted the Jews. Still, at times passions flared high enough to embolden interests and threaten the Imperial peace. It nonetheless held in some fashion for about sixty years.

---

34   Weyrauch, *Konfessionelle Krise*, 229.
35   Johann Jakob Rabus, *Christliche bescheidne und wolgegründts ablähnung/der vermeindten Bischoffs Predigt . . . im Münster zu Strassburg*, fol. 30r. I am grateful to Lorna Jane Abray for this text. The term "epicurean" means in this context one who advocates laissez faire and not coercion in religious matters.

3. THE EMPIRE IN THE ERA OF RELIGIOUS WARS

The first decade of life under the Religious Peace witnessed a stronger spirit of political collaboration than the Empire had known for generations. One powerful reason was the Ottoman threat, which "posed an important consolidating force in the Empire."[36] The wheel had come full circle. Just as the coincidence of the Protestant challenge and the Ottoman advance had weakened Imperial governance under Charles V, their divergence after 1555 bolstered governance under his brother and his nephew. During these years work resumed on the improvement of political institutions, a revival, as it were, of the Imperial reform begun in the years between 1486 and 1495. Looking back from the death of Emperor Maximilian II in 1576, one might judge the Protestant reformation's disruption of Imperial governance to have been a mere episode in an eighty-year process of state formation.

Beginning in the later 1550s, six improvements in Imperial governance stand out:

1. In 1556 the six Imperial electors formed at the initiative of Ferdinand a permanent association, which acted as an executive committee of the Imperial Diet and mediated between emperor and estates;
2. In the Imperial Diet in issues related to religion, majority rule was replaced by separate confessional caucuses (*itio in partes*);
3. Imperial justice was strengthened by reforms in 1555 of the Imperial Chamber Court, which heard more than twice as many cases (19,300) in the second half of the sixteenth century as it had in the first half (about 9,900); it was further improved in 1559 by giving fixed form to the emperor's prerogative court (Imperial Aulic Council);
4. A new assembly of deputies, a kind of working committee of the Diet, first called to Worms by Ferdinand in 1564, drafted laws and in general enhanced the authority of the emperor and the circles;
5. The Imperial Circles, strengthened between 1564 and 1567, began to become active in supplying the military forces and financial means required for police work and for military efforts against the Ottomans;
6. The Imperial estates began to vote generous subsidies and to require their subjects to pay them. The Imperial Tax Collector, an office created in 1566, actually collected 80 percent of the nearly 30 million gulden levied between 1576 and 1606, a miraculous level compared to what the Diet had granted to Charles V.

The political effect of external wars on Imperial solidarity depended very much on who was fighting whom and where. Some wars promoted cooperation. The Hussite Wars of the fifteenth century come to mind, and so do the Ottoman Wars of the later sixteenth.[37] The Northern Wars of the last third of the sixteenth century also promoted the sense of a common Imperial policy. In 1558 a Muscovite invasion of Livonia disrupted at one blow the Baltic region's balance of power.[38] The Swedish and Danish kings called on the emperor for aid, as did Lübeck and other northern trading cities, plus the Hohenzollerns, whose grip on the duchy of Prussia stood at risk. In 1559–60 the Imperial Diet discussed but did not grant aid to the northern cities. Three years

36 Winfried Schulze, *Reich und Türkengefahr im späten 16. Jahrhundert. Studien zu den politischen und gesellschaftlichen Auswirkungen einer äußeren Bedrohung*, 366.
37 On the Ottoman Wars see Chapter 16.
38 The Baltic land of Livonia is now divided between Latvia and Estonia.

later the Seven Years' War of the North (1563–70) erupted between Denmark and Sweden for control of the Baltic. Emperor Maximilian II, concerned for Imperial influence in the north and the German cities' trade there, tried to arbitrate between them, though without help from the estates, who showed themselves as disinterested in foreign affairs as their predecessors had been in the time of Maximilian I. The diplomacy that led to the Peace of Stettin in 1570 reveals the conflict of interests that prevented Maximilian from gaining greater authority in the north. As Holy Roman emperor he strove to end a war that threatened the Empire's internal order and economic prosperity and to play the peacemaker on a wider European stage. As head of the House of Austria he aimed to exploit the peace between Sweden and Denmark in order to extend his own influence in the Baltic. Maximilian's initiatives failed because "the emperor never clearly defined common aims around which the Imperial estates could rally," and because "the Empire largely lacked either the will or the ability to project power beyond its borders."[39] His great-grandfather and namesake would have understood.

The wars that did threaten the Imperial Peace were the religious wars in western Europe, which broke out in France in 1560, and in the Low Countries in 1568. Pitting Protestants against the Catholic monarchs of France and Spain respectively, these struggles attracted men, money, and diplomatic support from the German powers to both sides, though principally to the rebels. Many German Protestants, especially those of the Reformed faith, deeply sympathized with the French and Dutch Calvinists who sought their aid. Most Lutheran princes, on the other hand, backed August of Saxony's policy of collaboration with the Catholic emperor to guard the Peace by isolating the Empire from the western wars. In 1568–69 came the principal test of this policy. At the beginning of the Dutch Revolt against the king of Spain, William of Orange-Nassau had withdrawn to his Nassau kinsmen on the Middle Rhine.[40] In the spring of 1568, aided by a number of other German princes, William assembled German mercenaries to invade the northern Netherlands and wrest them from the Spanish regent.[41] His actions sent a wave of apprehension and rumor through the Empire, and other western princes mobilized, some to support him, others to support the French Calvinists (Huguenots).[42] One prince who responded to the appeals from the west was Duke Wolfgang of Zweibrücken (1526–69), a Wittelsbach prince of the Palatine line, who promised to bring 6,000 cavalry and 16,000 infantry to fight alongside the Huguenots. His mobilization unleashed wild rumors of an impending "priests' war" against the Rhenish bishoprics. Wolfgang protested that he intended not "to cause trouble for any obedient estate or member" but to "promote the Holy Empire's welfare" by driving French royal troops from the occupied bishoprics of Metz, Toul, and Verdun in Lorraine.[43] Drawing cavalry from as far away as Mecklenburg and Pomerania, Wolfgang formed his army – 20,000 strong – west of the Rhine

---

39 Jason Lavery, *Germany's Northern Challenge: the Holy Roman Empire and the Scandinavian Struggle for the Baltic, 1563–1576*, 144.
40 Because William the Silent cuts such a heroic figure in Dutch national historiography, it is easy to forget that he was an Imperial count (of the line of Nassau-Dillenburg) and had been a page at the Habsburg court in Brussels. William was reared a Lutheran, converted to Catholicism when he came to Charles V's court, and kept his own religious counsel as head of the revolt against Spain.
41 Fernando Alvarez de Toledo (1507–82), Duke of Alba.
42 The nickname "Huguenots" for French (Calvinist) Protestants first appeared in 1560.
43 Maximilian Lanzinner, *Friedensicherung und politische Einheit des Reiches unter Kaiser Maximilian II. (1564–1576)*, 163.

around New Year's 1569 and joined forces with William of Orange in Alsace. Strasbourg's magistrates reported to Emperor Maximilian II that a French royal army also was headed their way, and that the coming battle would be "the final decline and ruin" of the land.[44] The crisis encouraged new measures by the Swabian and Franconian Circles to suppress foreign recruitment, though to little effect.

What linked the French to the Netherlandish situation was the growth of the Geneva-centered Reformed faith, commonly called "Calvinism."[45] At this time, the 1560s and 1570s, it posed a serious danger to the Empire's confessional balance of power. In 1561 Elector Palatine Frederick III (r. 1559–76), called "the Pious," announced his adherence to the Reformed faith. His capital at Heidelberg rapidly became both a gathering point for Reformed clergymen and others from various lands and a center of communications with co-religionists in western kingdoms. Because the Religious Peace made no provision for tolerating a second Protestant confession, Reformed Christians in the Empire represented themselves as disciples of Luther, who differed from Lutherans only in their wish to continue his reformation. This claim, given the Imperial estates' near universal desire to avoid reopening the Religious Peace, may have seemed plausible. When the Diet assembled at Augsburg in 1566, however, Duke Christoph of Württemberg (b. 1515, r. 1550–68), Frederick's cousin and exact contemporary, publicly denounced the "heretical catechism" promoted at Heidelberg.[46] When Frederick disputed the charge, the Lutheran princes swallowed their skepticism and reasoned that if Frederick were condemned, "the persecutions in France, Spain, the Netherlands and other similar places would grow at once by heaps, and that by a condemnation [of Frederick] we should be guilty of shedding their blood."[47] By refusing to face the issue at hand – two Protestant confessions or one? – they added a handy arrow to the Catholic quiver. For the next half-century the Reformed faith lived in the Empire as virtually Lutheran, a fiction challenged by many Lutheran clergymen but only rarely by the prince. The rise of the challenge of the Reformed faith nonetheless cemented the Lutheran estates' support for the Religious Peace and for their leader, August of Saxony.

4. THE SAXONYS – ORDER AND REVOLUTION

Elector August I of Saxony (r. 1553–86) was born in the mining town of Freiberg as second son of Duke Henry, called "the Pious," who had taken Albertine Saxony over to the Protestant faith. After his brother Maurice fell in battle in 1553, August succeeded to the electorate at age twenty-two. A more sober dresser than his foppish father, the red-headed prince was nearly as handsome, despite his close-cropped hair, pronounced widow's peak, and thrusting chin. In maturity, as he gradually assumed the obligatory barrel-like corporation of a German prince, August's face became fleshy, and his curly, forked beard gave way to a full one. A hard, sober, and reserved

44 Lanzinner, *Friedensicherung*, 165.
45 While "Calvinism" is the textbook term for this faith and its churches, in German usage the term "Reformed" is generally preferred both by the historians and by the churches.
46 The *Heidelberg Catechism* is a Protestant confession configured as 129 articles of questions and answers. Approved at Heidelberg in the Palatinate in 1563, it was subsequently approved by synods at Wesel, Emden, Dort, and The Hague. It is officially honored today by Reformed churches in Germany, the Netherlands, Canada, and the USA.
47 Henry J. Cohn, "The Territorial Princes in Germany's Second Reformation, 1559–1622," 146.

ruler of little inner warmth or geniality, August ruled from Dresden for thirty years over the old lands of his Albertine line plus those his brother's treachery had carried away from their Ernestine cousins in 1547.

While the days of great Saxon expectations now lay in the past, in August the lands found an able and attentive lord. He strove to pay off Maurice's debt to the tune of 1.7 million gulden, promoted agriculture by consolidating large blocks of land for systematic exploitation, expanded the ducal domain, and sponsored experiments with foreign agricultural methods. He and Electress Anna (1532–85), a Danish royal princess, enjoyed traveling about to inspect the countryside, acting like the principal farmers of the land.[48] They imported colonists, new breeds of cattle, hogs, and sheep, and new strains of cereals. Annual incomes from the ducal domain rose from 250,000 gulden in the 1560s to 400,000 gulden by August's death in 1586.

Saxony's jewel box, the mines of the Erzgebirge, attracted August's "special inclination, pleasure, and desire."[49] His ruthless concentration of the mining sector even saw a smelter erected on the grounds of Dresden Castle. Yet the Saxon mines, already past their peak, showed declining yields after 1540. So did the manufacture of bleached linens at Chemnitz, the other branch in which capitalist entrepreneurs had been most successful and technological progress most advanced. These were hard times, too, for the Saxon peasants, as the nobles, now fully recovered from the late medieval depression, consolidated their power over the land, pushed the burghers out of the territorial government, and built new castles everywhere. Thanks to what is sometimes called "refeudalization," Saxony, once the east in the west, was now becoming the west in the east.

Maurice had been a prince of European stature, ally to the emperor and to the French king, and an Imperial commander in Hungary. August, by contrast, was a provincial Saxon prince who held rigidly to two policies: loyalty to Emperor Maximilian II (and to the anti-Spanish faction at the Imperial court), and unrelenting expansion of his power over his own lands. Between 1559 and 1565 he swallowed the three Saxon episcopal *Hochstifte*, Meissen, Naumburg, and Merseburg, and picked off further lands from his Ernestine cousins.

"Father August," he was called, and his wife was "Mother Anna." They truly deserved these names. Anna, who at sixteen had married August at Torgau in 1548, sewed, washed, and churned butter, bore fifteen children, and dosed the survivors and her husband when ill. To her August handed over entire branches of the court's business, but her great passion was medicine, a field in which she accomplished a good deal and about which she exchanged letters with famous physicians. Some courtiers, unhappy with Anna's management, began to grumble. One of them groused about a "gynocracy," and Kaspar Peucer (1525–1602), court physician and Melanchthon's son-in-law, imprudently wrote in 1573, "if we had Mother Anna with us, we'd have no worry, for we'd soon get the master as well."[50] When this letter was intercepted, it brought down the wrath of both mother and father on the heads of a

---

48 Anna was the daughter of King Christian III (b. 1503, r. 1536–59) of Denmark.

49 Rudolf Kötzschke and Hellmut Kretzschmar, *Sächsische Geschichte. Werden und Wandlungen eines Deutschen Stammes und seiner Heimat im Rahmen der Deutschen Geschichte,* 221.

50 Gustav Wustmann, "Geschichte der heimlichen Calvinisten (Kryptocalvinisten in Leipzig. 1574 bis 1593)," 14. The crack about "gynocracy" was made by the Pomeranian jurist Georg Cracow (1525–75), councilor to Elector August.

group of leading court officials. They had chosen a bad moment to grumble, for just then began the shift in August's policy toward the intra-Lutheran religious schism.

Elector August differed, a master of Saxon history wrote, "from the majority of his princely contemporaries in his outspoken aversion to the Protestant confessional quarrels over doctrine that characterized these decades."[51] All the more ironical, then, that he should have been responsible for the consolidation of a fully fledged Lutheran confession in the Empire. In his early years he tended in the direction of the moderate party of "Philippists" rather than the hardline orthodox party of what will be called "Real Lutherans," for whom the usual term is "Gnesio-Lutherans."[52] Although the latter party agitated for a restoration of the Ernestine Saxon line, defeated and heavily dispossessed in 1547, August had other fish to fry during the two decades that followed his brother's death in 1553. He built up his ties to Vienna and his support for the emperor's policy of protecting the Religious Peace. He defended this policy at Augsburg in 1566, when a Reformed (Calvinist) presence first surfaced in the Princes' Chamber of the Imperial Diet in the person of Elector Palatine Frederick III, and he later opposed Frederick's agitation for German Protestant powers to send money and men to the Protestant fighting forces in the French and Netherlandish Wars of Religion.

During these years, the later 1560s, August committed himself neither to one side nor the other of the internecine Lutheran strife, nor did he take up the struggle against the Reformed incursion into the Empire. One reason he refused to act was that he had serious business at home. It concerned the security of his own Albertine line of the Wettin dynasty and its hold on the Saxon electorate and lands that Duke Maurice had won for the line in return for supporting Charles V in the Smalkaldic War. Two decades passed before August, Maurice's brother and heir, descried an opportunity to complete the ruin of his Ernestine cousins.

Head of the Wettin dynasty's Ernestine line, Duke John Frederick II (1529–95), called "the Middler," was the eldest of three sons of the dispossessed Smalkaldic chief, Elector John Frederick. The duke was eighteen years old when his father lost the battle of Mühlberg, the electoral title and lands to Maurice, and his own freedom. The son, who had to share the rump Ernestine lands with two younger brothers, carried an unhappy portmanteau full of deep resentment, great expectations, and meager means. One of the best-educated German princes of this or any other time – he could read Hebrew, Greek, and Latin – John Frederick proved a stubborn, imprudent, and recklessly ambitious ruler. He fairly thirsted for revenge on August, longed for the recovery of the lost electorate and lands, and dreamed of championing the true faith as Holy Roman emperor.

Although the Wettins of Saxony were not in fact a royal dynasty, their rapid ascent to power as Imperial prince-electors had awakened, already under Frederick the Wise, thoughts of a Wettin on the Imperial throne. It was said that at Frankfurt in

51 Kötzschke and Kretzschmar, *Sächsische Geschichte*, 231.
52 In conventional usage, "Philippist" refers to Philip Melanchthon and his followers, who were held by opponents to be advocates of compromise with the Catholics in doctrine and the emperor in politics and/or with the Reformed confession. The other party is called "Gnesio-Lutheran," in which the Greek prefix means "true" or "authentic." Because the latter term means little in English, except to the experts, I choose to call them "Real Lutheran," which seems to me to express both this party's claim to be the only authentic interpreters of Luther and their ultra-realistic sense of God's rule over the world.

Figure 12. Elector Frederick the Wise and Luther under the Cross

1519, the elector of Trier came to Frederick's quarters one night, "unexpected and unannounced, and pled with him to accept the Empire." Frederick, "though he had a number of votes, perhaps three, for himself as king of the Romans, declined the Holy Roman Empire with more honor than shown by those who pursued it."[53] Thereafter God piled mark upon mark of favor on the Saxon electors as agents of the miraculous restoration of His Word. From the Wittenberg workshop of the Cranachs, father and son, poured a rich wave of images of Frederick the Wise, John the Constant, and his successor, John Frederick I, in sacral settings, praying before the crucified Savior or witnessing God's interventions in the world of man, often in christomimetic settings and poses. Images of Solomon, David, Constantine, Charlemagne, and the great Ottonian and Hohenstaufen emperors swirled in a rich, visual stew of the Wettins' alleged sacrality and very real expectations.

John Frederick II came to maturity in the heated atmosphere of a new Biblical age filled with God's mighty power, only to see his father imprisoned, himself and his brothers expropriated, and his dynasty at one stroke disgraced and reduced to the level of a third-rate power. The wounded prince turned to the Real Lutherans, some of them veterans of the defiant defense of holy Magdeburg against the emperor and Elector Maurice.

What the resentful, ambitious young hothead lacked, money, he found in the form of French livres, 30,000 per year, when he entered the French king's service in 1558. But he needed more, a lot more, and soon he found a man who boasted he could supply

53 Ingetraut Ludolphy, *Friedrich der Weise, Kurfürst von Sachsen, 1463–1525*, 217.

funds sufficient to make all things possible. Before he entered John Frederick's service, the Franconian knight Wilhelm von Grumbach (1503–66) had a well-deserved reputation for lawlessness, ambition, and ferocity. During the campaign of 1552 Grumbach had rampaged across Franconia, in reward for which his feudal lord, the prince-bishop of Würzburg, declared his episcopal fiefs in escheat. The knight was not a man to be crossed, and while the first two previous attempts failed, his assassin shot the bishop dead on 15 April 1558. Then, like other German nobles who fell afoul of the law or acquired too many enemies, he took refuge in France. In 1559 the outlaw returned to plead his case before the Diet and, when rejected, entered John Frederick's service. The two men, prince and knight, soon became one in a desperate desire to recover their heritages and take vengeance on those who had deprived them of what was rightfully theirs.

In their quest for funds John Frederick and Grumbach spared no possible source: new taxes, debt collection, private credits, alchemy, and treasure hunting. In 1562 Grumbach, old and cunning in the ways of intrigue, found the perfect tool to bind the gullible prince to his own purposes. While a Grumbach agent was searching Thuringia for information about the fabulous "spring-root," a magical tuber which led its possessor to buried treasure, he stumbled across another instrument. Grumbach, informed of the find, asked John Frederick to come posthaste to inspect the newly discovered key to great wealth. "Your Princely Grace should therefore lay aside all of your affairs, however large they may be," Grumbach urged, "go to Gotha," and "do not tell any power on earth of these matters."[54] In a room in Castle Grimmenstein at Gotha, the prince met his new savior, Hansi Henkel (d. 1567), a thirteen-year-old shepherd who spoke with angels. His angelic friends were small fellows dressed in white with black caps, each with a burning torch in one hand. In the other they held white rods, with which, they told Hansi, they could open the earth and return to their underground home. They were, in fact, miniature, magical miners. They would help the duke discover a buried treasure, which, once raised, would fill his financial needs at a single stroke.

Plans and fantasies, salted with Lutheran theological controversies, enveloped John Frederick's court. There was a Sickingen-like plot to rouse the free knights of the German lands to rebellion, there were schemes to aid putative allies in Lorraine, to help the Swedish king against King Frederick II (r. 1558–88) of Denmark, and to overthrow Elector August and recover the lost lands and titles.[55] Hansi, the angels' friend, came as a godsend to the intriguers. For nearly five years, the boy put to his angels questions supplied by the duke and Grumbach: how to assassinate Emperor Ferdinand at a great distance (a magical bullet fired into the air in Saxony would kill Ferdinand at such distance), how to overthrow Elector August, and, above all, how to raise the fabulous treasure. Hansi relayed the angels' answers. Meanwhile, Grumbach made his strike. In 1563 he attacked Würzburg, seized and plundered the city, and

---

54 Staatsarchiv Coburg, LA A 2021, fols. 275^{r-v}. My thanks to Peter E. Starenko for this document.
55 Behind the Lorraine-Swedish-Saxon intrigue against Frederick of Denmark and August of Saxony originally stood two daughters of the deposed Danish king, Christian II (r. 1513–23). Frederick's sister, Anna, was August's wife and electress of Saxony. The duke and Grumbach fell in with this fantastic plot in 1558 and stuck to it until the end of the duke's reign and Grumbach's life in 1567, long after the Lorraine connection had fizzled. My thanks to Peter E. Starenko for information on this bizarre, little-known affair.

compelled chapter and bishop to restore his hereditary fiefs. This led to his renewed outlawry, and in November 1566, when John Frederick failed to give him over, he, too, was outlawed. August, appointed executor of the Imperial decrees of outlawry, seized the day. He invaded his cousin's lands and besieged Gotha's castle, the surrender of which put duke, knight, and the angels' friend into August's clutches. The prince was carried off in exile to Styria, where he died many years later. Hansi and Grumbach went to their deaths. August recouped his costs, around 100,000 gulden, and took four Ernestine districts in pledge, only one of which was ever returned.

Thus ended the deadly rivalry that had begun at Leipzig in 1485 with the fateful partition of the Saxon lands between two brothers, Ernest and Albert. The Protestant reformation shaped their descendants' fortunes: the junior, Albertine line at Dresden betrayed the Protestant cause in 1547, gained the electoral title and lands, and became the Empire's leading Protestant power; the senior, Ernestine line protected Luther and his reformation and suffered losses of title and lands, humiliation, exile, and a future as third-raters. From the Albertines would spring a line of kings, from the Ernestines a long, many-branched line of princelets.

John Frederick II and August of Saxony were third cousins, kinsmen of Elector Fredrick the Wise, whose mantle as preserver of the Empire and champion of the new faith descended with the electorate to the Albertine line. John Frederick was cut from a different cloth, his mind colored by an apocalyptic spirit the evangelical movement had reawakened with dreams of royal ascendancy and an unrelenting desire for vengeance. His temper is captured in one of the most curious artifacts, a sketch of a flag to be made for John Frederick's campaign to seize and reform the Holy Roman Empire in a Protestant sense. It bears the evangelical motto, V.D.M.E. (God's Word endures forever), but also the image of the Bundschuh, the peasant boot, which had flown on the Upper Rhine between 1493 and 1517 and again in 1525.[56] In the dreams and plans of John Frederick II, stoked by Wilhelm von Grumbach, the repressed reformation as revolution returned for a final reprise. Then it passed into oblivion, along with Grumbach and Hansi Henkel, the boy who spoke with angels.

In the early 1570s, free at last from the Ernestine rivalry, August was free to put the Lutheran house in order. His wrath rose not only in defense of his bride, but also against his own councilors. The elector had decided to shift sides against the Philippist party and toward the Real Lutherans, who from their stronghold at the University of Jena hammered away at the "crypto-Calvinists." These dissembling Calvinists in Lutheran guise, they alleged, aimed to create a pan-Protestant party by compromising with Calvinist views of the Lord's Supper and many other aspects of Christian doctrine and ritual practice. They or their partisans even spread the rumor that August had converted to Rome. When this came to Mother Anna's ear, she knew what to reply. The rumor, she wrote to a friend, was "just as true, as that the Turkish emperor accepted the Christian faith and the pope likewise the Lutheran doctrines."[57] The rumor was spawned by "some Illyrian, agitating, bellicose preachers, who have caused all of the trouble and disunity between rulers and subjects."[58]

---

56 This image I also owe to Peter E. Starenko, who intends to publish it.
57 Katrin Keller, "Kurfürstin Anna von Sachsen (1532–1585): Von Möglichkeiten und Grenzen einer 'Landesmutter,'" 278.
58 Keller, "Kurfürstin Anna," 278. "Illyrian" refers, of course, to Matthias Flacius.

August's shift toward an uncompromisingly orthodox Lutheran party came to light in 1572 with the fall of the Saxon Philippists. The leading suspects at court were arrested and subjected to trials conducted with great cruelty, sometimes for years on end, under the personal supervision of Father August and Mother Anna. The chancellor died under torture in 1575. Peucer, the court physician, moldered for twelve years in prison before his release. A purging wind swept through the court, the church, and the universities at Leipzig and Wittenberg. Whoever would not condemn Calvinism and all its works and pomps went to jail or into exile. Later, it turned out that the Reformed infiltration of church and universities had been greatly exaggerated. August encouraged similar purges at other Lutheran courts and promoted a doctrinal reunification of Lutherans in an orthodox sense. From a meeting he sponsored at Torgau in 1576 emerged a union formula, the Formula of Concord, which he had circulated among the princely courts of the Empire's central and northern lands.[59]

The elector's sponsorship of Lutheran orthodoxy's victory crowned his long reign. It rallied, on the one hand, the Lutheran estates to his policy of working within the Religious Peace and avoiding participation in the western religious wars. It sealed, on the other, a policy of internal consolidation, unity, and centralization that suppressed internal religious dissent and made August the unchallenged head of the Empire's Protestant party and Saxony the Empire's archetypal Protestant state. It also made possible the emergence of a fully fledged Lutheran confession.

5. IMPERIAL CATHOLICISM — EMPEROR MAXIMILIAN II

The triumph of Lutheran ideas of order over Lutheran apocalyptic dreams preserved the Religious Peace. August's partnership with two emperors, Ferdinand I and Maximilian II, was secured by their policy of moderation. They inherited this policy from Charles V, who in his more benign moods had sought ways to bring the princes together without compromising the Catholic faith. Ferdinand pursued this policy more consistently and more ably, because, whatever he thought, there was no other way to preserve the Empire. Since his experience at Passau in 1552 and especially at Augsburg in 1555, Ferdinand had "pursued a solid accord between the two 'religious parties,' even though he was aware of 'scruples' of his brother, the emperor, with the goal that this policy should be the basis for his tenacious goal of a peaceful restoration of religious unity."[60] When the Diet deliberated, his representatives would seek compromises on disputed questions in the Princes' House, upon which in the final phase the king would personally try to reach "a result acceptable to all parties, which would stabilize the Empire's peace without wrecking the path to religious unity."[61] That this goal seemed to him reachable, far more than it did to his two successors, is to be explained, perhaps, by the fact that he had experienced the moment of the early 1540s, when religious comity and unity against the Empire's foes had seemed close enough to smell. At Worms in 1557 he organized a religious colloquy in the style of 1539–41, though this one foundered not on Catholic-Protestant disagreements but on intra-Protestant strife. Ferdinand invited the Protestants to Trent, where the council

---

59 See Chapter 13.
60 Ernst Laubach, *Ferdinand I. als Kaiser. Politik und Herrscherauffassung des Nachfolgers Karl V.*, 738.
61 Laubach, *Ferdinand I.*, 739.

was still in session, but they refused to send envoys. Justly so, because in their view the proceedings seemed to take little or no note of their beliefs, concerns, and needs. There were those who thought Ferdinand should join the kings of France and Spain to force Trent in an anti-Roman direction, but Ferdinand held to the course his elder brother had laid in. His continuing loyalty to Rome was one of the greatest policy coups of Giovanni Cardinal Morone (1509–80), Rome's top expert on German affairs. The council's course of reform better suited Rome's policies, however, than it did the Empire's peace. Disappointed and discouraged, Ferdinand died at Vienna on 25 July 1564, the feast of St. James, national patron of Spain, the land of his youth.

Unlike his father, young Maximilian was a German prince through and through, a throwback to his great-grandfather and namesake. This he proved by drinking, eating, and roistering in the notorious manner of the German courts. This was one reason he won his father's mistrust. Another was his mediocre record during four years of service at the court of his uncle, Emperor Charles V. Maximilian's relations with his father were permanently strained, which is perhaps why Ferdinand decided, against dynastic law and tradition, to divide the Habsburgs' heritage among his three sons. The emperorship, Bohemia, Hungary, and the two Austrias came to Maximilian; Tyrol and Outer Austria, with its capital at Innsbruck, to Archduke Ferdinand (1529–95), his father's favorite; and the Inner Austrian duchies (Styria, Carinthia, and Carniola) to Archduke Charles (1540–90), who ruled from Graz. The Austrian lands were not fully reunited until 1665.

The most contested issue about Maximilian has always concerned his religion. It was also the most disturbing element in Maximilian's relationship to his wife, Maria (1528–1603), daughter of his uncle Charles and therefore his own first cousin. That he was influenced by Protestant beliefs cannot be doubted, and during the 1550s many Catholics held him to be a "patent heretic."[62] His toying with the idea of a Protestant monarchy for the German lands is conceivable but not probable, though in August 1560, four years before his father died, Maximilian asked his Protestant friends "what he could expect from them."[63] After perfunctory replies from princes who doubtless dreaded the renewal of religious strife, Maximilian kept his peace, and in February 1562 he swore to his male kinsmen that he wished to live and die a Catholic. It was the counsel of prudence, for on this decision depended his electability to the Roman (German) crown in that year, his succession to the Imperial one in 1564, and the prospects of his and Empress Maria's children with respect to the Spanish succession. The mental illness of Don Carlos (1545–68), King Philip II's son, was an open secret, and in 1563 Maximilian sent two of his sons to the Spanish court to be educated, possibly as future kings of Spain.

Maximilian's continued adherence to the policy of Imperial Catholicism has often been ascribed to crypto-Protestant religious views or simply to his timidity as a monarch. Yet there was another reason, until recently hardly noticed, for holding to his father's policy. Its name was "Calvinism," the political potential of which Ferdinand had already seen. In 1563, the year of the *Heidelberg Catechism*, the emperor had written to its sponsor, Elector Palatine Frederick III, and warned him not to desert the Confession of Augsburg. The introduction of Calvinism, he wrote

---

62 Lutz, *Das Ringen*, 354.
63 Lutz, *Das Ringen*, 354.

(on 13 July), must lead to a further "abandonment, break-up, and obfuscation in religion."[64] Like his father, Maximilian II grasped the danger this faith presented to a monarchy, the chief legitimacy of which depended on a sacrality that, in turn, derived from its ancient symbiosis with the Church of Rome. Quite apart from other considerations, this is quite enough to explain why, on grounds of policy alone, no Habsburg monarch could seriously contemplate apostasy. It is simply anachronistic, therefore, to assume that their policy's principal goal, an Empire reunited in religion, was foolish, unrealistic, or utopian. Formulated under Charles V, the principle of Imperial Catholicism and its policy of conciliation continued under Ferdinand I, Maximilian II, and, at least in his first years, Rudolph II.

6. THE SCHISM AND THE EMPIRE'S FUTURE

The effort to save Imperial public life from permanent schism was never a concern of the Imperial dynasty alone. From the earliest days following the Diet of Augsburg in 1530, some Imperial electors and princes had engaged themselves, fitfully, it is true, with the pacification of religious strife and the restoration and preservation of Imperial political life. Fifteen years after the Diet of 1530, the interplay of political opposition and negotiation had disclosed "how essentially minimal was the remaining consensus between the confessions concerning peace and law and order and thereby laid bare the full extent of the ongoing disintegration."[65] Gradually, the neutral powers of this era, the Palatine and Brandenburg electors and the duke of Cleves-Jülich, who had badly underestimated the depth of the schism, joined the opposition party and thereby helped to create a situation that led to and shaped the Religious Peace of 1555. In such circles there had nonetheless emerged a political ideal of the Empire, "obligation to which was both ethical – Erasmian – in a general sense and grounded in religion."[66]

In the decades following the Peace and Charles's abdication, a certain routine returned to Imperial public life. Over the next two decades, a much stronger sense of collegiality and correspondingly dense communications developed among the Imperial electors, who, except for the Palatine elector, aimed at collaboration rather than opposition. Yet the Reformation's great mortgage remained, and "the electoral college's position of leadership became deeply threatened, whenever confessional partisanship exerted an enduring influence on the patterns of political communication."[67] The electors' role complemented the activities of the Diet and other representative assemblies, allowing Imperial public life to continue thickening, at least to some degree, along the line the reformation movements had interrupted between 1520 and 1555. The growth of business before the two Imperial supreme courts, the rising willingness to grant taxes, the rising activity of some Imperial Circles, and the creation of new institutions all testify to this general restoration of Imperial public life. This quickening of Imperial political life coincided, of course, with the last wave of

---

64 Laubach, *Ferdinand I.*, 739.
65 Albrecht Pius Luttenberger, *Glaubenseinheit und Reichsfriede. Konzeptionen und Wege konfessions-neutraler Reichspolitik 1530–1552 (Kurpfalz, Jülich, Kurbrandenburg)*, 714.
66 Luttenberger, *Glaubenseinheit*, 724.
67 Albrecht Pius Luttenberger, *Kurfürsten, Kaiser und Reich. Politische Führung und Friedenssicherung unter Ferdinand I. und Maximilian II.*, 450.

Protestant advances and the nadir of Catholic fortunes in the Empire. Absent a change in the constellation of political forces these asymmetrical fortunes promoted, the future must complete the transformation of the Holy Roman Empire into a Protestant polity.

The new energy did not exhaust itself in the practical politics of the Imperial estates. The Empire was growing in soul as well as strengthening in body, that is to say, the new situation encouraged a new conceptualization of the Empire as a partic-ular, secular polity. The changes that took place during the twenty years between the abdication of Charles V and the death of his nephew, Maximilian II, can be followed in the writings of the publicists, Catholic and Protestant, between whom, however, "a general asymmetry . . . can hardly be overlooked."[68] The Catholics continued to regard the Empire as a universal monarchy partnered with a universal Church, essentially the medieval dualism of *imperium* and *sacerdotium*. The Protestants, by contrast, tended to see the Empire as a German national monarchy on an aristocratic-corporate foundation. In this they built upon the pioneering historical-national vision of the German Renaissance humanists. Taken together, the two views reflect both differences of structure between the two Imperial faiths and their different fortunes in the time of Maximilian II. The Protestant advance had not yet slowed; the Catholic recovery had not yet begun. The differences between the Catholic universal and the Protestant national view remained even when political attitudes with respect to the need for peace, harmony, and law and order were very similar. This can be seen by comparing two writers, a Catholic bishop from Saxony and a Protestant general from Swabia.

Julius Pflug (1499–1564), an Italian-educated Saxon nobleman, was the last Cath-olic bishop of Naumburg (r. 1542–64), the Saxon see of which he could not take possession until after the war of 1546–47.[69] Pflug belonged among the flexible church-men to whom the policy of Imperial Catholicism and stability made sense. Following the Smalkaldic War, he secretly corresponded with Melanchthon and other Protes-tants and took part in discussions that led to the two Interims, Augsburg and Leipzig. Pflug was above all a politician of negotiated restoration, who believed until his death in the possibility of restoring the Catholic Church in the Empire through a union policy built on concessions to the Protestants.

In service to this cause Pflug produced what has been called "a Catholic-monarchical vision of a renovated Empire."[70] A veteran Imperial politician, he cast his vision of a restoration of the Empire in the form of a humanist address, such as one might hold before an Imperial Diet. Pflug's employment of the moralizing idea of history as the schoolmaster of life (*historia magistra vitae*) also places the bishop in the mainstream of later German humanist thought. His basic device is to contrast a highly idealized picture of a strong, communal German past with the present day, in which the Protestant advance coincides with a late stage of decline. "Our people were then so firmly bound to one another," he writes of earlier times, "they so respected the emperor and the fatherland, that they scarcely ever hesitated to put themselves in

---

68   Alexander Schmidt, *Vaterlandsliebe und Religionskonflikt. Politische Diskurse im Alten Reich (1555–1648)*, 177.
69   The three Saxon sees, Naumburg, Merseburg, and Meissen, were secularized but not absorbed by the electors of Saxony.
70   Schmidt, *Vaterlandsliebe*, 201.

the greatest kinds of danger or even to sacrifice their lives. Just as nothing was more important than to live with honor and serve the fatherland well, so nothing was more hated than to live disgracefully or to abandon the fatherland."[71] The key to this morality of the past, Pflug writes, was that so long as the Germans remained united by religion, "our people loved the fatherland and preferred the common good to their private conveniences."[72] Religious division – the bishop's central point – brought moral degeneration, and the Peasants' War, the Smalkaldic War, and the Princes' War of 1552 followed directly from the religious schism. The Religious Peace of 1555 had scarcely interrupted this decline.

Pflug's remedy for German decline is predictable: end the schism. This would require his fellow Catholics to admit their own faults but hold fast to their obligations to Empire and Church. Beyond this point, the bishop advocated a national program to lead the nobility and the common people back "to virtue" (*ad virtutem*) and to promote the rule of virtuous men whose lives will be both useful and honorable. Behind this (admittedly very ideal) program lay a humanist's appreciation of ancient Greek civic life. And behind that lay a bishop's desire to strengthen loyalty to an emperor who seemed the last, best hope for the Catholic Church in the Empire.

From Julius Pflug to Lazarus von Schwendi (1522–84), a whole generation or more passes by in a moment. A Swabian nobleman's bastard ennobled at age two, Schwendi studied at Basel and Strasbourg and at twenty-four entered the emperor's service. It was a career-making move. Schwendi fought for the emperor in 1546–47 against the Smalkaldeners, in 1552 in Lorraine against France, in the Netherlands, and later as supreme commander against the Ottomans in Hungary. In the fall of 1568, newly created baron, he received permission to retire to Hohenlandsberg Castle in the Alsatian Vosges. His Imperial master, however, gave him no rest, and Schwendi served as Maximilian's trusted advisor on political as well as military affairs.

In 1574 Schwendi composed for Maximilian a long memorial on the Empire's situation and prospects. He believed that in a world faced with uncertainty and corruption governing a land was like commanding a ship through storms, "namely, one must regard and make allowance for time, just like the turbulence of the wind, and pay attention to and tolerate many things in order better to move ahead and preserve the ship of the common good from injury and ruin."[73] Switching now to a medical metaphor, Schwendi says that all human matters, "not only the natural also those which concern reason and presumption" – both in governance and in religion – "are subject to all kinds of imperfections, corruptions, and abuses, just as "in the natural body occur internal weaknesses, diseases, aging and finally total change."[74] This is the language of Machiavelli, of course, among whose readers Schwendi belonged.

Schwendi's acknowledgement of change as a universal experience helps to explain why, unlike Pflug, who appealed to ancient German glories and universal values, Schwendi sees both progress and regress in German history. For perhaps 2,000 years, he writes, "so long as human memory stretches . . . Germany has possessed this advantage over other nations and peoples . . . that it has always been protected and

---

71 Schmidt, *Vaterlandsliebe*, 212, n. 52.
72 Schmidt, *Vaterlandsliebe*, 212.
73 Lazarus von Schwendi, *Des Lazarus von Schwendi Denkschrift über die politische Lage des Deutschen Reiches von 1574*, 5.
74 Schwendi, *Des Lazarus von Schwendi Denkschrift*, 6.

preserved from all kinds of foreign power and servitude by its great inner strength, manliness, and loyal solidarity, all rooted in great zeal and desire for freedom."[75] Yet these qualities also gave rise to feuds, banditry, and other violent ways. During the past 100 years, a more civilized way of life promoted by the growth of learning, schools, especially printed books, and highly reasonable acts of the recent emperors, "has softened this old, hard, too brash German manner and promoted greater peace, more law and order, and a more moderate way of life."[76] Through this civilizing process, however, "German devotion, consensus, and obedience to the common good and the authority of the Empire and the German emperorship have been not a little diminished."[77]

In Schwendi's view, the times had changed. The changes began in Maximilian I's time with attacks on Rome and the clergy and demands for a reformation, to which neither pope nor clergy responded, even though (in his overestimate) "up to two-thirds or three-quarters of all land and money in Germany came into clerical hands."[78] Then came the spark, the preaching of the great indulgence against which Luther first raised his voice. All things doubtless happened according to the judgment of God on high that more changes should be made, but then came political disorder, "namely, the intervention of foreign nations in the Empire's governance, from which arose soon two great evils and damages to the German Nation."[79] These were the freedom-loving Germans' unwillingness to be ruled by foreigners, notably by Emperor Charles V, and the desire of foreign nations to exploit the Imperial regime for their own purposes.

Schwendi directs his argument toward one principal goal: a strong monarch for a German nation whose spirit of solidarity has been weakened, in some cases even neutralized, by the religious schism. The failure of Charles V's settlement after the Smalkaldic War, which Schwendi approves, had left the Empire open to foreign, chiefly Spanish, exploitation.[80] How to overcome this weakness? The answer is religious unity, by which Schwendi means not striving for a (to him hopeless) unity in doctrine and practice but the promotion of a Christianity conducive to stronger governance of the entire German nation by its king-emperor. Schwendi's goal thus resembles Pflug's, but with a difference, for the general argues for both a national monarchy and a national church.

Schwendi's political realism marks him as what in France in this generation was called a "politique," one of those moderate Catholics who opposed the forward policy of the Catholic League and favored a tolerant royal policy for the sake of peace. The term also had the connotation of favoring a church more or less national in the Gallican sense. In the Empire, of course, the policy of Imperial Catholicism resembled, at least by Maximilian II's time, this French idea fairly closely. There was one great difference. A German of whatever confession had little or no grounds for

---

75   Schwendi, *Des Lazarus von Schwendi Denkschrift*, 7.
76   Schwendi, *Des Lazarus von Schwendi Denkschrift*, 7–8.
77   Schwendi, *Des Lazarus von Schwendi Denkschrift*, 8.
78   Schwendi, *Des Lazarus von Schwendi Denkschrift*, 9.
79   Schwendi, *Des Lazarus von Schwendi Denkschrift*, 9.
80   Following Charles V's abdication, Schwendi served King Philip of Spain against the French in the Low Countries, where he came into contact with both William of Orange and the Duke of Alba. Perhaps out of anti-Spanish sentiment formed at this time, he resigned his post and in 1564 took service in the Imperial army.

accepting the French Catholic politiques' easy assumption that toleration would preserve the Catholic Church as the principal church of their nation.

In his recommendations concerning the monarchy and religion, Schwendi captured with canny precision the problem of making a strong monarchy in a polity divided by religion. For the general the central fact is not either religious party's religious claims, but the fall of the Catholic faith he sees plunging to extinction before his eyes. At the present time, he observes, the German nobility "is almost entirely favorable to the altered [evangelical] religion," while "the common man no longer has any regard for the old ways and ceremonies of the Roman clergy, except to the degree that his ruler binds him to them."[81] This had all happened in a single lifetime. Fifty years before, the mendicant orders had enjoyed great authority and respect among the common people; now they had nearly been extinguished. The monasteries were empty, indulgences were almost universally scorned, as were pilgrimages, miraculous images of the saints, Masses for the dead, and Purgatory. Almost nowhere were new foundations being made, and no one wanted any longer to donate anything to the monasteries or the clergy. In sum, "the people's mind no longer favors . . . the old Roman system, which is losing its basis day by day."[82]

The only policy Maximilian needed to follow in religious affairs, his general recommends, is one of neutrality, for "nothing about governance evokes greater assent from and has more influence on the people than the perception and belief that the ruler intends to be even-handed, sincere, and upright."[83] The emperor needs only to halt the attacks on Catholic clerical jurisdictions and properties, forbid all religious persecution in word and deed, and suppress all polemics between the two parties. The rest will come in the course of things. Otherwise, if nothing is done, a great papal-Spanish conspiracy will try to reverse the changes, extirpate the evangelical religion, and return the Empire to the Roman obedience.

Schwendi and other advocates of a via media "were thus ready to make concessions concerning the freedom of conscience and worship, because they believed that internal peace would be thereby better secured than by an attempt to restore confessional unity by force."[84] Schwendi's imagination of the Holy Roman Empire as a Protestant German kingdom locates his vision at the peak of Protestant expansion in the German lands. The old church's only hope, he thinks, is a spilling over of the Spanish tyranny from the Netherlands into the rest of the Empire. This did not happen, but neither did the future the Swabian general envisaged for his emperor. For one thing, "both the territorial rulers and the emperor and his advisor were convinced that even a limited freedom of worship and conscience would challenge the structure of lordship and the internal order of the entire body politic."[85] Schwendi's counter policy of deconfessionalization was compatible neither to this conviction nor to the "fundamental decision of 1555 for an Imperial governance based on the liberties of the estates."[86] Second, Schwendi did not sufficiently appreciate the significance of the splitting of the German Protestants, now already well begun, into two

---

81 Schwendi, *Des Lazarus von Schwendi Denkschrift*, 18–19.
82 Schwendi, *Des Lazarus von Schwendi Denkschrift*, 20.
83 Schwendi, *Des Lazarus von Schwendi Denkschrift*, 24.
84 Lanzinner, *Friedensicherung*, 309.
85 Lanzinner, *Friedensicherung*, 310.
86 Lanzinner, *Friedensicherung*, 311.

mutually hostile parties, Lutheran and Reformed. Third, the general had no inkling of the Catholic revival that was preparing as he wrote, and even less of the direction from which the new threat would come – not Spain, but Italy. For these reasons, within a decade his advice became obsolete.

The fate of these proposals to sacrifice the dream of religious unity to the equally unrealistic dream of Imperial unity illustrates how fundamentally the confessionalization of the Holy Roman Empire represented its rulers' prime goal of preserving the Empire via a further empowerment and hardening of the political order that had developed before the Protestant reformation. The confessions were not religions, they were not churches, but they were large bodies, intermediate between the estates and the Empire. By means of them the Empire absorbed and to the degree possible neutralized the Protestant reformation's threat to destroy the Empire. Confessionalization was necessary, if the Empire were to survive this experience.

7. THE "SECOND REFORMATION" OF GERMAN CALVINISM

A decade before Schwendi drafted his memorandum for the emperor, the Reformed faith entered the Empire's public life. It had initially been planted in the German lands by Netherlandish refugees who settled at Aachen, Metz, and Trier, and on the Lower Rhine and the North Sea coast at Emden and Bremen. Its role in Imperial public life, however, began with the faith's adoption by the Palatinate, and over the next thirty years it gained further strength from the religious wars in France and in the Netherlands. This success created a self-confidence that rose to a peak in the early 1590s. Looking back from the 1620s, the Silesian clergyman Abraham Scultetus (Schultheiß, 1566–1625), once court preacher at Heidelberg and later at Prague, described the mood of those days:

> I cannot fail to recall the optimistic mood which I and many others felt when we considered the condition of the Reformed churches in 1591. In France there ruled the valiant King Henry IV, in England the mighty Queen Elizabeth, in Scotland the learned King James, in the Palatinate the bold hero John Casimir, in Saxony the courageous and powerful Elector Christian I, in Hesse the clever and prudent Landgrave William, who were all inclined to the Reformed religion. In the Netherlands everything went as Prince Maurice of Orange wished, when he took Breda, Zutphen, Hulst, and Nijmegen. . . . We imagined that an *aureum saeculum*, a golden age, had dawned.[87]

Within twelve months, "the elector of Saxony, the count palatine, and the landgrave all died, King Henry deserted the true faith, and all our golden hopes went up in smoke."[88]

Meanwhile, the Reformed faith had penetrated three major Protestant territories – the Palatinate, Saxony, and Brandenburg – and gained ground in Silesia. By 1620 two of the lay electors, Brandenburg and the Palatinate, were Calvinists, as were, or recently had been, a whole series of other princes and Imperial counts.[89] Yet these formed but a remnant of the German-speaking Calvinism that might have been, had

87 Cohn, "Territorial Princes," 135.
88 Cohn, "Territorial Princes," 135.
89 Five Silesian dukes, the prince of Anhalt, the count palatine of Zweibrücken, the landgrave of Hesse-Cassel, and seventeen Imperial counts (among them Nassau, Mörs-Neuenahr, and Dhaun-Falkenstein). Cohn, "Territorial Princes," 135–40, with map.

princely attempts to bring Reformed religion to Electoral Saxony, Brandenburg, Baden-Durlach, and Schleswig-Holstein not foundered on Lutheran resistance. The story of Reformed Protestantism as an independent force in German history is therefore very much a tale of what might have been. The faith presented itself to the German lands as not a new faith but an enhancement and extension of Luther's reformation. Luther's heirs thought differently.

The most obvious difference between the Reformed faith in the German lands and its counterparts in the French kingdom and the Dutch Republic was its strict subordination to princes. It was, in fact, more thoroughly dominated by rulers – this often surprises – than was its Lutheran counterpart. In a few lands, true, notably in the Lower Rhenish duchies of Cleves-Jülich and in East Frisia, Reformed churches established presbyterian governance in the Franco-Dutch manner as prescribed by the Synod of Emden in 1571. The typical Reformed church in the Empire, however, was organized strictly along Heidelberg lines, ruled from above by the prince and his lay officials.

The refugees who had streamed in from various lands since the late 1550s made Heidelberg the hub of the German Reformed network. Its ancient university (est. 1386) became the center of a German Reformed academic network that included the universities at Marburg (Hesse) and Frankfurt an der Oder (Brandenburg), academies at Herborn (in Nassau) and Bremen, and a score of secondary schools of the first rank. As prince-regent at Heidelberg, Count Palatine John Casimir (1543–92) campaigned in coordination with Huguenot operations in France and maintained a broad network of diplomatic ties to the rest of Calvinist Europe. Along the Rhine valley, Heidelberg's influence converged with that of Dutch Calvinism, a process clearly visible in the district known as the Wetterau, which lay on the river's right bank.

The Wetterau was dominated by a federation of Imperial counts, none of them powerful enough to act against their princely neighbors, the Hessian landgrave and the Elector Palatine. The first counts to identify themselves with the Reformed faith were Count John VI of Nassau-Katzenelnbogen (b. 1536, r. 1559–1605) and Count Louis of Sayn-Wittgenstein (1532–1605), followed in 1582 by Count Conrad of Solms-Braunfels (1540–92).[90] The shift from Lutheran to Reformed practices, like the original advance of evangelical religion, was an act of state performed without popular consent. In these small territories, as generally, lay officials took a leading role in Reformed church affairs, and in the later 1580s the counts organized a common general synod for the churches of their lands. Count John led the way, other members of the Wetterau federation followed. Lacking the military power of greater princes, these petty rulers seized upon other measures – bureaucratization of governance, schools, Dutch immigration, and mercantilist economic policies – to discipline and benefit their peoples.

The Nassau duchies became the Reformed faith's second secure center in the German lands. In Nassau-Dillenburg worked Wilhelm Zepper (1550–1607), professor of theology at Herborn and Inspector in the church. It was he who made in 1596 the leading argument for his faith as not a new confession but a purification of Luther's

---

90 The last-named married in 1559 Countess Elizabeth of Nassau-Dillenburg (1542–1603), a sister of Count John VI.

work, a "second reformation." The two pillars of the church's "spiritual structure," he declares, are its "teaching on faith" and its "teaching on life."[91] The first reformers had had "so much to do" to reform "doctrine, the violent intrigues, and insane behavior of the pope and his crew," that they lacked time to reform the way of life.[92] In those days "they did not rightly understand the matter of discipline," but now that the Gospel rightly understood has been secured, Zepper thought, the time had come for "a right reformation of the chief matter of our Christianity, that we establish, according to the order and command of Our Lord, Jesus Christ, the pure teaching of the Holy Gospel and the correct usage of the Holy Sacrament and the authentic, external forms of worship."[93]

Any Lutherans who read Zepper's remarks knew what he meant, for in the Empire the Reformed faith grew almost entirely at Lutheran expense. The Lutherans, understandably, reacted against being relegated to the role of honorable but obsolete pioneers and resisted the newcomer as best they could. They did so doggedly in the Palatinate, the official religion of which changed with dizzying frequency. Protestant (i.e., Lutheran) religion had not been explicitly established there until the rule of Elector Ottheinrich (b. 1502, r. 1556–59), whose death without heir brought the succession to Frederick III, the introducer of Reformed religion at Heidelberg. His elder son, Louis VI (r. 1576–83), reestablished Lutheranism and required his university professors to sign the Formula of Concord, but his younger son, John Casimir, reestablished Reformed practice during his regency (1583–92). This second Reformed establishment was upheld by the electors until well after 1648. No other German land experienced so many changes of confession as did the Palatinate. It was the supreme playground of the principle: whose the rule, his the religion.

The revolving confessional policy of Heidelberg was one thing, coercing the subjects was another. Many of the clergymen and other refugees who clustered at the court were aliens who lacked the slightest attachment to the territory. At least two of them, it was discovered, were antitrinitarians, of whom one was executed in 1572 and the other died a Muslim at Istanbul. The Palatinate was in fact a land of mixed religion. Lutherans gagged at the Calvinist requirement of leavened bread in the Lord's Supper; Calvinists fumed at Lutherans' attachment to so many rags and tags of defeated "popery." Resistance to Calvinism remained strongest in the Upper Palatinate (north of Bavaria), where in 1592, responding to harsh measures from Heidelberg, burghers lynched two Calvinist officials. In the German lands, therefore, the Reformed faith lived a mortgaged life as an unwanted suitor to its Lutheran counterpart, which reacted with loathing to every protestation of its loyalty and love. This contest, which reached a peak in the 1590s, was well underway when Maximilian II died in 1576.

8. AN EMPEROR'S END

To the end of his days Emperor Maximilian II concealed his religious convictions from his family, from his friends and advisors, from the common people, and, one

91 Paul Münch, "Volkskultur und Calvinismus. Zu Theorie und Praxis der 'reformatio vitae' während der 'Zweiten Reformation,'" 296.
92 Münch, "Volkskultur und Calvinismus," 296.
93 Münch, "Volkskultur und Calvinismus," 296–7.

must add, from future historians. Every action, every opinion he offered on religion retained the color of policy. Long plagued by ill health, he also feigned illness to cover neglect of his religious duties, and at one point in 1572 he had heard no sermons for six months at a stretch. Despite Empress Maria's entreaties, Maximilian's majordomo refused to supply him with a reliably Catholic confessor. Devout, though she sometimes neglected her religious duties, Maria was happiest in the company of her Bavarian in-laws at Munich, then the only politically important center of the Catholic cause. Although a bull of Pope Pius IV (r. 1559–65) granted the emperor and his children a dispensation to take Communion under either one or both kinds, Maria declared that she would rather see her sons dead than receive Communion in the irregular way. Maximilian gave way, "as he always has done," wrote the Spanish ambassador, but he continued to delay the First Communions of his three sons until the summer of 1575.[94] Eventually, even King Philip of Spain, Maria's brother, lost patience and gave up on Maximilian's religion as a hopeless project.

By then Maximilian was dying. He kept up with his pleasures as best he could but not very well, and when he passed forty-nine – a dangerous "threshold" year, his astrologers warned – he told his congratulators that "for me, every year is a threshold year."[95] He was suffering from recurring pains in his loins, kidney stones, gout, and palpitations of the heart, and at age forty-six for months on end, he was able to take, at most, four to six steps at a time in his bedroom. Still, an emperor is not his own man, and as the recent truce with the Ottoman sultan began to crumble, he had to call the estates to Regensburg to ask for money. The Diet opened on 25 June 1576 with few princes in attendance. They seemed sulky, and the religious issues, which Maximilian had hoped to finesse, came very soon to the fore. The Ecclesiastical Reservation, which protected Catholic bishoprics and abbeys from alienation by prelates who converted, would have to stand, he told the Protestants; the Ferdinandine Declaration, which guaranteed certain rights to Protestants living in ecclesiastical states, would also stand, he told the Catholics.

By early October nothing was settled. Five physicians quarreled incessantly at the dying emperor's bedside, though in accordance with the era's pluralistic medical culture, he was also treated by Magdalena Streicher, a healer from Ulm. To the last the emperor refused to have a will drawn up, to confess his sins, or to take the Catholic last rites, and for a time he would not even see Bishop Lambert Gruter (r. 1573–82) of Wiener Neustadt. Although he answered affirmatively to the bishop's question whether he repented of his sins and wished to die within the church, he did not say which church. Perhaps he believed to the last – plenty of people did – that the schism would soon be over. Perhaps he did not care. In the morning of 12 October, feast of St. Maximilian the Martyr, the emperor died. Bishop Gruter declared that he had passed into the company of the blessed, but the dissembling emperor's mystery remains intact to this day.

Death gave Emperor Maximilian no more peace than he had gained in life. Although his son and heir, Rudolph II (b. 1552, r. 1583–1612), was informed of his father's wish to be interred in St. Stephen's Cathedral at Vienna, the son – to save expense, it was whispered – decided for St. Vitus's Cathedral at Prague. Instead of

94 Paula Sutter Fichtner, *Emperor Maximilian II*, 212.
95 Fichtner, *Emperor Maximilian II*, 214.

getting a funeral monument of his own, to which as emperor he was entitled, Maximilian was to be buried alongside his parents, but the platform supporting their sarcophagi proved too small and had to be raised and enlarged. In death, as in life, he was plagued by instability, including his own. The funeral was held at Prague, but in St. James's Church, and that not until Maximilian was five months dead. None of his siblings appeared, though his sons did. A mood of impending change was in the air. A rumor flew about that Rudolph, spurred by his mother and the Jesuits, was about to attack the Bohemian Utraquists, and during the funeral someone cried out that a second purge of Antwerp, a second St. Bartholomew's Day, was about to unfold at Prague. Rudolph, standing at his father's bier, drew his dagger, but someone stayed his hand. The tomb in St. Vitus's Cathedral took a curious form. At its center lies Emperor Ferdinand I in august majesty; on the left is Empress Anna of Hungary; and on the right is a small Maximilian – there was no space for a larger image – who gestures toward an Imperial orb. He is either grasping for it or pushing it away.

Maximilian II was the last Imperial monarch who had lived before Luther died. Born in 1526, when the first Diet of Speyer finessed the issue of the religious schism, he was twenty when the Smalkaldic War began in 1546; thirty when his father succeeded in 1556; and nearly forty when he came to the throne in 1564. On all major fronts – the Ottomans, the religious schism, the European wars, and his personal religious attitude – he decided, as the Imperial estates had done at Speyer in 1526, not to decide. He was a monarch trapped in an unfinished reformation. His personal inclinations may have been evangelical, but an emperor's policy could only be Catholic, for it gained legitimacy from the pope and support in the Diet from the Catholic bishops and abbots. The situation was most delicate, for the Empire's religious geography was still very much in flux. The zones of greatest uncertainty lay in the southeast, where the Protestant nobles of the Austrian lands seemed to be following the Bohemian path, and in the northwest, where a chain of Catholic bishoprics stretching from Cologne and Münster to Osnabrück and Hildesheim lay squeezed between German Protestant princes and the Protestant Dutch Republic. The entire northeast was Lutheran, while the largest principalities of the southwest, Lutheran Württemberg and the Reformed Palatinate, also lay in Protestant hands. Given these uncertainties, the least dangerous policy for Maximilian II was to defend the Imperial *convivencia* of 1555. By this logic he had lived; in this conviction he died.

Part IV

Confessions, Empire, and War, 1576–1650

> The laws of God, therefore, are none but the laws of nature, whereof the
> principal is that we should not violate our faith, that is, a commandment to obey
> our civil sovereigns . . . who are therefore the supreme pastors, and the only
> persons whom Christians now hear speak from God – except such as God
> speaketh to, in these days, supernaturally.
>
> Thomas Hobbes

The Protestant reformers set out to reform churches; their disciples created confessions. Luther's revolutionary theology aimed to restore and did redraw relationships between the temporal and the spiritual realms in such a way that neither individual salvation nor the world's governance would be frustrated from achieving its respective object – the soul's reunion with God and the keeping of the world's peace. The key, so they believed, was the Church's submission to the Word in the form of true doctrine. Get this right, and – Satan's designs notwithstanding – the rest would fall into place. Whether because his tumultuous life left him no peace, or because he was a political innocent, Luther failed to work out in detail how the task should be accomplished. Each of his dicta for reordering a liberated Church's relationship to temporal authority preserved the stopgap character with which the reordering had begun.

Reflection on this outcome unveils a paradox: Martin Luther was the godfather of European Protestantism but not its creator. The religious community that came to be called – and to call itself – "Lutheran" expressed a collision between his radical theology and the political realities of the German lands. With one hand, Luther conveyed to Christian rulers authority over the church in this world and removed the foundation of the Catholic Church's power, the priesthood, by universalizing it. With the other hand, he denied to the Christian rulers the possibility of ultimate and exclusive authority over the world, including the soul, without which, as Hobbes taught and Rousseau confirmed, a new seamless fusion of spiritual authority and material power could not be formed. The ad hoc flavor of ecclesiastical institutions in the German Protestant world reflects this lack of fit between the idea of the Church and the forms of the churches.

From this unconformity arose the bitter internal strife that burst forth after Luther's death and ended a whole generation later with the creation of the Lutheran confession. The first of the confessions that formed during those years, it was also the most German. Not because it expressed some unique quality of a German soul, but because it most conformed to the political structures of the German lands. This meant that, absent absolutist rule, princes or magistrates ruled their churches, but they did not command the doctrinal formulae and liturgical usages that made Lutheranism a confession rather than a mere congery of local churches.

The German reformation's history has often been told as the tale of a devout and peaceful Lutheranism attacked by two aggressive foreign powers, the Roman papacy and French-born Calvinism. Deconstructing this legend has been one of Reformation scholarship's most important achievements since the 1960s. In its place today stands a quite different story, sometimes called "the confessionalization thesis." It holds that the three German confessions – Lutheran, Catholic, and Reformed – developed together from the 1570s as a system in which each developed characteristics that became, mutatis mutandis, common property of all. The German term "confession," used in this sense, means a large, transterritorial, readily identifiable, and more or less disciplined community identified by its formalized canon of belief, its "confession," but also by distinctive liturgical practices. Among them there emerged a politically determined *convivencia*, or coexistence, which the Peace of Westphalia in 1648 restored upon ending the Thirty Years War.

These chapters aim to show that all religious change in this era was mixed in success, that major changes required generations to achieve, and that the interactions and strife among the three confessions may be seen as a normal pattern of action, reaction, and exchange among them. Their creation, preservation, and restoration reveals an intensification of public life in the Empire, a subjection to law that, one by one, came either to include once-persecuted groups, Jews and Anabaptists, and allowed the most persecuted, the witches, to slip gradually below the judicial horizon. The Empire's creeping culture of toleration (tolerance is quite another issue) arose from the combination of religious plurality with the Empire's character as a polity. It grew up in an era that, traditional pictures to the contrary, witnessed a great deal of political consolidation without much centralization. The limits of this culture show themselves not so clearly in its failure to prevent war in 1618 as in its reactivation right in the midst of the Thirty Years War. The peace signed at war's end confirmed the reformed church(es) in a reformed Empire. It was an odd kind of realization of Emperor Sigismund's project nearly 250 years before. Yet the result looked nothing remotely like what that monarch might have imagined, for if the Empire remained a unity, though a diminished one, the church remained one only in the sense that the three confessions enjoyed equal status under the Imperial law.

Part IV opens with chapters on integration, one on the creation and progress of the two Protestant confessions (Chapter 13), and the other on the Catholic reformation (Chapter 14). There follows a contrasting chapter on other groups and their exclusion from public life (Chapter 15). The general narrative resumes with an account of the erosion of public life during the opening years of the seventeenth century (Chapter 16) and of the Thirty Years War (Chapter 17). A final chapter (Chapter 18) offers a brief look forward as far as the twentieth century.

13

Forming the Protestant Confessions

> And I saw an angel flying through the midst of heaven. He had an eternal
> gospel to proclaim to those who sit and dwell on earth, to all heathen and
> races and languages and nations. And he said with a loud voice: Fear God and give him
> honor, for the time of his judgment has come. Worship the one who has made heaven
> and earth, the seas and the springs of water. And another angel followed
> and said: "She has fallen, she has fallen, Babylon, the great city, for she has made
> drunk all the heathen with the wine of her harlotry." This angel . . . was
> Dr. Martin Luther.
>
> Johannes Bugenhagen

The Protestant reformation grew under the sign of the Last Day. "In these last days of
this transitory world," declares the preface to the *Book of Concord* (1580), "the
Almighty God, out of immeasurable love, grace, and mercy for the human race,
has allowed the light of his holy gospel and his Word that alone grants salvation to
appear and shine forth purely, unalloyed and unadulterated out of the superstitious,
papistical darkness for the German nation, our beloved fatherland."[1] These words
define Luther's principal legacy to his heirs: our lives are lived in the struggle between
God and the Devil for mastery of man and the world.

Before he was known beyond his university and his order, Luther, speculating on
the prophecies of the end of time (Rev. 20), proposed "that the true Antichrist according to Paul is reigning in the Roman Curia."[2] He accused "the Romanists" of making
"the pope a vicar of the Glorified Christ in heaven. . . . These are certainly the proper
works of the real Antichrist."[3] The events of the next five years – Luther's escape from
Worms (1521), the Peasants' War (1525), the Ottoman invasions of Hungary (1526, 1529),
and the sack of Rome (1527) – fed this belief. In a village near Wittenberg, Luther's
friend Michael Stifel (1487–1567) predicted from his pulpit – prematurely as it turned out –
that the world would end on 19 October 1533 at precisely eight o'clock in the morning.

1 Robert Kolb and Timothy J. Wengert, eds., *The Book of Concord: The Confessions of the Evangelical
  Lutheran Church*, 5.
2 Roberto Rusconi, "Antichrist and Antichrists," in Bernard McGinn, ed., *Apocalypticism in Western
  History and Culture*, 311–12.
3 Rusconi, "Antichrist and Antichrists," 312.

Luther may have been apocalyptic, but he was no chiliast – no Müntzer, no Hoffman, no Jan Beukelszoon. The world would end in God's good and unfathomable time. His views became the Lutheran view, and in 1530 the Confession of Augsburg (Article 17) condemned those who spread "Jewish opinions, that before the resurrection of the dead the godly men will take possession of the kingdom of the world, while the ungodly are suppressed everywhere."[4] Just as God's saving grace did not transform but negated human nature, God's apocalyptic time did not fulfill but negated human history. Meanwhile, Satan and his demons were everywhere, in Rome, of course, but also in every home and workshop. In the latter decades of the sixteenth century, an entire genre of "devil literature" flourished among Lutherans. Just as Sebastian Brant and Erasmus had seen the world's follies as the work of fools, these writers attributed them to the devils who accompanied humans in every walk and at every moment of life. There were beer devils, hair devils, oven devils, trouser devils, and shoe devils, devils to be responsible for anything and everything that went wrong in daily life.

The domestication of demons did not intensify but softened both the terrible apocalyptic sense of cosmic struggle and the anxieties of a world newly deprived of blessing, the classic prophylactic against evil in general and demons in particular. In a world beset, the Christian's practical task remained the pursuit of peace. In domestic and local settings he could do this personally, but for the world at large God had established civil authority, princes and magistrates.

1. LUTHER'S REFORMATION AND THE STATE

"If I, Dr. Martin Luther, had never taught or done anything else," Luther wrote in 1533, "than to illuminate secular government or authority and make it attractive, for this one deed the rulers should thank me. . . . Since the Apostles' time no theologian or jurist has more splendidly and clearly confirmed, instructed, and comforted the temporal rulers than I, by special divine grace, was able to do."[5] For him temporal authority was God's instrument to punish wickedness, preserve peace, and – Luther's chief interest – build and guard the Church in this world. Luther thus gave his blessing to the process, begun in the fifteenth century, by virtue of which German magistrates and princes appropriated command of the visible church in their lands. The pioneers of the German state-church were the magistrates of larger Imperial cities; not far behind them came the rulers of Saxony, Württemberg, and Hesse. Luther and his disciples did not create the new order so much as they removed restraints on it. Their christening of the prince as God's magistrate was implicit in Luther's call in 1520 to "the Christian nobility" to adopt right of reformation (*ius reformandi*), which the Imperial Diet sheepishly wrote into law in 1526. Two years later the Saxons set to work, as the elector mandated a visitation of his lands' churches, much as every bishop was bound to do. Other princes and some magistrates followed, and from their efforts evolved the German Protestant state-church, the Reformation's most durable

---

4 Kolb and Wengert, eds., *The Book of Concord*, 51.
5 Martin Luther, *D. Martin Luthers Werke. Kritische Gesamtausgabe. Schriften*, vol. 38: 102, line 30, to 103, line 9.

creation. It intermeshed far more efficiently with the Empire's dispersed governance than the Catholic papal/episcopal Church had ever done.

The translation of Luther's rapturous early hymns to Christian freedom into stern Protestant litanies of obedience has encouraged many to view the entire affair as a lost revolution. It is true that Luther advocated a free, congregationally governed church and that he continued to do so long after he recognized its impracticality. "Whoever has been called is ordained and should preach to those who have called him," he wrote privately in 1535, "that is the ordination of our Lord God."[6] Yet a free church meant "false brethren," as he called the dissenters – Anabaptists and spiritualists – whose ghosts haunted his reformation.

Just as important for Luther's shift, however, were the shocking conditions, especially in the villages, uncovered by the Ernestine Saxon visitation of 1528. "Dear God, help us!" he exclaimed a year later in the preface to his *Shorter Catechism*:

> What misery I have seen! The common man, especially in the villages, knows absolutely nothing about Christian doctrine, and unfortunately, many pastors are practically unfit and incompetent to teach. Nevertheless, they are all called Christians, have been baptized, and enjoy the holy sacraments even though they can recite neither the Lord's Prayer, the Apostles' Creed, nor the Ten Commandments. They live just like animals and unreasoning sows.[7]

Many laymen, as Johann Geiler had observed, hated their clergy. "Peasants, burghers, and nobles naturally hate pastors," reported a Saxon visitation commission to the elector in 1535, and "in many places the servants of the Word are held in such contempt, that unless this attitude is improved, few men will be willing to enter."[8]

Conditions were, if anything, worse in the cities, those nurseries of the early movements for the Gospel. At the end of 1531 Strasbourg's preachers complained to the magistrates "how many people in this city, in the inns and shops, in the squares, on the boats, and in the streets, blaspheme and dishonor most terribly the same Christian doctrine that our lords have confessed before His Christian Majesty and we have taught most faithfully."[9] Two years later, in his annual sermon before the city's magistrates, Caspar Hedio described the Gospel's rocky road in his city:

> Like the ass by the lion, the preacher is lamentably ripped and torn by the ungrateful, carnal world. One fellow cries, [the preachers] court the authorities, thinking thereby to protect and defend the Gospel. A second says, they preach and court the magistrates so that the latter will throw this or that fellow into the tower and imprison him there. A third shouts, those who do not believe as we do should be driven out. And a fourth [says], we want to establish a new papacy. . . . These others say . . . faith should be free, that is, each should act and live as seems best to him [or even that] temporal authority should not extend its office over Christian things and religion.[10]

6 Susan C. Karant-Nunn, *Luther's Pastors: The Reformation in the Ernestine Countryside*, 56.
7 Susan C. Karant-Nunn, *The Reformation of Ritual: An Interpretation of Early Modern Germany*, 67.
8 Karant-Nunn, *Luther's Pastors*, 54.
9 Manfred Krebs et al., eds., *Elsaß, parts 1–4: Stadt Straßburg 1522–52*, vol. 1: 357, ll. 17–21.
10 Krebs et al., eds., *Elsaß*, vol. 2: 262, ll. 26–32 (14 January 1534). The sermon was part of the annual ceremonies on *Schwörtag*, when new magistrates were installed and the citizens renewed their civic oath.

Popular anticlericalism continued right through and into the new order. "Yes, it is an injurious, poisonous, hasty thought Satan now inspires," Hedio lashed out at the preacher's enemies, "so that he can create an entry to and open a window on all the conspiracies, sects, and errors, saying, the authority should not oversee religious matters."[11] What is sometimes called "the victory of the Reformation" had not brought a triumph of the Gospel, and the task of establishing the new faith through routine evangelization would require decades, perhaps generations.

Everything depended on agency, on replacing the (admittedly lax) authority of the Church with some other agency. Early on, Luther had recognized with his brilliance the unbridgeable gap between his original ecclesiological ideal, congregational initiative, and practical necessity. In *On Temporal Authority and Whether It Ought To Be Obeyed* (1523), he had confessed with rue the dashing of his earlier confidence in princes, some of whom were using their freedom to persecute his followers. "They are thereby presumptuously setting themselves in God's place," he fulminates, "lording it over men's consciences and faith, and schooling the Holy Spirit according to their own crackbrained ideas."[12] Luther, to whom it hardly occurred that a good Catholic might have said the same of the evangelical princes, decided that "we must provide a sound basis for the civil law and sword so no one will doubt that [he is] in the world by God's will and ordinance."[13] His ingenious solution was his doctrine of the Two Kingdoms: in the "kingdom of God" dwell "the true believers who . . . need no temporal law or sword, . . . because the righteous man of his own accord does all and more than the law demands"; in the "kingdom of the world" live "the unrighteous," who "need the law to instruct, constrain, and compel them to do good."[14] For the two kingdoms God established two regimes, "the one to produce righteousness, the other to bring about external peace and prevent evil deeds. Neither one is sufficient without the other."[15] Despite his reputation for subservience to authority, Luther had few illusions about princes. "Since the beginnings of the world," he writes, "a wise prince is a mighty rare bird, and an upright prince even rarer. . . . They are God's executioners and hangmen: his divine wrath uses them to punish the wicked and to maintain outward peace."[16] Good or wicked, their authority comes directly from God.

Whether Church or church, it had for Luther no special authority of its own, for "the government of priests and bishops is not a matter of authority or power, but a service and an office, for they are neither higher nor better than other Christians. Therefore, they should impose no law or decree on others without their will and consent, . . . [for] Christians can be ruled by nothing except God's word."[17] This means that the real existing ("visible") church belongs, despite its commission by Christ, to the temporal realm and must submit to the ruler. This logic drove Luther in 1528 to invent the notion of the prince as an "emergency bishop" who leads the church's reconstruction with love rather than force.[18]

11 Krebs et al., eds., *Elsaß*, vol. 2: 263, ll. 8–11.
12 Martin Luther, *Luther's Works*, vol. 45: 84.
13 Luther, *Luther's Works*, vol. 45: 85.
14 Luther, *Luther's Works*, vol. 45: 88–9.
15 Luther, *Luther's Works*, vol. 45: 91.
16 Luther, *Luther's Works*, vol. 45: 113.
17 Luther, *Luther's Works*, vol. 45: 117.
18 In his preface to the "Instruction for the Visitors of the Parishes in the Electorate of Saxony" of 1528.

It was therefore not only reasonable but also necessary that the Protestant clergy became salaried civil servants, comparable to lawyers, physicians, and military commanders. Yet they did not surrender religious authority so easily. They soon discovered that their duties, prescribed by God's law, required the authority to discriminate, not between the saved and the damned – this remained God's work alone – but between those who obeyed and those who flouted God's laws. The only sanction at their disposal was to admit to or exclude from the sacrament of the Lord's Supper, which soon put them at loggerheads with Protestant magistrates and officials. In city after city, the issue came to a head, and the magistrates, who often believed that the preachers were arrogating power to themselves, taught them better. Having rejected one pope in distant Rome, no prince or magistrate would contemplate obeying "new popes" at home.

This clerical dilemma and the need that drove it decided the political fate of the Protestant clergies. The reformers, having begged princes and magistrates to tear down the idolatrous papal religion and build a new and godly church in its place, had no credible argument for clerical authority to excommunicate. How could those who had struggled against religious coercion justify religious coercion? At Strasbourg in 1534 a Tyrolean soap maker named Leupold Scharnschlager (d. 1563) put this point to the city's magistrates with exquisite eloquence. "You accept and press us," this brave fellow told the magistrates, "to abandon our faith and accept yours. That is just the same as when the emperor told you that you should abandon your faith and accept his. Now I speak to your consciences. Do you think it right to obey the emperor in such things? Ah, well, then you might also say that we ought to obey you in such things." If so, he mocked the magistrates, "you would be obliged to reinstate all the idolatry and the papist convents, also the Mass and other things."[19] Jacob Sturm knew that the Tyrolean had hit this nail on the head. "It would be a good thing," the stettmeister sighed, "if we could find a way to get the people to come to church and hear the Word of God," but since "faith is a voluntary act and a gift of God, little can be gained through laws."[20] If made and not enforced, such laws would only "prompt people to say that 'a new papacy has been established.'"[21] "Laws," he declared, "make hypocrites."[22] Still, this old Erasmian bowed to the logic he had helped to create and became the architect of persecution at Strasbourg. To leave religion unregulated, he thought, would open the gate to "all sorts of heretical sects, unnecessary argument, and contentious opinions about the faith" and lead "to considerable scandal and provocation of many Christians and to the destruction of civic peace and unity."[23]

This central contradiction of the Protestant reformation was never to be resolved, at least not in the age of reformations. No one could define more starkly than Sturm did the cruel contradiction between the individual's Christian freedom and the godly community's need for discipline, much less the prince's God-given authority over the church. The Protestant reformers chose the state's protection for themselves and the liberated Gospel, because the only alternative, the free congregation, they would not

19 Krebs et al., eds., *Elsaß*, vol. 2: 348, line 2, to 349, line 11.
20 Thomas A. Brady, *Protestant Politics: Jacob Sturm (1489–1553) and the German Reformation*, 110.
21 Brady, *Protestant Politics*, 110.
22 Brady, *Protestant Politics*, 111.
23 Brady, *Protestant Politics*, 111.

and could not accept. They were churchmen for whom the Church, if no longer the vessel of God's saving grace, was still the speaker of His saving Word. Without the ruler's aid, they believed, their mission could not be fulfilled.

2. FORMING THE LUTHERAN CONFESSION

The one power left to the Lutheran clergy was the determination of Christian doctrine, a task in such uncertainty and disarray at Luther's death in 1546 that an entire generation was consumed by theological quarrels among his heirs. In the 1570s a way to peace emerged from the sponsorship of radical Lutheran doctrine by modern Lutheran politics, and from this settlement the Lutheran confession was born. This persistent culture of polemic and contention laid open Luther's legacy to both competition from the Reformed faith and contest with a reforming Catholicism. The strife erupted from the convergence of three experiences: the loss of Luther's charisma, a flowering of radically apocalyptic agitation after the Smalkaldic War, and the Lutheran princes' commitment to the Imperial political *convivencia* forged in 1552–55.

Luther's persona, the movement's greatest asset in life, became its burden in death. In life he exercised a charismatic authority for the evangelical movement that finds no parallel in the Protestantism of his or any other day. He was "our revered father and our most beloved preceptor," wrote Melanchthon, "the horseman and chariot of Israel."[24] Erasmus Alber (1500–53), a priest's son from the Wetterau, Luther's student, and then pastor at Neubrandenburg in the duchy of Mecklenburg, composed a song about "the dear, pious Luther tender / the Germans' true prophet, / who correctly taught us God's Word."[25] Precisely this legacy came to lie in disarray. In May 1579, Cyriakus Spangenberg (1528–1604) of Nordhausen, a fierce foe of the moderate ("Philippist") party, wrote to Elector August that while "God did not send Luther to us Germans in vain, . . . [He] has let many learned theologians sink and fall to such a low estimate of the writings of this precious man, the true German prophet, Dr. Luther, that they read him very little and follow them not at all."[26]

Spangenberg did not overstate the gravity of his generation's situation. Among the "very dangerous situations and troublesome disturbances [that] arose in our beloved fatherland, the German nation, soon after the Christian death of that highly enlightened and pious man, Dr. Martin Luther,"[27] doctrinal controversy broke out into at least six distinct wildfires. The issues included antinomianism (whether the natural and Mosaic law binds Christians) and adiaphorism (whether matters of faith, doctrine, and practice can be separated into essentials and non-essentials); good works and salvation; the role of the will in conversion; the indwelling of Christ in the believer; and the sinful believer's possession of some power to do good. While the number and range of these disputes might suggest that Luther had settled nothing, his heirs tended to believe that he had settled everything, and that controversy must arise from perverse will, as it had in bygone controversies with Zwingli and the Anabaptists. At the center of the storms stood "the authority of the living teacher transformed into the written authority of the corpus of his works," which underwent a

24 Robert Kolb, *Martin Luther as Prophet, Teacher, Hero: Images of the Reformer, 1520–1620*, 36.
25 Kolb, *Martin Luther*, 37.
26 Cyriakus Spangenberg to Elector August of Saxony, 23 May 1579, in Kolb, *Martin Luther*, 47.
27 Kolb and Wengert, eds., *The Book of Concord*, 5, preface.

"quasi-papalization."[28] This underestimates the problem, for while popes speak when they must and more or less in one voice, the immense corpus of Luther's works spoke continuously, often in discordant voices.

Behind each of these doctrinal controversies lay the issue of religious and political compromise with the Catholics. Beginning in the years of Protestant defeat, 1547 to 1552, this issue split the Lutheran community into the radical and moderate parties, respectively Real Lutherans and Philippists.[29] The rupture's roots went back to Charles V's defeat of the Protestants in 1547 and his proclamation in the following year of a provisional (hence the name, "Interim") religious settlement until the general council at Trent should publish its decisions. The Interim's crucial doctrinal article did not rule out the evangelical teaching on justification, and it permitted clerical marriage and utraquism (communion under both kinds). Strasbourg's Martin Bucer signed it – under duress, he later claimed – and the Wittenberg theologians around Philip Melanchthon seemed at least unwilling to reject an even more moderate version (called the "Leipzig Interim"). But when Elector Maurice moved to enforce this settlement in Saxony, all hell broke loose.

The Saxon estates and the Catholic bishop of Meissen rejected the Leipzig text, while a party of Lutheran theologians began a fierce campaign against it. Among the resisters' leaders were several Saxons who possessed the very best Lutheran credentials: Nikolaus von Amsdorf (1483–1565), the reformer of Magdeburg and Goslar, and sometime Protestant bishop of Naumburg, and Nikolaus Gallus (Hahn, 1516–70), a native of Anhalt and Wittenberg graduate, who in 1549 was called to the pastorate of St. Ulrich in Magdeburg. Amsdorf, one of the few nobles among the Lutheran clergy, rendered his judgment: "Whoever obeys the INTERIM, worships not God but the Devil and his minions."[30] The most strident voice belonged to Matthias Flacius Illyricus (Matija Vlačič, 1520–75), a Germanized Italo-Croat who had come in 1541 to Wittenberg. To Flacius's party, their old teacher Philip Melanchthon now seemed an apostate.

Now there must be war to the knife, Magdeburg against Wittenberg. To the Real Lutherans, compromise with the Catholics, whether on rites or doctrines, meant returning to the Roman yoke, to filthy idolatry, to the arms of the Antichrist. In their uncompromising ferocity the Magdeburgers revived the spirit of the 1520s. Their propaganda machine came to be called "Lord God's chancery" (*Herrgotts Kanzlei*), a remarkable battery of writers who poured forth a steady stream of printed invective against pope, general council, emperor, and Elector Maurice. It was, in word if not in deed, a revolutionary moment, and it brought forth a rich, frenzied tide of words in a spirit unheard since the 1520s, except perhaps in Luther's last diatribes against pope and Jews. The flood of words bespoke a mental world steeped in the apocalyptic temper that hovered over the Empire during the years between the Interim (1548) and the Treaty of Passau (1552). That mental world was "a monument of words" – just as Luther's had been.[31]

At the very center of this fierce war of words was a struggle for the possession of Luther himself. The Magdeburgers interpreted his life not from his tower experience,

28 Kolb, *Martin Luther*, 33.
29 For the meanings of the party names, see Chapter 12, 219–20.
30 Bodo Nischan, *Lutherans and Calvinists in the Age of Confessionalism*, 7.11.
31 Thomas Kaufmann, *Das Ende der Reformation: Magdeburgs "Herrgotts Kanzlei" (1548–1551/2)*, 430.

the key moment for modern interpreters, but from his death. Only at this moment did the true meaning of his prophetic mission reveal itself, just as Christ's death on the cross fully revealed His saving mission. Looking back from 1549, Flacius remembered the aged prophet:

> See, this is our old venerable father in Christ, the authentic man of God and true Elijah, who, as an undaunted hero, fought confidently and blessedly against the Antichrist and all heretics and idolaters [literally: followers of Baal]. Today or tomorrow the Lord God will take him from us, but we will remain behind. We immature children of weak faith and little wisdom will easily be attacked . . . by the defiant foes of God and divine truth; and some of us will be despicably seduced and oppressed.[32]

To Flacius and his fellows "closeness to Luther was synonymous with closeness to the authentic Biblical message, to the divine origin of the reformation, and to salvation."[33] In his unmasking of the pope as the vicar not of Christ but of Antichrist, Luther had marked off the world into two sides: Christ and His true believers versus the Antichrist and his apostates, whose instrument was the Interim. Luther had taught that every day is *potentially* the Last Day; the Magdeburgers believed that today or tomorrow is *surely* the Last Day, on which will end the fourth and last world monarchy, the (Holy) Roman Empire, just as Daniel had foretold.[34]

This second great struggle for God and against Satan at Magdeburg reprised the Anabaptist kingdom at Münster in both its apocalyptic vision and its doom. Its destroyer was Elector Maurice, the "Judas of Meissen." Having betrayed the Protestant cause in 1547, in the fall of 1550 he mounted in the Empire's service a siege of Magdeburg, the New Jerusalem of the Real Lutherans. Once his troops took the city, the wily Maurice turned his coat once more, allied with the king of France, and humiliated the emperor. His brother and successor, Elector August, swung back toward Vienna and helped Emperor Ferdinand I (r. 1556–64) to negotiate the Religious Peace of 1555. August became thereby the principal Protestant broker of the Imperial *convivencia*, a role he held through the reigns of Ferdinand and of Maximilian II (r. 1564–76).

3. PAX LUTHERANORUM

The Real Lutherans lost every battle, but they won the war. The terms of Lutheran doctrinal unity, when it came, vindicated their contention that to compromise with Rome meant to betray God's Word. The Formula of Concord took shape in 1577, one year after Lazarus von Schwendi had predicted the imminent disappearance of Catholicism from the German lands. Ironically, while it canonized Real Lutheran theology, it also affirmed by its very character August's policy of collaboration with the emperor to preserve the Imperial *convivencia*.

Two things made possible the victory of radical theology and moderate politics within the Lutheran party. First, Elector August's ruin of his Ernestine cousins and

---

32 Kaufmann, *Das Ende der Reformation*, 430.
33 Kaufmann, *Das Ende der Reformation*, 433.
34 The reference is to Daniel 7, which tells of the dream of King Belshazzar of Babylon, in which the four world monarchies – later identified as Assyrian, Persian, Greek, and Roman – appear to him.

his adoption in 1574 of the Real Lutheran line removed the Saxon rivalry as a political catalyst of theological strife and made it possible for the Lutheran estates and clergy to unite under a common statement of faith, the Formula of Concord, and a common political chief, August of Saxony. Second, the entry of Calvinism onto the German stage posed riddles for which the Real Lutherans' worldview had no answer and provocations which they could not resist, as their old Lutheran foes seemed to merge with the newcomers in a firm alliance against Luther's legacy. Philippists and Calvinists did agree, it is true, that the Real Lutherans were ensnared by old errors, most notably the dualist heresy of Manichaeism. Cyriakus Spangenberg, a hardened warrior in these fights, defended himself in 1579 to Elector August. He told how Luther, "that man of God," had "predicted this cross that I must now bear on behalf of his teaching. . . . God be praised and thanked, Who has kept me from departing even a hand's breadth from the true, pure, Lutheran teaching."[35] His (Lutheran) enemies, however, "who have well learned from the Calvinists, say: O, Luther was a man, who could also err! If Luther were living now, he would change many things in his books."[36] Yet it is they who have abandoned Luther's way, fallen into more than twenty obviously Manichaean errors, and contradicted Luther's Catechism on no fewer than 174 points.

Well before Spangenberg poured out these grievances, intra-Lutheran peace was already on track. A new generation of Lutheran clergymen, too young to have known Martin Luther, had meanwhile come to maturity, and they were more concerned with defending Luther's churches against Calvinists and Catholics than with fighting other Lutherans. In 1577 a number of them drafted the Formula of Concord at Bergen Abbey near the walls of Magdeburg. Its final redaction, the *Book of Concord*, appeared in 1580, precisely thirty years after the signing of the Confession of Augsburg. As the Lutheran peace spread, it both dampened the apocalyptic fires set by Luther – and stoked to great heat by the Magdeburgers – and rallied theologians from both sides of the old Lutheran divide.

Nothing could have been more appropriate than the restoration through words of a communion based on the Word. The *Book of Concord* aimed, its preface announced,

> not to manufacture anything new through this work of concord, nor to depart in either substance or expression to the smallest degree from the divine truth, acknowledged and professed at one time by our blessed predecessors and us, as based on the prophetic and apostolic Scripture and comprehended in the three Creeds, in the Confession of Augsburg presented in 1530 to Emperor Charles of kindest memory, in the Apology that followed it, and in the Smalkaldic Articles and the Large and Small Catechisms of that highly enlightened man, Dr. Luther.[37]

The signatories affirmed their desire "to live in genuine peace and unity with [their] colleagues, the electors, princes, and estates in the Holy Roman Empire and also with other Christian potentates."[38] Doctrinal unity and political peace, the *Book of Concord* was a hard-won stroke of genius. Its list of signatories shows how far the faith

35 Heinrich Rembe, ed., *Der Briefwechsel des M. Cyriakus Spangenberg*, 121, Cyriakus Spangenberg to Elector August of Saxony, 23 May 1579.
36 Rembe, ed., *Der Briefwechsel des M. Cyriakus Spangenberg*, 121.
37 Kolb and Wengert, eds., *The Book of Concord*, 15.
38 Kolb and Wengert, eds., *The Book of Concord*, 15.

had advanced in the fifty years. In 1530 the Confession of Augsburg had been signed by 1 elector, 6 princes, and 2 cities; in 1580 the *Book of Concord* (which included the Confession) bore the signatures and seals of 3 electors, 20 other princes, 28 counts and barons, 35 urban regimes, and 8,000 Protestant pastors. Out of their pledges not to break the restored fellowship, the Lutheran confession – in both senses of the term – was forged. Of course, the one generation that had passed since Luther's first public act was nothing compared to the many generations it would take to animate the civic and territorial churches and alter the habits and beliefs that had been centuries in the making.

4. RECONSTRUCTING CHURCHES

The foundations of the Protestant confessions lay in the structures of their particular churches. Their formation depended on a culture of collaboration between clergies and regimes and the latter's appropriation – with clerical approval – of the episcopal duty of visitation, the regular inspection of local churches that formed the sine qua non of ecclesiastical governance. Protestant visitations were pioneered in Ernestine Saxony, Nuremberg, and Brandenburg-Ansbach. The first complete model for the governance of a territorial church appeared in 1559 in the duchy of Württemberg. Its simple structure provided oversight by a synod, in which sat ducal councilors and the church's four superintendents-general, while under the latter stood superintendents for the duchy's twenty-three districts, and below them the local pastors and their congregations.

More widely influential in Lutheran lands was the church ordinance issued for Electoral (Albertine) Saxony in 1580. This law placed the church's governance under the authority of the elector's privy council (est. 1574) and in the everyday custody of the Superior Consistory and its central financial office (est. 1586). The consistories were staffed by pastors and lay councilors in equal numbers under a lay president. Leipzig and the three former prince-bishoprics (Meissen, Merseburg, and Naumburg) each received its own consistory. Although derived from the (Ernestine) Saxon church organized in Luther's time, the Albertine constitution was far more complex and, in the end, more unified.

It is surprising, given the fierce doctrinal battles between the Lutheran churches and their Reformed rivals, how little the two confessions differed in the governance of their respective territorial churches. When the Reformed (Calvinist) faith began to penetrate the German lands around 1560, it rejected the presbyterian church order favored by western European Calvinists and instead adapted Lutheran models to more centralized territorial church governance under strong lay control. The most influential Reformed model came from Heidelberg, the Palatine elector's capital and the seat of his university.

Elector Frederick III's highly authoritarian ordinance arose from a struggle between representatives of two Reformed traditions. The Ecclesiastical Council (*Kirchenrat*) favored separate clerical authority in the manner of Geneva, while the elector's High Council (*Oberrat*), wanted the church brought directly under the ruler's "regime" (*Polizei*) in the manner of Zurich. At first the clerical party got the upper hand and tried to introduce a Genevan-style clerical-and-lay consistory with powers of excommunication. After a long battle, however, the advocates of lay

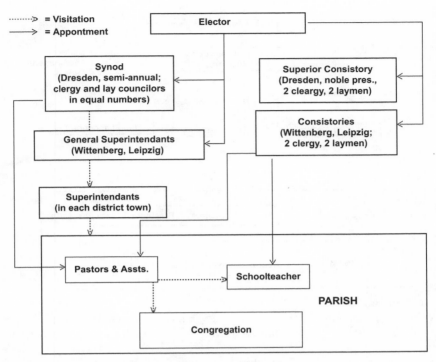

Figure 13.   Lutheran Church Governance: Albertine Saxony, 1580
Source: Hubert Jedin, Kenneth Scott Latourette, and Jochen Martin, eds., *Atlas zur Kirchengeschichte. Die christlichen Kirchen in Geschichte und Gegenwart*, 74.

control beat the clericals and established a complete fusion of ecclesiastical discipline with electoral authority. The struggle thus ended with a victory of Zurich over Geneva.

The logic of this Reformed experiment was stated with great clarity by the Swiss physician Thomas Erastus (Lüber, 1524–83), a peasant's son from near Baden in the Aargau. Called in 1558 to Heidelberg's faculty of medicine, he lost his post when the Palatinate was taken back into the Lutheran faith under Elector Louis VI (r. 1576–83). Erastus correctly saw, in the fulcrum of clerical authority, the power of excommunication, a power the clergy could not claim if – as both Zwingli and Luther had taught – the Church has no authority of its own. He blamed "excommunicatory fever" for the view that "some certain presbyters should sit in the name of the whole church and should judge who were worthy or unworthy to come unto the Lord's Supper."[39] This view is without Biblical warrant, he argues, because there is no reason "why the Christian magistrate at the present day should not possess the same power God commanded the magistrate to exercise in the Jewish common-wealth. Do we imagine that we are able to continue a better constitution of Church

---

39   Robert Lee, ed., *The Theses of Erastus Touching Excommunication*, 160–2, thesis lxxiii.

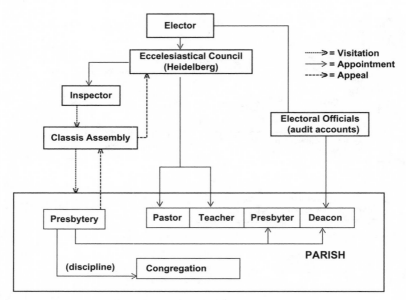

Figure 14.   Reformed Church Governance: The Palatinate, 1563
Source: Hubert Jedin, Kenneth Scott Latourette, and Jochen Martin, eds., *Atlas zur Kirchen-geschichte. Die christlichen Kirchen in Geschichte und Gegenwart*, 75.

and State than that?"[40] Therefore, Erastus concludes, "Wherever the magistrate is godly, there is no need of any other authority under any other pretension or title to rule or punish the people – as if the Christian magistrate differed nothing from the heathen."[41]

Erastus represents the ultimate redaction of the logic inherent in the territorialization of churches. Anomalies could exist, such as the presbyterian churches planted by Dutch exiles at Emden, the chief town of East Frisia, and a few other places. Yet the Palatine church supplied a Reformed version of the principle that the lay ruler stands between God and the church. "We have finally recognized and undertaken to fulfill Our divinely ordained office, vocation, and governance," the *Heidelberg Catechism*'s preface announces,

> not only to keep peace and order, but also to maintain a disciplined, upright, and virtuous life and behavior among Our subjects, furthermore . . . to instruct them and bring them . . . to the righteous knowledge and fear of the almighty and His sanctifying Word as the only basis of all virtues and obedience, and also unflinchingly and with gladness of heart to help them gain eternal and temporal well-being, to the best of Our abilities.[42]

No king of England, Denmark, or Sweden ever claimed more.[43]

40   Lee, ed., *The Theses of Erastus*, 160–2, thesis lxxiii.
41   Lee, ed., *The Theses of Erastus*, 160–4, thesis lxxiv.
42   R. Po-chia Hsia, *Social Discipline in the Reformation: Central Europe, 1550–1750*, 34–5, slightly altered.
43   By one of history's tricks the term "Erastianism" survives only in the history of the Church of England.

5. THE REFORMED CONFESSION – A SECOND REFORMATION?

The Reformed faith came to the German lands as a second reformation, a reformation of the Protestant reformation. But it was also a new faith, a very much transformed version of the faith that had spread three decades earlier from the German lands to France, the Low Countries, and the British kingdoms. In the 1560s it returned as a vigorous, militant, internationally connected movement, bent on completing the purgation of the German churches and gathering their support in the wars against the minions of Rome.

German Lutherans, skeptical about Reformed adherents' claims, tended to see in them not welcome brethren from the west but agitators who sought to revive the Eucharistic quarrel that had split the infant Protestant movement. The new "false prophets" (Matt. 7:15–20 and 24:24) were old Sacramentarians, and Satan, their chief, wore a long black robe in the Genevan style. Into this battle the Lutheran polemicists called on forces from the increasingly popular genre of devil books. In his flamboyantly named *Serpens Antiquus: The Old Snake as the Sacramental Devil* of 1580, Johann Schütz counts thirty-seven assistant devils. "The Devil," he writes, "is relying not solely on Turks and Papists to do his work, but this time is using primarily the Sacramentarians to deprive us cunningly and maliciously of God's saving word thereby moving Christ even further away from us than the old church had ever done."[44] Better Rome than Geneva?

The main phase of the Reformed Lutheran conflict lasted one long generation. It reached a first peak around 1590 with the struggle in Saxony and a second greater one in 1610 with the struggle in Brandenburg. Then came the great German war. By the 1630s some rapprochement had begun, promoted intellectually "by Reformed irenicism, politically by the Catholic victories and carnage of the Thirty Years' War."[45] The conflict concentrated in a belt that stretched from the Palatinate, Nassau, and Hesse in the west across to Anhalt, Saxony, and Brandenburg in the east. Nowhere did it capture or even attempt to capture an intact Catholic land.

The lands of two Protestant electors, Saxony and Brandenburg, became principal arenas of this struggle. In both lands the trouble began at the center, at the elector's court. At August's death in 1586 the Electoral Saxon regime passed to his son, Christian I (b. 1560, r. 1586–91), a weak prince whose chancellor, Dr. Nikolaus Crell (1551–1601) of Leipzig, was able to unite all bureaus of government in his own capable hands. Crell initiated an authoritarian reform of a typically Reformed, centralizing kind. First, he unified the central regime and ceased to call the territorial diet. Second, he dropped the mandatory swearing of pastors on the Formula of Concord, purged the court clergy, dissolved the consistories, issued a new prayer book, catechism, and hymnal, and (secretly) ordered a new Bible translation – all in a Calvinist sense. And third, Crell advocated a military alliance of all Protestant estates, an end to August's political partnership with the emperor, and the forging of new contacts with French

---

44 Nischan, *Lutherans and Calvinists*, 7.11.
45 Nischan, *Lutherans and Calvinists*, xiii.

Calvinist leaders. Alas for Crell, his young prince's death in 1591 left as successor a minor under the guardianship of a strict Lutheran kinsman. Now the Saxon estates counterattacked. Crell was arrested and, following ten years of incarceration on a dubious trial, executed at Dresden in 1601. By then the restoration in Saxony was well underway. The church was returned to orthodoxy; the alliance with the emperor was renewed; and in 1608 the Saxon elector refused to join the Palatine and Brandenburg electors in founding the Protestant Union.

The Brandenburg case is altogether more illuminating. It shows how, even against a strong prince and a determined Reformed elite, a second reformation could be defeated by resistance from the subjects.[46] Brandenburg's first reformation had begun after the death in 1539 of Elector Joachim I. The next year his son and heir, Joachim II Hector (b. 1505, r. 1539–71), began a new era in Brandenburg's history under the Hohenzollern dynasty. A cautious lord, Joachim introduced in 1540 what has been described as "the most Catholic of all the German Protestant [church] orders," Lutheran in its core doctrines but heavily Catholic in liturgy, especially in its strong view of the Real Presence in the Lord's Supper and in its retention of the episcopal office.[47] Like Maurice of Saxony, in the Smalkaldic War, Joachim sided with the emperor and left his Protestant allies in the lurch. Thereafter, as in Saxony, over the decades the Brandenburg churches settled down into Lutheran ways. Joachim's new church order of 1572 instructed pastors to follow "the writings and books of the blessed Doctor Martin Luther, because through God's providence he restored the unadulterated pure doctrine." "God's word and Luther's doctrine," declared the inscription on a memorial coin of 1564, "will never pass away."[48]

By the end of the sixteenth century, Brandenburg's "soft reformation" – Lutheran doctrine and many Catholic practices – formed a reasonable target, more promising than Saxony had been, for a Reformed second reformation. The Reformed theologians held that Luther had made the beginning, but only the beginning, of a restoration of true Christian doctrine, godly worship, and a truly Christian way of life. Abraham Scultetus played a central role in the initial program of a new reformation for Brandenburg's church. He later described the Reformed view of the Protestant reformation: "In our times, alongside and after Luther, Melanchthon, Zwingli, Oecolampadius, God raised up many other splendid men, who condemned the papal idolatry more and more successfully and explained the Scriptures more and more fully."[49] Most Lutherans, steeped by now in a belief that Luther had been *the* prophet of reformation, would never accept this evolutionary concept of how God had caused His Word to be proclaimed anew and caused His Church to be purified.

46 In early modern times the Mark Brandenburg comprised the following lands west to east: the Altmark (today the northern part of the state of Saxony-Anhalt) and to its north Prignitz (historically a buffer zone between Brandenburg and Mecklenburg, today the northwest of the state of Brandenburg); the Mittelmark (including Berlin) and to its north the Uckermark (today the northeastern part of the state of Brandenburg); and the Neumark (today in western Poland). Each of its constituent parts possessed its own territorial estates. East Prussia, a land of the Teutonic Knights, was secularized in 1525 by the Grand Master, a Hohenzollern prince. It came to a personal union with the Mark Brandenburg under Elector John Sigismund in 1618.

47 Bodo Nischan, *Prince, People, and Confession: The Second Reformation in Brandenburg*, 21.

48 Nischan, *Lutherans and Calvinists*, 205.

49 Nischan, *Lutherans and Calvinists*, 207.

Brandenburg's second reformation began at the very highest level. In 1608 the electoral office passed to Joachim II's great-grandson, Margrave John Sigismund (b. 1572, r. 1608–19). Reared in the strictest version of Real Lutheranism, he began to have doubts during a visit in Heidelberg. The young margrave may have become a secret Calvinist at Heidelberg around 1606, but back at Berlin he played the nicodemite. His youngest brother openly converted to the new faith at Pentecost, 1609. John Sigismund did not immediately follow suit, though at Berlin the old, passive, pro-Imperial, and ultra-Lutheran policies of earlier days were coming under criticism.

By the 1590s the Catholic revival – protected by Catholic dynasties, advised by the papacy, and supported by the Jesuits – was beginning to press the politically isolated Lutheran leaders back on the defensive. Some continued to denounce popish idolatry and Calvinist heresy with equal vigor, but others were being drawn toward solidarity or even collaboration with the activist Reformed party at Heidelberg.[50] This change suggested at least the possibility of mutual tolerance and even collaboration between the two Protestant confessions. At Berlin this possibility became more attractive in view of the Hohenzollern expectancy on parts of Cleves-Jülich, whose prince had died, childless and mad, in 1609.[51]

At the same time the war of words between Reformed and Lutheran theologians was heating up. Their differences had come to focus on the Eucharist or Lord's Supper and in particular whether and how Christ was present in its elements. The differences between the Lutheran and the Reformed teaching on the Eucharist have often been regarded as minimal and the conflicts they gave rise to as based on quibbles. In the Confession of Augsburg (Article 10) of 1530, Lutheran theologians attempted to steer carefully between the Zwinglian doctrine of representation and the Catholic doctrine of the Mass as a propitiatory sacrifice. What Luther and others wrote, however, centered more on practice than on explanation. Take Luther's *Small Catechism*: "What is the Sacrament of the Altar? Answer: It is the body and blood of our Lord Jesus Christ under the bread and the wine, instituted by Christ himself for us Christians to eat and to drink."[52] The explanation comes three questions later in the answer to the question as to how salvation can be given through the physical eating and drinking of the elements: "Eating and drinking certainly do not do it, but rather the words [of Jesus] that are recorded: 'given for you' and 'shed for you for the forgiveness of sins.' These words, when accompanied by the physical eating and drinking, are the essential thing in the sacrament."[53] The Lutheran teaching, therefore, rested on the separation "between the absolute necessity of the biblical text and the adiaphora of a whole range of practices" adopted for various territorial principalities and Imperial cities.[54]

When the *Heidelberg Catechism* declared a normative Reformed teaching on the Eucharist, it aimed precisely at the distinction between the essential text and the inessentials of practice. Unlike Zwingli at Zurich, John Calvin had taught both

---

50 This is a convenient name for those German princes, politicians, professors, and pastors who favored closer relations with and even support of the Protestant leaders and forces in the Netherlands and in France.
51 See Chapter 16, 366.
52 Kolb and Wengert, eds., *The Book of Concord*, 362.
53 Kolb and Wengert, eds., *The Book of Concord*, 363.
54 Lee Palmer Wandel, *The Eucharist in the Reformation: Incarnation and Liturgy*, 116.

the uniqueness of Christ's sacrifice on the cross (vs. the Mass) and the physical, not just spiritual presence of Christ in the Eucharist. He also criticized the Lutheran teaching of consubstantiation and the ubiquity of Christ's glorified body nearly as sharply as he did the Catholic doctrine of transubstantiation and sacrifice. As if to arm themselves to conquer for the Reformed faith the ground already claimed by Luther's disciples, the men who produced the *Heidelberg Catechism* (1563) significantly escalated Calvin's critique of Lutheran teaching on the Eucharist.[55] The new teaching "separates the sign [the elements] absolutely from Christ's body – there will be no commingling of bread and body, wine and blood – and concentrates on the singularity of the sacrifice Christ made on the cross."[56] Bread and wine become "tokens" of Christ's body and blood instead of Calvin's "signs." The polemical intent of this formulation is obvious, for it removed from the elements and the rite the cloak of "inessentials" (*adiaphora*) and made correct administration of the Eucharist a mark of its validity.

Such was the doctrinal and rhetorical background to the Eucharist's central role in the eruption of the new Eucharistic quarrel – a parody of that between Luther and Zwingli – in the northern German homelands of the Lutheran faith. Unlike doctrine, which could be parsed one way or another, the ritual of the Eucharist proclaimed unambiguously what it meant.

In Brandenburg the Lutherans and the Reformed clashed head to head as in no other major Protestant territory. The conflict's temper is suggested by the very informative title of a tract (anonymously published) authored by Simon Ulrich Pistoris (1570–1615), a noble Brandenburg jurist: *Twelve Important and Well-Founded Reasons Why the Reformed Evangelical Churches Cannot Accept Dr. Luther's and his Successors' Interpretation of Christ's Words in the Lord's Supper.* Pistoris argues that the Lutheran doctrine, which he contemptuously calls "ubiquity," endangered the entire Protestant reformation by making the sacrament into a miracle and thereby restoring the Roman Mass and other blasphemies. "Luther still had derived his views from the darkness of the papacy," he declares, "and thus had inherited all the errors and false opinions of the papal doctrine of transubstantiation. . . . Unwittingly he had thus become a pillar and prop of the papacy."[57] This assault on Real Lutheran theology threatened the entire clerical establishment of Brandenburg.

A change of confession by a German prince began with a public reception of the Lord's Supper according to the rite of his new faith. Elector John Sigismund did this on Christmas Day 1613, and he declared his desire for a new and final reformation of Brandenburg's church. And this is what happened, or, rather, was planned, organized, and executed by members of the electoral court, theologians – including Abraham Scultetus, Heidelberg's chief agent for external missions – called in for this task, professors at the land's university at Frankfurt an der Oder, and native clergy who desired to make this turn. The entire operation was conceived and carried out from

55 The *Heidelberg Catechism* became the doctrinal standard for the German Reformed churches. It was also taken in 1568 by refugees returning to the Netherlands, where it was adopted by the Dutch Reformed Church at the Synod of Dort in 1618–19.
56 Wandel, *The Eucharist in the Reformation*, 206.
57 Nischan, *Prince, People, and Confession*, 84. Pistoris was the son of Simon Pistoris, who had been chancellor to Elector August of Saxony, and one of the "crypto-Calvinists" purged by August. The son was a prominent jurist in Berlin and a member of the Reformed community there.

the top down in the Heidelberg manner. The Brandenburg enterprise was far better organized, more determined, and much better staffed than its abortive counterpart in Saxony. Had the Lutheran churches been passively obedient, as they have often been described, and had history been aware of Brandenburg's Prussian destiny, which it could not have been, the enterprise should have succeeded.

The mighty struggle over Brandenburg's soul pitted the elector (and his brothers) and his advisors and court against a clergy which, despite accusations of tolerating, even advocating, popish superstitions and idolatry, enjoyed backing from many nobles and pastors and not a few ordinary subjects. In the end the Reformed advance failed to conquer Brandenburg's church, though it retained the allegiance of the elector and his court. A deal was struck. The prince and his court would practice according to the Reformed rite, while most of the rest of Brandenburg would worship as Lutherans and hold to the Formula of Concord and the Real Presence. In foreign policy, to be sure, Brandenburg continued to be drawn toward the Protestant party of action and away from Dresden's political influence, a tendency that was to have important consequences for the two states' policies during the Thirty Years War. But the church settlement in Brandenburg remained as it was made: a Calvinist/ Reformed dynasty and court in a Lutheran land.

The story of Brandenburg's second reformation confirms the importance of ritual and sacral presence to the planting of a Protestant identity among the people. "For many Lutherans the elevation, the rite of the real presence, now certainly had become a matter on which no concessions were possible."[58] The acceptance of the Real Presence – how explained, is another matter – formed the strongest link between their people and the Lutheran pastors who bravely defied Elector John Sigismund and his new advisors. In Brandenburg Lutheranism continued as it had begun, with a defense of the Real Presence.

Lutheran sacrality did not, however, simply maintain the old Catholic sacrality differently explained, as if in these lands nothing had changed between the Wilsnack Blood and the Reformed second reformation. In the realm of ritual, God was not present in the same way as before, and it did the believer no good to see, touch, or be in the presence of images and other objects. "The single and singular exception to this was the Savior's physical presence in the Lutheran Eucharist."[59] Yet even this remnant aroused the Reformed polemicists to attack the Real Presence with aggressive fury and the Lutherans to defend it with equal passion. In the eyes of one party, to surrender the Real Presence was to deny the entire Christian faith; to the other party its retention threw the door open wide to the restoration of papal superstitions and idolatry. In Brandenburg and other Lutheran lands, belief in the Real Presence, whether trans- or consubstantiated, validated the sensibility that supplied their clergy with a confidence in their own duty to defy, if necessary, the powers of this world.

Drawing this line in the sand meant that German Protestantism would live in two distinct confessions, held together, if at all, by their common hostility to Rome. In these struggles the chief issue was truth, and although some clergymen adopted moderate positions between the two extremes, for those at the poles the opposition

---

58 Nischan, *Lutherans and Calvinists*, 5.21.
59 Karant-Nunn, *The Reformation of Ritual*, 191.

was total. Abraham Scultetus described in these words the passing in 1604 of the ultra-orthodox Lutheran Cyriakus Spangenberg. "In this year Cyriakus died at Strasbourg," he wrote, "a learned theologian and historian who was nearly eighty years old. I want to remember him here, because with him the horrible doctrine of Flacius concerning the substantiality of sin died and was buried. Cyriakus would have sooner lost his post and everything he had than given up this doctrine. So far as I know, after his death no one could be found who would defend this Manichaeism."[60]

The prominence of such condemnations and harsh feelings in the clerical polemical literature tends to obscure how totally the recognition of such absolute truths depended on political success at the center. In Saxony the Reformed reformation failed because it did not gain and hold the center, the elector and his court. In Brandenburg, where it did conquer the center, it made but fitful progress among the pastors and their people. While in France, Scotland, and the Low Countries the Reformed faith established itself independently of the authorities and then mobilized an important part of the population, "Germany's second reformations depended above all on decisions taken by territorial rulers in consultations with their leading councillors and most influential theologians."[61] Typically, they aroused resistance, which increased over the years, so that by the early seventeenth century territorial churches could no longer be converted from the Lutheran to the Reformed faith. The process can be observed in miniature in the northwestern German county of Lippe, where the Lutheran burghers of Lemgo, the principal town, defended their communal liberties and their by now traditional religion against the centralizing counts.

The success or failure of conversion projects depended far less on the confessions involved, Reformed or Lutheran, than on two other contingencies. First, the more time that had passed since the initial Protestant reformations, the more difficult it became to convert whole lands. Second, Lutheran clerical corps, bound in solidarity by endogamy and a common education, were sometimes able to defend their custody of the people's religious life, even against a prince of the same faith. The Lutheran pastors of Rostock did this for years against the Lutheran dukes of Mecklenburg.

The German experience of Protestant confessional formation and conflict relativizes the widely held modern view that Reformed religion or Calvinism possessed an inherent affinity for anti-authoritarian politics, republicanism, or even revolution. Such convergences did sometimes occur, notably in the republic of Graubünden. While the Protestant clergy here initially adopted the conventional evangelical position – Christians owed the magistrates obedience and counsel – after 1572, when the republic's elites tried to exclude the clergy from politics, the pastors counterattacked. They pointed to the republic's communal structure and to its Protestant majority as reasons why the common man was in fact the true magistrate. One of them even described Graubünden as a "democracy."[62]

60 Abraham Scultetus, *Die Selbstbiographie des Heidelberger Theologen und Hofpredigers Abraham Scultetus (1566–1624)*, 46.
61 Philip Benedict, *Christ's Churches Purely Reformed: A Social History of Calvinism*, 202.
62 Randolph C. Head, "Rhaetian Ministers, from Shepherds to Citizens: Calvinism and Democracy in the Republic of the Three Leagues, 1550–1620," 55n. 2.

6. FORMING A NEW CLERGY

Having disqualified or ousted much of the old clergy, the Protestants invented a new clergy as a kind of laity. Its domestication into a lay society structured by marriage, family, and household was the laity's final triumph over the clergy. The new clergy formed, however, a special kind of group, a sector of the burgher elites characterized by a written culture, specialized training, and subsistence from salaries rather than from benefices.

The Protestant reformation had begun as a clerical revolt against clerical authority. The first generation of new clergy sprang from the old, and the notion of the average preacher as an articulate layman was an illusion nourished by skillful propaganda.[63] The early preachers of evangelical religion were mostly well-educated Catholic clergymen from the towns. Of 176 evangelical clergymen known to have been active in the Empire between about 1520 and about 1550, some 87 percent had been Catholic secular priests (42 percent), monks (32 percent), or schoolteachers (13 percent). They were also town-bred, as most (87 percent) sprang from the middling and upper burghers, and the rest from the urban poor, the peasantry, or the nobles. They were educated men. Of those whose education is known, 94 percent had attended university, more than a third at Wittenberg, that forcing house of evangelical clergy for an immense region stretching from Thuringia to Livonia.

The immense task of recruiting competent clergy proceeded much faster in the cities, of course, than in the villages, where the purging of old and the installation of new clergy took many years, even decades. Of 1,117 men ordained at Wittenberg between 1537 and 1550, 84 percent gave their former occupations as teachers, secretaries, students, or church officials. One had been a peasant. The ordination of nearly 80 new pastors annually at Wittenberg suggests how great was the need, as does the decision to remove only those pastors (about one-sixth in Ernestine Saxony) who were most obdurately Catholic or unrepentantly corrupt. The demands of other lands, from Nuremberg to Denmark, combined to overstrain Wittenberg's resources. "Truly," Luther wrote to his prince in 1541, "at present we have almost exhausted our school in order periodically to send people out, and the boys left here are not yet mature."[64] The conversion of Albertine Saxony in 1539 immediately worsened the problem, and for a time schoolteachers and even laymen had to be pressed into service.

The medieval Catholic Church had half-solved the problem of clerical reproduction by inventing the universities. The Protestant churches completed the solution by creating the legitimate clerical household. In this, as in so many things, the Protestants enhanced one late medieval tendency – clerical endogamy – but suppressed another – clerical celibacy. Once the stain of illegitimacy disappeared, and clergymen could openly choose their children's mothers, the clergy could become largely self-reproducing. In each city and principality a version of the classic Protestant "pastors' church" was formed. Clerical endogamy became well established between 1585 and 1630 in the duchy of Brunswick-Wolfenbüttel and the city of Brunswick.

63 The following figures come from Robert W. Scribner, "Preachers and People in German Towns," in Robert W. Scribner, *Popular Culture and Popular Movements in Reformation Germany*, 123–43.
64 Karant-Nunn, *Luther's Pastors*, 12, and the figures on ordinations at 9–11.

Table 4. The Formation of a Pastors' Church in the Duchy of Brunswick-Wolfenbüttel
and the City of Brunswick, 1585–1630 (percentages)

	Duchy	City
1. Pastors' Sons as Pastors	21.7	36.6
2. Pastors' Daughters as Pastors' Wives	16.4	44.1
3. Pastors' Sons and Sons-in-Law as Pastors	77.5	72.8

Source: The figures come from Luise Schorn-Schütte, *Evangelische Geistlichkeit in der Frühneuzeit, deren Anteil an der Entfaltung frühmoderner Staatlichkeit und Gesellschaft, dargestellt am Beispiel des Fürstentums Braunschweig-Wolfenbüttel, der Landgrafschaft Hessen-Kassel und der Stadt Braunschweig*, 479–88.

While the city of Brunswick led this concentration, within three generations the duchy took over the lead. In Württemberg, the best studied Lutheran land, some 63 percent of the sixteenth-century Lutheran pastors of known social origin (about 20 percent of 2,716) were pastors' sons. A similar pattern could be found in Hesse-Cassel and in the northern duchy of Oldenburg. Clergy begat clergy, as pastors encouraged their sons to take up their own calling and their daughters to marry men of the cloth. It was an efficient mode of social reproduction, since many a candidate for ordination acquired his initial skills from growing up in a pastor's home, learning the ins and outs of his future role, and feeding his interests and ambitions by browsing in his father's library.

Boys were prepared in Latin schools for the university and in the university for the pastorate. Although the early Protestant publicists mocked the old priests for ignorance and prided themselves on supplying the people with a learned clergy, the evidence speaks against them. In most dioceses and principalities, during the sixteenth century the average level of education of the clergy fell from fifteenth-century levels. In Ernestine Saxony before the Reformation, around one-half had studied at the university, over the next two decades this dropped to between a quarter and a half.[65] The decline reflected a general fall in university attendance during the evangelical movement's heyday. The aggregate number of students in German-speaking universities (excluding Basel and Vienna) fell from a high of 5,687 in 1506/10 to a low of 1,135 in 1521/25. It did not recover its former level during the course of the sixteenth century, though during the following half-century it rose to 8,000.[66]

Although it initially depressed university studies, in the longer run the Protestant reformation accelerated the rising importance of university education, and not only for clergymen. Before the Protestant reformation some sixteen universities were operating in the Holy Roman Empire, of which half were converted into Protestant institutions (excluding Prague, then in Utraquist hands). Beginning with Landgrave Philip's Marburg in 1527, nine new Protestant institutions of higher learning came into being during the next 100 years, making a total of seventeen. In the main, the new universities replicated the faculty structures of the old – theology, law, medicine, and

---

65 Comparisons must be relativized by the incompleteness of the data and by differences between relatively greater and lesser access to universities.
66 The figures come from Rainer Müller, *Geschichte der Universität. Von der mittelalterlichen Universitas zur deutschen Hochschule*, 52, 60.

arts – though legally they were purely territorial institutions, for few of the new Protestant universities acquired an Imperial charter.[67] All but two became Lutheran. The exceptions were Heidelberg, the only old university to become Reformed, and Herborn, founded for Nassau in 1584.

The Reformation profoundly altered the patterns of university study in the Empire's Protestant lands.[68] For one thing "the Reformation brought immense popularity to the universities of the German Empire, until then neglected by students of other countries."[69] This popularity attached to the Protestant universities alone, for although German-speaking Catholics attended foreign universities in great numbers, their own institutions attracted few students from other parts of Europe. Neither confession nor geography determined all choices of a university. German Protestants streamed into those Italian universities – notably Padua and Siena – whose tolerant policies catered to an ultramontane clientele, and many others into those of France, well known for their lax standards. Felix Platter (1536–1614), Thomas's son, admitted that it would have been more "honorable" for him to have studied medicine at home in Basel rather than resorting to Montpellier, for it was common knowledge that French universities claimed, "we take their money and send them off to Germany as ignorant as they came."[70]

Different patterns of study also marked the cultural characters of the two Protestant confessions. Lutheran theology remained a German subject, little influenced by foreign academic cultures, whereas Reformed theology drew German-speaking students to foreign universities, especially to Leiden (founded in 1575), the rise of which put all other Protestant universities in the shadows. The cultural divide between a highly international Reformed and a deeply German Lutheran discipline of theology marked the two confessions' relations powerfully, perhaps more powerfully, than did their explicit doctrinal differences.

How the study of theology translated into clerical careers is difficult to say, because "doubtless the least-known aspect of the university system is what happened to students after they had left the university."[71] One reason for the decline of the numbers of theological students in the wake of the Protestant reformation was an absolute fall in numbers of clergy in Protestant lands, including the German ones. Yet even in the longer run, theology and the church lost ground with respect to law and the state, although the social and cultural consequences of this shrinkage did not become apparent until after 1650.

The success of Protestant territorial and civic churches depended absolutely on the formation of a clerical corps which, secure in its status, set its hand to the plows of admonition, discipline, and comfort to shepherd the formation of a devout laity conscious of its obligations to God, the temporal rulers, and the pastors. No Protestant polity, probably, was better situated to achieve this end than was the city-state of Basel. To serve the urban parishes and the twenty-seven village churches, the

67 Exceptions include Marburg (1541), Strasbourg (1621), and Altdorf (1623, Nuremberg's university).
68 The Catholic counterpart of this movement is discussed in Chapter 14, 309.
69 Hilde de Ridder-Symoens, "Mobility," in Hilde de Ridder-Symoens, ed., *Universities in Early Modern Europe (1500–1800)*, 421.
70 De Ridder-Symoens, "Mobility," 433.
71 Willem Frijhoff, "Graduation and Careers," in de Ridder-Symoens, ed., *Universities in Early Modern Europe (1500–1800)*, 406.

magistrates founded a college specifically to train local boys for the ministry – much like a post-Tridentine Catholic seminary – and reserved a majority of the university scholarships (33 by 1624) for theology students. These steps led within a couple of generations to "the creation of an increasingly homogenous and territorialized pastoral corps."[72] Whereas in 1529 only eight of the twenty-eight rural pastors had entered the university, by 1609 half of them possessed master's degrees. Almost all of the clergy were sons of Baselers, often related by blood or marriage. "The result of such close, continual contact was the formation of a remarkably uniform and insular group of men who served the Basel church."[73]

Education in a clergyman was generally considered a good thing by the burghers, perhaps less so by the farmers. One Basel pastor was rebuked in 1601: "[You] may want to expound in detail on the significance of the Jewish priests' clothing but the illiterate won't be able to understand it; it is more necessary to preach on Christ, on rebirth, faith, and other useful things."[74] Another reported that he had preached on the Acts of the Apostles in mid-week sermons for the past five and one-half years and had reached only the book's fourteenth chapter. A second pastoral duty, catechetical work, met the difficulty that rural folk considered the catechism an unwelcome innovation. As the work went on, however, conditions improved, and by the 1580s the rural visitations reported that parishioners diligently attended Sunday sermons, and children – but not adults – came diligently to catechism classes.

Even in Basel's church, possibly the best-served in the Protestant German lands, the pastor's lot was not always a happy one. In 1605 Pastor Heinrich Strüblin described his work:

> I began twenty years ago to explain [the Decalogue] in the weekday sermons, pointed out the errors of the popes and others, and began to teach the youth the right division. And although I have had to listen to and swallow many absurdities from young and old, as if I've introduced some novelty and so forth, I didn't quit and I let such talk go in one ear and out the other and continued for as long as God has given me his grace and his Spirit. In this way I brought a few boys and girls to my side (and gradually have brought around the rest, God be praised), and since then both young and old, and even the parents, have been well-pleased and content.[75]

Many rural pastors – and by no means only Protestants – would have nodded their heads at the causes of Strüblin's underlying tone of weariness – Sunday services and mid-week sermons in a poorly filled church, children missing catechism, backsliding and backbiting, and other disappointments.

How well did these efforts succeed? Following a generation of historians' debate on this question, the provisional answer must be: less success than its admirers contend, more than its critics allow. The key points are the following. First, evangelization was never a one-way experience, in which the pastor taught and the parishioners learned or resisted learning. The creation of a more devout laity (Protestant or Catholic) required decades, even generations of discussing "the same discourse in which alternative

72 Amy Nelson Burnett, "Basel's Rural Pastors as Mediators of Confessional and Social Discipline," 73.
73 Burnett, "Basel's Rural Pastors," 73.
74 Burnett, "Basel's Rural Pastors," 76.
75 Burnett, "Basel's Rural Pastors," 78.

strategies, misunderstandings, conflicting goals and values are threshed out."[76] Second, success in these terms required a conscientious and well-trained clergy of considerable stamina and great patience, possessed of both a sufficient cultural familiarity with their flocks to get and keep their attention and a sufficient cultural distance to guard themselves from complete rustication. Third, under post-Reformation conditions in confessionally mixed regions, instruction was always both positive – in the church's teachings and practice – and negative – against the rival church's teachings and practice. It was nonetheless possible over the long run to transform Catholics into Protestants (and vice versa), though the longer the confessional era went on, the stronger became the engrained barriers to conversion. The very favorable conditions at Basel offer an illustration of the sticking power of able evangelization. In 1585 several villages that had lain under the city's protection were returned to their lawful lord, the prince-bishop of Basel (who did not, of course, reside at Basel). When the bishop attempted to reintroduce the Mass, the villagers resisted, though they did recognize him as their legitimate temporal lord. Slow, steady pressure achieved results, however, and with the replacement of the Protestant clergy and village officials with Catholic ones, "it took a generation before a strongly Catholic identity could be established in these villages."[77]

7. REFORMING THE LAITY – DISCIPLINING MARRIAGE

If education was the key to reforming the clergy, the household was the key to reforming the laity. It was the target of the new disciplinary regimes that prescribed when one should attend church and who might take the Sacrament; who might marry whom, when, and with whose permission; what were the consequences of adultery, fornication, and bearing illegitimate children; what penalties fell on those who cursed, swore, blasphemed, habitually got drunk, missed divine worship, or disrespected the pastor; and what attitude one ought to display toward the ruler and his officials.

At the heart of the immense effort to further Christianize the common people lay the family. The Christian household began with marriage – more precisely, with betrothal – the key to regulating all other behavior. In a society that had abolished celibacy, paternity – domestic, political, and divine – as Luther correctly saw, bound earth and heaven together. The household was the nursery of virtue and the cell of society, just as the Hessian pastor Erasmus Alber (ca. 1500–53) expressed in verse: "A wise and virtuous piece of advice:/Many pious burghers living without vice/Are the strongest walls of all against any disaster,/Protecting the city better than those of stone and plaster."[78]

The Church recognized marriage as a sacrament that man and woman conferred on one another and as a natural institution that involved all sorts of temporal matters, such as inheritance and other property issues. Marital litigation therefore came sometimes before civil courts and often before episcopal courts, and the Protestant withdrawal from episcopal jurisdiction created a need for a new judicial authority over the newly desacramentalized institution of marriage. The cities, as usual, blazed the way

---

76 David Warren Sabean, *Power in the Blood: Popular Culture and Village Discourse in Early Modern Germany*, 29–30.
77 Burnett, "Basel's Rural Pastors," 79.
78 Joel F. Harrington, *Reordering Marriage and Society in Reformation Germany*, 26.

into the future. Zurich early on created a purely civic marriage court; Strasbourg did the same; other cities followed.

The Protestant reformers aggravated perceptions of a crisis of marriage both by highlighting an absence of sexual control as a primary cause of clerical misconduct and by attacking the plain utility of celibacy as a way of life. Their recognition of the married state as the only acceptable condition for adult Christians became the anchor point of Protestantism's patriarchal ideology. The important thing was to regulate marriage as the founding moment of new households, the enabling act of social reproduction. This aim, not granting relief through divorce with the right to remarry, stood at the center of the new Protestant marriage law.

The social pressure for reforming marriage is readily understood. The canon law defined a valid marriage as a contract between two persons, who, being of proper age and free of specific impediments, could confer the sacrament on each other by exchanging vows and then physically consummating their union. Parents, who naturally opposed the latitude this rule gave to young love wanted parental consent to be made a condition of a valid marriage. Reformers, Protestant and Catholic alike, responded to this desire. Protestants declared marriage to be a civil matter and Catholics declared the presence of witnesses and a priest a condition for a canonically valid wedding. The Protestants brought the wedding into the household, the Catholics into the church. Each remedy responded to the perennial parental wish to control children's marriages by means of the same prophylactic: public weddings. Both Church and State understood the parental understanding that sexual discipline and social reproduction went hand in hand. There were a few, perhaps, who failed to grasp the need for a reformed discipline. Had they visited the courts, whether civil, as in Protestant Basel, or ecclesiastical, as under the bishop of Constance, they would have met many a young female plaintiff with babe in arms, or on the way, who pled for the baby's father to be forced to make good on his pledge. The preventative for such cases was publicity, the public performance of marriages before witnesses in the church with the approval of parents and others. A Saxon law of 1557 stated this motive with perfect clarity:

> And because some [people] get themselves married at home in their houses, courts [*Höfe*], even under the sky and not in the church, from which all manner of impropriety follows, from now on except when necessary the marriage and giving together or blessing of the bride and the groom shall take place nowhere other than in the church before the Christian community [*gemeine*], and with the prior knowledge of both parties' parents, guardians, or next of kin.[79]

In the villages, where enforcement fell on the pastors, changes to marriage practices came very slowly. They depended on the keeping of registers of marriages, births, and deaths, for what was not recorded could not be effectively policed, and on the householders' consent and support. The times were favorable, for the pressure of rising populations on the land was intensifying parental desires to control their children's futures, if not their hearts. More than in any other social milieu, in the village, because of its size, communal nature, and atmosphere of familiarity, courtship and marriage assumed the character of a natural sacrament, a visible sign of the social miracle that transformed unreliable young people into socially responsible householders.

79 Karant-Nunn, *The Reformation of Ritual*, 17.

How the new discipline of marriage planted itself can be followed in the small Franconian territory of Hohenlohe, where the first Lutheran visitation occurred in 1556 and new marriage courts were not put into place before 1600. Well before then the new rules were changing lives. In 1550 Lienhard Dietz's daughter was serving as a maid in the household of a prosperous miller at Künzelsau. When the miller's son secretly promised to marry her, she slept with him, assuming that they were now married – which, according to the old church's law, they were – and bore a child out of wedlock. The Lutheran pastor who took the case to the court claimed that a soldier, not the miller's son, was the baby's father. Under the old marital regime, of course, the woman would have been a respectable housewife; under the new she became a "whore."

Gradually, the new marriage regime's logic sank in, even among young folk. At a festival held at Ingelfingen in 1579, Ursula Schneider rejected Hans Streckfus' invitation to dance, saying, "I could not take any man without my mother's knowledge and consent, or I would bring a curse down on her house." But the sexual practices of rural youth were tenacious, and in the evenings after weddings and festivals, a Hohenlohe pastor observed, "young servants get together in barns and other places without regard for male or female sex."[80] Young people clung to the permissive old regime of marriage formed by mutual consent, mutual promises, and sexual intercourse, which young women alleged as a defense until well into the following century. They got no mercy from the courts, for between 1550 and 1680 the courts in Hohenlohe-Langenburg[81] terminated all contested engagements in which youths did not have their parents' explicit permission to marry, and they punished youths for engaging in premarital sex by jailing them for a week or two. Their parents mostly agreed with the farmer who told the court that every child "must seek the parent's consent beforehand, because, if one or another of his own children contract a marriage on his own, he would give them neither a *heller* nor a penny for their dowries for the rest of this life."[82] Parents and judges alike knew all the tricks. One court dismissed a marriage claim with the remark that poor girls and their fathers often tried to trap "wealthy peasants" into marriage.[83]

It was principally the villagers themselves who enforced the new order. Their concept of how sexual conduct related to success turned on the notion of honor, and persons who dishonored themselves pulled their whole families after them into shame and ill repute. This was especially true of women, on whose sexual behavior the family's integrity and future depended in an obviously special way. Disobedient, undisciplined women were frequently the targets of savage abuse and taunts by the married matrons, the chief enforcers of patriarchal values and marital discipline. An unfortunate target of their mockery was a woman of Ingelfingen who in 1629 found herself mobbed by the women of the town, "who did all kinds of bad things, shouted almost the entire day at her, and made her to suffer."[84] The women suspected that she had slept with a number of men and wanted to know how far the dishonor had spread and, incidentally, who had slipped into her bed.

80 Thomas W. Robisheaux, *Rural Society and the Search of Order in Early Modern Germany*, 107.
81 Since 1551/53 the lands had been divided between two lines, Hohenlohe-Neuenstein-(Langenburg) and Hohenlohe-Waldenburg.
82 Robisheaux, *Rural Society*, 109.
83 Robisheaux, *Rural Society*, 111–12.
84 Robisheaux, *Rural Society*, 114.

On the other hand, the discipline often clashed with local custom, especially where the latter sanctioned sexual intercourse before the public wedding. In Franconia this practice was known as "windowing" after the intended's right to slip through his betrothed's window and spend the night in her bed. Until the vows were solemnized, of course, the parents could still deny the couple permission to marry, though this was more difficult if the woman had become pregnant. Consider what happened to Margarethe Volker. Her suitor, the son of a local tenant farmer, began to make nightly visits to her room. She feared for her honor, she said, because she knew that she could never marry him. She asked him "to leave her in peace," as she later told the marriage court, "because I am poor, have no bed or anything else to offer, and even if he wanted to marry me, his parents and brothers and sisters would never consent to it." The young fellow nonetheless charmed her, declaring "that he wished the devil would take him if he slept with a girl and did not honor her with marriage," for she was "rich and beautiful enough for him, and she, not his parents, would have to live with [him]."[85] Eventually, she consented, or half-consented, or perhaps he raped her, but the court refused her desperate plea to approve the marriage. Margarethe and her family were disgraced.

Disciplining began with marriage-brokering and the betrothal agreement. The farmers placed very great weight on the promise to marry, on the exact words used, and on the subsequent agreement about money and land. As one farmer in Hohenlohe said, "I asked whether he [the groom] could match the dowry and he replied, yes, he would gladly do so . . . and we gave each other our hands on the marriage."[86] Once an agreement was reached, the male relations met in the village tavern, where they cemented the family alliance with one or more ritual drinks. From this point on, the marriage was considered licit, and though the pastor had to read the bans from the pulpit on three successive Sundays, the bond could now be broken only by the marriage court. In practice, village custom mixed freely with Lutheran solemnity, gaiety with stern piety, and the pastors and magistrates rarely approved of but could hardly suppress the three-day festivals with which well-off Franconian peasants celebrated weddings. A wedding began on Saturday with the families' exchange of gifts; it continued on Sunday with "morning soup," the wedding ceremony in church (for those sober enough to attend), and serious feasting and dancing over the next eight hours or so; and it ended on Monday with pranks and mockery by the unmarried young folk. "All kinds of deviltry and frivolity are practiced by young people on the wedding guests," one pastor complained, "in which the wedding day and holy matrimony are not honored, but scorned and desecrated."[87] Not even Catholics at carnival time were worse. "When two single youths marry," Hohenlohers said, "they put property and blood together."[88] And, they might have added, all enjoyed a good time.

The state, more interested in property than in blood, collaborated with the church to guard the household unit and its reproducibility from such evils as hasty marriage, sexual infidelity, promiscuity, marital strife, and rebellion. Its interest was especially intense in regions of impartible inheritance, such as Franconia, where the indivisible farms remained large enough to pass from generation to generation and prosperous

85 Robisheaux, *Rural Society*, 115.
86 Robisheaux, *Rural Society*, 117.
87 Robisheaux, *Rural Society*, 118–19.
88 Robisheaux, *Rural Society*, 121.

enough to bear a share of the state's fiscal burdens. The state promoted this order by inscribing the customary inheritance regime into territorial law. The jurists who worked for the counts of Hohenlohe saw in impartibility the key to preserving order and prosperity in the countryside, for, as Chancellor Johann Christoph Assum (1561–1651) of Hohenlohe-Langenburg wrote in 1634, "no peasant is allowed to divide his farm among his children, to sell to two of them a half part without the permission of the state or the lord."[89] If partition were freely allowed, he thought, within twenty years the farms would become so parcelized that no family could support itself. The state must therefore protect impartibility against the land hunger of growing populations.

These Franconian stories illustrate a collaboration of rural householders, church, and state that was replicated, with variations, in other Protestant German states. The parents chiefly aimed to protect the household's honor and to secure the orderly and intact transmission of the family substance from one generation to the next. The church sought to enforce a (reformed) Christian understanding of marriage that would help partners toward security and happiness in this world. And the state hoped to protect the prosperity of and orderly succession to farms of sufficient size and prosperity to bear regular taxation.

The reformation of marriage in the German lands thus wove together the stories of rural social development, religious reform, and state-building. While the church possessed an agent, the pastor, in most villages, neither he nor lay officials could accomplish much without the collaboration of the principal householders, those couples who were fortunate enough to be "housed," that is, inheriting (in contrast to their sometimes "unhoused" siblings). This combination of disciplinarians was crucial to rural success everywhere, not just in Franconia and not just in Protestant lands. In the Catholic Waldviertel of Upper Austria, too, the consolidation of rural order during the sixteenth and the early seventeenth century rested on an alliance of archducal regime and the housed peasants against the unhoused, who were often the non-inheriting siblings of the heirs.

8. PROTESTANT EVANGELIZATION

Over the longer run, Protestant religion succeeded in the German lands by embedding its message in the self-reproducing cultures of ordinary people. Confessionalization, which created the apparatus for this process, required decades, generations even, of dedicated labor, often with disappointing results by a mostly dedicated corps of university-educated pastors. The swiftest progress came in the cities, small country towns, and nearby villages, the slowest in the deep countryside.

Tradition and custom formed formidable barriers to the new order. Their tenacity and the new clergy's way of dealing with them can be examined in the story of the holy springs of Hornhausen. This village lay in the *Hochstift* of Halberstadt, a little over 53 miles northwest of Martin Luther's birthplace at Eisleben. On St. Frederick's Day (5 March), 1646, one hundred years and two weeks after Luther's death, the first of twenty-five springs appeared in the middle of the village. Pastor Friedrich Salchmann (d. 1648) reports that some schoolboys discovered a "spring of grace . . . in the form of a round sinkhole about three ells (about 11 feet) in diameter, right in the

89 Robisheaux, *Rural Society*, 144.

middle of the village," where "no spring had been suspected."[90] Immediately the springs were found to have healing properties, and in the following weeks, as more and more springs appeared, news of their power spread like wildfire through the heartlands of Protestant Germany. On 1 August an anonymous informant recounted his conversation with a party returning home to Dresden with their health restored: "And they brought with them some bottles of water from the wondrous springs of healing and health, of which I drank some, and they reported that at the springs were gathered some 12,000 persons, among them General Torstenson and the king of Poland."[91] Pilgrims, great and small, flocked to Hornhausen, whose healing waters performed miraculous cures. Even Queen Christina of Sweden (1626–89, r. 1632–54), Gustavus Adolphus's daughter and heir, came to Hornhausen.[92]

Lots and lots of humble folk, too, came on pilgrimage to the holy springs. Christoph Müller of Dresden, who had come by boat and had to be carried ashore to the springs, "drank the water for only two days and then stood upright on his legs;" a tailor from Neustädtel, blind for eight years, could see well with his eyes after drinking from the first spring for three days.[93] And so it went, miracle after miracle effected by the holy springs' water, the fame of which spread by word of mouth and a small flood of handy printed pamphlets. The crowds are described as constantly praising God for this gift of restored health and relief from longstanding disabilities and conditions. Pastor Salchmann, something of an amateur scientist, catalogs around 170 different ailments cured by the springs' water and names 122 different places from which pilgrims came to Hornhausen. Most of the places lie in Thuringia, Saxony, or Brandenburg, which rules out the possibility that the pilgrims were mostly recusant Catholics still under the spell of popish superstition.

The scenes at Hornhausen described by observers remind one of the crowds that gathered to hear the Drummer of Niklashausen in 1476, those who flocked to the shrine of the Virgin at Altötting in Bavaria around this same time, those who came to revere the Holy Blood at Wilsnack, or those who come on pilgrimage to Lourdes or Knock today. Clearly, the phenomenon had to be explained. Pastor Salchmann, while he finds precedents in the ancient authors, places his main emphasis on God's providential care for and gift to fallen humanity. "As a compensation for the Tree of Life, God established other means of healing for the sustenance and restoration of physical health" by giving "plants, herbs, . . . and other created things a healing and healthful power by means of which – if only humans do not sin against the Tree of Discovery, that is, the law and command through which alone God proclaims His will – the lost human powers may to some degree be replaced and restored."[94] In all the cures he

90 Friedrich Salchmann, *Historischer Bericht von den Hornhausischen Befund-Brunnen / Wann dieselbe entstanden worden / Vnd was der Wunderthätige GOtt biß anhero Denckwürdiges durch dieselbe gewürckt hat. Zur Ausbreitung der Ehren Gottes / mit sonderm Fleiß beschrieben*, 4. Hornhausen lies today in the state of Sachsen-Anhalt.

91 *Deutlicher Bericht / Aus Etlichen andern Schreiben und Mündlichen Bericht / Von Heil-Brunnen zu Hornhausen / Die grossen Wunder und Wercke des HERRN zusammen getragen und in Druck befördert.*, (1646), 2. The Swedish fieldmarshal-general Lennart Torstensson (1603–51) was forced to resign his command in 1646 because of gout, the presumable cause of his pilgrimage to Hornhausen. I cannot explain the presence of "the king of Poland."

92 Gustavus Adolphus's only suviving, legitimate child, she converted to Catholicism, abdicated, and in 1654 settled in Rome.

93 *Deutlicher Bericht*, 3–4.

94 Salchmann, *Historischer Bericht*, 3.

sees God's own work through natural means and describes how he led the gathered pilgrims in prayer. His "history of cures" recounts many instances of miraculous healing.

Others saw the miraculous springs in a more problematical light, and, indeed, had the clergymen belonged to the Reformed rather than the Lutheran faith, one can imagine them denouncing the whole phenomenon as gross idolatry. The other possibility was to accept the cures as inexplicable miracles but to spiritualize their meaning. Pastor Balthasar Balduin (1605–52) came to Hornhausen with a party from his congregation in Zwickau. On Pentecost Sunday he preached outdoors before "many thousands of eyes," taking his texts from the story of Jesus's conversion of Zaccheus the tax-collector (Luke 19) and His healing of the man born blind at the pool of Siloam (John 9). Balduin launches his sermon with an attack on the Catholic use of holy water and the "fantasy" of its power to take away sins. On the contrary, he says,

> The springs of Christ's eyes give us blessed water, which is the true holy water, so that our sins may be cleansed by washing away. All other water which flows from human hearts and comes from their eyes cannot expunge or oppose the slightest misdeed, and even if a sinner could cry tears of blood, . . . not the slightest spark of hellfire could be washed away. . . . Come, you poor, sad, and troubled Christian hearts, take living consolation from this spring of Christ's tears.[95]

If Pastor Balduin's effort to Christianize the holy springs of Hornhausen seems contrived, it is worth remembering that the Protestant clergy, Lutheran and Reformed, faced a problem more profound than the quarrels over doctrine and liturgy between the confessions. To Protestant pastors, the possibility of their flocks accepting a realistic view of the infusion of material nature by divine grace represented a lapse into "popery."

In the countryside the Protestant clergy faced conditions similar to those that had made the old religion, at least in their eyes, "materialistic," "superstitious," and "idolatrous." The Catholic priests had offered a well-understood power of blessing and healing that meshed with the peasants' own understanding of the apotropaic (protective) powers of sacraments, rituals, saints, and their own magical practices. In the main, rural religion linked the visible community of work, life, and death to the spiritual world that could both promote and guard the vital communal solidarity of the village and protect its members against evils both natural and supernatural. It helped the peasants to confront Nature, at once their source of livelihood and the greatest source of threat. The coming of Protestant religion seemed to some peasant communities a deprivation of protection and a hostile threat to their traditions. In mid-November 1528, a confrontation took place between some upland rural subjects of the city of Bern and the Bernese magistrates who had mandated religious reforms. When the magistrates sent evangelical (Protestant) preachers to their districts, the uplanders ejected them, reinstalled their own priests, restored the Mass, refused tithes, and declared their will "not to be driven from the old faith and their liberties."[96]

---

95 Balthasar Balduin, *Threnen-Brunnen Christi und seiner Gläubigen Beym Gnaden- Heil- und Wunderbrunnen zu Hornhausen im Stifft Halberstatt gelegen/ mildiglich vergossen/ Als am 10. Sontag nach dem Fest der heiligen Dreyeinigkeit/ aus ... Luc. 19. die Threnen unsers Heylandes ... geflossen ... in einer Thränen- Trost- und Trawer-Predigt zusammen gefasset*, C2b–C3a.

96 Rudolf Dellsperger, "Zehn Jahre bernischer Reformationsgeschichte (1522–1532). Eine Einführung," 47.

Mediation having failed, the Bernese magistrates commanded the peasants to "uproot the Mass, burn and destroy the images, break up and destroy the altars, and drive out the priests immediately, [or they would] do it with might and main and acts of force."[97]

From a village perspective, Protestant and Catholic reformers were engaged in the same enterprise – the transformation of traditional belief and practice to conform with new interpretations – though with somewhat different expectations.[98] Both aimed at improving their flocks' moral discipline, but while the Protestants were bent on repressing idolatry – they meant much of traditional Catholic religious life – the Catholics placed the intensification of this same "idolatry" – sacraments, images, shrines, and processions – at the center of their program. It was in principle a battle between individualized/spiritualized grace and socialized/sensualized grace.

As Luther had begun to recognize during the Saxon visitation of 1528, he and his colleagues had embarked on a labor that would last for generations. Luther's own personal experience was no helpful model of change, because for most people change came not as the blinding light had come to Saul of Tarsus on the road to Damascus but as a slow testing of the clergy's assertions by individual and collective experience. In the more remote corners of the land, this might take a very long time. The poor village of Ödenwaldstetten in the limestone uplands of the Swabian Jura lay under the lordship of the Catholic abbot of Zwiefalten, whose temporal guardian was the Lutheran duke of Württemberg. When the parish priest died in 1558, and Abbot Nikolaus Buchner of Zwiefalten asked the duke for permission to install another "Mass priest," Duke Christoph decided that the time had come to bring the Gospel to that village. Two candidates, after inspecting the post, refused the pastoral call because "they could not detect that the mayor, officers, and jurors have any special love for the holy Gospel. Also, they found a very small, cramped, crumbling . . . manse, in which no clergyman could possibly live with wife and children. And in the little church they found all sorts of papist trash, which the people continue to honor."[99] The villagers, needing a clergyman, sought the aid of the Lutheran superintendent, Dr. Johann Otmar Mayländer (Epple) of Urach, who deprecated their wish to remain Catholic and provided them, at best, with occasional services by the pastor of another village. When Mayländer visited the village at Pentecost 1559, he was astounded to see the villagers in solemn procession, led by a volunteer Catholic priest from a nearby village, who, when addressed in Latin, did not or could not reply. The superintendent admonished the villagers to leave off their papistical ways and to remove wax ex-voto gifts from the church, in which Lutheran preaching had been going on for over a year. What tipped the village toward the new faith was the abbot's failure to pay for reconstruction of the manse. Yet the new Lutheran pastor at Ödenwaldstetten

---

97 Dellsperger, "Zehn Jahre," 45.
98 On this, at least, the modern scholarship is largely of one mind. The idea that Protestant and Catholic reformers engaged in a common civilizing process, sometimes called "acculturation," lies, since around 1970, at the heart of the discussion. See Craig Harline, "Official Religion–Popular Religion in Recent Historiography of the Catholic Reformation," 239–62. The German version, called "confessionalization," places more emphasis on institutions and behavior than on culture, but its basic concept is the same.
99 Eberhard Fritz, *Dieweil sie so arme Leuth: Fünf Albdörfer zwischen Religion und Politik 1530–1750. Studien zur Kirchengeschichte der Dörfer Bernloch, Eglingen, Meidelstetten, Oberstetten und Öden-waldstetten*, 40.

experienced a strange parody of what rural priests had gone through a generation before. He found that some of his flock continued to hear Mass and take the sacraments in nearby Catholic villages. Only around 1610 were local voices for a Catholic priest stilled, and far into modern times, it was told, Ödenwaldstetters nodded to the spot on the church's outside wall, where the image of the Virgin had once stood. Not until 1750, when Ödenwaldstetten passed from the rule of Zwiefalten to that of Württemberg, was a typical fusion of official and local religion achieved. In the countryside, the Protestant reformation was not a historical moment but a generations-long process.

9. THE HARVEST OF THE PROTESTANT REFORMATIONS

The term "confession" as used in this account engages an interpretation, called the "confessionalization thesis," which came to the fore thirty years ago. It regards the confession as a large, translocal, and supra-territorial religious community, which is marked by distinctive doctrines, liturgical practices, and relatively hard boundaries to other confessions, and enjoys an especially intimate relation with the rulers. The experience of confessional formation encompassed "the rise of early modern confessional churches as institutions, also the 'formation of confessions' in the sense of a prominence accorded to religious-cultural systems that can be clearly distinguished from one another by their doctrine, ceremonies, spirituality, and . . . the everyday culture of their people."[100] In this vision, the three German confessions – Reformed, Lutheran, and Catholic – resemble three trains headed on parallel tracks for the same destination of modernity but on offset schedules.

The German Protestant reformations cannot be understood solely from their part in forming the old confessional order. What did they do? The core of their work had a fundamentally different form from that of the Catholic renewal, which set in during the sixteenth century's waning decades. It undertook the building of new local churches that were coterminous with the new territorial principalities and Imperial cities, not with the old ecclesiastical provinces and dioceses. Around this central work the two Protestant communions constructed transpolitical shells, confessions, marked by conformity in doctrine and, to a lesser degree, in ritual practice. Underpinning these constructions, two social adaptations created a favorable basis for this peculiarly Protestant arrangement between local churches and confessions. In this milieu the new clergy, in its form as a semi-caste of skilled laymen so markedly different from its Catholic counterparts, led the adaptation of Christian society to the most powerful social institution of the age, the nuclear household. These impressive achievements, which Lutheran and Reformed shared even as they locked in combat, had no real counterparts in the church of the Catholic counterreformation. The two formed, indeed, the Empire's only true confessions.

This work of the Protestant confessions may seem humble when compared with Protestantism's roles in other interpretations, such as the restoration of Biblical

100   Heinz Schilling, "Die Konfessionalisierung von Kirche, Staat und Gesellschaft – Profil, Leistung, Defizite und Perspektiven eines geschichtswissenschaftlichen Paradigmas," in Wolfgang Reinhard and Heinz Schilling, eds., *Die katholische Konfessionalisierung. Akten eines von Corpus Catholicorum und Verein für Reformationsgeschichte veranstalteten Symposions, Augsburg 1993*, 4.

Christianity, the movement toward modern nation-states, and the liberation of the human spirit and thought from obsolete traditions and superstitions. These tend to obscure the tremendous inventiveness and courage it required to build new churches on ground from which the old ones had been razed. This long labor can be appreciated, however, once the blinders of anachronism have been laid aside.

14

Reforming the Catholic Church

Did, therefore, the faith or the Church perish? [Although] on account of
our sins – faith, obedience, and finally the holy sacrifice have been taken away
from many cities and territories, they nevertheless remain healthy and unimpaired
with others.

Theodor Loher, O. Cart. (1534)

If the German Protestant reformers' charges were to be taken at face value, it was highly improbable that the Catholic Church should ever recover, impossible that it should begin to do so within a generation of Luther's death. Yet, just in the 1570s, as Lazarus von Schwendi was ringing the old church's death knell, new life was stirring. By 1600 the Catholic revival was fully underway in the German lands; by 1620 the Protestants lay on the defensive in many places; and by 1630 the Protestant cause seemed defeated by the triumphs of Catholic arms, the emperor's will to restore his church, and the vigor of Catholic evangelization. Divine providence is inscrutable, however, the reason of history cunning, and soon Protestant reformation and Catholic reformation lay locked in a stalemate which would endure for 150 years.

In the Holy Roman Empire the Protestant reformation was a German event, the Catholic reformation was an international event. The term "Catholic reformation" most often refers to the activities of Catholic groups for religious renewal in Italy and Spain during the fifteenth and early sixteenth centuries, later in other countries. A second term, "Catholic counterreformation," is applied to Catholic defensive measures and efforts to recapture lands lost to the Protestants.[1] The recovery of Catholicism, like the advance of Protestantism, required both serious complementary programs of self-reform and aggressive action against the opponent. The Catholic revival drew aid from lands of intact Catholicism, chiefly Italy and the southern Netherlands, in the forms of personnel, education, books, new forms of piety and devotion, money, and, most precious of all, a confidence in the Church's ability to heal itself. The movement started slowly but, buoyed by external aid, it built up speed with remarkable vigor, especially considering how desperate the old faith's situation had only recently been in the German lands.

---

1 This book retains both terms. A third term, "early modern Catholicism," has been suggested to replace them both. While vague in content, it is flexible enough to include the Catholic expansion outside Europe.

I. THE ORDEAL OF THE IMPERIAL CHURCH

At the beginning, despite Emperor Charles V's proud retort to Luther at Worms in 1521, the Imperial church's leadership stood in shambles. On 12 March Duke Ernest of Bavaria described the wild scene. "Things are very bad among the princes," he wrote,

> some are strongly on his [Luther's] side, some not. Yet all agree that we should tell the Holy See not to oppress our province [*nostram provinciam*]. Many, even most, of the lay princes submit their grievances not only against the Holy See at Rome but also against their own bishops [*ordinarios*]. There is also report that the bishops will also submit grievances against the lay princes, though I don't know if this will happen. I am afraid that nothing good will come of this. How it continues, stands in God's hand.[2]

During the following quarter-century many Catholics despaired of the Church's future. Some thought, of course, that advances outside Europe compensated for the losses in the Empire. Theodor Loher (d. 1554), subprior of St. Barbara's Carthusian monastery at Cologne, took comfort from the fact that the German schism could no more destroy the faith or the Church than the Greek schism or the Muslim conquests had done. As God had been "able to arouse other sons of Abraham even in the most distant nations," under His guidance a similar advance is "just now happening in America, Cuba, New Spain, and in other regions, populations, and languages of Great Asia through the Spaniards. And what is happening in Ethiopia, Arabia, Persia, India, and on the surrounding southern isles through the Portuguese?"[3]

Many German Catholics took the opposite view. In 1538 the see of Hildesheim came into the hands of the Thuringian Valentin von Tetleben (1488/89–1551), an experienced Roman string-puller whom the shock of reformation had converted into a sober reformer. After five years at Hildesheim, a see already robbed of most of its *Hochstift* and now practically under siege by neighboring Protestant princes, Tetleben wrote to Rome, "I and my church are slain."[4] He hardly exaggerated. His successor at Hildesheim was Duke Frederick of Schleswig-Holstein (1529–56), the king of Denmark's son and a Protestant who gained the see with the emperor's approval. Neither priest nor bishop, the sybaritic duke never entered his cathedral, "ate and drank like a common man," and died in 1556 of venereal disease.[5] By mid-century, the canniest observers at Rome knew that the Imperial church's very survival lay in the balance. Giovanni Cardinal Morone reported from the Diet of Augsburg in 1555 that Rome could only allow "the thing" – the Imperial church – to collapse and hope for a better future.[6] By 1566 even Rome was losing hope, and Pope Pius V (r. 1566–72) was heard to say that "most [of the bishops] are concerned only for protecting their temporal interests."[7]

---

2 Georg Pfeilschifter, ed., *Acta reformationis catholicae Germaniae concernantia saeculi XVI. Die Reformverhandlungen des deutschen Episkopats von 1520 bis 1570*, vol. 1: 420–1. Duke Ernest was at this time administrator of the prince-bishopric of Passau.
3 Sigrun Haude, *In the Shadow of "Savage Wolves": Anabaptist Münster and the German Reformation during the 1530s*, 67–8.
4 Georg May, *Die deutschen Bischöfe angesichts der Glaubensspaltung des 16. Jahrhunderts*, 292–3.
5 May, *Die deutschen Bischöfe*, 295.
6 Heinrich Lutz, *Christianitas afflicta: Europa, das Reich und die päpstliche Politik im Niedergang der Hegemonie Kaiser Karls V. (1552–1556)*, 361.
7 Eike Wolgast, *Hochstift und Reformation. Studien zur Geschichte der Reichskirche zwischen 1517 und 1648*, 316.

Absent fundamental reforms, wrote the Dutch Jesuit Peter Canisius (Kanys, 1521–97) a decade later, "it will be impossible both to keep the Catholics from apostasy and to win back the heretics."[8] Reform as the precondition of recovery became the cantus firmus of the Catholic reformation.

At the darkest moment broke a great storm over the German north. In 1563 its duke took Brunswick-Wolfenbüttel, the last surviving Catholic dynastic principality in the region, over to Lutheranism. With that the episcopal dominos began to fall. In elections held in 1566–67 the Catholics lost four sees to more or less openly Protestant candidates. Added to the earlier secularization of seven territorial (non-princely) sees, the new losses nearly wiped out the Church in the Empire's north-central and north-eastern reaches. Pockets of Catholics held out, of course, particularly in and around the cathedral chapters and some abbeys, long the pillars of Catholic rural life. Yet the Benedictines and Cistercians lost very many houses during the first thirty years of the Protestant reformation, the female branches more than their male counterparts (62 percent vs. 43). With the monks and nuns went innumerable shrines, not to mention rural pastoral work supplied via monastic incorporations of benefices.

To stem this Protestant tide the Catholic forces needed four things: first, a program of Catholic reform; second, the protective power of Bavaria and later Austria;[9] third, a renovation of the prince-bishoprics remaining in Catholic hands; and, fourth, support from the intact Catholicism of other lands, chiefly Italy.

The first step, framing a program, began to occupy Catholic leaders almost immediately after the Diet rose at Worms in 1521. As a first reaction, in 1522 Duke George of Saxony simply ordered his officials to arrest all monks and ex-priests who were teaching "the unChristian doctrines of Martin Luther or his disciples" or "giving the Holy Sacrament in both kinds, . . . so that we may punish them as they deserve."[10] Yet calmer heads knew that coercion without reform would not restore the situation. In 1523 Duke William IV of Bavaria placed reform of the Catholic clergy at the center of the problem: "The common people in our principality openly let it be known they wish to kill all the priests, and they give the following reason, among others: that in these days the priests behave so unpriestlike, irregularly, and ignorantly, that it would be impossible and against the Christian faith to tolerate them any longer."[11] Simply suppressing the heretics would not do, and reform had to begin with undisciplined priests. This idea gained programmatic form in early July 1524 at Regensburg, where the papal legate met with representatives of Archduke Ferdinand, the dukes of Bavaria, and eleven southern prince-bishops.[12] They agreed that "the damnable heresy" was caused "partly by the irregular clerical way of life, and partly by a growing unwillingness to tolerate the clergy's abuses of the holy laws and the rules for the clergy."[13] From this program – defending the faith through reform of the clergy – subsequent ideas did not much depart. By 1528 even Archduke (now king) Ferdinand, a stranger to these lands, acknowledged that "the new, unChristian sects, especially

8 Albrecht Pius Luttenberger, ed., *Katholische Reform und Konfessionalisierung*, 313.
9 Neither of the two Catholic dynasties in the Empire's francophone lands, Lorraine and Savoy, played any role in the German lands.
10 Luttenberger, ed., *Katholische Reform*, 179.
11 Pfeilschifter, ed., *Acta reformationis catholicae*, vol. 1:7.
12 Salzburg, Trent, Regensburg, Speyer, Strasbourg, Augsburg, Constance, Basel, Freising, Passau, and Brixen/Bressanone.
13 Luttenberger, ed., *Katholische Reform*, 217.

Anabaptism," were spreading in his lands because "there is lacking good instruction of the poor common folk."[14]

Good ideas did not staunch the old faith's wounds. Catholic hopes reached a low point in 1530 with the failure of Charles V's policy of conciliation; they were little raised by the emperor's military victory in 1547; and they fell to a new low with his defeat in 1552. How long could they sink? Until the program of Catholic reform gained political protection from the German Catholic dynasties. Only Bavaria and Austria could supply protection comparable to that which Saxony and Hesse had afforded the young Protestant movement.

2. BAVARIA — WELLSPRING OF CATHOLIC RESURGENCE

Bavaria, Rome's most loyal German daughter, produced the earliest and most important model of Catholic reformation for the German lands. It evolved from a struggle between the Bavarian nobles, early adopters of the new faith, and their duke, earliest and most strenuous defender of the old. The real work of reconstruction began under Duke Albert V (b. 1528, r. 1550–79). When he enrolled at Ingoldstadt, a university under strong Jesuit influence, someone glossed his registration entry: "Bavaria's only hope, who because of wisdom and his unshakable desire to protect the Catholic Church in his own lands and in other lands of the Empire, was called Albert the Wise and Strong-willed."[15] At first, to be sure, he supported the Habsburg policy of conciliation pursued by his father-in-law, Emperor Ferdinand I, but at Augsburg in 1566 he changed course and emerged as the head of the strongly Catholic party in the Imperial Diet. Albert's instruction of 1568 for his son, Duke William V (b. 1548, r. 1579–93), formulates the Catholic forward policy: "Principally, however, when dealing with religion, my dear son should take care to act with zeal and seriousness, and that nothing should be treated with deliberate forbearance. Experience shows that in the past forbearance has caused much apostasy in matters of faith."[16]

For the next one hundred years, Munich pursued the policy it had invented, the Bavarian way of counterreformation: centralization of religious and state affairs against the territorial nobility's resistance, repression of heresy and nonconformity, concessions and privileges from Rome, vigorous activity by the religious orders (first and foremost the Jesuits), a demonstrative style of dynastic piety, and a new pedagogy of religious discipline. Duke Albert V expelled the Lutheran nobles from the Bavarian diet and required his officials to swear to the Tridentine profession of faith,[17] and he called the Jesuits to his university at Ingolstadt. At Munich he had built for them the church of St. Michael, the first church in the German lands built in the new Italian style (modeled on Il Gesu in Rome) and the supreme symbol of the dynasty's loyalty to the old faith in a new dress.

14 Luttenberger, ed., *Katholische Reform*, 198.
15 Georg Wolff, ed., *Die Matrikel der Ludwig-Maximilians-Universität Ingolstadt-Landshut-München, part I: Ingolstadt*, 542.
16 Heinrich Lutz and Walter Ziegler, "Das konfessionelle Zeitalter, Part 1: Die Herzöge Wilhelm IV. und Albrecht V.," 387.
17 This was the *professio fidei tridentini*, called the "Creed of Pope Pius IV," one of the four official creeds of the Roman Catholic Church.

The implementation of a reform policy for Bavaria lay chiefly in the hands of laymen, because all the bishops' seats lay outside Bavarian territory.[18] This did not deter the duke from creating in 1556 a Council for Spiritual Affairs, whose members supervised appointments to ecclesiastical offices, managed visitations, audited church finances, oversaw the university, schools, and libraries, and censored the printing and sale of books. Still, if the Catholic duke were to govern the church on a territorial basis, as his Protestant colleague of Saxony did, his reach had to include the dioceses in which his lands lay. He began with Freising, Munich's diocese, to which succeeded in 1566 Duke Ernest of Bavaria (b. 1554, r. 1566–1612) at the age of twelve. When Ernest gained the see of Cologne (r. 1583–1612), Freising became in effect a Bavarian territorial bishopric, the affairs of which were administered through the Spiritual Council at Munich. The council introduced the typical Tridentine reforms: episcopal visitations of the collegiate churches, monasteries, and parishes, promotion of the Jesuits, and the founding of an episcopal seminary. Freising became in effect a Bavarian territorial bishopric. Similar programs were introduced, though later and more slowly, against Protestant resistance in Eichstätt and Regensburg. In the huge diocese of Passau, which stretched down the Danube almost to Vienna's gates, little could be done so long as the Habsburg policy of Imperial Catholicism held sway.

The counterreformation also made Bavaria a principality of Imperial rank. The great coup came at Cologne, where in 1583–85 the incumbent archbishop, who aimed to turn Protestant and keep his lands, was driven out. Duke William then maneuvered his brother, Ernest of Freising, into the see. Cologne became the base for stabilizing the Catholic position in the Imperial northwest, and Bavarian Wittelsbach princes occupied the see for the next 180 years.

To consolidate Bavaria as the fountainhead of Catholic reformation in the German lands was the life's work of William V's eldest son, Maximilian I (b. 1573, duke 1597–1651, since 1623 Imperial elector). By some margin the most gifted Imperial prince of his generation, Maximilian was the very model of a counterreformation ruler. His father left him a land impressive by its antiquity and compactness, in which the mainly Protestant nobles had already been beaten. By now the duke possessed a regime over the church stricter and more efficient than any Protestant prince, Lutheran or Calvinist, ever achieved. Furthermore, his predecessors had outdone the Protestant dynasties – Saxony, Brandenburg, Brunswick, and Denmark – in promoting kinsmen into prince-bishoprics right across the old Imperial heartlands from Regensburg to Cologne.

Maximilian promoted the idea of his Bavaria as a holy land, a spiritual matriarchy under its patroness, the Virgin Mary, to the sanctity of which everyone, especially women, was meant to contribute. From this patronage Bavaria drew "an idiom of meaning, behavioral prescriptions, and moral orientations through which rulers as well as ruled acquired and experienced their respective subjectivities."[19] This was a startlingly singular enterprise among a German (and a European) aristocracy obsessed with masculine images of belligerence and sexual prowess.

There was nothing of belligerent raison d'etat in the "paternal admonition" Maximilian composed in 1639 for his three-year-old son and heir, Ferdinand Maria (b. 1636, r. 1651–79). Fully aware that he would not live to see his child come to majority

---

18 Salzburg, Freising, Passau, Regensburg, Bamberg, Eichstätt, Augsburg, and Chiemsee (see Map 4).
19 Ulrike Strasser, *State of Virginity: Gender, Religion, and Politics in an Early Modern Catholic State*, 174.

(Maximilian was then sixty-five years old), he drew up a kind of political testament organized under the headings of three classes of duties: to God, to himself, and to his subjects. God, the instruction begins, is the sole Lord and Ruler over all things. "Piety," Maximilian writes, "consists in having a pure sense for and understanding of things divine, that is, in the fear, love, and service of God. Piety confirms the kingdom."[20] Therefore, "you will do right and well, if you never abandon either the Catholic, Roman Church or our ancient, traditional faith."[21] To himself, the elector continues, the prince must apply the correct measure for his spirit, his soul, and his body. He must practice thrift, avoid anger, avoid the inclinations of the flesh, and "flee above all drunkenness, the fount of all vices."[22] Finally, the prince must "sustain his subjects with goodness rather than ruin them with severity," for "excessive punishment should be as obnoxious to a prince as a corpse is to a physician. The true art and genuine praiseworthiness of a ruler consists in sustaining one's subjects with goodness rather than harming them with strictness."[23] Maximilian's list of advices to his little son is a specifically Catholic instruction. Unlike the Lutheran patriarchal ideal – God the Father, the prince as father (of the land), and the father of the household – Maximilian's is a matriarchy, in which a female, the Virgin Mary, reigns over and directly sustains the people through the male prince. The Marian cult became an important matter of state: "In the guise of identity, morality, and culture, religion apparently shaped the sociopolitical and sexual order as well as gender relations in Bavaria long after . . . the Thirty Years' War."[24]

3. COUNTERREFORMATION AND CATHOLIC REFORMATION IN INNER AUSTRIA

In the sprawling, weakly governed Austrian lands, the new faith could not be so easily hindered, much less countered, as in compact, relatively centralized Bavaria. When the golden age of Bavarian Protestantism began to dim in the 1560s, the star of its Austrian counterpart was on the rise. The Austrian lands divided into two zones, a strongly Catholic west – Tyrol and Vorarlberg – and the five duchies of the east, in each of which the provincial nobility took like ducks to water to the Protestant faith in its Lutheran version. In land after land, they consolidated their power in the territorial diet, bargained edicts of toleration from their Habsburg princes, and deployed their religious liberties to advance and protect their faith in castle or town. According to the Peace of 1555, of course, the archdukes possessed the same right of reformation enjoyed by the Lutheran elector of Saxony and the Catholic duke of Bavaria. Yet the politics of conciliation continued into the 1590s and allowed the Protestant power to become quite strong.

Emperor Ferdinand I had partitioned the Austrian lands among his three sons, of whom the eldest, Maximilian II, partitioned them again between his two sons, Rudolph and Matthias. It was not at Vienna but at Graz, one of the two Habsburg satellite courts, that the Austrian counterreformation began. Its model came fresh from Bavaria.

20 Heinz Duchhardt, ed., *Politische Testamente und andere Quellen zum Fürstenethos der frühen Neuzeit*, 120.
21 Duchhardt, ed., *Politische Testamente*, 120.
22 Duchhardt, ed., *Politische Testamente*, 121.
23 Duchhardt, ed., *Politische Testamente*, 125.
24 Strasser, *State of Virginity*, 178.

The process began in the clustered duchies of Inner Austria – Styria, Carinthia, and Carniola – under Archduke Charles (b. 1540, r. 1564–90) and his Bavarian wife, Mary (1551–1608). Unlike Bavaria, where the bishops sat in more or less secure positions beyond the dukes' jurisdiction, these duchies possessed territorial bishoprics with tiny or no *Hochstifte*, which made possible the close coordination between archducal and episcopal effort that characterized Inner Austria's counterreformation.

The most notable of Inner Austria's reforming bishops was Martin Brenner (1548–1616, r. 1585–1615) of Seckau/Graz.[25] He was not an Austrian but a Swabian, a butcher's son from Dietenheim, south of Ulm. Schooled in that Protestant city, he then studied philosophy at Dillingen, the bishop of Augsburg's new university, and theology at Ingolstadt and a series of Italian universities (from one of which he received a doctorate). Brenner's way to the see of Seckau (consecrated 5 May 1585) was smoothed by familiar connections to the powerful Fugger and Montfort families, and by his service with the archbishop of Salzburg. At Graz, Brenner found relatively good preconditions for reform: a strongly Catholic prince and court, a resident papal nuncio, and a Jesuit college (raised by Pope Sixtus V in 1586 to a university).

Under pressure from his vassals, Archduke Charles had granted in 1572 a liberty, called a "Religious Pacification," in which he confirmed to the nobles of the three Inner Austrian duchies the free exercise of religion, the sponsorship of preaching, and the founding of schools. This charter, similar to those issued in other Austrian lands, had then been confirmed to the territorial diet held at Bruck an der Mur (north of Graz) in 1578. The revocation of this charter was an obvious opening move in any campaign to restore the old faith. Meeting in mid-October 1579 at Munich, Archduke Charles, Duke William, and Archduke Ferdinand, ruler of Tyrol and Outer (western) Austria, framed a plan for restoring the Catholic faith in Inner Austria. They agreed that the existing concession must be abolished, not by summary revocation but by a gradual campaign of undermining the right to free exercise of religion. The nobles, after all, had abused the archducal concessions by extending the privilege to commoners, seeking thereby "not only to suppress the Catholic religion but also to free themselves from the obedience they owe."[26] When the nobles protested, the archduke should call upon "the Religious Peace and employ it with no less vigor than other Imperial princes do."[27] He must seek alliances with neighboring princes, ask the pope for a subsidy and the Spanish king for aid, and strengthen Graz Castle's garrison. At the same time, Protestants must be purged and replaced by Catholics at the archducal court and in the district governorships, and the bishops should be pressed through papal channels to found seminaries and implement the other Tridentine reforms. This very comprehensive plan for a Catholic reform, both offensive and defensive, in the three Inner Austrian duchies closely follows earlier (1577) Bavarian proposals for Vienna and Upper and Lower Austria.[28]

More than a decade passed before these proposals began to be implemented in Inner Austria. Protestant resistance proved one impediment, but another was a grave

25 This see had been founded at Seckau Abbey in Styria. Most of its bishops, who were also vicars of the duchy of Styria, resided at Graz.
26 Luttenberger, ed., *Katholische Reform*, 335.
27 Luttenberger, ed., *Katholische Reform*, 335.
28 The titles and geographical terms used here may be confusing. All of the Habsburg princes bore the title of archduke, but the term "archduchies" refers only to Upper and Lower Austria. Charles, therefore, was an archduke of Austria but duke of Styria, Carinthia, and Carniola.

scarcity of priests. In Brenner's diocese of Seckau, as elsewhere, the only hope lay in recruiting them from other lands – Bavaria, Swabia, Italy, and Slovenia – many of them graduates of Jesuit schools in their native regions. Foreign Jesuits had been at work in the Austrian lands since the early 1580s. Peter Canisius brought a small band of his Jesuit brethren to Vienna, where they founded a college, and then to Prague, where they did the same. By the time of Canisius's death in 1597, there were also Jesuit houses at Graz in Styria, Innsbruck in Tyrol, and Olomouc/Olmütz in Moravia. These schools produced the first generation of native Catholic clergy for the Habsburg dominions, many of whom came from modest origins.

In the sixteenth century's final years, Bishop Brenner's hour struck. He and the secular authority working together purged Graz's municipal council and the churches of Protestants. With the capital secure, he organized Reformation Commissions to deal with the provinces. These flying columns were composed of an archducal councilor, a secretary, and a captain of the guard.[29] From late in 1599 they harried the Protestants, seeking to bring them back into the Catholic fold. The commissions replaced the parish ministers with Catholic priests, pulled down Protestant houses of worship, and closed Protestant schools. They began in the small towns and proceeded into the countryside, employing as a shock weapon of choice a kind of "super reformation" of long (three-to-four hours at a time), highly polemical preaching. The finale played out back at Graz, where in high summer 1600 some 10,000 Protestant books were burnt. The entire operation then moved into the neighboring duchy of Carinthia, where Bishop Brenner's program of intensive preaching met fierce Protestant resistance at Klagenfurt, the provincial capital. The commissions then rolled on into the third Inner Austrian duchy, Carniola, where a similar program, headed by the bishop of Llubljana/Laibach but organized with Brenner's aid, restored Catholicism within about five years.

As Catholic leaders had recognized as early as the 1520s, coercion without self-reform was a fruitless enterprise. Bishop Brenner disciplined his concubinarian and married priests – clerical marriage was common in these lands – with the same ruthless efficiency that he employed against Protestants, except that his own priests could not escape through emigration. The laity, too, felt the new yoke, as Brenner introduced a typical Tridentine discipline: mandatory Communion in one kind, enforcement of the Easter duty, and the replacement of the Salzburg liturgical texts with Roman ones.

Within just over a decade, the Inner Austrian counterreformation's main phase broke the Protestants' resistance. The main weight fell on burghers, who were confronted with the common choice of the age – conform or emigrate – while the nobles continued to enjoy their religious privileges until 1628. They outlasted Bishop Martin Brenner, whom ill health forced to resign his see in 1615. The Swabian butcher's boy had become a star of the Austrian counterreformation. He was long remembered by Protestants for his "tyrannical, papistical persecution of the Holy Gospel,"[30] and by his own Catholic people as a hammer of heretics. Inspired by the earlier successes in Bavaria, his reclamation of the Inner Austrian duchies' churches set the stage for the tougher struggles in Upper and Lower Austria.

29   A flying column is a small military unit assembled for a particular mission and often of combined arms.
30   Karl Amon, *Die Bischöfe von Graz-Seckau, 1218–1968*, 265.

4. THE STRUGGLE FOR UPPER AND LOWER AUSTRIA

In the two lands of the archduchy, Upper and Lower Austria, since the 1570s the counterreformation depended on "the collaboration between the Catholic rulers and the reform efforts within the Catholic church."[31] Austrian Protestantism was chiefly a castle-and-town faith which depended for political protection on the nobles acting through the provincial estates. In the archduchy it never commanded more than half the pastorates, and the majority of these were castle chaplaincies. In the villages the new faith made much weaker headway, not least because the archducal regime won over the leading farmers by guaranteeing inheritance rights in this zone of impartible inheritance. Then, too, the revival of the rural abbeys, which began in the 1580s, supplied initial bases for the old faith's recovery in the countryside. Finally, in the villages the Catholic cause was likely helped by the Protestant nobles' role in crushing the great rural insurrection in 1594–97 in both parts of the archduchy.

Like the spread of the new faith, the recovery of the old depended very greatly on social and political geography. Ultimately, in both parts of the archduchy the success of the Protestant religion depended on its appeal to castle and town, but most of all on the lesser nobility.[32] They were strongest in Upper Austria, where their powerful network maintained good relations with their Protestant neighbors across the border in Bohemia. In Lower Austria the situation was more complex. Here the new faith did well among the nobles, but it also attracted many burghers of Vienna, where the Imperial court resided until 1583, when Emperor Rudolph II moved it to Prague.

Apparently very strong, since the 1590s the Protestant position, especially in Lower Austria, began to be weakened by the gradual movement of noble families from the faith of their parents back to that of their grandparents. The main reason for this reconversion was not direct coercion but the standing of the Habsburg court and regime as the only source of patronage and preferment for military and civil offices, for pensions and honors, and for ennoblements and improvements in rank. Vienna housed the bureaus of government that recruited a constant stream of university-educated jurists into service; Vienna controlled the military forces along the Hungarian frontier with the Ottomans; and at Vienna's Imperial chancery rank and improvement in rank were to be had for a price. Gradually, the policy of Catholic preferment, pioneered at Innsbruck and Graz and perfected at Vienna, placed Protestant noble families under severe pressure to sacrifice religious preference to their children's' prospects.

The power of this attraction is difficult to overestimate. All over Europe in this age, royal and princely courts were becoming the principal centers of noble culture and advancement. In the Austrian lands, where the Protestant faith had grown strong in conditions of provincial rustication, noble parents now "wanted their sons to internalize modes of behavior and schemes of appreciation that distinguished them from commoners and prepared them for court life."[33] At court they would learn the self-control and the physical grace that were expected, as Prince Karl Eusebius von

31 Markus Reisenleitner, *Frühe Neuzeit, Reformation und Gegenreformation. Darstellung – Forschungs-überblick – Quellen und Literatur*, 116.
32 As in some other lands, in Austria the nobility consisted of two strata, the barons and the untitled nobles, each of which had its own chamber in the provincial diets.
33 Karin J. MacHardy, "Cultural Capital, Family Strategies and Noble Identity in Early Modern Habsburg Austria 1579–1620," 56.

Liechtenstein (1611–84) wrote to his son, in "high social circles."[34] At the courts, too, letters more than arms had become the preferred path to noble success. Among the Lower Austrian nobility in 1620, two-fifths of the upper and one-fifth of the lower nobility had studied at university. Just as significant, newly ennobled families not only sent a higher proportion of their sons to universities than the old families did, they supplied almost all of those who pursued their studies through to a doctorate in law. The pursuit of cultural competence and competition for rank swelled the importance of the offices and favors at the courts of the relatively poor and (except for Vienna) sparsely populated Austrian lands. Thus did the social and geographical context magnify the power of Catholic preference to erode the political solidarity of provincial Protestant nobilities.

At Vienna the Habsburg policy of conciliation, now a generation old, barred the way forward to serious efforts for a Catholic revival. Since 1530 with only brief exceptions, the emperors had felt compelled to trade concessions to the Lutherans for their support in the Ottoman Wars. "Our city of Vienna," Ferdinand I had written in 1546, "is almost a frontier town against them [the Turks] .... Vienna is important and vital not only for the hereditary dominions, but also for all Christendom and the German nation."[35] The Ottoman problem, as much as his own inscrutable religious views, had convinced Emperor Maximilian II in 1568 to grant the two noble estates (upper and lower) the right to worship in their castles and houses. As in other Habsburg lands, the nobles exploited legal loopholes to justify Lutheran worship in other places, including Vienna, where it was formally forbidden. By this time, "Habsburg religious policy had done nothing less than permit the exercise of Protestantism in Vienna as well as Lower Austria."[36] At court, meanwhile, flourished an ideology of unity and compromise, which to loyal Catholics seemed nothing more than a disguise for Lutheranism.

The first serious attack on this situation came from the pen of Georg Eder (1523–87), a Bavarian jurist who had arrived at Vienna in 1550. Here he rose quickly through the university (he served eleven times as rector) and the emperor's court to become at age forty a judge in the Imperial Aulic Council. Eder, a layman, won fame and notoriety as a public defender of the Catholic faith. In twelve books he challenged the reigning policy at Vienna, which placed him at "the coalface of the implementation of Catholic reform at precisely its most important moment."[37] There he became "the most vociferous and effective opponent of the irenic faction."[38]

Eder saw in the lax, irenic atmosphere at court the root of the problem, in its alteration the key to change. "I myself know the ways and characters of men," he wrote, "even of those who hold government. I know their counsels, and they are all carried by deception .... I see nothing of hope, unless Caesar immediately rushes against these evils."[39] Eder's most notorious attack on the irenic faction and policy,

34 MacHardy, "Cultural Capital," 55.
35 Elaine Fulton, *Catholic Belief and Survival in Late Sixteenth-Century Vienna: The Case of Georg Eder (1523–87)*, 24.
36 Fulton, *Catholic Belief and Survival*, 25.
37 Fulton, *Catholic Belief and Survival*, 17.
38 Howard Louthan, *The Quest for Compromise: Peacemakers in Counter-Reformation Vienna*, 127. Eder later observed that as many as 3,000 persons were still going out from the city on Sunday to hear a Lutheran preacher. Catholics, of course, were doing the same in cities ruled by Protestant princes.
39 Fulton, *Catholic Belief and Survival*, 84.

his *Evangelical Inquisition* (*Evangelische Inquisition*), was printed at Dillingen in 1573.[40] The author was so bold (or incautious) as to present a copy to Emperor Maximilian himself, who immediately ordered it confiscated and forbade Eder ever again to write on religion. The chief spur to this reaction was Eder's attack on the "court Christians" (*Hofchristen*) as dissemblers who disguised their religious beliefs for the sake of preferment. Some he described as blowing "like weathervanes: with the Catholics, they are Catholic; with the Lutherans, they are Lutheran."[41] Worse, yet, the book seemed to ridicule the emperor's piety, his policy, and, worst of all, his authority. This was no ordinary book by no ordinary man, and the furor over it arose in part from the fact that "to the international Catholic community, Georg Eder was nothing less than a doctor of the Church," a layman who with papal and episcopal approval sought to instruct laity and clergy alike in the tenets of their own faith and in their own German language.[42] He wished to expose the heretics, who "are Lutheran, tomorrow Calvinist; the day after that Schwenkfeldian, soon Anabaptist, and finally Muslim."[43]

Eder's attack on the situation at Vienna won him friends at Pope Gregory XIII's court at Rome, where someone proposed the appointment of the freshly widowed Eder as the new bishop of Gurk.[44] This was never done, and Eder left Vienna for the one Catholic capital – Munich – where his service to the Church would not be resented. He left behind a city and a land in which the religious question would continue to be agitated for another three decades.

A generation passed before Vienna found able clerical leadership in the person of Melchior Khlesl (b. 1552, r. 1598–1630), whose biography is a microcosm of the Austrian counterreformation.[45] The son of a Viennese baker and his wife, Khlesl was reared as a Lutheran but converted under the influence of Jesuit sermons. After ordination he represented the bishop of Passau at the Imperial Aulic Council in Vienna, of which see he became bishop in 1589.[46] He well knew what he faced, for less than a decade earlier he had written to Duke William of Bavaria in deepest despair. "The well-meant reformation I planned makes no progress," he writes, "when I try to punish a bad priest, especially in the emperor's parishes, they have their protectors at the court to help and advise them against me."[47] Khlesl reflected on the stream of bad priests coming out of Bavaria to seek benefices in Austria: "I often secretly complain to God, my Lord in heaven, and feel no more desire to remain any longer bound to this wearisome, embattled office."[48] With reform of the clergy, the foundation of every Catholic reform, he despaired of success: "I've been able to do very little with

40 That it was printed in the bishop of Augsburg's residential town, not in Vienna, suggests the reception Eder expected for this work.
41 Fulton, *Catholic Belief and Survival*, 88.
42 Fulton, *Catholic Belief and Survival*, 91.
43 Fulton, *Catholic Belief and Survival*, 92.
44 Gurk in Carinthia was one of the three small Inner Austrian sees (the others were Seckau and Lavant) that had originally been founded at abbeys. The bishop resided at Klagenfurt.
45 Erwin Gatz and Clemens Brotkorb, eds., *Die Bischöfe des Heiligen Römischen Reichs 1448 bis 1648. Ein biographisches Lexikon*, 367–70.
46 Passau, the Holy Roman Empire's largest diocese (42,000 km²), extended down the Danube past Vienna to the borders of Hungary and southward into the Alps. Before 1500 it was divided into two, and in 1469 two very small dioceses, Vienna and Wiener Neustadt, were carved out of the eastern part.
47 Luttenberger, ed., *Katholische Reform*, 515.
48 Luttenberger, ed., *Katholische Reform*, 515.

the godless concubinaries (except for a few, thank God, whom I've been able with His help to reform). I write, I speak, I command, and I do with them as I might, but it is all in vain.''[49] The only remedy for this dire situation, a full coordination of secular and spiritual rulers in a program of Catholic reformation, seemed a hope beyond hoping. Then, in 1608, a new horizon seemed to open when the bitter quarrel between the emperor and his brothers forced Rudolph to cede the archduchy to his brother, Matthias (b. 1557, r. 1612–19). The Austrian Protestant estates, emboldened by the strife, demanded from him a patent of religious toleration comparable to the one Rudolph had issued for the Bohemian estates in 1609. Matthias now stood at a fork in the road with respect to religious policy. Down one path lay a continuation of the old policy of conciliation; down the other lay Catholic reform and counterreformation. Matthias chose not to choose. Bishop Khlesl of Vienna, his chief advisor on religion, had been won over to a policy of conciliation by the need for Protestant votes in the Imperial election of 1612 and – the old reason – by his belief that the Ottomans were more dangerous than the Protestants. This policy held until the Bohemian revolt began in 1618.

The histories of reformation and counterreformation in the Austrian lands display a common pattern. First came the spread of the new faith among the provincial nobles and then from their towns into the burghers' towns. In time it became strong enough to wring religious liberties from the Habsburg prince. In response, the archdukes turned one after the other to a policy of Catholic reform in the Bavarian style. They began by favoring Catholics for offices and inviting preachers and teachers, above all Jesuits, into their lands. Imperial law, the foundation of the Empire's religious peace, lay on their side. There was coercion, of course, as there had been in the Protestant reformation: suppression of worship, expulsion of clergymen, appropriation of ecclesiastical incomes and properties, and placing the minority before the choice between conformity and exile. The two reformations differed, however, in efficiency. The Catholic leaders enjoyed the benefit of a model supplied by ducal Bavaria, the most highly developed territorial state in the Empire. Its relevance, however, was limited, for beyond Bavaria and Austria, there remained only two other significant Catholic dynasties, Lorraine and Savoy, neither of which played a significant role in the German lands' affairs.[50] In the parts of the Empire where the Catholics retained something to renew and save, the Bavarian model hardly applied. In such places Catholic leadership lay in the hands of that inherently problematical figure, the Imperial prince-bishop.

5. IMPERIAL BISHOPS AND CATHOLIC REFORMS

An informed observer who gazed at the Catholic situation in the German lands around 1575, and who reflected on the Council of Trent's principle that the bishops were the keys to Catholic reform, had to agree with Lazarus von Schwendi that the end was near. Bavaria stood alone, a stone wall against the Protestant tide. Yet a closer

---

49 Luttenberger, ed., *Katholische Reform*, 515.
50 There was in addition the duchy of Cleves-Jülich, an unintegrated group of four lands on the Lower Rhine with its capital at Düsseldorf. Its ruling dynasty became extinct in the agnatic line in 1609. The last two dukes, one of dubious sanity and the other seriously disturbed, played no roles in the Catholic revival.

look found other grounds for hope. In the episcopal cities of the south and west (Würzburg, Bamberg, Mainz, Salzburg), the Protestants had discovered very hard ground in which to plant their faith. Unable to call on princes and magistrates to overthrow "the papacy" – the entire panoply of Catholic rites, teachings, authority, and property – the small Protestant communities in these cities mostly fell victim to relatively low degrees of coercion. In the episcopal cities "the reformation movement even failed to develop beyond preaching activities or – in the second half of the sixteenth century – the Protestants remained at best temporarily tolerated dissidents without legal protections or formal organization."[51]

An appreciation for the prince-bishoprics' potential as leaders of Catholic reform was not an easy thing to teach, even to well-wishing foreigners. One who tried just that was the Jesuit Adam Contzen (1571–1635), a native of Monschau in the Eifel near Aachen and confessor to Maximilian I of Bavaria. He was a man, who "very much saw himself dealing with the real world, and he dreaded being written off as a utopian."[52] Dealing with the real world gave him an understanding of the Empire to be found in no book. "How many Italians," he sighed, "believe that the bishops of Germany resemble them in their external government? They are comparing fir trees to tamarisk bushes.[53] How many imagine that the Empire is a vast city? A certain gentleman asked if the Empire had many villages."[54] Italian churchmen must learn, he adds in a pithy marginal gloss, "German bishops are princes, Italians are not."[55] It was a difficult lesson, made no easier by Italian prejudices against the Germans. Almost a century after Contzen's little lecture, the Neapolitan philosopher Giambattista Vico (1688–1744) solemnly explained the German peculiarity: "In Germany, which was clearly the most savage and ferocious of the European nations, there came to be almost more clerical sovereigns – bishops or abbots – than there were secular ones."[56] An improvement but still mistaken.

A realistic assessment of the Catholic cause in the German lands depended on a correct grasp of the Empire's peculiar institutions, first and foremost the Imperial prince-bishopric. In time, contrary to Adam Contzen's impression, the Roman Curia did learn something about German peculiarity and how to exploit it. Its officials had first to learn that German princely dynasties were far more autonomous than their Italian counterparts, and that Roman confirmation of a bishop-elect who either was or might become a Lutheran led sooner or later to a permanent loss of the see. This happened with some frequency during the 1550s and early 1560s, but soon thereafter Rome began to balk at continued collaboration with the emperor's policy of paying off Protestant princes with feudal investitures of their kinsmen and clients. It was reasonable to assume that, as the papal legate wrote in 1566 from the Diet of Augsburg, the emperor and the Diet would never adopt, much less enforce, the decisions of

51 Hans-Christoph Rublack, *Gescheiterte Reformation. Frühreformatorische und protestantische Bewegungen in süd- und westdeutschen geistlichen Residenzen*, 124.
52 Robert Bireley, *The Counter-Reformation Prince: Anti-Machiavellianism or Catholic Statecraft in Early Modern Europe*, 139.
53 In other words, apples to oranges.
54 Adam Contzen, *Politicorum libri decem in quibus de perfectae reipubl. forma, virtutibus, et vitiis, institutione civium, legibus magistratu ecclesiastico, civili, potentia republicae; itemque seditione et bello, ad usum vitamque communem accomodate tracature*, 418.
55 Contzen, *Politicorum libri decem*, 418.
56 Giambattista Vico, *New Science. Principles of the New Science Concerning the Common Nature of Nations*, 464.

Trent. Nor, for that matter, the Ecclesiastical Reservation to the peace of 1555. This was alarming, the more so because, with the Dutch Revolt against the king of Spain, the Protestant powers formed a threat to the great arc of prince-bishoprics that stretched across the northern plain from Cologne and Münster eastward to Osnabrück and Hildesheim. Absent a strategy, the northwest would go the way of the northeast, where the old church lost three archbishoprics (Bremen, Magdeburg, and legally extra-Imperial but German-ruled Riga) and nineteen bishoprics.[57]

What was to be done? Against the collective wills of cathedral chapters, nothing at all. In the short run the only hope lay in encouraging the cathedral canons to elect princes from Catholic dynasties, which for a time meant a Bavarian, chiefly one Bavarian, Ernest, Duke Albert V's son. He was elected to Freising in 1566 (at age twelve), Hildesheim in 1573, Liège in 1581, Cologne in 1583, and Münster in 1585. The church's need found its first rescue specialist in this unlikely pluralist, who devoted himself to gambling, to magic, and to Gertrud von Plettenberg (d. 1608). The times made Ernest a vital link in the Rome-Munich-Brussels-Madrid axis that in time helped to save most of the northwestern prince-bishoprics for the Catholic faith.

If no way could be found to rally the electoral chapters to the cause of reform, the promotion of princely sybarites would never be more than a makeshift. What distant Rome *could* do was supply the chapters with superior candidates. The central agency for this project, the German College at Rome, had been founded in 1552 following Giovanni Morone's recommendation to Ignatius Loyola (1491–1556). Those who "are intensely interested in the saving of Germany," Morone writes, "see in this college the surest and almost only means to support the tottering and – alas that we should have to say so, of many places at least – the collapsed Church in Germany."[58] The German College became the cornerstone of Rome's efforts to recruit, train, and return to the German lands young men whose social backgrounds made them acceptable to the chapters, but whose formation made them loyal to the church. By the 1580s this policy raised, inevitably, the issue of favoring nobles as recruits. The Jesuits, urban men mostly, opposed noble preference, but the head of the German Congregation, the Curia's body responsible for church affairs in the Empire, favored it. He was none other than Cardinal Morone, who had meanwhile survived a long, bitter process for heresy before the Roman Inquisition. Morone got his way, and thereafter the college's inscriptions show a marked increase in nobles and a corresponding decrease in commoners.

Why did Morone favor nobles? Perhaps because of his superior knowledge of German conditions. It stemmed partly from his work as a papal legate in the Empire, of course, but he also had a superb informant in Peter Canisius, who spent forty-five years in the German missions. In the summer of 1576 Canisius drafted for Morone a long memorial on the German problem. The central issue, Canisius writes, is not heresy as such but "a total ignorance of the faith, and ignorance of and contempt for the Church," which is preserved by the fact that "not only is the life of the laity corrupt, but also that of the entire clergy and above all the prelates and the religious

57 Riga with its suffragan sees of Samland, Ermland, Pomesanian, and Kulm; Magdeburg with Brandenburg, Havelberg, Merseburg, and Naumburg; and Bremen with Lübeck, Ratzeburg, and Schwerin. The Catholics also lost Halberstadt and Verden from the province of Mainz, Schleswig from Lund, and the exempt sees of Kammin and Meissen.
58 Ignatius Loyola to Claude Le Jay in Bavaria, July 1552, in Ignatius Loyola, *Letters of St. Ignatius Loyola*, 259.

orders."[59] This situation "is almost impossible of remedy, because the lower and upper clergy do not recognize the Roman Church as the mother and chief of all churches, nor do they listen to its teachings and admonitions."[60] The only solution, Canisius believes, "is to ensure a good education for young Germans in the various seminaries," above all in the German lands, where the costs will be lower than in Rome.[61] Reform thus could not be simply imported, it would have to occur not inspite of the Imperial church's historic structures but through them. Canisius recognized that the key lay in the noble canons' right to elect bishops from their own ranks: "As I've said, the bishops are customarily elected from the decayed class of nobles."[62] Given the adverse conditions, however, "at the present time it is not possible to remove the nobles from the cathedral chapters or to reform them from top to bottom."[63] At best Rome could only demand that no more noble heretics be admitted to the chapters, and that the Protestant canons be excluded from taking part in future episcopal elections. The chapters had to be instructed that in the future Rome would not confirm irregularly elected bishops.

"Decayed" the nobles may have been, but Catholic reformers could neither deprive the cathedral chapters of their electoral rights nor dispossess the regional nobilities who dominated most of them. Once purged of Protestants, the nobles would become a likely source of Catholic churchmen. Unlike the princely dynasties, the nobles had no designs on the *Hochstifte*, since they were not state-formers; unlike the commoners, the nobles enjoyed local political influence through their dense familial networks and corporate associations. Given the Empire's weak monarchy and the conflicted character of Habsburg policy, a convergence between Rome's goals of reconstruction and recovery and the nobles' goal of preserving their independence, the noble preference was a quite rational strategy.

Ultimately, of course, episcopal reform depended on the bishops' devotion to duty and strength of will. Yet the old German problem remained: the dioceses needed spiritual leaders; the *Hochstifte* needed able princes. What could happen if the bishop were neither is illustrated by the seven occupants of the see of Paderborn between 1508 and 1616: a well-intentioned but timid prelate; a pluralist who became Lutheran and tried to keep the *Hochstift* as his own; a pious but helpless seventy-year-old of exemplary life; a half-Protestant pluralist installed with Brunswick's support; a reforming bishop of a Tridentine stripe; a sybaritic pluralist and not-so-secret Protestant who secretly married his mistress; and, finally, a nobleman of chaste lifestyle, energy, and learning, who proved an able bishop and a strong prince.

The history of drift came at a stiff price. About half the diocese of Paderborn was permanently lost to neighboring Protestant princes; much of the local population became Lutheran; the monasteries lay in ruins. The seventh bishop, Count Dietrich von Fürstenberg (b. 1546, r. 1585–1618), put a stop to this drift with a double program of repression and evangelization.[64] On the one hand, he expelled Protestant preachers

59 Luttenberger, ed., *Katholische Reform*, 313.
60 Luttenberger, ed., *Katholische Reform*, 313.
61 Luttenberger, ed., *Katholische Reform*, 314.
62 Luttenberger, ed., *Katholische Reform*, 318.
63 Luttenberger, ed., *Katholische Reform*, 318.
64 Dietrich von Fürstenberg came from a Westphalian family, unrelated to the more celebrated southern family of this name. He also introduced into his territories trials for witchcraft, especially of members of the clergy.

from the urban parishes, closed the Protestant schools, forbade public Protestant worship, and told the Protestants to make their Easter duty or emigrate (though this was rarely enforced). On the other, he jailed disobedient priests, convened a diocesan synod, sponsored a catechism in the Westphalian (Low German) tongue, and got the Jesuit college (est. 1585) raised to the rank of university.

The experience of Paderborn emphasizes two elements vital to episcopal rescue operations, the chapter and the *Hochstift*. Where chapters stood against the initial Protestant tide, they conserved the see's resources and became the staging bases for Catholic renewal and reclamation. Where the *Hochstift* remained intact, a capable and energetic bishop could suppress openly Protestant religious life, discipline the Catholic priests, and begin the catechizing of the Catholic laity. The result might very much resemble the reformation of a typical Protestant principality, a Saxony or a Württemberg, although it had the advantages of support from a vast Catholic Church, a well-defined program, more consistent laws, and superior administrative techniques.

Between the worldly prelates of an earlier day and the austere counterreformation bishops of a later time appeared hybrids, princely in their lifestyles, reforming in their policies. A superior example of the type was Wolf Dietrich von Raitenau (1559–1617), a reforming archbishop of Salzburg (r. 1587–1612). Son of an Imperial general and nephew of Pope Pius IV (r. 1559–65), Wolf Dietrich studied at Pavia and at the German College in Rome. He entered Holy Orders after the canons of Salzburg elected him to the see. Pope Sixtus V (b. 1521, r. 1585–90) urged him "to break the strikes of the heretics and turn their deadly shots back on them."[65] In October 1587 Wolf Dietrich entered Salzburg to find his church in a ripe state of decay. He called not on his Jesuit teachers but on the Capuchins, a new Italian branch (est. 1525) on the Franciscan tree; he initiated the transformation of Salzburg into a showplace of the new Roman ("baroque") style; and he disciplined his clergy and consulted neither cathedral chapter nor territorial estates. In policy, therefore, Wolf Dietrich was a counterreformation prelate; in lifestyle he was something more traditional. He fathered ten children by Salome Alt (1568–1633), the lovely daughter of a Salzburg magistrate, and sought in vain for permission from Rome to marry her. Emperor Rudolph II nonetheless ennobled Salome and her children, "to whom she has given birth by a prominent churchman," raising them into the Imperial nobility and absolving the children of "all stain and disability of their illegitimate birth."[66]

Already in Wolf Dietrich's time, the Empire began to see prince-bishops who more nearly fit the Tridentine ideal. Easily the most notable of them was Julius Echter von Mespelbrunn (b. 1545, r. 1573–1617), who occupied the see of Würzburg for nearly forty-five years. A Franconian nobleman like most Würzburg bishops, Julius went to the Jesuits at Cologne, studied at Louvain, Paris, Angers, and Pavia, and became at age twenty-two a canon and six years later bishop at Würzburg. He lived a regular life, performed his religious duties, disciplined his clergy, evangelized his laity, treated his Jewish subjects with severity, and repressed his Lutheran ones. A builder in every sense of the word, Julius founded a hospital for the mentally ill that has been called both "revolutionary" and "a dramatic Counter-Reformation statement."[67] Julius

65 Heinz Schilling, *Aufbruch und Krise. Deutschland 1517–1648*, 285.
66 Schilling, *Aufbruch und Krise*, 286.
67 H. C. Erik Midelfort, *A History of Madness in Sixteenth-Century Germany*, 371.

Echter represents most clearly an Imperial prince-bishop of the post-Tridentine type. In the longer view, the appearance of such prelates at a crucial moment helps to explain why most of the centers of modern German Catholicism (Munich is the great exception) were in early modern times not secular capitals but old episcopal cities – Cologne, Trier, and Mainz; Münster, Paderborn, and Osnabrück; Würzburg, Bamberg, and Fulda. Their magnificent baroque cathedrals and palaces testify to the prince-bishops' vital role in the Catholic recovery. Yet little of their work would have endured, probably, had they not enjoyed protection from the houses of Bavaria and Austria and support and services from abroad, chiefly from Italy.

6. ROME, ITALY, AND THE GERMAN LANDS

The Protestant reformation in the German lands was a German affair. Its roots lay in a powerful religious seriousness, especially among clergy and burghers, in a disappointment by failed reform initiatives and lax episcopal leadership, and in a national pride wounded by the Italians and especially by Rome. While Martin Luther's revolutionary theology gave the movement an initial opening, its enduring successes came from the actions of the princes, urban magistrates, and clergy who provided military protection, political leadership, and pastoral service.

The Catholic reformation in the German lands was an international affair. Its German roots lay in a dogged loyalty of many clergy and laity to their ancestors' faith and in the opposition to Protestantism of a few rulers, notably the Bavarian dukes. Its programs and execution depended very heavily, however, on its ties to and support from the lands of intact Catholicism, above all Italy. The Council of Trent provided an agenda; the (mostly Italian) religious orders provided networks of exchange for news, ideas, techniques, and personnel; Rome supplied candidates for high offices, a diplomatic network, and norms and forms of standardization in religious practice.

By 1563, when the Council of Trent rose for the last time, Rome's view of the situation of the Catholic Church could hardly have been more disheartening. The English church had left the Roman communion; the French church was threatened by a vigorous and well-armed Calvinist movement; the Scandinavian north was lost, the Polish kingdom stood in danger, and much of Hungary lay under Ottoman rule. In the German lands the Protestant advance continued, untrammeled by the Religious Peace of 1555. In the German north, except the northwest, the last Catholic outposts were gone; in the south and west the old church held out in the ecclesiastical principalities and in Bavaria, but it lay desperately under siege in Austria, Bohemia, and Hungary. While by century's end the general situation appeared somewhat better, the main work of reform, Tridentine or not, still lay ahead, some of it well beyond the Peace of Westphalia. Even in the early phases, however, Rome and Italy played important parts in supporting the programs in the German lands.

At Rome serious backing for a counterreformation in the German lands began with the election in 1566 of the 62-year-old Italian Dominican Michele Ghislieri as Pope Pius V (r. 1566–72). He not only sponsored the Roman catechism (1566), a reformed breviary (1568), and a Roman missal for use by all dioceses and orders (1570), but he strongly supported the efforts of Carlo Borromeo (1538–84), the Milanese archbishop, to promote Catholic recovery in Switzerland. His successor,

Gregory XIII (r. 1572–85), had lived through the entire course of the Protestant reformation. This pope understood that reform in the German lands depended on,
among other things, the advancement of that most un-Tridentine prelate, Ernest of
Bavaria, and he improved communications with the Imperial church by establishing
permanent papal nunciatures (embassies) at Lucerne (1579), Graz (1580–1622), and
Cologne (1584). His most spectacular reform, however, was the completion of a
fifteenth-century project to reform the Julian calendar. The new Gregorian calendar,
which eliminated ten days (5–14 October 1582) and changed the counting of leap years,
was quickly accepted by the German Catholic principalities but not by the Protestants. For a long time Imperial institutions, such as the Imperial Chamber Court, had
to follow both calendars, so that the common feasts – Christmas, Easter – had to be
observed twice. The German Protestant rulers did not accept the "papist" calendar
until 1700.

By far the most important external aid to Catholic reform came from new societies
and orders dedicated, even more than the medieval mendicants had been, to active
service in the world. The same purpose also gripped women, though they were
hindered, if not entirely blocked, from active service by the Council of Trent's decree
that women's communities must be cloistered. Among the male communities, pride
of place belonged to the Jesuits and the Capuchins.

The Society of Jesus was the most remarkable creation of the Catholic reformation. A small band of students, who had gathered at Paris, came in 1540 to Rome,
where Pope Paul III approved its rules. Over the next generation it exploded at a pace
unprecedented except in the mendicant friars' expansion during the thirteenth
century. The Jesuits' activities stretched around the world from Spain and Paraguay
to the markets of Manila and Macão to the great courts of Catholic Europe to quiet
places in Mayo, Lancastershire, and Moravia. Of all their undertakings, some of the
greatest successes were registered in the Holy Roman Empire, sometimes called the
"domestic Indies," perhaps old Christendom's most taxing mission field.

The Jesuits tended "to understand the Reformation as primarily a pastoral problem. They saw its fundamental causes and cures related not so much to doctrinal
issues as to the spiritual condition of the persons concerned."[68] What the cloister
had been to the great orders of the High Middle Ages, the school became to the
Jesuits. They organized schools for the sons of princes, nobles, and burghers, as well
as for scholarship boys; they ran colleges and universities for future scholars and
priests. Their balanced pedagogy mobilized the emotions by means of constant competition and by grounding the instructor's authority in the affections of the pupil; it
encouraged individuality through games, sport, and theater; and it formed the intellect via the study of ancient languages and an emphasis on spiritual independence.
Schools run according to the Jesuit pedagogy attracted both students of great promise
and sons of great families. At the same time, their Marian congregations, prayer
confraternities dedicated to the Virgin, proved highly successful in the schools and
universities but also in the professions (such as law) and among women. The congregation's members were encouraged to frequent reception of the sacraments,
undertake charitable work among the poor, perform catechetical instruction, distribute religious literature, and bury the dead.

68   John W. O'Malley, *The First Jesuits*, 16.

The first Jesuits came to the German lands in the early 1540s. The Savoyard Peter Faber (Pierre Favre, 1506–46), one of Ignatius's original companions, founded the first German house at Cologne in 1544. Others followed at Dillingen (seat of Augsburg's bishop), Mainz, and Würzburg, where Bishop Julius Echter von Mespelbrunn asked the Jesuits to staff his new university. By the 1560s the Jesuits were an important force in the German lands, and decade by decade the numbers of members, schools, and graduates rose until the outbreak of the Thirty Years War. Whereas in the mid-1560s there had been about 273 Jesuits in the Empire, by the 1620s their numbers had grown to nearly 2,500, organized in three provinces (Rhenish, South German, and Austrian).

Through their schools, congregations, and preaching, Jesuits played the central role in the work of Catholic reclamation in the German lands. They were patient but persistent. Typical, perhaps, was their work at Fulda, an ancient Benedictine abbey on the eastern edge of the modern state of Hesse, descended from a foundation by St. Sturm, St. Boniface's disciple. The Imperial prince-abbots of Fulda ruled a considerable territory, but in the town a majority of the burghers had become Protestants. Then came the Jesuits, who during the 1570s and 1580s pursued a patient pastoral strategy. They made no attempt to press their message on the burghers, the knights, or the monks but confined themselves to waiting until their help was called for and then tailored their actions to specific local needs. At Fulda, as in many other places, the Jesuits counted among their flocks numbers of boys and young men who became Catholic converts during their school days.

As the Jesuits spread across the Empire, they planted schools in town after episcopal town. In 1610 Prince-bishop Dietrich of Paderborn raised the Jesuits' Latin school to a school of philosophy and theology for the formation of priests, which he financed from his own means. In 1616 Pope Paul V (r. 1605–21) privileged this institution to grant academic degrees on the model of Dillingen in the diocese at Augsburg, and Paderborn became in turn a model for establishments at Osnabrück and Münster. The Jesuits' religious and pedagogical colonization of the German lands developed on a vast scale. From the beginning to 1615, at least seventy Jesuit stations, residences, and schools were established in the German lands (including six in Switzerland), eleven more in the Bohemian lands, and no fewer than thirty in the Low Countries.[69]

The Jesuits, more than any other organization, supplied the Catholic cause in the German lands with what it most needed, a secular clergy of the kind reformers had been demanding since the Council of Basel: priests more learned, more spiritual, and more faithful to their pastoral duties than their predecessors had been. Jakob Rehm (d. 1618), a Vorarlberger who was rector of the Jesuit college in Ingolstadt, remarked around 1600, "In twenty years the Catholic religion in Germany will experience such a growth and will affect so many conversions from every social class that, with the lack of secular clergy, our own will not suffice to bring all the wandering sheep into Christ's flock."[70] Lazarus von Schwendi had predicted in 1574 the old church's imminent demise; Rehm predicted a quarter-century later the old church's triumph.

69 Hubert Jedin, Kenneth Scott Latourette, and Jochen Martin, eds., *Atlas zur Kirchengeschichte. Die christlichen Kirchen in Geschichte und Gegenwart*, 78. The concentration of Jesuit foundations in the southern Netherlands reflects the region's role as the principal center of Catholic reformation north of the Alps. They trained priests not only for the German lands but also for the British Isles.

70 Anton Huonder, *Deutsche Jesuitenmissionäre des 17. und 18. Jahrhunderts: Ein Beitrag zur Missionsgeschichte und zur deutschen Biographie*, 14. I owe this text to Luke S. Clossey.

If the Jesuits were the engineers of the Catholic reformation, the Capuchins were its blue-collar workers. Their order founded in Italy in the 1520s, they dedicated themselves to St. Francis's original ideals, poverty and simplicity of life, and to evangelizing the common people. In the 1570s they broke out of the peninsula and during the next half-century formed nineteen provinces in France, Spain, the southern Netherlands, and the German lands. In numbers the Capuchins outdid even the Jesuits, rising from 8,803 members in 1600 to 16,967 in 1625.[71] The founding dates of their provinces in the Empire tell the tale of their spread: Switzerland (1581), Tyrol (1593, with Bavaria and part of Swabia); Austria-Bohemia (1600), Styria (1609, with Croatia), and Cologne (1611, with most of the German northwest).[72]

Capuchin friars specialized in work among the country people and the urban poor, milieus in which the Jesuits were not very successful. Some Catholic bishops preferred them to the Jesuits because "they seemed less haughty, less likely to stir Protestant antagonisms, and closer to the people and popular religion."[73] When the prince-bishop of Speyer called the Jesuits into his *Hochstift* just before the Thirty Years War, these urbane priests met their match. Far from desiring to be reformed by preachers, Catholic or Protestant, the farmers stuck to the old ways of a communal Catholicism deeply veined with the non-Christian elements that appalled the Jesuits as much as they had Luther. Against their resistance the Jesuits made little headway. After the Peace of Westphalia, a new bishop called in the Capuchins, who enjoyed success where the Jesuits had failed. Much the same division between reformed and traditional Catholicism developed in the episcopal town of Münster, once the site of the notorious Anabaptist kingdom. When the bishop invited the Jesuits to evangelize the city, many of the burghers preferred to keep to the comfortably communal and – to reformers' eyes – superstition-ridden ways of an older time. One major sign of this divide between the new and the revitalized old Catholicism can be seen in Bavaria, where the Jesuits gained great influence in Munich and in the university at Ingolstadt but played little or no role in the great flowering of Bavarian shrines and pilgrimage culture that so effectively armored Bavarian Catholicism against heterodoxy.

The rivalry between Jesuits and Capuchins thus promoted an effective division of labor between highly educated, city-bred clergy who could not reach the farmers and demotic friars who could. The Capuchins took easily to the custody of popular religion – too easily, many educated German Catholics believed – and in the Alpine lands they acquired fame as exorcists and managers of evil spirits.

7. JESUITESSES – WOMEN AND CATHOLIC REFORMS

The prospect of spreading the true faith and thereby transforming religious lives inspired Protestants and Catholics alike, figures as diverse as Abraham Scultetus and Georg Eder, the one a Reformed clergyman, the other a Catholic layman. In very many respects, the Protestant and the Catholic reformations unfolded as

71 John Patrick Donnelly, "Catholic Reformation: The New Orders," in Thomas A. Brady, Heiko A. Oberman, and James D. Tracy, eds., *Handbook of European History, 1400–1600. Late Middle Ages, Renaissance, Reformation*, vol. 2: 296. Like the other early modern missionary orders, their great age was the eighteenth century.
72 Jedin, Latourette, and Martin, eds., *Atlas*, 79.
73 John Patrick Donnelly, "Catholic Reformation: The New Orders," in Brady, Oberman, and Tracy, eds., *Handbook*, vol. 2: 295.

programs of evangelization promoted and protected by rulers. There is therefore some wisdom, laying aside the deep structural differences, in seeing the entire process in terms of a pace-setting Protestant and a responding Catholic effort. Yet this image is not useful with respect to gender. Initially, Catholic reformers were tempted to follow the Protestant suit by retaining a celibate male clergy but dissolving the female clergy, thereby implicitly consigning women to the household alone. This had been recommended in 1537 by Pope Paul III's reform commission, a body loaded with stars and future stars of the Catholic reformation. They, or their majority, clearly thought that religious women had become a liability to the Church, because Protestant attacks on the convents as brothels had "turned the behavior of religious women, and not the conduct of religious men, into the primary measure for gauging the theological credibility of Catholics and Protestants."[74] The commission therefore recommended that the female convents be forbidden to accept novices, which meant that within a generation they would disappear.

When the Council of Trent dealt with the issue of women's convents, its decision, though in principle less radical than the recommendation of 1537, proved severely restrictive even when not strictly enforced. The council chose enclosure over suppression. It mandated abolition of unregulated women's communities, enforcement of strict enclosure, placement of the communities under male supervision, and mandated enclosure for previously uncloistered female – but not the male – groups called "tertiaries."[75] These decisions "laid the doctrinal grounds for re-creating nunneries in the image of male-headed households," undermined the ancient principle of equality of nuns and monks, drew "sharper boundaries . . . between the sacred and the profane [and] . . . designated women as threats to as well as guardians of boundaries."[76]

The stricter separation of genders is readily apparent in the new religious orders. Many of the great medieval religious orders, the older (Benedictines, Cistercians, Carthusians) and the newer ones (Franciscans, Dominicans, Carmelites) alike, possessed both male and female branches. Most new orders (Jesuits, Barnabites, Theatines, Oratorians, and Camillans) were, by contrast, not only strictly male, they also enjoyed a greater freedom from the duties of communal life for the sake of working in the world. The women's communities, old or new, enjoyed no such freedom. Protestant and Catholic reformations alike saw pastoral service, the clergy's chief duty, as an exclusively male activity.

To a degree unprecedented in Catholic history, the Catholic reformation awakened a desire among Catholic women to do pastoral work in the world. Whether directly inspired by the Jesuits, when such women formed uncloistered communities, as Ignatius and his companions had done, they came to be called "Jesuitesses." In spirit they were just that, for they wished to dedicate themselves to pastoral life in the world, a life of prayer, to be sure, but above all to teaching. However small and local their beginnings, if they grew in numbers, sooner or later they would come to face disapproval against which neither episcopal nor Jesuit patronage could protect them. Such was the fate of the two principal groups of Jesuitesses in the German lands, the Ursulines and the English Ladies.

---

74 Strasser, *State of Virginity*, 70.
75 Tertiaries are members of religious orders who live outside of the community according to a modified version of the order's rule.
76 Strasser, *State of Virginity*, 75.

The Jesuitesses came not from the center, Rome, but from the northern margins, the southern Netherlands and England. In 1578 the Cologne diarist Hermann Weins-berg (1518–97) recorded the Netherlandish beginnings in that city:

> Elisabeth Horn, my brother's wife, and the spinster from Delft, who fled from Holland to Cologne and were tenants in my house, were good Jesuit followers. They went early in the morning to church, attended many sermons, read a great deal, and at table they were always debating and talking about reform.[77]

Cologne was the right place, for it had become a great fortress of the old faith in a region swirling with Lutheran, Anabaptist, and Calvinist refugees and missionaries. "It alone of all the imperial cities never experienced a crisis of faith, nor deviated from the path of Catholic orthodoxy."[78]

Cologne was St. Ursula's city. She was believed to have been an ancient British princess who had led 11,000 virgins on pilgrimage to Rome. On the return trip Attila's Huns massacred them at Cologne, where their relics were preserved and revered. The ten women who in 1606 formed a community of Ursulines – they met and worshiped at the saint's church – had come from Aachen, fleeing the plague. Their Society of St. Ursula had originally no connection to the Italian order of Ursulines founded at Brescia in 1535 by Angela Merici (1474–1540).[79] Its purposes, however, were remark-ably similar, for, as the local Jesuit college's rector reported to Rome, they dedicated themselves to works of piety and love of neighbor, notably "teaching to the ignorant God's commandments and the way to salvation."[80] Besides communal prayer and Mass and comforting the sick and the dying, they concentrated on catechizing chil-dren, on which account the Cologne group was nicknamed "Catechism Sisters."

The women of St. Ursula's society understood themselves to be laywomen bound by a vow to the celibate life and devoted to good works. A dispute about the admis-sibility of married women to their company – some feared the "women of the world" would neglect religious duties – was settled in 1623 by a local Jesuit official in favor of the celibates. Upon this major step in the transformation of this female community into a religious order followed the introduction of corporate governance and the religious habit, and by 1646 the native and the newly arrived "true" Ursulines (Meri-ci's group) merged into a single order. Eighty-three years had passed since the council fathers at Trent had decreed claustration for religious women.

Meanwhile, another group of Jesuitesses had arrived from the Low Countries. They were English, and their leader was Mary Ward (1585–1645), daughter of recusant Catholic gentry in Yorkshire. Leaving England in 1606, she had landed at Saint-Omer in Flanders, one of the greatest melting pots of Catholic religious exiles. Wanting to aid the Catholics of her native land, she did not know how to begin, and when she returned to England in 1609 she still was undecided between the contemplative and the active life. Mary later described her indecision in a letter to the papal nuncio at Cologne and noted that "enclosure and the perfect observance of poverty were the

77   Anne Conrad, *Zwischen Kloster und Welt: Ursulinen und Jesuitinnen in der katholischen Reformbe-wegung des 16./17. Jahrhunderts*, 113.
78   Robert W. Scribner, "Why Was There no Reformation in Cologne?" in Robert W. Scribner, *Popular Culture and Popular Movements in Reformation Germany*, 217.
79   The famous teaching order of Ursulines descends from Merici's community.
80   Conrad, *Zwischen Kloster und Welt*, 114.

two special points I aimed at in whatsoever order I should undertake."[81] Enlightenment came at a moment, her "Glory Vision" it came to be called, when "something
very supernatural befell me . . . I was abstracted out of my whole being, and it was
shown to me with clearness and inexpressible certainty that I was not to be of the
Order of St. Teresa,[82] but that some other thing was determined for me."[83] Soon after,
she learned what this thing was.

Mary's decision was, in her biographer's words, "to adopt the Institute of the
Society of Jesus for her congregation."[84] Others, whether friendly or hostile, called
them "the English Ladies," and by 1616, when they had sixty members and an empty
treasury, Mary took the fateful step of going to Rome to seek approbation from Pope
Gregory XV (r. 1621–23). Already the waters there had been poisoned against her by
the swirling, back-biting, mean-spirited politics of the English exiles, many of them
bitterly hostile to the Jesuits. The documents sent to Rome named Mary and her
companions "garrulous little females" whom some call "runaway nuns and apostolic
viragoes."[85] In 1625 fell the hardly surprising blow: the English Ladies' Italian houses
were ordered dissolved and further foundations forbidden.

In the following year an undaunted Mary Ward, who possessed nothing if not
courage, departed Rome for not the Low Countries but an entirely new mission field –
the German lands. She and her companions walked via Tyrol to Bavaria and then to
Austria, Upper Hungary (Slovakia), and Bohemia. They had come to the German
lands at the right moment, for in the mid-1620s the Catholic position in the Empire
stood at its zenith. No less a figure than the Jesuits' Father-General had supplied them
with "kind recommendations" to the confessors – all three Jesuits – of Emperor
Ferdinand II, Empress Eleanor (1598–1655), and Elector Maximilian I.[86]

The new Jesuitesses made their first German conquest at Munich, where in Maximilian's time the Jesuits held sway. Upon the Ladies' arrival the elector paid their
bills, gave them a furnished house, and settled 2,000 gulden per year on them as
provision for ten persons. They opened a school for girls, the first of its kind in
Munich, and began to teach the four Rs (the usual three plus religion), Latin, French,
Italian, and various handicrafts. They were quickly swamped with pupils – 465 girls
taught by ten sisters – and Mary wrote off to the Netherlands about her pressing need
for twenty more teachers, but good ones, "for God will not be served with other than
good ones."[87]

Even before the Munich school opened, Mary was off again, this time bound for
Vienna. There she laid her cause before the emperor, who responded by offering
quarters for her work. This done, she traveled downriver to Bratislava, capital of
Habsburg Hungary (now Slovakia), and then on to Prague in the summer of 1628.
In all three Habsburg capitals she either founded or attempted to found new houses
for her community. Nothing quite like this English whirlwind or the schools it
planted had ever been seen in the Catholic German lands.

81 Margaret Mary Littlehales, *Mary Ward: Pilgrim and Mystic, 1585–1645*, 54.
82 Mary had considered joining the Carmelites.
83 Littlehales, *Mary Ward*, 56.
84 Henriette Peters, *Mary Ward: A World in Contemplation*, 309.
85 Peters, *Mary Ward*, 341, quoting Dr. Matthew Harrison, rector of the English College at Douai.
86 Peters, *Mary Ward*, 431. Empress Eleonora, of the house of Gonzaga in Mantua, married Ferdinand in
    1622 after the death of Empress Maria Anna of Bavaria (1574–1616).
87 Peters, *Mary Ward*, 436.

The triumph was brief, for two years later all came crashing down, as misfortune piled on bad luck. First, a turn of policy set Jesuit opinion at the highest level in Rome against the Ladies, which cooled relations with the Jesuits in Munich and caused Mary to wonder, "What a world is this, when one good must hinder another!"[88] Second, at Vienna the return of Bishop Khlesl from his Roman detention inspired him to begin the campaign of denunciation that paved the way to the Ladies' downfall. In mid-1628 a Roman congregation ordered the papal nuncios in Naples, Vienna, and Brussels to suppress houses of the "Jesuitesses."[89] Then, on 31 January 1630, Pope Urban VIII (r. 1623–44) issued a bull which contained an authoritative Roman decision against the Ladies, alluding to them in the harshest language and condemning them "not for any substantial failings but simply because they were women, and therefore beings of inferior intellectual capacity."[90] Urban declared the so-called Jesuitesses' organization to be null and void, suppressed their communities, and forbade their members to reassemble. Over the following years Mary was several times arrested and interrogated, but in a final interview with the pope she was acquitted of the charge of heresy. Meanwhile, while most of the Ladies' communities were suppressed, the new one at Rome and the one at Munich (under electoral protection) survived. Otherwise, the great commission revealed by Mary's Glory Vision was over. In the fall of 1637 Mary Ward set off for the Low Countries, took ship for England, and returned to her native Yorkshire, where she died in extreme poverty in January 1645.

Mary Ward's story illustrates how women were caught up in a wave of evangelizing zeal that passed through the Catholic lands after 1600. Like the male Jesuits, she saw the Church as her true country, and her biography dramatically displays the flow of ideas and persons across national, linguistic, and political boundaries in a Catholic world deeply wounded, though not broken, by the great schism. The most striking thing about Mary and her English Ladies was that, forbidden to evangelize in the apostate kingdom of England, they went wherever they could work freely, and when that was forbidden, they moved on. From the Spanish Netherlands via Rome they entered the German lands as true Jesuitesses, hardened for the fight against ignorance, indifference, and error. Their German successes and their Roman failures tell much about the desperate need of the nearly wrecked Imperial church and about the limits of Roman willingness to abandon prejudice-armored tradition for that church's sake.

The work of Jesuits and Jesuitesses depended on their confidence in the power of truth, that is, of the Word, of enlightenment through education. In this they did not differ much from their Protestant rivals, who also aimed to shape a laity that was devout, disciplined, lettered, and loyal.

8. CATHOLIC EVANGELIZATIONS

In the earliest days the Catholic reformation bishops and their officials, at least those in the larger dioceses, hardly knew what was happening in the small-towns and rural

88 Littlehales, *Mary Ward*, 159. How serious this change of the Society's policy was to be can be judged by the fact that the Society's General forbade the Jesuits to give them the Last Sacrament. The Ursulines suffered the same fate.
89 The first Roman congregations, committees of cardinals assigned specific functions in the papal administration of the church and the Papal State, were established by Pope Sixtus V in 1588. Mentioned here is the Congregation for the Propagation of the Faith (i.e., missions), created by Pope Gregory XV in 1622.
90 Peters, *Mary Ward*, 566.

parishes. The first step to knowledge, as in Luther's Saxony in the late 1520s, was a visitation to assess the state of things. Many a Catholic visitor would have sympathized with, had he read it, Luther's cry of despair about the condition of religion among the common people. Still, in some places the visitation records reveal gradual progress, just as they do for Protestant territorial churches. In the summer of 1579 the bishop of Würzburg's visitors met with the chapter (assembly of pastors) of the deanery of Karlstadt in Franconia.[91] They arrived as the assembled priests were singing vespers, upon which the visitors read their credentials. Next followed a Mass, including a sermon by the chapter's dean, Pastor Johann Amersbach of Schwäbisch Gmünd, and a procession to the local hospital. Then the visitation proper began in the church's sacristy. First, a formal acceptance of the Tridentine profession of faith was required of those "who had not yet done so in this chapter."[92] A survey of the twenty-nine priests present revealed that twenty-two were living with women (concubines), and twelve had fathered children, while the others were served by a mother, a sister, or an elderly woman. Some admitted that they seldom confessed their sins, another that he never did, even though he did say Mass. Among the ten priests who reported suspiciously low numbers of "disobedient" householders in their parishes, one was singled out: "He has seven disobedient householders, whom the provost of the cathedral [the chief visitor] warned to [practice] the Catholic religion, and if they refused to accept Catholicism, they should quit the place."[93]

When the priests were asked about their parishioners, several problems emerged. One was that the local civil official (at Schwäbisch Gmünd) encouraged the people to "go out," that is, attend Lutheran services in the countryside, and prevented the pastor from punishing them. He told the priest that "they should go where they wish, for it would violate his conscience to bar anyone from the true, pure faith."[94] As for the clergy, it was found that eight pastors had refused to attend the visitation, another walked out during the proceedings, and three others were simply absent (though one of those, a neophyte, did arrive late, having heard of the meeting at the last moment, he said). The visitation closed with a summary by the chief visitor – the Fleming Dr. Typotius, cathedral cantor of Würzburg – of the findings, "especially concerning concubinage," and a warning that, "on pain of episcopal disfavor, the priests must give up that sin, behave in an honorable and priestly fashion, and plant Catholicism by teaching and example."[95] In addition, before the chapter dispersed, each must pay his outstanding debt to the bishop. After dinner the visitors rode back to Würzburg.

Sixteen years later, in the summer of 1595, officials from Würzburg came again to visit the deanery of Karlstadt. The long, interesting record of their findings conveys an entirely different tone than does the report of 1579. Parish by parish it surveys the deanery, this time measuring them not by households but by numbers of communicants. The survey also attends to the physical condition of the parish churches, a hint that the Catholic reformation had come to stay. There are reports of gifts by better-off residents for the repair and refurbishing of churches and their adornments, often

91 A deanery was a subunit of an archdeanery (or directly of a diocese). The assembly of its parish priests was called a "chapter" or "rural chapter" (*Landkapitel*). See Chapter 2, 16.
92 Luttenberger, ed., *Katholische Reform*, 435.
93 Luttenberger, ed., *Katholische Reform*, 436.
94 Luttenberger, ed., *Katholische Reform*, 436.
95 Luttenberger, ed., *Katholische Reform*, 437.

by initiatives from local officials – mayors and churchwardens (*Heiligenmeister*) – and with gifts from other laymen for these purposes. At Sundtheim there was a very severely damaged roof to repair; the windows were in such bad condition that "Mass cannot be properly celebrated when the wind blows a bit. The honorable and learned fiscal, Dr. Urbanus, . . . not only saw this but himself experienced that when His Honor celebrated at the right side altar in the choir, a rising wind presented the danger that the wind might blow the Host away."[96]

Comparable problems and deficiencies are cataloged. At Sundtheim there is "a very old, badly painted" retable to renovate, for which some burghers, including some Würzburgers resident in the village, have offered money. The churchwarden will collect 50 gulden for this purpose; the district official (*Amtmann*) will also contribute with the bishop's permission; and "the burghers are willing to contribute through gifts and taxes, according to their means."[97] Only after these notices of the local church's needs does the report deal with the spiritual state of the faith at Sundtheim, which is less heartening: "Catechism is taught every Sunday, but the youth, who most need it, don't come . . .. They [the youth] stay away from the Holy Mass, and only few attend, mostly women."[98] At Fuchstadt (297 communicants), some confess their sins, including the mayor and his sons, and the sexton, though he has not taken Communion, has promised to confess next Sunday. At Langendorff (550 communicants) things are better, the sacraments are properly administered, catechism is held at midday, and vespers are sung on Saturdays and Sundays, and the schoolmaster does his job. And so it goes, things being a bit better in this village, rather worse in the next, and in most a mixture of encouraging and discouraging signs. At Cressthal (350 communicants), for example, on weekdays the pastor has to say a "dry Mass,"[99] because they've not enough wine. The midwife will not swear her oath (to baptize infants according to the Catholic rite), but other matters are in order. All in all, a very mixed scene, but some lights can be seen in what sixteen years ago were very dark skies. Fewer Lutherans are reported, and there has been some progress against superstitions. At Binssfeldt, where the pastor is in any case neglectful of his duties, the farmers refused to forgo the traditional fire dance on St. John's Day, which went on until midnight, even though the next day was a Sunday.[100]

Such pictures could be replicated from comparable records from most Catholic dioceses, though the rhythm of push and pull among people, priests, and bishop varied in times of onset and measures of progress, regress, and stalemate. Force was used, but mainly in Lutheran places threatened with conformity to Catholicism. This happened mostly during the Thirty Years War, though the efforts were successful only where and when the will and the means to coerce coincided. Success required three steps: first, placement of Catholic priests in the parishes; second, persuasion of the people to the new religion; and third, legal restrictions on dissenters and waverers.

Success also required the collaboration of civil and ecclesiastical authorities, though their union in the same hands – the prince-bishops – was no guarantee of

96 Luttenberger, ed., *Katholische Reform*, 456–7.
97 Luttenberger, ed., *Katholische Reform*, 457.
98 Luttenberger, ed., *Katholische Reform*, 457.
99 The dry Mass (*missa sicca*) is a common form of devotion when a real Mass cannot be said. Offertory, Consecration, and Communion are then omitted.
100 The feast of St. John the Baptist (24 June). The widespread practice of lighting fires (especially on hilltops) and leaping over them on St. John's Eve (not without drink being taken) is still alive.

success. When the Rhine Palatinate fell to the Catholic armies in the early 1620s, the prince-bishop of Speyer recovered in principal his ecclesiastical authority over the churches of some Palatine districts. In this principality the rural people were experts in changing and refusing to change religion, as their forebears had been several times dragged back and forth between the Lutheran and Reformed faiths. The bishop had little if any success in converting the villagers back to the oldest faith. He failed for three reasons. First, the Palatine farmers had been Protestants for more than two generations, so Catholic practices came as an innovation rather than a restoration, and "it is never easy to impose new practices on an unwilling population."[101] Second, at Speyer there was never the will at the top – the bishop and the cathedral chapter – to use sufficient force to alter the situation. And third, many Catholics, churchmen and laymen, "were highly skeptical of reformed Catholicism."[102] In the end, while the exercise of force might win for the Catholic reformers, as it had for the Protestants, the opportunity to evangelize the common people, only patient, often dishearteningly unprofitable, and persistent work over generations could make the programs of evangelization stick.

When all of these and other forms of friction and inertia are combined with the end around 1650 of war and overt political conflict over religion, it becomes understandable, even necessary, to identify the Catholic reformation as not only older than the counterreformation but also by far more powerful and enduring. When did the Catholic reformation end? At different times and places, can be the only answer, depending on where one looks, but in hardly any case earlier than the second half of the eighteenth century. Then and not before, the great evangelizing of the common people, which the Protestants had initiated, came to its close. In the German lands, as in transalpine Catholic Europe as a whole, "the distribution still observable today of regions which have remained faithful to Catholicism reproduces, more or less, the map of the most intense and most numerous missions of the age of the Enlightenment."[103]

Important similarities can be discovered between the Protestant and Catholic reformations in the German lands. Among them are a general aim of reform to produce or at least encourage the formation of a dedicated and disciplined clergy and a devout and disciplined laity; a close collaboration with, and sometimes a fusion of, temporal and spiritual authority; an end to superstition and to the free-wheeling, wildly variegated religious life of the past; and a perceived need for hard, fast boundaries to mark off the true from the false churches. Against these must be set not only the obvious institutional, doctrinal, and liturgical differences among the confessions but also a fundamental difference in the tasks the communities assumed. The Protestant reformation claimed to be a restoration of true, that is primitive, Christianity as had existed in the Apostles' time but had subsequently been obscured, perverted, and even abandoned. Underneath this claim to break with the past lay, of course, a perennial resort to medieval learning and law to solve practical problems, such as

---

101 Marc R. Forster, *The Counter-Reformation in the Villages: Religion and Reform in the Bishopric of Speyer, 1560–1720*, 145.
102 Forster, *The Counter-Reformation*, 145.
103 Louis Châtellier, *The Religion of the Poor: Rural Missions in Europe and the Formation of Modern Catholicism, c. 1500–c. 1800*, 236.

the disposition of ecclesiastical properties. The Protestants nonetheless wanted to take as little as possible from the old church into the future.

The Catholics' situation was fundamentally different and, in the event, immeasurably more difficult. For, while the Protestants faced a church being deeply shaken, the Catholics had to rebuild a church shaken to its foundations, and to do so without surrendering its claims to be, as Charles V had declared at Worms in 1521, the legitimate and true legatee of all the centuries of belief and practice since the days of Christ Himself. They undertook this with the aid of men (and, against the church's norms, some women) no less dedicated and devout than the Protestant reformers and their disciples, but, unlike the latter, without benefit of the unquestionable authority of (in principle) an utterly unmediated Biblicism. Then, too, their church already labored under a reputation for corruption and resistance to reform, the Protestants at least had to create their own, new reputation in this respect.

It is thus a mistake to pose the churches as parallel formations, except in their public guise of confessions. Both formed new shells as participants in the public life of the Empire, but however religious the confessions may have been, they were never even tantamount to, much less identical with, the churches that formed their infrastructures. This distinction illustrates both the confessions' linkage to the Empire's public life, its politics, and suggests why they were so deeply disturbed and altered by the Empire's death.

15

Limits of Public Life – Jews, Heretics, Witches

Hath not a Jew eyes? Hath not a Jew hands, organs, dimensions, senses,
affections, passions?
William Shakespeare, *The Merchant of Venice*

All Protestantism, even the most cold and passive, is a sort of dissent.
Edmund Burke

Witchcraft celebrates / Pale Hecate's offerings; and withered murder, /
Alarumed by his sentinel, the wolf, / Whose howl's his watch, thus with his
stealthy pace, / With Tarquin's ravishing strides, toward his design / Moves like a ghost.
William Shakespeare, *Macbeth*

The rapid growth, large followings, and powerful leaders of the confessions in the
German lands vastly expanded the limits of public life, that is, the boundaries between
those who possessed defensible rights and those who did not. The massive, overwhelming scope of the religious division defied the traditional remedy for heresy,
which was judicial prosecution with three possible outcomes: acquittal, recantation,
or death. The Peace of Augsburg transformed heresy from a spiritual crime into a
question of temporal obedience, to be enforced – or not – at the temporal ruler's
pleasure. This law averted the terrible spectre of a general civil war by accepting the
lesser evil of a political toleration of religious differences. The Empire remained, on
the one hand, a Catholic polity that tolerated those of the emperor's direct subjects
who adhered to the (Lutheran) Confession of Augsburg. This is why the Calvinists,
who appeared on the scene only five or so years later, had to present themselves as
Lutherans with a difference. On the other hand, no territorial prince, Catholic or
Protestant, was required to tolerate subjects who refused to conform to his religion.
These dissenters were not arrested and prosecuted, but they could be forced to choose
between conformity or exile. On this new *convivencia* depended the future of Imperial public life.

Three categories of persons stood in turn at or even outside the bounds of the
Imperial *convivencia*'s redefinition of the limits of public life: Jews, non-protected
heretics (chiefly Anabaptists), and witches. Each group in its time was demonized as

"enemies of God," each passed in its own time more or less rapidly from demonization into formal or tacit toleration. Their experiences in the German lands suggest that the question commonly posed by the historians of toleration – why should deviant groups have been persecuted? – should be reversed: Why should they have been tolerated? And, once persecuted, why and how did they come to be tolerated by, or just beyond, the age of reformations' end? Although these questions cannot be answered globally, a comparison of their fates helps us to understand how the age of reformations redefined the boundaries of Imperial public life.

1. GERMAN JEWRY FROM PERSECUTION TO *CONVIVENCIA*

The history of the Holy Roman Empire's Jews between 1500 and 1650 displays two principal tendencies. First, and more important from the standpoint of Jewish history, is the movement of Ashkenazic Jewry out of the Empire's old-settled lands along the Rhine and the Danube into the vast spaces of Poland, Lithuania, and the Baltic. Second, within the Holy Roman Empire the gradual improvement of legal security encouraged both a growth of Jewish populations and a stabilization of their distribution that was to characterize the German-speaking world until well into the modern era. These two tendencies define the prehistory of what has been called "the zenith of Jewish influence in early modern Europe."[1] Looking forward from the situation of the Empire's Jews around 1500, no one could have foreseen this outcome.

During the generations between the terrible massacres around 1350 and the beginnings of the German Reformation, German-speaking preachers (chiefly Franciscans), writers, and craftsmen cast into image and text a repertory of anti-Jewish images, epithets, and libel, some of which would retain currency beyond the early modern era. It was the classic time of accusations of Jewish usury, Jewish desecration of hosts, and Jewish ritual murder of Christians. In 1453 all these threads came together in a massacre at Breslau that followed inflammatory sermons by the Franciscan friar Giovanni da Capistrano (1386–1456). He could not have imagined that one day the same hateful images would be turned against the mendicant friars.

By 1500 the princes and magistrates no longer needed to borrow from Jews what they could borrow from Christian creditors. The common people still harbored resentments of the Jews, and the better-off classes saw the wisdom of sending away unneeded Jews whose presence remained a temptation to riots and lynchings. Unlike in the western kingdoms that had expelled their Jews – England, France, Spain – over the sixteenth-century the Empire's legacy of persecution softened into a limited toleration and a certain degree of political integration. The strengthening of the Imperial monarchy since the later fifteenth century played a part in this change.

The reception of Roman law may also have eased to some degree the integration of Jews. When the Swabian jurist Johannes Reuchlin (1445–1522) was asked in 1511 whether Hebrew books should be confiscated, he replied no, because the Empire's Jews had the rights of "Roman citizens," which they shared with the Christians, though without relief from the dishonor to which Christ's death rightfully condemned them. Reuchlin's thinking belongs to a wider process of thinking about Jews in a newly practical way. The issue came to a head in 1544 at the Diet of Speyer, where

1 Jonathan I. Israel, *European Jewry in the Age of Mercantilism, 1550–1750*, 123.

Charles V issued a general charter of protection for Jews from acts against their synagogues and schools, unsubstantiated charges of ritual murder, and deprivation of goods and liberty on the public roads. This mandate, many times renewed (the last in 1712), eventually improved Jewish access to the Imperial courts. Even though territorial laws continued, more or less in violation of Imperial mandates, to place special restrictions on Jews, by the early seventeenth century the preference for regulation rather than expulsion provided Jewish communities with a new degree of security. The Giessen jurist Theodor von Reinkingk (1590–1664) formulated the new situation into a norm: "The Jews, if they live quietly and peacefully, are to be tolerated and may not be expelled."[2]

The routinizing of jurists' views on the Jews around 1500 mirrors the simultaneous decline of Catholic churchmen's interest in either Jewish theology or Jewish conversion. While the Protestant Reformation formed "in many respects, part of a longer and on-going trend of marginalization of the Jews," it also witnessed a new process of Jewish *political* integration, which began under Charles V.[3] Among the Protestant reformers there developed, however, a countercurrent of interest in Jewish religious ideas and of emphasis on religious difference. In the Protestant lands the new theology had contradictory implications for the Jews. On the one hand, devaluation of the sacraments weakened interest in the old blood libel and accusations of host desecration, which persisted longer in the Catholic lands. On the other, the Jewish refusal to convert, against his expectations, led Martin Luther to revitalize the old anti-Judaism among the Lutheran clergy. When Elector John Frederick I proposed in 1536–37 to expel the Jews from his Saxony, the Jewish leader Josel of Rosheim (ca. 1476–ca. 1554) castigated "that priest named Martin *Lo Tohar* – may his body and soul be bound up in hell," whose writings "so inflamed the rulers and peoples against us that it was well nigh impossible for the Jews to maintain themselves."[4] Josel went to the Smalkaldic League's assembly at Frankfurt in 1539 where, he said, "I [was able to] refute the arguments of Luther and Bucer and their followers [with proofs] from our Holy Torah."[5] In 1543 Luther's prince, Elector John Frederick, backslid and expelled the Saxon Jews. Simultaneously, Luther published his notorious tract, *On the Jews and Their Lies*, in which he condemned the Jews for refusing to accept the refurbished Gospel from his mouth and pen. He did not carry the day. Josel noted that Elector Joachim II of Brandenburg (b. 1505, r. 1535–71), in whose father's time thirty-eight Jews had been burnt alive at Berlin, had kept his word to tolerate them. While occasional expulsions occurred in northern lands until the end of the sixteenth century, Luther's harsh polemics did not generally reverse the movement toward a stabilization of the Jews' legal situation.[6]

The new climate both encouraged an Imperial awareness among some Jewish leaders, who hoped the emperor would shelter the Jews from the arbitrariness of princely policy and legislation, and led them to form new political institutions

2 J. Friedrich Battenberg, *Die Juden in Deutschland vom 16. bis zum Ende des 18. Jahrhunderts*, 16.
3 Dean Bell, "Jewish Settlement, Politics, and the Reformation," in Dean Phillip Bell and Stephen G. Burnett, eds., *Jews, Judaism, and the Reformation in Sixteenth-Century Germany*, 434.
4 Joseph (Josel) of Rosheim, *The Historical Writings of Joseph of Rosheim, Leader of Jewry in Early Modern Germany*, 329.
5 Rosheim, *The Historical Writings*, 329.
6 Only in one major Protestant territory, Hesse, did many Jews live.

quite unlike the older translocal Jewish institutions, which had been purely religious and/or economic. In 1529 at Günzburg in Upper Swabia, at a meeting of Jewish leaders who were alarmed by an accusation of ritual murder at Pösing in the Bavarian Forest, Josel of Rosheim, a remarkable Alsatian rabbi-turned-merchant, had been selected as a spokesman and given the title of "Commander [or Governor] of All Jewry in the German Nation."[7] It was a shrewd move. Whereas in former times emperors had frittered away to princes and cities the regalian right of Jewish protection in return for a tax, under Charles V a new policy of royal intervention began to appear.

Josel, who had attended Charles's coronation at Aachen in 1520 and had met Ferdinand at Prague in 1528, took up his new charge with alacrity. In 1530 he saw the two monarchs again at Innsbruck on their way to Augsburg. The story that Jews were spying for the Ottomans, he told the monarchs, was false, to which Charles responded by renewing his grandfather's charter of protection for the Jews. Dissatisfied with the charter's terms, Josel followed the emperor's train to Augsburg where, during the great Diet, he was called upon to debate publicly Anthonius Margaritha (b. ca. 1490), son of a prominent Regensburg rabbi and a Christian convert. In his freshly minted account, *The Whole Jewish Faith*, Margaritha had set out to expose Judaism as an un-Biblical religion, dangerous to the Christian faith, and he argued against Imperial protection and for the expulsion of the Jews from the Empire. Josel appeared before the emperor and estates on 25 June 1530 to defend his people against three accusations: the Jews slandered Christ and Christianity; the Jews proselytized Christians; and the Jews sought to destroy Christian rulers. He describes the outcome in his terse style:

> In that same year 5290 (1530) there was an assembly of all the princes of the Empire and the nobles, as well as countless ladies, in order to establish preventive laws and regulations, and the princes and nobles intended to abolish usury. At that time, with God's help, I stood firm, and I obtained from the Emperor the renewal of our privileges from the Emperor Sigismund. The accusers were silenced and there was peace in the land for a little while.[8]

Margaritha was by no means Josel's only problem, for when the emperor returned in 1530, the movement against usury and big business – "monopolies" – flared up again. It augured, as it always had, danger for the Jews and their livelihoods. Nineteen free cities had petitioned the diet against the Jews and decried the disorder and suffering they caused through alleged sharp practices, heavy interest, and traffic in stolen goods, which were protected by the courts and the territorial rulers. As none any longer needed the Jews, the urban envoys told Charles, he should either drive all the Jews from the South German lands or at least forbid them to take usury and force them to earn their living by honest work.

At Augsburg the voices raised for expulsion of Jews or severe restrictions on their businesses evoked two responses. On 12 August, Charles V issued a new charter of

---

7 Arno Herzig, *Jüdische Geschichte in Deutschland von den Anfängen bis zur Gegenwart*, 91. Here Josel bears a title that means "commander," that is, a deputy of the sovereign. At a later time he calls himself "governor" (*Regierer*) of all Jewry, a title that emphasizes his own authority. See further in this chapter.

8 Rosheim, *The Historical Writings*, 321–2.

rights in which he confirmed for all of the Empire's Jews the rights King Sigismund had issued to them in the Alsatian Imperial cities in 1433. Three months later, Josel drew up *Articles and Regulations*, which, in the name of Imperial Jewry, formulated rules and restrictions on Jewish business transactions. Addressed to the Imperial estates, it forbids, among other things, any Jew to lend money to a Christian at compound interest, or a Jewish community's council (*parnasim*) to refuse justice to any Christian who submits a complaint against any Jew. Josel tells why he undertook this task: "In my capacity as emissary of all the Jews I have been informed that several Jews in the Holy Empire and also in the principalities and various lands are behaving in many matters in an inappropriate manner, thereby causing unfair damage and losses to you and your subjects."[9] When he heard of these problems, says Josel, he wrote to the Jewish communities "and demanded emphatically that they, collectively and individually, or their authorized delegates, come to me at Augsburg during the meeting of the Diet."[10] They did so, and with the delegates' aid "I could decide upon and draw up on behalf of the Jewish community, a suitable ordinance for the Jews in the cities, the market-places, and the villages, as is detailed below."[11]

Although Josel finished this document too late for consideration by the Diet, he did so in the common way that representatives of Imperial estates brought complaints and requests before the emperor and the assembled estates. His action suggested that the Jews were a kind of general – non-territorial – Imperial estate that encompassed all Imperial subjects having a particular legal status. His language reveals his awareness of his role both as a representative of Imperial Jewry and a kind of Imperial official who could undertake to see that his people obeyed the rules he and their representatives – not the Diet – had prescribed for them. "Therefore, for the aforesaid reasons," he closes, "I, Josel, the Jew of Rosheim, governor of all Jewry in the German lands, together with other delegates of the Jews here at Augsburg, have resolved, explicitly and clearly to publish these articles in all the localities, and to observe them as is fitting."[12]

It was clear to Josel that the path to real security for the Jews ran to the emperor, not to the Diet, in which common political reason would always struggle against particular interests. He was hampered in this effort by the long absence of Charles V, who left the Empire after the Diet of 1530 and did not return until 1541. Then Josel's mission resumed. In 1544 Charles V as "supreme lord and judge"[13] over the Jews, commanded that, in the absence of believable witnesses, no Jew, male or female, should be arrested, tortured, robbed, or executed, and all charges (of ritual murder) against Jews must be referred to him alone. The Imperial police ordinance of 1548 confirmed the estates' exercise of regalian authority over the Jews, but it also regulated the usury question by permitting interest at 5 percent. Charles's successors through Rudolph II continued his policy and thereby strengthened hopes for Imperial protection of Jewish rights. Rudolph resided at Prague, the chief center of Ashkenazic Jewry in the late sixteenth century. Apparently well disposed to Jewish protection, in 1595 he quashed an action at Hildesheim that prosecuted Jews for incest

9 Rosheim, *The Historical Writings*, 383.
10 Rosheim, *The Historical Writings*, 383.
11 Rosheim, *The Historical Writings*, 383.
12 Rosheim, *The Historical Writings*, 387.
13 Herzig, *Jüdische Geschichte*, 91–2.

who contracted levirate marriages and attempted "to guarantee legal protection for their Jewish customs."[14] Still, Imperial police laws could be better enforced in the small territories of Imperial knights, counts, prelates, and cities than in the princely territorial states. When the landgrave of Hesse-Darmstadt proposed in 1626 to drive the Jews from his lands, the Imperial Chamber Court forbade him to do so. The landgrave, asserting that his princely "superiority" included a comprehensive "regalian right to admit [and expel] Jews," did so anyway.[15]

Over the course of the sixteenth century, royal patronage enabled Jewish tendencies toward estate formation to expand on the basis of the Jews' own communal institutions of government. The early modern Jewish community operated through a variety of communal institutions, of which the individual community council, "comprised generally of wealthy and scholarly members," functioned as "in a certain sense a 'state' within a 'state.'"[16] Above them developed regional councils and an elaborate network of courts of law. Jews also resorted to secular courts, though a Jewish synod held at Frankfurt in 1603 decided that "anyone who sues his neighbor in secular courts shall be compelled to free him from all the charges against him, even though the Courts decided in favor of the plaintiff."[17]

The tendency toward formation of a Jewish general estate in the Empire thus built on an elaborate tradition of self-governance, the further development of which required continuing royal patronage. This relationship reached a critical point shortly after 1600 in an affair that brought down on the Jews the emperor's disfavor and charges of treason. The trouble erupted in 1604 at Bonn, when Levi, a local Jew, was accused by some other Jews of treason against Elector Ernest of Cologne. Levi, whom Ernest had named in 1598 as overseer of all the Jews in his *Hochstift*, was accused by some other Jews of abuse of his office. He had damaged the Jews in general, caused the death of a Jew, committed tax evasion, and forged documents in the elector's name. In return, Levi accused his opponents of committing high treason against the emperor and the Imperial estates, and produced as evidence a set of Jewish regulations, which a group of Jewish notables had drafted at Frankfurt in 1603, and which his accusers had signed. The drafters of these ordinances, he alleged, violated Imperial authority by rejecting the jurisdiction of Christian courts of law. The Frankfurt assembly of 1603 had drawn up thirteen regulations, of which eleven concerned ritual matters of purely Jewish interest. The other two, however, dealt with genuinely political matters. The first established a system of five appellate courts (Frankfurt, Worms, Friedberg, Fulda, and Günzburg) to exercise appellate jurisdiction over the local Jewish communities; the second levied a general property tax to be paid monthly by all Jews. With these measures, the assembly "issued a police-ordinance comparable to those of other authorities in this era. Precisely this led to charges against them, since at this time questions of legislative competence and the right to tax were among the principal political issues."[18]

The Frankfurt ordinances never became law of any kind, and they came to light only because of their use as weapons of opportunity in the lawsuits. The charges of

14 Herzig, *Jüdische Geschichte*, 94.
15 Battenberg, *Die Juden in Deutschland*, 14.
16 Dean Phillip Bell, *Jews in the Early Modern World*, 95.
17 Bell, *Jews in the Early Modern World*, 107.
18 Birgit E. Klein, "Die Frankfurter Judengasse: jüdisches Leben in der frühen Neuzeit," 163.

high treason, however, eventually brought the affair before the Imperial regime at Prague. This city housed not only the emperor and his court, which had moved from Vienna in 1583, but also the Empire's largest, richest Jewish community. Its leaders had their own ideas about who possessed the right to speak for and exercise jurisdiction over the Empire's Jews, "because here is the highest rabbinical school under His Imperial Majesty."[19] The rivalry between west and east, Frankfurt and Prague, contributed, therefore, to the sharp rejection of all claims to general authority over the Jews, which the Imperial Aulic Council issued in the emperor's name. The Jews must acknowledge, it declared, that the Jews have been granted neither a territory nor a superior jurisdiction, but only a provisional authority. They therefore remain subject to emperor and Imperial estates. The grounds of this decision were perhaps less a desire to punish Jews than an insistence on the principle that the possession of a territory is the prerequisite for principal authority. No territory, no authority. This judgment on an intra-Jewish quarrel grown into a matter of Imperial concern placed a grave question before the nearly eight decades of progress toward Jewish self-administration as an Imperial estate.

By this time, around 1600, some 35–40,000 Jews (0.2 percent of the population) resided in the Empire, a number that could have fit comfortably within the walls of Cologne or Nuremberg. Their distribution was very uneven. Nearly a third lived in several larger communities (Prague, Vienna) or dispersed through the southeast. Very few lived in the northeast, where the princes had expelled their Jews since the 1490s, leaving only a few small communities. A good many more resided in the northwest, including the Low Countries, where few Jews had lived in earlier times; and about 3,000 lived in small and tiny communities in the southwestern lands. In the heartland of Imperial Jewry, the west central region (Mainz and the Middle Rhine, Hesse, the Franconian bishoprics, and the Wetterau), an unbroken tradition of Jewish urban life had survived the late medieval dispersals, and in the sixteenth century it experienced a truly remarkable growth.

At Frankfurt the Jewish community underwent an astonishing transformation. It rose in numbers from 110 in 1463 to 900 in 1569 to about 3,000 in 1610, at which point about 15 percent of the city's population consisted of Jews.[20] Just as great was the growth in Jewish wealth. Figure 15 shows the Jewish taxpayers as a percentage of Christian taxpayers, based on the civic property tax between 1566 and 1607. It shows that the relative increase of Jewish taxpayers affected all three tax categories, but it was particularly great in the middle stratum, those having declared taxable wealth worth between 900 and 4,000 gulden.

Always in the past, of course, prosperity had brought danger to the Empire's Jews. These Frankfurt figures suggest potential for a quickening of the old envy of Jewish success. They also heighten our sense of the threat created by prosperity without political power to protect its beneficiaries. By 1600 the norms of law and order had strengthened in comparison with earlier times: outright lynching of Jews had nearly disappeared, expulsions had become rare, and discrimination somewhat lessened. An urban riot or insurrection, a rare occurrence in these days, could nevertheless produce a dangerous moment for the local Jews. This happened in the mid-1610s, when the last

19   Klein, "Die Frankfurter Judengasse," 169.
20   Bell, *Jews in the Early Modern World*, 50.

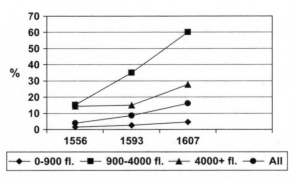

Figure 15. Taxpayers at Frankfurt am Main, 1556–1607 (Jews as a percentage of Christians)

old-style popular actions against Jews occurred at Frankfurt and Worms, homes to the largest Jewish communities in the Empire.

The insurrection at Frankfurt takes its name, "the Fettmilch rising," from Vinzenz Fettmilch (d. 1616), an immigrant gingerbread baker and a Calvinist. He became the popular leader of what began in 1613 as a classic late-medieval guild revolt against Frankfurt's patrician magistrates, always a dangerous situation for a city's Jews. Initially, the protests centered on the rights of citizens, who were kept more ignorant of them, it was alleged, than the Jews were of their own rights. Originally simply an argument, this claim potentially shifted the sights of discontent from the magistrates to the city's Jews. In 1614 new protests erupted, this time targeting usury, Jews, and "foreigners" (mainly Dutch merchants), who were accused of being cat's-paws for the regime.[21] Under the chieftainship of Fettmilch, who called himself "the new Haman,"[22] the rebels terrorized both the magistrates and Imperial arbiters and demanded expulsion of the city's Jews. On 22 August 1614 the baker of gingerbread led a large mob into the ghetto, where, having removed the old people and the children to the cemetery, they fought a street battle with armed Jews. Two Jews and one Christian were killed. Overpowered, the Jews withdrew, leaving their homes to be plundered by Fettmilch's followers. Meanwhile, 1,380 Jews fled Frankfurt by water, some up and some down the Main River.

When Imperial intervention put an end to Fettmilch's rising, there were no winners. The patrician political monopoly was broken in favor of the merchant and professional classes; the craft guilds lost their liberties; and Fettmilch and six co-conspirators were beheaded in Frankfurt's Horse Market. Their heads, mounted on iron spikes next to a city tower, were still to be seen there in Goethe's day. The Jews also lost, though not everything. At the emperor's command they were readmitted to Frankfurt in 1616 but limited to 500 households and to twelve weddings per year.

At Worms the story was much the same, beginning with an invasion of the ghetto on Easter Monday 1615 and ending with the Jews' return with their old privileges in

21 From the mid-sixteenth century onward, Frankfurt hosted one group of (Protestant) refugees after another, among whom were English who came during Mary's reign and a good many Dutch and German Calvinists.
22 This Calvinist knew his Bible. Haman (6th century BC?) and his wife plotted the deaths of all the Jews in Persia (Est. 3–7).

1616. In both cities, Emperor Matthias's intervention made the difference. German Jewry's course from lynching to expulsion to limited toleration with discrimination had largely been run. There was no thought of equality between Jews and Christians, nor did the Jewish minorities get free of the routine humiliations and insults that were (and are) fixed features of living as semi-strangers. To an increasing degree, however, the Empire's Jews were able to turn to the courts to seek protection of the rights they enjoyed by law. Outright coercion and expulsion of Jews grew ever less frequent, as the expanding regime of law and the courts secured them a place within, if still on the edges of, public life.

2. FROM PROSECUTION TO EXILE — HERETICS

For 300 years judicial prosecution had been the instrument of choice against heretics. It remained so in the German lands until the later sixteenth century. As in most of trans-alpine Europe, suspects were prosecuted not by the Church but by the civil autho-rities and courts, who were relatively unhampered by such niceties of canon law as defense counsels, restrictions on judicial torture, and the ability of convicted heretics to save their lives – the first time – by retracting their errors. Civil authorities, by contrast, sometimes tried suspects before summary courts and sometimes had them killed with-out trial. The Swabian League's assembly declared on 27 February 1528 that Anabaptists should be executed even if they recanted – men by the axe and women by water – and by fire if they did not. An Imperial decree of 1530 prescribed the death penalty for Anabaptists and "Sacramentarians" – presumably Zwinglians – on whom the main weight of repression in any case fell. German-speaking sectarians[23] accounted for most trials and executions for heresy during the sixteenth century. How many were lynched is uncertain, and the known figures for executions almost certainly understate the toll.

Table 5 gives the numbers of Anabaptists known, from Anabaptist martyrologies and from other sources, to have been executed in the German lands prior to the Thirty Years War. The total of 845 should be accepted as a minimum.[24] The persecution of Anabaptists, especially during the first three decades after the Peasants' War, con-centrated in the Empire's southern regions – from the Main valley southward – where more than 90 percent of the verified executions took place. The manner of execution is known for around half the cases: 56 percent were beheaded, the remainder were burned at the stake or drowned in about equal numbers.

The Anabaptists' time "under the cross" was brief. Most of the executions – 80 percent – occurred in a seven-year wave between 1527 – two years after the Peasants' War – and 1533, and nearly half fell in the years 1528–29. The wave ended with the Anabaptist kingdom at Münster in 1533–34, and thereafter the tempo of executions rapidly declined, though imprisonment, trial, and execution remained significant if diminishing threats, especially in southern Catholic lands, down to the eve of the Thirty Years War. More than half the executions occurred in Habsburg hereditary lands, chiefly in Austria and Tyrol, followed by Bavaria and Salzburg. Whereas the

---

23 "Sectarian" and "sect" have here the sense fixed by Ernst Troeltsch: religious communities unrecog-nized, whether or not by choice, by temporal authority.

24 Their compiler believes that the records of possibly 200 to 300 executions of Anabaptists have been lost, which would bring the figure, though not the geographical distribution, very close to those of the martyrologies. Clasen, *Anabaptism*, 370.

Table 5. Executions of Anabaptists in the German Lands, 1525–1618

Region	Anabaptist Sources	Certain	Probable
Switzerland	28/0	30	43
Habsburg lands	732/706	408	5
Southeast	153/124	113	9
Franconia	68/38	30	5
Swabia	120/81	41	46
Rhine Valley	75/55	22	17
Thuringia & Fulda	19/19	71	3
Uncertain	0/0	0	2
Total	1,195/1,051	715	130

Source: Rearranged from Claus Peter Clasen, *Anabaptism: A Social History, 1525–1618: Switzerland, Austria, Moravia, South and Central Germany*, 370. The figures from Anabaptist sources come from two different martyrologies.

modern literature on Anabaptism (especially Switzerland, Swabia, and Strasbourg) gives the southwest pride of place, the tale of martyrs played out chiefly in the southeast. The Catholic rulers of the southeast distinguished themselves by their readiness to ignore the protections of canon law and to have Anabaptists tried as rebels.[25] In Bavaria a ducal law of 1527 reserved to the duke the right to condemn even those who had recanted and taken the Sacrament. In Lower Austria in the same year, the provost was ordered to proceed against obdurate Anabaptists "without the solemnity of law;"[26] when the same was ordered in Tyrol, the regime at Innsbruck and the courts replied that such procedures were contrary to Tyrolean traditions and liberties. Eventually, in 1534 King Ferdinand admitted that most Anabaptists were not rebels, and thereafter the harsh Austrian policy toward Anabaptists softened.

Outside the southeast, authorities proved less inclined to execute Anabaptists, with or without trial, though the Bernese remained especially severe. In the north, by contrast, Anabaptists were rarely executed. Of fifty-seven accused Anabaptists arrested at Cologne in June 1565, only one suffered death. Even in the Low Countries, where heretics were tried before ecclesiastical courts, the toll remained much lower than in the southern lands. Of the estimated 1,120 to 1,600 cases handled by the Netherlandish inquisitor Pieter Titelmans, who spent twenty years hunting heretics during the mid-sixteenth century, only 127 (7.9 to 11.3 percent) led to executions. This figure agrees roughly with execution rates in other parts of Europe.[27]

Many Anabaptists sought peace and security in Moravia and elsewhere in the east, and many others, more than were executed, were reabsorbed into the locally dominant faith. Protestant clergymen worked very hard to understand why some were alienated from the newly reformed churches and how they might be brought over to the truth. It gradually became clear that it was no easy task to determine who was a sectarian and who was merely dissatisfied with prevailing religious standards. The history of Anabaptism tends to be cast in terms of constituted communities

25 Civil courts could try them either for heresy or for treason, and there was no reprieve for recantation of heresy.
26 Clasen, *Anabaptism*, 377.
27 Brad S. Gregory, *Salvation at Stake: Christian Martyrdom in Early Modern Europe*, 80.

and successions of leaders, but many, possibly most, of those who shared some of the beliefs and attitudes of the communities joined them either temporarily or not at all.

In some places dissenters were simply identified and told to leave. At Strasbourg the leading suspects were interrogated before a civic synod of pastors and magistrates, guild officials, and the obdurate were expelled. In territories the situation was more difficult, for once the authorities began to doubt the wisdom or justice of persecution, the full extent of the problem emerged of discriminating between dissatisfaction and dissent.

One such land was Hesse, where dissent was investigated and known dissenters expelled but not tried. Matthis Lotz, a miner who lived in a village near Marburg, was among those interrogated in 1535 after the Münster affair, in the suppression of which Landgrave Philip had been quite active. Matthis replied that though he had not been rebaptized, he rejected infant baptism, on which account he had separated himself from the official church. To the secular authorities, on the other hand, he acknowledged his duty to obey. When asked about Anabaptists, Matthis is recorded as saying,

> he doesn't know what to say, he had not spoken with any of them. When it should be like what is said of those in Münster – that one man has two or three wives or other things – he could not view that as right. He also said, he knows of no [true] church, and that is why he does not attend sermons, because at present the disreputable and the sinners are neither driven from the church nor excommunicated.[28]

Although Matthis's expressed dissatisfaction with the state of the Church led him to reject baptism, the principal mark of membership in the Church, by his own account he took no part in the sectarian reconstitution of the Church through rebaptism. His views, he affirmed, came not from sectarians but from God Himself, and "He knows nothing at all of rebaptism or the dogmas of its followers."[29]

The story of Matthis Lotz suggests a fundamental truth about sixteenth-century religion: the seeds of dissent, particularly Anabaptist dissent, fell on favorable ground among many who were alienated from the official church for one reason or another. A good many who were attracted to and even joined Anabaptist congregations recanted their views under coercion or the threat thereof. Some disappeared into quietism or unbelief, others hovered on the edges of or even rejoined the established church. Many who shared the Protestants' criticism of the old church declined to join the new.

This situation contained a special danger for the Protestants, because Catholics often argued that Anabaptism and rebellion were the ultimate destination toward which Lutheranism and Zwinglianism were but way-stations. Furthermore, the Protestants, dissenters themselves and rebels against what they believed a false religion, found it harder than Catholics did to advocate repression. At Strasbourg the two leading churchmen, Wolfgang Capito and Martin Bucer, admired the Anabaptists for the fervor of their faith and the purity of their lives. Capito even held that in all essential teachings the Anabaptists agree with other Christians. By 1533, however, Bucer saw that their tolerant attitude was hurting both the clergy's position in the

---

28 Günther Franz, ed., *Urkundliche Quellen zur hessischen Reformationsgeschichte*, vol. 4: 82. My thanks to Ellen Yutzy Glebe for this and the following translations from this text.
29 Franz, ed., *Urkundliche Quellen*, 4: 82.

city and the city's relations with the Lutheran princes. He therefore asked the magistrates to purge the city of dissenters from the established church. Recalcitrants were banished, and those who returned could be imprisoned, though not executed.

This dilemma made Protestant clergy and rulers less likely than were their Catholic counterparts to employ judicial repression against sectarians. This does not mean that all Catholic rulers hunted heretics with the zeal shown in Austria and Bavaria. The prince-archbishop of Salzburg did, but the prince-bishop of Augsburg declined to follow his Bavarian neighbor's example, and in the Palatinate, still a Catholic land at this time, the elector revealed his doubts by consulting eight universities about executing heretics.

Among the Protestants the soft policy of Strasbourg and Hesse did not predominate. Most leading Protestant reformers advocated repression, though in 1531 the Nuremberg pastors explicitly rejected it. Some Protestants objected even to imprisonment of Anabaptists, for "assent to truth should be free, without terror, through the Word of God."[30] Luther had originally been of this opinion – faith cannot be coerced – but Thomas Müntzer and the Peasants' War changed his mind. As late as 1528 he still held that hell was in itself sufficient retribution for heresy, but two years later he equated Anabaptists with rebels, as the Catholics generally did, and recommended their execution. Yet he and Philip Melanchthon remained uneasily in favor of expulsion for recalcitrant dissenters and of execution only for those who returned. This became a general attitude in Protestant lands, and only Electoral Saxony – Luther's land – and the County Palatine of Zweibrücken retained the death penalty prescribed for heresy by Roman and reiterated by Imperial law.

Anabaptists were a small and humble folk. The great heresies in the German lands, in each other's eyes, were the Protestant and Catholic faiths, the enormous size of which had forced the rulers to create a new version of Imperial public life as the best alternative to wars of religion. The Protestant reformation made religion a matter of conscience – not of individuals but of the princes and magistrates, whom the Religious Peace of 1555 allowed to undertake at will a religious cleansing of their lands or cities. This political solution placed the Empire in the middle of a European spectrum of religious coercion that ran with declining severity from west to east. To the west (excepting the Dutch Republic) lay a zone of more coercive regimes, some of which – France, Savoy, and England (especially in Ireland) come to mind – exercised what amounted to state terror. In the eastern kingdoms – Poland-Lithuania, Bohemia, and Hungary – predominated more or less uneasy *convivencias*.

The German princes and magistrates made practical use of their rights under the law of 1555 in various ways and to bewilderingly various degrees. In some of the larger free cities there was discrimination but little coercion, even though the magistrates, too, possessed the right to require conformity. At Ulm the Catholic minority was tolerated; at Strasbourg more or less secret Catholic Nicodemites held magistracies, and the magistrates tolerated Dominican women's convents and even sent their Protestant daughters to be educated (and occasionally converted) by the nuns.[31]

The will to cleanse appeared less strongly among Protestant rulers than among the Catholics, who made the most consistent efforts "to enforce as a principle of state the

---

30 Clasen, *Anabaptism*, 384.
31 Amy E. Leonard, *Nails in the Wall: Catholic Nuns in Reformation Germany*, 107–29.

mono-confessionalism guaranteed by the Religious Peace of Augsburg of 1555."[32] Among the many reasons for this difference should be mentioned the late onset of the Catholic reformation after almost two generations of largely defensive measures, the predominance of bishops among the Catholic princes, an incomparably effective international network of support, a tradition of religious coercion unbroken since the Middle Ages, and the relatively clear doctrinal and disciplinary program framed by the Council of Trent. Where the Protestants pioneered, therefore, the Catholics followed, but more efficiently and with more persistent measures. Everywhere the programs of religious cleansing left behind pockets of quiet dissenters and numerous Nicodemites.[33]

Looked at in a European context, the Imperial Religious Peace's great peculiarity was its restriction of the right to tolerate or coerce to a certain class of rulers, the Imperial estates.[34] While local *convivencias* did exist de facto in the German lands, nothing in the Empire came close to the remarkably complex regime of coexistence in the Lithuanian city of Vilnius. Here around 1600 there lived in relative peace Roman Catholics, Greek Catholics, Ruthenian Orthodox, Lutherans, Calvinists, and Jews.[35] In the Empire officially prescribed *convivencias* existed and persisted only in four southern free cities (called "parity cities") – Augsburg, Dinkelsbühl, Biberach, and Ravensburg – where Protestant majorities lived with Catholic minorities under bi-confessional regimes.

In the absence of external interference, *convivencias* encouraged the gradual accretion of codes of behavior that dampened overt conflict between the communities. They cast some real doubt on the almost universal belief of writers and politicians that a city divided in religion was a house built on sand. The fear of religious strife was nonetheless realistic enough, especially in the early decades of the Reformation, when no one could say how far differences would undermine such basic social institutions as marriage, feudal and business contracts, fraternal fellowships in the guilds, and neighborhood associations. The long coexistence of Christians and Jews, more or less punctuated by moments of aggression by the majority against the minority, may have somewhat prepared burghers for acquiring the mental and moral agility needed to preserve a sense of common fortune in the face of stark differences of belief.

While religious differences retained their potential for humiliation and violent aggression, they also generated self-limiting codes of everyday behavior, not by eliminating public signs of difference but by converting them into symbolic forms. The burghers in particular created striking symbolic markings of differences, most elaborately in the southern parity cities. Protestant Augsburgers named their sons Johannes; the Catholics preferred Maria for their daughters. The two different calendars also supplied easily readable confessional markers. Gradually, the codification of signs created what one investigator has called "the invisible boundary," which endured in some places and in some respects right down into the twentieth century. An Augsburg story from the eighteenth century illustrates perfectly how the

32 Arno Herzig, *Der Zwang zum wahren Glauben. Rekatholisierung vom 16. bis zum 18. Jahrhundert*, 9.
33 See Chapter 13. Nicodemites (the coinage is contemporary) were those who conformed to the established religion but practiced another, usually proscribed one, in secret. Nicodemus was the Pharisee who came to Jesus by night (John 3: 1–2).
34 The exceptions are discussed in Chapter 12.
35 I am grateful to David Frick for this information.

boundary worked in practice. Franziska Ludovika Meter, a Catholic, laid as condition for her resumption of cohabitation that her Lutheran husband should acknowledge her rights, first, to pray "aloud in the Catholic manner," to attend Mass, and to wear her Bavarian bonnet (*Riegelhaube*), which no Protestant woman would have done.[36]

Convivencias created space for dissent but also for personal religion, which could exist beneath and alongside – as well as within – the churches. Investigations conducted by Augsburg magistrates at the end of the sixteenth century reveal the depth, if not the extent, of resistance to the full confessionalization of society. In December 1598 they interrogated local artisans whom they suspected of Anabaptist activity. One of them, the goldsmith David Altenstetter (1547–1617), age forty-eight, was questioned about his failure to attend church. He replies that:

> he has heretofore been unattached in religious matters, for although born in a Catholic place, he later moved to Switzerland, where the Zwinglian faith is established. But after he came to Augsburg, he sometimes heard . . . the preachers of the Confession of Augsburg [i.e., Lutherans] and sometimes the Catholic preachers. He nonetheless joined neither religion, but if he has to join one, he will become a Catholic, though he will first need proper instruction in that faith.[37]

The goldsmith adds that sometimes he goes to services of one confession or the other, and though he likes "the cathedral preacher better than the Confession of Augsburg's preachers," on Sundays usually he stays home or goes for walks.[38] The reason is that "because the theologians of the Catholic religion and that of Augsburg have so stridently attacked one another, he has joined neither the one nor the other."[39] He was baptized as a child, not as an adult, and he denies any contact with or even knowledge of conventicles of any kind.

Three days later, Altenstetter is again interrogated, and again he asserts his detachment. No one, he hopes, "will force him, based on what he has said, to choose precipitously either the one religion or the other" and to learn more about the Catholic religion. If this wish is denied him, however, "he must accept the Confession of Augsburg, because he has at the present time insufficient instruction about the Catholic religion.[40]

This seeker, as a later age might have called him, knew his own mind and went his own way, which took him not into the constituted dissent of forbidden Anabaptism but to a benign but not uncritical neutrality between the confessions. His testimony illustrates an apparent paradox: whereas the coexistence of two religious communities in one city hastened the hardening of the cultural boundaries between them, it did not wipe out the space for individual choice.

Altenstetter objected, and surely many others with him, to the polemical preaching by the clergy, whatever their confession. Polemical speech and printed writings were the two great instruments of confessional competition and boundary policing.

---

36 Etienne François, *Die unsichtbare Grenze: Protestanten und Katholiken in Augsburg 1648–1806*, 189n. 92.
37 Bernd Roeck, ed., *Gegenreformation und Dreißigjähriger Krieg 1555–1648*, 105.
38 Roeck, ed., *Gegenreformation*, 106.
39 Roeck, ed., *Gegenreformation*, 107–8.
40 Roeck, ed., *Gegenreformation*, 108.

Once upon a time, the Protestants had had the better of the war of words and images, but by the turn of the century they were meeting their match in the Catholic polemicists. Provocation was built into the routines of everyday religious life, and harsh words formed a staple of the faithful's diet. Martin Luther had composed a hymn, "Lord preserve us in Your Word" (*Erhalte uns Herr bei deinem Wort*), first published in 1543, which opens with these lines:

> Lord, preserve us in Your Word
> Protect from murderous Pope and Turk,
> Who hate Jesus Christ, Your only Son,
> And seek to throw Him off His throne.[41]

A generation later, the Lutheran pastor Cyriakus Spangenberg included this piece in his collection of hymns. He glossed the title – "A Song for Children to Sing against the Two Archenemies of Christ and His Holy Churches, the Pope and the Turk" – with an explanation. "The Turk," he declares, stands for "tyrants and brutal men, who act with violence against the clear truth of the gospel," while the name "Pope" covers

> the entire antichristian horde of the papists, such as bishops, cardinals, monks, priests, and nuns, plus all false teachers, seducers, and false-tongued folk, such as Interimists, Adiaphorists, Sacramentarians, Anabaptists, Calvinists, Osiandrists, Schwenckfelders, Stancarists, Servetians, Sabbatarians, Davidists, Majorists, Synergists, etc., and all others who err grievously in one or more articles of Christian doctrine, defend their errors, and persecute, insult, or abuse true teachers and seduce many unsuspecting folk.[42]

Spangenberg seems to call for unremitting, bloody war between the confessional communities, but he did not, and this is the point. Long lists of heretics inspired no one to act. Indeed, one can say more generally that, depending on circumstances, the ritual exchange of violent words and heavy accusations may well have reduced the impulse toward violent deeds.

This culture of differentiating reproach, insult, and condemnation was not symmetrical. For the Catholics, of course, the dissenting faiths were equally objectionable. Although the Lutherans regarded the Catholics in the same way, the spread of the Reformed faith in Lutheran lands from the 1560s and 1570s posed a new and more immediately dangerous challenge. The Reformed clergy, after all, professed to be good disciples of Luther, perhaps even better than the Lutherans. This claim hardly fooled most Lutheran clergy, whose typical reaction is captured by a Pomeranian hymn composed in 1585:

> Lord, take the Calvinists with their deceit and spite,
> And make them scuttle away like crabs!
> Cast down their crafty tricks
> And melt their counsels like the snow.

41 In a tamer modern version the second line ("Und steure deiner Feinde Mord") reads in English (by Catherine Winkworth) "Curb those who fain by craft or sword."
42 Ernst Walter Zeeden, *Konfessionsbildung: Studien zur Reformation, Gegenreformation, und katholischen Reform*, 333–6. The anti-Catholic names refer to persons, the others to particular Protestant or Spiritualist doctrines.

So that Your dear true Christian band
May praise You throughout all time.[43]

At the height of the intra-Protestant struggle between 1570 and 1600, relations between Lutheran and Reformed Christians were sometimes as bitter as those between Protestants and Catholics. Electress Anna of Saxony warned her daughter, Elizabeth, not to attend Reformed services with her husband, the Elector Palatine, and when Elizabeth's baby was born dead, Anna wrote to her that the child was better off dead than a Calvinist.[44]

Even strongly constituted *convivencias* could be disrupted when differences related to religion impinged on public life. Such was the case with the quarrel between the old and new calendars. In the fall of 1582, Pope Gregory XIII introduced an improved ("Gregorian") calendar that shortened the month of October by ten days: Thursday, 4 October 1582 (Julian), was followed immediately by Friday, 15 October 1582 (Gregorian).[45] Lutheran publicists took up the challenge. The Württemberg court preacher Lucas Osiander (1534–1604) attacked it as a tyrannical violation of Christian liberty and opined that the pope would do better to reform "the errors, abuses, and terrible conditions in the papist church."[46] In vain did the astronomer Johann Kepler (1571–1630), himself a Lutheran, defend Gregory's calendar, writing that "many proposals were made, but I don't know whether a better way could be found than the one introduced by the pope."[47] At Vienna the Tyrolean Jesuit Georg Scherer (1540–1605) joined the fray and did his part to make the calendar affair into a polemical donnybrook. While the calendar was promptly adopted or rejected in countries having exclusive official religions, such as Spain or England, it caused much trouble in the German lands, especially in the small states and most of all in parity cities. The trouble only began with the difficulties of doing business across confessional boundaries and the chaos threatened in organs of the Imperial government, notably the Imperial Chamber Court. Far worse were the threatened and real effects in confessionally mixed cities, where the celebration of the great Christian feasts on different days pointed up the claims of each confession to possess and practice the true faith.

Convivencias might be made tough by habit, but they were inherently vulnerable to certain kinds of challenges. Strong, offensive words were the order of the day, but the calendar affair was much more than a battle of words. Magistrates in the four parity cities – Augsburg, Dinkelsbühl, Biberach, and Ravensburg – did attempt to introduce the new calendar, something the Protestant territorial states did not do until a century later. Nowhere did the move rouse a more terrific storm than at Augsburg, by this time the Empire's largest city. In January 1583 the magistrates declared their intention to introduce the new calendar if the prince-bishop of Augsburg did. This notice unleashed a tornado of words from the city's Lutheran preachers, who accused them of violating the peace of 1555, to which the magistrates responded by citing Luther's and Melanchthon's counsels to obedience. The Catholics stood firm, the

43 Zeeden, *Konfessionsbildung*, 334.
44 For a more general treatment of Lutheran-Reformed relations, see Chapter 13.
45 See Chapter 14.
46 Hildegard Traitler, *Konfession und Politik. Interkonfessionelle Flugschriftenpolemik aus Süddeutschland und Österreich (1564–1612)*, 143. He was the son of the theologian Andreas Osiander (1498–1552), a (losing) participant in a post-Luther doctrinal controversy.
47 Roeck, ed., *Gegenreformation*, 102.

Protestants were split, and appeals for support to powerful nearby princes, Catholic Bavaria and Protestant Württemberg, enlarged the bitterness and violent potential of the quarrel.

Meanwhile, at Augsburg every important feast day became an occasion to stir the pot anew, for the struggle was threatening to change the conditions of the city's *convivencia* and turn enmity and disdain into open confessional hostility. Protestants sauntered through the streets on the old calendar's feasts, while their Catholic fellow artisans had to work, just as Catholics did on the new calendar's corresponding feasts. The butchers, an almost exclusively Protestant trade, refused to slaughter in preparation for the Catholic feasts, so the bishop's officials went short on meat. In response, the Baumeister, a high magistrate, withdrew licenses from six Protestant butchers and redistributed them to foreign butchers from the surrounding lands. Then, in mid-1584 the struggle took on a whole new dimension, as a rift opened between the clergy and the magistrates over the calling of new preachers.

In May 1584 the Imperial Chamber Court at Speyer tossed a spark into this powder keg by confirming the magistrates' right to introduce the new calendar into Augsburg because it was a "secular and political matter."[48] After several Protestant magistrates were dismissed from office, the Protestant clergy began to work their flocks up to a fury. Nothing like this had happened since the days of the Interim a generation ago, as the city rolled toward a test of power between the city council and the Protestant clergy backed by their people. The matter came to a head on 4 June 1584, when the city council deposed and banished the agitating Lutheran pastor Georg Mylius (Müller, 1548–1607). After a mob snatched him at a city gate and brought him to safety, news ran like wildfire through the city, and a great crowd – butchers and weavers in the van – pushed its way to city hall. Shots were fired by the council's guards, shots followed from hotheads in the crowd, and one magistrate was hit. "It is never a good thing," muttered one artisan, "now City Warden Rehlinger has a boat full of blood, the city guardian is shot at but not yet hit, and things continue so."[49] It was a reprise of the Schilling affair of 1524, only this time at least 3,000 Augsburgers fled the city.

In the end the Catholic magistrates called the Protestant clergy to parlay. Augsburg's deep culture of negotiation and compromise favored a peaceful settlement. The proposed terms allowed Protestant churches to celebrate Pentecost by the old calendar, if they would otherwise accept the new one. The pastors balked, arbiters circulated, committees formed, and documents were prepared. The Catholics blamed Mylius and the Protestant churchwardens; the Protestants, unsurprisingly, blamed the magistrates, Catholic overrepresentation in the city council, and the great Catholic trading families. In the following year, 1585, the magistrates proceeded to action against the militants, the "true hearts," who claimed to speak for Protestant Augsburg. The regime banished those who would not accept the agreement and warned the preachers to obey. The latter called on the leading Protestant powers to support them, but in the end the magistrates prevailed. "It remains to note," wrote the Protestant chronicler Paul von Stetten (1731–1808), "that following this agreement, the burghers'

---

48 Paul Warmbrunn, *Zwei Konfessionen in einer Stadt: Das Zusammenleben von Katholiken und Protestanten in den paritätischen Reichsstädten Augsburg, Biberach, Ravensburg und Dinkelsbühl*, 362.
49 Warmbrunn, *Zwei Konfessionen*, 367n. 47.

trust in the magistracy as well as in the clergy grew much stronger and long endured."[50] Half of his judgment is true, for the calendar affair did consolidate the Protestant citizenry behind their clergy but not behind the magistrates.

The Thirty Years War put Augsburg's *convivencia* to two great tests, the first when the Imperial army came in the 1620s, the second when the Swedes came in 1632. Each confession failed its respective test and seized the chance to rule the city alone. Still, reason encased in custom is tough, and after the war the old order could be restored to live on for the rest of the Empire's existence. Living with people you don't like, or of whose religion or race you disapprove, is a learned skill. There were persons, however, with whom very many in this age were unwilling to live on any terms. This applied above all to a category of persons who, unlike the Jews, the Anabaptists, the Protestants, and the Catholics, formed a real community only in the imaginations of those who feared them. They were witches.

3. PURGING SATAN'S SERVANTS – WITCHES

Witchcraft was the capital crime of manipulating supernatural forces to do harm, for profit or vengeance, to another person or persons. When late medieval inquisitors turned their attention from heresy to witchcraft, it was an inconceivable, even mysterious phenomenon that supplied no concept of itself. How to understand it at all? The answer preferred by the investigators was diabolism: the witches formed a kind of counter-church of Devil-worshippers. The diabolic theory supplied the first means of understanding witchcraft as more than simply a random practice.

As the new idea migrated from the western Alps toward the Rhine, it challenged and supplanted older notions of witches as evil spirits who roamed the countryside and disturbed people in their dreams. The idea spread because it could explain for the first time a thing, witchcraft itself, the existence of which almost everyone accepted. Yet this semi-theological conception never meshed with the judicial process in a completely satisfactory way, for the same pressure to rationalize and explain that produced the diabolic theory, also contributed to growing skepticism about the possibility of uprooting the crime by questionable judicial means. Here, as in so many other movements of the time, popular sentiments collaborated with learned theory, with the result that the latter gained eventual supremacy over the former but was itself radically changed. The collaboration lasted for about 200 years from the later fifteenth to the later seventeenth century. Its main phase, the great early modern witch-panic,[51] was surprisingly brief, lasting roughly from 1580 to 1660.

According to the diabolic theory, Satan formed his church, the witches, by means of pacts with individuals on whose flesh he put an indelible fingerprint – a parody of baptism – to mark them as his own. It was not easy to understand, and never became easier, why his flock was predominantly female. They were not so at first, and in the early prosecutions in the Jura Mountains of western Switzerland, the accused were predominantly male. This was just one of the many problems examined by a contemporary book on the subject, the *Hammer of Witches* (Latin: *Malleus Maleficarum*;

50 Warmbrunn, *Zwei Konfessionen*, 374.
51 An unsatisfactory term for what happened, but no other term serves as well. "Witch hunt," for example, applies chiefly to the actual prosecutors and judges and by extension to their demonological theorists.

German: *Hexenhammer*), first printed at Strasbourg in 1487. Its author was Heinrich Institoris (Kramer, ca. 1430–1505), an Alsatian Dominican who specialized in the study and prosecution of witches. In this he was active from the end of the 1470s in the ecclesiastical provinces of Mainz, Cologne, Trier, Salzburg, and Bremen.[52] He wrote his notorious book following several failed attempts to prosecute witches in Upper Swabia and in Tyrol, where the burghers of Innsbruck repulsed him and the bishop of Brixen/Bressanone declared him mad. The *Hammer* was Institoris's vindication, perhaps also his revenge. Although a great, messy farrago of legend, lore, and experience, it became famous because of its utility and its demotic qualities. Institoris's book supplied a theory (or at least an idea) of the crime of witchcraft. He associated it with women; and it promised help to the civil courts, which in Institoris's day still employed oral procedure and non-evidentiary methods of proof.

To have practical value, Institoris's book required a pre-existing demand for new means of protecting the common good from witches. The key lay in an analogy between the ancient witchcraft and the new diabolic heresy. Institoris reports that in 1480 he was called to a place near the Upper Swabian Imperial city of Ravensburg, where "a very savage hailstorm was stirred up, and for a distance of one [German] mile it crushed the produce, crops and vineyards. . . ."[53] The matter was reported, "the popular outcry necessitating an inquisition," since most of the burghers believed that witchcraft was at work. Institoris went to the town and "conducted an inquisition . . . for half a month. The trail led to two persons in particular (though the number of other suspects was not small)."[54] Next day one of them, a bath-attendant named Agnes, was interrogated by the mayor and the magistrates. Under torture before witnesses, "she asserted her innocence during the first onslaught with the spirit not of a woman but of a man," but when freed from her chains, "she freely revealed all the crimes she had committed."[55] Because there were no witnesses to her apostasy or to her carnal commerce with an incubus, only a confession could condemn her. Both Agnes and the other accused woman having confessed, they "were burned to ashes on the third day." While contrite Agnes embraced the cross, "eager to die in order to escape the Devil's injuries," her fellow condemned woman, who had lived for twenty years with her incubus, disdained to do the same.[56]

The Ravensburg trial reveals that in 1480, a hundred years before the onset of the great witch-panic, in the southern German lands the connection between the traditional fear of witchcraft as harm to neighbors had begun to fuse with the diabolic idea. Still, by Institoris's account only one act, the defendant's confession, gave any evidentiary substance to the theory, and slight substance at that. The hailstorm concerned local folk more than did the demonologists. The process itself had not made clear why service to Satan, apostasy, and sex with a demon should be linked to crop damage, no more than why women should be especially attracted to the service of Satan. As for disbelief in witchcraft, "out of ignorance of the hidden causes,"

52 The book was printed under the names of Institoris and another Dominican, Jacob Sprenger (ca. 1435–95), Institoris's colleague as inquisitor-general, who seems to have had no interest in witchcraft, as distinct from heresy.
53 Henricus Institoris, O.P., and Jacobus Sprenger, O.P., *Malleus Maleficarum*, vol. 2: 335.
54 Institoris and Sprenger, *Malleus Maleficarum*, vol. 2: 335–6.
55 Institoris and Sprenger, *Malleus Maleficarum*, vol. 2: 336.
56 Institoris and Sprenger, *Malleus Maleficarum*, vol. 2: 338.

Institorus declares that this error "is refuted by all the Doctrines ... [and] it is attacked more strongly by St. Thomas when he condemns it as heresy, saying that this error is rooted in heresy. . . ."[57] As for the women, Institoris opines, a woman is intellectually like a child and "more carnal than a man."[58] "Everything is governed by carnal lust," he judges, "which is insatiable in [women]."[59] Villagers, who knew a lot about lust, presumably didn't need the inquisitor's citations to Terence, Lactantius, and Cato to demonstrate that most of those suspected of malefice were older women. And malefice, not anthropology, was clearly their main concern. Collaboration did not mean agreement, and this distinction, a recognized practice and a shaky theory, ran right through the great age of witch hunting.

To characterize the European explosion of witch hunting between 1580 and 1660 as a "witch-panic" is incomplete but not misleading. During this period at least 110,000 persons were prosecuted (many more were accused) for the crime of witchcraft, of whom something fewer than half were convicted for the crime. Around three-quarters of the victims were women. The sudden eruption and just as sudden subsidence of the wave puzzled contemporary observers as much as it does modern historians. The Burgundian demonologist-judge Henri Boguet (1560–1619) estimated that there were 300,000 witches in France and 1.8 million in all of Europe, and that they were multiplying like worms in a garden. His estimate was modest compared to the imaginings of an eighteenth-century German lawyer who boosted the figure to 9 million.

Although the historians have stripped the witch-panic of many fantasies, an overall explanation remains elusive. Theories range from the fabulous to the sober to the amusing. Witch hunting was a persecution of an ancient, pre-Christian religion; a war of men against women; a campaign of Church and State for social control; a subjugation of rural, oral culture by urban, literate culture; a tool of the Catholic counter-reformation; a mass delusion caused either by ergotism during the "Little Ice Age" or indulgence in tea made from hallucinogenic plants.[60] There are so many theories because no one idea seems to correlate the data, and the more the overall problem is studied, the more bewildering it grows. The most stabilizing factor seems to have been the strength of the State. The heartlands of the witch-panic lay in the western tier of the German-speaking and the eastern sector of the French-speaking lands. In this zone, practically devoid of strongly centralized governance, the issue came relatively slowly to resolution and the greatest numbers of prosecutions and executions occurred. The reverse is true for strongly governed lands, probably because here the growing skepticism of judges, lawyers, and others about prosecuting for witchcraft could more easily influence the administration of law. What eventually halted the witch-panic was not only that the skeptics – about judicial efficacy, rarely about witchcraft itself – made a strong case, but also that the skeptical officials, judges, and clergymen could do something about it. A second consistent factor is social milieu, for witches were accused in the countryside and the small towns, but not in the large cities.

57 Institoris and Sprenger, *Malleus Maleficarum*, vol. 2: 143.
58 Institoris and Sprenger, *Malleus Maleficarum*, vol. 2: 117.
59 Institoris and Sprenger, *Malleus Maleficarum*, vol. 2: 122.
60 Ergotism is a form of poisoning produced by eating grain infected with a fungus. Under the name "St. Anthony's fire," it has been advanced as a explanation of bewitchment.

The German lands formed by far the greatest cauldron of the witch-panic. They contributed between a third and a half of the persons executed for witchcraft in Europe – more than 22,000 and perhaps as many as 30,000 souls. Temporally, the panic in the German lands conformed to the European pattern: a first peak in the late 1580s and 1590s, a second between 1618 and 1630, and a third in the 1660s. Thereafter the whole process began to decline until the early eighteenth century. Politically, too, the witch-panic in the German lands resembled the European pattern, for the strength of governance seems to have been decisive in the movement's shape. Table 6 shows current estimates based on the internal boundaries of today's German Federal Republic.

Translating these figures into early modern political geography reveals two major zones of witch hunting. The zone of relatively few trials and executions encompasses the Lower Rhenish area (Cleves-Jülich), the northern and eastern parts of the northern plain (Electoral Brandenburg, Electoral Saxony, but not Mecklenburg), and Bavaria.[61] The second zone of relatively many executions and trials covers Lorraine, the Rhenish electoral states (Trier, Cologne), Westphalia, Nassau, Swabia, and Franconia. Large, well-consolidated territorial states prosecuted and executed few witches relative to their sizes and populations; highly fragmented lands in the Empire's old heartlands prosecuted and executed many. The well-consolidated southeast (Bavaria, Salzburg, and Austria) executed far fewer persons (ca. 1,800) than did the highly fragmented southwest and Franconia (ca. 8,000). Even within the fragmented regions, large states (Württemberg, Hesse, and Cleves-Jülich) were less active than small ones. The Palatinate, which lay in the same region as the great witch hunting prince-bishoprics – Bamberg, Würzburg, Mainz, Cologne, Trier – declined to prosecute witches at all.

Confession is another guide to the patterns. In principle, the Catholic theorists of witchcraft were more severe than the Protestants. Perhaps this happened because of the shock the Catholic Church had received from the Protestant reformation, for German Catholic severity certainly did not reflect the general thinking of the Catholic experts. In the Mediterranean lands of intact Catholicism, Spain and Italy, the inquisitorial courts acted earliest to stop prosecuting persons accused of witchcraft. In the German debates about witchcraft, Protestant authors tended to be more open to change, Catholic ones more bound to tradition. The rest of the picture is quite mixed. Convinced demonologists, such as the Catholic Martin Del Rio (1551–1608), an Antwerp-born Jesuit of Spanish descent, saw no problem in prosecuting witches as agents of a vast diabolic conspiracy. Convinced skeptics, such as the Protestant physician Johan(n) Weyer (1515–88), a Netherlander, counseled caution concerning accusations of witchcraft because the crime could not be prosecuted fairly under accepted procedural norms. The skeptical position first surfaced in legislation, however, in Catholic Bavaria, where it influenced the witchcraft law of 1611, "the most detailed law ever drafted on this subject."[62] In the small Lutheran duchy of Saxe-Coburg during the 1620s, opponents of prosecution borrowed from the Catholic skeptics in Munich, while proponents took arguments from a Jesuit. Arguments aside, in practice the Catholic states executed many more witches than did their Protestant counterparts. Of the thirteen Imperial lands having the most deaths, ten were Catholic (seven ecclesiastical, three secular), two Calvinist, and one Lutheran. The Catholic

---

61 Note that Northern Bavaria in Table 6 refers not to the historic duchy but to eastern Franconia.
62 Wolfgang Behringer, *Mit dem Feuer vom Leben zum Tod: Hexengesetzgebung in Bayern*, 11.

Table 6. Executions for Witchcraft in the German Lands

Land	Executions
Baden-Württemberg	3500
Northern Bavaria (Franconia)	4500
Southern Bavaria (Old Bavaria, Swabia)	1500
Hesse	2000
Saarland	500
Rheinland-Pfalz	2000
North Rhine-Westphalia	4000
Schleswig-Holstein & Hamburg	500
Lower Saxony & Bremen	1500
Mecklenburg-Hither Pomerania	1000
Brandenburg & Berlin	500
Saxony, Saxe-Anhalt, Thuringia	1000
Total	22,500

Source: Wolfgang Behringer, ed., *Hexen und Hexenprozesse,* 193, based on the present political geography of the German Federal Republic, which excludes the Austrian lands, Switzerland, the Franche-Comté (Imperial Burgundy), the Spanish Netherlands, and the Dutch Republic.

lands on this list accounted for four-fifths of known executions.[63] Among the Protestant polities, the pendant to the Catholic prince-bishoprics among witch hunting lands were the Imperial counties under Reformed rulers.

Strength of states and confession are thus two determinants of the intensity of witch hunting in the German lands. The study of German witchcraft trials has yielded another unambiguous if startling factor: popular pressure from the villages and small towns, the classic theaters of witch hunting. In the town of Siegen (Nassau) in the 1650s, the magistrates lobbied for the prosecution of witches, who made "compacts with the Devil, using forbidden spells against both men and animals, robbing milk from cows by magical means, making human skin hard and impenetrable, magically closing boxes and chimneys ... and all sorts of other magical things that are practiced all over the place." Such practices "are to be regarded as a powerful skill, against which soon no one will be able to protect and guard his children and servants."[64] The magistrates' blending of the diabolic concept with ordinary malefice suggests the prescience of Heinrich Institoris. It was widespread by this time. Practices such as "forbidden things, ceremonies, and illicit charms," declared a 1591 mandate in Trier, "open the door for the Hereditary Enemy to sow his cursed seed."[65] Collecting the grease from the church bells on New Year's Eve and mixing it with fat to heal the

---

63   Wolfgang Behringer, *Hexen: Glaube, Verfolgung, Vermarkung,* 61. At the head of the list is the duchy of Lorraine (2,700 deaths), followed by the ecclesiastical polities of Cologne (2,000), Mainz (2,000), Würzburg (1,200). Reformed Bern and Lutheran Mecklenburg each had around 1,000 deaths. These are the principal Protestant polities. I have omitted one entry for Mainz, which appears twice on Behringer's list.

64   Gerhard Schormann, *Hexenprozeße in Deutschland,* 105–6.

65   Schormann, *Hexenprozeße in Deutschland,* 106.

wounds of man and beast might be an idle superstition, or it might be a sign of Satan's service. This is local knowledge: witchcraft was a local matter generalized only as an idea. While "the rulers had no special interest in trials for witchcraft, the rural population established a veritable inquisition."[66] If this is so, then those are right who hold that the witch-panic arose from a "great hatred" in everyday life.

Most witch hunts began with local accusations, which developed pressure from below. Their multiplication in a weakly governed polity created the stuff of the great panics, which arose not only in ecclesiastical polities, well-known centers of witch hunting, but also in popularly governed lands. There is a very striking case that drives the point home. For years the Habsburg regime in Innsbruck refused demands to hunt witches from the federated communes of the Prättigau, a region now in Switzerland bordering on the Austrian province of Vorarlberg.[67] Between 1649 and 1652 the valley federation bought its freedom and joined the free republic of Graubünden (now a Swiss canton), whereupon its three tribunals of self-appointed judges embarked on a wild campaign against witches, called the "Great Witch-killing" (*Groos Häxatöödi*). This campaign "occurred because of pressure from the peasant communities, 'so that the evil will be exterminated.'"[68] Between 1652 and 1660 the courts sentenced, without reference to Roman law or theology, more witches to death than were executed in the much larger, neighboring Vorarlberg. In the neighboring county of Vaduz, the count had nearly 10 percent of the entire population killed, a level never reached in the two busiest witch hunting polities of the Empire, the duchy of Lorraine and the electorate of Cologne. Finally, the emperor dispossessed the count and imprisoned him for life.[69]

The collaboration of rulers with local communities explains much, but every answer raises a new question. If behind most of the witch-panic lay "the great hatred" between neighbor and neighbor, what explains its timing? Two answers offer themselves: first, local populations suffered long-term disruptions of their lives by the market, overpopulation, land hunger, war, and famine; second, local populations took advantage of stronger governance to rid themselves of an ancient evil their ancestors had been forced to suffer. The first explanation fits the profile of the iron century between 1560 and 1650, the second suggests a continuation of the sixteenth-century movement for good government. Possibly, both are right. The pressure of intra-village competition went back to the decades before the Peasants' War of 1525, the programmatic expressions of which demanded stronger governance, law, and order. As conditions deteriorated from the mid-century on, when the recovery was creeping to its end, mounting competition within the villages and small towns heightened suspicion among neighbors, a search for culprits, and a new appeal to the rulers to eliminate the enemy within. The "great hatred" in the villages targeted mostly old women living alone, their apparent weakness suspected as a disguise for illicit strength. When this local hatred flared into a true panic, however, persons of any social rank could be pulled into the maelstrom of fear, passion, and revenge. Did

---

66 Eva Labouvie, *Zauberei und Hexenwerk: Ländlicher Hexenglaube in der frühen Neuzeit*, 58.
67 If not exactly a peasant republic, except for the towns of Davos, Klosters, and Landquart, the self-governing Prättigau was a federation of rural communes.
68 Behringer, *Hexen: Glaube*, 60.
69 Vaduz was given in fief to the princes of Liechtenstein, in whose hands it remains.

this compensate virtually for the real social divide in the villages? We shall never know.

All of these elements come together in Barbara Jung's story, which contains elements found in many others. At the end of August 1631, a court at Dillenburg in the Protestant county of Nassau heard two witnesses against Barbara Jung of Donsbach, a widow. One of them, Krein (Katharina) Immel by name, deposed that Barbara had come from Nantzenbach, so "she knew nothing about the woman's family, and that most of the neighbors, including small children,"[70] suspected Barbara of sorcery. Krein added that Barbara once gave her a piece of cake, which was soft and covered by thumbprints. In view of Barbara's reputation, Krein thought better of eating it, and back at home she threw it into the hog trough. An hour and a half later the swineherd came in to report that one of the hogs, earlier healthy enough, had fallen ill. When Krein went out to see, she found it dead. In her anger she remembered how the death of her black calf a year ago had already aroused her suspicions of Barbara Jung. This story follows the classic popular tradition: witches do harm to neighbors.

Now the snake of sex reared its head as Krein's unmarried sister, Barbara Immel, age twenty-five, testified that four years ago Barbara Jung had a (sexual) relationship with Hermann Ningel. So violently did Hermann's wife rail at Jung as a witch that the pastor had to intervene and admonish both women. Soon, the village children were calling Barbara Jung a witch. Now we have Institoris complete: everything springs from carnal lust.

The next witness, Jost Vesch, age sixty and Barbara Immel's godfather, confirmed her account. Barbara Jung, he said, came to Donsbach about forty years ago (around 1591) and lived there in good reputation for about a dozen years. For the past twenty or so years, however, she was rumored to be a witch. He did not know how this talk started, "only that she is quarrelsome and also lives by herself."[71] Twelve years ago, Vesch was stealing water from Barbara Jung's meadow. Coming into the field, she spied him hiding in the grass and shouted, "Say, fellow lying there, you mind me or you'll be sorry. I have black eyes fixed on you."[72] A few days later Vesch's legs swelled up with great pain – proof positive that she had cast a spell on him. Now the story has become classic: a solitary old woman takes vengeance for an injury. What does not appear in the trial record, however, is anything about Satan, devil-worship, demon lovers (Hermann Ningel is a quite ordinary fellow), shape-changing, flying through the air, or witches' sabbaths. Yet another missing thing is suspicion of the most intimate relationships. In 1629 Ottilie Kneip from Hirschberg in Cologne territory was reported to have cursed her own daughter as a witch. "Well," replied the daughter, "if so, you yourself have made me one."[73] This story ended with Kneip's death as a witch.

Educated people who dealt with accusations, prosecutions, and executions of witches knew about its flowering in the sour soil of slight, insult, backbiting, gossip, slander, and revenge. Accuser and accused almost always knew one another, and often there was already bad blood between them. Friedrich Spee (1591–1635), who in his anonymously printed *Cautio Criminalis*, the most widely read seventeenth-century

70 Schormann, *Hexenprozeße in Deutschland*, 95.
71 Schormann, *Hexenprozeße in Deutschland*, 97.
72 Schormann, *Hexenprozeße in Deutschland*, 98.
73 Schormann, *Hexenprozeße in Deutschland*, 99.

book on prosecutions for witchcraft, thought this background poisoned witchcraft trials from the outset. A native of Kaiserwerth in Cologne territory, where his father had been castellan, Spee became a Jesuit. At Würzburg, where he served as prison chaplain – he was also a poet of note – Spee ministered to some 200 convicted witches and accompanied them to their deaths. Toward the end of his book, Spee pours out his belief that prosecutions for witchcraft led inexorably to executions.

Spee's analysis fits with great precision the modern picture of the great witch-panic as an especially German affair, and among the Germans more a Catholic than a Protestant affair. It was also, though he does not say so, among the German Catholics more an affair of prince-bishops in the old Imperial heartlands (Trier, Cologne, Würzburg, Bamberg) than of the dynastic principalities such as Bavaria, where skepticism about the prosecutions first surfaced in the law. Spee found especially terrible the contrast within the Catholic world with respect to prosecution and executing for witchcraft:

> Certainly the Italians and Spaniards, who by nature seem to be more prone to speculating and meditating on these matters and clearly see how large a crowd of innocent people would also be carried off if they copied the Germans, rightly abstain and entrust to us alone the duty to burn – we who prefer to trust in our own zeal rather than be satisfied with the teaching of Christ our Lawgiver.[74]

Spee utterly detested the processes that transformed local attitudes and mentality in the demonization of neighbors by neighbors. "It is incredible what superstitions, jealousies, lies, slurs, mutterings, and the like there are among the common people in Germany," he laments,

> particularly (it is embarrassing to say) among the Catholics, which the authorities do not punish nor preachers reproach, and which first arouse the suspicion of magic. All divine punishments which God threatens in the Holy Scriptures are committed by witches. God no longer does anything, nor nature, but everything is done by witches.[75]

"Thus everyone shouts with great passion," Spee adds, "that the authorities should therefore investigate the witches – of which they themselves created so many with their own tongues."[76] At first the authorities did not know where to begin, because without proofs they hesitated on grounds of conscience to proceed, but after two or three admonitions they began the trials. The common people howl that the delays warrant suspicion, and princes, advised by who knows whom, say the same, for "in Germany it is a serious matter to offend the princes and not obey them immediately."[77] When at last the judges go to work, having no proofs against her – Spee names his figurative victim "Gaia" – they turn to circumstance and rumor. If her manner of life is evil, that is how witches are; if good, well, witches commonly try to appear virtuous. From this point, the fatal path from evil tongues to the scaffold is complete, according to Spee, its ending only a matter of time.

74 Friedrich Spee, *Cautio Criminalis, or a Book on Witch Trials*, 52.
75 Spee, *Cautio Criminalis*, 214.
76 Spee, *Cautio Criminalis*, 214.
77 Spee, *Cautio Criminalis*, 215.

Mass witch trials tended to occur in small towns, where the culture of denunciation could multiply by chain reaction into genuine panics, from the fury of which no one was safe. Based on his experience at Würzburg, a notorious center of witch hunting, Friedrich Spee concludes,

> from this a particular COROLLARY follows which should be noted in red. If we constantly insist on conducting trials, no one of any sex, fortune, condition, or rank whatsoever who has earned himself even one enemy or slanderer who can drag him into the suspicion and reputation for witchcraft can be sufficiently safe in these times.[78]

Spee's denunciation of mass trials was based on personal experience. The most notorious sites of mass trials were the episcopal towns of "priests' alley" (Bamberg, Würzburg, Mainz, Cologne, and Trier), in and around which between 1626 and 1630 there occurred a series of sweeping hunts for witches. In the north German lands, where witch trials were relatively rare, the prosecution and killing of witches was sometimes called "Würzburg work."[79] In 1589 a Strasbourgeois reported that "in the bishopric of Trier nearly 300 persons have been burned for sorcery. In one village were burned all the women except two. . . . Among the 300 were many elderly cooks [housekeepers] of priests. Many others took off and got away."[80] Among the causes of complaint the informant notes the bitter poverty of these poor folk and, presumably, their ordained husbands.

The largest witch hunts took place in "priests' alley" – some 2,000 victims – and scoured the elector of Cologne's territory in 1630. This event, which shocked Friedrich Spee into writing against the trials, has been interpreted as a pure campaign of extermination engineered from above by Elector-archbishop Ferdinand, Duke William V of Bavaria's son. Closer examination reveals, however, that here, as in the villages, the initial impulses for prosecution came from below, which explains why the campaign began only after Ferdinand had been ten years in office. The pattern of local initiative is known from other places right across the Main, Rhine, Mosel, Nahe, and Saar valleys, where citizens' initiatives formed in the towns to press the authorities to action. "The hunting of witches was popular," a noted scholar writes, and "in the largest hunts the people were the driving force."[81]

Lastly, there come the children. Of all the problems that plague historians of the German (and European) witch-panic, the severest by far is the participation of children in the witchcraft trials. In the earliest phases children appear chiefly as victims of witches, murdered and eaten, as was said of such accused monsters as the Cologne midwife Enn Volmers and Gregor Agricola, pastor of Hatzendorf in Styria. Later, after 1600, children appear as accusers of witches and later as themselves accused of this crime. In the panic's last phase, large groups were sometimes prosecuted on the accusations of children. Such phenomena not only tax the powers of comprehension of modern historians, they intensified the beliefs of contemporary educated

78 Spee, *Cautio Criminalis*, 221.
79 Behringer, ed., *Hexen und Hexenprozesse*, 186.
80 Behringer, ed., *Hexen und Hexenprozesse*, 204.
81 Behringer, ed., *Hexen und Hexenprozesse*, 189.

observers, lawyers and pastors, that what could not be explained should not be prosecuted. In their skepticism, not in doubts about the reality of witchcraft itself, the will to end the prosecutions was formed.

The witch-panic, probably, will never yield its secrets entirely to the historian's skill with sources and analytical tools. The puzzle it presents, especially in the German lands and above all in the mass trials, is why apparently harmless women elicited such murderous hatred, often from their neighbors, how they could have been treated so cruelly, and, further, why people could fear that old women were plotting to root out the Christian faith. In the mass trials, of course, the hatred escaped all controls to course inexplicably and irresistibly through the social order, taking down men as well as women, rich as well as poor, and high church officials as well as helpless old women, not to mention children. Yet in everyday witch hunting, especially in its classic German landscapes, a majority of the trials arose from accusations by persons known to the older women they accused, and the most common accusations concerned not greed or sexuality – contrary to Institoris – but fertility: the getting, birthing, and rearing of children by women. The protection of reproduction made sense to people "who were already worried about how their society could reproduce itself in an age of limited resources," when "men and women tried to control fertility by waiting, delaying the age at which they married or even giving up the hope of marriage if they had insufficient resources to set up their own household."[82]

How deeply one must probe into emotions and even the unconscious in order to find the binding elements between such worries and the deep fears that led people in real numbers to accept the witches' world as a counter-cosmos is a matter of historians' debates. What is certain is that every obvious and some hardly serious global explanations – population, economic breakdown, Reformation and/or Counterreformation, climate, and narcotics – have been tested and failed to account credibly for the data derived from the trial records. What is probable, on the other hand, is that a whole panoply of such larger tendencies and events can be tagged as having contributed to the creation of environments and attitudes more favorable to blaming, hunting, and executing witches than the preceding era was or the succeeding era would be. What were these? They included stiffer competition for land and livelihood, greater chances for success and survival of householders and lesser ones for most others, and the reformations' upsetting of long traditional senses of a cosmic order lying securely in God's hand and of belief in blessing as a sovereign against many kinds of evil. In a nutshell, the conditions of the German lands around 1600 required larger, more secure solidarities and better protections of law and the common good than either churches, states, or their hybrids could supply.

The reformations did not create this situation, but they diverted energies and commitments from it into other channels. "The very fragmentation of political and legal authority in Germany made it possible for panics to get out of hand, while the intensity of the religious struggles ... nourished a kind of moral fundamentalism that saw the Devil's hand at work in all opponents."[83] The religious changes and quarrels intensified the sense of a need for stronger, more effective governance that animated

82 Lyndal Roper, *Witch Craze: Terror and Fantasy in Baroque Germany*, 8.
83 Roper, *Witch Craze*, 18.

the Imperial reform, Church reform, and the Peasants' War. Practically speaking, authority arises from consent more than from force, and all the great forces of the age had shared in weakening both. The old Imperial church had neglected its pastoral duties and hardly tried to put its house in order.

In this respect Protestant reformation and Catholic counterreformation worked as the two parts of a bellows. The former promoted an apocalypticism that signaled a weakened faith in sacrament and blessing; the latter relapsed into its own heritage of coercion in matters of belief. In the German lands the global problem was that the religious struggles overstrained the small, weak states that had crystallized in the Empire and created a tremendous spiritual mortgage on the churches' capacities for coping with the great, traditional task of combining the salvation of souls with the good of the world. The formation of confessions was an ad hoc solution to the radical disruptions of the interface between religion and politics. The old confessional order did not segregate the religious communities but enabled them to share traits, both noble and ignoble, while they remained distinct.

4. THE ENTROPY OF RELIGIOUS COERCION

Jews, heretics, witches – while it is profitless to lump them together as faces of a general "other," it can be fruitful to bring their stories together for the light they can shed on public life in the early modern German lands. The grounds, chronologies, and methods employed against them differed substantially, to be sure, from group to group. The sixteenth century saw a marked decline of the prosecution of Jews for the traditional crimes of murder and host desecration. Expulsions also became rarer, perhaps because of the new forms of Jewish protection, first in the Empire, then in the territorial states. The new statutes gave the Empire's Jews a fixed legal status including right of residence, though they did not end discrimination.

The treatment of heretics – chiefly Anabaptists – developed along quite different lines. At first, like the Jews in earlier centuries, they suffered lynching and summary justice, but unlike the Jews they continued to be prosecuted through most of the sixteenth century. Meanwhile, the Peace of 1555 politically neutralized the line between real orthodoxy and real heresy, between Protestants and Catholics. In this atmosphere, from the 1570s prosecution of the now rusticated Anabaptists gradually lost its appeal.

If the witches are considered (for the sake of argument) a virtual confession, which is how the demonologists construed them, their inclusion suggests an interesting pattern of chronological succession. The persecution of Jews in the German lands largely came to a halt during the first third of the sixteenth century, despite occasional expulsions and one failed assault on the Empire's largest community; that of Anabaptists went on for about fifty years and then receded; and the hunt for witches became a flood in the 1580s and lasted for about eighty years. Around 1520, as prosecutions of Jews on the traditional grounds ceased, the persecution of Anabaptists as heretics was just beginning; around 1570, as the execution of Anabaptists began to decline, the great witch-panic was beginning. It is tempting to string the stories together in a tale of coercive intolerance – from Jews to Anabaptists to witches. Still, the radically different geographic patterns and social milieus of persecution counsel serious skepticism.

In themselves Jews, heretics, and witches had little or nothing in common. What they did share were certain relationships to the world on the edges of which they lived. For one thing, each was perceived to pose a threat to the Christian common good, and contemporary German attitudes favored the view that the rulers and their courts should as custodians of that welfare move against its enemies. To those who urged rulers in this direction, all three were "enemies of God." On the other hand, all three stories offer evidence of the same, slow thickening of governmental power and judicial restraint that brought each successive story of marginalization and persecution to a gradual close. Their comparative history belongs, therefore, to the story of state-formation at all levels of the Empire, the chief agents of which were not pastors and theologians but lawyers, judges, and professors of law. Over the course of 150 years, they were principally responsible for the entropy of religious coercion in the early modern Empire.

The social milieus of the three stories display more differences than similarities. They differ markedly in socially specific attitudes toward the targets of coercion. The common people disliked the Jews for both economic and cultural reasons; the rulers found the Jews useful. The common people had little interest, though it was probably positive, in the Anabaptists; the rulers regarded them as rebels and splitters. The common people, finally, hated witches as malevolent neighbors; the rulers saw both accused and accusers as disturbers of order in the villages and towns.

Making one story from the three highlights the confessional differences that distinguish this age in the German lands' histories. During the sixteenth century both ideological attacks on and physical expulsions of Jews were considerably less common in Catholic than in Protestant territories; Anabaptists were persecuted more vigorously in Catholic than in Protestant states; and while Catholic theories of demonology may well have remained less skeptical than Protestant ones, the willingness or unwillingness to prosecute for witchcraft does not seem to have been confessionally specific. In all three enterprises, the old Imperial heartlands of the south and west were more deeply engaged than were regimes in the more recently colonized German lands – roughly, very roughly, the old Catholic Empire against the newer Protestant Empire. What do these facts suggest? The Catholics, once the first, paralyzing shock of the Reformation was over, had a full command of past practice and past thinking. The Protestants, by contrast, had to sort through their traditions – religious, theological, and legal – and to determine what was tainted by Romanism and must therefore be discarded, and what was not. This need promoted uncertainty about practice on many subjects besides coercion, notably on the disposition of church properties. Moreover, it is understandable why, theology aside, Protestant authorities, themselves condemned as "heretics," might prove more skeptical about prosecuting for heresy and less comfortable in making the analogy between heresy and witchcraft.

The three stories' outcomes are also quite different. The new degrees of legal protection transformed the German Jews into an honorary confession, whose rights were in principle guarded by Imperial and eventually by territorial statutes. The Anabaptists, by contrast, were driven into the dark corners and cracks of the confessional order, except in the Dutch Republic, where they lived as a kind of miniature confession. The witches, however, conceived as a counter-church of Devil-worshippers, had never been a community and did not become one. When the witch-panic came to a close, witches remained what they had been, targets of local discrimination and fear but no longer of the law. By around 1700, with occasional local exceptions, "enemies of God" no longer resided in the German lands.

16

Roads to War

Incensed with indignation Satan stood
Unterrified, and like a comet burned
That fires the length of Ophiuchus huge
In the Arctic sky, and from his horrid hair
Shakes pestilence and war.

John Milton

"There is no more friendship on this earth, and each person has become Devil to the other."[1] When Theobald Höck (b. 1572), a poet of Palatine origin who served as secretary to a powerful Bohemian nobleman, made his lament in 1601, he might have been speaking for – or about – the man who both reigned over and embodied the German lands in this age of iron. From 1583, when he moved his court to Prague, Emperor Rudolph II sat in seclusion in an interior chamber of Hradschin/Hardčany Castle above the city. Outside, an apparently leaderless Empire was sliding into chaos. Rudolph, who suffered from a serious mental disorder, was the most eminent of the Empire's rich crop of "mad princes." "For long stretches mentally ill," Rudolph was "so disordered and irrationally frightened that he let imperial business slide for months and years, so depressed that he thought himself bewitched and even attempted suicide."[2] He was nonetheless Holy Roman emperor and king of both Bohemia and Hungary and, at least to his kingdoms' Catholics, principal protector of the Church Universal.

At the court of this long-lived, somber ruler clustered politicians, scholars, and artists who represented every organized faith and none. Attracted by an atmosphere compounded of Habsburg Imperial Catholicism, late Renaissance humanism, political universalism, and esoteric learning, Catholics from the Empire and from southern Europe and Melanchthonian Protestants flocked to the court. They shared "the belief in a single universal authority and the total, all-embracing conception of society," which might "preserve the mental and political unity of Christendom, to avoid religious schism, uphold peace at home, and deliver Europe from the Ottoman menace."[3]

1 R. J. W. Evans, *The Making of the Habsburg Monarchy, 1550–1700: An Interpretation*, 278.
2 H. C. Erik Midelfort, *A History of Madness in Sixteenth-Century Germany*, 128.
3 Evans, *The Making of the Habsburg Monarchy*, 284.

In retrospect, the contrast could not have been greater between this vision and the realities of Rudolph's 36-year reign (1576–1612): a slow breakdown of the Imperial *convivencia*; a deterioration of his relations with both the Catholic Church and the Lutheran princes; and an intra-dynastic Habsburg "brothers' quarrel." Against these trends worked the Rudolphine engagement in the Long War (1593–1606), the last of the sixteenth-century's Ottoman Wars. The war had its political uses, for the shadow of "the Turk," as the Ottomans were collectively named, reminded the Christian parties of a common heritage and a common fortune.[4]

The expansion of Ottoman power into east central Europe was for western Christians one of the most shocking events of the sixteenth century. It created an enduring image of the Ottomans as a race of warriors, armed and handsome in the Renaissance style but cruel and inspired by implacable hatred for Christians and their God. This initial image from the 1520s still lived on in the days of the Long War. In 1595 David Teucher, a rural schoolteacher outside Breslau, looked back seventy years to the Ottoman invasion of Hungary in 1526 and saw in the Ottoman power a never-ending threat to his world:

> The Turk has arisen,
> With mighty hand and many men,
> To visit on us fire and death,
> Trusting to his own cruel ways,
> And trumpeting that his power and great spirit,
> Will throw down the gospel of Jesus Christ.
> He denies that You, Lord Jesus Christ,
> Are the Father's true begotten Son,
> Then, too, does he refuse,
> To own the everlasting Holy Ghost,
> The true God, Three-in-One
> He wants to snatch from us.[5]

The feeling that the Grand Turk, as the Ottoman sultan was called, was God's rod of punishment for Christian sins, and that, paradoxically, Christians must resist him by supporting the emperor's military efforts, intensified the pressure on the Imperial estates not to leave the emperor and his armies in the lurch. In the midst of the Long War, the Augsburger Peter Waldner drew the connection between German divisions and Ottoman power:

> Because the Empire's princes are so contentious
> The Turk has become so powerful.
> There is no peace in Christendom,
> So that he grazes where he will.
> He knows well how things stand,
> That there is no peace in Christendom.[6]

4 "Turks" was the conventional European name for the Ottomans, corresponding to the Muslims' use of "Franks" for western Christians.
5 Winfried Schulze, *Reich und Türkengefahr im späten 16. Jahrhundert. Studien zu den politischen und gesellschaftlichen Auswirkungen einer äußeren Bedrohung*, 55–6.
6 Schulze, *Reich und Türkengefahr*, 61n. 9.

As Machiavelli had noted in Emperor Maximilian I's day, the German lands possessed plenty of soldiers and plenty of money, even though the princes could prevent their mobilization à la française. In the 1590s there were still soldiers and money, and the Ottoman threat reminded Germans that if before God they stood as two parties, one orthodox Christian and the other heretical, in confronting the Grand Turk they were all Christians. And, as sixteenth-century European warlords could attest, the Germans were also a martial race.

I. THE MILITARY REVOLUTION IN THE GERMAN LANDS

The fame of the Germans, Johannes Cochlaeus had declared in 1512, rests on two things: their discovery of the printing press and their prowess in war. In his time the renaissance of heavy infantry, pioneered by the Swiss, was already running full bore in the German lands. The typical military figure of the day was the mercenary infantryman, called "lansquenet" (*Landsknecht*), with his slit trunks and tunic, broad-brimmed and plumed hat, whiskers, sword and pike, swaggering style, and his appetite for other people's goods and women. Trained to fight in heavy, deep formations – pike, sword, and gun, supported by cavalry and artillery – he trailed his pike to Italy, Burgundy, the Low Countries, and Hungary in search of booty, fame, and adventure. Figure 16 shows how the Nuremberg artist Hans Sebald Beham portrayed such a fellow around 1535.

Some Germans admired these rough fellows, others did not. In Maximilian I's time, wrote the ex-Franciscan pamphleteer Johann Eberlin von Günzburg (ca. 1470–1533), "a new order of soulless people grew up called the Landsknechte, . . . [who] have no respect for honor or justice," who practice "whoring, adultery, rape, gluttony, drunkenness, . . . stealing, robbing, and murder," and who live "entirely in the power of the devil, who pulls them about wherever he wants."[7]

The lansquenet, this reckless, dangerous fellow, was both harbinger and instrument of a new era of war-making by royal and princely warlords. His immediate employer and commander belonged to another new species, the German military enterpriser, who raised troops on credit to make possible wars no one could truly afford. Step by step through the Italian Wars and the religious wars in France and the Low Countries, war-making became a complicated bundle of command control, organization, money, guns, and men. They linked the armies of the Italian Wars and the great royal war machines of the Old Regime.

The German military enterpriser was a broker of war, a creditor of kings and princes, an employer of troops, and a maker and breaker of fortunes. Unlike a modern financier of war, he risked both his capital in extending credit and his life in commanding troops in the field. His colonels and their officers were subcontractors who recruited under the warlord's license to fill up their regiments. The prime German recruiting grounds for infantry lay in the south (Tyrol, Vorarlberg, Upper Swabia, the Upper Rhine), while the north (the Lower Rhine, Westphalia, Lower Saxony) supplied most of the mercenary cavalry.

The debut of the lansquenet and the military enterpriser on Europe's battlefields signaled the beginnings of what historians now call the "military revolution." It had

7 Keith Moxey, *Peasants, Warriors, and Wives: Popular Imagery in the Reformation*, 96.

Figure 16. Lansquenet

three principal elements: greater firepower and corresponding changes in infantry tactics; dramatic growth in the size of armies; and improved artillery and fortifications. At the tactical level, the growing popularity of the musket promoted a shift from massed to linear formations, which maximized mobility and minimized casualties from enemy fire, and required new levels of discipline and drill. By 1600 German and Dutch commanders were codifying the new ways and spreading them among the other German states.

With the new tactics came two other centrally important innovations. One was a radically new type of fortification, the "Italian track" (*trace italienne*). In contrast to the high, towered walls of medieval castles and cities, the new arrangement presented the attackers with low, solid, angular bastions linked by short, strong curtain walls, and overlapping fields of fire. The second change was the growth of armies. Charles V's grandparents had taken Granada in 1492 with fewer than 20,000 men; he had commanded some 100,000 in Hungary in 1532 and 150,000 before Metz in 1552; and by the 1630s each major belligerent in the Thirty Years War was maintaining about 150,000 troops in the Empire.

These new ways for fighting appeared in the German lands before 1600, though it took another generation before they displaced the pitched battle with long, drawn-out campaigns of attrition made up of marches and counter-marches and much raiding and skirmishing by small units. During 1631–32 – a supreme example – the Swedish king's main army covered 1,600 kilometers (1,000 miles) and fought but four pitched battles. The new way of war gradually banished the battle of decision from the battle-field. "[Nowadays] war is dragged out for as long as possible," remarked the Italian political writer Giovanni Botero (ca. 1544–1617) in 1605, "and the object is not to smash but to tire; not to defeat but to wear down."[8] This certainly applied to the Long War in Hungary, which at the moment he wrote was winding down to its end.

2. THE SPECTER OF THE TURK

From the mid-1520s onward, the Empire's Ottoman problem and its religious schism marched together. In time the Ottoman presence in Hungary provided the Protestant princes with a tactic that became a new policy: no taxes without concessions on religion. "The matters of religion and of the Turks," wrote an observer in 1542, "neither can, may, nor should be divided and separated from one another, for one always brings up the other, and one always either helps or hinders the other."[9] Some saw the Ottomans as a Habsburg problem, others recognized that the Habsburg lands – Hungary, the eastern Austrian lands, and Bohemia – formed just the forward line of defense for other lands.

From one Ottoman siege of Vienna in 1529 to another in 1683, the Imperial/Habsburg-Ottoman wars in Hungary lasted for more than a century and a half. They began during the reign of Sultan Süleyman I (b. 1494, r. 1520–66), called "the Magnificent" by westerners but "the Law-Giver" by his own peoples. His armies fought Imperial forces in Hungary between 1529 and the peace of 1547, which was renewed in 1562 and 1590. This first round went to the sultan, for during the long peace that preceded the Long War, the Holy Roman emperors acknowledged his overlordship of Hungary and paid him 30,000 Venetian ducats per year in tribute.

The wars' rhythm alternated periods of serious campaigning (1526–47, 1593–1606, 1663–83) with long truces (1547–93, 1606–63). War and peace formed, in effect, a long stalemate unbreakable either by the emperor, who could not raise sufficient fighting forces to take the offensive, or the sultan, who could not master the logistical problems of pushing further westward. Between major campaigns the respective positions were held by two heavily fortified systems of defense, on the Habsburg side called

8 Geoffrey Parker, *The Military Revolution: Military Innovation and the Rise of the West, 1500–1800*, 61–2.
9 Winfried Schulze, *Deutsche Geschichte im 16. Jahrhundert 1500–1618*, 65.

"the military frontier" and manned by Croats, Vlachs, and Serbs who were both free farmers and resident warriors. Raids, sometimes in force, were a constant experience, but so was trading across the frontier. In addition, each ruler had his nemesis, for the Habsburg-Ottoman conflict resembled a grand pas de quatre of the two principals and their respective partners – France in the Empire's rear, Persia in the Ottomans'.

When the peace was broken in Hungary, it was usually by raids in strength on one side or the other. One such incident occurred in 1592, when Emperor Rudolph sent a large force to the front, the operations of which led to the Long War. The war fell at a favorable time, the height of the Diet's willingness – a fruit of the Imperial *convivencia* – to support the Imperial war effort in Hungary far more generously than in the past. The Imperial forces regained Esztergom/Gran, seat of the Catholic primate, but they lost Pest once again and were beaten badly by the Ottomans. Much as in the Thirty Years War, victories on both sides led to little permanent advantage, and by 1606 both sides were ready for peace. In the treaty of Zsitvatörök (11 November 1606), which ended the Long War, the sultan renounced his claim to precedence over and right to receive tribute from the emperor, who in turn conceded Ottoman suzerainty over the tributary principalities north of the Danube – Transylvania, Wallachia, and Moldavia.[10] The sultan had other fish to fry in Poland, Persia, the Crimea, Anatolia, Venice, and Russia; Rudolph already faced the political crisis that would push the Empire into a generation of hardly remitting war. What might have happened, conditions permitting, had the Ottoman sultan mounted a major attack while the Habsburg rulers were engaged against the Bohemians, the Protestant Germans and Danes, the Swedes, and the French, makes an interesting speculation.

The Ottomans as "the Turk" captured imaginations in the German lands. Since the taking of Constantinople in 1453, images of them had run the full gamut from practical butchers and destroyers to an apocalyptic specter. From the time of Maximilian I, the Grand Turk took pride of place among the dangerous villains whose menace justified each new emperor's every plea to the Imperial Diet for money. The tax law of 1495 was passed "in order to preserve law and order in the Holy Empire and to resist the enemies of Christ, the Turks, and other foes of the Holy Empire and the German Nation."[11] The preamble to the Public Peace of 1495 is more precise in placing the Ottomans at the very center of attention. "We now see what constant attacks are being made, and long have been made, against Christendom," it speaks in the royal voice,

> whereby many kingdoms and rulers of Christian lands have been subjected to unbelievers, so that they now rule right up to the boundaries of the Holy Empire and have in recent times both notably increased their depredations against the cities, lands, and properties held by Our Holy Father the pope and the Roman churches and violently seized other lands and jurisdictions of the Holy Empire.[12]

---

10 The treaty of peace for twenty years was signed by envoys of Sultan Ahmed I and of Archduke Matthias. Zsitvatörök lies near a former mouth of the Zsitava River, which flows into the Danube. The place was in what was then called Habsburg Hungary or Royal Hungary and is today the Republic of Slovakia. By this treaty the Ottomans recognized the Habsburgs as "Roman Emperors" rather than just "Kings of Vienna."

11 Hanns Hubert Hofmann, ed., *Quellen zum Verfassungsorganismus des Heiligen Römischen Reiches Deutscher Nation 1495–1815*, 28–31.

12 Hofmann, ed., *Quellen*, 2, ll. 19–28.

The heavy losses caused by Ottoman attacks on "both the Holy Empire and all of Christendom" would continue "if, after timely and broad consultation, a stable, binding condition of law and order is not established, maintained, and enforced in the Empire."[13] Those were two powerful arguments – internal German disorder and external Ottoman tyranny – for stronger rule, larger forces, and heavier taxation. Maximilian's Ottomans thus succeeded to the role of Sigismund's Hussites, for the Hussite Wars had occasioned the first Diet-like assemblies and the first levying of military taxes. With this difference: Maximilian never found the right moment for actually campaigning against the Ottomans. He resembled the beggar who repeatedly pleads for help to return to his distant home but who, alms in his pocket, never begins the journey.

Sultan Süleyman converted this posturing into genuine fear in 1526, when he took his army into Hungary and killed its king and nobles. In the darkest days of defeat began the golden age of German political pamphleteering. The Germans learned quickly, and, from the siege of 1529 on, nobody repeated Enea Silvio's disparagement of the Ottomans as effeminate, weak, and unwarlike. "It is incredible," wrote Justus Jonas (1493–1555), one of Luther's colleagues, "that the Turk is in Austria and that he could possibly have such an enormous force before Vienna."[14]

It is a commonly repeated error that the Europeans in general and the Germans in particular regarded the Ottomans as simply a cruel, implacable, unfathomable, and mysterious "Other." The images of the Ottomans that circulated in the German lands between the invasion of Hungary in 1526 and the beginning of the Thirty Years War in 1618 broadcast fantasies, to be sure, but also a good deal of knowledge about the Ottomans. Four themes dominated their output. One theme was ethnographic: the Ottomans as a semi-familiar, semi-exotic people. The second theme was military and political: the Ottoman sultan was the most powerful warrior of the age, able by turns to make war and peace with the Christian rulers and occasionally to become their ally. The third theme was moral: the Turk was a tyrant who cruelly misused, enslaved, or slaughtered his Christian captives. The fourth theme was theological: Turk and pope were twin servants of the Antichrist, enemies of God sent to prepare the world in general and Christians in particular for these Last Days.

The ethnographic images of the Ottomans began with soldiers, drawing details from other soldiers' and travelers' accounts, and moved on into other subjects. Illustrators showed Ottomans' dress, weapons, and animals as exotic but nonetheless generally familiar. The conventional marks of an Ottoman warrior are visible in a 1529 woodcut by Niklas Stoer (d. 1563), who portrays an Ottoman cavalryman as he might have appeared on the plains of Hungary clad in a turban-wound helmet and long gown, holding a saber and shield, and mounted on a fine horse in Ottoman harness.[15]

A woodcut of the same year by the Nuremberg illustrator Erhard Schoen (ca. 1491–1542) shows two Ottoman lancers and two prisoners. The troopers ride well mounted in eastern dress and weapons, their lances flying the crescent of

13 Hofmann, ed., *Quellen*, 2, ll. 28–34.
14 Carina Lee Johnson, "Negotiating the Exotic: Aztec and Ottoman Culture in Habsburg Europe, 1500–1590," ch. 4.
15 Max Geisberg and Walter L. Strauss, *The German Single-Leaf Woodcut, 1500–1550*, vol. 4: 1338.

Dans Guldenmundt.

Figure 17. Ottoman Trooper

Islam, while the (Christian) captives plod behind, tethered and sad, the face of one turned wistfully back toward home.[16]

The next year Schoen showed the other side of the coin: German lansquenets, one with a captured saber on his shoulder, lead away Ottoman infantrymen (one a Janissary), while in their midst stride exotic eastern beasts – a dromedary and a two-humped Bactrian camel.[17]

16 Geisberg and Strauss, *German Single-Leaf Woodcut*, vol. 4: 1192.
17 Geisberg and Strauss, *German Single-Leaf Woodcut*, vol. 4: 1199. Dating from the fourteenth century, Janissaries were elite Ottoman infantry who served as the sultan's household troops and bodyguard.

Figure 18. Two Turks with Four Captives

The second, military-political, image of the Ottomans, the Grand Turk as a great power, spread through depictions of sultans, armies, battles, and buildings, all favorite subjects for German illustrators. Portraits of each sultan were sold in the German lands. The early portraits of Süleyman and his father, Selim I (b. 1470, r. 1512–20), show their subjects as exotic but not outlandish. A generation later there appeared a very fine portrait, probably of Selim II (r. 1566–74). It was attributed to Melchior Lorck

Figure 19. Lansquenets with Camel, Dromedary, and Turkish Captives

358

Figure 20. Portrait of Sultan Selim II

(1527–ca. 1589), a Danish subject from Flensburg who worked in the great cities of the German south and in Italy. In it the sultan wears a four-tiered helmet-crown (the pope's crown had but three), each tier studded with pearls, and all surmounted by a splendid plume.[18]

During the latter third of the sixteenth century, the ideas encouraged by these first two themes, the ethnographic and the military-political, gained textual support from

18 Walter L. Strauss, *The German Single-Leaf Woodcut, 1550–1600: A Pictorial Catalogue*, vol. 2: 615, incorrectly identified as a portrait of Sultan Süleyman II (r. 1687–91).

the Latin letters of Ogier Ghiselin de Busbecq. A Netherlander from Walloon Flanders, Ogier served as Emperor Ferdinand I's envoy to the Sublime Porte (the Ottoman court) from 1555 to 1562. From the first encounter he found the Ottomans – especially the fearsome Janissaries – to be courteous, interesting, and in many ways admirable. Ogier was especially struck by the Ottomans' apparent honoring of merit only, not birth. He commented, too, on the Ottomans' skill at adaptation. On a visit to the sultan's headquarters in Cappadocia, he notes:

> no single man owed his dignity to anything but his personal merits and bravery; no one is distinguished from the rest by his birth and honour is paid to each man according to the nature of the duty and offices which he discharges. Thus there is no struggle for precedence, every man having his place assigned to him in virtue of the function which he performs.[19]

Because everything is assigned on the basis of ability and merit, not rank or birth, "the Turks succeed in all that they attempt and are a dominating race and daily extend the bounds of their rule."[20] "Our method," he wryly adds, "is very different; there is no room for merit, but everything depends on birth; considerations of which alone open the way to high official position."[21] Comparison, the broad gateway from strangeness to familiarity, worked its spell on Ogier as on many other European Christians who traveled in the Ottoman lands as free men.

This is not to say that Ogier looked upon Ottoman civilization uncritically. It was a warlike civilization, he thought, and the sultan was a great and standing danger to his neighbors. "Soleiman stands before us," he wrote,

> with all the terror inspired by his own successes and those of his ancestors; he overruns the plains of Hungary with 200,000 horsemen; he threatens Austria; he menaces the rest of Germany; he brings in his train all the nations that dwell between here and the Persian frontier . . . he spreads far and wide the terror of his name.[22]

No nation on earth, Ogier adds,

> has shown less reluctance to adopt the useful inventions of others; for example, they have appropriated to their own use large and small cannons and many other of our [the Christians'] discoveries. They have, however, never been able to bring themselves to print books and set up public clocks. They hold that their scriptures, that is, their sacred books, would no longer be scriptures if they were printed; and if they established public clocks, they think that the authority of their muezzins and their ancient rites would suffer diminution.[23]

Comparison cuts both ways.

The third, moral, theme, the Turk as cruel tyrant, appeared in many depictions of Ottoman atrocities in the wars and raids along the central European front. It was reinforced by pamphlets, sermons, and captive narratives, a special literary genre in

19   Ogier Ghiselin de Busbecq, *The Turkish Letters of Ogier Ghiselin de Busbecq*, 59.
20   Busbecq, *Turkish Letters*, 60.
21   Busbecq, *Turkish Letters*, 60–1.
22   Busbecq, *Turkish Letters*, 239.
23   Busbecq, *Turkish Letters*, 135.

which former captives described their sufferings and sexual abuse at the hands of their Ottoman captors. Here fantasy could take flight in suggestions of the Turk's notorious lust. A pamphlet about the battle of Mohačs in 1526 tells of "nearly 1100 virgins" who were forced into the harem to be raped, "and those who would not obey were all stabbed to death."[24] Nor were young men and boys safe, for the sultan "has almost exclusively handsome boys around him, which he uses for his special purposes, just like women, . . . and this shameful crime of sodomy . . . with boys, women, and irrational beasts is quite general."[25]

The image of the Ottoman captive's life as "bestial servitude,"[26] a favorite with the pamphleteers, was nuanced by eyewitness accounts. Urban Sagstetter (ca. 1529–73) from Lower Austria, who was bishop of Gurk (r. 1556–73), administrator of the see of Vienna (1563–68), and court preacher to Emperor Ferdinand I, preached in moderate language about his experiences. Captured near Vienna in 1529 as a three-year-old child, Urban lived for years as an Ottoman slave. He spoke of "the misery, the suffering, the severe captivity and bestial servitude, the hard and most menial work, the unbearable hunger and deprivation, the blows and beatings, the torture and the punishment, all of which the poor, miserable Christian captives must suffer under this tyrant."[27] Yet though cruel, his captors were not demonic, and he recommended getting along with them, so long as it stopped short of apostasy. One important survival skill was language, for one must speak to the enemy "so you can ask him either to spare your life or to ameliorate the conditions of your imprisonment."[28] Urban's printed sermons and accounts by other survivors represented Ottoman civilization as in many respects unfamiliar but not incomprehensible.

While the fourth, theological, theme, the Turk as apocalyptic destroyer, goes back to western Christian reactions to the fall of Constantinople in 1453, it gained theological weight only in the worldview of the Lutheran reformation. No one contributed more to its fashioning than did Martin Luther himself. At first he favored missions over an anti-Ottoman crusade, but he did this in 1518, when peace reigned on the western fronts. The western policy of Süleyman I changed his mind, as two writings of 1529 reveal, in a characteristically theologized way. In the first (*On War against the Turks*), he takes the position that fighting the Ottomans is the emperor's business, and Christians should not think that by taking part they are answering the pope's call or defending the Gospel. In writing on this subject, Luther says,

> What motivated me most of all was this: They undertook to fight against the Turk in the name of Christ and taught and incited men to do this as though our people were an army of Christians against the Turks, who were enemies of Christ. This is absolutely contrary to Christ's doctrine and name. It is against his doctrine because he says that Christians shall not resist evil, fight, or quarrel. . . . It is against his name because there

24 Johnson, "Negotiating the Exotic," ch. 4.
25 Johnson, "Negotiating the Exotic," ch. 4.
26 Johnson, "Negotiating the Exotic," ch. 4.
27 Johnson, "Negotiating the Exotic," ch. 4.
28 Johnson, "Negotiating the Exotic," ch. 4.

are scarcely five Christians in such an army, and perhaps there are worse people in the eyes of God in that army than are the Turks.[29]

The emperor and the princes should be told (by a papal legate at a Diet!) that "God gave and commended Germans and the Empire to you, so that you will protect, rule, advise, and help. Nay, no 'should' but 'must' by pain of losing your souls' salvation."[30] For while it is true that the Ottomans serve the Devil, Christians should fight the devilish Ottoman god with prayer and penitence. "If the emperor were supposed to destroy the unbelievers and non-Christians" – a grandly typical shot – "he would have to begin with the pope, bishops, and clergy."[31] Luther's central point in this first writing was motivation: Christians may and should fight, but only as rulers and subjects, not as Christians.

In the autumn of 1529, as Vienna lay under Ottoman siege, Luther went over to a fully apocalyptic view of the matter that united foes, Turk and pope, as servants of the Devil in a great apocalyptic clash. In a second writing (*A Military Sermon against the Turks*) he announces the Ottoman advance as a sign of the Last Days, when Christ will come again to annihilate Gog and Magog and free all His people. Pope and Turk work for Satan, one with spiritual means, idolatry, the other with corporeal means, the sword. The Turk, therefore, is "the Devil's last and worst [act of] wrath against Christ," upon which follow judgment and hell.[32] "If we fall under the Turk," Luther wrote, "we go to the Devil; if we remain under the pope, we go to hell."[33]

Luther's assimilation of the Ottoman invasion of Hungary to his own crusade against the papacy took on visual form in the woodcuts of Mathis Gerung (ca. 1500–70). One of them shows in the foreground two Ottoman soldiers cutting down unarmed Christians; in the middle ground the pope, accompanied by soldiers, a bishop, and a demon, is persecuting refugees; and above it all sits Christ enthroned in a cloudy crescent, while before him two angels exhibit on a banner the scene of His crucifixion. The meaning is clear: pope and Turk persecute God's faithful and His poor, but above them sits Christ in supreme judgment.[34]

Gerung's second woodcut portrays the same theme more explicitly: above, Christ preaches the Word of God to Christians, while below the pope and the sultan drive wagons that carry the infidels and the Catholics into hell.[35]

The pope looks out to his people on the shore, the emperor, cardinals, bishops, and monks; the sultan looks toward the opposite shore at his troops, who march, Christian heads on their lances, under the Prophet's banner. Here Luther's concept is complete: pope and sultan, false Christianity and demonic Islam, Europe and Asia, spiritual sword and temporal – the enemies of God doomed to defeat.

In the decades between the Habsburg-Ottoman peace of 1547 and the outbreak of the Long War in 1593, consciousness of the Ottomans became routinized in German culture. It was by no means a single, inky darkness, filled with the screams of

29 Martin Luther, *Luther's Works*, vol. 46: 165.
30 Luther, *Luther's Works*, vol. 46: 186.
31 Luther, *Luther's Works*, vol. 46: 186.
32 Martin Luther, *D. Martin Luthers Werke. Kritische Gesamtausgabe. Schriften*, vol. 30.2: 162 ll. 19–21.
33 Luther, *D. Martin Luthers Werke. Schriften*, vol. 30.2: 195, line 31, to 196, line 1.
34 Strauss, *The German Single-Leaf Woodcut 1550–1600*, vol. 1: 305.
35 Strauss, *The German Single-Leaf Woodcut 1550–1600*, vol. 1: 314.

Figure 21. Ottomans Kill Christians; the Pope Persecutes the Poor

Christian victims, as is sometimes alleged. It contained, on the contrary, various shapes, various colors, various threads, of which the Lutheran apocalyptical vision was by no means the most prominent. The dominant impression, to be sure, was one of menace. Yet in Vienna realism in these matters was compelling. The Ottomans were a very great power but still a great power with whom one could negotiate and make peace. The Habsburg monarchs had done so in 1533, in 1545–47, and again in 1606.

Figure 22. Pope and Sultan in a Wagon

The Treaty of Zsitvatörök restored a kind of equality between the two great emperors and regulated the main points at issue in Hungary. Informed persons at the European courts knew that at the Ottomans' backs still stood the shah of Persia, a Habsburg ally of opportunity. It was not foolhardiness, therefore, that caused Emperor Ferdinand II's advisors to decide to go to war over Bohemia in 1618. They gambled on the sultan's will to keep the peace, and the luck of the draw was with them. The peace of 1606 endured for two whole generations.

3. THE IMPERIAL *CONVIVENCIA* AND CATHOLIC RESURGENCE

A long tradition encourages us to see the decade before the outbreak of the Thirty Years War as a time of worsening conditions, deepening confessional strife, and a breakdown of the Imperial *convivencia*. Much evidence speaks for this view. Certainly, economic times were hard. Population growth and the economic recovery had ceased around 1550; price inflation was depressing real wages; a financial crash in the early 1570s had carried away important South German firms and fortunes; and by century's end economies were sliding into full stagnation, the worst for two hundred years. Even the climate had turned contrary. Whether because of sunspots or for some other reason, declining mean summer temperatures reached a nadir around 1600, bringing depressed yields and the return of famine.

The Empire's political climate seemed to resonate with the real climate's "Little Ice Age." The Imperial *convivencia* established in 1555 began to slip away. Yet as tempting as the idea of a long, irresistible slide into the Thirty Years War may be, it does not fit the facts very well. The Peace of 1555 had been signed as the Protestant cause was still advancing toward its zenith in the 1570s. Thereafter, a growing capacity of the Catholics to defend their faith signaled the end of such hopes.

Four incidents during the 1580s and 1590s tested but did not break the Peace. First, the Cologne affair of the 1580s challenged the Ecclesiastical Reservation, the codicil to the Religious Peace, which the Protestants contested. This decree prohibited incumbents who turned Protestant from retaining their Catholic offices and benefices. While generally effective in the south, events in the see of Cologne tested its enforceability in the strategically vital northwest. Cologne, an archbishopric with a substantial *Hochstift*, also carried an electorate, Protestant possession of which would yield a Protestant majority in the college of Imperial electors. The affair began in 1577 with the election of Gebhard II Truchseß von Waldburg (1547–1601), a Swabian noble and avid pluralist, whose uncle had been prince-bishop of Augsburg. Gebhard had a problem. He was in love with "the lovely Mansfelder," a Protestant deaconess named Countess Agnes of Mansfeld-Eisleben (1551–1637). In 1582 he announced his conversion to the Reformed faith, and in the following year he and Agnes were married. Well and good, but instead of surrendering his see, he intended to retain both it and the electoral title. Rome excommunicated him, and threats of war were heard, but in the event Gebhard's backers – the Elector Palatine and the Dutch Republic – stood down. The new Catholic bishop-elect, Ernest of Bavaria, took possession backed by Spanish and Bavarian troops. The fighting ended without decision, and in 1589 Gebhard resigned and went with his wife into a wandering life of exile. The "Cologne War," while not an important military conflict, served notice that the Catholics would surrender no more prince-bishoprics in the north. Bavarian incumbents at Cologne would see to that.

The Strasbourg affair, second of the political conflicts that strained the Imperial *convivencia*, began in 1592 with the death of Bishop Johann IV (r. 1569–92). He had struggled for Catholic reform, called the Jesuits to found a school at Molsheim, and excluded those excommunicated Protestant canons who also held canonries at Cologne. Johann's passing led to a double election, the Protestant majority choosing a Brandenburg prince, the Catholic minority a duke of Lorraine. Forces were mustered, some fighting occurred, and in the end the balance of forces shifted in favor of the Catholics. Emperor Rudolph (who wanted the see for his own nephew) enfiefed the Catholic claimant, in 1604 the Brandenburger and the Protestant canons were bought off, and shortly thereafter the see came into Habsburg hands.

The third conflict tested the Ferdinandine Declaration, a second codicil to the Peace of 1555. Contested by the Catholics, it deprived Catholic ecclesiastical princes of the right to force their dissenting subjects to choose between conformity and emigration. The test case arose at Würzburg, where Julius Echter von Mespelbrunn became the incumbent in 1573. In Julius his Protestant vassals found themselves overmatched. In short order he reclaimed Würzburg's *Hochstift* by paying off the land's debts and redeeming many districts mortgaged to Protestant nobles. In 1577, when Julius banished their preachers, the Protestants protested the move as illegal. Holding his ground, Julius undertook a major campaign of evangelizing his subjects, about 100,000 of whom returned to Catholicism. Two years later, defying the Declaration, Julius ordered the recusants to leave Würzburg territory, and he made the order stick against a storm of Protestant protests and polemics.

The fourth conflict concerned the rights of religious minorities in free cities, which, except for four southern cities, the Religious Peace did not protect. It unfolded at Aachen, the northwestern free city that for centuries hosted the coronations of Roman (German) kings. In 1560, when three Protestant congregations existed at Aachen, the Catholic city council barred Protestants from the magistracies. By 1574, however, the Protestants had got a foothold in the council and forced nullification of the law of 1560, and by 1580 they felt strong enough to declare religious toleration in the city. These changes led to severe internal conflicts and intensified the intrigues of foreign powers, notably at Brussels and at Düsseldorf (Cleves-Jülich). After mediation failed, the case was referred to Prague, where, with his customary energy, Emperor Rudolph let it drag on for more than a decade. Eventually, an Imperial mandate restored control of Aachen to the Catholics, though it could not be fully enforced until the mid-1610s. Neither the Protestant Union nor the Dutch Republic intervened.

These four incidents illustrate how the reversal of Catholic fortunes and Protestant reluctance to break the Peace preserved the Imperial *convivencia*. At Cologne and Strasbourg the Catholic dynasties (Bavaria, Austria, Lorraine) successfully protected the Catholic interpretation of the Ecclesiastical Reservation. At Würzburg Bishop Julius successfully asserted the Catholic rejection of the Ferdinandine Declaration and treated his dissenting subjects as every lay prince had the right to do. And at Aachen the local Catholics regained control of their city because of the emperor's (desultory) enforcement of the Religious Peace's provision for Imperial free cities. Taken together, the four cases formed a string of defensive successes that bolstered Catholic hopes and deepened Protestant fears.

By 1600 the Protestants had split into two separate parties. While the Lutheran princes swallowed much unpleasantness and danger to preserve the Imperial *convivencia*, the Reformed party, urged by their confessional brethren in France and the Low Countries, were pressing German Protestants to help the international struggle against Rome. The Lutherans held the key to the Peace, for although they became more unified after the Formula of Concord (1576), they did not become politically stronger. If the Imperial situation should unravel and merge the German situation with the international confessional struggle, Calvinists against Catholics, the Lutherans would be caught in the middle. This is why their political leaders did not contest the Catholic recovery with arms, no more than they would, unless forced by necessity, during the Thirty Years War.

4. ARISTOCRATIC POLITICS AND CONFESSIONAL STRIFE

The Imperial *convivencia* had arisen from a political sleight-of-hand that finessed an uncompromisable religious conflict into a compromisable political one. It depended on a political asymmetry in the Imperial Diet between a larger, more diffuse Catholic party and a smaller, more compact Protestant one. The Catholics possessed the monarchy and majorities in the electoral college and the Princes' Chamber of the Diet, but, with two powerful exceptions (Austria and Bavaria), the principal aristocratic dynasties were Protestants.[36] The asymmetry of this configuration was compensated by abandoning majority rule for parity rule in what were called "religious matters." The successful overcoming of the four crises of the 1580s and 1590s without serious fighting ought to have hardened the *convivencia* and would have done so, perhaps, in the absence of other disturbing forces.

From the west, to be sure, ripples from the French and the Netherlandish religious wars continually refreshed old grievances and hatreds. Still, the structures of Imperial public life continued to function well until the last years of the new century's first decade. Then began a disruption that certainly did help to open the road to war by paralyzing the institutions of Imperial governance. Yet it did not arise, as has often been alleged, spontaneously from the confessional parties in the Diet. The somnolence and indecision of the Imperial monarchy in the latter part of Rudolph II's reign played an important weakening role, of course, because his dilatory and inconsistent rule confused, exasperated, worried, and angered the princes on both sides of the confessional divide. The result was an entropy of Imperial constitutional life. The absence of leadership aggravated an attrition of the trust on which depended the Diet and the Imperial Chamber Court, the weakening of which deprived public life of regular forums for negotiating conflicts. Yet such institutions were not the Empire's only political assets. The princes, who in some sense constituted the Empire, also commanded an ancient aristocratic culture of direct negotiation and arbitration among dynasties. This culture proved its undiminished strength in the prewar era's most dangerous conflict, a struggle over the succession to the Lower Rhenish duchies of Cleves-Jülich.[37]

The last native ruler of these lands, John William (1562–1609), was "by nature and complexion melancholy and depressed," his physicians declared in 1589.[38] When he died childless in 1609, two Lutheran princes, Elector John Sigismund of Brandenburg and Count Palatine Wolfgang William (1578–1653) of Neuburg, advanced claims to the lands through their wives. At first everything went well. In July 1609 the claimants' envoys met at Duisburg, where the territorial estates accepted their joint rule (*condominium*) and swore obedience to both "until one of our principals be declared by

36 The dukes of Lorraine, though Imperial princes, took little or no part in Imperial political life.
37 Cleves-Jülich (in German the two names are reversed) denotes a composite state of five parts: the duchies of Cleves, Jülich, and Berg, plus the counties of Mark and Ravensberg. Its capital lay at Düsseldorf. The entire complex straddled the Rhine along the modern Dutch-German border and up the Rhine toward Cologne.
38 H. C. Erik Midelfort, *Mad Princes of Renaissance Germany*, 99.

agreement or by law the sole rightful successor to these lands."[39] The estates set the condition, however, that the joint rulers:

> sustain, preserve, and protect the Roman Catholic and the other Christian religion, which both in the Holy Roman Empire and in these principalities and the county of Mark are everywhere publicly practiced and exercised. Further, that no one is to be disturbed, molested, annoyed, or distressed in his conscience or worship.[40]

In Cleves-Jülich a settlement based on the Religious Peace of 1555 was entirely unrealistic. One of the legal faiths, Roman Catholicism, was getting stronger, while the other, Lutheranism, was losing ground to both the legal Catholic and the illegal Reformed faith. The latter's strength was emphasized by the organization of a synod at Duisburg for the combined Reformed churches of Cleves, Jülich, and Berg. They called for counsel from Abraham Scultetus, who was trawling in these disturbed waters, "and I was happy to show up there, where certain canons and rules were made concerning the uniformity of doctrine and church usages, which down to the present day are still beneficial to these churches."[41] Then, in 1613/14 a hammer blow fell on the condominium in the form of a double conversion, John Sigismund to the Reformed and Wolfgang William to the Catholic faith. These acts immediately transformed the Cleves-Jülich affair from a regional, intra-Lutheran issue into a general European one. The Dutch Republic and the Protestant Union sided with the Brandenburger, the Spanish regime at Brussels and the Catholic League backed the Neuburger. What would have been, two generations ago, just another aristocratic succession dispute, in these times threatened to disrupt the Twelve Years Truce (1609–21) between Spain and the Dutch Republic and plunge the entire northwest into a transregional conflict. In the midst of this affair, the old emperor died.

Left to themselves, the two claimant princes proceeded in the traditional way. Adopting the German aristocracy's customary preference for negotiation and aided by French and English mediation, they came to an agreement. The Treaty of Xanten (12 November 1614) maintained the fiction of joint rule but in fact partitioned the five principalities. Cleves and Jülich became the first Hohenzollern outpost in the west; Mark, Berg, and Ravenstein strengthened the Catholic position in the northwest.[42] And there, at least for the time being, the matter rested.

The peaceful outcome of the Cleves-Jülich succession crisis showed that the Empire could regulate its conflicts even when rising confessional blood had neutralized its chief organs, the Diet and the Chamber Court. But only with great luck, for alternatives had already begun to form. In 1608–9 two large, armed, confessionally specific associations came into being. On the initiative of Prince Christian of Anhalt-Bernburg (1568–1630), governor of the Upper Palatinate and principal councilor to the Palatine Elector, Protestant powers assembled in May 1608 at Ahausen near

39 Gottfried Lorenz, ed., *Quellen zur Vorgeschichte und zu den Anfängen des Dreissjährigen Krieges*, 112.
40 Lorenz, ed., *Quellen zur Vorgeschichte*, 113.
41 Abraham Scultetus, *Die Selbstbiographie des Heidelberger Theologen und Hofpredigers Abraham Scultetus (1566–1624)*, 53.
42 Wolfgang William, ruler of a northern Bavarian principality created in 1505 to compensate the losers in the Bavarian War, was the nephew of the elector-archbishop of Cologne. This very artificial conglomerate was never reunited.

Nördlingen to found the Protestant Union.[43] They indicted the times for a general degradation of the Public Peace and of threats and acts of violence, such that no estate could any longer feel secure. If these things continued, "the ancient constitution of the Empire will be tossed onto the trash heap," from which "the final destruction of all law and order and welfare, also the ruin of all peaceful life in the Holy Empire may be expected."[44] The Protestants denied any desire to withhold from the emperor his due loyalty, but they insisted on their determination "to oppose with a necessary and just defense, and in a manly way, those who intend to burden or trouble them in violation of the common law, Imperial laws and statutes, and especially the established and oft-confirmed Public Peace."[45] It was a reprise of Smalkalden in 1530–31. Some Protestant princes and cities stood aloof from the Union, but those of the highly fragmented south and west flocked to its ranks.

The Catholic League formed at Munich on 10 July 1609 as a response to the Union. Around Duke Maximilian I of Bavaria, its head, engine, and financier, there assembled mostly southern prince-bishops. In him, not in the emperor, they recognized the rock that anchored the Catholic cause in the south.[46] The Catholic League's treaty resembled the Union's in its stated purpose of defending "the sound Imperial constitutions and (other) laws, and especially the religious and secular peace [of 1555], which were accepted by the estates in order to maintain peace, order, and unity" against "misunderstandings" and "violent attacks and actions."[47] The signatories saw their motive as "solely to defend and maintain the true Catholic religion" and to preserve "a general peace and order in the Empire, and therefore the common good [*publicum bonum*]."[48]

The Empire's legal structure aside, a comparison of the League and the Union reveals the fundamental inequality of the two confessions' status and self-understanding. On one side stood a Protestant party that was only a party, an aristocratic association of the classic type, in which estates large and small gathered for mutual aid and protection. On the other side stood a Catholic party which was more than a party, a pillar of the Catholic empire, in which Duke Maximilian stood proxy for the decrepit emperor as protector of the Imperial episcopacy. Union and League faced one another as self-proclaimed defenders of Imperial public life and the common good, but also as potentially hostile powers outfitting themselves for the ever more probable end of the Imperial *convivencia*. Each had its allies or potential allies outside the German lands, the Union with the Dutch Republic and France (with whom it signed an alliance in February 1609), the League with Spain. The situation seemed to many then, and has seemed to many modern historians, a tinderbox waiting for the right match. This is deceptive, for when the war began, it came not on this western front but in the east, in the kingdom of Bohemia. Its cause was not the rise of

43 Members were Prince Christian of Anhalt for the Elector Palatine, Count Palatine Philip Louis of Pfalz-Neuburg, Margrave Christian of Brandenburg-Bayreuth (Kulmbach), Duke John Frederick of Württemberg, Margrave Joachim Ernest of Brandenburg-Ansbach, Elector John Sigismund of Brandenburg; Landgrave Maurice of Hesse; and the cities of Nuremberg, Strasbourg, and Ulm.
44 Lorenz, ed., *Quellen zur Vorgeschichte*, 68.
45 Lorenz, ed., *Quellen zur Vorgeschichte*, 69.
46 Members were Duke Maximilian I of Bavaria; Count Jacob Fugger of Kirchberg-Weissenhorn; prince-bishops of Würzburg, Augsburg, Constance, Strasbourg and Passau (Archduke Leopold of Austria), and Regensburg; prince-prelate of Ellwangen; and prince-abbot of Kempten.
47 Lorenz, ed., *Quellen zur Vorgeschichte*, 104.
48 Lorenz, ed., *Quellen zur Vorgeschichte*, 107, art. 4.

confessional strife in the German lands but a struggle between king and nobles for the rule of that kingdom.

5. THE HABSBURGS AND THEIR BOHEMIAN PROBLEM

The Thirty Years War did not begin with a breakdown in Imperial governance. The Sarajevo of 1618 lay not in Austria or any other German land, arguably not even in the Holy Roman Empire. In Bohemia the Religious Peace of 1555 was not law. The kingdom possessed its own, much older *convivencia*. Since the end of the Hussite Wars, it comprised a plurality of religious communities – Utraquists, Catholics, and the Unity of Brethren[49] – de facto and to some real degree de jure.

The situation in Bohemia differed in major ways, therefore, from those in the eastern Austrian duchies. In the latter the Habsburg rulers certainly did possess the right of reformation, even if the Protestant nobles and Imperial policy long conspired to make it irrelevant. This combination foundered when Habsburg policy began to apply to the Austrian lands the rights that the Religious Peace confirmed to all Imperial princes. Imperial law trumped provincial liberties, though only because the dynasty discovered in favoring Catholics for patronage a key to breaking noble power in the various Austrian duchies. It might seem reasonable, at least from the point of view of Innsbruck, Graz, and Vienna, that such policies be extended to the kingdom of Bohemia, but that is not how the Bohemian conflict began. It had initially little or nothing to do with a program – what some would call "absolutist" – to create religious unity from above in the western European style. Rather than a religious war of the western kind, it began as a continuation of the Hussite Wars.

In the kingdom of Bohemia between the end of the Hussite Wars and around 1500 had consolidated the first religious *convivencia* of what would become (in retrospect) a recognizably east central European kind. While historians have very probably romanticized the Bohemian *convivencia* (as others have its medieval Iberian counterpart), taken by itself the evidence for a peaceful plurality of religions is impressive. In 1596 Enrico Cardinal Caetani (1550–99) passed through Moravia on his way to Poland, to which he had been named legate *a latere*. After crossing the frontier at Mikulov, the cardinal's party stopped at Austerlitz,

> a place full of so many and various heresies and sects that some say in the same house the father could believe one and his son another. There the wife could be of one persuasion in matters of faith and her husband of another, so it was not surprising that 64, perhaps even 70 kinds of heresy could be found. But of Catholics there was not a single one.[50]

Fynes Moryson (1566–ca. 1617), an English traveler in Bohemia, reported much the same conditions, though he was far less surprised than was the Roman nobleman. "I founde [the emperor's] subiectes in Bohemia more differing in opinions of Religion," he recorded, "yet to converse in strong amity and peace together, without

49 The English term for the Unity of Brethen, dissenters from the Utraquist establishment, is "Moravian Brethren."
50 Jan Polišenský, *The Thirty Years War*, 53. He quotes this passage from an official diary in the Caetani family archive.

which patience a turbulent spirit could not live in those partes."[51] Such locally ordered *convivencias* were fairly common in east central Europe, whereas they had difficulty maintaining themselves in the German lands and were practically unknown in western Europe (except the Dutch Republic).

Establishing and preserving a *convivencia* depended far less on the idea of religious tolerance than on the sense of security that permitted parties to negotiate differences where they were negotiable, and to tolerate them where they were not. Much the worst intercommunal bloodlettings in this era were provoked by rulers as manipulators, invaders, conquerors, colonizers, and expellers of peoples.[52] It may be true that Bohemia's peace depended on collaboration between Catholics and Utraquists, which since around 1500 formed "a firm foundation ... for the maintenance of religious peace and the calm furthering of domestic affairs of state."[53] Yet the Bohemian order had been created after the Hussite Wars by a dominant nobility under relatively weak kings. The chief threat to it came from the Ottomans, hence the decision of 1527 to elect Archduke Ferdinand, a powerful Habsburg prince, to succeed the king who had fallen on the field of Mohačs. While this realistic settlement held for most of the following three-quarters of a century, both the resurgence of Roman Catholicism and the growing role of Utraquism as a legal Trojan horse for Protestants placed new pressures upon it, much as the Catholic resurgence and the Reformed advance tended to threaten, it would seem, its Imperial counterpart.

The disruption of the Bohemian *convivencia* began during the last years of Emperor Rudolph with the Habsburg "brothers' quarrel" (*Bruderzwist*). His eldest brother, Archduke Matthias, backed by their younger brothers, aimed to force his eldest brother to cede the rule of Hungary, the Austrian lands, Moravia, and Bohemia, plus an expectancy of the Imperial crown. Matthias met with total success. A Jewish chronicler in Prague reports that in mid-April 1608, Archduke Matthias came into Bohemia accompanied by

> great numbers of brave men mounted on steeds [Esther 8: 10, 14] and armed infantry from the [ranks of] the warriors [Num. 31: 49] of the countries of Austria, Moravia, Hungary, and Tartary. They did great damage to this city, stealing, rampaging, killing, and burning – inflicting damage of more than four times one hundred thousand [gulden?]. Duke Matthias desired to rule over the countries of Bohemia, Hungary, Moravia, and Austria by force. Our ruler, the emperor, may he be exalted, also gathered a great force from the cities of Bohemia, and a force of about twenty thousand brave armed soldiers came here, to Prague. And we were extremely disturbed.[54]

Satisfied by Rudolph's cessions, Matthias and his forces returned to Vienna.

Rudolph died on 20 January 1612, only months after his last remaining kingdom, Bohemia, passed into Matthias's hands. For sixty years – the longest Imperial reign in

51 "Of Bohemia touching Religion," in Fynes Moryson, The fourth Part of an Itinerary/written by Fynes Moryson gent:/first in the Latine tongue and then/by himself translated into English/Continuing/The discourse uppon several heads/through all the Dominions he passed/in his travell described in the former/three Parts, Corpus Christi College Oxford Ms. XCIV (Book III, p. 326). My thanks to Howard Louthan for this text.
52 This is true of St. Bartholomew's Day in 1574 in France, the rising in the Valtellina in 1620, the Ulster rising in 1641, and Savoyard action against the Waldensians in 1655.
53 Polišensky, *Thirty Years War*, 24.
54 Abraham David, ed., *A Hebrew Chronicle from Prague, c. 1615*, 59–60.

history – he had more or less preserved the Habsburg policy of Imperial Catholicism despite the Reformed challenge and the Catholic revival. His final assertion of the traditional policy was a masterpiece, a veritable time-bomb for his fraternal tormentors. Rudolph's "letter of majesty" (*Majestätsbrief*) of 9 July 1609 declared his special grace for "the Utraquist estates,"[55] confirmed their right of self-administration and their equal standing with the Catholics, and guaranteed freedom of religion to all subjects. Agreements were then reached on the regulation of ordination of priests, management of parishes and cemeteries, and division of tithes. Formally, therefore, the Bohemian *convivencia* resembled its Imperial counterpart extended to much broader sectors of the population, but with a difference: unlike the exclusion of Calvinists from the Imperial Religious Peace, the Bohemian arrangement confirmed both Lutherans and Calvinists as de jure Utraquists. While Rudolph's charter appeared to grant general religious freedom, it masked the old question of Bohemian sovereignty – king or estates? If a Habsburg king were to threaten or seem to threaten the Bohemian *convivencia*, he would be opposed by the united forces of the old dissenting faith and two new, Protestant ones.

Matthias did not, could not, stabilize this situation. The third son of Maximilian II and Maria of Spain (Charles V's daughter), Matthias was personally open and good-tempered, but his long wait in the shadows had frustrated his ambition and wounded his pride. At his succession he had but seven years to live, and his marriage to a cousin in 1611 produced no heir. Next in line stood Archduke Ferdinand of the Styrian line (b. 1578, r. 1619–37), eldest son of Charles, Emperor Ferdinand I's son (1540–90). Ferdinand II possessed neither Rudolph's stolidity nor Matthias's volatility. More Wittelsbach than Habsburg in his firm principles and strong religious commitment, he represented a forward, Bavarian-style Catholic policy rather than the Imperial Catholicism of his grandfather, father, and brother. According to the dynasty's customary law, Matthias had no choice but to promote Ferdinand's succession to the Bohemian throne. When the Bohemian Diet met at Prague in June 1617, most of the estates agreed to accept Ferdinand as their king, providing he would first confirm the religious status quo. When Ferdinand announced that he would comply, both his path to the throne and the Bohemian *convivencia* seemed secure.

The disruption of the Bohemian succession can only be described as a (preventive) coup d'état, which announced itself by reprising the defenestration of Prague in 1419. On 23 May 1618 representatives of the Bohemian estates assembled in Prague Castle, where they learned of Emperor Matthias's refusal to allow an action the Protestants maintained was lawful under the 1609 letter of majesty. They seized two royal governors, Vilem Slavata (1572–1652) and Jaroslav Borzita of Martinicz (1582–1649) – monarchists and strong Catholics – and, in Slavata's own words, "pitilessly precipitated two governors of His Majesty, the highest officers in Bohemia, out of the window into a deep valley."[56] Martinicz, tells Slavata, "since in flying down he ceaselessly called out the names 'Jesus, Maria,' sank to earth as gently as if he were sitting down, so that through the intercession of the Virgin Mary and the protection of God the

---

55 Bernd Roeck, ed., *Gegenreformation und Dreißigjähriger Krieg 1555–1648*, 149.
56 Henry Frederick Schwarz, *The Imperial Privy Council in the Seventeenth Century*, 344–5. The remaining quotes in this paragraph are also from this source. Slavata, a convert from Protestantism, opposed the settlement of 1609. He later became a bitter opponent of Albrecht von Wallenstein, who was his kinsman.

terrible fall did not harm his health . . . in spite of his heavy body."[57] One of the defenestrators, a knight named Ulrich Kinsky, shouted as Martinicz was falling, "We shall see whether his Mary helps him."[58] But then Kinsky looked down out of the window, and, seeing the victim unhurt, exclaimed, "I swear to God, his Mary did help him."[59] So, if the report is to be trusted, did the rubbish heap onto which he fell. Slavata, less fortunate, hit his head on a rock, but he, too, survived to thank the Virgin for her saving miracle.[60]

The Bohemian insurrection began at Prague on the day of defenestration. A committee of the Diet now assumed power. With some reluctance the Silesian and Lusatian estates followed suit, though the Moravians refused, and the Hungarian diet agreed to the coronation of Ferdinand (he was already crowned as king of Bohemia). As the confrontation worsened, a call went out from Prague to all enemies, current and prospective, of the Habsburg dynasty. Immediately, the politico-religious lines began to tangle, as Christian of Anhalt (1568–1630) persuaded the Catholic but anti-Spanish duke of Savoy to finance a mercenary force to fight for the Bohemians. At Vienna, Bishop Melchior Khlesl, Matthias's chief advisor and an advocate of negotiation, found himself under arrest on orders from Ferdinand, who began to assemble his own forces for war. With Matthias's death on 20 March 1619 the curtain rose on a new era. It looked weirdly similar to what had happened at Prague two hundred years earlier.

The Bohemian conflict brought down the Imperial Religious Peace for only one reason: the Bohemian king was also Holy Roman emperor. Given the weakened state of Imperial public life, perhaps the next religious conflict in the German lands would have overstrained the *convivencia* and led, without Bohemian instigation, to another German religious war. What seems clear today is that Imperial public life, as it had developed since the fifteenth century and as it had been modified and hardened by the Peace of 1555, and the formation of confessions possessed long-underestimated capabilities for the regulation of conflict.

The Thirty Years War was not the outcome of an irresistible plunge toward a great religious war in the German lands. Its chief causes were contingent causes, and the most serious of them resided in the Habsburg dynasty's rule and misrule, in its policies and the paralysis, and in the impossibly disparate and contradictory characters of the lands and peoples it governed.

57 Schwarz, *The Imperial Privy Council*, 345.
58 Schwarz, *The Imperial Privy Council*, 345.
59 Schwarz, *The Imperial Privy Council*, 345.
60 Klaus Bussmann and Heinz Schilling, eds., *1648. War and Peace in Europe. Münster/Osnabrück 24.10.1998–17.1.1999*, vol. 2: 337. The traditional detail of their falls being cushioned by a dungheap seems to be an embellishment.

17

The Thirty Years War

Through the *Peace of Westphalia* the Protestant Church had been acknowledged as an independent one – to the great confusion and humiliation of Catholicism. This peace has often passed for the palladium of Germany, as having established its political constitution. But this constitution was in fact a confirmation of the particular rights of the countries into which Germany had been broken up. It involves no thought, no conception of the proper aim of a state.

G. W. F. Hegel

The Thirty Years War ended centuries of the German lands' relative isolation and brought their age of reformations to a close. It began as a double reprise: the Bohemian revolt against Emperor Ferdinand II in 1618 reprised the Hussite revolt against Sigismund 200 years before; the ensuing war between the emperor and German Protestant princes emulated the German wars of religion between 1546 and 1552. German history contained no precedents, however, for the massive, repeated, and decisive intrusions of foreign military powers – Denmark, Sweden, and France – which transformed a German civil war into the most complex of struggles.

Historians commonly divide the Thirty Years War into four phases, each named for the principal military antagonist of the emperor and the Catholic League:

1. the Bohemian War (1618–23), from the Bohemian revolt against Emperor Ferdinand II through the Catholic League's occupation of the Rhine Palatinate and Lower Saxony;
2. the Danish War (1625–29), from the Danish intervention to the Edict of Restitution;
3. the Swedish War (1630–35), from the Swedish invasion to the Peace of Prague; and
4. the French War (1634–48), from the French invasion of the Empire to the Peace of Westphalia.

From the German lands' perspective, however, the central issue was "the constitution of the Holy Roman Empire and – inseparable from this question – the balance of political and religious forces in central Europe."[1] In this perspective, the picture of four discrete phases of conflict dissolves into a three-act German drama with a huge supporting cast. Act I still begins in Bohemia, but it develops into an

---

1 Ronald G. Asch, *The Thirty Years War: The Holy Roman Empire and Europe, 1618–48*, 3.

opportunistic attempt to reform the Empire in a Habsburg, monarchical, and Catholic sense, and it ends with the Edict of Restitution of 1629. Act II opens with the Swedish invasion of 1630 and the Protestant victories that persuade emperor and princes, Catholic and Protestant, to restore the Imperial constitution; it closes with the Peace of Prague signed in 1635. Finally, Act III brings the French into the field and creates a military stalemate which ends only in 1648 with the Peace of Westphalia. This replotting produces a drama with turning points at 1630 and 1635. Its outcome represents a German victory inside a European failure, for while the Empire reconstituted itself, Europe steamed ahead into 150 years of international wars.

I. THE BOHEMIAN WAR TO THE IMPERIAL WAR

The war opened in the summer of 1619, when the Bohemian rebels took the military initiative and sent an army under Count Henry Matthew of Thurn (1567–1640) on the march toward Vienna. The Austrian Protestants rejoiced, and one of them, it is said, grabbed King (soon to be emperor-elect) Ferdinand's sleeve and told him to give in. Soon, however, a Habsburg victory made Ferdinand's position secure enough to travel in July to Frankfurt for his Imperial election and coronation. He did not apply for papal confirmation.

At this point came the fateful step that escalated an Austro-Bohemian tit-for-tat into a genuine insurrection. On 31 July 1619 the Protestant estates of Bohemia formed a "Bohemian Confederation" and deposed Ferdinand as king. "King Ferdinand," the rebels declared, "was elected and crowned Bohemian king against the liberties and privileges of this kingdom and in an irregular manner."[2] Five days later, they crowned as their new king Elector Frederick of the Palatinate (1596–1623), who decided against his Heidelberg advisors' counsel that "acceptance would begin a general religious war."[3] Alas, in this senior lay Imperial elector and head of the Protestant Union the Bohemian estates had elected "a man who had never seen either a battle or a corpse . . . a prince who knew more about gardening than fighting."[4] The "Winter King" – so he was mocked for his reign's brevity – accepted the Bohemian crown only on the strong persuasion of Christian of Anhalt and Electress Elizabeth (1596–1662), an Anglo-Scottish princess of the house of Stuart, who possessed the iron her husband lacked.

When the new royal couple arrived at Prague on the last day of October 1619, the Palatine councilor Ludwig Camerarius (1573–1651) wrote to Heidelberg that "King Matthias or Ferdinand never received such honor, for the public rejoicing of many persons beggars description . . . and the Prague burghers alone spent 50,000 gulden on the occasion."[5] Well and good, but then Camerarius discovered that "the treasury is utterly empty, and everything's so ruinous that I find the pope's quip – 'this prince may well find himself in a labyrinthine war' – quite apt with respect to the government as well."[6] The ubiquitous Abraham Scultetus, who had come from Heidelberg with his prince, undertook a purging of the churches, beginning with the royal chapel, an act for which his critics called him, as he records, "an iconoclast, an atheist without

2 Gottfried Lorenz, ed., *Quellen zur Vorgeschichte und zu den Anfängen des Dreissjährigen Krieges*, 369.
3 Geoffrey Parker, *The Thirty Years' War*, 47.
4 Parker, *The Thirty Years' War*, 47.
5 Lorenz, ed., *Quellen zur Vorgeschichte*, 421.
6 Lorenz, ed., *Quellen zur Vorgeschichte*, 421.

religion, a persecutor of the pious and the godfearing."[7] His Calvinist zeal to purify St. Vitus's Cathedral soon gave Praguers pause for thought about how the Bohemian *convivencia* might fare under a Calvinist king whose German preachers had never been forced to tolerate dissent.

Of more immediate concern to the king's German councilors were the empty treasury and the queen's behavior. "So long as the English hussy [Elizabeth] does not change people's minds," Camerarius wrote home, "the situation is well in hand. Having to wait for her at meals and for churchgoing, plus other petty rudenesses, gives offense, and the Bohemian women are offended in particular by an uncovered breast."[8] Prague was not Heidelberg, much less London. Frederick and Elizabeth were crowned at St. Vitus's on 3 November 1619.

A major confrontation now seemed unavoidable, just as had happened in Sigismund's day, for once the Bohemians allied with the nobles of Upper and Lower Austria, Ferdinand probably had no choice. His position was good. The Protestant Union and the kings of France and England declined to support the Bohemian rebels; the German Lutheran princes, no friends to Calvinists, were bought off with a promise that they could keep the secularized bishoprics in the north; and in May 1620 the Protestant Union and the Catholic League signed a pact of non-aggression. With the Bohemian forces now isolated, the League's army under Johan Tserclaes, Count Tilly (1559–1632) moved on the Austrian rebels, united with the Habsburg troops, and in September 1620 crossed with them into Bohemia. Meanwhile, Elector John George I (b. 1585, r. 1611–56) honored his deal with Ferdinand by invading the Bohemian crownlands of Lusatia and Silesia, which fell almost without a shot fired, while Spanish troops moved in to occupy the Rhine Palatinate. In early November, Tilly decided to assault the rebels' fortified position on White Mountain, a rise near Prague, which fell easily after an hour's fighting. Now fugitives, the Winter King and his queen fled westward toward the Rhine.

White Mountain, commonly seen as a clash between Bohemian patriots and German invaders, was actually a mêlée of peoples. Christian of Anhalt's memorandum on the lost battle breaks down the Imperial order of battle as follows: Neapolitans, Walloons, South Germans, Lower Saxons, and Nassauers in the infantry, and Germans, Bohemians, Netherlanders, Florentines, and Austrians in the cavalry. Against them – the League army's battle order is lost – stood Bohemians, Moravians, Germans, and Austrians. The combined Imperial-Bavarian League force is estimated at 32,400 foot, 7,550 horse; the Bohemians had 10,100 foot and 11,000 horse. The Catholic army was ethnically more mixed, and its much higher ratio of infantry to cavalry – 4.3:1 versus 1:1 for the Bohemian side – made it more modern as well.

Duke Maximilian of Bavaria, whose support had made the Imperial-League victory possible, thought it should be exploited with caution. In mid-January 1621 he opposed making a general and thorough program of religious reformation in a Catholic sense. In view of the current instability in Bohemia, he writes, "such a reformation should be put on hold, though the Catholics should regain possession of what

7 Abraham Scultetus, *Die Selbstbiographie des Heidelberger Theologen und Hofpredigers Abraham Scultetus (1566–1624)*, 80. It is worth pointing out that Scultetus's passages on his activities in Prague are deeply defensive and apologetic, laced with typical Reformed condemnations of the veneration of images as idolatry. His printed sermons, he reports with some satisfaction, were as roundly attacked at Lutheran Tübingen, Wittenberg, and Leipzig as at Catholic Mainz and Ingoldstadt.
8 Lorenz, ed., *Quellen zur Vorgeschichte*, 422.

they formerly had."[9] Calvinist worship should be forbidden and existing anti-Catholic measures nullified. The remaining tasks, "which at the present time and in present conditions cannot be accomplished, can be taken care of later, when everything has been brought to a better, more peaceful, and proper condition."[10] As for the future, the duke holds it "necessary that Spain and the house of Austria, whom this matter concerns directly and in principle, decide . . . how and in what form they want to go on with the war."[11] And the war did go forward, as mixed bodies of Imperial and Bavarian troops pursued noble rebels in both Upper Austria and Bohemia. Meanwhile, as the invasion of the west got underway, Maximilian reaped his reward from Ferdinand. The Palatine electoral office, declared forfeit by reason of treason, was conferred on Maximilian for life, and the eastern Palatine lands (Upper Palatinate), which lay on his northern border, came to him in perpetuity.

In Ferdinand II the Bavarian duke had found at last a Habsburg ruler to his own taste. No more of the unsteady temporizers who had ruled so long at Vienna or Prague. And no more conciliatory Imperial Catholicism, for Ferdinand was the first Habsburg monarch to adopt Munich's forward Catholic policy. Some found this emperor charming, mild-mannered, and self-reliant, others tough, inflexible, and too ready to heed his Jesuit confessors. All agreed, however, on the depth and vigor of his devotion to the Catholic religion and the model character of his personal and family life, in both respects a major change from the Habsburg courts of the previous sixty years.

Behind Ferdinand's policy lay no concept, much less one of what has been called "confessional absolutism." His pronouncements advance legalistic arguments about historic rights, the classic political language of the German lands (and of Bohemia). He had no clear concept of the unity of the Habsburg lands nor any program of governmental centralization. But he did have a clear sense of his right of reformation under the Religious Peace and, though his Imperial writ arguably did not run in that kingdom, he fashioned accordingly his plans for a settlement in post-White Mountain Bohemia. The process began with what was called a "Confiscations Court," which tried 1,500 Bohemian landowners and condemned almost half to lose all or part of their estates. Many other nobles and most towns also lost their lands, and by autumn 1623 their power of resistance was broken. Thus began a reconfiguration of the Bohemian kingdom's religions (the Austrian Protestants suffered similar treatment). For the Bohemian Catholics it was a second spring, for the Protestants a new winter.

As the dispossessed king and queen of Bohemia fled westward, behind them came Tilly and his army, sent to finish the war by seizing the Palatine lands and their capital at Heidelberg. In the west the Catholic forces faced three armies commanded by German Protestant princes. After Tilly defeated one of them, the foul-mouthed warrior-bishop Christian of Brunswick (1599–1626), all three scurried via Lower Saxony toward safety in the Dutch Republic with Tilly in pursuit. Meanwhile, in the conquered Palatine capital, the magnificent Heidelberg library was packed into 196 boxes and sent by Maximilian's order to Rome as a gift to the pope.[12]

9   Lorenz, ed., *Quellen zur Vorgeschichte*, 514.
10 Lorenz, ed., *Quellen zur Vorgeschichte*, 514.
11 Lorenz, ed., *Quellen zur Vorgeschichte*, 517.
12 This most important library of the German Renaissance consisted of both printed books and manuscripts. They were incorporated into the Vatican Library. About a quarter of the manuscripts, mostly in German, were returned to Heidelberg in 1816.

The invasion of the German north by a (mostly) southern, Catholic army was a triumphant sign of the solidarity between Elector Maximilian and Emperor Ferdinand. Nearly a century ago, Maximilian's great-grandfather had intrigued with the Protestant princes and the king of France against the royal election of Ferdinand, Charles V's brother. Now, the two leading Catholic dynasties stood as firmly united as they had earlier been at loggerheads. The divisions on the Protestant side, chiefly between Lutheran and Calvinist princes, meant that if the war now ended, it would be followed by a Catholic peace.

The Catholic military victories in the west and northwest drove the northern Protestant princes into a watch and wait posture of neutrality. They were well advised, for behind Tilly's forces, some 15,000 strong, a second Catholic army was on the march for the north. Ferdinand, unable to raise an army in his Austrian lands, had turned to the tried-and-true German solution, a military enterpriser. The man he found became the most celebrated of that breed. He was Albrecht Wenzel Eusebius von Wallenstein (Albrecht z Valdštejna, 1583–1634), a Bohemian noble long in Imperial service. An Utraquist born and Catholic by choice, he studied in the Jesuit school at Olmütz/Olomouc in Moravia and thereafter in numerous foreign universities – German, Dutch, English, French, and Italian. He read mathematics and astronomy, when he studied at all.

Wallenstein's true métier was war. Besides military experience, two things – money and connections – equipped him to become the leading Imperial general during the second half of the 1620s. Wealth from a first marriage and vast estates he acquired from the Bohemian confiscations made him a principal creditor to the Imperial treasury. Emperor Ferdinand, a contemporary reported, "called him loyalty itself, his friends could rely on him, the young nobles looked upon him as a father, strangers as a protector . . . the common people loved him and praised him as an ornament and glory of the Imperial Court."[13] Fortune smiled on this Wallenstein, the ultimate striving man, whose love of astrology (Johannes Kepler had cast his horoscope) may have convinced him that money and connections, aided by the stars, would realize all his dreams.

Wallenstein's moment arrived in July 1623, when Ferdinand commissioned him supreme commander of an Imperial army yet to be raised. By year's end he had 62,000 men in arms, four times Tilly's forces, under veteran officers, some Catholics, some Protestants. He marched them to the north, where he and Tilly were able to coordinate attacks on the Protestant forces. The highpoint came in August 1627 at Lutter in southeastern Lower Saxony, where they defeated the Danish king's forces. More than a year earlier, Christian IV of Denmark (b. 1577, r. 1588–1648) had brought an army of about 20,000 men southward with the idea of saving his fellow Protestants (as Duke of Holstein he was also an Imperial prince). After Lutter, the two Catholic armies ravaged Lower Saxony and the Jutland peninsula. Christian, a broken man, saved his lands by means of a humiliating peace with the emperor (May 1629).

By 1629, when Catholic armies stood on the Baltic shore, the clearing of the north was complete. Wallenstein's army, now 130,000 strong, stood ready to keep it so. How the victors should now exploit their victory divided councilors at Munich

---

13 Franz Christoph von Khevenhüller, in Henry Frederick Schwarz, *The Imperial Privy Council in the Seventeenth Century*, 242.

and Vienna into militant and moderate parties. The rulers' Jesuit confessors – Adam Contzen at Munich and the Luxemburger Wilhelm Lamormaini (1570–1628) at Vienna – pressed for an aggressive policy of Catholic restoration. Against their counsel the moderates argued that some concessions should be made to the Protestant princes of Saxony and Brandenburg, hitherto neutral in the war, so as not to provoke them into taking up arms for the Protestant cause.

At this zenith of Catholic success, the militants won out at both courts. Emperor Ferdinand, emboldened by the Catholic victories in the field, issued on 6 March 1629 the Edict of Restitution. It ordered a general restoration to Catholics of ecclesiastical lands in the Empire. The Protestant powers must disgorge lands they had taken from the Catholic Church since 1552: two archbishoprics (Bremen and Magdeburg), twelve bishoprics, and more than 100 abbeys. The edict sought to settle the outstanding issues by declaring the Catholic interpretation of the Religious Peace of Augsburg (1555) to be correct, the Ecclesiastical Reservation (prelates who converted lost their offices) to be valid, and the Ferdinandine Declaration (protection for Protestant subjects of prince-bishops) invalid. The emperor would dispatch his commissioners around the Empire to reclaim all the archbishoprics, bishoprics, monasteries, hospitals, and endowments the Catholics had possessed in 1552 and restore them without further process to Catholic hands.

While the militants won the debate for the time being, enforcing the Edict of Restitution proved difficult in the heavily Protestant north, though less so in the south. The small Franconian town of Kitzingen had been mortgaged by the prince-bishop of Würzburg to the Hohenzollern margraves of Brandenburg-Ansbach, who had introduced Lutheranism. In January 1629, following the Catholic victories, Prince-bishop Philipp Adolf von Ehrenberg (b. 1583, r. 1623–31), a notable hunter of witches, redeemed the mortgage. When he came to Kitzingen on 10 January to receive the burghers' homage, the bishop entered the church, "held mass and demanded the keys to the parish [church], hospital and Etwashäuser church. After that the first popish sermon was held in the parish church on 11 January."[14] Nearly a thousand Kitzingen burghers chose exile over conformity. But this was not the end. Before the change, Master Claus, the stonemason, dreamt that after Würzburg bishop's arms replaced those of Hohenzollern margraves on the church tower, "it seemed that a man came in the air from the direction of Schweinfurt [from the north] *leading a lion*, and he gave the Würzburg arms a kick so that they clattered to the churchyard below."[15] Later on, when the king of Sweden entered the town following the battle of Breitenfeld, Master Claus was asked "whether *the man with the lion* has now arrived and whether he could recognize him [as the king of Sweden]. Master Claus [on seeing the picture] straightaway said, 'Yes, that's him.'"[16] This little story suggests how desperate things had become. German Protestants, their own princes having failed them, greeted the Swedish champion as their sole hope.

The Catholic triumph proved as brief as it was great, for it helped to provoke both the Swedish and later the French interventions in the German war. The Swedish invasion in 1630 began the changes that eventually forced a reversal of the Catholic

14   Gerhard Benecke, ed., *Germany in the Thirty Years War*, 46.
15   Benecke, ed., *Germany*, 46, emphasis in the original.
16   Benecke, ed., *Germany*, 46, emphasis in the original.

party's expectations and hence its policy. At the very moment when Gustavus Adolphus landed on the Pomeranian coast, the electors or their envoys, assembled at Regensburg, were being pressed by the emperor to join the Spanish efforts against the Dutch Republic and to elect his son as Roman king. When his confessor, Lamormaini, heard the Catholic electors' price, Wallenstein's dismissal, he "closed his eyes and replied . . . the Edict must stand firm, whatever evil might finally come from it. It matters little that the emperor, because of it, loses not only Austria but all of his kingdoms . . . provided he save his soul, which he cannot do without the implementation of the Edict."[17] Yet if the restoration were to succeed, the Catholic armies had to hold their positions in the north, and the best man for the task, Wallenstein, was now skulking in his tent. At this critical moment, even before King Gustavus Adolphus (b. 1594, r. 1611–32) broke camp for the march south into Saxony, the Catholic position began to crumble. It would never recover. Fortune, as Machiavelli famously wrote, proved indeed a fickle mistress.

2. THE ENTERPRISE OF WAR — FINANCES AND FORCES

"Money is the sinews of war." Whatever Wallenstein's meteoric rise owed to his abilities, its very possibility depended on the truth encapsulated by this maxim, borrowed from the ancient Romans. It expressed "an entirely new view of the nature and meaning of capital."[18] The new realism about power and money, which had spread through the German lands before 1600, reflected a new interest in government and war as rational enterprises. At the beginning of the Long War against the Ottomans, the Strasbourg jurist Georg Obrecht (1547–1612) practically reduced the practice of government to the getting, conserving, and deployment of money. "When a ruler wishes to protect, guard, and defend himself and his subjects from unjust force," he is reported to have said in 1590, "he must above all else possess and be armed with large sinews of war."[19]

For kings as for farmers, money was a necessary but unreliable good. The general devaluation of money since the 1570s had arisen from complex causes: economic disorders, population growth, increasing rates of extraction, rising stocks of bullion, and perhaps climatic deterioration. Prices soared, real incomes fell. By 1600 copper miners' wages in the county of Mansfeld sank below subsistence; in the southern Netherlands urban wage workers were paying as much as 80 percent of their incomes just to feed their families; and near the Upper Swabian city of Memmingen around 1600, rents were falling and prices rising.[20] Conditions continued to worsen in the early 1620s, the "Clipper and Nipper Era" (*Kipper- und Wipperzeit*), as official debasement and private fraud enabled profiteers, from local cheats up to Wallenstein, to coin money from the plight of the already and the soon to be poor.[21]

17 Parker, *The Thirty Years' War*, 101.
18 Michael Stolleis, *Pecunia Nervus Rerum. Zur Staatsfinanzierung der frühen Neuzeit*, 68.
19 Georg Obrecht, *Fünff Underschiedliche Secreta Politica von Anstellung, Erhaltung und Vermehrung guter Policey*, Preface. In the sixteenth-century slang, "nervus" was also a slang expression for "prick."
20 Based on information from Robert Dees, to whom my thanks.
21 This name alludes to the practice whereby sound coins were sorted out, melted down, and reminted into coins of the same face value but of lesser value by weight.

The crisis also tightened the marriage of finance and command control on which military entrepreneurship rested. It threatened the stability of all belligerent powers, it fueled the near universal practice of living off the land, and it grew worse as the war went on. After 1635 logistical and financial difficulties promoted a stagnation of military techniques and a decline in the size of battle armies, and by the 1640s even main field armies rarely numbered more than 20,000 effectives. "Strategic thinking had become crushed between the sustained growth in army size and the relative scarcity of money, equipment, and food. In the age of the military revolution, the skill of individual governments and generals in supplying war often became the pivot about which the outcome of armed conflict turned."[22] Even major battles seldom yielded decisive effects.

As the war dragged on, fighting armies faded into paper armies. Only a small fraction stood in the field, while the rest garrisoned fortresses, protected capitals, patrolled (and fleeced) subordinate theaters, and requisitioned provisions. Militarily peripheral operations accounted for most of war-making's costs. Take the year 1632, which saw three major battles – Rain (Bavaria), the Alte Veste (near Nuremberg), and Lützen (Saxony). None engaged more than a fraction of the total troops on each side, none was decisive. In November, when he deployed for the battle of Lützen, Gustavus Adolphus more or less commanded 183,000 soldiers: 62,000 scattered over northern Germany in 98 permanent garrisons; 34,000 in Sweden, Finland, and the Swedish Baltic provinces; and 66,000 operating independently in various parts of the Empire. This left the king in command of a mere 20,000 men, at the head of whom he fought and died. In the same year the Imperial-League forces were similarly dispersed: 18,000 men at Lützen, 40,000 more in other operations, and 43,000 tied down in garrisons. By war's end the majority of the Swedish army was tied down in 127 garrisons all over Germany. The war's typical operation was not the pitched battle but what a French general called merely "fights, encounters, skirmishes, ambushes, and occasional battle, minor sieges, assaults, escalades, captures and surprises of towns."[23]

Weak finance brought weak command control. Some 1,500 individuals are known to have been active as contractors at some time during the war. Between 1630 and 1635, perhaps 400 of them raised and maintained fully equipped regiments, brigades, and even whole armies on behalf of governments lacking the resources to do the job for themselves. Some enterprisers served causes, others served chiefly themselves, and the war coined, as wars will, the suffering and destruction of some into the good fortune (and profit) of others. Henrik Holck (d. 1633), a Dane in Imperial service, left his native land a poor man and returned in 1627 rich enough to pay 50,000 thalers for an estate on the island of Funen. Hans Christoph von Königsmarck (1600–63) began as a minor Brandenburg noble and died as field marshal general and count with assets worth almost 2 million thalers. Wallenstein was able to advance more than 6 million thalers to the emperor between 1621 and 1628. In 1637 the Protestant condottiere Bernard of Saxe-Weimar (1604–39) estimated his personal fortune at 450,000 thalers.

War was a business from top to bottom. Although a soldier's wage scarcely exceeded a farmhand's pay, no warlord, however rich, could pay an army indefinitely

22 Parker, *The Thirty Years' War*, 43–4.
23 Parker, *The Thirty Years' War*, 41.

from his own resources. Instead, cash from his treasury went to repay his enterpriser, who served as both creditor and field commander. In the field every officer could act as a contractor. In his classic novel, *Adventurous Simplicissimus*, H. C. von Grimmelshausen compares an army on payday to a flock of birds in a tree. Those on the topmost branches "were at their best and happiest when a commissary-bird flew overhead and shook a whole panful of gold over the tree to cheer them; for they caught as much of that as they could and let little or nothing at all fall to the lowest branches so that, of those who sat there, more died of hunger than of the enemy's attacks."[24] The birds lower down – the rank and file – had to find sustenance from other sources. The simplest method was looting, of course, but much favored was a form of extortion known as "arson protection" (*Brandschatz*). A trooper rode into a village, called out the elders, and promised not to burn the village if its people produced a ransom in cash or in commodities. In return, the officer might give the village a letter of protection guaranteeing that it would not have to pay again forces from the same side. In contested zones, naturally, protection money had to be paid to both sides.

From ransom and extortion it was but a short step to the full-fledged "contributions system," pioneered by the Dutch but adopted almost universally by occupying armies. A contribution was a regular tax levied by the army on all communities within a certain radius of its encampments. In the hands of a skilled and ruthless commander, a Wallenstein, contributions could supply the troops' every need – food, clothing, lodgings, munitions, transport – on a schedule worked out between the regimental and company clerks and the local magistrates. What local sources could not supply, merchants brought to the armies. Dutch and German generals bought Swiss cattle and English cloth. Wallenstein organized the regular delivery of beer, bread, clothing, and other necessaries from his own extensive estates in Bohemia. By the 1640s, most military administrators reckoned to supply two-thirds of their troops' wages in kind rather than cash.

Two items were especially difficult to supply. One was artillery, a good train of which could add 50 percent to a campaign's costs and which was therefore usually stockpiled by the governments themselves. A second item was horses, which were expensive and vulnerable. Armored heavy cavalry had disappeared from European armies by the late sixteenth century, and in many forces the number of mounted men made up but 10 percent of the total effectives. When France went to war against the Habsburgs in 1635, orders went out to raise 132,000 infantry but only 12,400 cavalry, though at this time experts reckoned the ideal ratio to be about 4:1. This was good news, for a trooper required about three new mounts per year, sometimes more. The Thirty Years War was an equine holocaust. The Imperial General Ottavio Piccolomini (1599–1656) had seven horses shot from under him on a single day at Lützen. In the same battle was mortally wounded Gustavus Adolphus's magnificent charger called "Streiff" (his value was reckoned at 1,000 thalers). By war's end, crash breeding programs in England, France, and Spain were sending the armies a reliable, sufficient supply of horses.

Like horses, men came through the market. No one who could pay, whether king, prince, government, or contractor, had much trouble hiring at need the men required.

24 Hansjakob Christoffel von Grimmelshausen, *The Adventurous Simplicissimus*, 35 (Bk I, ch. 16).

Conscription existed only in Sweden from around 1600. It was ruthlessly methodical rule, which compelled all males over fifteen to register and parishes to provide, equip, and feed ten eligible male parishioners for the king's use. Most of the conscripted Swedes and Finns went straight from the farm to the fray.

All other armies relied on volunteers, mostly true or would-be professionals. Why did they sign up? We know something about the motives of the Scots, about 25,000 of whom went over the sea between 1626 and 1632 to fight for the Protestant cause in Danish and/or Swedish service. Some went simply to gain experience or to have a hand in the action in Germany. Sir James Turner (1615–86), who fought as a teenager for both Denmark and Sweden, confesses that he went abroad because "a restless desire [had] enter'd my mind to be, if not an actor, at least a spectator of these wars which at that time made so much noise over all the world."[25] More complex were the motives Robert Monro (ca. 1590–ca. 1675), chief of the Clan Mackay, ascribed to the men who followed him to the battlegrounds of Central Europe. They went, he wrote, for travel, adventure, and military experience under an illustrious leader, but also to defend the Protestant faith and to vindicate the claims and honor of Elizabeth Stuart, their king's sister (and the Winter King's wife).

The most striking thing about the soldiers of the Thirty Years War is the variety not so much of their motives, which were mixed enough, as of their origins. "Military expatriation," a fancy name for sending hired troops outside their native land, was the common practice of the age. Some peoples had more martial renown than others. Cardinal Richelieu (Armand Jean du Plessis, 1585–1642), the French king's first minister, had a low opinion of French troops and wanted the fighting forces to be 50 percent foreigners. No French army came anywhere near this figure, though between 1635 and 1664 perhaps 25,000 Irish fought for France alongside numerous German and Swiss regiments. The war drew units and individuals from far away – Croatia, Hungary, Italy, Scotland, and Ireland – but it also circulated the peoples among the armies. The Dutch Republic relied very heavily on foreigners, especially French, English, Germans, and Scots, while the Swedes swept up all nationalities.

The most sought-after military commodity was the veteran, and it was standard practice for the victor to take captured soldiers en masse into his own ranks. In time, of course, the veterans became more numerous. In the ranks of one well-documented Bavarian regiment, the veterans rose from 15 percent in 1624 to 66 percent in 1647. The circulation also made all armies multilingual and multi-confessional. Such mixing awakened misgivings in some observers, such as Sir James Turner, who in his *Memoirs* criticized the commanders and governments who "swallowed without chewing, in Germanie, a very dangerous maxime, which militarie men there too much follow: which was, that so we serve our master honestlie, it is no matter what master we serve."[26] True enough, for absorbing defeated units necessarily mixed loyalties to commanders, regiment, and religion. One Bavarian regiment mustered in 1644 men from sixteen different peoples, among them fourteen Turks. No matter what the origins of individual units, the rhythms of victory and defeat made every army into an ethno-linguistic omnium gatherum.

25 Parker, *The Thirty Years' War*, 174.
26 Parker, *The Thirty Years' War*, 175.

In such conditions, how did the officers and men on the battlefield tell the contending sides apart? The modern solution, uniforms, first came into use during the Thirty Years War. In 1645 an Imperial general, Count Matthias Gallas (1584–1647), placed an order with Austrian clothiers for 600 uniforms for his men, for which he supplied samples of the exact material and specified the color (pale gray). He also sent samples of powder horns and cartridge belts to be manufactured in numbers by Austrian craftsmen. Generally, though, regiments wore the color of the army in which they were serving: Habsburgs (Spanish and Austrian) red, Swedes yellow, French blue, and Dutch orange.

Soldiers and even whole units, therefore, might serve on both sides and shift sides several times – if they lived so long, for commanders were ever on the search for veterans. The chief reason for the rapid turnover of fighting forces was very high mortality. It has been estimated that in early modern European warfare, each year one out of every four or five enlisted soldiers died on active service, and that total deaths from other causes exceeded deaths in battle by a factor of about ten. This is probably too high, as records for the Spanish Army of Flanders suggest annual losses from all causes, including desertion, of under 20 percent. But battle losses could be very high. Johann von Werth (1591–1652), a Silesian commander in the Bavarian army, wrote of the battle of Freiburg in 1644 that "in the twenty-two years I have been involved in the carnage of war, there has never been such a bloody encounter [as this]."[27] This battle consumed about 5,000 per side.

Sieges destroyed men as well as walls. During the blockade of Stralsund in 1628, the Scottish Mackays were under fire for six weeks continuously and out of a total of 900 men, 500 were killed and 300 wounded. When the Swedes besieged and took the Brandenburg town of Frankfurt an der Oder in 1631, the Imperial defenders lost 3,000 and the Swedes 800 men. The dead, reports Colonel Robert Monro of the Mackays, "were not buried fully in six dayes, in th'end they were cast by heapes in great ditches, above a hundred in every Grave."[28] It is no wonder there were so many deserters. In 1622 an Italian deserter from the Spanish siege of Bergen-op-Zoom was asked, "Where have you come from?" "From Hell" (*D'infierno*), he replied.[29] Afflicted by desertions, casualties, and disease at rates that could reach perhaps 20 percent per month, whole regiments just melted away before their colonels' eyes.

An iron law of warfare decreed that, whatever a soldier's motive for going to the wars, he deserved booty as well as his pay.[30] The simplest way to booty was to fleece civilians under threat of arson, torture, and death. Villages in war zones and especially along main roads were looted many times. Traveling merchants were also soft targets. In January 1638 a convoy of Augsburg and Nuremberg merchants with seven wagons on the way home from the Leipzig fair was ambushed by about 200 troopers. They demanded 500 pounds in cash, and when the convoy rashly offered less than 100 pounds, it was immediately attacked and plundered. The troopers killed several merchants, seized 80 horses, and destroyed everything they could not carry away. This

27 Parker, *The Thirty Years' War*, 240, n. 8.
28 Robert Monro, *Monro, His Expedition with the Worthy Scots Regiment Called Mac-Keys*, 161.
29 Geoffrey Parker, *The Military Revolution: Military Innovation and the Rise of the West, 1500–1800*, 55.
30 Parker, *The Thirty Years' War*, 58.

was Nuremberg's seventh wagon train to be lost in a twelve-month period, and sixteen more such incidents were recorded before war's end.

Keeping armies in the field through ad hoc military government of occupied regions required the commanders to discourage, if not suppress, opportunistic plundering of the region's producers. This required discipline, something in very short supply. In December 1629 Wallenstein issued a disciplinary order for the Imperial army, "since we were informed, what sort of severe disorders have occurred in the winter quarters."[31] In winter quarters, of course, dispersed armies came into their closest contact with the civilian population and were least subject to the effective control by the commanders. Wallenstein's ordinance goes on to specify what cash and supplies each soldier was due per day and per week and confirms that these payments should come only to the troops who stayed in quarters, while those who left quarters were on their own. Officers must not make exaggerated estimates of their requirements or otherwise try to enrich themselves from the supply system. Soldiers must not leave their units: "It is always forbidden that any trooper or foot soldier leave quarters and go into the countryside without a pass from his officer."[32] Nothing shall be taken – so runs the ordinance's chief theme – more than the fixed amounts of contributions, neither by marauding soldiers or defrauding officers. As for the farmers, "officers must protect the farmers while they work in the fields and not allow them to be hindered in any way in their work."[33]

Were such measures ever enforced? Well, sometimes they were, and loot and requisitioned horses were returned to the farmers. On occasion, draconian measures were used in all armies to enforce discipline. Wallenstein was thought so severe that the men nicknamed him "Gallowstone" (*Galgenstein*) and "the hanging duke." His men deserted in droves.

3. THE HUMAN FACE OF WAR – SOLDIERS AND SAVAGES

The classic image of the Thirty Years War's ravages on the common people derives from a scene in Grimmelshausen's novel. Simplicissimus tells how marauding soldiers sack the farmstead and rob, rape, and slaughter his adopted family: "In a word each had his own device to torture the peasants, and each peasant had his several tortures."[34] While it has been intermittently fashionable among historians to dismiss local reports of atrocities as self-interested exaggerations, a sounder judgment holds that their "rhetoric of death and destruction" is indeed "sensitive to both the rhythm of the war itself and the opportunities provided by the expansion of language."[35]

None but kinfolk and neighbors and their pastors mourned the plundered and slaughtered peasants, but burghers sometimes had recourse. An account of the Swedish occupation of the Moravian city of Olmütz/Olomouc from 1642 until 1650 records the casual violence that attended occupations of towns: executions, forced contributions, and random acts of violence. When one householder refused to feed a marauding officer who invited himself to dinner, the officer cut him on his head with a

---

31 Gerhard Schormann, *Der Dreißigjährige Krieg*, 115.
32 Schormann, *Der Dreißigjährige Krieg*, 115.
33 Schormann, *Der Dreißigjährige Krieg*, 115.
34 Grimmelshausen, *The Adventurous Simplicissimus*, 9 (Bk I, ch. 4).
35 John Theibault, "The Rhetoric of Death and Destruction in the Thirty Years War," 275.

dagger, for which the attacker was later tried by a military court. Once, when the drunken Swedish commandant ordered all the cannon on the city walls to fire and all gunners to fire into the air, he danced with the citizens' wives in the street. When one citizen refused to allow this, he grew furious, had the man placed before a cannon, and ordered it to be fired. "All the captains and officers present," tells the town clerk, "were shocked and disgusted, though none said anything, until Lieutenant Winter persuaded him to withdraw the order, and the tragedy was avoided."[36]

Not all occupying armies devoted themselves to limitless predation. The Veste Recklinghausen, a small place in the prince-archbishopric of Cologne, lay in Imperial hands between 1636 and 1638. When local people complained of robberies and thieving, Alexander von Velen (1599–1675) ordered his officers to arrest the thieving soldiers or, if they resisted, to shoot those caught red-handed, even though the offenses were alleged against property only and not persons. At Recklinghausen as at Olmütz, the greatest burden on the people was not the soldiers' atrocities but the permanent contributions systems of occupying forces.

Contributions were demanded, not asked, and terrible events could follow refusals to pay. The logic of reprisals was formulated at the beginning of the 1620s with great precision by Count Palatine Johann Casimir of Zweibrücken (1584–1638), the Swedish king's brother-in-law, who referred to "the great destruction to the countryside, which arises from failure to pay the troops."[37] Gustavus Adolphus seems to have discovered with surprise that, immediately upon landing in the Empire, his army's discipline fell in direct proportion to his inability to pay. For this reason, the Peace of Prague of 1635 ordered the Imperial estates to pay their troops regularly, "in order to reestablish the military discipline [*die Disciplina Militaris*] and to prevent further excesses and irregularities, which in wartime result from the lack of sufficient pay."[38] Ability to pay depended on contributions, and whatever the soldiery's normal level of violence against civilians, it was bound to increase when hunger drove unpaid occupying soldiers to help themselves. Still, poverty and starvation were the soldiers' most reliable pay. Abbot Maurus Friesenegger (1595–1655) of Andechs, southwest of Munich, describes an Imperial unit being mustered in 1633: "When the Italian-Spanish [*welsch-spanisch*] regiment was mustered on 30 December, it was a sight to behold. Many companies had barely half their men, who had black and yellow faces, skeletal bodies half-clothed in rags, or wrapped in women's garments, looking the very picture of hunger and misery."[39]

Ragged, hungry, diseased – such troops were nonetheless more than equal to the business of destroying isolated farmsteads and plundering undefended villages. Thousands of the Empire's villages replicated the experience of Reichensachsen in the landgraviate of Hesse-Cassel, which felt the full brunt of the war from 1623, when Tilly's Croatian cavalry – greatly feared for their ferocity – reduced its 172 hearths to 72.[40] There followed two rounds of plague in 1629 and 1635, and when the mayor of a nearby village gathered his commune in 1639 to assess the village's condition, they

36 Schormann, *Der Dreißigjährige Krieg*, 117.
37 Schormann, *Der Dreißigjährige Krieg*, 118.
38 Schormann, *Der Dreißigjährige Krieg*, 118.
39 Quoted by Schormann, *Der Dreißigjährige Krieg*, 118.
40 It is worth mentioning that in the sources "Croats" (*Crabatten*) often means Imperial light cavalry who, like Croatian horsemen, were used for scouting and other auxiliary operations.

reported that the fifteen remaining households (of a pre-war 82) could muster by way of livestock two cows, no sheep or horses, one ox, and no pigs. It was natural for people to exaggerate damages to ward off higher military taxes, but more often the suffering was real enough. "Anno 1642," Lorenz Ludolf, the pastor of Reichensachsen, wrote in his parish register, hidden away from all other eyes, "all the misery continued just as bad as in the previous year, so that the despair pressed all the harder ... whoever has not himself seen and lived through such circumstances cannot believe what I note here."[41] Ludolf's lament was echoed by Pastor Klöggel, his counterpart at Ödenwaldstetten in the Swabian Jura. "From 1634 onward," he wrote in Latin in his baptismal register,

> when the Imperials and the Bavarians fought and decisively defeated the Swedes and their allies on the battlefield near Nördlingen, famine, disease, and the sword raged unchecked. And Germans saw around them nothing in the face of the poor, troubled peasants but enslavement of their villages, wicked threats from hostile military bands and violent men, plundering, empty, unplowed fields, bands of robbers, bloodletting, pillaging, arson, rape, wickedness, and disorder.[42]

Against such laments may be set, of course, the many islands of calm, such as Heilsbronn Abbey in Franconia – where the local annals record few incidents of physical violence during the war years.

To plunder a village was routine, to sack a great city was a soldier's dream. The most notorious sack, Magdeburg in May 1631, rose in magnitude and horror above all the routine atrocities. Because possession of the city was vital to the Imperial-League forces' position in the Elbe valley, Tilly's army attacked it on 20 May 1631. The troops stormed a bastion, broke into the city, and commenced fighting in the streets. The magistrate Otto Gericke (1602–86, later: von Guericke), a future mayor of Magdeburg and discoverer of the vacuum, recorded what he saw and heard on that terrible day. "When General Pappenheim had gotten a considerable number of men over the wall at Reustadt and into the city streets," he wrote, "fire spread everywhere, the city was finished."[43] The wall was broken, and Pappenheim's troopers rode right into the city and opened the gates to Tilly's waiting men, among whom Gericke counts Hungarians, Croatians, Poles, Italians, Spaniards, French, Walloons, north Germans, and south Germans – the war's typical ethnic stew. Many thousands of burghers were murdered, according to Gericke, and Magdeburg, for more than 650 years the proud seat of an archbishop, disappeared in a tremendous blaze. Fleeing the flames, the Imperials evacuated the city, and "the surviving residents with their wives and children were driven away as captives by the enemy. . . . Those women, girls, daughters, and female servants who had no men, parents, or relations to pay their ransoms or to seek mercy from the higher officers,

---

41 Theibault, "The Rhetoric of Death," 271.
42 Eberhard Fritz, *Dieweil sie so arme Leuth: Fünf Albdörfer zwischen Religion und Politik 1530–1750. Studien zur Kirchengeschichte der Dörfer Bernloch, Eglingen, Meidelstetten, Oberstetten und Ödenwaldstetten*, 91.
43 Bernd Roeck, ed., *Gegenreformation und Dreißigjähriger Krieg 1555–1648*, 298. The general referred to is Count Gottfried Heinrich of Pappenheim (1594–1632), a Bavarian noble who since White Mountain commanded cavalry in the Catholic forces. He is remembered in the colloquial expression, "We know our Pappenheimers," which exists in German, Flemish, and Czech. It refers to someone who is performing exactly (whether well or poorly) as expected.

were very unfortunate, for some of them were raped and shamed, others became concubines."[44] The corpses were dumped into the Elbe.

Gericke's estimate of 20,000 dead and wounded at Magdeburg flew across the Protestant world like wildfire, spread by at least 20 newsletters and nearly 250 pamphlets. Some made martyrs of the dead, others dramatized the events in sexual terms as Tilly's rape of a chaste maid, Magdeburg. Long after his death, Count Tilly's reputation was dogged by opprobrium for the sack, though he had in fact wanted Magdeburg intact. One pamphlet, called *Tilly's Testimony*, sang after his death (at the battle of Rain on the Lech, 20 April 1632): "Here lies Tilly the tyrant / Who took the city of Magdeburg / By assault and by treachery / And many an innocent Christian's blood / He spilled in his terrible fury."[45] To this writer the great Swedish victory at Breitenfeld in 1631 brought God's vengeance for the "innocent Magdeburg blood / That cries up to heaven."[46] The sack of Magdeburg, the most sensationalized event of the Thirty Years War, lent a new, bitter edge to confessional enmities. Among Protestants arose the cry, "Magdeburg quarter," no mercy to Catholics.

No one may judge that one person's suffering is more meaningful than another's, except to the sufferer. Yet sufferings are collective as well as individual, and a majority of the war's civilian deaths were caused not by atrocities but by disease. Epidemic disease, especially bubonic plague, shadowed the armies and the hordes of refugees from town to town and district to district. The most terrible wave of illnesses coursed through the German lands between 1632 and 1640. People fled their homes, perhaps a million of them at any one moment, to take refuge in the fortified towns and cities, where death reaped among them more terribly than it would have in their native villages.

Were the population losses truly catastrophic – long the historians' question – or mere blips in the ordinary patterns of mortality? Today's answer sorts the German lands into four groups. The first, lands that lost about half their people, forms a band across the Empire from northeast to southwest: Pomerania and Mecklenburg through Thuringia into the Palatinate, the Upper Rhine valley, and Württemberg. The latter land's population fell from 450,000 in 1618 to 100,000 in 1634, recovering to only 120,000 by 1645 and not regaining its pre-war level until 1750. The second group comprises lands that lost between a third and a half: Brandenburg, Magdeburg, Hesse, Franconia, Bavaria, Swabia, Alsace, and Lorraine. The third group, the Bohemian lands (Bohemia, Moravia, Silesia, Lusatia), lost between a tenth and a third. Finally, the fourth group consists of lands – the northwest, Austria, Switzerland – that lost fewer than a tenth of their pre-war populations. The average losses, something like 40 percent in the countryside and 33 percent in the towns and cities, were not made good after the war until three peaceful generations had passed.

For more persons than not, the war brought on financial crisis. Crushing war debts, disruptions of production and trade, and the vast system of military requisitions and taxes combined to depress the prices of land and grain. The crisis hit the villages, as it always did, harder than the cities. It did not cause extensive permanent abandonments of land or of settlements, as the great depression 300 years before had done, but it did stimulate mobility and redistributions of rural property, which

44 Roeck, ed., *Gegenreformation*, 299–300.
45 Werner Lahne, *Magdeburgs Zerstörung in der zeitgenössischen Publizistik*, 164.
46 Lahne, *Magdeburgs Zerstörung*, 164.

sometimes enabled landless survivors to acquire land. It was perhaps the last time in German history when poor but industrious rural people could rise through their own efforts alone – alone, that is, aided by price conjunctures and high mortalities.

New farmers nonetheless faced high costs, for where lease prices fell most steeply, military operations and contributions had most damaged the rural infrastructure. This meant heavy costs in new buildings, clearing overgrown fields, and new tools and livestock, not to speak of contributions to the armies. Such costs, plus the general depression of grain prices across Europe, kept war-related social mobility within modest bounds. Regional studies all agree on the very high levels of farmers' indebtedness. In the Oberes Zenngrund west of Nuremberg, rural tax revenues fell by 82 percent, more than 50 percent of the farms were untenanted but deeply indebted, and many remained unworked into the 1650s, because the outward flow of capital and the debts made them unobtainable or unattractive. The great problem, as in the American South after the Civil War, was the lack of money. Families who wanted land and were willing to work it simply had not the purchase price or the capital needed to restore the farms to working order. A ruined farm with overgrown fields, for example, which had sold in 1614 for 500 gulden, could in 1648 be had for 37 gulden. Under such conditions, neither the landless rural people nor the strong farmers could seize much advantage from the opportunities presented by the war. Despite the population losses, therefore, the war brought no general social transformation.

No document reveals more forcefully or more poignantly the common people's experience of the Thirty Years War than does the journal (*Zeytregister*) kept by the Swabian cobbler Hans Heberle (1597–1677). He and his family worked a small farm at Neenstetten, a village 18 kilometers north of Ulm on the edge of the Swabian Jura. Heberle survived hunger, dearth, and exile, lost seven of his children (four to the plague of 1634–35), and died in 1677 at the age of eighty. The great comet of 1618 inspired him to begin keeping a journal of noteworthy events. "In 1618," he writes, "a great comet appeared in the form of a great and terrible rod, which was visited upon us by and through God because of our sinful lives, which we have richly earned in the past and continue daily to earn."[47] The next year Emperor Ferdinand II "began war in Bohemia, which land he subjugated and forced into his religion, and the same in the following years with the lands of Brunswick, Mecklenburg, Lüneburg, Brandenburg, Pomerania, Gotland, Austria, Moravia, the Lands above the Enns [Upper Austria], Silesia, the Rhine Palatinate, yea, almost all of Germany, more than I can tell or describe."[48] One of the remarkable features of Heberle's record is the degree to which this humble man, who lived in a tiny place in a poor, upland region of the German southwest, followed with interest the great events of the time. He kept himself informed, we may infer, by reading broadsheets and pamphlets. The general debasement of coinage and inflation of prices around 1622 did not escape him, and he learned of "fiery balls from heaven" falling in Württemberg from a "public announcement, which," he records, "I read myself."[49]

Heberle often got fairly precise, accurate accounts of the great events of the day. He recognized the importance of the Edict of Restitution, by which "the ecclesiastical

---

47 Hans Heberle, *Der Dreissigjährige Krieg in zeitgenössischer Darstellung: Hans Heberles "Zeytregister" (1618–1672), Aufzeichnungen aus dem Ulmer Territorium. Ein Beitrag zu Geschichtsschreibung und Geschichtsverständnis der Unterschichten*, 93.
48 Heberle, *Der Dreissigjährige Krieg*, 94.
49 Heberle, *Der Dreissigjährige Krieg*, 110.

properties were restored to the Catholics against the wishes of the Protestants, who opposed it strongly but in vain."[50] Then, suddenly, God sent the Lion of the North. "If the Swedish king had not opposed the emperor in the field," Heberle believes, "the German princes would have been finished. Alone, they were too weak and couldn't have overcome the crafty crowd. But God, Who can end and change everything, buried them in the grave they themselves had dug."[51] He records that at Ulm, where he had taken refuge, the Protestants held a feast of thanksgiving, "for it is precisely one hundred years since the Protestant confession was submitted at Augsburg . . . to the great Emperor Charles V. . . . During the morning and noon sermons the Confession of Augsburg was read publicly by the pastor from the pulpit, so that everyone would know what the confession is and what it contains."[52]

The Swabian cobbler identifies with impressive accuracy the war's two turning points, 1629 with the Edict of Restitution and the Swedish intervention and 1635 with the Peace of Prague. Oddly enough, he does not seem to have heard of the Swedish king's death in 1632, for he reports in 1635 that "the emperor had beaten the Swede fairly well and driven him back, so that he thought to leave the Empire altogether, but he went only to the coast in Farther Pomerania."[53] He nonetheless does record accurately the Peace of Prague: "The emperor and the Saxon made peace at Prague, for the Saxon was the head of the Protestants. The emperor believed that when he captured the head, he would have the entire Protestant Union, which is what happened."[54] The emperor also confirmed the Ulmers' liberties, so that "they will be left secure and uncoerced concerning the free exercise of their religion, their form of government, and their rights, liberties, and laws as of old, . . . 'O God, we praise Thee' [*Te Deum laudamus*] was sung in all the churches, and the bells were rung for an hour, and at the end all the city's artillery was fired from all bastions at once."[55]

The promise of peace was a false dawn, for in the southwest "many thousands died of violence, starvation, and disease. The hunger, you see, drove many poor folk to eat nasty and disgusting things, indeed, all sorts of improper things, such as dogs and cats, mice and dead cattle, and horseflesh. And flesh from dead carcasses thrown away by the renderer – horse, dog, and other animals – was taken away. Indeed, people quarreled over it and thought it fine stuff."[56] In one sermon an Ulm pastor commented on the deaths of more than 15,000 persons: "among them 5,672 beggars, 4,033 peasants and foreigners, and 168 orphans. . . . Wasn't that terrible? Yes, I believe it was the evil of all evils, for I have not only heard about it but saw it and heard it with my own eyes and ears."[57] Worse was to come, as the war rebounded with renewed vigor though to less effect, as armies – Imperial, League, Spanish, Swedish, and French – swept back and forth across the region. Heberle reports a story from the siege of Breisach on the Rhine by Bernard of Saxe-Weimar's French army in 1638. Within the beleaguered fortress, after the horses, oxen, calves, sheep, dogs, and cats had been eaten, dark rumors began to fly: a captured soldier died and eaten by fellow prisoners;

---

50 Heberle, *Der Dreissigjährige Krieg*, 129.
51 Heberle, *Der Dreissigjährige Krieg*, 130.
52 Heberle, *Der Dreissigjährige Krieg*, 130.
53 Heberle, *Der Dreissigjährige Krieg*, 162. Heberle corrects this error in an entry for 1649.
54 Heberle, *Der Dreissigjährige Krieg*, 162.
55 Heberle, *Der Dreissigjährige Krieg*, 162–3.
56 Heberle, *Der Dreissigjährige Krieg*, 161.
57 Heberle, *Der Dreissigjährige Krieg*, 162.

two corpses in the cemetery carved up and consumed; three children eaten in one day; a piemaker's son lured in and butchered by soldiers; eight prominent burghers' children disappeared in one day. Finally, when on a December day another prisoner died, "the others lying about fell upon the body, ripped it with their teeth, and ate the corpse raw."[58]

Hans Heberle's record provides one of the very few running accounts of a common man's experience of the Thirty Years War. No one who reads it will ever again sneer that the infamous "horrors of the Thirty Years War" sprang from the imagination of novelists and historians. The Swabian cobbler has it right, for the ordeal of these terrible years did not consist only, perhaps not chiefly, of random acts of robbery, rape, and murder by marauding soldiers, though these occurred aplenty. War's greater terror came in irresistible forms: wild inflation of prices, terrible plagues, famine and starvation, and the devastation of whole regions by armies who lived "off the land." Such experiences, except in some favored regions, were those of the common people during the Thirty Years War.

4. THE PROTESTANT CAUSE – GUSTAVUS ADOLPHUS AND WALLENSTEIN

Act II of the Thirty Years War gave the palm to the Protestant forces, as Act I had done to the Catholics. It opened with the Swedish king's invasion of the German lands. His stay was brief – he landed on Pomerania's shore in July 1630, won an overwhelming victory in September 1631 at Breitenfeld, ravaged the Catholic south, and fell in battle at Lützen in April 1632 – but Gustavus Adolphus's 21-month campaign changed the war in two ways. First, the Swedish intervention broke (for good, as fortune would have it) the brief domination by Imperial-League forces of the heavily Protestant German north and saved the Protestant princes from having to bow to the emperor's will. Second, the king's arrival and victories raised the spirits of the German Protestants, who saw in Gustavus Adolphus God's champion come to save His people after their own princes had failed. No other participant in the war, Protestant or Catholic, achieved the honor of sainthood.[59]

Gustavus II Adolphus of the house of Vasa was born in December 1594 to King Charles IX (b. 1550, r. 1604–11) and Duchess Christina of Holstein-Gottorp (1573–1625). Having come of age in a Sweden flanked by two rivals, Denmark to the west and Poland to the east, he decided to enter the German war after the debacle in Lower Saxony. There is no reason to speculate about his chief motives: to roll back the Imperial advance into the northern German lands and to protect the German Protestants. Gustavus, to be sure, was not devout in the way that Ferdinand and Maximilian of Bavaria were, but he did push the case for Protestant solidarity. "It is a fight between God and the Devil," he told a Brandenburg envoy, "there is no third choice."[60]

Opportunities – foraging and contributions – not strategic concepts dominated the Swedish king's war. In twenty years of campaigning in the German lands, his

---

58 Heberle, *Der Dreissigjährige Krieg*, 175.
59 For Gustavus Adolphus are named a German Protestant association for missionary work in Catholic lands, an American college, and numerous American Lutheran churches.
60 Michael Roberts, *Gustavus Adolphus*, 153.

armies won only one decisive battle, Breitenfeld in September 1631. This sufficed to establish forever the king's reputation as the field commander who best understood the military potential of the age. He employed linear formations of highly disciplined infantry who could maneuver and fire rapidly; closely coordinated heavy and light cavalry; and light, mobile field artillery to enhance the firepower of his musketeers.

The king's battle of decision came in Saxony in summer 1631. Count Tilly hoped that a demonstration of force there might convince Elector John George (1585–1656) to remain neutral or even to emulate his neighbor of Brandenburg's shift toward the emperor and the Catholics. Conversely, the Swedish king aimed to pressure the northern Protestant princes and peoples to join him in his campaign to drive Tilly's Leaguers backward and southward: "Awake, awake, dear friends / All of you who are not yet Swedish."[61] The king's immediate goal was to clear the foe from Saxony. When the two armies met in September 1631 at Breitenfeld, a few miles northwest of Leipzig, their deployments for battle displayed two different tactical concepts. Tilly arranged his infantry in large formations, each of which showed a front of about 150 and a depth of ten men – mostly pikemen supported by musketeers. It was an improved version of the classic sixteenth-century formation, its flanks guarded by the cavalry. The Swedo-Saxon army, by contrast, formed up in lines only five pikemen or six musketeers deep, an arrangement that enabled the king to match Tilly's front and keep some troops in reserve. Around noon the battle began with the obligatory cannonade – the Swedes fired around four shots to the foe's one – and then came the serious work. Seven times Pappenheim's heavy cavalry charged the Swedish right and were as many times thrown back by firepower. On the other flank, Imperial cavalry drove off the Saxon horse, whereupon most of Tilly's infantry made an oblique march to smash the Saxon infantry as well. With 40 percent of the enemy forces beaten, Tilly next prepared a devastating flank attack on the remaining Protestant forces. At this moment Gustavus Adolphus ordered his infantry to refuse the right flank, which deprived Tilly's infantry of their main target and allowed the Swedish guns to enfilade their position.[62] A charge of the Finnish cavalry drove off the rest of the Imperial horse, and the Swedish artillery pounded the Catholic army off the field.

Breitenfeld was the first of the Thirty Years War's three decisive battles.[63] The Imperial-League army, having lost 60 percent, had only 6,000 men left, while the Swedes after absorbing their prisoners came away stronger than before. The king now headed his army toward the Catholic south, plundering "priests' alley" along the River Main as he went:

> Triumph! Victory! The Lion from the North
> Has at last taken vengeance and put you to flight,
> You fat monks in Priests' Alley!
> Run, flee your strong hideaways.[64]

---

61 Johannes Burkhardt, *Der Dreißigjährige Krieg*, 229.
62 Refusing a flank means to pull one end of the line back in oblique formation while concentrating one's forces to attack the enemy on the other flank. It is meant to lure an enemy attack on the weakened end of the line. The maneuver was later famously a favorite of King Frederick II of Prussia.
63 The others were Lützen in 1632, a strategic victory but a tactical defeat for the Swedes, and Nördlingen in 1634, a decisive Catholic victory.
64 Burkhardt, *Der Dreißigjährige Krieg*, 228.

At Würzburg his men took the great fortress of Marienburg, some of whose treasures found their way, following warlords' universal practice, back to Uppsala.

After Breitenfeld Cardinal Richelieu decided to ally with both sides, with the Swedish king for "restitution of the suppressed Estates of the Empire"[65] and with Elector Maximilian, whom he hoped to split away from the emperor. Both at Munich and at some Protestant courts the sentiment was growing in favor of a new, bi-confessional party of estates, a third force to restore the Empire's political order. Among the Lutheran princes there was more or less stiff resistance to moving with the flow of Protestant fortunes into the Swedish king's arms. When Margrave George of Hesse-Darmstadt (1605–61), a Lutheran, put the question – the Swedish king or the emperor? – to his councilors in 1632, his theologians replied that an alliance with the Catholic emperor was less objectionable than one to which Calvinists were party, especially when the latter included George's own cousin, Landgrave William of Hesse-Cassel (1602–37). In the end, however, George yielded to the same logic that brought John George of Saxony into the Swedish party. At this point, no amount of nostalgia for the old Imperial order could stand against the Swedish tide. To some at Vienna the Imperial cause seemed lost, as one courtier wrote: "We cry 'Help, Help,' but there is nobody there."[66]

In 1632 the Swedish storm reached the south and broke over Bavaria. When Tilly tried to stop the king at Rain on the Lech, he lost both the battle and his life. Up the Lech valley the Swedes rolled, entering Augsburg to the rejoicing of the Lutheran burghers and the terror of the Catholics. From this base Gustavus Adolphus staged his invasion of Bavaria, driving Maximilian and his court from Munich northeastward over the Danube. When Gustavus entered Munich on 17 May, the hapless Winter King at his side, he spared Maximilian's residence but plundered the arsenal of its cannon. The Swedish troops ravaged Bavaria almost at will, though less terribly than other troops did. Or so alleged some Bavarian peasants who later on asked Maximilian to bring the Swedes back because, however bad these heretics were, the Imperial soldiers were worse.

With Tilly dead and his army defeated, Ferdinand had either to capitulate or to recall the disgraced Wallenstein. This most wondrous of all German military entrepreneurs responded with customary energy after his restoration to supreme command in April 1632. Wallenstein's army moved from Bohemia northward to invade Saxony, where he made the worst mistake of his military career. Assuming that the campaigning season was over for the year, he began to disperse his troops into winter quarters. Two days later, the Swedes appeared at Lützen, southwest of Leipzig, and caught Wallenstein with only 19,000 men assembled. A full day's brutal fighting left both armies exhausted, but when Wallenstein decided to retreat to Bohemia, leaving behind baggage, artillery, and some 6,000 dead, the Swedes held the field. As the price of the victory, their king and commander, who scorned to wear armor, lay among the dead with three bullets through his leather coat.

Lützen cancelled Breitenfeld, and henceforth only a fresh foreign intervention could tip the scales to one party or the other. Commonly celebrated for his modernity

---

65 Parker, *The Thirty Years' War*, 107.
66 Gerhard von Questenberg to Albrecht von Wallenstein, 23 April 1631, in Parker, *The Thirty Years' War*, 117.

in military affairs, Gustavus had been in one crucial aspect a throwback to the old way of war: like a barbarian chieftain, a king in the Dark Ages, or a medieval emperor, he had led his army in person and from the saddle. At his death Chancellor Axel Oxenstierna (1583–1654) began his long service as both Swedish commander in the German lands and chief regent for the dead king's daughter, Queen Christina (1626–89, r. 1632–54). By nature a shrewd, cautious man, the chancellor abandoned the dead king's grandiose political ambitions and took as his main war aim an adequate compensation for the Swedish crown's sacrifices. Lacking sufficient charisma to rally the German Protestant princes, Oxenstierna watched his army sink into ever deeper dependence on French subsidies.

Wallenstein's failure at Lützen began his fall. Now his secret enemies' murmurs became audible at Munich, Vienna, and lesser Catholic courts. Later victories in 1633 did nothing to stop his critics' mouths, even when it seemed as if he had nearly restored the Empire's military balance of power. The end came on 25 February 1634, when Wallenstein was assassinated by Imperial officers under commission from Vienna. The plot's origins are still obscure, not least because, as one conspirator noted, "Put briefly, dissimulation is the alpha and omega of this business."[67] By this time both Munich and Madrid wanted Wallenstein dismissed, and at Vienna there were some – Lamormaini was one – who believed that the general was planning to take the Imperial army over to the Protestant side. The general's doom was sealed, a secret decree of outlawry was prepared. It notified "our Imperial army and all of its officers and commanders, higher and lower, also the soldiers" that they were relieved of "all obligations that bind them to the aforementioned general."[68] When this document was published, three weeks later, it was clear to all that any resistance by Wallenstein would be dealt with as high treason. The general backed water and moved his troops up to Eger/Cheb in Bohemia's western tip, ostensibly to begin a new campaign.

The game was up, for already in the plot were some of his own officers, including his commandant at Eger, Colonel John Gordon (d. 1648) of Aberdeenshire. Wallenstein seems to have favored Scottish and Irish officers, several of whom he stationed on Bohemia's vulnerable western borders. On the way to Eger there rode with the commander an Irish colonel, Walter Butler (d. 1634) of Tipperary, who, alas, was in touch with Gordon. In the plot with them was a third officer, Walter Leslie (1606–67), also from Aberdeenshire, who had come over in 1624 to fight for the Dutch Republic, later served either the Danes or the Swedes, and then transferred to the Imperial army.[69] Upon their arrival, the general, Butler, and a few others were admitted to Eger Castle. Leslie then had to give Wallenstein the emperor's letter of dismissal and listen to the general's raging fury at the news. Next day, Butler persuaded Gordon to let some of his Irishmen into the castle. The three conspirators then invited Wallenstein's four loyal commanders to a dinner of snails and pike, at the end of which the conspirators called in Butler's men and watched them slay the loyal officers. Later

67 Ottavio Piccolomini to Johann Graf von Aldringen, in Golo Mann, *Wallenstein, His Life Narrated*, 801.
68 Roeck, ed., *Gegenreformation*, 332.
69 The lists of Wallenstein's officers compiled in 1633 contain names of 37 "Latins" (including 18 Italians and 16 French speakers), 3 Spaniards, 56 from the Empire (including Bohemians), 9 Hungarians or Croats, 3 Danes, 3 from the British Isles, and 1 Swiss. David Worthington, *Scots in the Habsburg Service, 1618–1648*, 155.

that evening, thirty or so Irishmen, Gordon reported, entered Wallenstein's chamber "with the cry 'Rebels! Rebels!' and found His Princely Grace [Wallenstein] in his nightshirt, leaning on the table. He said nothing more than 'Ah, mercy!' to which the captain [William Devereaux] replied, 'You damned, oath-breaking, old rascal of a traitor,' and skewered him with a partisan between his breasts. He fell immediately and died."[70]

To be slaughtered like a hog, and that by Irishmen, was a mean end for this gifted adventurer, a believer in the stars and in his own destiny, who had dreamed of becoming (and remaining) an Imperial prince.[71] It was a pipe dream, for while military success could lead to great wealth, the authority to govern required legitimacy more than ability. A Wallenstein might have founded a dynasty, but only if the entire structure of Imperial authority had collapsed, a possibility the Imperial princes, Catholic and Protestant, feared more than anything else.

Nothing was more improbable than that a military collaboration between the two Habsburg monarchies would reverse the Catholic paralysis, yet this is what happened. In the summer of 1634, as disagreements, suspicion, and lack of funds plagued the Protestant allies, the Catholic star began to rise again. Under Matthias Gallas, who had fought with the Spanish in Flanders, Savoy, and Italy, the Imperial army began to recover. After his forces beat off the Saxons in Bohemia, his ability to block a new Swedish invasion of Bavaria largely healed the breach between Munich and Vienna. When the Protestants withdrew back northward, King Ferdinand of Hungary (b. 1608, r. 1625–57 in Hungary, 1637–57 in the Empire), heir-apparent to the Imperial throne, marched the Imperial army westward to besiege the Protestant city of Nördlingen. Against him came two Protestant armies, the Saxons under Bernard of Saxe-Weimar (1604–39) and the Swedes commanded by Gustav Horn (1592–1657), Chancellor Oxenstierna's son-in-law. Before they could unite to relieve the siege, an army of Spanish regulars arrived, having marched all the way from Milan. At their head rode Cardinal-Infante Fernando (1609/10–41), a Spanish royal prince, (never ordained) archbishop of Toledo, governor of the Habsburg Netherlands, and King Ferdinand's third cousin. In the face of this combination Bernhard and Horn foolishly decided on a night assault, the riskiest of all offensive moves. In the night of 6–7 September their men attacked the besieging Catholic armies, fell afoul of their own baggage and guns, and were driven off with terrible (4:1) casualties.

This tremendous Imperial victory stopped the Protestant advance as Breitenfeld had stopped the Catholics four years earlier. Without aid the Swedes were finished. Oxenstierna wrote in November 1634 to his sole remaining general, "I will struggle no longer, but drift where the tide may take me. . . . We are hated, envied, harassed" and such fortunes "make me weary of my life."[72] Hope nonetheless rose once more on the wind from the west. "The House of Austria wishes to subjugate all Germany," Oxenstierna declared, "extirpating liberty and the Reformed religion. So in this extremity we must look to France."[73]

---

70 Roeck, ed., *Gegenreformation*, 337–8. A partisan is a type of pole weapon.
71 Following his victories in the far north, Wallenstein had been named duke of Friedland (Bohemia) and Mecklenburg, prince of Sagan (Silesia), and Admiral of the North and Baltic Seas.
72 Michael Roberts, *From Oxenstierna to Charles XII: Four Studies*, 86.
73 Roberts, *From Oxenstierna*, 86.

Over this strategy the German Protestant princes divided along confessional lines. Oxenstierna's strongest supporter was a Reformed ruler, Landgrave William of Hesse-Cassel, called "the Constant." Among the Lutheran princes, by contrast, the Nördlingen disaster purged the will to fight on. Elector John George and Landgrave George of Hesse-Darmstadt already stood in negotiations with the emperor, whose advisors saw that peace must be made before a French intervention revived the Protestant cause. In February 1635 Ferdinand put the question to his theologians, only a few of whom voted with Lamormaini against peace.

By spring, when the Brandenburg elector climbed aboard peace's bandwagon, the iron was hot for striking. On 30 May 1635 the emperor and John George signed the Peace of Prague. The treaty defines the issues: "How and to what degree a Christian, general, honorable, just, and secure peace can be reestablished in the Holy Roman Empire; how . . . the blood-letting within it might be ended; and [how] the dear fatherland of the most honorable German Nation might be preserved from total ruin."[74] On the great stumbling block to peace, the ecclesiastical properties, they struck a compromise. What the Protestants had held before 1552/55, they would retain; what else they had held on 1 November 1627, they could retain for the next forty years; all properties taken after that date were to be restored to Catholic hands; and the entire settlement would be revisited within forty years by a committee of negotiators "in equal numbers."[75] The Saxon elector pressed for free exercise of religion where it had existed before 1612, but the emperor could not be moved, and the Peace of Prague confirmed application of the principle of 1555 – "whose the rule, his the religion" – to all German lands.

Whether the Peace of Prague represented the victory of Habsburg "confessional absolutism" or a broad-gauged project to restore the pre-war Imperial constitution remains a matter of debate. Crucial to the treaty's success was a projected military reform, the unification of all forces except garrisons (and the Saxon army) in an Imperial army under the emperor's supreme command but financed by the Imperial estates – precisely what Emperor Maximilian I had longed for but never got. This time Maximilian of Bavaria played the spoiler, for he refused to surrender control of his own forces, which had done as much as, perhaps more than, the Imperial armies to gain the Catholic victories. He agreed with the Protestants and with the emperor, however, that all must unite against the foreign powers, Sweden and France.

The Peace of Prague came about because of a general desire for a restoration of the old order, and only two German Protestant belligerents, Bernard of Saxe-Weimar and William of Hesse-Cassel, refused to sign the treaty. The peace of 1635 nevertheless dramatized the subterranean power of the old political culture of compromise and negotiation enabled by real concessions and untroubled by dictates of principle. If politics had once sufficed to provide security, it did so no longer, for under seventeenth-century conditions the Empire could not achieve and secure peace absent the collaboration of the foreign powers. This loss of control was the price of "German liberty," the aristocratic-corporate power that diverted the Empire from taking the western way to absolutist governance. Gained, on the other hand, was a cooling of confessional discord, as dreams of an Empire united under God began to recede into

74 Roeck, ed., *Gegenreformation*, 343.
75 Roeck, ed., *Gegenreformation*, 345.

the past. They would never revive in the old forms and never in the old intensity until the Holy Roman Empire had passed into history.

Whatever it signified, Prague proved a paper piece. Its unrealistic military aims persuaded the new emperor – Ferdinand III (b. 1608, r. 1637–57) – to moderate his war aims. Chief among them was no longer victory but the avoidance of defeat. Thus it was that in the war's final phase, the German notables were not warriors of the stripe of Tilly or Wallenstein, nor were they confessional warhawks like the Catholic Lamormaini or the Calvinist landgrave of Hesse-Cassel. They were diplomats, men of the stripe of the Styrian noble Maximilian von Trauttmansdorf (1584–1650), who emerged as a power in the Imperial regime at Vienna. He would guide the battered Habsburg ship through the final phase's heavy seas into the diplomatic harbor of Westphalia.

5. END GAME – THE FINAL PHASE

If the war's Act I can be described, in Hegel's language, as a Catholic thesis and Act II a Protestant antithesis, Act III produced not a synthesis but stalemate and exhaustion. Just as, according to Karl Marx, a mode of production does not produce revolution until all of its economic possibilities are exhausted, so the Thirty Years War produced no peace until all of its military resources were exhausted. This capacity for war to escape political reason and to reproduce itself in a seemingly automatic way reveals how far mid-seventeenth-century military technology and logistics had outrun command control and diplomacy. The stalemate could not be mastered, and the German lands now became hostages to the international war in which the chief belligerents were Spain, France, and the Dutch Republic.

When King Louis XIII (b. 1601, r. 1617–43) declared war on Spain in May 1635, French forces were already operating in the Empire, sent to block Imperial forces from crossing the Upper Rhine into Alsace and the Palatinate. Eleven months later, when war was declared on the emperor, Richelieu, who mistrusted Oxenstierna as "a bit gothic and very wily," chose Bernard of Saxe-Weimar to command the French army on the Rhine.[76] Bernard, promised four times as much as the Swedes were paying, agreed to serve. Although weak in hardened troops and experienced commanders, the French forces came into the German war relatively fresh and backed by the second strongest royal finances in Europe (after the Ottomans). Despite initial French failures in the Low Countries, the Valtellina, the Franche-Comté, Alsace, and on the Middle Rhine, French commanders and troops gradually learned the modern way of war. Their seizure of three strong places along the Rhine – Ehrenbreitstein (near Coblenz), Philippsburg (near Karlsruhe), and Breisach (below Freiburg im Breisgau) – gave them superior bases from which to continue the war.

Now the Protestant cause of earlier times became a strictly anti-Habsburg cause, and perhaps already at this time Europe's religious wars, the Reformation's legacy, yielded place to what is sometimes named "the Age of the Great Powers." The commanding events of this final phase took place beyond the German lands. One of them was the battle fought on 19 May 1643 before Rocroi, a small fortified town in the Noise valley of the Ardennes region. Although the French and Spanish armies

76 Parker, *The Thirty Years' War*, 133.

were well matched in size and composition, the French cavalry turned the Spanish left and surrounded the infantry. When the tough Spanish squares refused to yield – their German, Walloon, and Italian comrades had already given up – French artillery and cavalry charges ground them to pieces. Rocroi ended the myth of the invincibility of Spanish infantry, unbeaten for more than a century, and initiated the French bid for military hegemony in Europe.

As the Empire's German-speaking lands became a secondary theater of an international war, leadership of the anti-Habsburg cause there remained chiefly in Swedish hands. When peace came, the alliance's garrisons and field armies belonged 58.2 percent to the Swedes, 27.5 percent to the French, and 14.3 percent to Hesse-Cassel, whose regent, the remarkable Amelia Elisabeth of Hanau-Münzenberg (1602–51, regent 1637–50), maintained a field army about 20,000 strong. The German Protestant powers thus commanded at the end a mere one-seventh of the (real and honorary) Protestant forces in the Empire.

This endless, grinding conflict away from the main theaters of the war was not at all what Oxenstierna had envisaged when he stepped into command after Lützen. He never considered the German lands his primary target. "The Polish war is our war," he wrote in the mid-1630s, "win or lose, it is our gain or loss. This German war, I don't know what it is, only that we pour out blood here for the sake of reputation, and have naught but ingratitude to expect."[77] The Swedes, who had to eat, drink, and ride just like other armies, could not afford to be nice about whether they took or bought from Protestants or Catholics. Hans Heberle, the Swabian cobbler and a Protestant, tells how after he and his neighbors heard news of the Swedish defeat before Nördlingen in 1634, "we did not long hesitate. Whoever could, got out, so we could reach Ulm on the same day. We were in peril, for the [Catholic] enemy was breathing down our throats. The Swedes, too, did nothing for us. Whatever they could pick up of ours during their flight, they took along, so that we were in peril from both sides."[78]

Oxenstierna, ever the ultra-realist, lacked all faith that the German Protestants, who had greeted Gustavus Adolphus as their deliverer from the Catholic tide, would be steadfast in their gratitude. "We must let this German business be left to the Germans," he thought, "who will be the only people to get any good of it (if there is any), and therefore not spend any more men or money here, but rather try by all means to wriggle out of it."[79] Drawing his Swedish units northward toward the coast, he hoped to leave the rest of the struggle to German Protestant forces. Long before this time, the Swedish army had ceased to be Swedish in anything but name, and at Uppsala a defeatist mood reigned. "Amnesty is honourable," a Swedish councilor sighed, "compensation is useful; but the contentment of the soldiery is essential."[80] Finally, in 1638 France abandoned its waiting game, gold began to flow, and 14,000 new reinforcements arrived from Sweden. In return – a high price – the chancellor had to commit the army to fight alongside France for the war's duration. That would be almost precisely a decade.

77 Parker, *The Thirty Years' War*, 140.
78 Heberle, *Der Dreissigjährige Krieg*, 150.
79 Axel Oxenstierna to the Swedish Council of State, 7 January 1635 in Parker, *The Thirty Years' War*, 140.
80 Parker, *The Thirty Years' War*, 143.

With the reconfigured alliances stabilized, the war slogged on, and in some regions it seemed as if the plundering and killing would continue until the Last Day. Englishmen who traveled through the Empire in the late 1630s found vast regions devastated, populations disappeared or reduced to beggary, remaining populations so jumpy they panicked at the approach of strangers, and the roads plagued by nameless forces turned bandit. In 1639 the Swabian Lutheran Johann Valentin Andreae (1586–1654), pastor at Calw in Württemberg and in his youth an author of Rosicrucian works, lamented that since 1630 he had lost two-thirds of his communicants, among them five intimate and thirty-three other friends, twenty relatives, and forty-one clerical colleagues. "I have to weep for them," he wrote, "because I remain here so impotent and alone. Out of my whole life I am left with scarcely fifteen persons alive with whom I can claim some trace of friendship."[81]

By 1640 the stalemate persuaded Emperor Ferdinand to call the Imperial electors to Nuremberg, where he proposed that an Imperial Diet be called, the first since 1613. It did meet for a while, but without result. Once again the secularized church lands formed the sticking point, and even the emperor's renunciation of the Edict of Restitution brought no progress. The war was no longer a German war, and the Germans could not end it.

By New Year of 1643 pressure on the emperor to treat for peace had become difficult to resist. Maximilian of Bavaria urged peace with France, and the sudden collapse of Spanish power in the Low Countries added weight to his arguments. So did resentment of the war among populations in France, Sweden, and the Empire. In January 1644 envoys of many German princes assembled at Frankfurt to discuss German issues and decide how to negotiate together with the foreign powers. Soon, negotiations began among the belligerents headquartered at Münster for the Catholic powers, Osnabrück for the Protestants. For several years yet they were stalled by the emperor's refusal to allow the German princes, his vassals, to take part individually, but at the end of August 1645 he conceded to them the right to make war and peace (*ius belli ac pacis*) – and hence to represent themselves. When the Dutch Republic's envoys arrived at Münster seeking a peace with Spain, the cast of characters was complete. The Catholic delegations at Münster totaled 176 plenipotentiaries (nearly half of them lawyers) acting for 194 rulers, ranging in size from the 200-person strong French delegation down to individuals who represented minor princes. Meanwhile, the fighting went on, if more desultorily than before. Adam Adami (1610–63), a Benedictine who was acting for the prince-abbot of Corvey and the Swabian Imperial prelates, commented laconically on the situation: "In winter we negotiate, in summer we fight."[82]

In 1648 at last, the 5-year-long negotiations came to a conclusion. The treaties of Münster and Osnabrück are together known as the Peace of Westphalia. Their provisions for the Empire looked remarkably like a restoration of the old Imperial governance, including the Religious Peace of 1555. The *ius reformandi* of all Imperial estates – including the free cities and the Imperial knights – was confirmed, though all confessional minorities settled in 1624 or earlier acquired the right to live in peace. New Year's Day 1624 was fixed as the reference point (*Normaljahr*) for the permanent

81 Parker, *The Thirty Years' War*, 148.
82 Parker, *The Thirty Years' War*, 160.

possession of ecclesiastical properties. The Peace also revised the Empire's current confessional configuration by including the Reformed (Calvinist) faith. Most important as a guarantee of the Imperial peace was the treaties' secular character. The pope was not party to the negotiations at Münster, and when his nuncio, Fabio Chigi (b. 1599, r. 1655–57),[83] protested both treaties' terms, most of the Catholic estates turned a deaf ear.

The peace introduced two important innovations into Imperial governance. First, although the Imperial estates might deal with foreign powers, they were forbidden to wage war against the emperor, and the right to declare war and sign treaties was reserved to emperor and estates acting jointly. Second, the election of Future emperors prior to a vacancy (*vivente imperator*) was forbidden. The Imperial monarchy remained an institution sacral in principle, at least for the Catholics, but secular in fact. In this way the interim character attributed to the peace in 1555 – "until a final Christian agreement on religion"[84] – passed into history. And so the truce of 1555 became the peace of 1648,[85] hardening further the late medieval political reform that produced a large country without centralized governance. Nor would it ever enjoy a single, national religion, for the Empire overcame its religious schism by building the old confessional order into its own public life.

Westphalia's territorial settlements seem relatively modest for such a long, bitter, and bloody war. The peace awarded France the Habsburg possessions and the free cities (except Strasbourg and Mulhouse/Mühlhausen) in Alsace and confirmed French titles to the three prince-bishoprics (Metz, Toul, and Nancy) of Lorraine, which had lain under French occupation since 1552. Swedish gains were also substantial. While Oxenstierna had demanded all of Pomerania, which clearly would violate the Hohenzollern right to succeed the native dynasty (extinct in 1637), France backed the claims of Elector Frederick William (b. 1620, r. 1640–88) of Brandenburg. Sweden thus gained only western Pomerania and the episcopal territories, which put the mouths of the major north German rivers under Swedish influence. By virtue of their respective gains, the French and Swedish monarchs each secured a seat in the Imperial Diet.

Two German princes, Bavaria and Brandenburg, came away clear winners. The peace confirmed to Maximilian and his heirs both the Imperial electorate and the eastern or Upper Palatinate, though the Rhine or Lower Palatinate went to the Winter King's heir. Frederick William of Brandenburg was rewarded with the eastern half of Pomerania, plus the bishoprics of Magdeburg and Halberstadt. Finally, two ancient sectors of the Holy Roman Empire, the Swiss Confederation and the Republic of the Seven United Netherlands, gained international recognition as fully independent countries.

If any belligerent power can be said to have won the war, it was France, a point on which the conventional view of the war is correct. Looking back 200 years later, Prudhon boasted with satisfaction, "the Treaty of Westphalia preeminently identifies

83 The future Pope Alexander VII (r. 1655–67).
84 Ruth Kastner, ed., *Quellen zur Reformation 1517–1555*, 526.
85 In retrospect, therefore, the peace of 1555 reminds one of Marshal Ferdinand Foche's comment upon reading the Peace of Versailles: "Ce n'est pas un traité de paix, c'est un armistice de vingt ans." Paul Reynaud, *Mémoires*, vol. 2: 457.

justice with the force of things, and will last forever."[86] For "justice" read "the strategic interests of France." With respect to the war's international scope, Westphalia confirmed its most important consequences, the shift in military paramountcy from Spain to France and the consolidation of the Old Regime's international system of negotiation and war. The Swedish gains by comparison proved ephemeral, for the impressive new Swedish position on the southern Baltic littoral crashed down in just over sixty years.

Hardly anyone in the German lands thought the religious outcome ideal – three versions of Christianity in one country – but the end to fighting and the political settlement were greeted with cries of relief mingled with laments for the dead, thanks to God, and admonitions to rebuild the land. One poet framed this hope in a polyphonic hymn of praise:

> Now venture forth on land and sea:
> You merchants and you traders;
> The roads are truly safe once more
> Free of bandits and of robbers.
> Now the golden power of peace
> Has swept away the caps of thieves
> And banished all our burdens. . .
> Now go forth with fresh, happy mien,
> You mowers and you harvesters!
> Build up once more both farm and house,
> O housefather and housemother.
> Blessed are they who nourish true,
> Who bring forth child and grandchild,
> To build up a whole new world.[87]

Up and down the Empire ran news of the Peace. It came to Upper Swabia, where the war, from the epidemics spread by soldiers in the early 1630s to a two-day siege by the combined French and Swedes in October 1646, had shattered forever the prosperity of "golden Augsburg."[88] The burghers' sufferings were chronicled by an anonymous pamphlet, *The Augsburg Larder*, in which the animals discuss their losses at the hands of starving Augsburgers. The cat says:

> The Augsburgers no longer need any cats
> Because the mice, which we used to catch,
> They now eat themselves. Even that's not enough,
> For they eat us cats as well. We are not free.[89]

When the "peaces of all peaces" was finally signed, Augsburg, now fallen from an international metropolis to a regional center, celebrated the restoration of the old confessional parity in public life, according to the rule of 1555, which would endure until the Empire was no more.

---

86   Pierre-Joseph Prudhon (1809–65), quoted by Fritz Dickmann, *Der Westfälische Frieden*, 7.
87   Heinz Schilling, *Aufbruch und Krise. Deutschland 1517–1648*, 460.
88   Bernd Roeck, *Als wollt die Welt schier brechen: Eine Stadt im Zeitalter des Dreissigjährigen Krieges*, 280–318.
89   Roeck, *Als wollt die Welt schier brechen*, 275.

Last of all, news of the Westphalian peace came to Hell. It arrived by "fast messenger," as Grimmelhausen's Simplicissimus tells, who related it to Lucifer:

> O great prince, the German Peace now concluded has cast nearly all Europe into a state of peace. Everywhere the sounds of "Glory to God in the Highest" and "O God, We Thank Thee" ring to the heavens, and now everyone will hustle to serve God under his own vine and his own fig tree.[90]

Did anyone demur? Some veteran soldiers, surely, who now looked forward to a life minus adventure and perhaps on even shorter commons than they had got in service. The arms manufacturers, almost certainly, plus the suppliers of horses, fodder, uniforms, and transport of all kinds to the fighting forces. But the rest, especially the little people, now facing the grinding task of rebuilding their lands, greeted war's end with relief, thanks, and rejoicing. "This year of 1649," wrote Hans Heberle,

> is a year of blissful, unheard-of jubilation and joy.... To God on high alone is the honor that now there is peace on earth in our Germany and in the entire [Holy] Roman Empire; among the emperor, Sweden, the French, and all kings, princes, counts, and cities; also villages large and small, hamlets, farmsteads, and wastelands; among rich and poor, young and old, wife and husband, woman and child; and the dear stock and horses – all rejoice and can enjoy the peace. Yea, even the dear fields and plowlands, which have for so long been fallow and barren, [rejoice] to be plowed and sown once more, so that we poor children of humankind can once again get our nourishment from them and so have our injuries healed and our sufferings stilled.[91]

The great German war was over. Its consequences would live on for many generations, but not forever.

90 Hansjakob Christoffel von Grimmelshausen, "Continuatio des abenteuerlichen Simplicissimi oder der Schluß desselben," ch. 2, in Hansjakob Christoffel von Grimmelshausen, *Werke*, 568.
91 Heberle, *Der Dreissigjährige Krieg*, 226.

18

German Reformations, German Futures

For most Germans now going to Berlin, our history starts in 1945 or with
the Holocaust. . . . We have developed a new national consciousness, one formed
from the terrible legacy of Auschwitz.

Hans Mommsen

The future is made of the same stuff as the present.

Simone Weil

In 1983, the year of Martin Luther's 500th birthday, Heiko Augustinus Oberman
chose a coign of vantage from which to set the reformer into the age of reformations
without veiling his significance for the modern era. He found such a site not beyond
but above both Luther's time and all others. "Surprisingly," Oberman wrote, "the
discoveries and experiences of a life marked by battle raging within and without make
him a contemporary of our time, which has learned to sublimate the Devil and
marginalize God."[1] If we are to understand such a Luther, he added, "we must read
the history of life from an unconventional perspective. It is history 'sub specie aeter-
nitatis,' in the light of eternity; not in the mild glow of constant progress toward
Heaven, but in the shadow of the chaos of the Last Days and the imminence of
eternity."[2] Yet Oberman also understood that however tellingly Luther the theologian might speak to the great issues of our day, they cannot be understood, much less
explained, except in terms of the ideas, issues, struggles, and solidarities of the age of
reformations. Luther had his time and place, we have ours.

This final chapter begins with a summation of the argument about German histories in the age of reformations. There follows a reflection on how this era might be
understood in relation to later times, now that it is liberated from the spell cast by
Leopold von Ranke, the historian who created German history in the age of the
Reformation.

---

1 Heiko A. Oberman, *Luther: Man between God and the Devil*, xix. The original (German) edition
  appeared in 1983.
2 Oberman, *Luther*, 12.

I. THE AGE OF REFORMATIONS

This book's central thesis is that the creation of the early modern Holy Roman Empire and the religious reform that produced the German confessional system form two phases of a single transformation of the medieval German lands into the early modern German world. The success of the political reform, the argument runs, simultaneously enabled the ensuing religious reform and assured its truncation and the divisions it produced. Reformation, when it finally came, proved revolutionary in concept and fragmenting in fact. Its settlements in 1555 and 1648 halted the political evolution of the Holy Roman Empire of the German Nation and coagulated the religious schism into the old confessional order. That order was an essential structure in the post-reformations Empire's public life, and was the age's most durable legacy to post-Napoleonic Germany.

The German lands embarked on this journey during the fifteenth century. Their social contours – population, complex social groupings, and mixed economies of farming, manufacturing, and trade – were for the most part unremarkably European (as discussed in Part I). Like other lands, they had survived a shrinkage of population, a recession of settlement, a depression of agriculture, manufacturing, and trade, and a general weakening of larger agencies of governance, including the Church. The German lands differed from some other realms, however, in how their governance recovered from the late medieval depression. This difference is crucial to our understanding the course of German histories over the next four centuries.

The German lands' age of reformations unfolded between 1400 and 1650 in three phases: political reforms (Part II), religious reformations (Part III), and formation of the old confessional order (Part IV). The first phase down to the 1520s transformed the medieval German feudal kingdom into the early modern Holy Roman Empire of the German Nation. It created a new kind of institutionalized public life simultaneously at both the Imperial and the territorial levels. The result was the stronger, more stable governing order under which Germans would live for 300 years. The monarchy formed its capstone, the chief vassals, the great Imperial princes spiritual and temporal, its pillars. They dominated the Imperial parliament (the Diet); they mediated the lines of authority and the power of enforcement that connected their own territorial subjects to Imperial governance. The growth of the territorial princes' dynastic power meant a corresponding political decline of the lesser Imperial estates – counts, nobles, and cities – and it promoted a new corporate politics suggested by the phrase, "emperor and Empire." The Empire thus participated in its own peculiar way in the general strengthening of governance in post-depression Europe. The new era's states came to possess a more definite legislative authority, administrative bureaucracies, heavier taxation, more powerful armies, and new controls over their particular churches. In the Empire, one condition of a successful monarchy was the unbroken Habsburg succession, which saved this royal dynasty from the fate of its predecessors, the Luxemburgs. Still, they could only rule in concert with their chief vassals, temporal and spiritual. Although this German form of cogovernance has commonly been branded a political failure, when tested it proved extremely tough and durable. Its broadly dispersed governance managed a vast, ramshackle web of authority that proved very strong in the defense of the status quo but very weak in the initiation of change. Its most notable success was the political management of the religious schism through the age of reformations, though at the cost of three decades of civil war.

The transformation's second phase – Protestant reformations – began with Martin Luther's public debut around 1520 and closed with the beginnings of the Catholic recovery in the 1570s and 1580s. Luther's challenge to the status quo fell on ground prepared by the long frustration of the religious reform projected by the general councils of Constance and Basel. It helped to awaken an intervention of ordinary people in public affairs, which erupted without precedent and subsided with few direct offspring. The religious reforms that followed were both enabled and constrained by the foregoing political reforms, which produced effects different from those of the royal-episcopal reforms conducted in other European kingdoms, both those that broke with Rome and those that did not.

It is possible to see in the success of Luther's revolutionary appeal to the German princes a consequence of the Imperial church's shirking of reform during the foregoing decades. Although the prince-bishops assumed a leading role in fashioning the Empire's new corporate politics of collaboration, representation, consultation, consent, and judicialization, they failed to mount a concerted reform of the Imperial church. Instead, they took the easy way of diverting the pressure for reform, not to speak of anticlerical resentment, southward toward Rome. One could conclude, therefore, that the combined success of Imperial reform and territorial state formation made impossible a reform of the Church according to the conciliar agendas set at Constance and Basel.

Martin Luther's words and the news of his heroic resistance to pope and emperor struck this logjam of reform like a mighty hammer. By separating the question of salvation from ecclesiastical authority, he issued a passport to the early reform movements. This radical theology spread through public opinion, a new kind of milieu stimulated by an inundation of printed words and images on an absolutely unprecedented scale. Its flooding tide struck an ecclesiastical world immobilized by its past and distracted by many preoccupations. The movement swept up both traditional anticlericalism and a newly virulent anti-Romanism, which, superheated by the Italian Wars, inspired priests and laymen as well as women to speak and act for the reform of religious life in their own hometowns.

The Protestant reformation's initial capital came not from the aristocracy or the nobles but from the burghers. They possessed a rich corporate political culture, relatively high literacy, an educated clergy, printing presses, magistrates vulnerable to popular pressure, and long traditions of quarrels with their bishops. Their reform movement developed with blazing speed and shocking demonstrations and expressions of disobedience to and defiance of authority. Though brief, this urban phase lasted long enough to ensure the security of reforming urban priests against their bishops.

The urban movements and the great German Peasants' War of 1524–26 overlapped chronologically and geographically, and they drank from the same streams of rumor, report, and agitation. Yet, although burghers and peasants sometimes collaborated, the rural movement differed fundamentally from its urban counterpart. The former aimed to undermine seigneurial power and to secure good government on a regional-territorial basis; the latter aimed to purify the churches. The Peasants' War thus may be seen as a culmination of the political reforms that had begun in the 1480s. It nevertheless cut deeply into the evangelical movement, because during and after 1525 the reformers had to dissociate themselves from insurrection. The revolution of 1525 forced the rulers' hands. Some believed that Luther had inspired the insurrection,

Confessions, Empire, and War, 1576-1650

others that his reformation was the best prophylactic against revolution. Given the emperor's absence and the Diet's paralysis, princes and, to a lesser degree, free cities' magistrates were left to encourage or retard the movement's expansion and to re-fashion the Imperial church, Catholic as well as Protestant, on a territorial basis.

Many dynastic rulers and magistrates of free cities opted for the new faith and joined the Protestant League of Smalkalden. Although in 1547 Emperor Charles V defeated them in the field, he proved himself unable to coerce the Protestant powers into ending the religious schism and had to fall back on conciliation and compromise. The Religious Peace of 1555 not only legalized the new faith, it gave Protestant mag-istrates and princes freedom to establish the new faith and suppress the old in many places, to grab ecclesiastical properties and even some bishoprics, and to recruit a new generation of Protestant clergymen. The addition of a third, Reformed, confession since 1560 complicated but did not fundamentally alter this outcome.

The transformation's third phase created the old confessional order of the German lands. It began around 1575 and ended in 1648 with the Peace of Westphalia. As the Protestant advance slowed, a powerful movement for Catholic renewal and restora-tion began to throw down roots and, propelled by massive external aid, to acquire momentum. The Catholic reformation sprang from the Protestant reformation's challenge to assure that the religious struggle would not end in a clear victory for one side, as it did in England, France, Scotland, Denmark, and Sweden.

The old German confessional order took shape during an era of deteriorating climate, demographic and economic stagnation, declining currencies, business fail-ures, weak emperors, a quarrelsome Diet, frenzied witch-hunting, European religious wars, recurring Ottoman pressure, three decades of civil war, and foreign invasion and occupation. When it was over, the religious geography of the German lands had taken the shape it would maintain until very recent times. When the Germans even-tually became a nation, they would possess not one but two national religions.

The German confessional order arose from a political agreement to disagree about religion. In its peculiarly two-tiered arrangement – general tolerance, particular intoler-ance – the Imperial *convivencia* built on the Empire's political evolution since the early fifteenth century. Its ethos promoted a general practice of regulating conflict and difference through arbitration and judicialization, a hallmark of Imperial governance until the end. The general movement away from persecution toward discipline is visible in the fortunes of marginal and persecuted peoples: the Empire's Jews came to enjoy a protected status (though not without discrimination), while Anabaptists (since the 1570s) and witches (since the 1660s) sank below the horizon of official repression.

Only the Thirty Years War seriously threatened this Imperial *convivencia*. First, at the end of the 1620s, military successes put total victory within the Imperial/Cath-olic forces' grasp. Next, the swift reversal of fortunes then shifted the war into an increasingly hopeless stalemate. When it broke, the Peace of Westphalia restored but hardly altered the Imperial *convivencia*. It may seem counter-intuitive to conclude that the religious conflicts of the sixteenth and seventeenth centuries strengthened the hybrid governance of the Holy Roman Empire of the German Nation.[3] Yet there is

---

3 I mean "hybrid" in two related senses: between the highly symbolic, personal, and unpredictably violent governance of earlier times and the highly real, institutional, and disciplining governance of modern times over much of Europe; and between the dispersed sovereignty of the reformed early modern Empire and the more concentrated sovereignty of western Europe's early modern kingdoms.

no other explanation for the survival of this complex polity through the great European wars between 1618 and 1789. It is not easy to imagine how, given the confessional stalemate, in the absence of a great military upheaval the post-Westphalian Empire could have been governed as a single polity in any other way.

2. FROM THE OLD CONFESSIONAL ORDER TO THE NEW CONFESSIONALISM

Three hundred and twenty years separated the Imperial reform's inception at the Diet of Frankfurt in 1486 from the Holy Roman Empire's end in 1806.[4] Since then, no newly founded German-speaking state has endured longer than two generations.[5] It makes poor sense, therefore, to ascribe statehood (*Staatlichkeit*) to the Holy Roman Empire of the German Nation as a kind of ancestor of any modern, German-speaking state. The persistence of names aside – Empire/*Reich*, emperor/*Kaiser*, diet/*Reichstag* – the concept of state supplies no direct, institutional bridge from early modern to modern German history. What continuity there was rested, rather, on the confessional culture of public life, which, though radically changed after 1803, formed the most important link between early modern and modern German histories.

State development aside, there are two views of the passage from German histories to German history that supply far more convincing grounds for arguing a continuity between them. First, there is the German lands' economic and social development from a feudal kingdom toward a national, capitalist democracy. On this very large scale, the historical-materialist argument has no rivals. It holds, as Friedrich Engels wrote, that "political, juridical, philosophical, religious, literary, artistic, etc., development is based on economic development," though in no fixed way, because, as he added, they "react upon one another and also upon the economic base."[6] Although this powerful principle has by no means lost its utility because of the apparent collapse of the political movement it was fashioned to serve, its scope is far too large to frame adequately the histories examined in this book.

The second view is that the German old confessional order formed a major strand of continuity between the age of reformations and modern Germany. This history can be comprehended in three phases.

1. the era of the Imperial *convivencia* (1555–1806), in which the confessions bound the Christian churches into an Imperial legal and political framework, promoted discipline, and habituated themselves to coexistence;
2. the era of confessionalist rivalry and competition (1815–1918), in which the religious communities, no longer sheltered or constrained by the Imperial *convivencia*, strove to maintain or even enhance their positions in conditions of rapid political and social change; and

---

4 Confusion sometimes arises about when the Holy Roman Empire ended. It was formally dissolved by Napoleon's decree in 1803, but the Diet did not complete the secularization and the reordering of lands and peoples until 1806.
5 Meant is a generation of the conventional length of thirty years. Counting the Second Empire (47 years), Weimar Republic (15 years), First Austrian Republic (20 years), Third Reich (12 years), German Democratic Republic (40 years), German Federal Republic (60 years), and Second Austrian Republic (64 years).
6 Friedrich Engels to H. Starkenburg, 25 January 1894, in Karl Marx and Friedrich Engels, *Selected Correspondence, 1846–1895*, 517.

3. the era of accommodation (1919 to the present), in which, despite the brief, violent interruption of 1933–45, the communities gradually made their peace with a secular state and with one another.

It is a serious error to think of the old confessional order as a frozen artifact of the deep past, incapable of adaptation or development. By the middle decades of the eighteenth century, the Imperial *convivencia* and the growth of state power over the churches made the confessional order simply a fact of life for many Germans. Gotthold Ephraim Lessing (1729–81) believed that impulses for change moved back and forth between the confessions like fermentation among wines in a cellar. "One sets the other in motion, and neither can move by itself," he wrote, and

> each of the mighty steps pioneered by the Protestant church through the Reformation, the Catholics soon followed. The papal influence on the State is no less benevolent than that of the Protestant Church. Truly, if the latter is not prevented from withdrawing further into itself and rejecting all heterogeneous things, one day it will stand just as far behind the papal church as it was ever ahead of that church.[7]

Less sanguine observers detected beneath the calm a potential for renewed conflict. In 1766 the jurist Friedrich Karl von Moser called the religious division an "irreversible reason why Germany is divided into two main parts" that renew from one generation to the next "the perverse and harmful concept of a double fatherland, of a Catholic and a Protestant Germany."[8]

In the shorter run, history falsified Lessing's vision and validated Moser's, for the Empire's end overturned the old confessional order and produced, within one generation, open strife between the confessions. The nineteenth century was not, as is sometimes alleged, a "second confessional age," but a post-*convivencia* age of confessionalism, of competition and enmity, as the decay of security destabilized the interconfessional boundaries. Although open strife began only one generation after Napoleon's fall, the event that precipitated the plunge toward the new confessionalism took place under his hegemony and at his will.

The most important consequence of the Empire's end was the secularization. This massive wave of expropriation was not confessionally symmetrical, for the Protestant losses to secularization were tiny compared to what happened to the Catholic Church. The great secularization of 1803–6 swept away the Catholic prince-bishoprics and abbeys, whose 10,000 km^2 of territory and 3.2 million persons (about a seventh of the Empire's population) were transferred to new, mostly Protestant, rulers.[9] Lost, too, were the monasteries and their schools, lands, libraries, and treasures, plunder that poured into princely treasuries and speculators' hands. The secularization completed what the Protestant reformation had begun. What followed, however, in contrast to Revolutionary France, was not a violent secularization of the State but a religious revival, which masked the first phase of political secularization and the removal of the churches from public life. "The German nineteenth century," wrote Thomas Nipperdey (1927–92), "is still a Christian age shaped by the churches.

---

7 Gotthold Ephraim Lessing, *Werke*, vol. 8: 713–15. My thanks to Michael O. Printy for the text.
8 Friederich Carl von Moser, *Von dem deutschen Nationalgeist*, 17–18.
9 Only one important Catholic state survived, Bavaria, which gained rule over large numbers of Protestants. Otherwise, the displaced peoples were Catholics, the new rulers Protestants.

Religion and church are matters of fact and a power which determines people's existence, consciousness, and behavior; and they remain of decisive importance for the State, society, and culture."[10] These conditions provided fuel and incentive for the culture of confrontation and competition that arose with the movement toward a new Germany.

In the post-Imperial era, the German-speaking peoples were evenly divided between the two confessions.[11] Then, the wars of 1866–70 made it possible to exclude Austria and thereby to reduce a near confessional parity to a 3:2 Protestant advantage. Yet even before, when a united Germany was but a notion on the horizon, the Protestants began to scent victory. In 1809, after Napoleon's defeat of Prussia, the theologian Friedrich Daniel Ernst Schleiermacher (1768–1834) opined that one might "allow the continued existence of Catholicism for the Latin peoples," so long as Protestants strove "with good conscience to spread the Reformation among the Germanic peoples as the form of Christianity most properly suited to them."[12] G. W. F. Hegel, his colleague at the new University of Berlin, went further to put the seal on the idea of an evolutionary, general supersession of medieval Catholicism by modern Protestantism. "It has been our fortune," Hegel declared in his university address in July 1830, "that the commands of religion agree with the State's idea of law."[13] The enormous Catholic minority in Prussia, one may infer from Hegel's views, would become just another German church of Protestant form and sensibilities. This domesticating project would require breaking down the practices and lines of authority that guarded the Catholic Church's autonomy vis-à-vis the State, principally, but not only, its relationship to the Roman papacy.

In Prussia the government's efforts to domesticate the Catholic clergy to the level of their Protestant counterparts collided almost immediately with realities. The first attempt came with the "Cologne Troubles" of 1837–39, in the course of which the Prussian state imprisoned the archbishop of Cologne, ostensibly for resisting official policy with respect to confessionally mixed marriages. The second came on the heels of the founding of the new German empire in 1871, when the Protestant government attempted to break the power of the Catholic hierarchy. This "battle for civilization" (*Kulturkampf*), the high point of the Protestant-national project of assimilation, inspired great hopes for a German national Christianity to partner the German national state. They rose to their peak in 1883, the 400th anniversary of Luther's birth, when the liberal historian Heinrich von Treitschke (1834–98) prophesied that "the confessional division approaches its end," for

> since the Roman Church has spoken its final word on papal infallibility, we feel more painfully than ever the gulf that separates the parts of our nation. To close this gulf, and thus to revitalize Protestant Christianity again, so that it will become capable of

---

10 Thomas Nipperdey, *Deutsche Geschichte 1800–1860. Bürgerwelt und starker Staat*, 403.
11 It is convenient, though not entirely accurate, to consider the two Protestant confessions, Lutheran and Reformed, as a single, Protestant confession with respect to public life. Here the tone was set by the Prussian Union of 1817 and administrative integration of the two confessions.
12 Werner Schuffenhauer and Klaus Steiner, eds., *Martin Luther in der deutschen bürgerlichen Philosophie 1517–1845*, 364.
13 Schuffenhauer and Steiner, eds., *Martin Luther*, 346. The occasion was the 300th anniversary of the Confession of Augsburg's submission to Emperor Charles V.

dominating our whole nation – this is a task which we acknowledge, and which later generations will fulfill.[14]

Alas, just as Treitschke sounded his note of triumph, the Prussian state had to abandon its failed program to domesticate the Catholic Church.

Only retrospect reveals why the great project failed to integrate the Catholics into a Protestant Germany. From post-Napoleonic times the German Catholics seemed internally divided and politically weak. The internal divisions turned on a whole bundle of issues, but principally on the German Catholic Church's independence from Rome and its degree of assimilation to a Germany increasingly dominated by Protestants. Explicitly or implicitly, confessional differences accompanied every argument about the Germans' future.

Religious contests are largely fought out in words and also in symbols, and the Protestant liberals made the most of the fact that Martin Luther had been a German. Down to the mid-nineteenth century, nationally minded German Catholics found no comfortable accommodation to a national future without submitting to Protestant claims to represent a German national faith. In 1825 the Catholic publicist Johann Joseph Görres (1776–1848) wrote: "Truly, it was a great, noble movement of the German people that produced the Reformation."[15] A dozen years later, the Swabian Joseph Sprissler (d. 1879), a (later defrocked) Catholic priest, went further in appreciating the reformer. "Luther was filled with the purest zeal and divinely inspired courage," he writes, "strict and blameless in his morals, in whom lived an implacable, high, and holy – we could say terrible – seriousness about Christian truth and morals, about religion and reform of the Church."[16] Another quarter-century passed until Johann Joseph Ignaz von Döllinger (1799–1890), Munich's renowned professor of Catholic theology declared: "Luther is the only founder of a religion the German nation has produced, and he is therefore also in his entire being, his aims and actions, in his talents and his actions, the true man of the people, the purest type of the German being."[17] The greater the zeal for national unity grew, the more excruciating became the pressure on Catholics, especially academics and the educated middle class, to join in. "To us alone among nations," Döllinger lamented, "has fate ensured that the sharp blade of ecclesiastical division would continually cut through us. Carved into almost equal parts, we can neither separate from one another nor really live properly together."[18]

---

14 Heinrich von Treitschke, "Luther und die deutsche Nation," 395–6. He alludes, of course, to the Vatican Council's declaration in 1870 of papal infallibility. I use "Protestant liberals" to mean not only members of the Liberal Party but also the cultural-religious liberals, almost all of whom were Protestants. Reversing the phrase into "liberal Protestants" would make it refer to a party in the intra-Protestant struggles of the age. They, too, are included in my use of "Protestant liberals." Today historians hardly doubt that the *Kulturkampf* was essentially a liberal project, many of the implications of which could apply as well to the Protestant churches.

15 Heinrich Bornkamm, ed., *Luther im Spiegel der deutschen Geistesgeschichte. Mit ausgewählten Texten von Lessing bis zur Gegenwart*, 328.

16 Bornkamm, ed., *Luther*, 341. Sprissler was removed from his pastorate because of his remarks against the Catholic Church in the Frankfurt Parliament of 1848.

17 Bornkamm, ed., *Luther*, 339.

18 Quoted in Georg Schwaiger, ed., *Zwischen Polemik und Irenik. Untersuchungen zum Verhältniß der Konfessionen im späten 18. und frühen 19. Jahrhundert*, 5.

Two things prevented the Catholic Church from being ravaged by the powerful logic of full assimilation into a Protestant German nation. First, despite external encouragement, Catholic schisms yielded meager results. The "New Catholicism" (later "German Catholicism") of the mid-1840s produced only a few hundred congregations. Although the conservative, assimilationist movement of "Old Catholics," who refused the Vatican Council's declaration of papal infallibility, gained perhaps 50,000 members, it, too, soon reached the limits of its potential. Neither movement cut very deeply into the bishops' solidarity with Rome or weakened the Catholic laity's support for their priests and bishops during the *Kulturkampf* of the 1870s. One secret to their success was that, when the struggle became fully political, the Catholic Church's disadvantage in numbers was more than balanced by its people's greater cohesion and the electoral efficiency of the Catholic Center Party.

The second reason for the frustration of the prophesies announced by Schleiermacher, Hegel, and Treitschke was the coming of that fairest child of the Industrial Revolution, the German Social Democracy. On the heels of the state's defeat in the *Kulturkampf* there followed a second failure, this of the campaign against the powerful new labor movement. By the early 1890s the bloom was disappearing from the euphoria of the past two decades, as educated Protestants seemed to find themselves caught between the old anvil of Catholicism and the new hammer of Social Democracy. In the early 1890s the philosopher Wilhelm Dilthey (1833–1911) lamented to his fellow Protestants, "It is not only elemental feelings but also their integrated intellectual systems that give the Social Democracy and Ultramontanism their predominance over all other political forces of our time."[19]

The Great War of 1914–18 destroyed the project for assimilating German Catholics into a Protestant Germany as definitively as it did the comparable British project for Ireland. Earlier than most, the Protestant historian Erich Marcks (1861–1938) recognized what was happening. In 1917, the war's darkest year for the Germans, the Luther jubilee prompted him to look back on the last great Luther jubilee (in 1883), which had "sounded a tone of attack and defense in which tremors of *Kulturkampf* echo still."[20] He compared it with his present day when, by contrast, in the midst of a national war, coexistence and cooperation must prevail. Protestantism and Catholicism, Marcks writes, present "the enduring coexistence and confrontation of two spiritual tendencies, which now live within a whole that yokes them in a grand, authoritative way: People and Fatherland. Forces of struggles they may have been, but also forces of vitality. So may it remain in our future: at once against, alongside, and with one another."[21] Marcks thus renounced the assimilationist project for a new order of partnership. He admitted that the Lutheran reformation, "with its unpolitical and self-absorbed spiritual interiority," caused "that split, a thousand times lamented, the curse of our German history. Truly!"[22] Yet the old confessional order also contributed to unity, for it "brought the Protestants from all Germany and the Catholics from all Germany together ... and was in the midst of division, ... a new solidarity."[23]

19 Wilhelm Dilthey, *Gesammelte Schriften*, vol. 2: 91. "Ultramontanism," an intentionally insulting synonym for "Catholicism," intended to emphasize the foreignness of papal authority.
20 Erich Marcks, *Luther und Deutschland. Eine Reformationsrede im Kriegsjahr 1917*, 1.
21 Marcks, *Luther und Deutschland*, 1.
22 Marcks, *Luther und Deutschland*, 20.
23 Marcks, *Luther und Deutschland*, 22.

The reformations' splitting of the nation meant, therefore, "a doubling of German life."[24] And so, in the dark cloud of division that had frightened Moser, irritated Hegel, and stirred up Treitschke, Marcks saw a silver lining of national unity enriched by diversity. He did not add, though it cannot have escaped him, that a partnership of the Christian confessions also might well settle the Social Democracy's fate.

The defeat in 1918 and the Weimar Republic that followed ended the competitive, militant phase of the German confessional order. It did not stop, of course, the powerful culture of criticism and condemnation, prejudice and discrimination, and epithet and insult that had formed since the Holy Roman Empire's passing. Some of this culture descended from the old confessional order, while other parts were new. Whereas the codes of tit-for-tat behavior in everyday life formed a relatively symmetrical exchange that gave each party its innings, the critiques and prejudices show an asymmetry that more nearly suggests the respective confessions' real strengths and weaknesses.

In mixed villages and towns, ritualized forms of symbolic aggression and humiliation strengthened local *convivencias* by marking boundaries that were important but not total. Margaret Lavinia Anderson relates a story set in the town of Kempen, which lies northwest of Düsseldorf and near the Dutch border.[25] On Good Friday, when Kempen's Protestants gathered in church to observe one of the holiest days of their church year, Catholic housewives gave their carpets their annual beating, producing a harsh, rhythmic competitor to the solemn harmonies of Bach. Meanwhile, their Catholic husbands were hauling dripping kegs of liquid manure (*Jauche*) to spread on their fields, from which a powerful aroma drifted into the church and distracted the assembled Protestants from their prayers. Anderson asks, "Was the annual offense to Kempener Protestants illegal? Certainly not. Was it intentional? Absolutely!"[26] The Kempeners were enacting one side of a very common ritual in the day-to-day life of local *convivencias*: on Good Friday the Catholic women beat their carpets; on Corpus Christi the Protestant women returned the favor.

The rules that regulated aggression in local life did not apply to the principal medium of intercommunal strife, printed words and images. This world of agitation on paper, in which ancient libels mixed with acute observations, pornography, and downright lies, waxed and waned with the temperature of relations between the confessional communities. If the experience of Württemberg was at all typical, the agitation rose to three peaks: around 1840 with the Cologne Troubles; in the 1870s and 1880s with the *Kulturkampf*; and around 1900, when the Protestant grip on national life was undergoing a major crisis. This rhythm suggests that the culture of intercommunal agitation in the modern era should not be seen as simply a throwback to the culture of confrontation in the old confessional order.

Very much the same is true of the two parties' characterizations and critiques of one another. Here everything turned on one central issue: the struggle for or against the formation of a German national religion. The situation and the sides determined that in a national forum the Protestant majority should normally play offense to the Catholic minority's defense. The inequality is deceptive, however, because the

24 Marcks, *Luther und Deutschland*, 29.
25 Kempen is noted as the birthplace of the fifteenth-century spiritual writer Thomas à Kempis.
26 Margaret Lavinia Anderson, *Practicing Democracy: Elections and Political Culture in Imperial Germany*, 319.

Catholic Church's superior organization and tighter cohesion largely made up for its numerical disadvantage. Still, in its great era between the 1840s and 1880s, the struggle was fundamentally not a direct test of strength between churches or confessions in the narrow sense but a campaign by German liberals "not just to defend our spiritual property," as one writer stated, "but to break the power of Rome on German soil."[27] The attackers saw in the Catholic Church both a barrier and a rival to their program, at once political, economic, cultural, and sexual, for the new Germany. "If we continue to place our public life under the aegis of the Center Party," warned a spokesman for the leading anti-Catholic association, "we will renounce the masculine ideal of independent morality and individual national character; we will show ourselves to belong to the degenerating nations."[28] It takes little imagination to see that the German liberals, though overwhelmingly Protestant in culture, made claims on public life that marked them as a modern counterpart to the old confessions. They represented not the Protestant churches and belief, which retained the pastoral, preaching, and liturgical goals and tasks of earlier centuries, but national culture. They had become, to give them the modern term that corresponds to "confession" in the old sense, a "milieu."[29]

In words, at least, the struggle for the German future cast itself as a version of the familiar nineteenth-century clash of civilization versus barbarism, good breeding versus degeneracy, and masculinity versus effeminacy, but also of an aggressive positive ideal versus its defensive negation. It was never symmetrical, for "Catholics did not appeal to national identity or to the logic of German history in order to justify confessional polemics."[30] The roots of their own intolerance and exclusivity lay "not in the national organization of political Catholicism, nor in the national ideology of German Catholics, but rather in local life, in integralist pressure on piety, and in the periodic encyclicals that emanated from Rome."[31] There is an aura of haunting reprise around this drama of a national Protestantism against a Catholicism at once local and international. Beyond words and feelings, however, nothing tied this modern struggle to the age of reformations. The conditions and the stakes were entirely new.

By the 1880s the project for a national religion had been defeated, though recriminations and resentments endured for another generation or more. Long after the political confrontations and literary battles subsided, the old stereotypes lived on as a folkloric knowledge. They belonged to those superstructural elements, which, as Ernst Bloch wrote, "continue to reproduce themselves in the cultural consciousness after their social bases have disappeared."[32] A recent mapping of stereotypes of this kind unearthed mostly fairly predictable versions of what can still be found in other countries of significantly mixed forms of Christianity. In Protestant eyes they

---

27 Helmut Walser Smith, *German Nationalism and Religious Conflict: Culture, Ideology, Politics, 1870–1914*, 58.

28 Smith, *German Nationalism and Religious Conflict*, 58.

29 A milieu in this sense is the culture in which the individual was reared and educated or has joined, including the people and institutions with whom the person interacts and feels solidarity. The term is widely used by historians of modern German politics and culture. That the Social Democracy also fashioned itself as a milieu, though not as a religion in the full sense, is a common observation in that literature.

30 Michael B. Gross, *The War Against Catholicism: Liberalism and the Anti-Catholic Imagination in Nineteenth-Century Germany*, 71.

31 Gross, *The War Against Catholicism*, 71.

32 Ernst Bloch, *Das Prinzip Hoffnung*, vol. 1: 176.

themselves are "German," while the Catholics are "un-German" and "unpatriotic," "Ultramontanists, Papists, and Romanists," "internationally connected revolutionaries," "pious and loyal to their church," "superstitious," "lazy, slovenly, and dirty," and "hypocritical, insincere, and untruthful." In Catholic eyes they themselves are "more religious, pious, and loyal to the church," and "bound to the Catholic Church as protector," while Protestants represent "moral decay," and they "oppress Catholics" and serve as "slaves of the State."[33]

This stew of stereotypes is now a cultural remnant in Bloch's sense. It mixes folklore from the old confessional order with memories, real or imagined, of injuries inflicted or threatened under the old confessional order and under new confessionalism. Together these layers form the detritus of two historic passages. The first, marked by dispossession at the end of the Holy Roman Empire, deeply injured German-speaking Catholicism. The second, marked by loss of a national dream at the end of the Great War, injured German-speaking Protestantism just as or even more deeply. The Catholics lost a past, the civilization they once had created, but the Protestants lost a future, the civilization they might have created. Thomas Nipperdey remarked on this fact. "One who was born a Protestant, as I was," he wrote in the Luther jubilee year of 1983, "and who does not take this to be an accident of birth but accepts it willingly, is inclined to set a high, positive value on the constitutive significance of Luther and Lutheranism for the history of modernity in Germany, for the formation of personality and behavior, of society and culture."[34] Nipperdey's elegiac tone suggests a closed book, a tale finished without resolution because the world has changed so radically as to rob the story itself of its point. They are all over now: the age of reformations, the age of confessionalization, and the age of confessionalism. Their chain was broken by the wreck of the German national dream, the vision of a single German people living in a spiritual-cultural unity that could best be characterized as not a church – it was never that – but the last confession.

The results of these changes are so obvious in today's Germany as to require little comment in detail. Following the twelve-year Nazi dictatorship, which attempted to install, under the name of "positive Christianity," a racist civil religion above the existing confessions, postwar German politicians remained ultra-wary of establishing a democratic civil religion and tended to leave the custody of morality in the churches' hands. Rolf Schieder explains how this functioned: "The German system of established churches and confessional competition has been responsible for the fact that the civil-religious division of labor between political and religious institutions is much more strictly managed than in the USA."[35] Yet this order is now breaking down. Since the unification of the two Germanys in 1990, around 30 percent of the citizens adhere to no organized religion, the levels of practice among those who do is falling steadily, and a growing fraction of Germany's population comprises non-Christian immigrants. However Germans of future generations deal with the issues these trends raise, it will not be in terms of confessions in the old sense.

33 Christel Köhle-Hezinger, *Evangelisch-Katholisch. Untersuchungen zu konfessionellem Vorurteil und Konflikt im 19. und 20. Jahrhundert vornehmlich am Beispiel Württembergs*, 99–105.
34 Thomas Nipperdey, "Luther und die Bildung der Deutschen," 27.
35 Rolf Schieder, *Wieviel Religion verträgt Deutschland?* 133.

3. THE RANKEAN SPELL AND THE AGE OF REFORMATIONS

The world into which these passages have brought the German speakers is one they clearly have in common with other Europeans, each people on the same track but with its own schedule. In important ways, this world is more distant from that of Leopold von Ranke than his was from the world of Luther, Loyola, and Calvin. Between Ranke and us stands what Nicholas Boyle has called "the Seventy-Five Years of War . . . from 1914 to 1989."[36] This terrible experience, followed by the challenges that a globalizing, market-based civilization is creating, has dropped a veil between us and those earlier times. More than anything else, this new barrier to understanding falsifies the long-held view of the Protestant reformation as the revolutionary birth moment of modernity. When Heinz Schilling proposes "We have lost the Reformation" as a "counter-thesis" to the idea of reformation-as-revolution, he suggests what the veil's descent means to our conception of German and European history.[37] The Reformation, to be sure, has suffered less loss of coherence from this stretching of history than has its one-time partner, the Renaissance. "The venerable Renaissance label," wrote William J. Bouwsma in 1978, "has become little more than an administrative convenience, a kind of blanket under which we huddle together . . . because . . . we have nowhere else to go."[38] This is not the case for the Reformation, nor is it likely to become so, for whereas the Renaissance's audience today is confined mostly to professors and art collectors, the Reformation retains a broad spectrum of attention both in and outside the Christian communities. Among them, liberated from Ranke's spell, the subject must find its future audiences.

Deep in Ranke's *German History in the Age of the Reformation* lies a mystery: history's original frustration of a belief in the Germans' future as a nation destined to be united by a purified Christianity. The Reformation was the era, he wrote, "in which the politico-religious energy of the German nation was most conspicuous for its growth and most prolific in its results."[39] Then began a great shift away from the Middle Ages, that "compound of military and sacerdotal government which forms the basis of all European civilisation from that moment,"[40] toward a new order based on the partnering of a spiritualized Christianity with autonomous national states. Hence, Ranke was utterly baffled by the power of the Catholic counterreformation – symbolized by the papacy – to frustrate this outcome in the Empire and thereby to produce a conundrum, "the division of our nation into two, mutually uncomprehending, and often mutually hostile halves."[41] Ranke and his disciples expected history to make good someday – and soon – what history had once got wrong. Surely, history, for them a normally opaque but occasionally transparent mask of God's providence, would not allow to endure what seemed a patently wrong turn.

Although Ranke's authority lost weight after 1918, his fundamental idea of the Reformation lived on well into the post-1945 era. While it hardly surprises to find this

36 Nicholas Boyle, *Who Are We Now? Christian Humanism and the Global Market from Hegel to Heaney*, 5.
37 Heinz Schilling, "Profiles of a 'New Grand Narrative' in Reformation History? Comments on Thomas A. Brady Jr.'s Lecture," in Thomas A. Brady, *The Protestant Reformation in German History*, 44.
38 William J. Bouwsma, "The Renaissance and the Drama of Western History," 3.
39 Leopold von Ranke, *Deutsche Geschichte im Zeitalter der Reformation*, vol. 1: 4 (Bk I, Einleitung).
40 Ranke, *Deutsche Geschichte*, vol. 1: 5 (Bk I, Einleitung).
41 Ranke, *Deutsche Geschichte*, vol. 2: 85 (Bk III, ch. 5).

so among traditional historians during the interwar decades, it is more striking to discover an essentially Rankean narrative alive in the writings of both a leading National Socialist historian, Günther Franz (1902–92), and the dean of Reformation historians in the German Democratic Republic, Max Steinmetz (1912–90). Each adopted a narrative of German history essentially Rankean in form, in which a German national movement frustrated in the sixteenth century comes to victory in later times.[42] Of course, their explanations of what happened differed radically from one another. Franz's crudely nationalistic interpretation held that the German Peasants' War aimed for a revolutionary national state free of the corrupting, alien influences of the Roman Church and the Roman Law. Still, the old narrative remains of a then frustrated, now vindicated German national revolution. "Today, at the end of the first successful revolution," Franz wrote in 1933, "the peasant has won in the Third Reich the position in national life for which he had already striven in 1525."[43]

The concept of Peasants' War and Reformation that emerged in the German Democratic Republic around 1960 had only one thing in common with Franz's view – the form of its narrative. It, too, reprised the Rankean narrative of a national revolution once lost but now won. In 1960 Max Steinmetz drafted thirty-four theses, in which he introduced or reintroduced (from Friedrich Engels) the concept of an early bourgeois revolution. So dominant did this concept become in writing on the Reformation and the Peasants' War scholarship in the GDR that "between 1960 and 1989 no publication on the Reformation era appeared which did not employ this term."[44]

"The early bourgeois revolution," reads the first of Steinmetz's theses, "which culminated in the Peasant War, represented the first attempt of the popular masses to create a unified national state from below."[45] The revolution was frustrated by an alliance between the feudal princes and the "feudal church" of Rome, the twin forces of reaction that together serve very nearly the same role in Franz's narrative. The frustration of revolution then shaped a Germany which remained long thereafter feudal and backward in both politics and religion. The early bourgeois revolution, which "reached its highpoint in the Reformation and Peasants' War (1517–25)," nonetheless remained "the most significant revolutionary mass movement of the German people until the November Revolution of 1918."[46] In effect, Steinmetz presented a Rankean vehicle driven by a historical-material motor.[47]

42 I allude to the Ranke of the early masterworks, *The History of the Popes* and *The German History*. They reflect his wrestling with the problem of revolution and order in history. Later, shocked by the Revolutions of 1848, he turned strongly anti-revolutionary and remained so. The consequences of this turn are visible in his histories of Prussia, France, and England, also in his later search for the secret of history in what he called "world history." Still, the chapters on Vatican I and the 1870 war, which he added to the final, revised edition of this work, strongly suggest the revival of hope for a resolution to the Christian/German conundrum he discovered during the 1820s and 1830s.

43 Laurenz Müller, *Diktatur und Revolution: Reformation und Bauernkrieg in der Geschichtsschreibung des "Dritten Reiches" und der DDR*, 1.

44 Müller, *Diktatur und Revolution*, 321. The concept's international reception was limited, because Marxist historians in other countries rarely accepted the German early bourgeois revolution into their accounts of the transition from feudalism to capitalism. It was perhaps somewhat better received outside such circles.

45 Robert W. Scribner and Gerhard Benecke, eds., *The German Peasant War of 1525–New Viewpoints*, 17.

46 Scribner and Benecke, eds., *The German Peasant War*, 9.

47 It bears mentioning that Friedrich Engels's *The Peasant War in Germany*, the ultimate source (via the writings of Alfred Meusel) of Steinmetz's concept, was published just six years after the final volume of Ranke's work appeared.

The views of Franz and Steinmetz represent the ultimate incarnations of the ghostly Rankean spell over the historical image of the age of reformations. Leopold von Ranke was a fine historian but, like most of his professional tribe, a poor prophet. His reflections on how politics and religion shaped the public life of the German lands are often insightful, but the world has changed too much to rely on him for wisdom about the present or the future. Instead of realizing his hope for a future Germany united in a national Christianity, the twentieth century threatened the very existence of nations. As for unity, the post-1945 experience set the final seal on the unstable confessional competition that had succeeded the old confessional order. Nowadays the confessions are being steadily driven to the margins of public life, as history strips them away from the churches that always stood behind them.

This is not to say that the post-Napoleonic history of Germany, or of Europe, has been a relentless, total secularization of all aspects of life, although that is certainly how it looked to twentieth-century observers from a vantage point in the interwar era. "We remind ourselves in the first place," wrote Franz Schnabel in the 1930s,

> that the decisive accomplishments that shaped the image of the nineteenth century did not lie in the areas of religion. The burgeoning renewal of religious and ecclesiastical sensibility did not endure, the dominant spirit of the nineteenth century remained entirely secular. The accomplishments, by means of which this spirit fundamentally transformed the face of the globe, were of a political, social, and scientific nature. It created the national, constitutional state, the capitalist social order, and the experimental science on which technology and industry depended. The nineteenth century produced nothing comparable to the great religious age of the Middle Ages or the Baroque era.[48]

While the picture may be more nuanced today, its outline is little changed. The contrast Hartmut Lehmann draws between the role of religion in European public life in 1800 and its role in 2000 fits Germany especially well. We must first of all understand, he writes, "that 200 years ago public space and public time were so clearly marked, unequivocally defined, and filled up in such measure that between them remained no space for other forms and other practices of religion," while today "public space and public time are no longer determined primarily by Christianity, so that the question, what do people believe at the end of the twentieth century, yields no clear answer."[49] The picture contains, of course, counter-tendencies, of which the most striking may be the post-Napoleonic religious revival, but when the view is limited to public life and the place of religion in it, Hartmut Lehmann's analysis, like Schnabel's before him, is surely correct. The role of vanguard along this track belonged in the past to the Protestants, while the Catholics followed, often uncertainly, in their wake. Today, however, the German Catholics are rushing at a much faster pace to pull even with the other Christian confession. A recent poll of German Catholics reveals that "only a quarter is convinced that faith in God will rise again; two-thirds believe that faith in God will decline even further; almost three-quarters of the Catholics polled predict that the importance of the Church and participation in its parishes will continue to decline."[50]

48 Franz Schnabel, *Deutsche Geschichte im neunzehnten Jahrhundert*, vol. 4: 5.
49 Hartmut Lehmann, *Protestantisches Christentum im Prozeß der Säkularisierung*, 15–16.
50 Hartmut Lehmann, *Säkularisierung. Der europäische Sonderweg in Sachen Religion*, 23–4.

The decline of the German confessions is replicating itself mutatis mutandis in other European countries. It does not mean the death of the Christian churches – churches are not confessions – nor the oft-prophesied death of religion in Europe. The more, however, religion detaches itself from its centuries-long role as co-guardian of public order, and the more it concentrates itself in private lives, the harder its long-term effects are to assess. This is surely the reason why the deployment of images, events, and persons from the post-medieval era of European Christianity in today's public life is declining so rapidly. The age of reformations is over, and so is the confessional era.[51] From that perspective alone, one might apply to that history what the Alsatian theologian Albert Schweitzer (1875–1965) famously said of the quest for the Historical Jesus. Once loosed from the bands "by which he had been riveted for centuries to the stony rocks of ecclesiastical doctrine, . . . [Jesus] does not stay: he passes by our time and returns to his own."[52]

What has happened to the histories of reformations can be called "historicization," setting history back into historical context. This means not disappearance but transvaluation. In Europe, obviously, we may expect that confessions, as distinct, historically bound forms of Christian religion from the age of reformations, will continue to decline as forces in public life. Their decline mirrors the sinking legitimacy of the nation-states. If the fall of confessions brings, however, the passing of a particular age of specifically European configurations of Christianity, it may also liberate the particular churches of Europe to find a new kind of history out in the vast global congery of milieus that has been called "the next Christendom."[53] "World Christianity at the beginning of the twenty-first century," Lehmann has written, "has its centers in Latin America and Africa, to some degree also in some countries of the Far East . . . but no longer in Europe."[54] In the once colonial worlds, the old values will find either transfiguration or oblivion. Almost a century has passed since Ernst Troeltsch wrote, "The present continually hovers before the backward-looking glance, because it is by the aid of analogies drawn from the life of today – however little this may be consciously before the mind – that we reach the causal explanation of the events of the past."[55] Troeltsch was right, although he could not have known how the future would change the meaning of "we." Nor can we.

51 This has just recently become startlingly obvious in the least likely corner of Europe, Northern Ireland, where in recent times the issues and symbols from the age of reformations have perhaps played a more important part in political life than they have in any other European state.
52 Albert Schweitzer, *The Quest for the Historical Jesus: A Critical Study of its Progress from Reimarus to Wrede*, 399.
53 Philip Jenkins, *The Next Christendom: The Coming of Global Christianity*, 166–7.
54 Lehmann, *Säkularisierung. Der europäische Sonderweg*, 25.
55 Ernst Troeltsch, *Protestantism and Progress: The Significance of Protestantism for the Rise of the Modern World*, 17.

Appendix

1. GERMAN KINGS AND HOLY ROMAN EMPERORS, 1350–1650

Charles IV (1347–78)
Wenceslas (1378–1410)
Sigismund (1410–37)
Albert II (1438–39)
Frederick III (1440–93)
Maximilian I (1493–1519)
Charles V (1519–56)
Ferdinand I (1556–64)
Maximilian II (1564–76)
Rudolph II (1576–1612)
Matthias (1612–19)
Ferdinand II (1619–37)
Ferdinand III (1637–57)

2. ECCLESIASTICAL ORGANIZATION OF THE HOLY ROMAN EMPIRE, ca. 1500

(abol. = abolished; archbp. = archbishopric; bp. = bishopric; diss. = dissolved; est. = established; ex. = exempt; reorg. = reorganized; sec. = secularized. Suffragan sees are indented under their provinces. The ordering of multiple names is governed solely by the form used in this book, usually the most common American usage.)

Mainz. Est. 2nd–4th c.; archbp. 782–1802; to Malines/Mechelen 1802

> Strasbourg (Straßburg). Est. 4th c.; to Mainz 1795; to Besançon 1802
> Worms. Est. ca. 4th c.; to Mainz 747; diss. 1806
> Speyer. Est. ca. 4th c.; to Mainz 747
> Chur. Est. 5th c.; to Mainz from Milan 843; ex. 1803
> Augsburg. Est. ca. 5th–6th c.; to Mainz 798
> Constance (Konstanz). Est. ca. 610; from Besançon 795
> Würzburg. Est. 741/42
> Eichstätt. Est. 741/48

Verden. Est. ca. 787; abol. 1631/48
Paderborn. Est. ca. 800/15
Hildesheim. Est. ca. 800/15; ex. 1824
Brandenburg. Est. 948; to Magdeburg 968
Havelburg. Est. 948; to Magdeburg 968
Prague (Prag, Praha). Est. 973; to archbp. 1344
Olmütz (Olomouc). Est. ca. 976/1063; to Prague 1344; to archbp. 1777
Bamberg. Est. 1007
Fulda. Est. 1752 ex.; to Mainz 1755

Cologne. Est. 2nd c.; archbp. 795

Liège (Lüttich, Leuk). Est. 4th c. at Tongern, 8th c. to Liège; to Cologne 795; to Malines/Mecheln 1802
Utrecht. Est. 695/96; to Cologne 795; archbp. 1559
Osnabrück. Est. ca. 772; to Cologne 795
Minden. Est. ca. 780; to Cologne 795; abol. 1643/48
Bremen. Est. ca. 787; to Cologne 795; to archbp. (with Hamburg) 848
Münster. Est. ca. 800

Trier. Est. ca. 1st–4th c.; archbp. ca. 800; 1802 to Malines/Mechelen

Metz. Est. 3rd–4th c.; to Trier ca. 800; to Besançon 1801
Toul. Est. 4th–5th c.; to Trier ca. 800; to Besançon 1801
Verdun. Est. 4th–6th c.; to Trier ca. 800

Salzburg. Est. 6th c.; reorg. 739; archbp. 798

Saeben. Est. 5th–6th c.; to Salzburg 798; seat of Brixen (Bressanone) since ca. 1000
Passau. Est. by 739; to Salzburg 798
Regensburg. Est. by 739; to Salzburg 798
Freising. Est. ca. 724/39; to Salzburg 798
Gurk. Est. 1072; seat of Klagenfurt since 1787
Chiemsee. Est. 1215
Seckau. Est. 1218; seat of Graz since 1786
Lavant. Est. 1225/28
Leoben. Est. 1786

Hamburg-Bremen. Est. 787/831; archbp. 838; abol. 1566/1648

Schleswig. Est. 947/48; to Lund 1104
Ribe (Ripen). Est. 947/48; to Lund 1104
Aarhus. Est. 947/48; to Lund 1104
Oldenburg. Est. 948/68; seat of Lübeck 1160; abol. 1588
Mecklenburg. Est. ca. 992/1158; seat of Schwerin since 1160; abol. 1555
Ratzeburg. Est. ca. 1062/1154; sec. 1554; abol. 1648

Magdeburg. Est. 968; sec. 1551; abol. 1680

Brandenburg. Est. 948; from Mainz 968; abol. 1539/65
Havelburg. Est. 948; from Mainz 968; abol. 1548/65

Merseburg. Est. 968/1004; abol. 1543/61
Meißen. Est. 968; ex. 1365/99; abol. 1581
Naumburg. Est. 968; seat at Zeitz since ca. 1030; abol. 1564

Gniezno (Gnesen). Est. 1000

Poznan (Posen). Est. ca. 968; to Gniezno ca. 1000
Cracow (Kraków). Est. ca. 984; to Gniezno 1000
Breslau (Wracłow). Est. ca. 1000; ex. 1821
Lebus. Est. 1123/24; sec. 1556; abol. 1648
Dorpat (Tartu). Est. 1211/24; from Lund 1255; abol. 1558
Kurland (Courland). Est. 1219; seat at Pilten; to Riga 1255; abol. 1560
Ösel-Wiek (Sarema). Est. 1228; to Riga 1255; abol. 1560/82
Kulm (Chełmno). Est. 1243; seat at Löbau; from Riga 1466
Pomesanien (Pomezania). Est. 1243; seat at Riesenburg; to Riga 1255; to Gniezno 1466
Ermland (Warmia). Est. 1243 as ex.; seat at Heilsberg; to Riga 1255; to Gniezno 1466

Riga. Est. 1201 under Hamburg-Bremen; archbp. 1255; abol. 1563

Dorpat (Tartu). Est. 1211/24; from Lund 1255; abol. 1558
Kurland (Courland). Est. 1219; seat at Pilten; to Riga 1255; abol. 1560
Ösel-Wiek (Sarema). Est. 1228; to Riga 1255; abol. 1560/82
Kulm (Chełmno). Est. 1243; seat at Löbau; from Riga 1466
Pomesanien (Pomezania). Est. 1243; seat at Riesenburg; to Riga 1255; to Gniezno 1466
Samland. Est. 1243; seat at Fischhausen; to Riga 1255; abol. 1525
Ermland (Warmia). Est. 1243 as ex.; seat at Heilsberg; to Riga 1255; to Gniezno 1466

Prague (Praha, Prag). Est. 973 under Mainz; archbp. 1344

Olmütz (Olomouc). Est. 976/1063 under Mainz; to Prague 1344; archbp. 1777
Leitomischl (Litomysl). Est. 1344; seat at Königgrätz since 1660/64

Exempt dioceses directly under Rome

Wollin. Est. 1140 as ex.; seat at Kammin since 1176/88; abol. 1544/1648
Vienna (Wien). Est. 1486/79 as ex.; archbp. 1722
Wiener Neustadt. Est. 1468/76 as ex.; to Vienna 1722; abol. 1785

3. THE IMPERIAL DIET, ca. 1600

Electoral Chamber (*Kurfürstenrat*): 3 spiritual (Mainz, Trier, Cologne) and 3 temporal (Saxony, Brandenburg, Palatinate) electors; the seventh elector, the king of Bohemia, had no seat in the Diet.

Princes' Chamber (*Fürstenrat*). Clerical bench = 3 archbps., ca. 24 bps., ca. 6 abbots; lay bench = dukes, margraves, landgraves, princes; 2 representatives each of the Imperial prelates and Imperial counts.

Cities' Chamber (*Städterat*). Approximately 65 Imperial cities, organized into Rhenish and Swabian benches.

4. THE SWISS CONFEDERATION (WITH YEAR OF ASSOCIATION)

1291. Unterwalden
1291. Uri
1291. Schwyz
1332. Luzern (Lucerne)
1351. Zurich
1352. Zug
1353. Bern (Berne)
1353. Solothurn (Soleure)
1386. Glarus
1406. Neufchâtel (Neuenburg)
1411. Appenzell
1415. Aargau
1416/76. Valais (Wallis)
1454. Fribourg (Freiburg im Üchtland)
1454. St. Gallen (St. Gall)
1460. Thurgau
1497/98. Graubünden (Liga Grischuna, I Grigioni, Grisons)
1501. Basel (Bâle)
1501. Schaffhausen
1512. Ticino (Tessin)
1515–1789. Mühlhausen (Mulhouse)
1519–1632. Rottweil
1519/26. Geneva (Genf)
1536. Vaud (Waadtland)

5. UNIVERSITIES IN THE HOLY ROMAN EMPIRE (WITH YEAR OF FOUNDING)

1348. Prague (Praha)
1365. Vienna
1381. Heidelberg
1388. Cologne
1392. Erfurt
1402–11, 1582. Würzburg
1409. Leipzig
1419. Rostock
1456. Greifswald
1457. Freiburg im Breisgau
1459. Basel
1472. Ingolstadt (to Landshut 1800, to Munich 1802)
1473. Trier
1476. Mainz
1477. Tübingen

1498, 1506. Frankfurt an der Oder
1502. Wittenberg
1527. Marburg
1544. Königsberg
1551–1804. Dillingen
1558. Jena
1576. Helmstedt
1576. Olmütz (Olomouc)
1584. Herborn
1586. Graz
1607. Giessen
1614. Paderborn
1618. Molsheim
1621. Rinteln
1622. Strasbourg
1622. Salzburg
1623. Altdorf
1630. Osnabrück
1632. Kassel
1632–56. Dorpat (Tartu)
1648. Bamberg
1655. Duisburg
1665. Kiel
1673. Innsbruck
1694. Halle
1702. Breslau
1734. Fulda
1737. Göttingen
1743. Erlangen (from Bayreuth 1743)
1760. Bützow
1780. Münster
1781. Stuttgart
1784. Lemberg (Lvov, Lwow)
1786. Bonn

Glossary

The glossary gives names (in English and German) and definitions of institutional and other terms mentioned in this book. The names are alphabetized according to their nouns.

Abbey, Imperial (*Reichsabtei*). A monastic community, male or female, the abbot/abbess of which held the Imperial rank of prince. Like the counts, they were collectively represented (by two votes) in the Imperial Diet.

Anabaptists (*Wiedertäufer, Täufer*). Members or followers of various small religious groups characterized by the practice of adult rather than infant baptism. They often rejected private property, taking oaths, and military service. Although varied in doctrine, they commonly rejected the teachings of the Protestant reformers.

Archdeanery (*Erzdekanat*). The principal unit of a diocese, further divided into deaneries, by which its secular clergy is organized into a corporate body with administrative powers. Its chief official is the archdeacon. *See* Deanery, Diocese.

Archdiocese (*Erzdiözese*). A diocese of special eminence and antiquity, whose bishop held this prestigious title. The archbishop governed a province consisting of his own diocese and those of other bishops (his suffragans), from whose courts cases came to him on appeal (and then further to Rome). *See* Diocese, Province.

Assembly, Imperial Representative (*Reichsdeputationstag*). Created by the Diet of Augsburg in 1555, in the Assembly sat envoys of the Imperial Estates; smaller than the Diet and called by the emperor to deal with specific issues, such as the enforcement of the Public Peace.

Bench (*Bank*). One of two (Rhenish and Swabian) divisions of the Cities' Chamber (*Städterat*) of the Imperial Diet; speakers of the two benches were respectively the senior envoys of Strasbourg and Nuremberg.

Benefice (*Pfrund*). The incomes attached to an ecclesiastical office, giving the bishop, abbot, parish priest, professor, or student a property right in law to the incomes, which are often derived from specified lands. The benefice, an early medieval creation, was the near universal instrument for financing the church from the Carolingian Age far into the early modern era.

Bishopric. *See* Diocese.

Bundschuh. An Upper Rhenish rural conspiracy originally formed in Alsace in 1493; it reappeared in the lands of the bishop of Speyer in 1513 and may have survived until the Peasants' War (1525).

Burghers (*Bürger*). Persons holding rights of citizenship in a town or city, either actively (male heads of household) or passively (their dependents); in a more general sense, townsmen.

Cathedral Chapter (*Domstift*). A college of beneficed clergymen (canons) attached to a diocese's principal church (cathedral), to which they owe religious service, and in the properties of which they hold individualized legal rights or benefices (canonries). In church law their principal function is to elect a bishop, though in the Empire they also participated in the government of the bishop's temporal holdings. Many, but not all, chapters practiced socially exclusive admissions.

Chamber (*Rat*). A chamber of a parliament or diet equivalent to the English "house." The Imperial Diet sat and voted in three chambers: electors (*Kurfürstenrat*), princes (*Fürstenrat*), and cities (*Städterat*). Territorial parliaments show a variety of arrangements in the number and social composition of their chambers.

Church (*Kirche, ecclesia*). In the most general sense, the Church Universal comprising all Christians, living and dead. Also the western or Roman/Latin Church or the churches of particular places, countries, and confessions.

Church, Collegiate (*Stiftskirche*). A church possessing a chapter, a college of beneficed priests to perform its religious services. In the Empire entry to such colleges was often restricted to nobles, and the religious duties were commonly performed by salaried vicars.

Circles, Imperial (*Reichskreise*). The ten, later twelve, administrative districts created by the reforms under Emperor Maximilian I; some circles began to function by the 1530s, mainly in highly fragmented regions such as Swabia, Franconia, and the Rhine Valley.

Cities, Imperial/Free (*Reichsstädte*). The cities that, by custom or by charter, had no lord but the emperor and thus possessed the right to sit in the Cities' Chamber (*Städterat*) of the Imperial Diet; around 1520 they numbered about 65.

Clergy, Regular (*Ordensklerus*). Those persons, men and women, of clerical status who lived in common under a rule (*regula*). They were obliged to celibacy and to poverty. There existed many more types of religious orders than today, ranging from the aristocratic military religious orders (Teutonic Knights, Knights of St. John) through the Benedictines and Augustinian canons and the mendicants (Dominicans, Franciscans) to unofficial local groups, such as the beguines.

Clergy, Secular (*Weltklerus*). Clergy who live in the world (Lat., *saeculum*), that is, not in community under a rule. They include most of the parish priests and vicars, plus the canons of cathedrals and other collegiate churches and almost all of the bishops, cardinals, and popes. The recruitment of bishops from the secular rather than the monastic clergy is one of the great differences between western or Latin Christendom and Eastern Orthodoxy.

Common Man (*der gemeine Mann*). A contemporary phrase for the common people, roughly equivalent to the English "commoner."

Common Penny. *See* Taxation.

Commune (*Gemeinde*). The sworn association of all full citizens (usually male heads of household) of a city, village, or district, who shared rights to the use of certain properties and obligations to defend one another.

Confession (*Konfession, confessio*). In the narrower sense a detailed statement of doctrine, such as the Confession of Augsburg. In a broader sense a religious community marked by adherence to such a document.

Confession, Augsburg (*Confessio Augustana*). The statement of twenty-eight articles of faith submitted by the Protestant estates to Emperor Charles V at the Diet of Augsburg in 1530. Together with other documents it forms the Formula of Concord (1576), which is the normative confession for the Lutheran communion.

Council, City (*Stadtrat*). The small council, usually the effective governing body of a German city. In some cities it was a monopoly of the patrician families, in many the seats were divided between patricians and guilds, and very occasionally (as at Basel) it was a guild monopoly.

Council, General/Ecumenical (*Generalkonzil*). The supreme representative body of the Church, beginning with the Council of Nicaea (323 A.D.). General councils met at Constance (1414–18), Basel/Ferrara/Florence (1431–39/49), Rome (Lateran V, 1512–17), and Trent (1545–49, 1551–52, and 1562–63).

Council, Imperial Aulic (*Reichshofrat*). The emperor's prerogative court founded in 1559 based on earlier forms; its jurisdiction overlapped in many affairs with that of the Imperial Chamber Court (*Reichskammergericht*). See Court, Imperial Chamber.

Council, Imperial Governing (*Reichsregiment*). A committee of Imperial estates–actually of their envoys–established to be the (temporary) Imperial executive body during the emperor's absence from the Empire; first organized in 1501 and again in 1521.

Court, Imperial Chamber (*Reichskammergericht*). The supreme court of the Holy Roman Empire, established 1495; attacked by the Protestants and suspended 1543–48; its judges, named by the emperor, electors, and Circles (*Reichskreise*), were professional jurists trained in Roman law. Since 1559 its jurisdiction was overlapped by that of the Imperial Aulic Council. See Council, Imperial Aulic.

Deanery (*Landdekanat*). The subunit of a diocese that stands between the archdeanery and the parishes. See Archdeanery, Diocese.

Declaration, Ferdinandine (*Declaratio Ferdinandea*). A codicil to the Religious Peace of Augsburg (1555), whereby Emperor Ferdinand I declared that Protestant dissenters in episcopal territories possessed certain rights of toleration (an exception to the rule of "whose the rule, his the religion"). It was contested by the Catholic Imperial estates.

Diet, Imperial (*Reichstag*). The parliament of the Holy Roman Empire, an assembly of the Imperial estates, called by the emperor or his deputy to advise and consent on matters of common concern. It was divided into three chambers (sing., *Rat*; pl., *Räte*) of electors, princes, and cities, and its decisions were incorporated into a recess (*Abschied*), which upon confirmation became Imperial law.

Diet, Territorial (*Landtag, Landschaft*). The parliament of a territorial principality, consisting of two or more corporately organized estates (*Landstände*) and with widely varying rights.

Diet, Urban (*Städtetag*). A separate meeting of the free and Imperial cities, attended by one to three envoys per city; usually held in the south and attended mainly by southern cities, plus Cologne.

Diocese (*Diözese*, also *Bistum*). The principal supra-local unit of church government, governed by a bishop who possesses both sacramental powers (*ordo*) by virtue of consecration and and jurisdiction (*iurisdictio*) by virtue of election (usually by the cathedral canons) and of papal confirmation. A diocese is divided into archdeaneries (only larger dioceses), deaneries, and parishes. Most dioceses are in a province governed by an archbishop. In the Empire, most but not all bishops also have temporal jurisdiction over territories (*Hochstifte*) which overlap but are never exactly coterminous with their dioceses.

Dynasty (*Dynastie, Haus*). A lineage in which the seniors (usually in the agnatic line) succeed to the rule of the Empire or a principality.

Electors, Imperial (*Kurfürsten*). The seven princes who, following the Golden Bull (1356), elected a King of the Romans and emperor-elect; they were the prince-archbishops of Mainz, Cologne, and Trier, the electors Palatine and of Brandenburg and Saxony, and the king of Bohemia. The Palatine electorate was transferred in 1623 to the duke of Bavaria, and an eighth electorate was created for the Palatinate at the end of the Thirty Years War.

Emperor (*Kaiser, imperator*). Ruler of the Roman Empire in the West, one of the two highest sacral offices in Christendom; also the title of a German king (literally, king of the Romans, emperor-elect) who has been crowned emperor by the pope; Frederick III was the last emperor to be crowned at Rome, and Charles V the last to be crowned by the pope. Although elective to the end (1803), since the fifteenth century the office was de facto hereditary in the Habsburg dynasty (House of Austria).

Empire, Holy Roman (*Heiliges Römisches Reich, imperium romanum*). Introduced in the tenth century, the name refers to the union of three kingdoms – German, Burgundian, and Italian – under a papally crowned emperor. By 1500 it was practically limited to the German-speaking lands, the Low Countries, and borderlands which spoke other tongues (French in the west, Italian in the south, and Hungarian and Slavic in the east).

Estates (*Stände*). The corporately organized subjects entitled to be consulted by the emperor (*Reichsstände*) or a territorial prince (*Landstände*), and who met as the parliament of the Empire (*Reichstag*) or a territory (*Landtag, Landschaft*). The term can also refer simply to the legal status of a person or group.

Evangelical (*evangelisch*). A name commonly adopted by adherents of the religious movement that arose in response to the teachings of Martin Luther and other reformers, also applicable more broadly to persons and groups (including Catholics) who emphasize the Bible as the standard of belief and practice. *See* Protestant.

Fief (*Lehen, feodum*). The general name for the lands and their attached labor obligations granted by a lord to a military servitor in return for faithful personal service. Created in the Frankish kingdom out of older institutions during the Early Middle Ages, the fief became the most widespread basis of the organization of Christendom's free warrior classes, spreading into the Empire during the 12th century.

German Lands (*Deutsche Landen*). The lands of the Holy Roman Empire including Switzerland but excluding the Netherlands after 1556. The kingdom of Bohemia (with Moravia, Silesia, and Lusatia) was an Imperial fief but not fully a part of the Empire. "Landen" is a now archaic plural of "Land."

Guild (*Zunft*). Originally a corporation of merchants and artisans organized for economic and religious purposes. In many German cities, the guilds gained representation in the civic regime, which meant that guilds as political organizations often came to contain unrelated crafts.

Hansa (*also:* **Hanseatic League**). A federation of trading cities in the trade zones centered on the North and Baltic seas. Headquartered at Lübeck, its merchants operated from London and Bruges to Novgorod. The Hansa encountered ever stiffer competition from the Dutch cities, which took the lead in the northern trade during the sixteenth century.

Hochstift. The territories held in fief from the emperor by a prince-bishop, in whose diocese they normally, but not necessarily, lay. By virtue of enfiefment, which followed election and papal confirmation, a bishop received these lands, over which he possessed temporal jurisdiction, including high justice. Commonly these lands are called "ecclesiasical territories."

Household (*Haus*). The basic social unit of life in town and countryside, also of nobles and princes. Widely employed in a figurative or analogical sense, so that a monastery is conceived as the abbess's household, the government as the king's household, etc.

Inheritance, Impartible (*Anerbenrecht*). An inheritance regime, whereby the property descends intact to one heir, in some regions to the eldest surviving son, in others to the youngest surviving son (East Frisia), and in still others to a child of the parents' choice (Bavaria). Normally, non-inheriting children receive a payment in lieu of inheritance.

Inheritance, Partible (*Realteilung*). Among German speakers the oldest form of inheritance regime, whereby each child inherits. Usually, but not always, real property is physically divided among the heirs.

Lansquenets (*Landsknechte*). German mercenary infantry, armed and drilled in the Swiss manner; first organized by King Maximilian around 1490; in the sixteenth century one of the most sought after mercenary forces by European warlords.

League, Catholic (*Katholische Liga*). A military alliance of Catholic Estates led by the Duke of Bavaria, founded in 1611; since 1618 involved in the Thirty Years War. *See* Union, Protestant.

League, Smalkaldic (*Schmalkaldischer Bund*). A military alliance formed in 1531 to protect Protestant interests and dissolved after its defeat by Charles V in 1547; under the dual command of the elector of Saxony and the landgrave of Hesse, it possessed a diet (*Bundesrat*) and a war council (*Kriegsrat*). Organized since 1535 into two chambers ("circles"), one northern under the Saxon elector, the other southern under the Hessian landgrave.

League, Swabian (*Schwäbischer Bund*). A peace-keeping and military alliance of free nobles, prelates, and cities (i.e., those subject only to the emperor), later joined by South and Central German princes; founded under Habsburg leadership in 1488 and periodically renewed until 1534; organized into two (since 1512 three) houses or chambers – nobles, cities, princes – under the presidency of one commander from each house, it possessed a court staffed by professional judges and an elaborate military system.

Netherlands (*also*: Low Countries). The seventeen provinces of the Burgundian Netherlands. The country formed after the revolt of 1576 is referred to as "the Dutch Republic."

Ordinance, Church (*Kirchenordnung*). In Protestant cities and territories a law issued to regulate church governance, clerical recruitment, worship, sacraments, religious instruction, and moral discipline.

Parish (*Pfarrei, Pfarrgemeinde*). The basic unit of religious life and of ecclesiastical organization in town and countryside; a creation of the medieval Church. The right to nominate (patronage) to the office of parish priest normally belonged to a patron, often a layman (usually a noble, prince, or king) or an ecclesiastical superior or corporation (such as an abbot, abbess, or collegiate chapter).

Peace of Augsburg, Religious (*Augsburger Religionsfriede*). A law passed by the Imperial Diet in 1555 whereby Lutheranism was to be tolerated alongside Catholics in the Empire. There were special rules for free cities, and a controversial corollary provided that Catholic prelates who coverted to Lutheranism must give up their offices. This law made the religion of a territory dependent on the prince, hence the formula, "whose the rule, his the religion" (*cuius regio, eius religio*). Essentially confirmed by the Peace of Westphalia in 1648.

Peace of Westphalia (*Westfälischer Friede*). General peace settlement in 1648 that ended the Thirty Years War. Actually two treaties, one drafted at Münster by the Catholic estates and foreign powers, the other at Osnabrück by their Protestant counterparts. The Peace confirmed the Religious Peace of 1555, adding the Reformed or Calvinist faith to the tolerated religions.

Peace, Public (*Landfriede*). A statute which established a special obligation to keep and enforce the peace. Such laws were originally (thirteenth century) issued by royal decree, later by decision of the emperor and the Imperial diet in a long series beginning in 1486.

Peasant (*Bauer*). The German term "Bauer" can be translated as "peasant" or "farmer," depending on whether dependence from a seigneur or cultivation of the soil is emphasized.

Prince (*Fürst*). A general term for lay aristocrats who hold the title of "Imperial Prince" and possess a customary right to sit in the Princes' Chamber (*Fürstenrat*) of the Imperial Diet. Besides its general meaning, also a hereditary title. Other princely titles were archduke (Austria only), duke, margrave, and landgrave. Sub-princely noble titles were count, baron, and Imperial knight.

Prince-Bishop (*Fürstbischof*). A bishop who is also, by virtue of being an Imperial vassal, secular ruler of a territory and possesses thereby a seat in the Princes' Chamber of the Imperial Diet. A prince-bishop's diocese and his territory overlapped but were not coterminous.

Principality (*Fürstentum*). The lands a prince held in fief from the emperor, in practice hereditary, though, unless dynastic custom dictated primogeniture, subject to partible inheritance at the testator's will.

Protestant (*Protestant, protestantisch*). In a narrower sense the German princes and cities that adhered to the protest entered at the Diet of Speyer in 1529 and who thereafter accepted the Confession of Augsburg. In a wider sense the adherents of the reformation movement that renounced the authority of the Roman papacy. *See* Evangelical.

Province (*Provinz*). The largest unit of the particular churches, governed by an archbishop who held jurisdiction over his dependent bishops (suffragans).

Recess (*Abschied*). The document in which were recorded the decisions of any assembly, including a body of estates.

Reformation, Right of (*jus reformandi*). The authority claimed by Protestant rulers (and also practiced by some Catholic ones) to reform the church. It was accorded most Imperial estates by the Religious Peace of 1555, though with some restrictions that were modified in 1648 by the Peace of Westphalia.

Reformed Church (*Reformierte Kirche*). The German counterpart to the Protestant churches of Switzerland, France, the Netherlands, and Scotland, from which it differs in its acceptance of the Lutheran Confession of Augsburg.

Religious Matters (*Religionssachen*). Suits and other matters touching religion, allegedly distinguishable from "secular" (*weltlich*) matters. The distinction lay behind the Protestants' attacks on the Imperial Chamber Court, though they were equally unable to agree on such distinctions in dealing with their own affairs.

Reservation, Ecclesiastical (*Geistlicher Vorbehalt, reservatum ecclesiasticum*). A codicil to the Religious Peace of Augsburg (1555), issued unilaterally by Emperor Ferdinand I, whereby bishops who convert to the Protestant religion must renounce their see, titles, and territories. It was contested by the Protestant Imperial estates.

Restitution, Edict of (*Restitutionsedikt*). An Imperial mandate of 1629, whereby Emperor Ferdinand II declared that all ecclesiastical lands, rights, and incomes secularized after a certain date must be restored to their Catholic owners. Repealed in 1648.

Restitution Suits (*Reformationsprozesse*). Judicial suits before the Imperial Chamber Court and other Imperial courts against Protestant princes and urban regimes who had confiscated or otherwise deprived Catholic clergy of their rights, incomes, and properties.

Swiss Confederation/Switzerland (*Eidgenossenschaft*). A sworn association formed in 1291 and many times renewed and expanded. Governed by an assembly (*Tagsatzung*) which met intermittently in a fixed place. Its members, free rural federations and city-states, included the full and the associated members (with their subject territories) but excluded the independent allied republics of Graubünden and Valais.

Taxation. The Imperial Diet, followed by those of the Swabian League and Smalkaldic League, normally granted taxes in units called "months" according to lists (*Matrikeln*) of assessments by alleged ability to pay; the grants were either emergency (*eilende*) or long-term (*beharrliche*) aids. To replace this form, the Imperial Diet experimented with a direct property tax, called the "Common Penny," in 1495, 1542, and 1543.

Territory, Episcopal. *See Hochstift.*

Territory/Territorial State (*Territorialstaat*). The common name for the institutionalized principalities that began to form out of the old, patrimonial holdings during the fifteenth and sixteenth centuries.

Union, Protestant (*Protestantische Union*). A military league of Protestant Estates, founded 1609; since 1618 involved in the Thirty Years War. *See* League, Catholic.

Vicar (*Vikar, vicarius*). Literally, a deputy of any kind. The term normally means one who is hired by a parish priest or a canon of a cathedral or other collegiate church to perform the religious duties of the office in the place of the holder of the benefice attached to the office. The vicar usually is unbeneficed and salaried.

Bibliography

Abel, Wilhelm. *Agricultural Fluctuations in Europe from the Thirteenth to the Twentieth Centuries*. London: Methuen, 1980.

Admont, Engelbert of. "On the Rise and End of the Roman Empire." In *Three Treatises on Empire*. Ed. Thomas M. Izbicki and Cary J. Nederman. Bristol: Thoemmes Press, 2000, 37–93.

Agricola, Johannes. *Die Sprichwörtersammlungen*. Ed. Sander Gilman. 2 vols. Berlin and New York: W. de Gruyter, 1971.

Althoff, Gerd. *Spielregeln der Politik im Mittelalter: Kommunikation in Frieden und Fehde*. Darmstadt: Primus, 1997.

Ammann, Jost. *Das Ständebuch: 133 Holzschnitte mit Versen von Hans Sachs und Hartmann Schopper*. Ed. Manfred Lemmer. Frankfurt: Insel Verlag, 1934.

Amon, Karl. *Die Bischöfe von Graz-Seckau, 1218–1968*. Graz: Verlag Styria, 1969.

Anderson, Margaret Lavinia. *Practicing Democracy: Elections and Political Culture in Germany*. Princeton: Princeton University Press, 2000.

Angermeier, Heinz, ed. *Reichstag von Worms 1495*. Ed. Historische Kommission bei der Bayerischen Akademie der Wissenschaften. Deutsche Reichstagsakten, mittlere Reihe. Deutsche Reichstagsakten unter Maximilian I., vol. 5. Göttingen: Vandenhoeck & Ruprecht, 1981.

Arnold, Klaus. *Niklashausen 1476. Quellen und Untersuchungen zur sozialreligiösen Bewegung des Hans Behem und zur Agrarstruktur eines spätmittelalterlichen Dorfes*. Saecula Spiritualia, vol. 3. Baden-Baden: Verlag Valentin Koerner, 1980.

Asch, Ronald G. *The Thirty Years War: The Holy Roman Empire and Europe, 1618–48*. New York: St. Martin's Press, 1997.

Aulinger, Rosemarie. *Das Bild des Reichstages im 16. Jahrhundert. Beiträge zu einer typologischen Analyse schriftlicher und bildlicher Quellen*. Schriftenreihe der Historischen Kommission bei der Bayerischen Akademie der Wissenschaften. Göttingen: Vandenhoeck & Ruprecht, 1980.

Balduin, Balthasar. *Threnen-Brunnen Christi und seiner Gläubigen Beym Gnaden- Heil- und Wunderbrunnen zu Hornhausen im Stifft Halberstatt gelegen/mildiglich vergossen/ Als am 10. Sontag nach dem Fest der heiligen Dreyeinigkeit/aus. Luc. 19. die Threnen unsers Heylandes. geflossen. in einer Thränen- Trost- und Trawer-Predigt zusammen gefasset*. Zwickau: Göpner, 1646.

Bast, Robert James. *Honor Your Fathers: Catechisms and the Emergence of a Patriarchal Ideology in Germany, c. 1400–1600*. Studies in Medieval and Reformation Thought, vol. 63. Leiden and New York: Brill, 1997.

Bastress-Dukehart, Erica. *The Zimmern Chronicle: Nobility, Memory and Self-representation in Sixteenth-century Germany.* Aldershot, Hants, England: Ashgate, 2002.

Bate, Heidi Eberhard. "The Measures of Men: Virtue and the Arts in the Civic Imagery of Sixteenth-century Nuremberg." Ph.D. Dissertation, University of California Berkeley, 2000.

Battenberg, J. Friedrich. *Die Juden in Deutschland vom 16. bis zum Ende des 18. Jahrhunderts.* Enzyklopädie Deutscher Geschichte, vol. 60. Munich: R. Oldenbourg Verlag, 2001.

Behringer, Wolfgang, ed. *Hexen: Glaube, Verfolgung, Vermarkung.* Beck'sche Reihe. Munich: C.H. Beck, 1998.

———. *Hexen und Hexenprozesse in Deutschland.* 3rd ed. Munich: DTV, 1995.

———. *Mit dem Feuer vom Leben zum Tod: Hexengesetzgebung in Bayern.* Munich: Hugendubel, 1988.

Bell, Dean Phillip. *Jews in the Early Modern World.* New York: Rowman & Littlefield, 2008.

Bell, Dean Phillip, and Stephen G. Burnett, eds. *Jews, Judaism, and the Reformation in Sixteenth-Century Germany.* Studies in Central European Histories, vol. 37. Leiden: Brill, 2006.

Benecke, Gerhard, ed. *Germany in the Thirty Years War.* London: Edward Arnold, 1978.

Benedict, Philip. *Christ's Churches Purely Reformed: A Social History of Calvinism.* New Haven: Yale University Press, 2002.

Berlichingen, Götz von. *Mein Fehd und Handlungen.* Ed. Helgard Ulmschneider. Forschungen aus Württembergisch Franken, vol. 17. Sigmaringen: Jan Thorbecke, 1981.

Bireley, Robert. *The Counter-Reformation Prince: Anti-Machiavellianism or Catholic Statecraft in Early Modern Europe.* Chapel Hill: University of North Carolina Press, 1990.

Black, Antony. *Council and Commune: The Conciliar Movement and the Fifteenth-century Heritage.* London: Burns & Oates, 1979.

———. *Monarchy and Community: Political Ideas in the Later Conciliar Controversy 1430–1450.* Cambridge Studies in Medieval Life and Thought, vol. 2, series 3. Cambridge: Cambridge University Press, 1970.

Blaschke, Karlheinz. *Sachsen im Zeitalter der Reformation.* Schriften des Vereins für Reformationsgeschichte, vol. 185. Gütersloh: Gerd Mohn, 1970.

Blickle, Peter. *Communal Reformation: The Quest for Salvation in Sixteenth-Century Germany.* Trans. Thomas Dunlap. Studies in German Histories. Atlantic Highlands, NJ: Humanities Press, 1992.

———. *Obedient Germans? A Contradiction.* Trans. Thomas A. Brady Jr. Charlottesville: University Press of Virginia, 1998.

———. *The Revolution of 1525: The German Peasants' War from a New Perspective.* Trans. Thomas A. Brady Jr. and H. C. Erik Midelfort. 3rd ed. Baltimore: Johns Hopkins University Press, 1985.

Bloch, Ernst. *Das Prinzip Hoffnung.* 2 vols. Frankfurt am Main: Suhrkamp, 1959.

Bloch, Marc. *The Historian's Craft.* Trans. Peter Putnam. New York: Alfred A. Knopf, 1953.

Boockmann, Hartmut. *Die Stadt im späten Mittelalter.* 3rd ed. Munich: C.H. Beck, 1994.

———. *Stauferzeit und spätes Mittelalter: Deutschland 1125–1517. Das Reich und die Deutschen.* Berlin: Siedler, 1987.

Bornkamm, Heinrich, ed. *Luther im Spiegel der deutschen Geistesgeschichte. Mit ausgewählten Texten von Lessing bis zur Gegenwart.* 2nd ed. Göttingen: Vandhoeck & Ruprecht, 1970.

Bossy, John. *Christianity in the West, 1400–1700*. Oxford: Oxford University Press, 1985.

Bouwsma, William J. "The Renaissance and the Drama of Western History." *American Historical Review* 84 (1979): 1–15.

Boyle, Nicholas. *Who Are We Now? Christian Humanism and the Global Market from Hegel to Heaney*. Notre Dame: University of Notre Dame Press, 1998.

Brady, Thomas A., ed. *Die deutsche Reformation zwischen Spätmittelalter und Frühe Neuzeit*. Schriften des Historischen Kollegs. Kolloquien, vol. 50. Munich: R. Oldenbourg, 2001.

———. "The Holy Roman Empire's Bishops on the Eve of the Reformation." In *Continuity and Change: The Harvest of Late Medieval and Reformation History. Essays Presented to Heiko A. Oberman on his 70th Birthday*, ed. Robert James Bast and Andrew C. Gow. Leiden: Brill, 2000, 20–47.

———. *Protestant Politics: Jacob Sturm (1489–1553) and the German Reformation*. Studies in German Histories. Atlantic Highlands, NJ: Humanities Press, 1995.

———. *The Protestant Reformation in German History*. Washington, DC: German Historical Institute, 1998.

———. *Ruling Class, Regime and Reformation at Strasbourg, 1520–1555*. Studies in Medieval and Reformation Thought, vol. 22. Leiden: E.J. Brill, 1978.

———. *Turning Swiss: Cities and Empire, 1450–1550*. Cambridge Studies in Early Modern History. Cambridge: Cambridge University Press, 1985.

———. "'You Hate Us Priests': Anticlericalism, Communalism, and the Control of Women at Strasbourg in the Age of the Reformation." In *Anticlericalism in the Late Middle Ages and Reformation*, ed. Peter Dykema and Heiko A. Oberman. Leiden: E.J. Brill, 1993, 167–207.

Brady, Thomas A., and Katherine G. Brady. "Documents on Communalism and the Control of Women at Strasbourg in the Age of the Reformation." In *Anticlericalism in the Late Middle Ages and Reformation*, ed. Peter Dykema and Heiko A. Oberman. Leiden: E.J. Brill, 1993, 209–28.

Brady, Thomas A., Heiko A. Oberman, and James D. Tracy, eds. *Handbook of European History, 1400–1600. Late Middle Ages, Renaissance, Reformation*. 2 vols. Leiden: Brill, 1994–95.

Brant, Sebastian. *Das Narrenschiff*. Ed. Manfred Lemmer. 2nd ed. Tübingen: Max Niemeyer, 1968.

Brecht, Martin. *Luther*. Trans. James L. Schaff. 3 vols. Philadelphia: Augsburg Fortress Press, 1985–93.

Brown, Peter. *Society and the Holy in Late Antiquity*. Berkeley and Los Angeles: University of California Press, 1982.

Brunner, Karl, and Gerhard Jaritz. *Landherr, Bauer, Ackerknecht. Der Bauer im Mittelalter: Klischee und Wirklichkeit*. Vienna, Cologne, and Graz: Böhlau, 1985.

Brunner, Otto. *Land and Lordship: Structures of Governance in Medieval Austria*. Ed. Howard Kaminsky and James Van Horn Melton. Philadelphia: University of Pennsylvania Press, 1992.

Bucer, Martin. *Deutsche Schriften*. Ed. Robert Stupperich. Gütersloh: Gerd Mohn, 1960–.

Buckwalter, Stephen E. *Die Priesterehe in Flugschriften der frühen Reformation*. Quellen und Forschungen zur Reformationsgeschichte, vol. 68. Gütersloh: Gütersloher Verlagshaus, 1998.

Burger, Heinz-Otto. *Renaissance, Humanismus, Reformation: Deutsche Literatur im europäischen Kontext*. Bad Homburg v. d. H., Berlin, and Zurich: Gehlen, 1969.

Burkhardt, Johannes. *Der Dreißigjährige Krieg*. Frankfurt: Suhrkamp, 1992.

Burnett, Amy Nelson. "Basel's Rural Pastors as Mediators of Confessional and Social Discipline." *Central European History* 33 (2000): 67–85.

Busbecq, Ogier Ghiselin de. *The Turkish Letters of Ogier Ghiselin de Busbecq.* Trans. Edward Seymour Forster. Oxford: Clarendon Press, 1927.

Bussmann, Klaus, and Heinz Schilling, eds. *1648: War and Peace in Europe: Münster/Osnabrück 24.10.1998–17.1.1999.* 2 vols. Munich: Bruckmann, 1998.

Bynum, Caroline W. *Wonderful Blood: Theology and Practice in Late Medieval Northern Germany and Beyond.* Philadelphia: University of Pennsylvania Press, 2007.

Capito, Wolfgang. *An den hochwirdigen Fürsten vnd herren Wilhelmen Bischoffen zu Straßburg vnd Landtgrauen zu Elsas. Entschuldigung.* Augsburg: Silvan Otmar, 1524.

Carlyle, Thomas. *Critical and Miscellaneous Essays.* Boston: Brown & Taggard, 1860.

Châtellier, Louis. *The Religion of the Poor: Rural Missions in Europe and the Formation of Modern Catholicism, c. 1500–c. 1800.* Trans. Brian Pearce. Cambridge: Cambridge University Press, 1997.

Chrisman, Miriam Usher. *Conflicting Visions of Reform: German Lay Propaganda Pamphlets, 1519–1530.* Studies in German Histories. Atlantic Highlands, NJ: Humanities Press, 1996.

Christian, William A., Jr. *Local Religion in Sixteenth-Century Spain.* Princeton: Princeton University Press, 1981.

Clasen, Claus Peter. *Anabaptism: A Social History, 1525–1618: Switzerland, Austria, Moravia, South and Central Germany.* Ithaca: Cornell University Press, 1972.

Cochlaeus, Johannes. *Brevis Germanie descriptio (1512) mit der Deuschlandkarte des Erhard Etzlaub von 1501.* Ed. Karl Langosch. Ausgewählte Quellen zur deutschen Geschichte der Neuzeit, vol. 1. Darmstadt: Wissenschaftliche Buchgesellschaft, 1960.

Cohn, Henry J. "The Territorial Princes in Germany's Second Reformation, 1559–1622." In *International Calvinism, 1541–1715,* ed. Menna Prestwich. Oxford: Clarendon, 1985, 135–65.

Conrad, Anne. *Zwischen Kloster und Welt: Ursulinen und Jesuitinnen in der katholischen Reformbewegung des 16./17. Jahrhunderts.* Veröffentlichungen des Instituts für Europäische Geschichte Mainz. Abteilung Religionsgeschichte, vol. 142. Mainz: Verlag Philipp von Zabern, 1991.

Contzen, Adam. *Politicorum libri decem in quibus de perfectae reipubl. forma, virtutibus, et vitiis, institutione civium, legibus magistratu ecclesiastico, civili, potentia republicae; itemque seditione et bello, ad usum vitamque communem accomodate tracature.* Mainz: I. Kinckius, 1621.

Cusa, Nicholas of. *The Catholic Concordance.* Trans. Paul E. Sigmund. Cambridge: Cambridge University Press, 1991.

David, Abraham, ed. *A Hebrew Chronicle from Prague, c. 1615.* Tuscaloosa: University of Alabama Press, 1993.

de Ridder-Symoens, Hilde, ed. *Universities in Early Modern Europe (1500–1800).* Ed. Walter Rüegg. A History of the University in Europe, vol. 2. Cambridge: Cambridge University Press, 1996.

Delbrück, Hans. *Geschichte der Kriegskunst im Rahmen der politischen Geschichte.* 6 vols. Berlin: G. Stilke, 1920–32.

Dellsperger, Rudolf. "Zehn Jahre bernischer Reformationsgeschichte (1522–1532). Eine Einführung." In *450 Jahre Berner Reformation: Beiträge zur Geschichte der Berner Reformation und zu Niklaus Manuel.* Bern: Historischer Verein des Kantons Bern, 1980, 25–59.

Deutlicher Bericht/Aus Etlichen andern Schreiben und Mündlichen Bericht/Von Heil-Brunnen zu Hornhausen/Die grossen Wunder und Wercke des HERRN zusammen getragen und in Druck befördert. n.p., 1646.

Dickens, A. G. *The German Nation and Martin Luther.* New York: Harper & Row, 1974.

Dickmann, Fritz. *Der Westfälische Frieden.* 6th ed. Münster: Aschendorff, 1992.

Dilthey, Wihelm. *Gesammelte Schriften.* 7th ed. 12 vols. Stuttgart: B.G. Teubner, 1957.

Dinzelbacher, Peter, ed. *Handbuch der Religionsgeschichte im deutschsprachigen Raum: Hoch- und Spätmittelalter,* vol. 2. Paderborn: Ferdinand Schöningh, 2000.

Dollinger, Philippe. *The German Hansa.* Trans. D. S. Ault and S. H. Steinberg. Stanford: Stanford University Press, 1970.

Duchhardt, Heinz, ed. *Politische Testamente und andere Quellen zum Fürstenethos der frühen Neuzeit.* Ausgewählte Quellen zur deutschen Geschichte der Neuzeit, vol. 18. Darmstadt: Wissenschaftliche Buchgesellschaft, 1987.

Duggan, Lawrence G. "The Unresponsiveness of the Late Medieval Church: A Reconsideration." *Sixteenth Century Journal* 9 (1978): 3–26.

Dürer, Albrecht. *Schriften und Briefe.* Ed. Ernst Ullmann. 6th ed. Leipzig: Reclam, 1993.

Dürr, Renate. *Politische Kultur in der Frühen Neuzeit. Kirchenräume in Hildesheimer Stadt- und Landgemeinden 1550–1750.* Quellen und Forschungen zur Reformationsgeschichte, vol. 77. Gütersloh: Gütersloher Verlagshaus, 2006.

Edwards, Mark U., Jr. *Printing, Propaganda, and Martin Luther.* Berkeley and Los Angeles: University of California Press, 1994.

Ehrenpreis, Stefan, and Ute Lotz-Heumann. *Reformation und konfessionelles Zeitalter.* Darmstadt: Wissenschaftliche Buchgesellschaft, 2002.

Engel, Pal. *The Realm of St. Stephen: A History of Medieval Hungary, 895–1526.* Trans. Tamas Palosfalvi. Ed. Andrew Ayton. London: I.B. Tauris, 2001.

Erasmus, Desiderius. *Collected Works of Erasmus.* Ed. R. J. Schoeck and B. M. Corrigan. 86 vols. Toronto: University of Toronto Press, 1974–.

Evans, R. J. W. *The Making of the Habsburg Monarchy, 1550–1700: An Interpretation.* Oxford: Clarendon Press, 1979.

Fabian, Ekkehart. *Die Entstehung des Schmalkaldischen Bundes und seiner Verfassung 1524/29–1531/35: Brück, Philipp von Hessen und Jakob Sturm.* 2nd ed. Tübingen: Osiander, 1962.

Fichtner, Paula Sutter. *Emperor Maximilian II.* New Haven: Yale University Press, 2001.

———. *Ferdinand I of Austria: The Politics of Dynasticism in the Age of the Reformation.* East European Monographs, vol. 100. Boulder: East European Quarterly, 1982.

Forster, Marc R. *The Counter-Reformation in the Villages: Religion and Reform in the Bishopric of Speyer, 1560–1720.* Ithaca: Cornell University Press, 1992.

Franck, Sebastian. *Germaniae chronicon: Von des gantzen Teutschlands, aller Teutschen völker herkommen, Name, Händeln, Guoten vnd bösen thaten, Reden, Räthen, Kriegen, Sigen, Niderlagen, Stifftungen, Veränderungen der Sitze, Reich, Länder, Religion, Gesatze, Policei, Spraach, völcker vnd sitten, Vor vnd nach Christi gebürt, Von Noe bisz auf Carolum V.* Frankfurt am Main: Christian Egenolff, 1538.

François, Etienne. *Die unsichtbare Grenze: Protestanten und Katholiken in Augsburg 1648–1806.* Abhandlungen zur Geschichte der Stadt Augsburg, vol. 33. Sigmaringen: Jan Thorbecke Verlag, 1991.

Franke, Annelore, and Gerhard Zschäbitz, eds. *Das Buch der hundert Kapitel und der vierzig Statuten des sogenannten oberrheinischen Revolutionärs.* Ed. Max Steinmetz. Leipziger Übersetzungen und Abhandlungen zum Mittelalter, series A, vol. 4. Berlin: Deutscher Verlag der Wissenschaften, 1967.

Franz, Günther, ed. *Quellen zur Geschichte des Bauernkrieges.* Ausgewählte Quellen zur deutschen Geschichte der Neuzeit, vol. 2. Darmstadt: Wissenschaftliche Buchgesellschaft, 1963.

———, ed. *Urkundliche Quellen zur hessischen Reformationsgeschichte.* 4 vols. Veröffentlichungen der Historischen Kommission für Hessen und Waldeck, vol. 11. Marburg: N.G. Elwert, 1951–57.

Friedensburg, Walter. *Der Reichstag zu Speier 1526 in Zusammenhang der politischen und kirchlichen Entwicklung Deutschlands im Reformationszeitalter.* Berlin: R. Gaertner, 1887.

Fritz, Eberhard. *Dieweil sie so arme Leuth: Fünf Albdörfer zwischen Religion und Politik 1530–1750. Studien zur Kirchengeschichte der Dörfer Bernloch, Eglingen, Meidelstetten, Oberstetten und Ödenwaldstetten.* Quellen und Forschungen zur Württembergischen Geschichte, vol. 9. Stuttgart: Calwer Verlag, 1989.

Fudge, Thomas A. *The Magnificent Ride: The First Reformation in Hussite Bohemia.* St. Andrews Studies in Reformation History. Aldershot: Ashgate, 1998.

Fulton, Elaine. *Catholic Belief and Survival in Late Sixteenth-Century Vienna: The Case of Georg Eder (1523–87).* Aldershot: Ashgate, 2007.

Gatz, Erwin, and Clemens Brotkorb, eds. *Die Bischöfe des Heiligen Römischen Reichs 1448 bis 1648. Ein biographisches Lexikon.* Berlin: Duncker & Humblot, 1996.

Geiler, Johann. *Die brösamlin doct. Keiserspergs vffgelesen von Frater Johann Paulin.* Strasbourg: Johann Grüninger, 1517.

——. *Die Emeis: Dis ist das buch von der Omeissen, und ouch her der kunnig ich diente gern.* Strasbourg: Johann Grüninger, 1516.

——. *Narnenschiff so er gepredigt hat zu straßburg in der hohen stifft daselbst. uß latin in tütsch bracht.* Trans. Johannes Pauli. Strasbourg: Johann Grüninger, 1520.

Geisberg, Max, and Walter L. Strauss. *The German Single-Leaf Woodcut, 1500–1550.* 4 vols. New York: Hacker Art Books, 1974.

Goethe, Johann Wolfgang von. *Sämtliche Werke: Briefe, Tagebücher und Gespräche.* 1st ed. Frankfurt am Main: Deutscher Klassiker Verlag, 1985.

Gollwitzer, Heinz, ed. *Reichstage von Lindau, Worms und Freiburg 1496–1498.* Ed. Historische Kommission bei der Bayerischen Akademie der Wissenschaften. Deutsche Reichstagsakten, mittlere Reihe. Deutsche Reichstagsakten unter Maximilian I., vol. 6. Göttingen: Vandenhoeck & Ruprecht, 1979.

Gregory, Brad S. *Salvation at Stake: Christian Martyrdom in Early Modern Europe.* Harvard Historical Studies, vol. 134. Cambridge, MA: Harvard University Press, 1999.

Grimmelshausen, Hansjakob Christoffel von. *The Adventurous Simplicissimus.* Trans. A.T.S. Goodrick. Lincoln, NE: University of Nebraska Press, 1962.

——. *Werke.* Bibliothek der Frühen Neuzeit, vol. I, part 1. Frankfurt am Main: Deutsche Klassiker Verlag, 1992.

Gross, Michael B. *The War Against Catholicism: Liberalism and the Anti-Catholic Imagination in Nineteenth-Century Germany.* Ann Arbor: University of Michigan Press, 2004.

Guicciardini, Francesco. *The History of Italy.* Trans. Sidney Alexander. New York and London: Macmillan, 1969.

Haller, Brigitte. *Kaiser Friedrich III. im Urteil der Zeitgenossen.* Wiener Dissertationen aus dem Gebiete der Geschichte. Vienna: Verlag des Wissenschaftlichen Antiquariats H. Geyer, 1965.

Hamm, Berndt. *The Reformation of Faith in the Context of Late Medieval Theology and Piety: Essays by Berndt Hamm.* Ed. Robert James Bast. Studies in the History of Christian Thought, vol. 110. Leiden: Brill, 2004.

Harline, Craig. "Official Religion–Popular Religion in Recent Historiography of the Catholic Reformation." *Archiv für Reformationsgeschichte* 81 (1990): 239–62.

Harrington, Joel F. *Reordering Marriage and Society in Reformation Germany.* Cambridge: Cambridge University Press, 1995.

Haude, Sigrun. *In the Shadow of "Savage Wolves": Anabaptist Münster and the German Reformation during the 1530s.* Studies in Central European Histories. Boston: Humanities Press, 2000.

Head, Randolph C. "Rhaetian Ministers, from Shepherds to Citizens: Calvinism and Democracy in the Republic of the Three Leagues, 1550–1620." In *Later Calvinism: International Perspectives*, ed. W. Fred Graham. Kirksville, MO: Sixteenth Century Journal Publishers, 1994, 55–69.

Heberle, Hans. *Der Dreissigjährige Krieg in zeitgenössischer Darstellung: Hans Heberles "Zeytregister" (1618–1672), Aufzeichnungen aus dem Ulmer Territorium. Ein Beitrag zu Geschichtsschreibung und Geschichtsverständnis der Unterschichten.* Ed. Gerd Zillhardt. Forschungen zur Geschichte der Stadt Ulm, vol. 13. Ulm: Stadtarchiv, 1975.

Heckel, Martin. *Gesammelte Schriften. Staat, Kirche, Recht, Geschichte.* 2 vols. Tübingen: J.C.B. Mohr (Paul Siebeck), 1989.

Hegel, Carl, ed. *Chroniken der deutschen Städte vom 14. bis ins 16. Jahrhundert.* 36 vols. Leipzig: S. Hirzel, 1862–1931.

Heimpel, Hermann. *Die Vener von Gmünd und Straßburg 1162–1447.* 3 vols. Veröffentlichungen des Max-Planck-Instituts für Geschichte, vol. 52. Göttingen: Vandenhoeck & Ruprecht, 1983.

Heine, Heinrich. *Deutschland. Ein Wintermärchen.* Historisch-kritische Gesamtausgabe der Werke, vol. 4. Hamburg: Hoffmann und Campe, 1985.

Heinisch, Reinhard Rudolf. "Das Bild Kaiser Friedrichs III. in der frühen Neuzeit." In *Kaiser Friedrich III. (1440–1493) in seiner Zeit. Studien anläßlich des 500. Todestags am 19. August 1493/1993*, ed. Paul-Joachim Heinig. Cologne, Weimar, and Vienna: Böhlau Verlag, 1993, 503–15.

Herlihy, David. *The Black Death and the Transformation of the West.* Ed. Samuel K. Cohn Jr. Cambridge, MA: Harvard University Press, 1997.

Hermann, Johannes, and Günther Wartenberg, eds. *Politische Korrespondez des Herzogs und Kurfürsten Moritz von Sachsen.* 5 vols. Berlin: Akademie Verlag, 1982–98.

Herzig, Arno. *Der Zwang zum wahren Glauben. Rekatholisierung vom 16. bis zum 18. Jahrhundert.* Göttingen: Vandenhoeck & Ruprecht, 2000.

———. *Jüdische Geschichte in Deutschland von den Anfängen bis zur Gegenwart.* Munich: C.H. Beck, 1997.

Hillerbrand, Hans J., ed. *The Reformation: A Narrative History Related by Contemporary Observers and Participants.* London: SCM Press, 1964.

Hlaváček, Ivan, and Alexander Patschovsky, eds. *Reform von Kirche und Reich zur Zeit der Konzilien von Konstanz (1414–1418) und Basel (1431–1449): Konstanz-Prager historisches Kolloquium (11.–17. Oktober 1993).* Constance: Universitätsverlag Konstanz, 1996.

Hödl, Günther. *Habsburg und Österreich. Gestalten und Gestalt des österreichischen Spätmittelalters.* Vienna, Cologne, and Graz: Böhlau Verlag, 1988.

Hoensch, Jörg K. *Kaiser Sigismund: Herrscher an der Schwelle zur Neuzeit 1368–1437.* Munich: Beck, 1996.

Hofmann, Hanns Hubert, ed. *Quellen zum Verfassungsorganismus des Heiligen Römischen Reiches Deutscher Nation 1495–1815.* Ausgewählte Quellen zur deutschen Geschichte der Neuzeit, vol. 13. Darmstadt: Wissenschaftliche Buchgesellschaft, 1976.

Hotz, Walter. *Handbuch der Kunstdenkmäler im Elsaß und in Lothringen.* Munich: Deutscher Kunstverlag, 1965.

Hoyer, Siegfried, and Bernd Rüdiger, eds. *"An die Versammlung gemeiner Bauernschaft." Eine revolutionäre Flugschrift aus dem deutschen Bauernkrieg (1525).* Leipzig: VEB Bibliographisches Institut, 1975.

Hsia, R. Po-chia. *Social Discipline in the Reformation: Central Europe, 1550–1750.* London: Routledge, 1989.

Hug, Johannes. *Quadrivium Ecclesie / Quatuor prelatorum officium / Quibus omnis status tum Secularis tum vero Ecclesiasticus subijcitur.* Strasbourg: Johann Grüninger, 1504.

Huonder, Anton. *Deutsche Jesuitenmissionäre des 17. und 18. Jahrhunderts: Ein Beitrag zur Missionsgeschichte und zur deutschen Biographie.* Freiburg im Breisgau: Herder, 1899.

Hutten, Ulrich von. *Deutsche Schriften.* Ed. Hans Mettke. 2 vols. Leipzig: VEB Bibliographisches Institut, 1972–74.

————. *Opera quae reperiri potuerunt omnia.* Ed. Eduard Böcking. 7 vols. Leipzig: Teubner, 1859–70.

Institorus, Heinrich, and Jacobus Sprenger. *Malleus moleficarum.* Trans. and ed. Christopher S. Mackay. 2 vols. Cambridge: Cambridge University Press, 2006.

Isenmann, Eberhard. *Die deutsche Stadt im Spätmittelalter, 1250–1500. Stadtgestalt, Recht, Stadtregiment, Kirche, Gesellschaft, Wirtschaft.* Stuttgart: Eugen Ulmer, 1988.

————. "Reichstadt und Reich an der Wende vom späten Mittelalter zur frühen Neuzeit." In *Mittel und Wege früher Verfassungspolitik*, ed. Josef Engel. Stuttgart Klett-Cotta, 1979, 9–223.

Israel, Jonathan I. *European Jewry in the Age of Mercantilism, 1550–1750.* 2nd ed. Oxford: Clarendon Press, 1989.

Jedin, Hubert, Kenneth Scott Latourette, and Jochen Martin, eds. *Atlas zur Kirchengeschichte. Die christlichen Kirchen in Geschichte und Gegenwart.* Freiburg: Herder, 1970.

Jenkins, Philip. *The Next Christendom: The Coming of Global Christianity.* Oxford and New York: Oxford University Press, 2002.

Johnson, Carina Lee. "Negotiating the Exotic: Aztec and Ottoman Culture in Habsburg Europe, 1500–1590." Ph. D. Dissertation. University of California, Berkeley, 2000.

Jörg, Joseph Edmund. *Deutschland in der Revolutionsperiode von 1522 bis 1526, aus den diplomatischen Correspondenz und Original-Akten bayrischer Archive dargestellt.* Freiburg im Breisgau: Herder, 1851.

Karant-Nunn, Susan C. *Luther's Pastors: The Reformation in the Ernestine Countryside.* Transactions of the American Philosophical Society, vol. 69, part 8. Philadelphia: American Philosophical Society, 1979.

————. *The Reformation of Ritual: An Interpretation of Early Modern Germany.* London: Routledge, 1997.

Kastner, Ruth, ed. *Quellen zur Reformation 1517–1555.* Ausgewählte Quellen zur deutschen Geschichte der Neuzeit, vol. 16. Darmstadt: Wissenschaftliche Buchgesellschaft, 1994.

Kaufmann, Thomas. *Das Ende der Reformation: Magdeburgs "Herrgotts Kanzlei" (1548–1551/2).* Beiträge zur historischen Theologie, vol. 123. Tübingen: Mohr Siebeck, 2003.

Keller, Katrin. "Kurfürstin Anna von Sachsen (1532–1585): Von Möglichkeiten und Grenzen einer 'Landesmutter'." In *Das Frauenzimmer. Die Frau bei Hofe in Spätmittelalter und früher Neuzeit,* ed. Jan Hirschbiegel and Werner Paravicini. Stuttgart: Jan Thorbecke, 2000, 263–86.

Kempis, Thomas à. *The Imitation of Christ.* Trans. Richard Whitford. Ed. Harold C. Gardiner S.J. New York: Doubleday Books, 1955.

Kerler, Dietrich, ed. *Deutsche Reichstagsakten unter Kaiser Sigmund. Erste Antheilung 1410–1420.* Ed. Historische Kommission bei der Bayerischen Akademie der Wissenschaften. Deutsche Reichstagsakten ältere Reihe, vol. 7. Munich: Oldenbourg, 1878–87.

Klein, Birgit E. "Die Frankfurter Judengasse: jüdisches Leben in der frühen Neuzeit." In *Schriftenreihe des Jüdischen Museums Frankfurt am Main.* Ed. Fritz Backhaus, Gisela Engel, Robert Liberles, and Margarete Schlüter. Frankfurt am Main: SocietätsVerlag, 2006, 161–70.

Köbler, Gerhard, ed. *Historisches Lexikon der deutschen Länder. Die deutschen Territorien vom Mittelalter bis zur Gegenwart.* 5th ed. Munich: C.H. Beck, 1995.

Köhle-Hezinger, Christel. *Evangelisch-Katholisch. Untersuchungen zu konfessionellem Vorurteil und Konflikt im 19. und 20. Jahrhundert vornehmlich am Beispiel*

Württembergs. Untersuchungen des Ludwig-Uhland-Instituts der Universität Tübingen, vol. 40. Tübingen: Tübinger Vereinigung für Volkskunde, 1976.

Kohler, Alfred. *Karl V. 1500–1558. Eine Biographie.* Munich: C.H. Beck, 1999.

Kolb, Robert. *Martin Luther as Prophet, Teacher, Hero: Images of the Reformer, 1520–1620.* Grand Rapids: Baker Books, 1999.

Kolb, Robert, and Timothy J. Wengert, eds. *The Book of Concord: The Confessions of the Evangelical Lutheran Church.* Minneapolis: Fortress Press, 2000.

Koller, Heinrich, ed. *Reformation Kaiser Siegmunds.* MGH Staatsschriften des späteren Mittelalters, vol. 6. Stuttgart: Anton Hiersemann, 1964.

Kottanerin, Helene. *Die Denkwürdigkeiten der Helene Kottannerin (1439–1440).* Ed. Karl Mollay. Wiener Neudrucke. Neuausgaben und Erstdrucke deutscher literarischer Texte. Vienna: Österreichischer Bundesverlag für Unterricht, Wissenchaft und Kunst, 1971.

Kötzschke, Rudolf, and Hellmut Kretzschmar. *Sächsische Geschichte. Werden und Wandlungen eines Deutschen Stammes und seiner Heimat im Rahmen der Deutschen Geschichte.* Frankfurt am Main: Verlag Wolfgang Weidlich, 1965.

Krebs, Manfred, Hans Georg (= Jean) Rott, Marc Lienhard, and Stephen V. Nelson, eds. *Elsaß, parts 1–4: Stadt Straßburg 1522–52.* 4 vols. Quellen zur Geschichte der Täufer, vols. 7–8, 15–16. Gütersloh: Gütersloher Verlagshaus, 1959–88.

Krieger, Karl-Friedrich. *Die Habsburger im Mittelalter von Rudolf I. bis Friedrich III.* Stuttgart: W. Kohlhammer, 1994.

Labouvie, Eva. *Zauberei und Hexenwerk: Ländlicher Hexenglaube in der frühen Neuzeit.* Frankfurt: Fischer Taschenbuch Verlag, 1991.

Laffan, R.G.D. "The Empire under Maximilian I, 1493–1520." In *The New Cambridge Modern History,* ed. G. R. Potter. Cambridge: Cambridge University Press, 1957, 194–223.

Lahne, Werner. *Magdeburgs Zerstörung in der zeitgenössischen Publizistik.* Magdeburg: Druckerei zum Gutenberg, 1931.

Lanzinner, Maximilian. *Friedensicherung und politische Einheit des Reiches unter Kaiser Maximilian II. (1564–1576).* Schriftenreihe der Historischen Kommission bei der Bayerischen Akademie der Wissenschaften, vol. 45. Göttingen: Vandenhoeck & Ruprecht, 1993.

Laon, Adalbero of. *Carmen ad Robertum regem.* Ed. Claude Carozzi. Les classiques de l'histoire de France au Moyen Age, vol. 32. Paris: Les Belles Lettres, 1979.

Laubach, Ernst. *Ferdinand I. als Kaiser. Politik und Herrscherauffassung des Nachfolgers Karl V.* Münster: Aschendorff, 2001.

Laube, Adolf, and Hans Werner Seiffert, eds. *Flugschriften der Bauernkriegszeit.* 2nd ed. Berlin: Akademie Verlag, 1978.

Lavery, Jason. *Germany's Northern Challenge: The Holy Roman Empire and the Scandinavian Struggle for the Baltic, 1563–1576.* Studies in Central European Histories. Boston: Brill, 2002.

Lee, Robert, ed. *The Theses of Erastus Touching Excommunication.* Edinburgh: Myles Macphail, 1844.

Lehmann, Hartmut. *Protestantisches Christentum im Prozeß der Säkularisierung.* Göttingen: Vandenhoeck & Ruprecht, 2001.

———. *Säkularisierung. Der europäische Sonderweg in Sachen Religion.* Ed. Hartmut Lehmann. 2nd ed. Bausteine zu einer europäischen Religionsgeschichte im Zeitalter der Säkularisierung, vol. 5. Göttingen: Wallstein, 2007.

Leonard, Amy E. *Nails in the Wall: Catholic Nuns in Reformation Germany.* Women in Culture and Society. Chicago: University of Chicago Press, 2005.

Lessing, Gotthold Ephraim. *Werke.* Ed. Herbert G. Göpfert. 8 vols. Theologiekritische Schriften I und II. Munich: Carl Hanser Verlag, 1970–79.

Lhotsky, Alphons. "Was heißt 'Haus Österreich'?" *Anzeiger der philosophisch–historischen Klasse der österreichischen Akademie der Wissenschaften 1956,* no. 11 (1956): 155–74.

Lietzmann, Hans, et al., eds. *Die Bekenntnisschriften der evangelisch–lutherischen Kirche, herausgegeben im Gedenkjahr der Augsburgischen Konfession 1930.* 2nd rev. ed. Göttingen: Vandenhoeck & Ruprecht, 1952.

Littlehales, Margaret Mary. *Mary Ward: Pilgrim and Mystic, 1585–1645.* Tunbridge Wells: Burns & Oates, 2001.

Lorenz, Gottfried, ed. *Quellen zur Vorgeschichte und zu den Anfängen des Dreissigjährigen Krieges.* Ausgewählte Quellen zur deutschen Geschichte der Neuzeit, vol. 19. Darmstadt: Wissenschaftliche Buchgesellschaft, 1991.

Louthan, Howard. *The Quest for Compromise: Peacemakers in Counter-Reformation Vienna.* Cambridge: Cambridge University Press, 1997.

Loyola, Ignatius. *Letters of St. Ignatius Loyola.* Trans. William J. Young. Chicago: Loyola University Press, 1959.

Ludolphy, Ingetraut. *Friedrich der Weise, Kurfürst von Sachsen, 1463–1525.* Göttingen: Vandenhoeck & Ruprecht, 1984.

Luther, Martin. D. *Martin Luthers Werke. Kritische Gesamtausgabe. Briefwechsel.* 15 vols. Weimar: Böhlau, 1930–78.

———. *D. Martin Luthers Werke. Kritische Gesamtausgabe. Schriften.* 61 vols. Weimar: Böhlau, 1883–1983.

———. *D. Martin Luthers Werke. Kritische Gesamtausgabe. Tischreden.* Ed. Karl Drescher. 6 vols. Weimar: Hermann Böhlaus Nachfolger, 1912–21.

———. *Luther's Works.* Ed. Jaroslav Pelikan and Helmut T. Lehmann. 55 vols. St. Louis and Philadelphia: Concordia Publishing House and Fortress Press, 1955–86.

———. *Three Treatises.* Trans. Charles M. Jacobs and James Atkinson. 2nd ed. Philadelphia: Fortress Press, 1970.

Luttenberger, Albrecht Pius. *Glaubenseinheit und Reichsfriede. Konzeptionen und Wege konfessionsneutraler Reichspolitik 1530–1552 (Kurpfalz, Jülich, Kurbrandenburg).* Schriftenreihe der Historischen Kommission bei der Bayerischen Akademie der Wissenschaften, vol. 20. Göttingen: Vandenhoeck & Ruprecht, 1982.

———, ed. *Katholische Reform und Konfessionalisierung.* Ausgewählte Quellen zur deutschen Geschichte der Neuzeit, vol. 17. Darmstadt: Wissenschaftliche Buchgesellschaft, 2006.

———. *Kurfürsten, Kaiser und Reich. Politische Führung und Friedenssicherung unter Ferdinand I. und Maximilian II.* Abteilung Universalgeschichte, Veröffentlichungen des Instituts für Europäische Geschichte Mainz, vol. 149. Mainz: Philipp von Zabern, 1994.

Lutz, Heinrich. *Christianitas afflicta: Europa, das Reich und die päpstliche Politik im Niedergang der Hegemonie Kaiser Karls V. (1552–1556).* Göttingen: Vandenhoeck & Ruprecht, 1964.

———. *Conrad Peutinger. Beiträge zu einer politischen Biographie.* Abhandlungen zur Geschichte der Stadt Augsburg, vol. 9. Augsburg: Verlag die Brigg, 1958.

———. *Das Ringen um deutsche Einheit und kirchliche Erneuerung. Von Maximilian I. bis zum Westfälischen Frieden 1490–1648.* Propyläen Geschichte Deutschlands, vol. 4. Berlin: Propyläen-Verlag, 1987.

Lutz, Heinrich, and Walter Ziegler. "Das konfessionelle Zeitalter, Part 1: Die Herzöge Wilhelm IV. und Albrecht V." In *Handbuch der Bayerischen Geschichte,* vol. 2, ed. Andreas Kraus. Munich: C.H. Beck, 1988, 324–92.

MacHardy, Karin J. "Cultural Capital, Family Strategies and Noble Identity in Early Modern Habsburg Austria 1579–1620." *Past and Present* 163 (1999): 36–75.

Machiavelli, Niccolò. *The Chief Works and Others*. Ed. Allan H. Gilbert. 3 vols. Durham, NC: Duke University Press, 1965.

Mangrum, Bryan D., and Giuseppe Scavizzi, eds. *A Reformation Debate: Karlstadt, Emser, and Eck on Sacred Images. Three Treatises in Translation*. Renaissance and Reformation Texts in Translation. Ottowa: Dovehouse Editions, 1998.

Mann, Golo. *Wallenstein, His Life Narrated*. Trans. Charles Kessler. New York: Holt, Rinehart and Winston, 1976.

Marcks, Erich. *Luther und Deutschland. Eine Reformationsrede im Kriegsjahr 1917*. Leipzig: Quelle & Meyer, 1917.

Marx, Karl. *Werke*. Ed. Hans-Joachim Lieber. 2nd ed. 6 vols. Darmstadt: Wissenschaftliche Buchgesellschaft, 1960–71.

Marx, Karl, and Friedrich Engels. *Collected Works*. 50 vols. New York: International Publishers, 1975–2004.

———. *Selected Correspondence, 1846–1895*. Trans. Donna Torr. New York: International Publishers, 1942.

Mau, Hermann. *Die Rittergesellschaften mit St. Jörgenschild. Ein Beitrag zur Geschichte des deutschen Einungsbewegung im 15. Jahrhundert*. Darstellungen aus der Württembergischen Geschichte, vol. 33. Stuttgart: W. Kohlhammer, 1941.

May, Georg. *Die deutschen Bischöfe angesichts der Glaubensspaltung des 16. Jahrhunderts*. Vienna: Mediatrix–Verlag, 1983.

McGinn, Bernard, ed. *Apocalypticism in Western History and Culture*. The Encyclopedia of Apocalypticism, vol. 2. New York: Continuum, 2000.

Melanchthon, Philipp. *Opera quae supersunt omnia*. 28 vols. Corpus Reformatorum. Halle: C.A. Schwetschke et filium, 1834–60.

Midelfort, H. C. Erik. *A History of Madness in Sixteenth-Century Germany*. Stanford: Stanford University Press, 1999.

———. *Mad Princes of Renaissance Germany*. Charlottesville: University Press of Virginia, 1994.

Minutoli, Julius von, ed. *Das kaiserliche Buch des Markgrafen Albrecht Achilles. Kurfürstliche Periode 1470–1486*. 2 vols. Quellensammlung zur fränkischen Geschichte, vol. 2. Berlin and Bayreuth: Schneider and Buchner, 1850.

Moeglin, Jean-Marie. *Dynastisches Bewußtsein und Geschichtsschreibung: Zum Selbstverständnis der Wittelsbacher, Habsburger und Hohenzollern im Spätmittelalter*. Schriften des Historischen Kollegs. Kolloquien, vol. 34. Munich: R. Oldenbourg, 1993.

Moeller, Bernd. "Kleriker als Bürger." In *Die Reformation und das Mittelalter. Kirchenhistorische Aufsätze*, ed. Johannes Schilling. Göttingen: Vandenhoeck & Ruprecht, 1991.

Moeller, Bernd, and Stephen E. Buckwalter, eds. *Die frühe Reformation in Deutschland als Umbruch. Wissenschaftliches Symposium des Vereins für Reformationsgeschichte 1996*. Schriften des Vereins für Reformationsgeschichte, vol. 199. Gütersloh: Gütersloher Verlagshaus, 1998.

Monro, Robert. *Monro, His Expedition with the Worthy Scots Regiment Called Mac-Keys*. Ed. William S. Brockington, Jr. London: Praeger, 1999.

Moser, Friedrich Carl von. *Von dem deutschen Nationalgeist*. Ed. Horst Denzer. Selb: Notos, 1766.

Moxey, Keith. *Peasants, Warriors, and Wives: Popular Imagery in the Reformation*. Chicago: University of Chicago Press, 1989.

Muldoon, James. *Empire and Order: The Concept of Empire, 800–1800*. New York: St. Martin's, 1999.

Müller, Laurenz. *Diktatur und Revolution: Reformation und Bauernkrieg in der Geschichtsschreibung des "Dritten Reiches" und der DDR*. Quellen und Forschungen zur Agrargeschichte, vol. 50. Stuttgart: Lucius & Lucius, 2004.

Müller, Rainer. *Geschichte der Universität. Von der mittelalterlichen Universitas zur deutschen Hochschule.* Hamburg: Nikol, 1990.

Münch, Paul. "Volkskultur und Calvinismus. Zu Theorie und Praxis der 'reformatio vitae' während der 'Zweiten Reformation.'" In *Die reformierte Konfessionalisierung in Deutschland–Das Problem der "Zweiten Reformation." Wissenschaftliches Symposion des Vereins für Reformationsgeschichte 1985,* ed. Heinz Schilling. Gütersloh: Gütersloher Verlagshaus, 1986, 266–90.

Nierenberg, David. *Communities of Violence: Persecution of Minorities in the Middle Ages.* Princeton: Princeton University Press, 1996.

Nipperdey, Thomas. *Deutsche Geschichte 1800–1866. Bürgerwelt und starker Staat.* Munich: C.H. Beck, 1983.

———. "Luther und die Bildung der Deutschen." In *Luther und die Folgen. Beiträge zur sozialgeschichtlichen Bedeutung der lutherischen Reformation,* ed. Hartmut Löwe and Claus-Jürgen Roepke. Munich: Christian Kaiser, 1983, 13–27.

Nischan, Bodo. *Lutherans and Calvinists in the Age of Confessionalism.* Variorum Collected Studies Series. Aldershot: Ashgate, 1999.

———. *Prince, People, and Confession: The Second Reformation in Brandenburg.* Philadelphia: University of Pennsylvania Press, 1994.

Notflatscher, Heinz. *Räte und Herrscher. Politische Eliten an den Habsburgerhöfen der österreichischen Länder 1480–1530.* Veröffentlichungen des Instituts für Europäische Geschichte Mainz, Abt. Universalgeschichte, vol. 161. Mainz: Philipp von Zabern, 1999.

Oakley, Francis. *The Western Church in the Later Middle Ages.* Ithaca and London: Cornell University Press, 1979.

Oberman, Heiko A. "The Long Fifteenth Century: In Search of its Profile." In *Die deutsche Reformation zwischen Spätmittelalter und Früher Neuzeit,* ed. Thomas A. Brady. Munich: R. Oldenbourg Verlag, 2001, 1–18.

———. *Luther: Man between God and the Devil.* Trans. Eileen Walliser-Schwarzbart. New Haven: Yale University Press, 1989.

———. *The Two Reformations: The Journey from the Last Days to the New World.* Ed. Donald Weinstein. New Haven: Yale University Press, 2003.

Obrecht, Georg. *Fünff Underschiedliche Secreta Politica von Anstellung, Erhaltung und Vermehrung guter Policey.* Ed. Bertram Schefold. Hildesheim: Olms-Weidmann, 2003.

Ogilvie, Sheilagh C. *State Corporatism and Proto-industry: The Württemberg Black Forest, 1580–1797.* Cambridge Studies in Population, Economy, and Society in Past Time, vol. 33. Cambridge and New York: Cambridge University Press, 1997.

O'Malley, John W. *The First Jesuits.* Cambridge, MA: Harvard University Press, 1993.

Ozment, Steven E. *When Fathers Ruled: Family Life in Reformation Europe.* Cambridge, MA: Harvard University Press, 1983.

Parker, Geoffrey. *The Military Revolution: Military Innovation and the Rise of the West, 1500–1800.* Cambridge: Cambridge University Press, 1988.

———. *The Thirty Years' War.* 2nd ed. London: Routledge, Kegan Paul, 1987.

Patschovsky, Alexander, ed. *Quellen zur böhmischen Inquisition im 14. Jahrhundert.* MGH, Quellen zur Geistesgeschichte des Mittelalters, vol. 11. Weimar: Hermann Böhlau, 1979.

Peters, Henriette. *Mary Ward: A World in Contemplation.* Trans. Helen Butterworth. Leominster: Gracewing, 1994.

Pfeiffer, Franz. "Volksbüchlein vom Kaiser Friedrich." *Zeitschrift für deutsches Altertum* 5 (1845): 250–68.

Pfeilschifter, Georg, ed. *Acta reformationis catholicae Germaniae concernantia saeculi XVI. Die Reformverhandlungen des deutschen Episkopats von 1520 bis 1570.* 6 vols. Regensburg: F. Pustet, 1959–74.

Piccolomini, Enea Silvio. *Germania and Jakob Wimpheling: "Responsa et replicae ad Eneam Silvium."* Ed. Adolf Schmidt. Geschichts-schreiber der Deutschen Vorzeit, vol. 104. Cologne: Böhlau, 1962.

Pirckheimer, Caritas. *Caritas Pirckheimer: A Journal of the Reformation Years, 1524–1528.* Trans. Paul A. McKenzie. Library of Medieval Women. Cambridge: D.S. Brewer, 2006.

Platter, Thomas. *Lebensbeschreibung.* Ed. Alfred Hartmann and Ueli Dill. 2nd ed. Basel: Schwabe & Co., 1999.

Plöse, Detlef, and Günter Vogler, eds. *Buch der Reformation. Eine Auswahl zeitgenössischer Zeugnisse (1476–1555).* Berlin: Union Verlag, 1989.

Prodi, Paolo. *The Papal Prince: One Body and Two Souls–the Papal Monarchy in Early Modern Europe.* Trans. Susan Haskins. Cambridge and New York: Cambridge University Press, 1987.

Quinn, Arthur J. *A New World: An Epic of Colonial America from the Founding of Jamestown to the Fall of Quebec.* Boston: Faber and Faber, 1994.

Rabus, Johann Jakob. *Christliche bescheidne und wolgegründts ablähnung/der vermeindten Bischoffs Predigt... im Münster zu Strassburg.* Cologne: Collen Cholinus, 1570.

Ranke, Leopold von. *Deutsche Geschichte im Zeitalter der Reformation.* Ed. Paul Joachimsen. 6 vols. Munich: Drei-Masken-Verlag, 1925.

Rapp, Francis. *Christentum IV: Zwischen Mittelalter und Neuzeit (1378–1552).* Die Religionen der Menschheit, vol. 31. Stuttgart: Kohlhammer, 2006.

———. *Les origines médiévales de l'Allemagne moderne: de Charles IV à Charles Quint (1346–1519).* Collection historique. Paris: Aubier, 1989.

———. *Réformes et reformation à Strasbourg. Église et société dans le diocèse de Strasbourg (1450–1525).* Collection de l'Institut des Hautes Études Alsaciennes. Paris: Ophrys, 1974.

Reinhard, Wolfgang, and Heinz Schilling, eds. *Die katholische Konfessionalisierung. Akten eines von Corpus Catholicorum und Verein für Reformationsgeschichte veranstalteten Symposions, Augsburg 1993.* Ed. Heinz Schilling. Gütersloh and Münster: Gerd Mohn and Aschendorff, 1995.

Reisenleitner, Markus. *Frühe Neuzeit, Reformation und Gegenreformation. Darstellung - Forschungsüberblick - Quellen und Literatur.* Ed. Helmut Reinalter. Handbuch zur neueren Geschichte Österreichs, vol. 1. Vienna: Studien-Verlag, 2000.

Rem, Wilhelm. "Cronica newer geschichte 1512–1527." In *Die Chroniken der deutschen Städte,* vom 14. bis ins 16. Jahrhundert, ed. Carl Hegel, vol. 25. Leipzig: B.G. Teubner, 1896, 1–268.

Rembe, Heinrich, ed. *Der Briefwechsel des M. Cyriakus Spangenberg.* Dresden: H.J. Naumann, 1887–88.

Reynaud, Paul. *Mémoires.* 2 vols. Paris: Flammarion, 1960–63.

Richental, Ulrich von. *Chronik des Constanzer Concils 1414 bis 1418.* Bibliothek des Litterarischen Vereins in Stuttgart, vol. 158. Tübingen: Litterarischer Verein in Stuttgart, 1882.

Roberts, Michael. *From Oxenstierna to Charles XII: Four Studies.* Cambridge: Cambridge University Press, 1991.

———. *Gustavus Adolphus.* 2nd ed. London: Longmans, 1992.

Robisheaux, Thomas W. *Rural Society and the Search of Order in Early Modern Germany.* Cambridge: Cambridge University Press, 1989.

Roeck, Bernd. *Als wollt die Welt schier brechen: Eine Stadt im Zeitalter des Dreissigjährigen Krieges.* Munich: C.H. Beck, 1991.

———, ed. *Gegenreformation und Dreißigjähriger Krieg 1555–1648.* Stuttgart: Reclam, 1996.

Rolevinck, Werner. *De Laude antiquae Saxoniae nunc Westphaliae dictae / Ein Buch zum Lobe Westfalens des alten Sachsenlandes.* Ed. Hermann Bücker. Münster: Aschendorff, 1953.

Roper, Lyndal. *The Holy Household: Women and Morals in Reformation Augsburg.* Oxford: Clarendon Press, 1989.

———. *Witch Craze: Terror and Fantasy in Baroque Germany.* New Haven: Yale University Press, 2004.

Rosheim, Joseph (Josel) of. *The Historical Writings of Joseph of Rosheim, Leader of Jewry in Early Modern Germany.* Trans. Naomi Schendowich and Adam Shear. Studies in European Judaism, vol. 12. Leiden: Brill, 2006.

Rott, Jean. *Investigationes historicae – Églises et société aux XVIe siècle – Gesammelte Aufsätze zur Kirchen– und Sozialgeschichte.* Edited by Marijn de Kroon and Marc Lienhard. Société savante d'Alsace et des régions de l'est, Collection "Grandes publications", vol. 32. Strasbourg: Librairie Oberlin, 1986.

Rublack, Hans-Christoph. *Gescheiterte Reformation. Frühreformatorische und protestantische Bewegungen in süd– und westdeutschen geistlichen Residenzen.* Spätmittelalter und Frühneuzeit. Tübinger Beiträge zur Geschichtsforschung, vol. 4. Stuttgart: Klett-Cotta, 1978.

Russell, Paul. *Lay Theology in the Reformation. Popular Pamphleteers in Southwest Germany, 1521–1525.* Cambridge: Cambridge University Press, 1986.

Sabean, David Warren. *Power in the Blood: Popular Culture and Village Discourse in Early Modern Germany.* Cambridge: Cambridge University Press, 1984.

Salchmann, Friedrich. *Historischer Bericht von den Hornhausischen Befund-Brunnen / Wann dieselbe entstanden worden / Vnd was der Wunderthätige GOtt biß anhero Denckwürdiges durch dieselbe gewürckt hat. Zur Ausbreitung der Ehren Gottes / mit sonderm Fleiß beschrieben.* Halberstadt: Andreas Kolwolt, 1646.

Sander, Paul, and Hans Spangenberg, eds. *Urkunden zur Geschichte der Territorialverfassung.* Ausgewählte Urkunden zur deutschen Verfassungs- und Wirtschaftsgeschichte. Stuttgart: W. Kohlhammer, 1922–26.

Schertlin von Burtenbach, Sebastian. *Leben und Taten des weiland wohledeln Ritters Sebastian Schertlin von Burtenbach.* Munich: Albert Langen, 1909.

Schieder, Rolf. *Wieviel Religion verträgt Deutschland?* Frankfurt am Main: Suhrkamp Verlag, 2001.

Schiess, Traugott, ed. *Briefwechsel der Brüder Ambrosius und Thomas Blarer 1509–1548.* 3 vols. Freiburg im Breisgau: Fehsenfeld, 1908–12.

Schilling, Heinz. *Aufbruch und Krise. Deutschland 1517–1648.* Berlin: Siedler, 1988.

Schmauss, Johann Jakob, ed. *Neue und vollständigere Sammlung der Reichs-Abschiede, welche von den Zeiten Kayser Conrads des II. bis jetzo auf den Teutschen Reichs-Tagen abegefasset worden.* 4 vols. Frankfurt: Ernst Koch, 1747.

Schmid, Peter. *Der Gemeine Pfennig von 1495. Vorgeschichte und Entstehung, Verfassungsgeschichtliche, politische und finanzielle Bedeutung.* Schriftenreihe der Historischen Kommission bei der Bayerischen Akademie der Wissenschaften, vol. 34. Göttingen: Vandenhoeck & Ruprecht, 1989.

Schmidt, Alexander. *Vaterlandsliebe und Religionskonflikt. Politische Diskurse im Alten Reich (1555–1648).* Studies in Medieval and Reformation Traditions, vol. 126. Leiden and Boston: Brill, 2007.

Schmugge, Ludwig. *Kirche, Kinder, Karrieren. Päpstliche Dispense von der unehelichen Geburt im Spätmittelalter.* Zurich: Artemis & Winkler, 1995.

Schnabel, Franz. *Deutsche Geschichte im neunzehnten Jahrhundert.* 4 vols. Freiburg im Breisgau: Herder, 1929–37.

Schnéegans, Louis, ed. *Code historique et dipomatique de la Ville de Strasbourg.* 2 vols. Strasbourg, 1845–47.

Schormann, Gerhard. *Der Dreißigjährige Krieg.* Göttingen: Vandenhoeck & Ruprecht, 1985.

———. *Hexenprozeße in Deutschland.* 2nd ed. Göttingen: Vandenhoeck & Ruprecht, 1986.

Schorn-Schütte, Luise. *Evangelische Geistlichkeit in der Frühneuzeit, deren Anteil an der Entfaltung frühmoderner Staatlichkeit und Gesellschaft, dargestellt am Beispiel des Fürstentums Braunschweig-Wolfenbüttel, der Landgrafschaft Hessen-Kassel und der Stadt Braunschweig.* Quellen und Forschungen zur Reformationsgeschichte, vol. 62. Gütersloh: Gütersloher Verlagshaus, 1996.

Schroeder, H. J., O.P., ed. *Canons and Decrees of the Council of Trent.* St. Louis and London: B. Herder, 1941.

Schubert, Ernst. "Albrecht Achilles, Markgraf und Kurfürst von Brandenburg (1414–1486)." In *Fränkische Lebensbilder,* vol. 4. Würzburg: Ferdinand Schöningh, 1971, 130–72.

———. *Einführung in die Grundprobleme der deutschen Geschichte im Spätmittelalter.* Darmstadt: Wissenschaftliche Buchgesellschaft, 1992.

———. "Vom Gebot zur Landesordnung. Der Wandel fürstlicher Herrschaft vom 15. zum 16. Jahrhundert." In *Die deutsche Reformation zwischen Spätmittelalter und Früher Neuzeit,* ed. Thomas A. Brady, Jr. Munich: R. Oldenbourg, 2001, 19–62.

Schuffenhauer, Werner, and Klaus Steiner, eds. *Martin Luther in der deutschen bürgerlichen Philosophie 1517–1845.* Berlin: Akademie-Verlag, 1983.

Schulte, Aloys. *Der Adel und die deutsche Kirche im Mittelalter.* 2nd ed. Kirchenrechtliche Abhandlungen. Stuttgart: F. Enke, 1922.

Schulze, Winfried. *Deutsche Geschichte im 16. Jahrhundert 1500–1618.* Frankfurt: Suhrkamp, 1987.

———. *Reich und Türkengefahr im späten 16. Jahrhundert. Studien zu den politischen und gesellschaftlichen Auswirkungen einer äußeren Bedrohung.* Munich: C.H. Beck, 1978.

Schütz Zell, Katharina. *Katharina Schütz Zell, vol. 2: The Writings. A Critical Edition.* Ed. Elsie Anne McKee. Studies in Medieval and Reformation Thought, vol. 69. Leiden: Brill, 1999.

Schwaiger, Georg, ed. *Zwischen Polemik und Irenik. Untersuchungen zum Verhältniß der Konfessionen im späten 18. und frühen 19. Jahrhundert.* Göttingen: Vandenhoeck & Ruprecht, 1977.

Schwarz, Henry Frederick. *The Imperial Privy Council in the Seventeenth Century.* Harvard Historical Monographs, vol. 53. Cambridge, MA: Harvard University, 1943.

Schweitzer, Albert. *The Quest of the Historical Jesus: A Critical Study of its Progress from Reimarus to Wrede.* Trans. W. Montgomery. New York: Macmillan, 1911.

Schwendi, Lazarus von. *Des Lazarus von Schwendi Denkschrift über die politische Lage des Deutschen Reiches von 1574.* Ed. Eugen von Frauenholz. Münchener Historische Abhandlungen, series 2, vol. 10. Munich: C.H. Beck, 1939.

Scott, Tom. "Germany and the Empire." In *The New Cambridge Modern History,* vol. 7, ed. Christopher Allmand. Cambridge: Cambridge University Press, 1998, 337–66.

———. *Society and Economy in Germany, 1300–1600.* European Studies Series. Houndsmill, Bassingstoke: Palgrave, 2002.

———. *Thomas Müntzer: Theology and Revolution in the German Reformation.* New York: St. Martin's, 1989.

Scott, Tom, and Bob (Robert W.) Scribner, eds. *The German Peasants' War. A History in Documents.* Atlantic Highlands, NJ: Humanities Press, 1991.

Scribner, Robert W. "Anticlericalism and the Cities." In *Anticlericalism in the Late Middle Ages and Reformation,* ed. Peter Dykema and Heiko A. Oberman. Leiden: E.J. Brill, 1993, 147–66.

————. *For the Sake of Simple Folk: Popular Propaganda for the German Reformation.* Cambridge: Cambridge University Press, 1981.

————. *Popular Culture and Popular Movements in Reformation Germany.* London: Variorum, 1987.

————, ed. *Germany: A New Social and Economic History, 1450–1630.* London: Edward Arnold, 1996.

————, and Gerhard Benecke, eds. *The German Peasant War of 1525–New Viewpoints.* London: George Allen & Unwin, 1979.

Scultetus, Abraham. *Die Selbstbiographie des Heidelberger Theologen und Hofpredigers Abraham Scultetus (1566–1624).* Ed. G. A. Benrath. Veröffentlichungen des Vereins für Kirchengeschichte in der Evangelischen. Landeskirche in Baden, vol. 24. Karlsruhe: Evangelischer Presseverband, 1966.

Seifert, Arno. "Das höhere Schulwesen – Universitäten und Gymnasien." In *Handbuch der deutchen Bildungsgeschichte, vol. I: 15. bis 17. Jahrhundert. Von der Renaissance und der Reformation bis zum Ende der Glaubenskämpfe,* ed. Notker Hammerstein. Munich: C.H. Beck, 1996, 197–377.

Sheehan, James J. *German History,* 1770–1866. Oxford: Clarendon Press, 1989.

Šmahel, František. *Die Hussitische Revolution.* Trans. Thomas Krzenck. 3 vols. Monumenta Germaniae Historica. Schriften, vol. 43. Hannover: Hahnsche Buchhandlung, 2002.

Smith, Helmut Walser. *German Nationalism and Religious Conflict: Culture, Ideology, Politics, 1870–1914.* Princeton: Princeton University Press, 1995.

Specklin, Daniel. "Les Collectanées." *Bulletin de la Société pour la Conservation des Monuments Historiques d'Alsace,* series 2 13–14 (1888–89): 157–360, 1–178.

Spee, Friedrich. *Cautio Criminalis, or A Book on Witch Trials.* Trans. Marcus Hellyer. Charlottesville: University Press of Virginia, 2003.

Spiess, Karl-Heinz. *Familie und Verwandschaft im deutschen Hochadel des Spätmittelalters – 13. bis Anfang des 16. Jahrhunderts.* Vierteljahrschrift für Sozial- und Wirtschaftsgeschichte. Beihefte, vol. 111. Stuttgart: Franz Seiner Verlag, 1993.

Stadtwald, Kurt. *Roman Popes and German Patriots. Antipapalism in the Politics of the German Humanist Movement from Gregor Heimburg to Martin Luther.* Travaux d'humanisme et renaissance, vol. 299. Geneva: Librairie Droz, 1996.

Stäudlin, Carl Friedrich. *Kirchliche Geographie und Statistik.* 2 vols. Tübingen: J.G. Cotta, 1804.

Steinmetz, Max. "Theses on the Early Bourgeois Revolution in Germany, 1476–1535." In *The German Peasant War of 1525: New Viewpoints,* ed. Bob Scribner and Gerhard Benecke. London and Boston: Allen & Unwin, 1979, 9–18.

Stolleis, Michael. *Pecunia Nervus Rerum. Zur Staatsfinanzierung der frühen Neuzeit.* Frankfurt: Vittorio Klostermann, 1983.

Strasser, Ulrike. *State of Virginity: Gender, Religion, and Politics in an Early Modern Catholic State.* Ann Arbor: University of Michigan Press, 2004.

Strauss, Gerald, ed. *Manifestations of Discontent in Germany on the Eve of the Reformation.* Bloomington: Indiana University Press, 1971.

————. *Nuremberg in the Sixteenth Century.* New York: John Wiley & Sons, 1966.

————. *Sixteenth-Century Germany: Its Topography and Topographers.* Madison: University of Wisconsin Press, 1959.

Strauss, Walter L. *The German Single-Leaf Woodcut, 1550–1600: A Pictorial Catalogue.* 3 vols. New York: Abaris, 1975.

Strieder, Jakob. *Studien zur Geschichte kapitalistischer Organisationsformen. Monopole, Kartelle und Aktiengesellschaften im Mittelalter und zu Beginn der Neuzeit.* 2nd ed. Munich and Leipzig: Duncker & Humblot, 1925.

Tennant, Elaine C. "An Overdue Revision in the History of Early New High German: Niclas Ziegler and the Habsburg Chancery Language." *Deutsche Vierteljahresschrift für Literaturwissenschaft und Geistesgeschichte* 55 (1981): 248–77.

Theibault, John. "The Rhetoric of Death and Destruction in the Thirty Years War." *Journal of Social History* 27 (1994): 271–90.

Tilly, Charles. *Coercion, Capital, and European States, AD 990–1992.* Studies in Social Discontinuity. Cambridge, MA: Blackwell, 1990.

———. "Reflections on the History of European State-Making." In *The Formation of National States in Western Europe*, ed. Charles Tilly. Princeton: Princeton University Press, 1975, 3–83.

———. "War Making and State Making as Organized Crime." In *Bringing the State Back*, ed. Peter B. Evans, Dietrich Rueschemeyer, and Theda Skocpol. Cambridge: Cambridge University Press, 1985, 169–91.

Tracy, James D. *Emperor Charles V, Impresario of War: Campaign Strategy, International Finance, and Domestic Politics.* Cambridge: Cambridge University Press, 2002.

———. *Erasmus: The Growth of a Mind.* Travaux d'humanisme et renaissance, vol. 126. Geneva: Droz, 1972.

Traitler, Hildegard. *Konfession und Politik. Interkonfessionelle Flugschriftenpolemik aus Süddeutschland und Österreich (1564–1612).* Frankfurt am Main: Peter Lang, 1989.

Treitschke, Heinrich von. "Luther und die deutsche Nation." In *Historische und politische Aufsätze*, vol. 4. Leipzig: S. Hirzel, 1897, 377–96.

Troeltsch, Ernst. *Protestantism and Progress: The Significance of Protestantism for the Rise of the Modern World.* Trans. W. Montgomery. Philadelphia: Fortress, 1986.

Vener, Job. "Avisamentum (1417)." In *Die Vener von Gmünd und Straßburg 1162–1447*, ed. Hermann Heimpel. Göttingen: Vandenhoeck & Ruprecht, 1983.

Vico, Giambattista. *New Science. Principles of the New Science Concerning the Common Nature of Nations.* Trans. David Marsh. 3rd ed. London and New York: Penguin, 1999.

Virck, Hans, Otto Winckelmann, Harry Gerber, and Walter Friedensburg, eds. *Politische Correspondenz der Stadt Straßburg im Zeitalter der Reformation.* 5 vols. Urkunden und Akten der Stadt Straßburg, part 2. Strasbourg and Heidelberg: Trübner and Carl Winter, 1882–1933.

Vogler, Günter. *Nürnberg 1524/25: Studien zur Geschichte der reformatorischen und sozialen Bewegung in der Reichsstadt.* Berlin: Deutscher Verlag der Wissenschaften, 1982.

Vogt, Wilhelm. *Die bayrische Politik im Bauernkrieg und der Kanzler Dr. Leonhard von Eck, das Haupt des Schwäbischen Bundes.* Nördlingen: Beck, 1883.

Voigt, Klaus. *Italienische Berichte aus dem spätmittelalterlichen Deutschland. Von Francesco Petrarca zu Andrea de' Franceschi (1333–1492).* Kieler Historische Studien, vol. 17. Stuttgart: Ernst Klett, 1973.

Wandel, Lee Palmer. *The Eucharist in the Reformation: Incarnation and Liturgy.* Cambridge: Cambridge University Press, 2006.

———. *Voracious Idols and Violent Hands: Iconoclasm in Reformation Zurich, Strasbourg, and Basel.* Cambridge: Cambridge University Press, 1995.

Warmbrunn, Paul. *Zwei Konfessionen in einer Stadt: Das Zusammenleben von Katholiken und Protestanten in den paritätischen Reichsstädten Augsburg, Biberach, Ravensburg und Dinkelsbühl.* Veröffentlichungen des Instituts für Europäische Geschichte Mainz, vol. III. Wiesbaden: Franz Steiner, 1983.

Weinrich, Lorenz, ed. *De reformando regni teutonici statu in medioaevo posteriore fontes selecta / Quellen zur Verfassungsgeschichte des Römisch-Deutschen Reiches im Spätmittelalter (1250–1500).* Ausgewählte Quellen zur deutschen Geschichte des Mittelalters, vol. 33. Darmstadt: Wissenschaftliche Buchgesellschaft, 1983.

———, ed. *De reformando regni teutonici statu in medioaevo posteriore fontes selectae / Quellen zur Reichsreform im Spätmitelalter.* Ausgewählte Quellen zur deutschen Geschichte des Mittelalters, vol. 39. Darmstadt: Wissenschaftliche Buchgesellschaft, 2001.

Weyrauch, Erdmann. *Konfessionelle Krise und soziale Stabilität: Das Interim in Straßburg (1548–1562).* Spätmittelalter und Frühe Neuzeit. Tübinger Beiträge zur Geschichts-forschung, vol. 7. Stuttgart: Klett-Cotta, 1978.

Wiesflecker, Hermann. *Kaiser Maximilian I. Das Reich, Österreich und Europa an der Wende zur Neuzeit.* 5 vols. Munich: R. Oldenbourg Verlag, 1971–86.

———. *Maximilian I. Die Fundamente des habsburgischen Weltreiches.* Vienna: Verlag für Geschichte und Politik, 1991.

Wiesflecker-Friedhuber, Inge, ed. *Quellen zur Geschichte Maximilians I. und seiner Zeit.* Ausgewählte Quellen zur deutschen Geschichte der Neuzeit, vol. 14. Darmstadt: Wissenschaftliche Buchgesellschaft, 1996.

Wiesner-Hanks, Merry, ed. *Convents Confront the Reformation: Catholic and Protestant Nuns in Germany.* Milwaukee, WI: Marquette University Press, 1998.

Wildefuer, Hans. *Die Hildesheimer Bischofschronik des Hans Wildefuer.* Ed. Udo Stanelle. Veröffentlichungen des Instituts für Historische Landesforschung an der Universität Göttingen, vol. 25. Hildesheim: August Lax, 1986.

Wilson, Peter H. *From Reich to Revolution: German History, 1558–1806.* Basingstoke: Palgrave, 2004.

Winkler, Heinrich August. *Der lange Weg nach Westen.* 2 vols. Munich: C.H. Beck, 2000.

Wolff, Georg, ed. *Die Matrikel der Ludwig-Maximilians-Universität Ingolstadt-Landshut-München, part I: Ingolstadt.* Ed. Götz Freiherr von Pölnitz. Die Matrikel der Ludwig-Maximilians-Universität Ingolstadt-Landshut-München, vol. 1, 1 (1472–1600). Munich: Universitätsbuchdruckerei C. Wolf & Sohn, 1937.

Wolgast, Eike. *Hochstift und Reformation. Studien zur Geschichte der Reichskirche zwischen 1517 und 1648.* Beiträge zur Geschichte der Reichskirche in der Neuzeit, vol. 16. Stuttgart: Franz Steiner Verlag, 1995.

Wopfner, Hermann, ed. *Quellen zur Geschichte des Bauernkriegs in Deutschtirol, part I: Quellen zur Vorgeschichte des Bauernkriegs, Beschwerdeartikel aus den Jahren 1519–1525.* Acta Tirolensia, vol. 3. Innsbruck: Wagner'sche Universitätsbuchhandlung, 1908.

Worthington, David. *Scots in the Habsburg Service, 1618–1648.* History of Warfare, vol. 21. Leiden: Brill, 2004.

Wrede, Adolf, ed. *Deutsche Reichstagsakten unter Kaiser Karl V.* Deutsche Reichstag-sakten, jüngere Reihe. Gotha: F.A. Perthes, 1896.

Wustmann, Gustav. "Geschichte der hemlichen Calvinisten (Kryptocalvinisten in Leipzig 1574 bis 1593)." *Neujahrsblätter der Bibliothek und des Archivs der Stadt Leipzig* 1 (1905): 1–94.

Zeeden, Ernst Walter. *Konfessionsbildung: Studien zur Reformation, Gegenreformation, und katholischen Reform.* Stuttgart: Klett-Cotta, 1985.

Zeiller, Martin. *Topographia Franconiae, das ist, Beschreibung und eygentliche Contra-factur der vornembsten Stätte und Plätze des Franckenlandes/und Deren die zum hochlöblichsten Fränkischen Craiße gezogen werden.* Frankfurt: Matthaeus Merian, [1648]. Reprint, Frankfurt: Frankfurt Kunstverein, 1925.

Ziehen, Eduard. *Mittelrhein und Reich im Zeitalter der Reichsreform 1356–1504.* 2 vols. Frankfurt am Main: Selbstverlag, 1934–37.

Zimmern, Froben Christof von. *Zimmerische Chronik.* 4 vols. Bibliothek des Litterarischen Vereins in Stuttgart, vols. 91–4. Tübingen: Litterarischer Verein in Stuttgart, 1869.

Zink, Burkhard. "Chronik des Burkhard Zink 1368–1468." In Carl Hegel, ed., *Chroniken der deutschen Städte vom 14. bis ins 16. Jahrhundert,* ed. Historische Kommission bei der Bayerischen Akademie der Wissenschaften, vol. 5. Leipzig: S. Hirzel, 1866, 1–509.

Zmora, Hillay. *State and Nobility in Early Modern Germany: The Knightly Feud in Franconia, 1440–1567.* Cambridge Studies in Early Modern History. Cambridge: Cambridge University Press, 1997.

Zwingli, Huldrych. *Huldrych Zwinglis sämtliche Werke.* Ed. Emil Egli and Georg Finsler. 14 vols. Berlin and Zurich: C.A. Schwetschke & Sohn and Theologischer Verlag, 1905–91.

Index

Abbreviations: archbp. = archbishop/archbishopric; b. = born; bp. = bishop/bishopric; d. = died; r. = reigned/ruled